CCIE Self-Study
CCIE Security Exam Certification Guide

Henry Benjamin

Cisco Press

Cisco Press
201 West 103rd Street
Indianapolis, IN 46290 USA

CCIE Self-Study
CCIE Security Exam Certification Guide

Henry Benjamin

Copyright © 2003 Cisco Systems, Inc.

Published by:
Cisco Press
201 West 103rd Street
Indianapolis, IN 46290 USA

Printed in the United States of America 2 3 4 5 6 7 8 9 0

Second Printing June 2003

Library of Congress Cataloging-in-Publication Number: 2002104850

ISBN: 1-58720-065-1

Warning and Disclaimer

This book is designed to provide information about the CCIE Security written exam. Every effort has been made to make this book as complete and as accurate as possible, but no warranty or fitness is implied.

The information is provided on an "as is" basis. The authors, Cisco Press, and Cisco Systems, Inc., shall have neither liability nor responsibility to any person or entity with respect to any loss or damages arising from the information contained in this book or from the use of the discs or programs that may accompany it.

The opinions expressed in this book belong to the author and are not necessarily those of Cisco Systems, Inc.

Trademark Acknowledgments

All terms mentioned in this book that are known to be trademarks or service marks have been appropriately capitalized. Cisco Press or Cisco Systems, Inc. cannot attest to the accuracy of this information. Use of a term in this book should not be regarded as affecting the validity of any trademark or service mark.

Feedback Information

At Cisco Press, our goal is to create in-depth technical books of the highest quality and value. Each book is crafted with care and precision, undergoing rigorous development that involves the unique expertise of members from the professional technical community.

Readers' feedback is a natural continuation of this process. If you have any comments regarding how we could improve the quality of this book, or otherwise alter it to better suit your needs, you can contact us through e-mail at feedback@ciscopress.com. Please make sure to include the book title and ISBN in your message.

We greatly appreciate your assistance.

Publisher	John Wait
Editor-in-Chief	John Kane
Executive Editor	Brett Bartow
Cisco Representative	Anthony Wolfenden
Cisco Press Program Manager	Sonia Torres Chavez
Cisco Marketing Communications Manager	Tom Geitner
Cisco Marketing Program Manager	Edie Quiroz
Managing Editor	Patrick Kanouse
Development Editor	Andrew Cupp
Project Editor	San Dee Phillips
Copy Editor	Marcia Ellett
Technical Editors	Gert De Laet, Anand Deveriya, Charles Resch, Gert Schauwers
Team Coordinator	Tammi Ross
Book Designer	Gina Rexrode
Cover Designer	Louisa Adair
Compositor	Octal Publishing, Inc.
Indexer	Brad Herriman

CISCO SYSTEMS

Corporate Headquarters
Cisco Systems, Inc.
170 West Tasman Drive
San Jose, CA 95134-1706
USA
www.cisco.com
Tel: 408 526-4000
 800 553-NETS (6387)
Fax: 408 526-4100

European Headquarters
Cisco Systems International BV
Haarlerbergpark
Haarlerbergweg 13-19
1101 CH Amsterdam
The Netherlands
www-europe.cisco.com
Tel: 31 0 20 357 1000
Fax: 31 0 20 357 1100

Americas Headquarters
Cisco Systems, Inc.
170 West Tasman Drive
San Jose, CA 95134-1706
USA
www.cisco.com
Tel: 408 526-7660
Fax: 408 527-0883

Asia Pacific Headquarters
Cisco Systems, Inc.
Capital Tower
168 Robinson Road
#22-01 to #29-01
Singapore 068912
www.cisco.com
Tel: +65 6317 7777
Fax: +65 6317 7799

Cisco Systems has more than 200 offices in the following countries and regions. Addresses, phone numbers, and fax numbers are listed on the **Cisco.com Web site at www.cisco.com/go/offices.**

Argentina • Australia • Austria • Belgium • Brazil • Bulgaria • Canada • Chile • China PRC • Colombia • Costa Rica • Croatia • Czech Republic
Denmark • Dubai, UAE • Finland • France • Germany • Greece • Hong Kong SAR • Hungary • India • Indonesia • Ireland • Israel • Italy
Japan • Korea • Luxembourg • Malaysia • Mexico • The Netherlands • New Zealand • Norway • Peru • Philippines • Poland • Portugal
Puerto Rico • Romania • Russia • Saudi Arabia • Scotland • Singapore • Slovakia • Slovenia • South Africa • Spain • Sweden
Switzerland • Taiwan • Thailand • Turkey • Ukraine • United Kingdom • United States • Venezuela • Vietnam • Zimbabwe

About the Author

Henry Benjamin, CCIE No.4695, holds three CCIE certifications, having attained Routing and Switching in May 1999, ISP Dial in June 2001, and Communications and Services in May 2002. He has more than 10 years experience with Cisco networks, including planning, designing, and implementing large IP networks running IGRP, EIGRP, BGP, and OSPF. Recently, Henry has worked for a large IT organization based in Sydney, Australia as a key Network Designer, designing and implementing networks all over Australia and Asia.

In the past two years, Henry has been a key member of the CCIE global team based in Sydney, Australia. As a senior and core member of the team, his tasks include writing new laboratory examinations and questions for the coveted CCIE R/S, CCIE Security, and CCIE C/S tracks, as well as the CCIE written Recertification Examinations. Henry has authored two other titles, "CCNP Practical Studies: Routing" (Cisco Press) and "CCIE R&S Exam Cram."

Henry holds a Bachelor of Aeronautical Engineering degree from Sydney University (1991).

About the Contributing Author

Gert De Laet, CCIE No. 2657, has both CCIE Security and Routing and Switching certifications. He has more than nine years of experience in internetworking. Gert currently works for the CCIE team at Cisco in Brussels, Belgium, as CCIE Proctor/Content Engineer and Program Manager for EMEA. He also holds an Engineering degree in Electronics.

Gert helped write Chapter 9 of this book and acted as a lead technical reviewer for the entire book.

About the Technical Reviewers

Anand Deveriya, CCIE No.10401, in Security and MCSE, has five years of LAN/WAN and network security experience with Cisco products. Currently, he is the Network Manager at Summerville Senior Living, where he designed and deployed their nationwide Frame Relay-based WAN network with VoIP. Additionally, he monitors the LAN/WAN security, penetration testing, and OS hardening. Prior to that, he was a network engineer with NEC, where he deployed scalable, secure, and redundant network backbone for dotcom and campus environments using Cisco routers, switches, PIX, and VPN products.

Charles Resch, CCIE No. 6582, currently works at Nuclio as a Senior Network Engineer, where he installs and configures management equipment to monitor customer networks. Among his projects are e-commerce sites with dual Cisco PIX Firewalls, Cisco Content Switch (CSS) load balancers, Intel and SonicWall SSL off-loaders, Cisco switches (HSRP-VLANs), and Cisco Secure Intrusion Detection Systems (CSIDS). Among other jobs, he has worked as a Senior Instructor at Information Technology Institute—Northwestern Business College, and as a Senior Internet Engineer at Globalcom Inc. He has extensive experience with Cisco hardware, Cisco IOS Software, numerous routed and routing protocols, and operating systems.

Gert Schauwers, CCIE No. 6924, has CCIE certifications in Security, Routing and Switching, and Communications and Services. He has more than four years of experience in internetworking. He is currently working for the CCIE team at Cisco in Brussels, Belgium, as CCIE Content Engineer. He has an Engineering degree in Electronics.

Dedication

This book is solely dedicated to two wonderful individuals whom I've had the pleasure of meeting on two occasions in my life. Without their inspiration and love for all humanity, I would not be here writing this book. I dedicate this book to His Excellency Monsignor, Claudio Gatti, and Marisa Rossi. I thank God for you.

"I am the Mother of the Eucharist. Know Jesus' word. Love Jesus, the Eucharist."

—Our Lady, Mary, Mother of the Eucharist

Questo libro è dedicato esclusivamente a due persone meravigliose che ho avuto il piacere di conoscere e incontrare in due occasioni nella mia vita. Senza la loro ispirazione e il loro amore per tutta l'umanità io non sarei qui a scrivere questo libro. Dedico questo libro a Sua Eccellenza Mons. Claudio Gatti e a Marisa Rossi.

"Io sono la madre dell'Eucaristia. Conoscete Gesù parola. Amate Gesù Eucaristia."

—Madonna, Maria, Madre dell'Eucaristia

Acknowledgments

I would like to thank the folks at Cisco Press for helping me and introducing me to this challenging project.

Brett Bartow, you are an amazing individual. Thank you for your wonderful insight and complete trust in me. Andrew Cupp, or Drew, as you are known to many of us, no bones about it, you are one of a kind; your editing and technical ability really astounded me, and without you, this book would not be the quality product it is now. No book on the market is as good as this one, thanks mate. Thank you for completing all the chapters with your wonderful touches. This book is better because of your input. The team at Cisco Press is an amazing family of hard-working people. It has been a true pleasure to be invited to write this book. Any inspired authors should only ever consider one publisher, Cisco Press. Thanks also to Tammi Ross, Tracy Hughes, and Ginny Bess for all your help. Thank you San Dee Phillips and Patrick Kanouse for your wonderful, final touches that made this book what readers see today.

The technical editors, Gert De Laet, Gert Schauwers, Anand Deveriya, and Charles Resch, provided valuable technical expertise and all have shown that they, too, can one day pursue a writing career, as I am sure they will in the near future. Gert De Laet, thank you, especially, for helping me write the security sections of Chapter 9. It was a real pleasure and honor to have you contribute to this book. Gert Schauwers, thank you for all the encouragement you gave me over the last twelve months. Loved that game of golf in San Jose.

Gert D. and Gert S., thank you for your true friendship.

To finish, I would also like to thank my wife, Sharon, and my one and only son, Simon (the spiderboy). I was always grateful to them both for understanding and knowing when I needed time to complete this project. I treasure my time with my family and my growing little boy who makes me proud to be his Dad. Simon, I love you to the sun, and keep going around forever and ever and watch out for the new Spider Boy movie. I also thank my Dad and Mum for bringing me up with such great examples, and my wife's parents (Nana and Mate, plus Princess) for their encouragement over the last six months. Uncle Albert, keep making those beautiful donuts and thank you for your encouragement. Thank you to my beautiful sister, Melanie, for her wonderful love throughout my life. This year you become a registered nurse and passed your exams with distinctions. What a wonderful sister you are. I am so proud of you, Mel. Thanks Mello Yello. Massimo Piccinini, my physicist friend in the most beautiful City of the World, Roma, thank you for the friendship and love over the past five years; you are a truly amazing friend (amico).

I want to thank my wonderful aunties who gave me wonderful encouragement over all the years they have known me. Thank you, Aunty Lyda and Alice.

Contents at a Glance

Table of Contents

Foreword

The CCIE program is designed to help individuals, companies, industries, and countries succeed in the networked world by distinguishing the top echelon of internetworking experts. In particular, the CCIE Security Certification is designed to identify network security experts.

The first step along the CCIE Security path is for individuals to take a challenging written exam designed to assess their knowledge across a range of technologies. If their scores indicate expert-level knowledge, candidates then proceed to a performance-based CCIE Security Certification Lab Exam.

Why Security Certifications?

Security is one of the fastest-growing areas in the industry. The expansive development of the Internet, the increase in e-business, and the escalating threat to both public- and private-sector networks have made security and the protection of information a primary concern for all types of organizations. An ever-increasing demand exists for the experts with the knowledge and skills to do it. Therefore, trained network security personnel will be required in the years to come.

Why CCIE Security?

CCIE Security distinguishes the top level of network security experts. The CCIE Security Certification enables individuals to optimize career growth, opportunity, and compensation by distinguishing themselves as being part of the network security experts of the world.

The CCIE Security Certification enables companies to minimize their risk by identifying the highest caliber of security personnel with the training and skills necessary to protect their critical information assets.

This book will be a valuable asset to potential CCIE Security candidates. I am positive individuals will gain extensive security network knowledge during their preparation for the CCIE Security written exam using this book. The book's main focus is providing an in-depth description of the various security features and an understanding of, and ability to navigate, the subtleties, intricacies, and potential pitfalls inherent to networking security. This book and accompanying CD-ROM contain many tools to strongly supplement your preparation for CCIE Security certification.

Good Luck!

Gert De Laet
Product Manager CCIE Security
Cisco Systems, Inc.

Introduction

The Cisco Certified Internet Expert Security Certification is an increasingly popular internetworking certification and one of the most popular security certifications in the world. Although CCIE certification builds on the foundation you might have established from the Cisco Certified Network Associate (CCNA) and Cisco Certified Network Professional (CCNP) certifications, there is no prerequisite to attempt to gain CCIE certification. However, attaining CCNA and CCNP certifications will help you understand Cisco subjects and testing strategies.

This book is designed to help you prepare for the CCIE Security written exam (Exam #350-018). It will also help prepare you for the CCIE Security Recertification exam (Exam #350-009).

Cisco released the Security CCIE track in 2001, and its popularity has grown to such an extent that Cisco is investing more heavily in this track than any other current CCIE track.

To achieve CCIE Security certification, you must pass a written exam and a one-day lab exam. To qualify for the CCIE Security lab examination, you must first successfully pass the written exam. Both examinations are difficult, and this book is primarily aimed at helping you prepare for the written exam. Chapter 9 includes a CCIE Security self-study lab that helps you with comprehensive preparation for the written exam and gives you an idea of the challenges you will face in the lab exam.

Cisco makes achieving CCIE Security certification intentionally difficult. No one book can prepare you for the exam. You should have extensive practical experience and consult many resources. This will give you a comprehensive look at all of the topics covered on the CCIE Security written exam (see Chapter 1). Use this book and the CD-ROM to confidently assess your level of preparedness for all of the topics covered on the exam.

The CCIE Security written examination is a two-hour, multiple-choice examination with a surprising amount of Cisco IOS Software configurations and scenario type questions. Some questions require only one answer while other questions require two or more.

The CCIE Security written exam is the first step you must take to attain CCIE Security certification.

This book provides you with the technical and practical knowledge to prepare for the CCIE Security written exam and enables you to obtain the skills required to fully appreciate what needs to be achieved on your journey towards one of the most sought-after certifications today.

Passing the written examination means that you have mastered the networking concepts and fundamental security topics necessary to build a complex, secure, and routable IP network using Cisco routers. This is a great skill and demonstrates to any employer that you are ready for any challenges that might be asked of you.

NOTE   The CCIE Security written exam is a computer-based exam with multiple-choice questions. The exam can be taken at any VUE testing site (www.VUE.com/cisco) or Prometric testing center (1-800-829-NETS, www.2test.com). The exam is 2 hours long and has 100 questions. Check with VUE or Prometric for the exact length of the exam. The exam is constantly under review, so be sure to check the latest updates from Cisco:

www.cisco.com/en/US/learning/le3/le2/le23/le476/learning_certification_type_home.html

---

NOTE	For more information on how to use this book and preparing for the CCIE Security exam, refer to Chapter 1, "Using This Book to Prepare for the CCIE Security Written Exam," and Appendix B, "Study Tips for CCIE Security Examinations."

Goals of This Book

This book's primary goal is to ensure that a CCIE Security candidate has all the technical skills and knowledge required to pass the written examination. Most Cisco certifications require practical skills and the only way to provide you with those skills is to demonstrate them in a working environment using common Cisco-defined techniques.

This book provides you with comprehensive coverage of CCIE Security exam topics, with minimal coverage of nonexam foundation topics. Ultimately, the goal of this book is to get you from where you are today to the point that you can confidently pass the CCIE Security written exam. Therefore, all this book's features, which are outlined later in this introduction, are geared toward helping you discover the IP routing challenges and security scenarios that are on the exam, helping you discover where you have a knowledge deficiency in these topics, and what you need to know to master those topics.

The accompanying CD is an invaluable tool that simulates the real exam and has a pool of over 300 questions. The CD can be used in study mode, which allows you to focus on certain topics and includes links to the electronic version of this book, or exam mode, which allows you to take a timed simulated exam.

Organization of this Book

Each chapter starts by testing your current knowledge with a "Do I Know this already" quiz. This quiz is aimed at helping you decide whether you need to cover the entire chapter, whether you need to read only parts of the chapter, or if you can skip the chapter. See Chapter 1 and the introduction to each "Do I Know this already" quiz for more details.

Each chapter then contains a Foundation Topics section with extensive coverage of the CCIE Security exam topics covered in that chapter. A Foundation Summary section that provides more condensed coverage of the topics and is ideal for review and study follows this. Each chapter ends with Q & A and Scenarios sections to help you assess how well you mastered the topics covered in the chapter.

Chapter 1, "Using This Book to Prepare for the CCIE Security Written Exam"

Chapter 1 covers details about the CCIE Security exam topics and how to use this book. The CCIE Security written exam blueprint is discussed in this chapter.

Chapter 2, "General Networking Topics"

Chapter 2 covers general networking technologies, including an overview of the OSI model, switching concepts, and routing protocols. The TCP/IP model is presented and explained with common applications used in today's IP networks. Routing protocols and sample configurations are presented to ensure that you have a good understanding of how Cisco IOS routes IP datagrams. Concluding this chapter is a discussion of some of today's most widely used WAN protocols, including PPP, ISDN, and Frame Relay. Keep in mind that the CCIE Security exam covers routing and switching topics as well as security topics. See the exam topics listed in Chapter 1 for more details.

Chapter 3, "Application Protocols"

Chapter 3 covers the principles of Domain Name System and TFTP file transfers. The most widely used applications such as FTP and HTTP are covered along with some of the more secure methods used to download information from the World Wide Web, such as Secure Shell and the Secure Socket Layer protocol. A challenging scenario is included to ensure that you have the IOS skill set to configure DNS, TFTP, NTP, and SNMP.

Chapter 4, "Cisco IOS Specifics and Security"

Chapter 4 covers the more advanced topics available to Cisco IOS routers. It covers in detail the hardware components of a Cisco router and how to manage Cisco routers. Common Cisco device operation commands are described and examples show how to manage Cisco IOS in today's large IP networks. Cisco password recovery techniques and basic password security are detailed to ensure you have a solid grasp of Cisco device operation. Coverage of standard and extended access lists and examples conclude this chapter.

Chapter 5, "Security Protocols"

Chapter 5 focuses on security protocols developed and supported by Cisco Systems and refined in RFCs, namely TACACS+, RADIUS, and Kerberos. Following sample configurations, the chapter covers encryption technologies and their use in today's vulnerable IP networks.

Chapter 6, "Operating Systems and Cisco Security Applications"

Chapter 6 covers today's most widely used operating systems: Windows and UNIX. The applications that run over these platforms are covered in more detail. Cisco Secure and Cisco Policy Manger are discussed.

Chapter 7, "Security Technologies"

Chapter 7 describes the basic security methods and evolution of the new secure networks, including packet filtering and proxies. The IP address depletion rates with IPv4 have led to NAT/PAT becoming increasingly popular; this chapter covers these topics along with sample IOS configurations.

The Cisco PIX is Cisco's trademark security device, and this chapter teaches you the architecture and configuration of these unique security devices. The IOS feature set and VPNs are covered to conclude this chapter.

Chapter 8, "Network Security Policies, Vulnerabilities, and Protection"

Chapter 8 reviews today's most common Cisco security policies and mechanisms available to the Internet community to combat cyber attacks. The standard security body, CERT/CC, is covered along with descriptions of Cisco IOS-based security methods used to ensure that all attacks are reported and acted upon. Cisco Security applications, such as Intrusion Detection System, are covered to lay the fundamental foundations you need to master the topics covered on the CCIE Security written examination.

Chapter 9, "CCIE Security Self-Study Lab"

Chapter 9 is designed to assist you in your final preparation for CCIE Security exam. Developed by one former (Sydney CCIE lab) and current CCIE proctor (Brussels CCIE lab) from the CCIE team, this chapter contains a sample CCIE security lab with full working solutions to ensure that you are fully prepared for the final hurdle, the CCIE laboratory examination. This lab is intended to challenge your practical application of the knowledge covered in the book, and it should give you a good sense of the areas you need to concentrate your study to prepare for the lab exam.

Appendix A, "Answers to Quiz Questions"

Appendix A provides the answers to the "Do I Know this Already" and Q & A quiz questions in each chapter. Explanations are included where appropriate.

Appendix B, "Study Tips for CCIE Security Examinations"

Appendix B describes some of the study tips and preparations steps you should consider before embarking on the long road to CCIE Security certification.

Appendix C, "Sample CCIE Routing and Switching Lab"

Appendix C is a bonus appendix designed to assist you in your final preparation for the CCIE Routing and Switching lab exam, and help you appreciate the level of difficulty found in any CCIE laboratory examination.

CD-ROM

The CD-ROM provides you with a sample testing engine that simulates the real examination with over 300 questions that will ensure that you have all the necessary knowledge to pass the first step in your journey. The robust test engine allows you to concentrate your study on particular topics, take full, timed exams, and refer to an electronic version of the text that explains each topic. Take the CD-ROM test and review all the answers so that you are fully prepared for the CCIE Security written exanimation.

Also on the CD-ROM are URL links and sample configurations used throughout the book. As a bonus, my first book, *CCIE Exam Cram*, is also included for those of you studying for the Routing and Switching examination, or who need to brush up on the Routing and Switching portions of the CCIE Security exams. Please enjoy this free bonus.

Command Syntax Conventions

Command syntax in this book conforms to the following conventions:

- Commands, keywords, and actual values for arguments are **bold.**
- Arguments (which need to be supplied with an actual value) are in *italics.*
- Optional keywords and arguments are in brackets [].
- A choice of mandatory keywords and arguments is in braces {}.

Note that these conventions are for syntax only.

Conclusion

Having many Cisco certifications myself, the joy and success I have achieved has significantly changed my life and that of my family. There are always challenges facing network engineers and, no doubt, becoming a certified Cisco professional meeting those challenges will drive you into acquiring skills you thought you never knew you could master.

I sincerely hope you enjoy your time spent with this book; it took over six months and long nights to complete to ensure you have the perfect companion through your journey to becoming CCIE certified.

When you succeed in attaining your certification, feel free to e-mail me at hbenjamin@optusnet.com.au so I, too, can enjoy your success.

CHAPTER 1

Using This Book to Prepare for the CCIE Security Written Exam

Cisco Systems offers many different varieties and levels of career certifications, including the three current CCIE certification tracks. This book helps prepare you for the written exam (#350-018) for the CCIE Security certification.

The CCIE program has existed for almost 10 years. The relative complexity of the CCIE examinations prompted Cisco to introduce associate and professional levels of certification to provide candidates a way to progress through the various levels of certification. Though many of these lower levels of certification have prerequisites to go along with the written exams, CCIE certification does not have any prerequisites. To become a CCIE, you need to pass two exams: a written exam and a one-day lab exam.

NOTE   For details on Cisco career certifications, visit www.cisco.com/en/US/learning/le3/learning_career_certifications_and_learning_paths_home.html.

By introducing these lower-level certifications, Cisco has maintained the complexity of the CCIE examinations. Passing any CCIE examination by reading only one book is still difficult. Being adequately prepared requires plenty of on-the-job experience and intense study. This book helps you prepare for the CCIE Security written exam by making you aware of the material you will be tested on, by helping you identify where you have knowledge gaps, and by providing you with practice and study tools, such as the sample exam on the CD-ROM.

NOTE   Although this book's primary goal is to help you prepare for the CCIE Security written exam, you will find some supplemental material that can help you begin to prepare for the CCIE Security Lab exam, too. For example, Chapter 9, "CCIE Security Self-Study Lab," includes a sample CCIE Security Lab written by qualified CCIE proctors.

The remainder of this chapter covers how you can use this book to prepare for the CCIE Security written exam. The next section covers some basic information about the exam, including a listing of the exam topics.

CCIE Security Certification

At this stage, you have decided to pursue CCIE Security certification, which requires you to pass a two-hour, 100-question, written qualification exam (#350-018) and a one-day lab.

NOTE   In addition to the CCIE Security certification, there are CCIE certifications for Routing and Switching and for Communications and Services. For information on these other CCIE certifications, see www.cisco.com/en/US/learning/le3/le2/le23/learning_certification_level_home.html.

After you successfully complete the written examination, you can take the one-day lab. You must wait at least one month after passing the written test before sitting for the lab exam.

The written test is designed to be difficult so that potential CCIE candidates are fully prepared and aware of the difficulty level of the lab.

The Cisco CCIE certification website at www.cisco.com/en/US/learning/le3/le2/le23/learning_certification_level_home.html contains further details about all the CCIE certification paths and exams, and information on possible new tracks when Cisco decides to release them to the public.

CCIE Security Written Exam Blueprint

This section includes the entire CCIE Security written exam blueprint (exam objectives) from the Cisco website and indicates the corresponding chapters in this book that cover those objectives.

Table 1-1 lists the CCIE Security written exam blueprint and where you can find the material covered in this book. As you can see, the blueprint places the objectives into eight categories.

Table 1-1   *CCIE Security Written Exam Blueprint (Exam Objectives)*

Topic Number	Objective	Chapter Covering the Objective
Security Protocols		
1	Remote Authentication Dial-In User Service (RADIUS)	Chapter 5
2	Terminal Access Controller Access Control System Plus (TACACS+)	Chapter 5
3	Kerberos	Chapter 5

Table 1-1   *CCIE Security Written Exam Blueprint (Exam Objectives) (Continued)*

Topic Number	Objective	Chapter Covering the Objective
4	Virtual Private Dialup Networks (VPDN/Virtual Profiles)	Chapter 5
5	Data Encryption Standard (DES)	Chapter 5
6	Triple DES (DES3)	Chapter 5
7	IP Secure (IPSec)	Chapter 5
8	Internet Key Exchange (IKE)	Chapter 5
9	Certificate Enrollment Protocol (CEP)	Chapter 5
10	Point-to-Point Tunneling Protocol (PPTP)	Chapter 5
11	Layer 2 Tunneling Protocol (L2TP)	Chapter 5
Operating Systems		
12	UNIX	Chapter 6
13	Windows (NT/95/98/2000)	Chapter 6
Application Protocols		
14	Domain Name System (DNS)	Chapter 3
15	Trivial File Transfer Protocol (TFTP)	Chapter 3
16	File Transfer Protocol (FTP)	Chapter 3
17	Hypertext Transfer Protocol (HTTP)	Chapter 3
18	Secure Socket Layer (SSL)	Chapter 3
19	Simple Mail Transfer Protocol (SMTP)	Chapter 3
20	Network Time Protocol (NTP)	Chapter 3
21	Secure Shell (SSH)	Chapter 3
22	Lightweight Directory Access Protocol (LDAP)	Chapter 3
23	Active Directory	Chapter 3
General Networking		
24	Networking Basics	Chapter 2
25	TCP/IP	Chapter 2
26	Switching and Bridging (including: VLANs, Spanning Tree, etc.)	Chapter 2
27	Routed Protocols	Chapter 2
28	Routing Protocols (including: RIP, EIGRP, OSPF, BGP)	Chapter 2

continues

Table 1-1   *CCIE Security Written Exam Blueprint (Exam Objectives) (Continued)*

Topic Number	Objective	Chapter Covering the Objective
General Networking (Continued)		
29	Point-to-Point Protocol (PPP)	Chapter 2
30	IP Multicast	Chapter 2
31	Integrated Services Digital Network (ISDN)	Chapter 2
32	Async	Chapter 2
33	Access Devices (for example, Cisco AS 5300 series)	Chapter 2
Security Technologies		
34	Concepts	Chapter 7
35	Packet filtering	Chapter 7
36	Proxies	Chapter 7
37	Port Address Translation (PAT)	Chapter 7
38	Network Address Translation (NAT)	Chapter 7
39	Firewalls	Chapter 7
40	Active Audit	Chapter 7
41	Content filters	Chapter 7
42	Public Key Infrastructure (PKI)	Chapter 7
43	Authentication Technologies	Chapter 7
44	Virtual private networks (VPN)	Chapter 7
Cisco Security Applications		
45	Cisco Secure UNIX	Chapter 6
46	Cisco Secure NT	Chapter 6
47	Cisco Secure PIX Firewall	Chapter 7
48	Cisco Secure Policy Manager (formerly Cisco Security Manager)	Chapter 6
49	Cisco Secure Intrusion Detection System (formerly NetRanger)	Chapter 6
50	Cisco Secure Scanner (formerly NetSonar)	Chapter 6
51	IOS Firewall Feature Set	Chapter 7
Security General		
52	Policies	Chapter 8
53	Standards bodies	Chapter 8

Table 1-1   *CCIE Security Written Exam Blueprint (Exam Objectives) (Continued)*

Topic Number	Objective	Chapter Covering the Objective
54	Incident response teams	Chapter 8
55	Vulnerability Discussions	Chapter 8
56	Attacks and common exploits	Chapter 8
57	Intrusion detection	Chapter 8
Cisco General		
58	IOS specifics	Chapter 4

How to Prepare for the CCIE Security Written Exam Using This Book

This book provides several tools designed to prepare you for the CCIE Security written exam. Each chapter helps you evaluate your comprehension of the exam objectives from the blueprint (see Table 1-1). In addition, this book includes a CD-ROM with a bank of over 300 sample exam questions you can use to take practice exams. The CD-ROM contains a good mixture of easy and difficult questions to mimic the content and questions asked in the real examination.

NOTE   For more information about the CCIE Security exams and for general tips on how to prepare for the exams beyond just using this book, see Appendix B, "Study Tips for CCIE Security Examinations."

The chapters open by identifying the exam objectives covered in that chapter. You can begin by taking the "Do I Know This Already?" Quiz to immediately evaluate how familiar you are with a subject. Then, use the quiz instructions in each chapter to decide how much you need to study the subject. If you need to learn a lot, start with the "Foundation Topics" section, which goes into detail about the objectives covered in that chapter. If your quiz results demonstrate that you already have a strong grasp of the subject, you can skip to the "Foundation Summary," "Q & A," and "Scenarios" sections at the end of the chapter. Each of these elements includes detailed instructions on how to best use it to prepare for the exam.

This book covers all the objectives in the CCIE Security written exam blueprint, but no one book can teach you everything you need to know for a CCIE exam. Although you can use this book to identify and fill in knowledge gaps, you might encounter areas where you feel less prepared than others. Consider supplementing your learning in these areas with practical experience, specific books on the subject, or on CCO (Cisco Connection Online).

In addition to the chapters in this book, the accompanying CD-ROM provides tools that can help you prepare for the exam. The CD-ROM includes over 300 sample questions that you can explore in a few modes. You can work through the questions in study mode. Study mode allows you to link to an electronic version of the book when you want more information on the particular topic covered in the question. In study mode, you can choose the topics and number of questions you want to work through.

Practice exam mode allows you to take a simulated exam with a time limit and randomly selected questions. At the end of the exam, you receive a score and a categorical breakdown of your performance. Use these results to identify areas of strengths and weaknesses, so you can use this book and other resources to fill in any knowledge gaps.

Using this book is one of the best steps you can take toward achieving the most sought after certification in the IT industry. You need to rely on your extensive experience to pass the exam, but this book can make your preparation focused and efficient. Do not give up, and keep studying until you become certified. When you do pass, please e-mail me at hbenjamin@optushome.com.au so that I can hear of your achievement.

Exam Topics in This Chapter

CHAPTER 2

General Networking Topics

This chapter covers general networking concepts listed in the CCIE Security blueprint for the written exam. The CCIE blueprint lists some example topics that define general networking, including switching, TCP/IP, routed and routing protocols, PPP, ISDN, and asynchronous communications.

The CCIE Security written exam contains approximately 50 percent security questions and approximately 50 percent general networking questions. This chapter prepares you for the general networking questions. Although the CCIE Security written exam blueprint lists some specific networking topics, it does not, for example, mention Frame Relay, which might appear on the exam. This chapter covers many of the listed and a few of the unlisted general networking topics.

Although these topics are not extensively defined in the blueprint, the CCIE Security written exam might include topics taken from the CCIE Routing and Switching written exam blueprint. This chapter endeavors to cover all bases and provide quality test examples to ensure that you are well prepared to tackle the general networking questions you encounter in the examination.

This chapter covers the following topics:

- **Networking basics**—The OSI model, concepts, and functions. Topics include the seven layers of the OSI model and common examples (TCP/IP).

- **Switching and bridging**—The process today's networks use to switch packets and traditional bridging methods. Virtual LANs, spanning tree, and Ethernet Channel are discussed.

- **Routing IP**—The most widely used routed protocol in today's Internet, IP, and the routing protocols available on Cisco routers, such as RIP, EIGRP, OSPF, and BGP. IOS commands and configuration examples demonstrate the power of routing IP on Cisco routers.

- **PPP, ISDN, Frame Relay, IP Multicast, and Async**—Two of the most widely used dialup protocols are PPP and ISDN. Frame Relay is covered briefly to ensure that you have a good understanding of the common terminology used in today's networks. IP multicast and async protocols are also covered.

"Do I Know This Already?" Quiz

This assessment quiz will help you determine how to spend your limited study time. If you can answer most or all these questions, you might want to skim the "Foundation Topics" section and return to it later as necessary. Review the "Foundation Summary" section and answer the questions at the end of the chapter to ensure that you have a strong grasp of the material covered. If you already intend to read the entire chapter, you do not necessarily need to answer these questions now. If you find these assessment questions difficult, read through the entire "Foundation Topics" section and review it until you feel comfortable with your ability to answer all these and the "Q & A" questions at the end of the chapter.

Answers to these questions can be found in Appendix A, "Answers to Quiz Questions."

1 Which layer of the OSI model is responsible for converting frames into bits and bits into frames?

  a. Physical

  b. Network

  c. Transport

  d. LLC sublayer

  e. Data Link

2 Routing occurs at what layer of the OSI model?

  a. Physical

  b. Network

  c. Transport

  d. LLC sublayer

  e. Data link

3 Bridging occurs at what layer of the OSI model?

  a. Physical

  b. Network

  c. Transport

  d. Data link

4 Which of the following is *not* part of the OSI model?

  a. Network layer

  b. Physical layer

  c. Operational layer

  d. Application layer

5 IP operates at what layer of the OSI model?

   a. Layer 1

   b. Layer 2

   c. Layer 3

   d. Layer 4

   e. Layer 5

   f. Layer 6

   g. Layer 7

6 On which layer of the OSI model is data commonly referred to as segments?

   a. Layer 4

   b. Layer 3

   c. Layer 2

   d. Layer 1

7 On which layer of the OSI model is data commonly referred to as packets?

   a. Layer 1

   b. Layer 2

   c. Layer 4

   d. Layer 3

8 Which layer of the OSI model transmits raw bits?

   a. Layer 1

   b. Layer 2

   c. Layer 3

   d. Layer 4

9 Which of the following protocols is *not* routable?

   a. IP

   b. IPX

   c. NetBEUI

   d. NetBIOS

10 Which of the following is *not* a required step to enable FastEther Channel (FEC)?

    a. Ensure that all ports share the same speed at 10 Mbps.

    b. Ensure that all ports share the same parameter such as speed.

    c. Ensure that all ports operate at 100 Mbps.

    d. Only eight ports can be bundled into a logical link or trunk.

11 How is FastEther Channel best defined?

    a. A bundle of 10-Mbps ports on a switch

    b. Another name for half duplex 100 Mbps

    c. Not available on Cisco Catalyst switches

    d. The ability to bundle 100 Mbps ports into a logical link

    e. Only supported with Gigabit ports

12 On what OSI layer does bridging occur?

    a. Layer 1

    b. Layer 2

    c. Layer 3

    d. Both Layer 1 and 2

13 In spanning tree, what is a BPDU?

    a. A break protocol data unit

    b. A routable frame

    c. A bridge protocol data unit

    d. A frame sent out by end stations

14 An incoming frame on a Layer 2 switch is received on port 10/1 on a Catalyst 5000. If the destination address is known through port 10/2, what happens?

    a. The frame is discarded.

    b. The frame is sent via port 10/2.

    c. The frame is broadcast to all ports on the switch.

    d. The frame is sent back via 10/1.

    e. None of the above.

15 Which of the following are the four possible states of spanning tree?

  a. Listening, learning, blocking, broadcasting

  b. Listening, learning, blocking, connecting

  c. Discovering, learning, blocking, connecting

  d. Listening, learning, blocking, forwarding

16 How many bits make up an IP address?

  a. 64 bits

  b. 48 bits

  c. 32 bits

  d. 24 bits

  e. 8 bits

17 Identify the broadcast address for the subnet 131.108.1.0/24.

  a. 131.108.1.1

  b. 131.108.1.254

  c. 131.108.1.255

  d. 131.108.1.2

  e. More data required

18 Convert the following address to binary:

131.1.1.1/24

  a. 10000011.1.1.1

  b. 10000011.00000010.1.1

  c. 10000011.1.1.01010101

  d. 10000011.1.1.11111111

19 How many subnets are possible in VLSM if the Class C address 131.108.255.0 is used with the subnet mask 255.255.255.252 in the fourth octet field?

    a. None

    b. 100

    c. 255

    d. 254

    e. 253

    f. 252

    g. 64

    h. 62

20 How many hosts are available when a /26 subnet mask is used?

    a. 254

    b. 62

    c. 64

    d. 126

21 How many hosts are available in a Class C or /24 network?

    a. 255

    b. 254

    c. 253

    d. 0

    e. More data required

22 You require an IP network to support at most 62 hosts. What subnet mask will accomplish this requirement?

    a. 255.255.255.255

    b. 255.255.255.252

    c. 255.255.255.224

    d. 255.255.255.192

    e. 255.255.255.240

23 Which of the following are multicast addresses? (Choose all that apply.)

   a. 224.0.0.5

   b. 224.0.0.6

   c. 221.0.0.5

   d. 192.1.1.1

   e. 131.108.1.1

24 Which of the following routing protocols does *not* support VLSM?

   a. RIPv1

   b. RIPv2

   c. OSPF

   d. EIGRP

   e. BGP

25 What is the source TCP port number when a Telnet session is created by a PC to a Cisco router?

   a. 23

   b. Not a known variable

   c. 21

   d. 20

   e. 69

26 What best describes the ARP process?

   a. DNS resolution

   b. Mapping an IP address to a MAC address

   c. Mapping a next-hop address to outbound interface on a Cisco router

   d. Both a and b

27 If two Cisco routers are configured for HSRP and one router has a default priority of 100 and the other 99, which router assumes the role of active router?

   a. The default priority cannot be 100.

   b. The router with a higher priority.

   c. The router with the lowest priority.

   d. Neither router because Cisco routers do not support HSRP; only clients do.

28 A Cisco router has the following route table:

```
R1#show ip route
     131.108.0.0/16 is variably subnetted, 17 subnets, 2 masks
C       131.108.255.0/24 is directly connected, Serial0/0
C       131.108.250.0/24 is directly connected, Serial0/1
O       131.108.254.0/24 [110/391] via 131.108.255.6, 03:33:03, Serial0/1
                         [110/391] via 131.108.255.2, 03:33:03, Serial0/0
R       131.108.254.0/24 [120/1] via 131.108.255.6, 03:33:03, Serial0/1
                         [120/1] via 131.108.255.2, 03:33:03, Serial0/
```

What is the preferred path to 131.108.254.0/24? (Choose the best two answers.)

a. Via Serial 0/0

b. Via Serial 0/1

c. None

d. To null0

29 IP RIP runs over what TCP port number?

a. 23

b. 21

c. 69

d. 520

e. None of the above

30 IP RIP runs over what UDP port number?

a. 23

b. 21

c. 69

d. 520

31 An OSPF virtual link should _____.

a. Never be used

b. Allow nonpartitioned areas access to the backbone

c. Allow partitioned areas access to the backbone

d. Not be used in OSPF, but in ISDN

32 What is the BGP version most widely used today?

  a. 1

  b. 2

  c. 3

  d. 4

  e. 5

  f. 6

33 What is the destination port number used in a Telnet session?

  a. 23

  b. 69

  c. 21

  d. 161

34 In what fields does the IP checksum calculate the checksum value?

  a. Data only

  b. Header and data

  c. Header only

  d. Not used in an IP packet

35 The TCP header checksum ensures integrity of what data in the TCP segment?

  a. The data only.

  b. The header only.

  c. The data and header.

  d. There are no TCP header checksums; IP covers the calculation.

36 ISDN BRI channels are made up of what?

  a. 1×64 kbps channel and one D channel at 64 kbps

  b. 2×64 kbps channels and one D channel at 64 kbps

  c. 2×64 kbps channels and one D channel at 16 kbps

  d. 32×64 kbps channels and one D channel at 16 kbps

37 What services can ISDN carry?

   a. Data only

   b. Data and voice only

   c. Voice and video

   d. Data, voice, and video

38 Place the following steps in the correct order for PPP callback, as specified in RFC 1570.

   1. A PC user (client) connects to the Cisco access server.

   2. The Cisco IOS Software validates callback rules for this user/line and disconnects the caller for callback.

   3. PPP authentication is performed.

   4. Callback process is negotiated in the PPP link control protocol (LCP) phase.

   5. The Cisco Access Server dials the client.

   a. 1, 2, 3, 4, 5

   b. 1, 3, 2, 5, 4

   c. 1, 4, 5, 3, 2

   d. 5, 4, 3, 2, 1

39 What hardware port is typically designed to connect a Cisco router for modem access?

   a. The console port

   b. The vty lines

   c. The auxiliary port

   d. The power switch

   e. The Ethernet interface

40 The AS5300 series router can support which of the following incoming connections?

   a. Voice

   b. Dialup users via PSTN

   c. ISDN

   d. All the above

Foundation Topics

Networking Basics—The OSI Reference Model

This section covers the Open Systems Interconnection (OSI) seven layer model theory and common examples. CCIE candidates must fully understand and appreciate the model because almost every routed protocol in use today is based on the architecture of the seven layer model. The OSI model was developed by a standards body called the International Organization for Standardization (ISO) to provide software developers a standard architecture to develop protocols (such as IP). For example, the OSI model allows a PC to communicate with a UNIX device.

NOTE   ISO developed the OSI model in 1984. Layers 1 and 2 are implemented in hardware and Layers 3 through 7 are typically implemented in software.

Table 2-1 displays the seven layers of the OSI model.

Table 2-1   *The OSI Seven Layer Model*

Layer Name	Layer Number
Application	Layer 7
Presentation	Layer 6
Session	Layer 5
Transport	Layer 4
Network	Layer 3
Data Link	Layer 2
Physical	Layer 1

The following sections cover each layer and provide protocol examples for each.

Layer 1: The Physical Layer

The physical layer consists of standards that describe bit ordering, bit transmission rates, connector types, and electrical and other specifications. Information at Layer 1 is transmitted in binary (1s and 0s). For example, the letter A is transmitted as 00001010. Examples of physical layer standards include the following:

- RS-232
- V.24
- V.35
- RJ-45
- RJ-12

Layer 2: The Data Link Layer

The data link layer focuses on getting data reliably across any particular kind of link. Flow control and error notifications are also functions of the data link layer. The data link layer applies to all access methods, whether they are LAN or WAN methods. Information being processed at this layer is commonly known as frames.

The IEEE further complicated matters by subdividing the data link layer into to sublayers: the Logical Link Control (LLC) sublayer and the MAC sublayer.

Figure 2-1 displays the IEEE definition compared to the ISO definition.

Figure 2-1   *IEEE Sublayers Versus ISO Definitions*

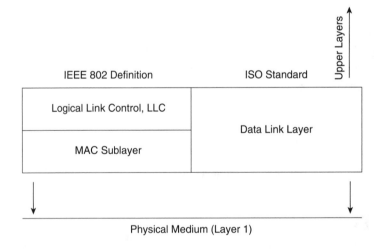

The LLC sublayer manages and ensures communication between end devices, and the Mac sublayer manages protocol access to the physical layer.

Examples of data link frame types include the following:

- ISDN
- SDLC
- HDLC
- PPP
- Frame Relay
- Ethernet Version II
- Spanning tree protocol
- NetBEUI

Layer 3: The Network Layer

The network layer determines the best path to a destination. Device addressing, packet fragmentation, and routing all occur at the network layer. Information being processed at this layer is commonly known as packets. Examples of network layer protocols include the following:

- Internet Protocol (IP)
- Open Shortest Path First (OSPF)
- Cisco's EIGRP routing protocol

Routing protocols (OSPF, EIGRP, and BGP, for example) provide the information required to determine the topology of the internetwork and the best path to a remote destination. A routed protocol is one that is transported by a routing protocol (such as RIP). For example, IP is a routed protocol that can be advertised by a number of routing algorithms, such as RIP, OSPF, and BGP.

NOTE   Connection-oriented and connectionless protocols are commonly used terms to describe Layer 3 and 4 (lower layers of the OSI model) protocols, such as IP or TCP.

A connection-oriented protocol, such as TCP, ensures delivery of all information, whereas a connectionless protocol, such as IP, only packages the data and sends it without guaranteeing delivery. Connection-oriented protocols exchange control information (also called Handshake) before transmitting data. A telephone call can be considered a connection-oriented service because the call is established before conversation can take place, much the same way that TCP sets up a data connection before data is sent. FTP is another example of a connection-oriented protocol. IP is an example of connectionless service.

Layer 4: The Transport Layer

The transport layer is responsible for segmenting upper-layer applications and establishing end-to-end connections between devices. Other transport layer functions include providing data reliability and error-free delivery mechanisms. Information being processed at this layer is commonly known as segments. Examples of transport layer protocols include the following:

- Transmission Control Protocol (TCP)
- Real-time transport protocol (RTP)
- User Datagram Protocol (UDP)

Layer 5: The Session Layer

The session layer performs several major functions, including managing sessions between devices and establishing and maintaining sessions. Examples of session layer protocols include the following:

- Database SQL
- NetBIOS Name Queries
- H.323 (Supports video as well; it is the packet switch voice standard)
- Real Time Control Protocol

Layer 6: The Presentation Layer

The presentation layer handles data formats and code formatting. The layer's functions are normally transparent to the end user because this layer takes care of code formats and presents them to the application layer (Layer 7), where the end user can examine the data. Examples of presentation layer protocols include the following:

- GIF
- JPEG
- ASCII
- MPEG
- TIFF
- MIDI
- HTML

Layer 7: The Application Layer

The application layer is closest to the end user, which means that the application will be accessed by the end user. This layer's major function is to provide services to end users. Examples of application layer services include the following:

- File Transfer Protocol (FTP)
- Telnet
- Ping
- Trace route
- SMTP
- Mail clients

TCP/IP and OSI Model Comparison

TCP/IP is the most widely used networking protocol and is often compared to the industry-defined OSI model.

Figure 2-2 displays the TCP/IP model in relation to the OSI model and where the protocol suite of TCP/IP lines up with the ISO standard. This comparison is provided to demonstrate that TCP/IP does not exactly conform to the OSI model. For example, the TCP/IP model has no Layer 5 or 6.

Figure 2-2   *OSI and TCP/IP Models*

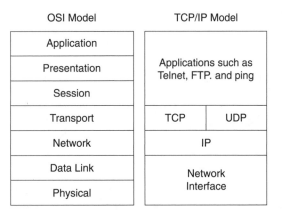

Example of Peer-to-Peer Communication

Each layer of the OSI or TCP model has its own functions and interacts with the layer above and below it. Furthermore, the communication between each layer's end devices also establishes peer-to-peer communication; this means that each layer of the OSI model communicates with the corresponding peer.

Consider the normal communication that occurs between two IP hosts over a wide-area network (WAN) running Frame Relay, as displayed in Figure 2-3.

Figure 2-3   *Peer-to-Peer Communication Example*

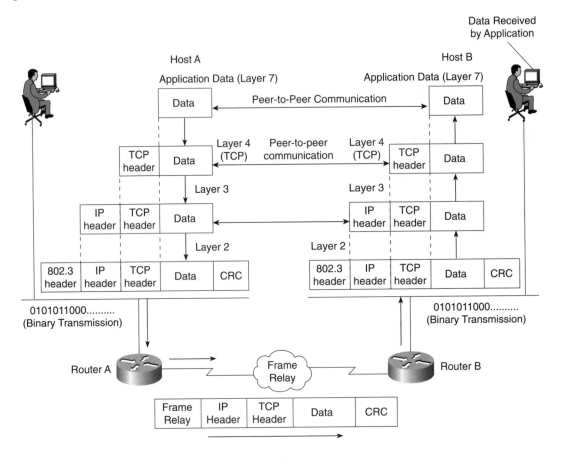

The data from one (Host A) is encapsulated inside a TCP header and passed down to Layer 3 (the IP layer) for address configuration, where an IP header is also added. Information included here is the source IP address and destination address. Layer 3 (the network layer) passes the data to the local router acting as the gateway via the Ethernet connection in raw binary.

Router A strips the 802.3 header and encapsulates the IP, TCP, and data in a Frame Relay packet for delivery over the WAN. A CRC is added here to ensure the packet is not corrupted over the WAN. Frame Relay is connectionless so, if an error occurs, it's up the to upper layers to retransmit; Frame Relay will not retransmit the packet. Similarly, HDLC (Layer 2 protocol) is connectionless and depends on upper layers to resubmit damaged data packets. PPP (connection-oriented), on the other hand, resubmits packets damaged in transmission over the WAN.

Router B receives the Layer 2 frames and strips the Frame Relay header/CRC and encapsulates the IP, TCP, and data frame back into an 802.2 header (with its own CRC; Ethernet checks only for errors and cannot repair them; once more, upper layers, such as TCP, ensure data delivery) for binary transmission across the Ethernet to Host B. The data is passed up the layers through IP, TCP, and finally to the application, where the application layer reads and acts upon the data.

The good news for security candidates is that Token Ring and legacy technologies are not covered in the written exam, so this chapter concentrates only on Ethernet switching. Before covering switching, the next section summarizes the evolution of Ethernet so that you are aware of the standards that have developed since Xerox first introduced Ethernet.

Ethernet Overview

Ethernet networks are based on a development made by Xerox, Digital, and Intel. The two versions of Ethernet are commonly referred to as Ethernet I and Ethernet II (or version 2).

Ethernet uses Carrier Sense Multiple Access Collision Detection (CSMA/CD) to transmit frames on the wire. In an Ethernet environment, all hosts can transmit as long as no other devices are transmitting. CSMA/CD is used to detect and warn other devices of any collisions, and colliding stations will use a back off algorithm and wait a random amount of time before trying again. Colliding devices send a jam signal to advise all stations that a collision has occurred. When a jam signal is sent (a jam signal is detected by all devices because the voltage is that of the combined colliding devices), all stations also stop transmitting. A device will attempt to transmit up to 16 times before a user is notified of the collisions; typically, an application error will inform the user that data could not be delivered. Microsoft's famous words are "Network is busy."

NOTE   The only time CSMA/CD is not used is in full-duplex connection because collisions are not possible when one pair of UTP is used to transmit and receive data. In other words, devices connected in full-duplex mode can send and receive data at the same time without the possibility of collision.

Table 2-2 lists some of the common Ethernet media specifications and the characteristics of each.

Table 2-2   *Ethernet Media Formats*

Media Type	Characteristics
10Base5	Maximum length: 500 m Maximum stations: 1024 Speed is 10 Mbps Minimum distance between devices is 2.5 m
10Base2	Maximum length: 185 m, using RG58 cable types and T connectors on all end stations Minimum distance between devices is 0.5 m Maximum devices per 185-m segment is 30 stations Speed is 10 Mbps
10BaseT	Based on UTP cabling Up to 100 m, better category cables longer One device per cable. Typically, only one device per segment with hubs or switches connecting all devices together Speed is 10 Mbps Physical topology star, logical topology bus
100BaseT	Same characteristics as 10BaseT but operates faster, at 100 Mbps Can be fibre, as well (100BaseFx); defined in IEEE 802.3U Physical topology star, logical topology bus
1000 GE	Gigabit Ethernet operating at 1000 Mbps Can run over fibre or UTP; frame formats and CSMA/CD identical to Ethernet standards Physical topology star, logical topology bus

*   The word BASE refers to Baseband signaling, which uses a single channel, as opposed to broadband, which uses multiple frequency channels.

Switching and Bridging

This sections covers Layer 2 devices that are used to bridge or switch frames using common techniques to improve network utilization, such as VLANs. The terms *switch* and *bridge* are used to mean the same technology.

Switching, or bridging, is defined as a process of taking an incoming frame from one interface and delivering it through another interface. Source stations are discovered and placed in a switch address table (called content-addressable memory [CAM] table in Cisco terms). Routers use Layer 3 switching to route a packet, and Layer 2 switches use Layer 2 switching to forward frames.

Switches build CAM tables when activity is noted on switch ports. Example 2-1 displays a sample CAM table on a Cisco Catalyst 5000 switch.

Example 2-1   *CAM Table or Bridge Table*

```
CAT5513 (enable) show cam ?
Usage: show cam [count] <dynamic|static|permanent|system> [vlan]
       show cam <dynamic|static|permanent|system> <mod_num/port_num>
       show cam <mac_addr> [vlan]
       show cam agingtime
       show cam mlsrp <ip_addr> [vlan]
CAT5513 (enable) show cam dynamic
* = Static Entry. + = Permanent Entry. # = System Entry. R = Router Entry. X = P
ort Security Entry


VLAN   Dest MAC/Route Des   Destination Ports or VCs / [Protocol Type]
----   ------------------   ------------------------------------------------------
36     00-10-7b-54-37-c6    8/13 [ALL]
35     00-09-43-3b-ac-20    8/5 [ALL]
101    00-01-02-00-4a-ff    1/1 [ALL]
1      00-01-02-00-4a-ff    1/1 [ALL]
102    00-03-e3-5e-ac-81    1/1 [ALL]
101    00-00-0c-92-0c-af    1/1 [ALL]
102    00-03-e3-53-7f-81    1/1 [ALL]
102    00-03-e3-5e-ae-c1    1/1 [ALL]
37     00-03-e3-63-55-80    8/9 [ALL]
102    00-03-e3-5e-a9-01    1/1 [ALL]
```

Example 2-1 displays a CAM table on a Catalyst switch with the CatOS command **show cam dynamic**. You can use other CatOS commands to view specific ports (**show cam dynamic 8/13** would show only devices discovered on port 8/13). Example 2-1 displays that the MAC address 01-10-7b-54-37-c6 is located via the port 8/13.

A Cisco switch populates the CAM tables as new devices send frames, so a switch bases all bridging decisions on source MAC address. When a device first sends a frame to a connected port on a switch, the switch adds the incoming source address to the CAM table. Any broadcasts received because the switch has no CAM entry are sent out all ports except the port the frame was received on. The switch then adds the source MAC address on the source port. Frames that are received as broadcasts are sent out all ports active in spanning tree.

NOTE   Transparent bridges can operate in two traditional modes. *Cut through switching* occurs when, after the destination MAC address is received, the switch immediately forwards the frame to the outgoing port. If a switch in cut through mode encounters a large number of frames with CRCs, the switch will drop down to store and forward mode. This technique is known as *adaptive cut-through*. *Store and forward switching* occurs when the entire frame is received before forwarding the frame. The CRC is checked to ensure that frames containing errors or CRCs are not forwarded. Cut-through switching is faster but the switch could potentially forward frames with errors because the CRC is not checked. The default mode is typically store and forward on Cisco switches. Routers can also be configured to bridge packets. The most common form of switch is adaptive cut-through.

Spanning tree is a Layer 2 protocol used to ensure a loop-free topology. A layer 2 loop is devastating to a network, as a frame will circulate the entire broadcast domain until all the switches eventually run out of memory because of the intensive broadcast storm that occurs. Broadcasts must be forwarded to all ports except the source port.

NOTE   A broadcast domain is defined as a group of all devices that receive broadcast frames originating from any device within the group. Broadcast domains are typically bound by routers because routers do not forward broadcast frames. Switches, on the other hand, must forward all broadcasts out all ports except the port the frame was received from.

Spanning tree is used when there are multiple LAN segments or virtual LANs (VLANs). A VLAN is a defined group of devices on one or more LANs that are configured (using management software, such as Catalyst switch code or CatOS) to communicate as if they were attached to the same wire when, in fact, they are located on a number of different LAN segments. VLANs are based on logical instead of physical connections and must be connected to a Layer 3 device, such as a router, to allow communication between all segments. To create a VLAN on a Catalyst switch, the CatOS command is **set vlan** *vlan id*. The *vlan id* is a number between 2 and 1005. By default, Cisco switches have vlan 1 already configured and cannot be removed for management purposes because protocols such as CDP and spanning tree will be active. You can disable CDP and spanning tree (not recommended in large switches networks).

Spanning tree is on by default on all Catalyst switches, and before data can be received or sent on any given port, Spanning tree protocol (STP) will go through a root bridge election phase. A root bridge election takes into account the bridge priority (value between 0 and 65535, default is 32768, and lower is better). If that value is equal in a segment with multiple bridges, the lowest MAC address associated with the bridge is elected as the root bridge.

| NOTE | Bridges communicate using frames called Bridge Protocol Data Units (BPDUs). BPDUs are sent out all ports not in a blocking state. A root bridge has all ports in a forwarding state. To ensure a loop-free topology, nonroot bridges block any paths to the root that are not required. BPDUs use the destination MAC address 01-08-C2-00-00-00 in Ethernet environments. |

Bridge Port States

Every bridge and associated port is in one of the following spanning tree states:

- **Disabled**—The port is not participating in spanning tree and is not active.
- **Listening**—The port has received data from the interface and will listen for frames. In this state, the bridge receives only data and does not forward any frames to the interface or to other ports.
- **Learning**—In this state, the bridge still discards incoming frames. The source address associated with the port is added to the CAM table. BPDUs are sent and received.
- **Forwarding**—The port is fully operational; frames are sent and received.
- **Blocking**—The port has been through the learning and listening states, and because this particular port is a dual path to the root bridge, the port is blocked to maintain a loop-free topology.

There are occasions when you do not want spanning tree to go through the steps mentioned above (listening, learning, and forward/blocking, which can take up to 45 seconds) but to immediately enter a forwarding state. For example, a PC with a fast processor connected to a switch does not need to test for any BPDUs (PCs do not run spanning tree), and the port on the Ethernet switch should enter a forwarding state to allow the PC immediate connectivity. This feature is known as *portfast* on Cisco switches. To enable portfast, use the Catalyst command **set spantree** *<spantree number>* **portfast** *<interface>* **enable**.

| NOTE | Concurrent Routing and Bridging/Integrated Routing and Bridging, Routing Information Fields, Source Route Bridging, and Source Route Translation Bridging are not covered in the CCIE Security written exam, and they are not part of the blueprint. |

FastEther Channel

FastEther Channel (FEC) is a Cisco method that bundles 100 Mbps FAST ETHERNET ports into a logical link. Because any redundant paths between two switches mean some ports will be in a blocking state and bandwidth will be reduced, Cisco developed FEC to maximize bandwidth use.

Figure 2-4 displays a switched network with two 100-Mbps connections between them. Because of STP, the link will be in a blocking state after the election of a root bridge, Switch A, in this case. Switch B will block one of the paths to ensure only one path (Switch A) to the root bridge. To purchase and enable a Fast Ethernet port is expensive, and to have it sitting in an idle position means wasted resources, so Cisco developed a method where Fast Ethernet ports could be bundled together and used concurrently (in other words, cheating spanning tree into believing that the two ports are one to send data from Switch A to Switch B with two 100-Mbps links instead of one).

Figure 2-4 *Spanning Tree Loop Avoidance*

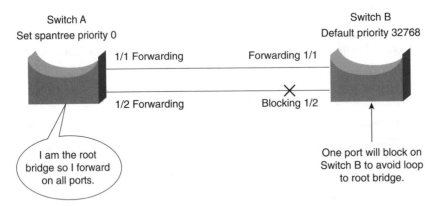

To enable FastEther Channel, the following steps are required:

Step 1 All ports that are part of FEC must be set to the same speed.

Step 2 All ports must belong to the same VLAN.

Step 3 Duplex must be the same, half or full, not a mixture.

Step 4 Bundle up to eight ports together.

Step 5 To set FastEther channel on a switch, the CatOS syntax is **set port channel**.

Step 6 To set FastEther Channel on a router, the IOS syntax is **channel-group** under the Fast Ethernet interface.

Step 7 You are allowed up to four FEC groups per switch. This could change with future Catalyst releases.

NOTE	A group of bundled ports running FEC is commonly known as a *trunk*. In switching terms, a trunk is a physical and logical connection between two switches.
	Inter-Switch Link (ISL) is a Cisco proprietary protocol that maintains VLAN information as traffic flows between switches and routers. ISL allows members of one VLAN to be located on any given switch. 802.1Q is an IEEE standard for trunking. You can use IEEE 802.1q in a multivendor environment.

Figure 2-5 displays the logical link when FEC is enabled between Switch A and Switch B.

Figure 2-5   *FEC: Logical Link or Trunk-Enabled*

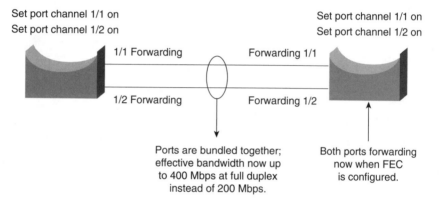

Internet Protocol

Internet Protocol (IP) is a widely used networking term that describes a network layer protocol that logically defines a distinct host or end system, such as a PC or router, with an IP address.

An IP address is configured on end systems to allow communication between hosts over wide geographic locations. An IP address is 32 bits in length, with the network mask or subnet mask (also 32 bits in length) defining the host and subnet portion.

Figure 2-6 displays the IP packet header frame format in detail.

Figure 2-6 *IP Frame Format*

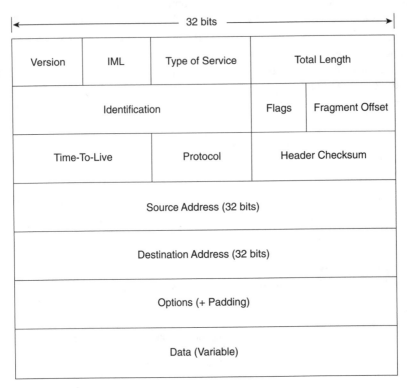

The following describes the IP packet fields illustrated in Figure 2-6:

- **Version**—Indicates the version of IP currently used. IPv4 is the most widely used version. IPv6 is also available. This version is not tested in the CCIE Security written exam yet, but will most likely be included in the future.

- **IP Header Length (IHL)**—Indicates the datagram header length in 32-bit words.

- **Type-of-Service (ToS)**—Specifies how an upper-layer protocol wants current datagrams to be handled and assigns datagrams various levels of importance. The ToS field (8 bits) defines the first 3 bits for precedence, of which there are eight possible values:

  — 000—Routine delivery

  — 001—Priority

  — 010—Immediate

  — 011—Flash

  — 100—Flash override

- 101—Critic

- 110—Internetwork control

- 111—Network control

Typically, IP packets are set with the value 000. The remaining 5 bits in the ToS are defined as follows:

- Bit 3—D bit defines normal or low delay.

- Bit 4—T bit defines normal or low throughput.

- Bit 5—R bit defines normal or low reliability.

- Bits 6 and 7—Not in current use.

- **Total Length**—Specifies the entire packet's length in bytes, including the data and header. The mathematically defined limit is calculated as 65,535 bytes (2^{16}–1).

- **Identification**—Contains an integer that identifies the current datagram. This field helps piece together datagram fragments (16 bits in length).

- **Flags**—Consists of a 3-bit field of which the two low-order (least-significant) bits control fragmentation. The low-order bit specifies whether the packet can be fragmented. The middle bit specifies whether the packet is the last fragment in a series of fragmented packets. The third, or high-order, bit is not used.

- **Fragment Offset**—Indicates the position of the fragment's data relative to the beginning of the data in the original datagram, which allows the destination IP process to properly reconstruct the original datagram.

- **Time-to-Live**—Maintains a counter that gradually decrements to 0, at which point the datagram is discarded. This keeps packets from looping endlessly. Cisco's implementation of the Cisco IOS Trace command works on TTL.

- **Protocol**—Indicates which upper-layer protocol receives incoming packets after IP processing is complete. For TCP, this value is 6; for GRE, it is 47; for ICMP, it is 1; and for OSPF, the value is 89; these are common uses in today's networks.

- **Header Checksum**—Helps ensure IP header integrity only and not the data field.

- **Source Address**—Specifies the sending node (32 bits).

- **Destination Address**—Specifies the receiving node (32 bits).

- **Options**—Allows IP to support various options, such as security. The Option field varies in length. Some options are Security, Loose Source Routing, Strict Source Routing, Record Route, and Timestamp.

- **Data**—Contains upper-layer information.

NOTE	A subnet is a network that is segmented by network administrators, allowing a hierarchical routing topology. Subnetting allows great use of IP address space using binary bits from the subnet mask. Examples of subnets appear later in this chapter. Routing allows communication between these subnets. The host address is a logical, unique address that resides on a subnet.

The Internet Engineering Task Force (IETF) standards body, which is a task force consisting of over 80 working groups responsible for developing Internet standards, has defined five address classes and the appropriate address ranges. Table 2-3 displays the five ranges.

Table 2-3   *Class A, B, C, D, and E Ranges*

Class of Address	Starting Bit Pattern	Range	Default Subnet Mask
Class A	0xxxxxxx	1-126, 127*	255.0.0.0
Class B	10xxxxxx	128-191	255.255.0.0
Class C	110xxxxx	192-223	255.255.255.0
Class D	1110xxxx	224-239	255.255.255.240
Class E	1111xxxx	240-255	Reserved

*   127.0.0.0 is reserved for loopback purposes. Other reserved addresses for private use as defined by RFC 1918 are as follows:
10.0.0.0-10.255.255.255
172.16.0.0-172.31.255.255
192.168.0.0-192.168.255.255

Soon after these ranges were defined and the Internet's popularity extended beyond the Department of Defense in the United States, it became clear that to ensure that a larger community could connect to the World Wide Web, there had to be a way to extend IP address space using subnetting. Subnetting allows an administrator to extend the boundary for any given subnet.

To understand an IP address and subnet portion, to determine how many hosts are available on a particular subnet, to learn how to best utilize an IP address space, consider the following example.

Suppose you are given the IP address 131.108.1.56 and the subnet mask is 255.255.255.0. This example will help you determine the subnet, how many hosts can reside on this subnet, and the broadcast address.

You can deduce the subnet for any IP address by performing a logical AND operation for the IP address along with the subnet mask.

NOTE A logical AND operation follows two basic rules. One is that positive and positive equal positive, and the second is that negative and either positive or negative equal negative. In binary (positive is 1 and negative is 0), 0 AND 0 is 0, 0 AND 1 is 0, 1 AND 1 is 1, and 1 AND 0 is 0.

Figure 2-7 displays the logical AND operation used to determine the subnet address.

Figure 2-7 *Logical AND Operation*

```
IP Address (131.108.1.56)        10000011.11001100.00000001.00111000
IP Subnet Mask (255.255.255.0)   11111111.11111111.11111111.00000000
Logical AND                      10000011.11001100.00000001.00000000
In Decimal                          131       108      1         0
```

The result of the logical AND operation reveals that the subnet address is 131.108.1.0. The subnet address is reserved and cannot be assigned to end devices.

To determine the number of hosts available in any given subnet, simply apply the formula 2^n-2, where n is the number of borrowed bits. This is best explained with examples. To determine the number of borrowed bits, you must examine the subnet mask in binary. For a default Class C network mask of 255.255.255.0, the last 8 bits represent the borrowed bits. For a Class C network, the number of hosts that can reside are $2^8-2 = 256-2 = 254$ hosts. You subtract 2 host addresses because host devices are not permitted to use the subnet address or the broadcast address. In IP, a broadcast address consists of all binary 1s. So, for this example, the broadcast address for the subnet 131.108.1.0 is 131.108.1.255 (255 in binary is 11111111).

Consider another example. Given the host address 171.224.10.67 and the subnet mask of 255.255.255.224, this example shows you how to determine the subnet and the number of hosts that can reside on this network.

To determine the subnet, perform a logical AND. Figure 2-8 displays the operation.

Figure 2-8 *LOGICAL AND Operation*

```
IP Address (171.224.10.67)         10101011. 11100000. 00001010. 01000011
IP Subnet Mask (255.255.255.224)   11111111. 11111111. 11111111. 11100000
Logical AND                        10101011. 11100000. 00001010. 01000000
In Decimal                            171       224       10        64
```

The subnet is 171.224.10.64. The number of hosts that can reside on this network with a subnet mask of 255.255.255.224 (or 11100000, 5 borrow bits) is $2^5-2 = 32-2 = 30$ hosts. You can apply this simple example to any Class A, B, or C address, and applying a subnet mask that is not the default or classful kind allows network administrators to extend IP address space and allow a larger number of devices to connect to the IP network.

Table 2-4 displays some common network subnets and the number of hosts available on those subnets.

Table 2-4 *Common Subnets in Today's Networks*

Decimal	Subnets	Hosts
252 (1111 1100)	64 subnets	2 hosts*
248 (1111 1000)	32 subnets	6 hosts
240 (1111 0000)	16 subnets	14 hosts
224 (1110 0000)	8 subnets	30 hosts
192 (1100 0000)	4 subnets	62 hosts
128 (1000 0000)	2 subnets	126 hosts

*Used commonly for point to point -ad WAN circuits when no more than two hosts reside.

Variable-Length Subnet Masks

A variable-length subnet mask (VLSM) is designed to allow greater use of IP address space by borrowing bits from the subnet mask and allocating them to host devices. To allow a greater number of devices to connect to the Internet and intranets, the standards body of various routing protocols designed an IP routing algorithm to cater to IP networks with a different subnet mask than the default used in classful networks.

NOTE   Routing algorithms that support VLSM are as follows:

- RIP Version 2

- OSPF

- IS-IS

- EIGRP

- BGP4

Additionally, Cisco IOS allows the use of any 0 subnets (for example, subnet 131.108.0.0/24) with the global IOS command, **ip subnet-zero**. This can be very useful for networks running out of IP address space.

To effectively use any IP address space, use the least number of subnet bits and least number of host bits. You could use a Class C mask or a mask that allows for 254 hosts. For a WAN link that will never use more than two hosts, this is a vast amount of wasted space. Applying different masks to cater to the exact requirement means that IP address space is not wasted unnecessarily.

Apply the formula to determine the best subnet to use to cater to two hosts on any given subnet and class of address. Remember that you must subtract two host addresses for the subnet address and broadcast address.

Applying the formula, you get $2^n - 2 = 2$, or $2^n = 4$, or $n = 2$ borrowed bits. You need to borrow only 2 bits from the subnet mask to allow for 2 host addresses. The subnet mask is 30 bits in length, or 255.255.255.252 in binary. This is represented as 11111111.11111111.11111111.111111100. The last 2 bits (00) are available for host addresses. The subnet is 00, the first host address is 01, the second is 10, and the broadcast address is 11.

TIP   Loopback interfaces configured on Cisco routers are typically configured with a host address using a 32-bit subnet mask. This allows, for example, a Class C network with 255 hosts among 255 different routers and conserves valuable IP address space.

Classless Interdomain Routing

Classless interdomain routing (CIDR) is a technique supported by BGP4 and based on route aggregation. CIDR allows routers to group routes together to reduce the quantity of routing information carried by the core routers. With CIDR, several IP networks appear to networks outside the group as a single, larger entity. With CIDR, IP addresses and their subnet masks are written as four octets, separated by periods, and followed by a forward slash and a two-digit number that represents the subnet mask. CIDR representation can be either a forward slash with a one-digit number or a forward slash with a two-digit number (for example, 131.108.1/24 or 131.0.0.0/8).

In the past few years, the expansion of the Internet has been phenomenal. Currently, the Internet uses more than 100,000 routes. From 1994 through 1996, the routing table increased from approximately 20,000 entries to more than 42,000. Currently, there are over 80,000 IP routing entries. How can network administrators reduce the large routing table size? Each routing entry requires memory and a table lookup by the router each time a packet is required to reach a destination. Reducing memory requirements and the time it takes to send a packet to the destination provides faster response times for packets to travel around the Internet.

CIDR helps to reduce the number of routing table entries and memory requirements. CIDR helps conserve resources because it removes the limitation of using the default mask (which wastes IP address space) and leaves the addressing up to the IP designer. Routers use CIDR to group networks together to reduce routing table size and memory requirements. CIDR is typically represented with the network number/bits used in the mask, such as 131.108.1.0/24, or the equivalent of 131.108.1.0 255.255.255.0. BGP and classless routing protocols use CIDR to reduce routing table entries, allowing faster lookup and less memory requirement on Cisco routers, for example.

Classful and Classless Routing Protocols

Routing protocols can also be classed or described as classful and classless.

Classful addressing, namely Classes A, B, and C (Class D is reserved for multicasts and Class E is reserved for future use), defines a set number of binary bits for the subnet portion. For example, a Class A network ranges from 1 to 127 and uses a subnet mask of 255.0.0.0. A Class B network uses the mask 255.255.0.0, and a Class C uses 255.255.255.0. Classful routing protocols apply the same rules. If a router is configured with a Class A address of 10.1.1.0, the default mask of 255.0.0.0 is applied, and so forth. This routing method does not scale well, so to design networks to better utilize address space, you have classless routing, which enables the network designer to apply different masks to Class A, B, and C networks to better utilize address space. For example, you can use a Class B network, such as 131.108.0.0, and apply a Class C mask (255.255.255.0 or /24 mask).

Classful routing protocol examples include RIP and IGRP. Examples of classless routing protocols are OSPF, IS-IS, EIGRP, and BGP. With classless routing, the ability to apply summarization techniques allows for a reduction in routing table size. Over 100,000 IP routing table entries exist on the Internet. Reducing the IP route table size allows for faster delivery of IP packets and lower memory requirements. BGP is commonly referred to as a path vector protocol. To accomplish CIDR, you must allocate subnets at the common bit boundary, ensuring that your networks are continuous. For example, allocating 131.108.0.0/22 in one location and 131.108.1.0/24 to another will result is a discontinuous allocation and will not allocate CIDR to work properly.

Transmission Control Protocol

Transmission Control Protocol (TCP) is the most widely used protocol today, and all Cisco certification exams will test your understanding of TCP/IP. This section covers TCP and how this connection-oriented protocol ensures efficient delivery of data across an IP network.

The TCP/IP model actually does not fully conform to the OSI model because IP was developed by the Department of Defense in the 1980s.

IP provides each host device with a 32-bit host address that is used to route across the IP network. TCP is a Layer 4 protocol that ensures data is delivered across any IP cloud by using mechanisms such as connection startup, flow control, slow start (a congestion avoidance scheme in TCP in which a host can increase the window size upon arrival of an acknowledgment), and acknowledgments. UDP is the connectionless protocol for applications such as a TFTP transfer.

TCP Mechanisms

Figure 2-9 displays the TCP header format.

Figure 2-9   *TCP Header Format*

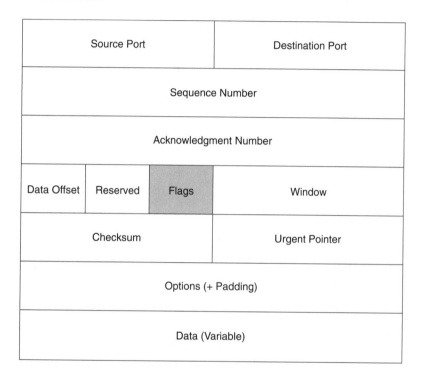

The following descriptions summarize the TCP packet fields illustrated in Figure 2-9:

- **Source Port and Destination Port**—Identifies points at which upper-layer source and destination processes receive TCP services (16 bits in length). Common destination ports include 23 for Telnet, 21 for FTP, and 20 for FTP data.

- **Sequence Number**—Usually specifies the number assigned to the first byte of data in the current message. In the connection-establishment phase, this field can also identify an initial sequence number to be used in an upcoming transmission.

- **Acknowledgment Number**—Contains the sequence number of the next byte of data that the sender of the packet expects to receive.

- **Data Offset**—Indicates the number of 32-bit words in the TCP header.

- **Reserved**—Remains reserved for future use.

- **Flags**—Carries a variety of control information, including the SYN and ACK bits used for connection establishment, and the FIN bit used for connection termination.

- **Window**—Specifies the size of the sender's receive window (that is, the buffer space available for incoming data).
- **Checksum**—Indicates whether the header was damaged in transit.
- **Urgent Pointer**—Points to the first urgent data byte in the packet.
- **Options**—Specifies various TCP options.
- **Data**—Contains upper-layer information.

A number of mechanisms are used by TCP to ensure the reliable delivery of data, including the following:

- Flags
- Acknowledgments
- Sequences numbering
- Checksum
- Windowing

NOTE   The Flags field is critical in a TCP segment. The field's various options include the following:

- **URG (U) (Urgent)**—Informs the other station that urgent data is being carried. The receiver will decide what to do with the data.

- **ACK (A) (Acknowledge)**—Indicates that the packet is an acknowledgment of received data, and the acknowledgment number is valid.

- **PSH (P) (Push)**—Informs the end station to send data to the application layer immediately.

- **RST (R) (Reset)**—Resets an existing connection.

- **SYN (S) (Synchronize)**—Initiates a connection, commonly known as *established*.

- **FIN (F) (Finished)**—Indicates that the sender is finished sending data and terminates the session.

To best describe how TCP is set up and established, consider a Telnet request from a PC to a Cisco router and follow the flags, acknowledgments, sequence, and windowing options.

Figure 2-10 displays a typical Telnet session between a PC and a Cisco router. The PC initializes a Telnet request using destination port 23 and an initial sequence number.

Figure 2-10 *Telnet (TCP) Packet Flow*

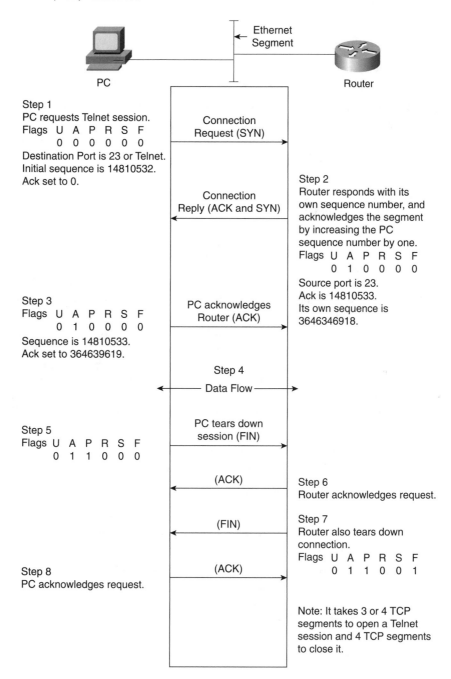

Ethernet
Segment

PC

Router

Step 1
PC requests Telnet session.
Flags U A P R S F
       0 0 0 0 0 0
Destination Port is 23 or Telnet.
Initial sequence is 14810532.
Ack set to 0.

Connection
Request (SYN)

Connection
Reply (ACK and SYN)

Step 2
Router responds with its
own sequence number, and
acknowledges the segment
by increasing the PC
sequence number by one.
Flags U A P R S F
      0 1 0 0 0 0
Source port is 23.
Ack is 14810533.
Its own sequence is
3646346918.

Step 3
Flags U A P R S F
       0 1 0 0 0 0
Sequence is 14810533.
Ack set to 364639619.

PC acknowledges
Router (ACK)

Step 4
Data Flow

Step 5
Flags U A P R S F
      0 1 1 0 0 0

PC tears down
session (FIN)

(ACK)

Step 6
Router acknowledges request.

(FIN)

Step 7
Router also tears down
connection.
Flags U A P R S F
       0 1 1 0 0 1

Step 8
PC acknowledges request.

(ACK)

Note: It takes 3 or 4 TCP
segments to open a Telnet
session and 4 TCP segments
to close it.

The following steps are then taken by TCP:

Step 1 A user on the PC initiates a Telnet session to the router.

The PC sends a request with the SYN bit sent to 1.

The destination port number is 23 (Telnet). The PC will also place an initial sequence number (in this case, random number 14810532) in the segment.

Step 2 The router responds with its own sequence number (such as, 3646349618) and acknowledges (ACK) the segment sent by the PC. The ACK will be the next expected sequence number generated by the PC; in this example, the ACK is numbered 14810533.

Step 3 The PC sends a segment that acknowledges (ACK) the router's reply. The first three steps are commonly known as the *TCP three-way handshake*. It is possible for four packets to start a session if a parameter needs to be negotiated.

Step 4 Data is transferred. The window size can be adjusted according to the PC or the router. The windows size, for example, might be four packets before an acknowledgment is required. The sender waits for an acknowledgment before sending the next four segments. The window size can change during a data transfer; this is commonly known as the *sliding window*. If, for example, a lot of bandwidth is available, the sender might resize the window to eight segments. Or the sender might resize the window to two segments during periods of high congestion. The ACK (acknowledge) sent by the receiver is the next expected segment. This indicates that all previous segments have been received and reassembled. If any segment is lost during this phase, TCP can renegotiate the time waited before receiving the ACK and resend any lost segments.

Step 5 After the PC completes the data transfer, the Telnet session is closed by sending a TCP segment with the FIN flag set to 1.

Step 6 The router acknowledges (ACK) the request.

Step 7 At this stage, the session is still open and the router could send data (this is known as *TCP half close*), but the router has no data to send and usually sends a segment with the FIN bit set to 1.

Step 8 The PC acknowledges the router's FIN request, and the Telnet session is closed. At any stage, the session can be terminated if either host sends a reset (RST flags in the TCP header); in this case, the session must be reestablished from scratch.

<table>
<tr><td>**NOTE**</td><td>You need to know the TCP process and how packets are sequenced and acknowledged. TCP acknowledgments specify the next expected segment from a sender. A TCP session requires three or four segments to start (known as three-way handshake) and four segments to shut down.</td></tr>
</table>

TCP Services

This section covers common TCP services or applications used in today's large IP networks:

- Address Resolution Protocol (ARP)
- Reverse Address Resolution Protocol (RARP)
- Dynamic Host Configuration Protocol (DHCP)
- Hot Standby Router Protocol (HSRP)
- Internet Control Message Protocol (ICMP)
- Telnet
- File Transfer Protocol (FTP)
- Trivial File Transfer Protocol (TFTP)

Address Resolution Protocol (ARP)

ARP determines a host's MAC address when the IP address is known. For example, to ping one device from another, the Layer 2 MAC fields require a destination MAC address. Because this is the first such request, a broadcast packet is sent across the wire to discover the remote host's MAC address. Figure 2-11 displays a scenario where PC1 wants to ping Host PC2.

Figure 2-11 *ARP Request*

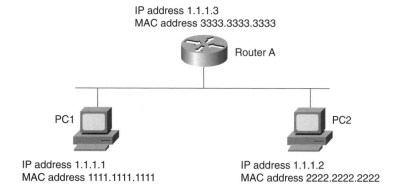

IP address 1.1.1.3
MAC address 3333.3333.3333

Router A

PC1

IP address 1.1.1.1
MAC address 1111.1111.1111

PC2

IP address 1.1.1.2
MAC address 2222.2222.2222

When PC1 sends a ping request to PC2 using the known IP address 1.1.1.2 (Layer 3), a broadcast Layer 2 frame is sent to the destination address FF-FF-FF-FF-FF-FF, and ARP (the ARP frame contains the source MAC address and the source IP address) is sent to all devices requesting the Layer 2 MAC address of the device configured with the IP address 1.1.1.2 (by sending a Layer 2 broadcast frame). PC2 responds to the ARP request with its source MAC address, 2222.2222.2222. PC1 now has PC2's MAC address and sends a packet to the destination address, 2222.2222.2222, and Layer 3 destination address, 1.1.1.2.

NOTE   A less common ARP term used in ARP terminology is a *gratuitous ARP*. A gratuitous ARP is an ARP request with its own IP address as the target address. It refreshes a device's ARP table entries and also looks up duplicate IP addresses. Routers are devices that can send a gratuitous ARP.

To view the IP ARP table on a Cisco router, the command is **show ip arp**. The IP ARP table from Figure 2-11 is displayed in Example 2-2.

Example 2-2 **show ip arp** *Command on Router A*

```
RouterA#show ip arp
Protocol  Address          Age (min)  Hardware Addr   Type   Interface
Internet  1.1.1.3                 -   3333.3333.3333  ARPA   Ethernet0
Internet  1.1.1.1               170   1111.1111.1111  ARPA   Ethernet0
Internet  1.1.1.2                94   2222.2222.2222  ARPA   Ethernet0
```

NOTE   If you've ever wondered why the first ping request on a Cisco router fails, it's because an ARP request is sent first when an entry is not present in the ARP table. Subsequent pings will have 100 percent success.

Reverse ARP

Reverse ARP (RARP) is when a device boots up without an IP address and requests an IP address. Reverse ARP is typically not used in today's networks, and is replaced by DHCP.

Dynamic Host Configuration Protocol

Dynamic Host Configuration Protocol (DHCP) is defined in RFC 1531 (latest RFC 2131) and provides a comprehensive method of allocating IP addresses, subnet mask, gateway address, DNS server, WINS servers, and many more parameters for IP devices.

DHCP clients send messages to the server on UDP 67, and servers send messages to the client on UDP 68. Cisco routers can also be configured for DHCP.

Example 2-3 configures a Cisco IOS router to allocate the entire range 131.108.1.0/24, with a gateway address 131.108.1.1, subnet mask 255.255.255.0, DNS servers 141.108.1.1 and 141.108.1.2, domain name cisco.com, and WINS (for Windows 2000 clients) server addresses 64.104.1.1 and 141.108.2.1. The lease should last forever, so the final command is **lease infinite**.

Example 2-3 *DHCP Configuration on Cisco IOS Router*

```
R1#sh running-config | begin dhcp
ip dhcp excluded-address 131.108.1.1

Interface Ethernet 0
ip address 131.108.1.1 255.255.255.0
!
ip dhcp pool DHCPpool
    network 131.108.1.0 255.255.255.0
    dns-server 141.108.1.1 141.108.1.2
    domain-name cisco.com
    default-router 148.16.36.6 148.16.36.3
    netbios-name-server 64.104.1.1 141.108.2.1
    lease infinite
```

To view the DHCP leases, use the IOS command **show ip dhcp server**. Example 2-4 displays the output taken from a router configured for DHCP.

Example 2-4 **show ip dhcp server** *Sample Display*

```
R1#show ip dhcp server
  DHCP server: ANY (255.255.255.255)
    Leases:    200
    Offers:    200      Requests: 400      Acks: 330      Naks: 230
    Declines:  0        Releases: 0        Bad:  0
```

Example 2-4 shows that 200 devices are currently allocated IP addresses, and over 400 requests were made.

Hot Standby Router Protocol

HSRP allows networks with more than one gateway to provide redundancy in case of interface or router failure on any given router.

HSRP allows router redundancy in a network. It is a Cisco proprietary solution from before the IETF defined Virtual Router Redundancy Protocol (VRRP). To illustrate HSRP, Figure 2-12 displays a six-router network with clients on segments on Ethernet networks, Sydney and San Jose.

Figure 2-12 *HSRP Example*

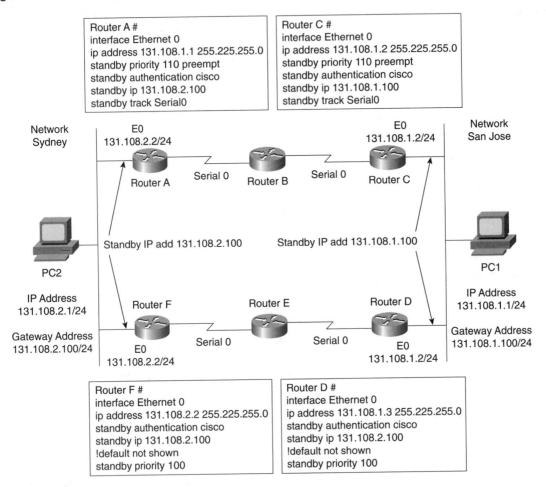

PCs are typically configured with only one gateway address. (Windows 2000/XP clients can take more than one but this still leaves a problem in that all devices must be configured for multiple gateways; the most scalable solution is to configure a single gateway on all devices and allow an intelligent network to provide redundancy where only a few devices require configuration.) Assume that PC1 is configured with a gateway address of 131.108.1.100. Two routers on the Ethernet share the segment labeled San Jose network. To take advantage of the two routers, HSRP will allow only Routers C and D to bid for a virtual IP address, and if any one router (Router C or D, in this example) fails, the operational router assumes the HSRP gateway address. Host devices typically have only a brief 100 to –200-millisecond interruption when a network failure occurs.

To illustrate how HSRP provides default gateway support, refer to Figure 2-12. In Figure 2-12, you can see a network with two local routers configured with an Ethernet interface address of 131.108.1.2/24 for Router C and 131.108.1.3/24 for Router D. Notice that both routers share a common Ethernet network. Assume that PC1 has been configured with a default gateway pointing to Router C. If Router C goes down or the Ethernet interface becomes faulty, all the devices must be manually reconfigured to use the second default gateway (Router D, 131.108.1.3/24). HSRP enables the network administrator to elect one of the two routers to act as the default gateway. If the elected router goes down, the second router assumes the IP default gateway. The IOS command **standby track** *interface-of-wan* under the Ethernet interface allows the router to monitor the WAN link. If the WAN link continuously fails past a threshold, the HSRP default router will decrease its priority to allow a more reliable WAN connection to provide a gateway. For example, in Figure 2-12, if the link between Routers C and B fails past a threshold, Router D can be configured to assume the HSRP address to provide a faster connection to the IP backbone network.

The steps to enable HSRP are as follows:

Step 1   Enable HSRP (required).

Step 2   Configure HSRP group attributes (optional).

Step 3   Change the HSRP MAC refresh interval (optional).

Table 2-5 illustrates the various required and optional commands to enable HSRP.

Table 2-5   *HSRP Commands*

IOS Command	Purpose
standby [*group-number*] **timers** [**msec**] *hellotime* [**msec**] *holdtime*	These required commands configure the time between hello packets and the hold time before other routers declare the active router to be down.
standby [*group-number*] **priority** *priority* [**preempt** [**delay** [**minimum** I **sync**] *delay*]] or **standby** [*group-number*] [**priority** *priority*] **preempt** [**delay** [**minimum** I **sync**] *delay*]	Sets the Hot Standby priority used in choosing the active router. The *priority* value range is from 1 to 255, where 1 denotes the lowest priority and 255 denotes the highest priority. Specifies that if the local router has priority over the current active router, the local router should attempt to take its place as the active router. Configures a preemption delay, after which the Hot Standby router preempts and becomes the active router. These commands are optional.

continues

Table 2-5 *HSRP Commands (Continued)*

IOS Command	Purpose
standby [*group-number*] **track** *type number* [*interface-priority*]	This optional command configures the interface to track other interfaces so that if one of the other interfaces goes down, the device's Hot Standby priority is lowered.
standby [*group-number*] **authentication** *string*	Selects an authentication string to be carried in all HSRP messages. Optional authenticator field allows only authenticated routers to offer HSRP.
standby use-bia [**scope interface**]	Configures HSRP to use the burned-in address of an interface as its virtual MAC address instead of the preassigned MAC address (on Ethernet and FDDI), or the functional address (on Token Ring).

Now configure Routers C and D in Figure 2-12 for HSRP, and ensure that Router C is the primary gateway address and that the PC is configured with a gateway address of 131.108.1.100. Router C is configured with a higher priority (standby priority 110 preempt) than the default 100 to ensure Router C becomes the default gateway for the hosts on the San Jose network; authentication is also enabled between the two gateway routers.

Example 2-5 displays the sample IOS configuration for Router C.

Example 2-5 *HSRP Configuration on Router C*

```
interface Ethernet0
 ip address 131.108.1.2 255.255.255.0
 standby priority 110 preempt
 standby authentication cisco
 standby ip 131.108.1.100
 standby track Serial0
```

Example 2-5 displays Router C configured with a virtual IP address of 131.108.1.100 and preempt, which allows Router C to assume the role if a failure occurs. The **track** command ensures that Serial0, or the WAN link to Router B, is monitored to make sure a flapping link does not cause bandwidth delays for users, such as PC1. For every tracked interface failure, the priority is reduced by 10 by default. The Cisco IOS default priority is set to 100. In this configuration, two failures must occur for Router D to assume the HSRP address (110–10–10=90<100).

Example 2-6 displays the sample IOS configuration for Router D. Configure Router D with an HSRP priority of 105 so that any one (1 not 2) failure on Router C will mean that Router D priority is higher than Router C. (Router C is set to 105; one failure and then it is set to 105–10=95<100.)

Example 2-6 *HSRP Configuration on Router D*

```
interface Ethernet0
 ip address 131.108.1.3 255.255.255.0
 standby authentication cisco
 standby ip 131.108.1.100
```

To view the status of HSRP, the IOS command is **show standby**. Example 2-7 displays the sample output when the IOS command **show standby** is entered in Router C.

Example 2-7 **show standby** *on Router C*

```
Router-C#show standby
Ethernet - Group 0
  Local state is Active, priority 105, may preempt
  Hellotime 3 holdtime 10
  Next hello sent in 00:00:01.967
  Hot standby IP address is 131.108.1.100 configured
  Active router is local
  Standby router is unknown expired
  Standby virtual mac address is 0000.0c07.ac00
  2 state changes, last state change 00:03:59
  Tracking interface states for 1 interface, 0 up:
    up Serial0
```

Router C is currently the configured gateway and is tracking Serial 0 for failures; every WAN failure decrements the priority value by 10. If a single failure occurs, the priority on Router C will drop to 95 (105–10=95), and Router D will immediately remain the default gateway until the interface on Router C has fully recovered. After the priority on Router C increments back to 105, Router C assumes the gateway function because preempt is enabled, as displayed in Example 2-54.

Example 2-8 displays the output of the **show standby** command on Router D.

Example 2-8 **show standby** *on Router D*

```
Router-D#show standby
Ethernet - Group 0
  Local state is Standby, priority 100,
  Hellotime 3 holdtime 10
  Next hello sent in 00:00:01.967
  Hot standby IP address is 131.108.1.100 configured
  Active router is local
  Standby router is unknown expired
  Standby virtual mac address is 0000.0c07.ac00
  2 state changes, last state change 00:03:59
```

Internet Control Message Protocol

Internet Control Message Protocol (ICMP) is a network layer (Layer 3) Internet protocol that reports errors and provides other information relevant to IP packet processing. ICMP is fully documented in RFC 792. ICMP's purpose is to report error and control messages.

ICMP provides a number of useful services supported by the TCP/IP protocol, including ping requests and replies. Ping requests and replies enable an administrator to test connectivity with a remote device.

Be aware that ICMP runs over IP, which means that there is no guarantee of delivery (because IP is a connectionless protocol). Example 2-9 provides a sample **ping** command in which an administrator wants to see if a remote device is reachable by sending the remote device a ping request from a Cisco router. By default, a Cisco router will send out a series of five ICMP requests whenever the **ping** command is issued. Example 2-9 displays a sample ping request to the remote IP address 131.108.1.1 on Router R2.

Example 2-9   **ping 131.108.1.1** *R2>ping 131.108.1.1*

```
Type escape sequence to abort.
Sending 5, 100-byte ICMP Echos to 131.108.1.1,
!!!!!
Success rate is 100 percent (5/5),
R2>
```

The **ping** command has a number of reporting mechanisms that run over ICMP. The exclamation point (!) indicates a successful reply. The **ping** command can also advise you, using a special code character, that the end device is not reachable, as depicted in Table 2-6.

Table 2-6   *Possible Test Characters When Using the* **ping** *Command*

Code	Description
!	Each exclamation point indicates the receipt of a reply.
.	Each period indicates that the network server timed out while waiting for a reply.
U	Destination unreachable.
N	Network unreachable.
P	Protocol unreachable.
Q	Source quench.
M	Could not fragment.
?	Unknown packet type.

NOTE	Cisco IOS provides a detailed version of the ping tool, which you can evoke by typing **ping** in the enabled mode. This command is known as the *extended ping command*.

Telnet

Telnet is an application layer protocol and part of the TCP/IP protocol suite. The TCP destination port number is 23 and commonly manages routers and switches, for example. Telnet is an insecure protocol, as data flows in plain text and the Telnet passwords can be sniffed. SSH is more secure for remote logins.

File Transfer Protocol and Trivial File Transfer Protocol

File Transfer Protocol (FTP) and Trivial File Transfer Protocol (TFTP) are application layer protocols (part of the TCP/IP protocol suite of applications). FTP is a connection-oriented protocol running over TCP. FTP uses two connections to maintain connectivity between two IP hosts; port 20 is used for server applications and port 21 for data transfer.

TFTP runs over UDP port 69 and is a connectionless-based protocol. TFTP commonly uploads IOS and configurations to a TFTP server. TFTP is regarded as the simple version of FTP. TFTP does not require any username/password combination to transfer data, as opposed to FTP, where a username and password are required before data can be transferred.

NOTE	Domain Name Server (DNS) is another common application that uses both TCP and UDP port 53.

Now that you fully appreciate the TCP/IP model, the next section covers routing protocols used to ensure TCP/IP data can be moved, or routed, from one location to another.

Routing Protocols

This section covers four main routing protocols:

- RIP
- EIGRP
- OSPF
- BGP

Before discussing the characteristic of each protocol, this section covers how routers (Cisco routers, in particular) generally route IP packets.

Routing is a process whereby a path to a destination host is selected by either a dynamic or static routing protocol. A routing protocol is an algorithm that routes data across the network. Each router makes routing decisions from host to destination based on specific metrics used by the operating routing protocol. For example, RIP uses hop count (commonly known as the network diameter) to decide what router interface the data is sent. A lower hop count is always preferred. OSPF, on the other hand, uses a cost metric; the lower the cost, the more preferred a path to the destination.

Routing IP across a network of Cisco routers requires IP address allocation to interfaces and then a static or dynamic routing protocol to advertise these networks to local or remote routers. After these networks are advertised, IP data can flow across the network. Routing occurs at Layer 3 (the network layer) of the OSI model.

By default, IP routing is enabled on Cisco routers. The command used to start or disable IP routing is [**no**] **ip routing**. By default, IP routing is enabled so you will not see this command by viewing the configuration. Consider a one-router network with two directly connected Ethernet interfaces as an introductory example. Figure 2-13 displays a two-port Ethernet router configured with two subnets.

Figure 2-13 *Connected Routes*

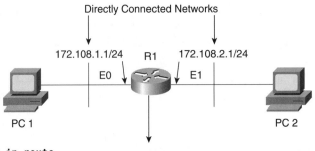

```
R1# show ip route
Codes C- connected, S- static, I- IGRP, R- RIP, M- mobile, B- BGP
D- EIGRP, EX- EIGRP external, Q- QSPF, 1A- OSPF inter area
N1- OSPF NSSA external type 1, N2- OSPF NSSA external type 2
E1- OSPF external type 1, E2- OSPF external type 2, E- EGP
i- IS-IS, L1- IS-IS level-1, L2- IS-IS level-2.*-candidate default
U- per-user static route, o- ODR
-
Gateway of last resort is not set
-
 172.108.0.0/24 is subnetted, 2 subnets
C  172.108.1.0 is directly connected, Ethernet0
C  172.108.2.0 is directly connected, Ethernet1
R1#
```

PC1 can communicate with PC2 as shown in Figure 2-13, because Cisco routers will route to directly connected interfaces.

The IOS command **show ip route** is used to view the IP routing table, and a number of symbols define how remote or local networks have been discovered. Table 2-7 defines the various symbols and their meanings. The Cisco Documentation CD defines the routing fields or codes as follows.

Table 2-7   **show ip route** *Defined**

Field	Description
O	Indicates protocol that derived the route. Possible values include the following: I—IGRP derived R—RIP derived O—OSPF derived C—Connected S—Static E—EGP derived B—BGP derived D—EIGRP EX—EIGRP external I—IS-IS derived Ia—IS-IS M—Mobile P—Periodic downloaded static route U—Per-user static route O—On-demand routing
E2	Type of route. Possible values include the following: *—Indicates the last path used when a packet was forwarded. It pertains only to the nonfast-switched packets. However, it does not indicate what path will be used next when forwarding a nonfast-switched packet, except when the paths are equal cost. IA—OSPF interarea route E1—OSPF external type 1 route E2—OSPF external type 2 route L1—IS-IS Level 1 route L2—IS-IS Level 2 route N1—OSPF NSSA external type 1 route N2—OSPF NSSA external type 2 route

continues

Table 2-7 · **show ip route** *Defined* (Continued)*

Field	Description

`172.108.0.0/24 is subnetted, 2 subnets`
`C  172.108.1.0 is directly connected, Ethernet0`
`C  172.108.2.0 is directly connected, Ethernet1`
`R1#`
	Indicates the address of the remote network.

`[160/5]`	The first number in the brackets is the information source's administrative distance; the second number is the metric for the route.
`via`	Specifies the address of the next router to the remote network.
`0:01:00`	Specifies the last time the route was updated in hours:minutes:seconds.
`Ethernet0`	Specifies the interface through which the specified network can be reached.

* *Part of this table taken from*
http://www.cisco.com/univercd/cc/td/doc/product/software/ios122/122cgcr/fiprrp_r/ind_r/1rfindp2.htm#102251,
all rights are reserved to Cisco.

By default, Cisco IOS assigns each routing protocol an administrative distance (AD) that indicates the trustworthiness of a routing entry if there is more than one path to a remote network running two or more routing algorithms. You can configure the AD value from the default with the **distance** *administrative-distance* IOS command if you want to manually choose RIP over OSPF, for example. The value for *administrative-distance* can be 1 to 255.

Table 2-8 displays the administrative distances enabled by default on Cisco routers.

Table 2-8 *Default Administrative Distances*

Route Source	Default Distance
Connected interface (or static route via a connected interface)	0
Static route	1
Enhanced IGRP summary route	5
External BGP	20
Internal enhanced IGRP	90
IGRP	100

Table 2-8   *Default Administrative Distances (Continued)*

Route Source	Default Distance
OSPF	110
IS-IS	115
RIP	120
EGP	140
EIGRP external route	170
Internal BGP	200
Unknown	255

For example, Table 2-8 demonstrates that an EIGRP (AD 90) route is preferred over a network entry discovered by RIP (AD 120) because the AD is lower, or more trustworthy.

NOTE   The IP address source and destination in an IP datagram does not alter, but the Layer 2 MAC source and destination do, for example, when PC1 sends a packet to PC2 in Figure 2-13. The TCP/IP software on PC1 identifies that the remote destination (172.108.2.0/24) is not locally connected and sends the Layer 3 frame to the local gateway address, 171.108.1.1/24. For the Layer 2 frame to transverse the local Ethernet, the destination Layer 2 Mac address must be that of the local router or gateway. PC2 resides on a different subnet, so the destination MAC address will be that of Router R1 (E0 burnt in address), or the default gateway address of 172.108.1.1. Router R1 will then strip the Layer 2 header and install its own Layer 2 header when the packet enters the network where PC2 resides. The Layer 2 header contains the source address (Layer 2) of R1 E1 and destination address of PC2's MAC address. The Layer 3 IP source and destination addresses do not change during the routing of the IP packet. The exception to changes in Layer 3 addressing is when Network Address Translation (NAT) is used.

Routing Information Protocol

Routing Information Protocol (RIP) is one the oldest routing protocols in use today.

RIP is a distance vector protocol. Table 2-9 defines the characteristics of a distance vector protocol.

Table 2-9   *Distance Vector Protocol Characteristics*

Characteristic	Description
Periodic updates	Periodic updates are sent at a set interval; for IP RIP, this interval is 30 seconds.
Broadcast updates	Updates are sent to the broadcast address 255.255.255.255. Only devices running routing algorithms will listen to these updates.
Full table updates	When an update is sent, the entire routing table is sent.
Triggered updates	Also known as Flash updates, these are sent when a change occurs outside the update interval.
Split horizon	This method stops routing loop. Updates are not sent out an outgoing interface from which the source network was received. This saves bandwidth, as well.
Count to infinity	Maximum hop count. For RIP, it's 15, and for IGRP, it's 255.
Algorithm	Example: Bellman-Ford for RIP.
Examples	RIP and IGRP.

RIP comes in two versions: RIPv1 (does not support VLSM) and RIPv2. Both versions of RIP automatically summarize at the network boundary (you can configure classful routing protocol, RIPv2, to support VLSM).

The following list summarizes RIPv1 characteristics:

- Distance vector protocol
- Runs over UDP port 520
- Metric is hop count (maximum is 15; 16 is unreachable)
- Periodic updates every 30 seconds
- Up to 25 networks per RIP update
- Implements Split horizon
- Implements triggered updates
- No support for VLSM or authentication
- Administrative Distance is 120

NOTE   Split horizon is a routing technique in which information about routes is prevented from exiting the router interface through which that information was received. Split horizon updates are useful in preventing routing loops. To enable split horizon, the IOS command is **ip split-horizon**. Split horizon on frame relay subinterfaces is enabled by default. Always use the IOS command **show ip interface** to determine if split horizon is enabled or displayed.

A triggered update is a method by which a routing protocol sends an instant message as soon as a network failure is detected. If a triggered update were not used, the only way the update would be sent would be via the normal update every 30 seconds, causing a delay in network convergence times. Split horizon is a favorite topic in CCIE lab exams.

Poison Reverse updates explicitly indicate that a network is unreachable rather than implying a remote network is unreachable by not sending that network in an update. Poison Reverse updates are intended to defeat routing loops in large IP networks.

Split horizon, Poison Reverse, and triggered updates are methods used by distance vector protocols to avoid routing loops.

RIPv2 was developed to enable RIP to support VLSM, so it is a classless routing protocol that also supports authentication. RIPv2 uses the same hop count and metric.

The following list summarizes RIPv2 characteristics:

- Distance vector protocol
- Runs over UDP port 520
- Metric is hop count (maximum is 15; 16 is unreachable)
- Periodic updates every 30 seconds
- Up to 25 networks per RIP update
- Implements Split horizon
- Implements triggered updates
- Supports VLSM (subnet mask carried in updates)
- Supports authentication
- Administrative Distance is 120
- Updates sent to multicast address 224.0.0.9
- Can set up neighbors to reduce broadcast traffic (send unicast updates)

To enable RIP on a Cisco router, the command required is **router rip**.

Consider a two-router topology running VLSM and RIP. Figure 2-14 displays two routers, named R1 and R2, with a /30-bit network used across the WAN. Loopbacks are used to populate the IP routing tables.

To start, enable RIP on both routers with the commands in Example 2-10. Version 2 must be enabled because you are implementing VLSM across the WAN links between R1 and R2.

Figure 2-14 *Practical Example of Routing RIP*

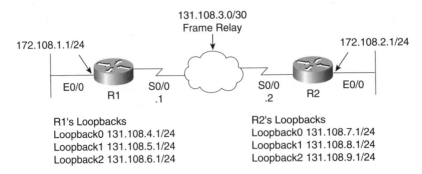

Example 2-10 displays the RIP configuration on R1. The same configuration commands are applied to R2.

Example 2-10 *IP RIP Configuration on R1*

```
router rip
 version 2
 network 131.108.0.0
```

View the RIP forward database with the command, **show ip rip database**.

Example 2-11 displays the output when **show ip rip database** is executed on R1.

Example 2-11 **show ip rip database** *Command on R1*

```
R1#show ip rip database
131.108.0.0/16    auto-summary
131.108.1.0/24    directly connected, Ethernet0/0
131.108.2.0/24
    [1] via 131.108.3.2, 00:00:12, Serial0/0
131.108.3.0/30    directly connected, Serial0/0
131.108.4.0/24    directly connected, Loopback0
131.108.5.0/24    directly connected, Loopback1
131.108.6.0/24    directly connected, Loopback2
131.108.7.0/24
    [1] via 131.108.3.2, 00:00:12, Serial0/0
131.108.8.0/24
    [1] via 131.108.3.2, 00:00:12, Serial0/0
131.108.9.0/24
    [1] via 131.108.3.2, 00:00:12, Serial0/0
```

Example 2-11 displays the directly connected routers and the four dynamically discovered routers via Serial0/0 to R2. To confirm that the entries are reachable, display the IP routing table on R1 and perform a few ping requests across the Frame Relay cloud.

Example 2-12 displays the IP routing table and the successful ping requests to the four remote networks.

Example 2-12 show ip route *and* ping *to R2*

```
R1#show ip route
Codes: C - connected, R - RIP,
     131.108.0.0/16 is variably subnetted, 9 subnets, 2 masks
R      131.108.9.0/24 [120/1] via 131.108.3.2, 00:00:00, Serial0/0
R      131.108.8.0/24 [120/1] via 131.108.3.2, 00:00:00, Serial0/0
R      131.108.7.0/24 [120/1] via 131.108.3.2, 00:00:00, Serial0/0
C      131.108.6.0/24 is directly connected, Loopback2
C      131.108.5.0/24 is directly connected, Loopback1
C      131.108.4.0/24 is directly connected, Loopback0
C      131.108.3.0/30 is directly connected, Serial0/0
R      131.108.2.0/24 [120/1] via 131.108.3.2, 00:00:01, Serial0/0
C      131.108.1.0/24 is directly connected, Ethernet0/0
R1#ping 131.108.2.1
Type escape sequence to abort.
Sending 5, 100-byte ICMP Echos to 131.108.2.1, timeout is 2 seconds:
!!!!!
Success rate is 100 percent (5/5), round-trip min/avg/max = 4/6/8 ms
R1#ping 131.108.7.1
Type escape sequence to abort.
Sending 5, 100-byte ICMP Echos to 131.108.7.1, timeout is 2 seconds:
!!!!!
Success rate is 100 percent (5/5), round-trip min/avg/max = 4/6/8 ms
R1#ping 131.108.8.1
Type escape sequence to abort.
Sending 5, 100-byte ICMP Echos to 131.108.8.1, timeout is 2 seconds:
!!!!!
Success rate is 100 percent (5/5), round-trip min/avg/max = 4/5/8 ms
R1#ping 131.108.9.1
Type escape sequence to abort.
Sending 5, 100-byte ICMP Echos to 131.108.9.1, timeout is 2 seconds:
!!!!!
Success rate is 100 percent (5/5), round-trip min/avg/max = 4/5/8 ms
R1#
```

Example 2-12 displays the four remote networks reachable by the Serial 0/0 and four successful ping requests (five replies to each remote network) to those interfaces on R2.

Stop R2 from sending R1 any updates via the Frame cloud to demonstrate the **passive-interface** command, **passive-interface Serial0/0**.

Example 2-13 displays the passive interface configuration on R2 serial0/0.

Example 2-13 *Passive Interface Configuration on R2*

```
R2(config)#router rip
R2(config-router)#passive-interface serial 0/0
```

R1's routing table now contains no remote entries from R2, which will still receive updates because the command affects only outbound updates. Example 2-14 confirms the missing routing RIP entries in R1's IP routing table.

Example 2-14 **show ip route** *on R1*

```
R1#show ip route
Codes: C - connected,
     131.108.0.0/16 is variably subnetted, 5 subnets, 2 masks
C       131.108.6.0/24 is directly connected, Loopback2
C       131.108.5.0/24 is directly connected, Loopback1
C       131.108.4.0/24 is directly connected, Loopback0
C       131.108.3.0/30 is directly connected, Serial0/0
C       131.108.1.0/24 is directly connected, Ethernet0/0
```

EIGRP

EIGRP is a Cisco-developed routing protocol that uses the same metric defined by IGRP multiplied by 256. The routing metric in EIGRP is based on bandwidth, delay, load, and reliability. The CCIE Security written exam does not test the candidates' understanding of EIGRP too greatly, so this section includes only the relevant topics for the exam.

EIGRP is a Cisco proprietary routing protocol that can be used to route a number of Layer 3 protocols, including IP, IPX, and AppleTalk. This section is concerned only with routing IP.

To ensure EIGRP is as efficient as possible, the following features were built into EIGRP:

- **Rapid convergence**—EIGRP uses the Diffusing Update Algorithm (DUAL) to achieve rapid convergence. A Cisco IOS router that runs EIGRP will ensure any redundant paths are stored and used in case of a network failure.

- **Reduced bandwidth usage**—By default, EIGRP uses up to 50 percent of available bandwidth, and this option can be changed with the IOS command **ip bandwidth-percent eigrp** *as-number percent*. By default, EIGRP uses up to 50 percent of the bandwidth defined by the **interface bandwidth** command. The interface command, **ip eigrp-bandwidth-percent** *<0-100%>*, can be used to change this value (a good method to use for the CCIE lab).

EIGRP is consider a hybrid routing protocol, meaning that EIGRP uses characteristics of both distance vector and link-state routing protocols to maintain routing tables.

EIGRP Terminology

EIGRP has a number of terms that must be understood by a candidate for the CCIE Security written exam. Table 2-10 defines some of the common terminology used in EIGRP.

Table 2-10   *EIGRP Terms*

Term	Meaning
Neighbor	A router in the same autonomous system (AS) running EIGRP.
Neighbor table	EIGRP maintains a table with all adjacent routers. To view the EIGRP neighbors, use the IOS command **show ip eigrp neighbors**.
Topology table	EIGRP maintains a topology table for all remote destinations discovered by neighboring routers. To view the topology table, the IOS command is **show ip eigrp topology**.
Hello	A packet used to monitor and maintain EIGRP neighbor relationships; they are multicast.
Query	A query packet that is sent to neighboring routers when a network path is lost; can be multicast or unicast.
Reply	A reply packet to a query packet; they are unicast.
ACK	Acknowledgment of an update packet, typically a hello packet with no data; they are unicast.
Holdtime	How long a router waits for a hello packet before tearing down a neighbor adjacency.
Smooth Route Trip Time (SRTT)	Time taken to send a packet reliably to an acknowledgment. SRTT is the average delta between the time a packet is sent and the arrival of the neighbor's acknowledgment.
Retransmission Timeout (RTO)	RTO is the time a router waits for the arrival of the neighbor's acknowledgment.
Feasible distance	Lowest metric to remote network.
Feasibility condition (FC)	A condition under which the sum of a neighbor's cost to a destination and the cost to this neighbor is less than current successor's cost.
Feasible successor	A neighboring router with a lower AD.
Successor	A neighboring router that meets the feasibility condition.
Stuck in Active (SIA)	An EIGRP router waiting for all acknowledgments from neighboring routers for all the queries sent.
Active	When a router is querying neighboring routers about a network path.
Passive	Normal route operation to a remote destination.

EIGRP Configuration Example

Configure a two-router EIGRP network with two Frame Relay links between two routers to demonstrate the redundancy mechanism with the EIGRP DUAL algorithm.

Figure 2-15 displays a two-router topology using the same addressing as the RIP example in Figure 2-14.

Figure 2-15 *EIGRP Configuration Example*

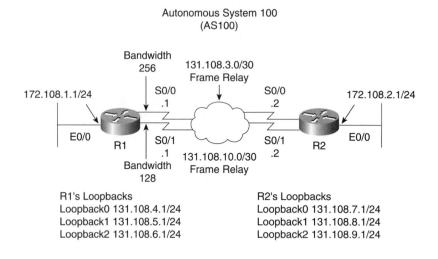

Routers R1 and R2 reside in AS 100, and to enable EIGRP on both routers, you need to start by configuring EIGRP. Example 2-15 displays the EIGRP configuration required on R1 and R2.

Example 2-15 *Enabling EIGRP in AS 100*

```
router eigrp 100
  network 131.108.0.0
```

The **network** command in Example 2-15 enables EIGRP to send and receive updates for interfaces configured with the Class B address, 131.108.0.0. EIGRP will automatically summarize.

Example 2-16 displays the IP routing table on R1.

Example 2-16 **show ip route** *on R1*

```
R1#show ip route
Codes: C - connected, D - EIGRP, EX - EIGRP external,
     131.108.0.0/16 is variably subnetted, 10 subnets, 2 masks
C      131.108.10.0/30 is directly connected, Serial0/1
```

Example 2-16 show ip route *on R1 (Continued)*

```
D        131.108.9.0/24 [90/10639872] via 131.108.3.2, 00:04:27, Serial0/0
D        131.108.8.0/24 [90/10639872] via 131.108.3.2, 00:04:27, Serial0/0
D        131.108.7.0/24 [90/10639872] via 131.108.3.2, 00:04:27, Serial0/0
C        131.108.6.0/24 is directly connected, Loopback2
C        131.108.5.0/24 is directly connected, Loopback1
C        131.108.4.0/24 is directly connected, Loopback0
C        131.108.3.0/30 is directly connected, Serial0/0
D        131.108.2.0/24 [90/10537472] via 131.108.3.2, 00:04:28, Serial0/0
C        131.108.1.0/24 is directly connected, Ethernet0/0
```

Example 2-16 displays four remote EIGRP entries (designated by D in the routing table) via the Serial interface Serial0/0. EIGRP has discovered these networks as the preferred path because the WAN bandwidth is 256 kbps as opposed to 128 kbps via Serial 0/1. To view the alternate paths, use the **show ip eigrp topology** IOS command to display backup paths.

Example 2-17 displays the output of the **show ip eigrp topology** command on R1.

Example 2-17 show ip eigrp topology *on R1*

```
R1#show ip eigrp topology
IP-EIGRP Topology Table for AS(100)/ID(131.108.6.1)
Codes: P - Passive, A - Active, U - Update, Q - Query, R - Reply,
       r - reply Status, s - sia Status
P 131.108.10.0/30, 1 successors, FD is 2169856
        via Connected, Serial0/1
        via 131.108.3.2 (11023872/1761792), Serial0/0
P 131.108.9.0/24, 1 successors, FD is 2297856
        via 131.108.3.2 (10639872/128256), Serial0/0
        via 131.108.10.2 (20640000/128256), Serial0/1
P 131.108.8.0/24, 1 successors, FD is 2297856
        via 131.108.3.2 (10639872/128256), Serial0/0
        via 131.108.10.2 (20640000/128256), Serial0/1
P 131.108.7.0/24, 1 successors, FD is 2297856
        via 131.108.3.2 (10639872/128256), Serial0/0
        via 131.108.10.2 (20640000/128256), Serial0/1
P 131.108.6.0/24, 1 successors, FD is 128256
        via Connected, Loopback2
P 131.108.5.0/24, 1 successors, FD is 128256
        via Connected, Loopback1
P 131.108.4.0/24, 1 successors, FD is 128256
        via Connected, Loopback0
P 131.108.3.0/30, 1 successors, FD is 2169856
        via Connected, Serial0/0
        via 131.108.10.2 (21024000/1761792), Serial0/1
P 131.108.2.0/24, 1 successors, FD is 2195456
        via 131.108.3.2 (10537472/281600), Serial0/0
        via 131.108.10.2 (20537600/281600), Serial0/1
P 131.108.1.0/24, 1 successors, FD is 281600
        via Connected, Ethernet0/0
```

Example 2-17 shows that the remote network 131.108.2.0 is via two paths, and because the feasible distance is lower through Serial 0/0, that path is injected into the routing table. If, for some reason, the link with Serial 0/0 on R1 fails, the alternate path will be chosen and inserted into the routing table, increasing convergence times.

When EIGRP loses a path to a remote network, it sends requests to neighboring routers for alternative ways to reach the failed network. The neighboring router that returns the most favorable routes is called the feasible successor; in Figure 2-15, that router is R2.

NOTE   The Cisco CD Documentation Codes State of this topology table entry are defined as follows:

- **P (Passive)**—No EIGRP computations are being performed for this destination.

- **A (Active)**—EIGRP computations are being performed for this destination.

- **U (Update)**—Indicates that an update packet was sent to this destination.

- **Q (Query)**—Indicates that a query packet was sent to this destination.

- **R (Reply)**—Indicates that a reply packet was sent to this destination.

- **r (Reply status)**—–A flag that is set after the software has sent a query and is waiting for a reply.

*Cisco Connection online was the source for this material, www.cisco.com/univercd/cc/td/doc/product/software/ios122/122cgcr/fiprrp_r/1rfeigrp.htm#1 025659.

OSPF

OSPF is a link-state routing protocol. Link-state protocols use Dijkstra's shortest path first (SPF) algorithm to populate the routing table. OSPF shares information with every router in the network. OSPF is a classless protocol and supports VLSM. Table 2-11 defines common OSPF terminology.

OSPF in a Single Area

When configuring any OSPF router, you must establish what area assignment the interface will be enabled for. OSPF has some basic rules when it comes to area assignment. OSPF must be configured with areas. The backbone area 0, or 0.0.0.0, must be configured if you use more than one area assignment. If your OSPF design has only one area, it can have any number.

Table 2-11 *Common OSPF Terms*

Term	Description
Hello packet	Exchanged by the routers for neighbor discovery and forming adjacency, neighbor keep-alive, and DR/BDR election.
Link state	Information is shared between directly connected routers. This information propagates unchanged throughout the network and is also used to create a shortest path first (SPF) tree.
Area	A group of routers and links that share the same Area ID. All OSPF routers require area assignments. All routers within an area have the same database. Link state flooding is limited to an area.
Autonomous system (AS)	A network under a common network administration domain running common routing protocols.
Cost (OSPF Metric)	The routing metric used by OSPF. Lower costs are always preferred. You can manually configure the cost of an interface with the **ip ospf cost** command. By default, the cost is calculated by using the formula, cost = 10^8/bandwidth.
Router ID	Each OSPF router requires a unique router ID, which is the highest IP address configured on a Cisco router or the highest-numbered loopback address. You can manually assign the router ID.
Adjacency	When two OSPF routers have exchanged information between each other and have the same topology table. Adjacency can have a number of states or exchange states: **Init state**—When Hello packets have been sent and are awaiting a reply to establish two-way communication. **Establish bidirectional (two-way) communication**—Accomplished by the discovery of the Hello protocol routers and the election of a DR. **Exstart**—Two neighbor routers form a master/slave relationship and agree upon a starting sequence that will be incremented to ensure that LSAs are acknowledged. **Exchange state**—Database Description (DD) packets continue to flow as the slave router acknowledges the master's packets. OSPF is operational because the routers can send and receive LSAs between each other. DD packets contain information such as the router ID, area ID, checksum, if authentication is used, link-state type, and the advertising router. LSA packets also contain information such as router ID, and additionally include MTU sizes, DD sequence numbering, and any options.

continues

Table 2-11 *Common OSPF Terms (Continued)*

Term	Description
Adjacency (*Continued*)	**Loading state**—Link-state requests are sent to neighbors asking for recent advertisements that have been discovered in Exchange state but not received. **Full state**—Neighbor routers are fully adjacent because their link-state databases are fully synchronized within the area. Routing tables begin to be populated.
Topology table	Also called the link-state table, this table contains every link in the entire network.
Designated Router (DR)	This router ensures adjacencies between all neighbors on a multiaccess network (such as Ethernet). This ensures that not all routers need to maintain full adjacencies with each other. The DR is selected based on the priority. In a tie, the router with the highest router ID is selected.
Backup DR	A Backup Designated Router is designed to perform the same functions in case the DR fails.
Link-state advertisement (LSA)	A packet that contains all relevant information regarding a router's links and the state of those links.
Priority	Sets the router's priority so a DR or BDR can be correctly elected.
Router links	Describe the state and cost of the router's interfaces to the area. Router links use LSA type 1.
Summary links	Originated by Area Border Routers, these links describe networks in the AS. Summary links use LSA type 3 and 4.
Network links	Originated by DRs. Network links use LSA type 2.
External links	Originated by autonomous system boundary routers; they advertise destinations external to the AS or the default route external to the AS.
Area Border Router (ABR)	Router located on the border of one or more OSPF areas to connect those areas to the backbone network.
Autonomous system boundary router (ASBR)	An ABR located between an OSPF autonomous system and a non-OSPF network.

The configuration steps to enable OSPF in a single area are as follows:

Step 1 Start OSPF with the command **router ospf** *process ID*. The process ID is locally significant to the router.

Step 2 Enable the interfaces with the **network** command. For example, to place the Network 131.108.1.0 in area 1, the IOS command is **network 131.108.1.0 area 1**.

Step 3   Identify area assignments.

Step 4   (Optional) Assign the router ID with the **router-id** *router-id* IOS command under the OSPF process.

NOTE   The following is a list of reasons OSPF (link-state) is considered a better routing protocol than RIPv1 (distance vector):

- OSPF has no hop count limitation. (RIP has a limit of 15 hops only.)

- OSPF understands VLSM and allows for summarization.

- OSPF uses multicasts (not broadcasts) to send updates.

- OSPF converges much faster than RIP because OSPF propagates changes immediately. OSPF is faster because it sends the link update and then calculates the local routing table. RIP calculates the local routing table and then sends an update.

- OSPF allows for load balancing with up to six equal-cost paths.

- OSPF has authentication available (RIPv2 does also, but RIPv1 does not).

- OSPF allows tagging of external routes injected by other autonomous systems.

- OSPF configuration, monitoring, and troubleshooting have a far greater IOS tool base than RIP.

Multiple OSPF Areas

An OSPF area is a logical grouping of routers and links by a network administrator. OSPF routers in any area share the same topological view (also known as the OSPF or database) of the network. OSPF is configured in multiple areas to reduce routing table sizes, which in return, reduces the topological database and CPU/memory requirements on a router.

Routing tables become very large even with just 50 routers.

Cisco recommends no more than 50 routers per area. The OSPF database is exchanged in full every 30 minutes, and if this database is too large, every time this occurs, the amount of bandwidth used over the network increases and can cause severe delays in sending user-based traffic because convergence times are increased.

Areas allow OSPF designers to limit and confine changes. Additionally, a number of predefined areas types help reduce the demand on routers, as displayed in Table 2-12.

Table 2-12   *Additional Area Types*

Area Type	Function
Stubby area	This area does not accept LSA types 4 and 5, which are summary links and external link advertisements, respectively. The only way to achieve a route to unknown destinations is a default route injected by the ABR.
Totally stubby area	This area blocks LSA types 3, 4, and 5. Only a single type 3 LSA advertising the default route is allowed. This solution is Cisco proprietary and is used to further reduce a topological database.
Not-so-stubby area (NSSA)	This area is used primarily for connections to an ISP. This area is designed to allow type 7 LSAs only. All advertised routes can be flooded through the NSSA but are blocked by the ABR. Basically, a type 7 LSA (if the P bit is set to one) is converted to a type 5 LSA and flooded through the rest of the network. If the P bit is set to 0, no translation will take place. Type 4 or 5 LSAs are not permitted. This advertisement will not be propagated to the rest of the network. NSSAs typically provide a default route.

Table 2-13 defines the challenges across various media types, such as Frame Relay and broadcast media.

Table 2-13   *OSPF over Various Media Types Using Cisco IOS Software*

Method	Description
Point-to-point nonbroadcast	Used typically for Frame Relay interfaces.
Point-to-point	This is the default mode for subinterfaces.
Point-to-multipoint	Used for multiple destinations.
Nonbroadcast	Nonbroadcast multiaccess (NBMA) mode.
Broadcast	Used in Ethernet and broadcast environments where the election of DR/BDR takes place. To define the DR, use the IOS command **ip ospf priority** *priority-number*. The *priority-number* is 1 to 255. The highest priority will be to elect the DR.

Ethernet is an example of where OSPF will elect a DR to minimize the OSPF updates over a broadcast medium. Each multiaccess OSPF network that has at least two attached routers has a designated router elected by the OSPF Hello protocol. The DR enables a reduction in the number of adjacencies required on a multiaccess network, which reduces the amount of routing protocol traffic and the size of the topological database, especially when more than two routers are deployed on this network segment.

Virtual Links

All OSPF areas must be connected to the backbone area (Area 0). Figure 2-16 demonstrates a topology where an area (Area 100) is not directly connected to the backbone.

Figure 2-16 *OSPF Area Assignment*

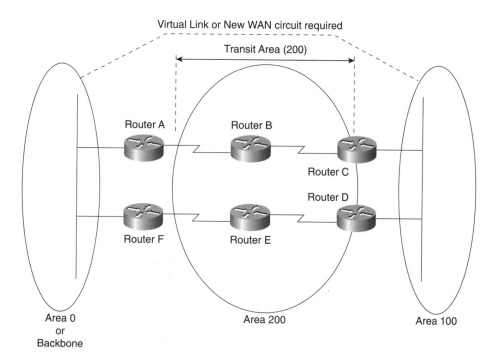

To ensure that Area 100 is reachable by the backbone, a virtual link can be configured over the transit area (200), and IP connectivity will be maintained. Virtual links are typically used in a transition phase (for example, when one company buys another and both companies use OSPF). Another solution to the problem depicted in Figure 2-16 is to install a physical link between Router C or Router D and the backbone core network.

OSPF Configuration Example

Figure 2-17 demonstrates a two-router topology. Figure 2-17 displays three OSPF areas with Area 2 partitioned from the backbone, necessitating a virtual link.

Figure 2-17 *Typical Cisco IOS OSPF topology*

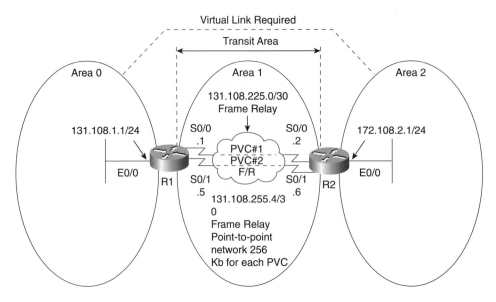

R1's Loopbacks in Area 0
Loopback0 131.108.2.1/24
Loopback1 131.108.3.1/24
Loopback2 131.108.4.1/24
Loopback3 131.108.5.1/24
Loopback4 131.108.6.1/24
Loopback5 131.108.7.1/24

R2's Loopbacks in Area 1
Loopback0 131.108.9.1/24
Loopback1 131.108.10.1/24
Loopback2 131.108.11.1/24
Loopback3 131.108.12.1/24
Loopback4 131.108.13.1/24
Loopback5 131.108.14.1/24
Loopback6 131.108.15.1/24

Example 2-18 displays the full working configuration of R1.

Example 2-18 *R1's OSPF Configuration*

```
!
hostname R1
enable password cisco
interface Loopback0
 ip address 131.108.2.1 255.255.255.0
 ip ospf network point-to-point
!
interface Loopback1
ip address 131.108.3.1 255.255.255.0
 ip ospf network point-to-point
!
interface Loopback2
 ip address 131.108.4.1 255.255.255.0
 ip ospf network point-to-point
```

Example 2-18 *R1's OSPF Configuration (Continued)*

```
!
interface Loopback3
 ip address 131.108.3.1 255.255.255.0
 ip ospf network point-to-point
!
interface Loopback4
 ip address 131.108.6.1 255.255.255.0
 ip ospf network point-to-point
!
interface Loopback5
 ip address 131.108.7.1 255.255.255.0
 ip ospf network point-to-point
!
interface Ethernet0/0
 ip address 131.108.1.1 255.255.255.0
!
interface Serial0/0
 bandwidth 256
 ip address 131.108.255.1 255.255.255.252
 encapsulation frame-relay
 ip ospf network point-to-point
!
interface Serial0/1
 bandwidth 256
 ip address 131.108.255.5 255.255.255.252
 encapsulation frame-relay
 ip ospf network point-to-point
!
router ospf 1
 router-id 131.108.7.1
 area 1 virtual-link 131.108.15.1
 network 131.108.0.0 0.0.7.255 area 0
 network 131.108.255.0 0.0.0.3 area 0
 network 131.108.255.4 0.0.0.3 area 0
!
end
```

By default, loopback interfaces are stub hosts in OSPF and are advertised as 32-bit hosts. The IOS command **ip ospf network point-to-point** advertises the loopback networks as /24 networks (in this case, you use /24 subnet mask). The Frame Relay connection is configured as point-to-point to ensure that no manual OSPF neighbor configuration is required to form OSPF neighbors. The virtual link is configured across the transit area, 1, to R2 router ID of 131.108.14.1.

Example 2-19 displays R2's full working configuration.

Example 2-19 *R2's OSPF Configurations*

```
hostname R2
enable password cisco
interface Loopback0
 ip address 131.108.9.1 255.255.255.0
 ip ospf network point-to-point
!
interface Loopback1
ip address 131.108.10.1 255.255.255.0
 ip ospf network point-to-point
!
interface Loopback2
 ip address 131.108.11.1 255.255.255.0
 ip ospf network point-to-point
!
interface Loopback3
 ip address 131.108.12.1 255.255.255.0
 ip ospf network point-to-point
!
interface Loopback4
 ip address 131.108.13.1 255.255.255.0
 ip ospf network point-to-point
!
interface Loopback5
 ip address 131.108.14.1 255.255.255.0
 ip ospf network point-to-point
!
interface Loopback6
 ip address 131.108.15.1 255.255.255.0
 ip ospf network point-to-point
!
interface Ethernet0/0
 ip address 131.108.8.1 255.255.255.0
 half-duplex
!
interface Serial0/0
 ip address 131.108.255.2 255.255.255.252
 encapsulation frame-relay
 ip ospf network point-to-point

interface Serial0/1
 ip address 131.108.255.6 255.255.255.252
 encapsulation frame-relay
 ip ospf network point-to-point
!
router ospf 1
 router-id 131.108.15.1
 area 1 virtual-link 131.108.7.1
 network 131.108.8.0 0.0.0.255 area 2
 network 131.108.9.0 0.0.0.255 area 1
```

Example 2-19 *R2's OSPF Configurations (Continued)*

```
network 131.108.10.0 0.0.0.255 area 1
network 131.108.11.0 0.0.0.255 area 1
network 131.108.12.0 0.0.0.255 area 1
network 131.108.13.0 0.0.0.255 area 1
network 131.108.14.0 0.0.0.255 area 1
network 131.108.15.0 0.0.0.255 area 1
network 131.108.255.0 0.0.0.3 area 0
network 131.108.255.4 0.0.0.3 area 0
end
```

Example 2-20 displays the IP OSPF routing table on R1.

Example 2-20 **show ip route ospf** *on R1*

```
R1#show ip route ospf
     131.108.0.0/16 is variably subnetted, 17 subnets, 2 masks
O       131.108.15.0/24 [110/391] via 131.108.255.6, 00:00:41, Serial0/1
                        [110/391] via 131.108.255.2, 00:00:41, Serial0/0
O       131.108.14.0/24 [110/391] via 131.108.255.6, 00:00:41, Serial0/1
                        [110/391] via 131.108.255.2, 00:00:41, Serial0/0
O       131.108.13.0/24 [110/391] via 131.108.255.6, 00:00:41, Serial0/1
                        [110/391] via 131.108.255.2, 00:00:41, Serial0/0
O       131.108.12.0/24 [110/391] via 131.108.255.6, 00:00:41, Serial0/1
                        [110/391] via 131.108.255.2, 00:00:41, Serial0/0
O       131.108.11.0/24 [110/391] via 131.108.255.6, 00:00:41, Serial0/1
                        [110/391] via 131.108.255.2, 00:00:41, Serial0/0
O       131.108.10.0/24 [110/391] via 131.108.255.6, 00:00:41, Serial0/1
                        [110/391] via 131.108.255.2, 00:00:41, Serial0/0
O       131.108.9.0/24  [110/391] via 131.108.255.6, 00:00:41, Serial0/1
                        [110/391] via 131.108.255.2, 00:00:42, Serial0/0
O IA    131.108.8.0/24  [110/400] via 131.108.255.6, 00:00:42, Serial0/1
                        [110/400] via 131.108.255.2, 00:00:42, Serial0/0
```

R1's routing table has the remote OSPF networks labeled as O IA because the network 131.108.8.0/24 is part of an area not directly attached to R1. Also, R1 is automatically load balancing across the two paths because the cost metric is the same (391). The administrative distance is 110 (the default).

NOTE   The election of the designated router in networks such as Frame Relay is important, and you must ensure the hub or core network router is the elected DR so that the hub router disseminates information to all spoke routers. To ensure the hub is the DR, you can disable the DR election process on edge routers with the IOS command, **ip ospf priority 0**.

Border Gateway Protocol

Border Gateway Protocol (BGP) is an exterior routing protocol used widely in the Internet. It is commonly referred to as BGP4 (version 4).

BGP4 is defined in RFC 1771. BGP allows you to create an IP network free of routing loops between different autonomous systems.

An autonomous system (AS) is a set of routers under the same administrative control.

BGP is called a path vector protocol because it carries a sequence of AS numbers that indicates the path taken to a remote network. This information is stored so that routing loops can be avoided.

BGP uses TCP as its Layer 4 protocol (TCP port 179). No other routing protocol in use today relies on TCP. This allows BGP to make sure that updates are sent reliably, leaving the routing protocol to concentrate on gathering information about remote networks and ensuring a loop-free topology.

Routers configured for BGP are typically called *BGP speakers*, and any two BGP routers that form a BGP TCP session are called *BGP peers* or *BGP neighbors*.

BGP peers initially exchange full BGP routing tables. After the exchange, only BGP updates are sent between peers, ensuring that only useful data is sent unless a change occurs.

Four message are types used in BGP4 to ensure that peers are active and updates are sent:

- **Open Messages**—Used when establishing BGP peers.
- **Keepalives**—These messages are sent periodically to ensure connections are still active or established.
- **Update messages**—Any changes that occur, such as a loss of network availability, result in an update message.
- **Notification**—Only used to notify BGP peers of any receiving errors.

Key BGP characteristics include the following:

- BGP is a path vector protocol.
- BGP uses TCP as the transport layer protocol.
- Full routing table is exchanged only during initial BGP session.
- Updates are sent over TCP port 179.
- BGP sessions are maintained by keepalive messages.
- Any network changes result in update messages.
- BGP has its own BGP table. Any network entry must reside in the BGP table first.
- BGP has a complex array of metrics, such as next-hop address and origin, which are called attributes.
- BGP supports VLSM and summarization (sometimes called Classless Interdomain Routing [CIDR]).

BGP4's ability to guarantee routing delivery and the complexity of the routing decision process mean that BGP will be widely used in any large IP routing environment, such as the Internet. The Internet consists of over 100,000 BGP network entries, and BGP is the only routing protocol available today that can handle and manage such a large routing table. The Internet (80,000+ routes) could not be functional today if BGP were not the routing protocol in use.

Before covering some simple examples, the next section describes BGP attributes.

BGP Attributes

BGP has a number of complex attributes that determine a path to a remote network. These attributes allow a greater flexibility and complex routing decision to ensure a path to a remote network is taken by the best path possible.

The network designer can also manipulate these attributes. BGP, when supplied with multiple paths to a remote network, will always choose a single path to a specific destination. (Load balancing is possible with static routes.) BGP always propagates the best path to any peers.

BGP attributes are carried in update packets.

Table 2-14 describes the well-known and optional attributes used in BGP4.

Table 2-14   *Well-Known and Optional Attributes*

Attribute	Description
Origin	This attribute is mandatory, defines the source of the path, and can be three different values:
	IGP—Originating from interior of the AS.
	EGP—Learned through an External Gateway Protocol.
	Incomplete—The BGP route was discovered using redistribution or static routers.
AS_Path	Describes the sequences of AS that the packet has traversed to the destination IP network.
Next Hop	Describes the next-hop address taken to a remote path, typically the eBGP peer.
Local Preference	Indicates the preferred path to exit the AS. A higher local preference is always preferred.
Multi Exit Discriminator (MED)	Informs BGP peers in other autonomous systems about which path to take into the AS when multiple autonomous systems are connected. A lower MED is always preferred.

continues

Table 2-14 *Well-Known and Optional Attributes (Continued)*

Attribute	Description
Weight	Cisco-defined, attribute-only attribute that is used in local router selection. Weight is not sent to other BGP peers, and higher weight value is always preferred. Weight is locally significant to the router and specifies a preferred path when more than one path exists. Cisco-only attribute.
Atomic Aggregate	Advises BGP routers that aggregation has taken place. Not used in router selection process.
Aggregator	The router ID responsible for aggregation; not used in the router selection process.
Community	Allows routes to be tagged and use a group of routes sharing the same characteristics. An ISP typically tags traffic from customers along with a route-map to modify the community attribute.
Originator ID	Prevents routing loops. This information is not used for router selection.
Cluster-List	Used in a route-reflectors environment. This information is not used for router selection.

There are two types of BGP sessions: internal BGP (IBGP) and external BGP (EBGP). IBGP is a connection between two BGP speakers in the same AS. EBGP is a connection between two BGP speakers in different autonomous systems.

IBGP peers also make sure that routing loops cannot occur by ensuring that any routes sent to another AS must be known via an interior routing protocol, such as OSPF, before sending that information. That is, the routers must be synchronized. The benefit of this added rule in IBGP TCP sessions is that information is not sent unless it is reachable, which reduces any unnecessary traffic and saves bandwidth. Route reflectors in IBGP ensure that large internal BGP networks do not require a fully meshed topology. Route reflectors are not used in EBGP connection. A BGP route reflector disseminates routing information to all route-reflector clients, and ensures that BGP tables are sent and that a fully meshed IBGP need not be configured.

The BGP routing decision is quite complex and takes several attributes into account. The attributes and process taken by a Cisco router running BGP4 are as follows:

1 If the next-hop address is reachable, consider it.

2 Prefer the route with the highest weight (Cisco IOS routers only).

3 If the weight is the same, prefer the largest local preference attribute.

4 If the local preference is the same, prefer the route originated by this local router (routes generated by **network** or **redistribute** commands).

5 Then prefer the route with the shortest AS Path.

6 If this is equal, prefer the route with origin set to originated (via BGP); IGP is preferred to EGP and then incomplete.

7 If the origin codes are the same, prefer the route with the lowest MED.

8 If the MED is the same, prefer EBGP over IBGP.

9 Then prefer the path that is the closest.

10 Finally, if all else is equal, prefer the path with the lowest BGP router ID.

Configuring BGP

To start the BGP process on a Cisco router requires the following command:

```
router bgp autonomous-system-number
```

To define networks to be advertised, apply the following command:

```
network network-number mask network-mask
```

You must be aware that the **network** command is not used the same way you apply networks in OSPF or EIGRP. With BGP, the **network** command advertises networks that are originated from the router and should be advertised via BGP. For more Cisco IOS examples of BGP, please visit Chapter 9, "CCIE Security Self-Study Lab."

To identify peer routers, apply the following command:

```
neighbor {ip-address | peer-group name} remote-as autonomous-system-number
```

NOTE	Route redistribution allows routing information discovered through one routing protocol to be distributed in the update messages of another routing protocol. Whenever redistribution is configured on Cisco routers, the routing metric must also be converted. For example, with redistribution from a RIP domain into OSPF, the RIP network inserted into OSPF requires an OSPF cost metric.

ISDN

Integrated Services Digital Network (ISDN) is a digital service that enables network users to send and receive data, voice, and video transmissions over a network. ISDN offers a variety of link speeds, ranging from 64 kbps to 2.048 Mbps. Many small- and medium-sized companies find that ISDN is a viable network solution.

Basic Rate and Primary Rate Interfaces

ISDN can be supplied by a carrier in two main forms: Basic Rate Interface (BRI) and Primary Rate Interface (PRI). An ISDN BRI consists of two 64-kbps services (B channels) and one 16-kbps signaling channel (D channel). An ISDN PRI consists of 23 B or 30 B channels, depending on the country. In North America and Japan, a PRI service consists of 23 B channels. In Europe and Australia, a PRI service consists of 30 B channels. A signaling channel (or D channel) is used in a PRI service and is a dedicated 64-kbps channel. The B channel sends data and the D channel primarily controls signaling.

NOTE   The effective throughput of a PRI service with 23 channels is 1.472 Mbps (23 × 64 kbps). With 30 B channels, the effective throughput is 1.920 Mbps (30 × 64 kbps). The International Telecommunications Union (ITU) defines the standards for ISDN. The specified standard is ITU-T Q.921.

ISDN Framing and Frame Format

The ISDN physical layer provides the ability to send outbound traffic and receive inbound traffic by transmitting binary bits over the physical media. The ISDN data link layer provides signaling, which ensures that data is sent and received correctly. The signaling protocol used in ISDN is called the Link Access Procedure on the D channel (LAPD).

ISDN Layer 2 Protocols

ISDN can use a number of Layer 2 encapsulation types. Point-to-Point Protocol (PPP) and high-level data link control (HDLC) are the only methods tested in the qualification exam.

NOTE   X.25 is not tested in the CCIE Security written exam.

HDLC

High-level data link control is a WAN protocol encapsulation method that allows point-to-point connections between two remote sites. Typically, HDLC is used in a leased-line setup. HDLC is a connectionless protocol that relies on upper layers to recover any frames that have encountered errors across a WAN link. HDLC is the default encapsulation on Cisco serial interfaces.

Cisco routers use HDLC encapsulation, which is proprietary. Cisco added an address field in the HDLC frame, which is not present in the HDLC standard. This field is used by Cisco devices to indicate the type of payload (protocol). Cisco routers use the address field in an

HDLC frame to indicate a payload type, but other routers or manufacturers that implement the HDLC standard do not use the address field. HDLC cannot be used to connect a Cisco router with another vendor.

Figure 2-18 displays the HDLC frame format, which shares a common format with the PPP frame format discussed in the next section.

Figure 2-18 *HDLC Frame Format*

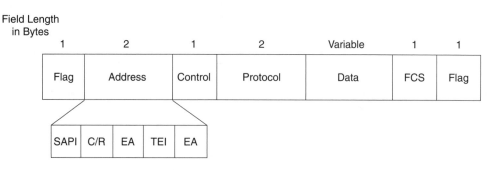

Point-to-Point Protocol (PPP)

PPP was designed to transport user information between two WAN devices (also referred to as point-to-point links). PPP was designed as an improvement over Serial Line Internet Protocol (SLIP). When PPP encapsulation is configured on a Cisco WAN interface, the network administrator can carry protocols such as IP and IPX, as well as many others. Cisco routers support PPP over asynchronous lines, High-Speed Serial Interfaces (HSSIs), ISDN lines, and synchronous serial ports. PPP has the added function of allowing authentication to take place before any end user data is sent across the link.

The following three phases occur in any PPP session:

- **Link establishment**—Link Control Protocol (LCP) packets are sent to configure and test the link.

- **Authentication (optional)**—After the link is established, authentication can ensure that link security is maintained.

- **Network layers**—In this phase, Network Control Protocol (NCP) packets determine which protocols are used across the PPP link. An interesting aspect of PPP is that each protocol (IP, IPX, and so on) supported in this phase is documented in a separate RFC that discusses how it operates over PPP.

Figure 2-19 displays the PPP frame format, which is similar to the HDLC frame format in Figure 2-18.

Figure 2-19 *PPP Frame Format*

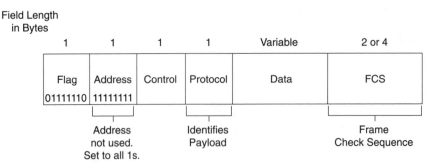

LCP

LPC is used to establish, configure, and test the link between two devices, such as Cisco routers. LCP provides the necessary negotiations between end devices to activate the link. After the link is activated, but while no data is yet flowing, the next phase(s) of the PPP session can take place—authentication (if configured) and the NCP.

Authentication

PPP supports authentication through Password Authentication Protocol (PAP) and Challenge Handshake Authentication Protocol (CHAP), with CHAP providing a more secure method of authentication. CHAP passwords are encrypted and safe from intruders because they are never actually transmitted on the wire. This technique, known as shared secrets, means that both devices know the secret (password), but they never talk about it directly. PAP passwords are sent in clear text; they are clearly visible on the wire.

NCP

PPP uses NCP packets to allow multiple network layer protocol types to transfer across WANs from point to point. IP Control Program (IPCP) allows IP connectivity, and IPXCP allows IPX connectivity.

Cisco IOS ISDN Commands

Cisco routers support ISDN. The commands most often used to enable data and voice communications over ISDN are listed in Table 2-15.

Table 2-15 *ISDN Commands*

IOS Command	Description
isdn caller *phone-number*	The number called by the router. The *phone-number* is the remote router's ISDN number.
isdn calling-number *calling-number*	The number of the device making the outgoing call; only one entry is allowed.
isdn switch-type	ISDN service provider switch type.

NOTE   Frame Relay is a Layer 2 protocol that provides connectionless delivery between devices.

Frame Relay, although not listed in the official blueprint for the CCIE Security written exam, has a few terms you should be aware of for the exam:

- **Forward explicit congestion notification (FECN)**—A bit set by a Frame Relay network to inform DTE receiving the frame that congestion was experienced in the path from source to destination. DTE receiving frames with the FECN bit set can request that higher-level protocols take flow-control action, as appropriate.

- **Backward explicit congestion notification (BECN)**—A bit set by a Frame Relay network in frames traveling in the opposite direction of frames encountering a congested path. DTE receiving frames with the BECN bit set can request that higher-level protocols take flow-control action, as appropriate. The ISP or WAN switches typically set FECN/BECN.

- **Data-link connection identifier (DLCI)**—A value that specifies a PVC or SVC in a Frame Relay network. DLCIs are locally significant. Globally significant DLCIs are used for LMI communication between Frame Relay switches.

IP Multicast

This section briefly covers the IP multicast areas of interest for the CCIE written test.

The multicasting protocol was designed to reduce the high bandwidth requirements of technologies, such as video on demand, to a single stream of information to more than one device. Applications include electronic learning, company share meetings (video on demand), and software distribution.

Multicasting can be defined as unicast (one to one), multicast (one to many), and broadcast (one to all).

Multicasting transmits IP packets from a single source to multiple destinations. The network copies single packets, which are sent to a subset of network devices. In IPv4, the Class D addresses ranging from 224.0.0.0 to 239.255.255.255 are reserved for multicast. Routing protocols, for example, use multicasting to send hello packets and establish neighbor adjacencies.

Table 2-16 displays some common multicast addresses and their uses.

Table 2-16   *Class D Multicast Address Examples*

Multicast Address	Use
224.0.0.1	All hosts on subnets
224.0.0.2	All multicast routers
224.0.0.5	All OSPF-enabled routers
224.0.0.6	All OSPF DR routers
224.0.0.9	RIPv2-enabled routers
224.0.0.10	All EIGRP-enabled routers

TIP   The Class D addresses used in multicast traffic range from 224.0.0.0 to 239.255.255.255.

Asynchronous Communications and Access Devices

An asynchronous (async) communication is a digital signal that is transmitted without precise clocking. The RS-232 session between a router and PC through the console connection is an example of async communications. Such signals generally have different frequencies and phase relationships. Asynchronous transmissions usually encapsulate individual characters in control bits (called start and stop bits) that designate the beginning and the end of each character.

For example, the auxiliary port on Cisco routers can be used to connect a modem and allow out of band (not via the network) management.

The Cisco AS5300 is an example of a device that supports both synchronous and async communication, such as voice, digital, and modem-based traffic (via a Public Switch Telephone Network [PSTN]).

The AS5300, or universal Access Server (AS), is a versatile data communications platform that provides the functions of an access server, router, and digital modem in a single modular chassis. The access server is intended for ISPs, telecommunications carriers, and other service providers that offer managed Internet connections. The AS5300 provides both digital (for example, ISDN) and analog access (dialup users using PSTN) to users on a network.

Figure 2-20 displays a typical scenario where clients, such as Internet dialup users with ISDN and analog phone lines (PSTN), can connect to the Internet using PPP.

Clients are supplied one number to call, and the AS5300 makes intelligent decisions based on the incoming call type, whether it be digital (ISDN) or analog (PSTN).

Figure 2-20 *AS5300 Typical Design Scenario*

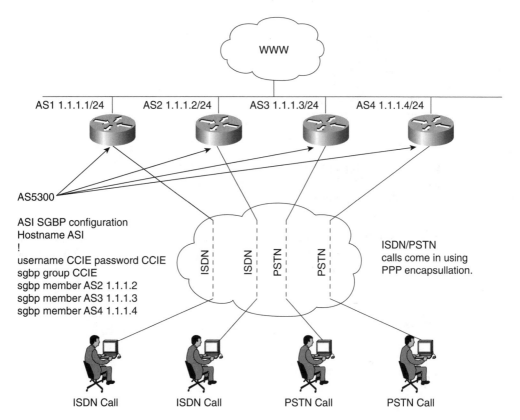

Users, such as clients with ISDN, call the dedicated number supplied by the ISP. The four AS5300s in Figure 2-20 can also share the load of incoming calls using Stack Group Bidding Protocol (SGBP), which is used when multiple PPP, or multilink PPP (MPPP), sessions are in use. When SGBP is configured on each Cisco AS5300, each access server sends a query to each stack group member. A stack group member is a router running the SGBP protocol.

Each router participating in SGBP then bids for the right to terminate the call. The router with an existing PPP session, for example, will win the bid; this allows the best bandwidth allocation to the end client, as both PPP sessions are terminated on the same router. If the PPP call is the first session to be terminated on the AS5300, the AS5300 with the lowest CPU usage will have a higher probability of terminating the call. Example 2-21 displays a typical IOS configuration when SGBP is enabled on the four AS5300 routers in Figure 2-21.

Example 2-21 *SGBP Configuration Example*

```
Hostname AS1
!
username CCIE password CCIE
sgbp group CCIE
sgbp member AS2 1.1.1.2
sgbp member AS3 1.1.1.3
sgbp member AS4 1.1.1.4
```

The following list explains the IOS commands used in Example 2-21.

- **username CCIE password CCIE**—Defines the username and password used for authenticating SGBP members. If the password is wrong, an error such as the following is presented on the console:

  ```
  %SGBP-1-AUTHFAILED: Member [chars] failed authentication
  ```

- **sgbp group CCIE**—Defines a named stack group and makes this router a member of that stack group. Use the **sgbp group** command in global configuration mode. To remove the definition, use the **no** form of this command.

- **sgbp member** *ip-address*—Specifies the host name and IP address of a router or access server that is a peer member of a stack group. Use the **sgbp member** command in global configuration mode.

Foundation Summary

The "Foundation Summary" is a condensed collection of material for a convenient review of key concepts in this chapter. If you are already comfortable with the topics in this chapter and decided to skip most of the "Foundation Topics" material, the "Foundation Summary" will help you recall a few details. If you just read the "Foundation Topics" section, this review should help further solidify some key facts. If you are doing your final preparation before the exam, the "Foundation Summary" offers a convenient and quick final review.

Table 2-17   *OSI Model*

OSI Name and Layer Number	Description
Application layer (Layer 7)	The application layer is closest to the end user, which means that the application is being accessed by the end user. This layer's major function is to provide services to end users. Examples of application layer services include the following: File Transfer Protocol (FTP) Telnet Ping Trace route SMTP Mail clients
Presentation layer (Layer 6)	The Presentation layer handles data formats and code formatting. This layer's functions are normally transparent to the end user because it takes care of code formats and presents them to the application layer (Layer 7), where the end user can examine the data. Examples of presentation layer protocols include the following: GIF JPEG ASCII MPEG TIFF MIDI HTML
Session layer (Layer 5)	The session layer performs several major functions, including managing sessions between devices and establishing and maintaining sessions. Examples of session layer protocols include the following: Database SQL NetBIOS Name Queries H.323 Real Time Control Protocol

continues

Table 2-17 *OSI Model (Continued)*

OSI Name and Layer Number	Description
Transport layer (Layer 4)	The transport layer is responsible for segmenting upper-layer applications and establishing end-to-end connections between devices. Other transport layer functions include providing data reliability and error-free delivery mechanisms. Information being processed at this layer is commonly known as segments. Examples of transport layer protocols include Transmission Control Protocol (TCP) and User Datagram Protocol (UDP).
Network layer (Layer 3)	The network layer determines the best path to a destination. Device addressing, packet fragmentation, and routing all occur at the network layer. Information being processed at this layer is commonly known as packets. Examples of network layer protocols include the following: Internet Protocol (IP) Open Shortest Path First (OSPF) Cisco's EIGRP routing protocol
Data Link layer (Layer 2)	The data link layer focuses on getting data reliably across any particular kind of link. Flow control and error notifications are other data link layer functions. The data link layer applies to all access methods, whether they are LAN or WAN methods. Information being processed at this layer is commonly known as frames. Example include the following: ISDN SDLC HDLC PPP Frame Relay Spanning tree protocol NetBEUI
Physical layer (Layer 1)	The physical layer consists of standards that describe bit ordering, bit transmission rates, connector types, and electrical and other specifications. Information at Layer 1 is transmitted in binary (1s and 0s; for example, the letter A is transmitted as 00001010). Examples of physical layer standards include the following: RS-232 V.24 V.35 RJ-45 RJ-12 10BaseT 100BaseT 1000BaseT Gigabit Ethernet

Table 2-18 *Ethernet Media Formats*

Media Type	Characteristics
10Base5	Maximum length 500 m. Maximum stations are 1024. Speed is 10 Mbps. Minimum distance between devices is 2.5 m.
10Base2	Maximum length 185 m, using RG58 cable types, T connectors on all end stations. Minimum distance between devices is 0.5 m. Maximum devices per 185 m segment is 30 stations. Speed is 10 Mbps. End points need termination.
10BaseT	Based on UTP cabling. Up to 100 m (longer for better category cables). One device per cable. Typically only one device per segment with hubs or switches connecting all devices together. Speed is 10 Mbps. Physical topology is star, logical topology is liner.
100BaseT	Same characteristics as 10baseT but operates faster, at 100 Mbps. Can be fibre, as well (100BaseFx). Defined in IEEE 802.3U.
1000 GE	Gigabit Ethernet operating at 1000 Mbps. Can run over Fibre or UTP. Frame formats and CSMA/CD identical to Ethernet standards.

Requirements for FastEther Channel

- All ports part of FEC must be set to the same speed.
- All ports must belong to the same VLAN.
- Duplex must be the same (half or full), not a mixture.
- Up to eight ports can be bundled together.
- To set FastEther channel on a switch, the CatOS syntax is **set port channel**.
- To set FastEther channel on a router, the IOS syntax is **channel-group** under the Fast Ethernet interface.

Table 2-19 *The States of Spanning Tree*

Bridge Port State	Description
Disabled	The port is not participating in spanning tree and is not active.
Listening	The port has received data from the interface and will listen for frames. In this state, the bridge receives only data but does not forward any frames to the interface or to other ports.
Learning	In this state, the bridge still discards incoming frames. The source address associated with the port is added to the CAM table. BPDU are sent and received.
Forwarding	The port is fully operational; frames are sent and received.
Blocking	The port has been through the learning and listening states, and because this particular port is a dual path to the root bridge, the port is blocked to maintain a loop-free topology.

Table 2-20 *Class A, B, C, D, and E Ranges*

Class of Address	Starting Bit Pattern	Range	Default Subnet Mask
Class A	0xxxxxxx	1 to 126, 127*	255.0.0.0
Class B	10xxxxxx	128 to 191	255.255.0.0
Class C	110xxxxx	192 to 223	255.255.255.0
Class D (multicast)	1110xxxx	224 to 239	255.255.255.240
Class E	1111xxxx	240 to 255	Reserved

> * 127.0.0.0 is reserved for loopbacks. Other reserved addresses for private use as defined by RFC 1918 are as
> follows:
> 10.0.0.0-10.255.255.255
> 172.16.0.0-172.31.255.255
> 192.168.0.0-192.168.255.255

Table 2-21 *Routing Protocol Classifications*

Routing Protocol	Class
IGRP	Distance vector (classful)
EIGRP	Hybrid (classless)
OSPF	Link-state (classless)
RIPv1	Distance vector (classful)
RIPv2	Distance vector (classless)
BGP	Path vector (classless)

Table 2-22   *TCP Flags Summary*

Flag	Description
URG (U)	Urgent—Informs the other station that urgent data is being carried. The receiver will decide what do with the data.
ACK (A)	Acknowledge—Indicates that the packet is an acknowledgment of received data, and the acknowledgment number is valid.
PSH (P)	Push—Informs the end station to send data to the application layer immediately.
RST (R)	Reset—Resets an existing connection.
SYN (S)	Synchronize—Initiates a connection, commonly known as *established*.
FIN (F)	Finished—Indicates that the sender is finished sending data and terminates the session.

Table 2-23   *TCP/IP Applications*

Application	Description
Address Resolution Protocol (ARP)	ARP maps an IP address to a MAC address.
Reverse Address Resolution Protocol (RARP)	RARP determines a host's IP address when the MAC address is known.
Dynamic Host Configuration Protocol (DHCP)	Dynamically provides IP addresses to TCP/IP hosts, subnet masks, and gateway addressing. Many other IP options can be assigned, as well.
Hot Standby Router Protocol (HSRP)	Redundancy gateway protocol, Cisco proprietary.
Internet Control Message Protocol (ICMP)	A network layer (Layer 3) Internet protocol that reports errors and provides other information relevant to IP packet processing. ICMP is fully documented in RFC 792.
Telnet	TCP/IP application layer protocol that enables remote management of TCP/IP hosts, such as routers or switches.
File Transfer Protocol (FTP)	TCP/IP application layer protocol that enables file transfer between TCP/IP hosts using a TCP, connection-orientated protocol.
Trivial File Transfer Protocol (TFTP)	TCP/IP application layer protocol that enables file transfers between TCP/IP hosts using a UDP, connectionless protocol.

Table 2-24   *Default Administrative Distances*

Route Source	Default Distance
Connected interface	0
Static route	1
Enhanced IGRP summary route	5
External BGP	20
Internal enhanced IGRP	90
IGRP	100
OSPF	110
IS-IS	115
RIP	120
EGP	140
EIGRP external route	170
Internal BGP	200
Unknown	255

Q & A

The Q & A questions are designed to help you assess your readiness for the topics covered on the CCIE Security written exam and those topics presented in this chapter. This format helps you assess your retention of the material. A strong understanding of the answers to these questions will help you on the CCIE Security written exam. You can also look over the questions at the beginning of the chapter again for further review. As an additional study aid, use the CD-ROM provided with this book to take simulated exams, which draw from a database of over 300 multiple-choice questions—all different from those presented in the book.

Select the best answer. Answers to these questions can be found in Appendix A, "Answers to Quiz Questions."

1 What are the seven layers of the OSI model?

_____

_____

_____

2 What layer of the OSI model is responsible for ensuring that IP packets are routed from one location to another?

_____

_____

_____

3 What mechanism is used in Ethernet to guarantee packet delivery over the wire?

_____

_____

_____

4 Name two physical characteristics of 10BaseT?

_____

_____

_____

5 What Catalyst command displays the bridging or CAM table on a Cisco 5000 series switch?

_____

_____

_____

6 What are the possible states of spanning tree?

_____

_____

_____

7 FastEther Channel (FEC) allows what to occur between Cisco Catalyst switches?

_____

_____

_____

8 What field in the IP packet guarantees data delivery?

_____

_____

_____

9 Name some examples of connection-orientated protocols used in TCP/IP networks.

_____

_____

_____

10 Given the address, 131.108.1.56/24, what are the subnet and broadcast addresses? How many hosts can reside on this network?

_____

_____

_____

11 How many hosts can reside when the subnet mask applied to the network 131.108.1.0 is 255.255.255.128 (or 131.108.1.0/25)?

_____

_____

12 Name five routing protocols that support VLSM.

_____

_____

_____

13 What is the destination port number used in a Telnet session?

_____

_____

_____

14 What TCP/IP services are common in today's large IP networks?

_____

_____

_____

15 What IOS command displays the IP ARP table on a Cisco IOS router?

_____

_____

_____

16 Cisco routers use what mechanism to determine the routing selection policy for remote networks if more than one routing protocol is running?

_____

_____

_____

17 What is the administrative distance for OSPF, RIP, and external EIGRP?

_____

_____

_____

18 Name five characteristics of distance vector routing protocols and provide two examples of routing protocols classified as distance vector.

_____

_____

_____

19 IP RIP runs over what protocol and port number when sending packets to neighboring routers?

_____

_____

_____

20 How many networks can be contained in an IP RIP update?

_____

_____

_____

21 Specify three main differences between RIPv1 and RIPv2?

_____

_____

_____

22 What is an EIGRP Feasible Successor?

_____

_____

_____

23 What is the metric used by OSPF?

_____

_____

_____

24 If OSPF is configured for one area, what area assignment should be used?

_____

_____

_____

25 What LSA types are not sent in a total stubby area?

_____

_____

_____

26 What IOS command disables an interface from participating in the election of an OSPF DR/BDR router?

_____

_____

_____

27 On an Ethernet broadcast network, a DR suddenly reboots. When the router recovers and discovers neighboring OSPF routers, will it be the designated router once more?

_____

_____

_____

28 What Layer 4 protocol does BGP use to guarantee routing updates, and what destination port number is used?

_____

_____

_____

29 What are ISDN BRI and PRI?

_____

_____

_____

30 What are the three phases that occur in any PPP session?

_____

_____

_____

31 Define what BECN and FECN mean in a Frame Relay network?

_____

_____

_____

32 Frame Relay DLCI values are used for what purpose?

_____

_____

_____

33 What is the IP address range used in IP multicast networks?

_____

_____

_____

34 What type of network environment typically uses an AS5300?

_____

_____

_____

Scenario

Scenario 2-1: Routing IP on Cisco Routers

Figure 2-21 displays a network with one Cisco router and two directly attached Ethernet interfaces. Use Figure 2-21 to answer the following questions.

Figure 2-21 *Scenario Diagram*

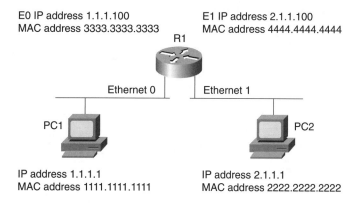

E0 IP address 1.1.1.100
MAC address 3333.3333.3333

E1 IP address 2.1.1.100
MAC address 4444.4444.4444

R1

Ethernet 0   Ethernet 1

PC1   PC2

IP address 1.1.1.1
MAC address 1111.1111.1111

IP address 2.1.1.1
MAC address 2222.2222.2222

1 In Figure 2-21, PC1 cannot communicate with PC2. What is the likely cause of the problem assuming that the router is configured correctly?

  a. Router R1 requires a routing protocol to route packets from Ethernet0 to Ethernet1.

  b. There is a problem with the IP address configuration on Router R1.

  c. The gateway address on PC1 is wrong.

  d. The gateway address on the router is wrong.

2 In Figure 2-21, what will be the ping response display when an exec user on Router R1 pings PC1's IP address for the first time? Assume that all configurations are correct.

  a. !!!!!

  b. !!!!.

  c. .....

  d. .!!!!

  e. .!!!!!

3 What IOS command was used to display the following output taken from Router R1?

```
Protocol  Address         Age (min)  Hardware Addr   Type   Interface
Internet  1.1.1.100          -       333.3333.3333   ARPA   Ethernet0
Internet  2.1.1.100          -       4444.4444.4444  ARPA   Ethernet1
Internet  1.1.1.1           10       1111.1111.1111  ARPA   Ethernet0
Internet  2.1.1.1           10       2222.2222.2222  ARPA   Ethernet1
```

a. **show ip arpa**

b. **show ip arp**

c. **show interface ethernet0**

d. **show interface ethernet1**

Scenario Answers

Scenario 2-1 Answers: Routing IP on Cisco Routers

1. **Answer: c. Cisco IOS routers will route between directly connected interfaces and, because PC1 cannot ping PC2 on another subnet, the PC1 gateway address must not be configured correctly.**

2. **Answer: d. The first request will fail because of the ARP broadcast. The subsequent pings (five in total: one for an ARP request and four successful replies) will reply successfully.**

3. **Answer: b. show ip arp displays the correct ARP address table for the devices in Figure 2-21.**

Exam Topics in this Chapter

CHAPTER 3

Application Protocols

This chapter covers some of today's most widely used application protocols.

This chapter covers the following topics:

- **Domain Name System (DNS)**—Topics in this section include how DNS is configured on Cisco routers and what port numbers are used when delivered across an IP network.

- **Trivial File Transfer Protocol (TFTP)**—This section covers TFTP's common uses, particularly on Cisco IOS-enabled routers. The process used to copy files to and from TFTP server is described.

- **File Transfer Protocol (FTP)**—This section covers FTP and the advanced mechanisms used in this connection-orientated protocol to ensure data delivery.

- **Other Application Topics**—Included are Hypertext Transfer Protocol (HTTP), Secure Socket Layer (SSL), Simple Network Management Protocol (SNMP), Simple Mail Transfer Protocol (SMTP), Network Time Protocol (NTP), Secure Shell (SSH), Lightweight Directory Access Protocol, and Active Directory. These sections cover some of the common configurations and IOS commands on Cisco routers that enable these applications.

NOTE   SNMP, although not listed officially on the Cisco website, is a possible topic in the written examination.

"Do I Know This Already?" Quiz

The purpose of this assessment quiz is to help you determine how to spend your limited study time. If you can answer most or all these questions, you might want to skim the "Foundation Topics" section and return to it later as necessary. Review the "Foundation Summary" section and answer the questions at the end of the chapter to ensure that you have a strong grasp of the material covered. If you already intend to read the entire chapter, you do not necessarily need to answer these questions now. If you find these assessment questions difficult, read through the entire "Foundation Topics" section and review it until you feel comfortable with your ability to answer all these and the "Q & A" questions at the end of the chapter.

Answers to these questions can be found in Appendix A, "Answers to Quiz Questions."

1 RFC 1700 defines what well-known ports for DNS?

 a. TCP port 21

 b. TCP port 23

 c. UDP port 21

 d. UDP port 53

 e. TCP/UDP port 53

2 What supplies DNS security?

 a. A default username/password pairing

 b. A TFTP directory

 c. A filename

 d. A domain name

 e. None of the above

3 What IOS command will stop a Cisco router from querying a DNS server when an invalid IOS command is entered on the EXEC or PRIV prompt?

 a. **no ip domain-lookup**

 b. **no ip dns-lookup**

 c. **no ip dns-queries**

 d. **no exec**

4 What does the following Global IOS configuration line accomplish?

```
ip host SimonisaCCIE 131.108.1.1 131.108.1.2
```

 a. Defines the router name as SimonisaCCIE

 b. Defines a local host name, SimonisaCCIE, mapped to IP addresses 131.108.1.1 and 131.108.1.2

 c. Configures the IOS router for remote routing entries 131.108.1.1 and 131.108.1.2

 d. Not a valid IOS command

 e. Configures the local routers with the IP address 131.108.1.1 and 131.108.1.2 on boot up

5 TFTP uses what predefined UDP port number?

   a. 21

   b. 22

   c. 23

   d. 53

   e. 69

6 What IOS command will copy an IOS image from the current system flash to a TFTP server?

   a. copy tftp image:

   b. copy flash tftp

   c. copy tftp flash

   d. copy tftp tftp

7 Suppose a client calls and advises you that an FTP data transaction is not allowing him to view the host's directory structure. What are the most likely causes of the problem? (Choose all that apply.)

   a. The client's username/password is wrong.

   b. The client's FTP data port is not connected.

   c. The host machine has denied him access because the password is wrong.

   d. A serious network outage requires that you reload the router closest to the client.

   e. An access list is stopping port 20 from detailing the directory list.

8 FTP runs over what Layer 4 protocol?

   a. IP

   b. TCP

   c. TFTP

   d. DNS

   e. UDP

9 HTTPS traffic uses what TCP port number?

   a. 21

   b. 443

   c. 334

   d. 333

   e. 343

10 SNMP is restricted on Cisco routers by what IOS command?

   a. **snmp-server enable**

   b. **snmp-server community** *string*

   c. **snmp-server** *ip-address*

   d. **snmp-server no access permitted**

11 TFTP protocol uses which of the following?

   a. Username/password pairs to authorize transfers

   b. Uses TCP port 169

   c. Uses UDP port 169

   d. Can use UDP/TCP and port 69

   e. None of the above

12 Which of the following statements is true regarding SSL?

   a. Every packet sent between host and client is authenticated.

   b. Encryption is used after a simple handshake is completed.

   c. SSL uses port 2246.

   d. SSL is not a predefined standard.

   e. SSL does not perform any data integrity checks.

13 What is the **HELO** SMTP command used for?

   a. To authenticate SMTP clients

   b. To identify SMTP clients

   c. This is an unknown standard

   d. The **HELO** command is used in SNMP (not SMTP)

14 POP3 clients can do what?

    a. Receive SNMP queries

    b. Send mail

    c. Send SNMP queries

    d. The POP3 protocol is a routing algorithm

15 NTP uses what well-known TCP port?

    a. 23

    b. 551

    c. 21

    d. 20

    e. 123

    f. 321

16 Secure Shell (SSH) is used to do what?

    a. Disable spanning tree on Catalyst 5000 switches

    b. Protect the data link layer only from attacks

    c. Protect the TCP/IP host

    d. Allow TCP/IP access to all networks without any security

    e. SSH is used only in the data link layer

17 Which of the following protocols can be authenticated? (Select the best four answers.)

    a. Telnet

    b. HTTP

    c. HTTPS

    d. Spanning tree

    e. TFTP

    f. FTP

18 What is the community string value when the following IOS commands are entered in global configuration mode?

```
snmp-server community publiC RO
snmp-server enable traps config
snmp-server host 131.108.255.254 isdn
```

a. ISDN

b. Config

c. publiC

d. public

e. Public

f. More data required

19 Which of the following best describes an SNMP inform request?

a. Requires no acknowledgment

b. Requires an acknowledgment from the SNMP agent

c. Requires an acknowledgment from the SNMP manager

d. Only SNMP traps can be implemented on Cisco IOS routers

20 What UDP port number will SNMP traps be sent from?

a. 21

b. 22

c. 161

d. 162

21 What TCP port number will an SNMP inform acknowledgment packet be sent to?

a. 21

b. 22

c. 23

d. 161

e. 162

f. None of the above

22 To restrict SNMP managers from the source network 131.108.1.0/30, what IOS command is required?

a.

```
ip http enable 131.108.1.1 131.108.1.2
```

b.

```
snmp community  131.108.1.1 131.108.1.2
```

c.

```
snmp-server community SimonisCool ro 4
  access-list 4 permit 131.108.1.0 0.0.0.252
```

d.

```
snmp-server community SimonisCool ro 4
```

e.

```
snmp-server community SimonisCool ro 1
  access-list 11 permit 131.108.1.0 0.0.0.252
```

Foundation Topics

Domain Name System

This section covers Domain Name System (DNS) and sample configurations used on Cisco IOS routers.

DNS's primary use is to manage Internet names across the World Wide Web. For users or clients to use names instead of 32-bit IP addresses, the TCP/IP model designers developed DNS to translate names into IP addresses.

DNS uses TCP and UDP port number 53.

In a large IP environment, network users need an easier way to connect to hosts without having to remember 32-bit IP addresses—that's where DNS comes into play. DNS provides a service that allows users to use a host's name in place of an IP Address to connect to hosts. When DNS services are running, the host's name is used to request its IP address from a DNS server. The DNS server is a host running the DNS service, and it is configured to do the translation for the user transparently. In other words, the user never sees the DNS request and host-to-IP address translation. The client simply connects to a host name, and the DNS server does the translation.

For example, the website www.cisco.com is translated to the IP address 198.133.129.25.

DNS is a distributed database where organizations can use a predefined name or extension to all their devices. Nations can use extensions to define hosts residing in their country. For example, the extension for Australia is defined as .au. To reach the Cisco website in Australia, a user would type www.cisco.com.au in a web browser.

A regulatory body called the Internet Registration Authority manages domain names.

Similar to DNS, Cisco routers can be configured to locally look up names so network administrator can simply type a name rather than an IP address. Local names can also be configured for devices.

To illustrate a local DNS lookup on a Cisco IOS router, look at the following Cisco router command that provides a host lookup. (Note: a router will not provide DNS server responses to client devices such as PCs or UNIX hosts.)

The following IOS command defines a local name to IP address:

```
ip host name [tcp-port-number] ip address1 [ip address2...ip address8]
```

You can assign more than one IP address to any given name.

Example 3-1 displays three hosts and their corresponding IP addresses.

Example 3-1 *Local IP Host Configuration on a Cisco Router*

```
ip host Router1 131.108.1.1
ip host Router2 131.108.1.2
ip host Router3 131.108.1.3
```

The three hosts, named Router1, Router2, and Router3 in Example 3-1, are translated into IP addresses 131.108.1.1, 131.108.1.2, and 131.108.1.3.

When a network administrator types in the host name, the router translates the name to an IP address. Example 3-2 displays a network administrator Telneting from router, R1, to the remote host, Router2.

Example 3-2 *Local DNS Translation*

```
R1#router2
Translating "router2"
Trying Router2 (131.108.1.2)... Open
User Access Verification

Password: *****
Router2>
```

When the network administrator types the name router2 (DNS names are not case-sensitive) at the exec prompt, the Cisco IOS router does a local host lookup for the name router2 and translates the address to 131.108.1.2.

What would happen if you typed a name that was not configured locally? Example 3-3 displays the sample output from a Cisco router when an unknown name (ccie, in this case) is typed at the exec prompt.

Example 3-3 *Name Translation for ccie*

```
R1#ccie
Translating "ccie"
Translating "ccie"
% Unknown command or computer name, or unable to find computer address
R1#
```

From the privileged exec prompt on Router R1 in Example 3-3, R1 does a local DNS lookup, discovers there is no DNS translation, and provides the shaded error message.

Scalability issues with local host configuration can become a nightmare with a large network. Thankfully, DNS servers can be placed around the network (typically in the core infrastructure) to ensure that only a few devices in the network require the full table of names and IP address translations. The World Wide Web has DNS servers that provide DNS mapping for websites.

NOTE   By default, Cisco routers search for a DNS server. To disable this feature, use the IOS command **no ip domain-lookup**. This stops the router from querying a DNS server whenever a name translation is required. This command is a definite time saver for the CCIE Security Lab exam.

To enable a Cisco IOS router to perform DNS lookup to a remote DNS server, the following steps are required:

Step 1   For local DNS entries, you must specify any local host mapping with the following IOS command (note that the **tcp-port-number** is used for connections on a different TCP port number other than the default, 23):

```
ip host name [tcp-port-number] ip address1 [ip address2...ip address8]
```

Step 2   Specify the domain name or a domain list (Cisco routers can be configured with multiple domain names) with the following IOS commands:

— **ip domain-name** *name* defines a default domain name that the Cisco IOS Software uses to complete unqualified host names.

— **ip domain-list** *name* defines a list of default domain names to complete unqualified host names.

Step 3   Specify the DNS server or servers with the following IOS command:

```
ip name-server server-address1 [server-address2...server-address6]
```

Devices such as PCs can also be configured for DNS servers and domain names. Example 3-4 configures a router named R1 with the domain name cisco.com. The domain name servers are 131.108.255.1 and 131.108.255.2.

Example 3-4   *DNS Configuration*

```
R1(config)#ip domain-name cisco.com
R1(config)#ip name-server 131.108.255.1
R1(config)#ip name-server 131.108.255.2
```

When a network administrator types a name (not a valid IOS command, of course), the Cisco router attempts to translate the name into an IP address, first from the DNS server with the IP address 131.108.255.1, and then from the DNS server 131.108.255.2.

Example 3-5 displays a successful DNS query and translation to the host named ccie (another Cisco router) from the DNS server 131.108.255.1.

Example 3-5   *DNS Query from the Exec Prompt*

```
R1#ccie
! Administrator types ccie
Translating "ccie"
! Query is sent to first configured DNS server
Trying CCIE (131.108.255.1)... Open
User Access Verification
Password: ****
CCIE>
```

NOTE   In Example 3-5, a Telnet connection requires a password authentication phase (and for all Telnet-based connections, for that matter). You can disable the Telnet login password on Cisco routers with the command **no login** under the VTY line configuration, as follows:

```
line vty 0 4
no login
```

Trivial File Transfer Protocol

Trivial File Transfer Protocol (TFTP) is a protocol that allows data files to be transferred from one device to another using the connectionless protocol, UDP. TFTP uses UDP port number 69.

TFTP is typically used in environments where bandwidth is not a major concern and IP packets that are lost can be resent by the higher layers (typically the application layer). TFTP has little security. In fact, the only security available to TFTP transfer is defining the directory on the host TFTP device and the filenames that will be transferred.

1 TFTP has no method to authenticate username or password; the TFTP packet has no field enabling the exchange of username or password between two TCP/IP hosts.

2 TFTP directory security (configurable on UNIX and Windows platforms) on the TFTP server is accomplished by allowing a predefined file on the server access. This allows the remote hosts to TFTP the file from the remote TFTP client. For example, to copy a configuration file from a Cisco router to a UNIX or Windows host, the file must be predefined on the TFTP server with the appropriate access rights defined.

Upgrading Cisco IOS images is a great example of when TFTP is useful; IOS images can be downloaded from a TFTP server to the Cisco router's system flash.

Cisco offers a free TFTP application protocol, available at the following URL:

www.cisco.com/public/sw-center/sw-web.shtml

Now, configure the Cisco application software, Cisco TFTP, to enable a Cisco router to download a version of IOS code.

Figure 3-1 displays the available options when configuring the TFTP application software.

Figure 3-1 *Cisco TFTP Application Software Options*

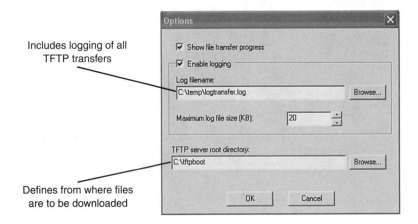

Includes logging of all
TFTP transfers

Defines from where files
are to be downloaded

The TFTP directory in Figure 3-1 is defined as c:\tftpboot. On the host TFTP server (in this case a Windows 2000 PC), the IOS images reside in the tftpboot directory at c:\tftpboot. This download directory option is a configurable option, and you can select any valid directory on the host TFTP server.

The file is located in the tftpboot directory. In this example, the IOS image is named c2600-js-mz.121-5.T10.bin.

To copy an IOS image from a TFTP server, the IOS command is **copy tftp flash**. Example 3-6 displays a TFTP request for the file c2600-js-mz.121-5.T10.bin from a TFTP server with an IP address of 150.100.1.253.

Example 3-6 *TFTP File Transfer*

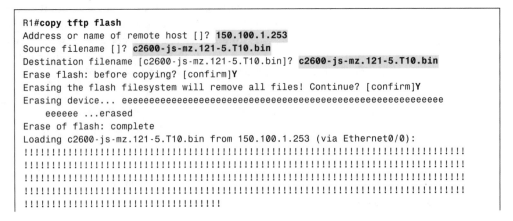

```
R1#copy tftp flash
Address or name of remote host []? 150.100.1.253
Source filename []? c2600-js-mz.121-5.T10.bin
Destination filename [c2600-js-mz.121-5.T10.bin]? c2600-js-mz.121-5.T10.bin
Erase flash: before copying? [confirm]Y
Erasing the flash filesystem will remove all files! Continue? [confirm]Y
Erasing device... eeeeeeeeeeeeeeeeeeeeeeeeeeeeeeeeeeeeeeeeeeeeeeeeeeeeeeeeeeee
    eeeeee ...erased
Erase of flash: complete
Loading c2600-js-mz.121-5.T10.bin from 150.100.1.253 (via Ethernet0/0):
!!!!!!!!!!!!!!!!!!!!!!!!!!!!!!!!!!!!!!!!!!!!!!!!!!!!!!!!!!!!!!!!!!!!!!!!!!!!!!!!!!!
!!!!!!!!!!!!!!!!!!!!!!!!!!!!!!!!!!!!!!!!!!!!!!!!!!!!!!!!!!!!!!!!!!!!!!!!!!!!!!!!!!!
!!!!!!!!!!!!!!!!!!!!!!!!!!!!!!!!!!!!!!!!!!!!!!!!!!!!!!!!!!!!!!!!!!!!!!!!!!!!!!!!!!!
!!!!!!!!!!!!!!!!!!!!!!!!!!!!!!!!!!!!!!!!!!!!!!!!!!!!!!!!!!!!!!!!!!!!!!!!!!!!!!!!!!!
!!!!!!!!!!!!!!!!!!!!!!!!!!!!!!!!!!!!!!!!!!
```

Example 3-6   *TFTP File Transfer (Continued)*

```
[OK - 11432808/22864896 bytes]
Verifying checksum... OK (0xBC59)
11432808 bytes copied in 106.126 secs (107856 bytes/sec)
R1#
```

The file (c2600-js-mz.121-5.T10.bin) is successfully copied and placed on the flash system on Router R1. The only two mechanisms for security permitted with TFTP are the filename and directory. TFTP has no mechanism for checking username and password. On a UNIX server where the TFTP server daemon is installed, the file to be copied must have the appropriate access rights. In UNIX, the **Touch** command is used to allow a TFTP request. For a Windows-based platform, the software must be configured to permit file creation on the Windows-based file system.

FTP, on the other hand, is a connection-based protocol, where username and password combinations are used to authorize file transfers.

File Transfer Protocol

File Transfer Protocol (FTP), an application layer protocol of the TCP/IP protocol suite of applications, allows users to transfer files from one host to another. Two ports are required for FTP—one port is used to open the connection (port 21), and the other port is used to transfer data (20). FTP runs over TCP and is a connection-oriented protocol. To provide security, FTP allows usernames and passwords to be exchanged before any data can be transferred, adding some form of security authentication mechanism to ensure that only valid users access FTP servers.

The advantages of FTP are the ability to list a remote FTP server's full list of directories and ensure that only valid users are connected. The file transfer progress can be displayed to the FTP client, as well. Many FTP applications are available, and the range of options is endless. For example, on the CCIE Security lab exam, the application Reflection 2000 can be used for Telnet and FTP. For more details on this application, visit www.wrq.com/products/reflection/.

NOTE   FTP connection issues are typically communicated by end users (FTP clients) as poor network performance when the problem might actually be a result of filtering the FTP data on port 20. For example, when a client successfully logs into an FTP server remotely but fails to list the remote FTP server's directory or to transfer files, this can indicate a problem with the FTP data port (via TCP port 20) or an access list problem on the remote network.

FTP clients can be configured for two modes of operation:

* Active mode
* Passive mode

Active FTP

Active FTP is defined as one connection initiated by the client to the server for FTP control connection. Remember that FTP requires two port connections through TCP ports 20 (data) and 21 (control). The second connection is made for the FTP data connection (where data is transferred), which is initiated from the server back to the client.

Active FTP is less secure than passive mode because the FTP server, which, in theory, could be any host, initiates the data channel.

Figure 3-2 displays the active FTP mode of operation between an FTP client and FTP server.

Figure 3-2   *FTP Active Mode*

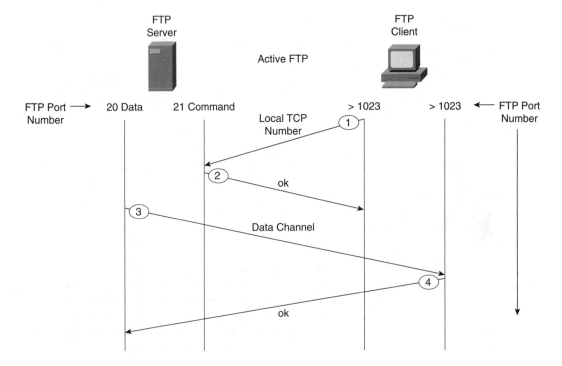

Figure 3-2 displays a typical FTP mode of operation between a client PC and FTP server in active mode. The following steps are completed before FTP data can be transferred:

1   The FTP client opens a control channel on TCP port number 21 to the FTP server. The source TCP port number on the FTP client is any number randomly generated above 1023.

2   The FTP server receives the request and sends an acknowledgment. FTP commands are exchanged between client and server.

3   When the FTP client requests a directory list or initiates a file transfer, the client sends a command (FTP **port** command). The FTP server then opens (initiates) a data connection on the FTP data port, TCP port 20.

4   The FTP client responds and data can be transferred.

Passive FTP

Passive FTP still requires a connection for the initial FTP control connection, which is initiated by the FTP client to the server. However, the second connection for the FTP data connection is also initiated from the client to the server (the reverse of active FTP).

Figure 3-3 displays a typical FTP mode of operation between a client PC and FTP server in passive mode.

Figure 3-3   *FTP Passive Mode*

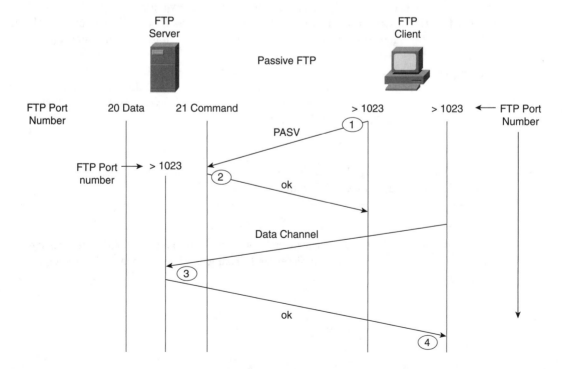

The following steps are completed before data can be transferred:

1   The FTP client opens a control channel on TCP port 21 to the FTP server and requests passive mode with the FTP command **pasv**, or **passive**. The source TCP port number is any number randomly generated above 1023.

2   The FTP server receives the request and agrees to the connections using a randomly generated, local TCP port number greater than 1023.

3   The FTP client receives the information, selects a local TCP number randomly generated and greater than 1023, and opens a data channel to the FTP server (on TCP greater than 1023).

4   The FTP server receives the FTP client's request and agrees to the connection.

In passive FTP, the client initiates both the control connection and the data connection. In active mode, the FTP server initiates the FTP data channel. When using passive FTP, the probability of compromising data is less because the FTP client initiates both connections.

Hypertext Transfer Protocol

Hypertext Transfer Protocol (HTTP), used by web browsers and web servers, transfers files, such as text and graphic files. HTTP can also authenticate users with username and password verification between client and web servers.

Cisco IOS routers can be configured from a browser client. By default, Cisco routers are disabled for HTTP server (HTTP is enabled by default on a few Cisco 1000 models, namely the Cisco 1003,1004, and 1005 model routers), and there have been issues with users entering certain hash pairs to gain access to configuration commands when HTTP has been enabled. Fortunately, the latest versions of Cisco IOS code have been strengthened, and users must now enter valid username and password pairings to gain access to the configuration options. HTTP authentication is not very secure, so Secure Socket Layer (SSL) was developed to allow a stronger method to authenticate HTTP users.

NOTE   For more details on the HTTP security vulnerability with Cisco IOS, please visit www.cisco.com/warp/public/707/ioshttpserver-pub.shtml

---

To view the router's home page, use a web browser pointed to http://*a.b.c.d*, where *a.b.c.d* is the IP address of your router or access server. If a name has been set via a DNS server, use http://*router-name*.

Figure 3-4 displays a sample HTTP request to a remote router with the IP address 10.66.32.5 displaying the request for a valid username and password. The default username is the Cisco router's local host name, and the password is set to the enable or secret password.

Figure 3-4   *HTTP Authentication on a Cisco Router*

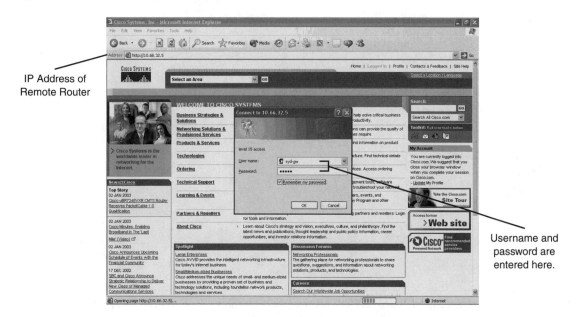

After the user is authenticated, the user enters the remote IP address or DNS name.

Varying forms of authentication for login can be set using the **ip http authentication** command. However, the default login method is entering the host name as the username and the enable or secret password as the password, as displayed in Figure 3-4.

After the user is authenticated with the correct username and password pairing, the user is permitted HTTP access. Figure 3-5 displays the options available after authentication.

After HTTP is authenticated, the available options are identical to the command-line interface (CLI) prompt. Depending on the configurable username and password pairing on the router, you will have certain privileged levels. For example, if you type the username as the local host name of the IOS router and the enable or secret password as completed in Figure 3-5, you will have privilege level 15, which is the same as the PRIV level on the CLI permitting all IOS commands. If the username/password pairing has a lower privileged level (via the **ip http authentication** command), the corresponding IOS command set will be available via HTTP. For example, a user with privilege level 5 will not have the option to reload the router.

Figure 3-5 *HTTP Web Page on a Cisco Router*

HTTP options; simply
click to expand IOS
command set.

Help Options

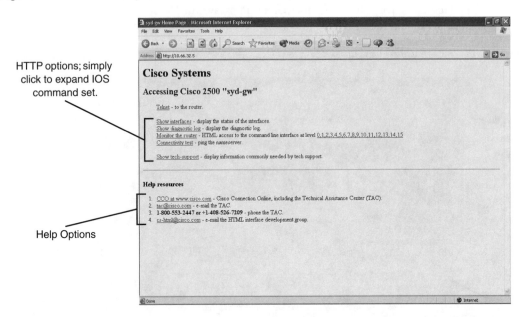

Secure Socket Layer

Secure Socket Layer (SSL) is an encryption technology for web host devices used to provide
secure transactions. For example, a secure transaction is required when clients enter their credit
card numbers for e-commerce via their browser. When the end user enters a web address via an
Internet browser, such as Internet Explorer, instead of entering HTTP: //*web address* in the
address window, the end user enters HTTPS://*web address*.

Secure Hypertext Transfer Protocol secure site, or HTTPS, transports HTTP-based traffic over an SSL connection and provides a stronger authentication mechanism than HTTP.

HTTPS runs over TCP port 443. SSL is defined in RFC 2246.

The SSL Handshake Protocol was first developed by Netscape Communications Corporation to provide security and privacy over the World Wide Web. The SSL protocol supports server and client authentication. The SSL protocol is application-independent, allowing protocols like HTTP, FTP, and Telnet to be layered on top of it transparently. In other words, it is a session layer-based protocol. Cisco has developed a number of content-based switches to accelerate this communication, such as the Cisco SCA 11000 Series Secure Content Accelerator. The Cisco SCA 11000 Series Secure Content Accelerator is an appliance-based solution that increases the number of secure connections supported by a website by offloading the processor-intensive tasks related to securing traffic with SSL. After an SSL session is established, no further authentication is required. Chapter 5, "Security Protocols," broadens this discussion on public security by discussing topics such as private and public keys, and how keys are exchanged through the Certificate Authority (CA) to ensure that SSL is secure.

Simple Network Management Protocol

Application layer protocol, Simple Network Management Protocol (SNMP), is used to manage IP devices. SNMP is part of the TCP/IP application layer suite. SNMP allows network administrators the ability to view and change network parameters and monitor connections locally and remotely. Managing network performance over a period of time is one of the major functions that SNMP provides.

There are three version of SNMP:

- SNMP Version 1 (SNMPv1)
- SNMP Version 2 (SNMPv2)
- SNMP Version 3 (SNMPv3)

Both SNMPv1 and SNMPv2 use a community-based form of security. The community string allows access to the SNMP agent and can also be defined by an IP address access control list and password.

To set up the community access strings to permit access to the Simple Network Management Protocol (SNMP) on a Cisco IOS router, use the **snmp-server community** global configuration command:

```
snmp-server community string [view view-name] [ro | rw] [number]
```

Table 3-1 describes this syntax.

Table 3-1   **snmp-server community** *Command Syntax Description*

Syntax	Description
string	Case-sensitive community string that acts like a password and permits access to the SNMP protocol.
view *view-name*	(Optional) Name of a previously defined view. The view defines the objects available to the community.
ro	(Optional) Specifies read-only access. Authorized management stations are able to retrieve only MIB objects.
rw	(Optional) Specifies read-write access. Authorized management stations are able to retrieve and modify MIB objects.
number	(Optional) Integer from 1 to 99 that specifies an access list of IP addresses that are allowed to use the community string to gain access to the SNMP agent.

SNMP servers collect information from remote devices known as SNMP agents. SNMP packets are sent and received by devices on UDP ports 161 (SNMP servers) and 162 (SNMP agents).

The Management Information Base (MIB) is a virtual information storage area for network management information consisting of collections of managed objects. Within the MIB are collections of related objects, defined in MIB modules. MIB modules are written in the SNMP MIB module language, as defined in STD 58, RFC 2578, RFC 2579, and RFC 2580. SNMP port 161 is used to query SNMP devices, and SNMP port 162 is used to send SNMP traps. SNMP runs over UDP and is secured by a well-known, case-sensitive community string.

SNMP Notifications

SNMP's key feature is the ability to generate notifications from SNMP agents.

Cisco routers can be configured to send SNMP traps or informed requests to a Network Management System (NMS) where a network administrator can view the data.

Figure 3-6 displays the typical communication between an SNMP manager and the SNMP agent (for example, a Cisco-enabled SNMP router).

Unsolicited notifications can be generated as *traps* or *inform requests*. Traps are messages alerting the SNMP manager to a condition on the network (sent by the SNMP agent). Inform requests (informs) are traps that include a request for confirmation of receipt from the SNMP manager. SNMP notifications can indicate improper user authentication, restarts, the closing of a connection, loss of connection to a neighbor router, or other significant events.

Figure 3-6   *Communication Between SNMP Manager and SNMP Agent*

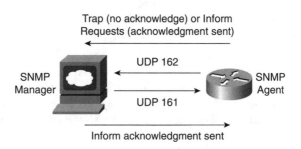

The major difference between a trap and an inform packet is that an SNMP agent has no way of knowing if an SNMP trap was received by the SNMP manager. An inform request will be sent continually until an acknowledgment is received by the sending SNMP agent.

Table 3-2 defines some of the common terminology used in SNMP.

Table 3-2   *SNMP Terminology*

Term	Description
Managed device	A network node that contains an SNMP agent and resides on a managed network. Managed devices collect and store management information and make this information available to Network Management Systems using SNMP.
Agent	A network management software module that resides in a managed device. An agent has local knowledge of management information and translates that information into a form compatible with SNMP.
Network Management System (NMS)	Executes applications that monitor and control managed devices.

NOTE   Managed devices are monitored and controlled using three common SNMP commands: **read, write,** and **trap.**

The **read** command is used by an NMS to monitor managed devices. The NMS examines different variables that are maintained by managed devices.

The **write** command is used by an NMS to control managed devices. The NMS changes the values of variables stored within managed devices.

The **trap** command is used by managed devices to asynchronously report events to the NMS. For example, Cisco IOS routers can be configured to report errors, such as emergencies alerts, to the NMS for urgent action, such as low memory resources or unauthorized access. When certain types of events occur, a managed device sends a trap to the NMS.

Management Information Base (MIB), a database of network management information, is used and maintained by a management protocol such as SNMP. The value of an MIB object can be changed or retrieved using SNMP commands, usually through a GUI network management system. Cisco supports a number of defined and proprietary MIB commands.

If the **snmp-server community** command is not used during the SNMP configuration session, it will automatically be added to the configuration after the **snmp-server host** command is used. In this case, the default password (*string*) for the **snmp-server community** is taken from the **snmp-server host** command. You must always set the community string manually; otherwise, your router could be left vulnerable to SNMP **get** commands.

Example 3-7 configures a Cisco IOS router for SNMP support.

Example 3-7   *Sample SNMP Configuration*

```
snmp-server community public RO
snmp-server enable traps config
snmp-server host 131.108.255.254 isdn
```

The IOS command **snmp-server community public RO** enables SNMP on a Cisco router. This command is also used to restrict access via SNMP. The community string is defined as public and acts as a password protection mechanism against unauthorized users. The community string is sent in every SNMP packet, so an incorrect community string results in no authorized access to the SNMP agent. The read-only attribute means that no configuration changes will be permitted via an SNMP.

The IOS command **snmp-server enable traps config** advises the NMS of any configuration changes. The IOS command **snmp-server host 131.108.255.254 isdn** alerts the host 131.108.254.254 of any ISDN traps. ISDN traps can include link flapping or high link usage, for example. (See Table 3-2 for a comprehensive list of traps.)

To specify the recipient of an SNMP notification operation, use the **snmp-server host** global configuration command. To remove the specified host, use the **no** form of this command.

```
snmp-server host host-addr [traps | informs] [version {1 | 2c | 3
    [auth | noauth | priv]}] community-string
    [udp-port port] [notification-type]
```

Table 3-3 expands the **snmp-server host** IOS command and presents the full range of options, including MD5 authentication.

Table 3-3 **snmp-server host** *Command*

Syntax Description	Meaning
host-addr	Name or Internet address of the host (the targeted recipient).
traps	(Optional) Sends trap messages to this host. This is the default.
informs	(Optional) Sends Inform messages to this host.
version	(Optional) Version of the SNMP used to send the traps. Version 3 is the most secure model because it allows packet encryption with the **priv** keyword. If you use the **version** keyword, one of the following must be specified: **1**—SNMPv1. This option is not available with informs. **2c**—SNMPv2C. **3**—SNMPv3. The following three optional keywords can follow the **3** keyword: **auth**—(Optional) Enables Message Digest 5 (MD5) and Secure Hash Algorithm (SHA) packet authentication. **noauth**—(Default) The noAuthNoPriv security level. This is the default if the [**auth** | **noauth** | **priv**] keyword choice is not specified. **priv**—(Optional) Enables Data Encryption Standard (DES) packet encryption (also called privacy).
community-string	Password-like community string sent with the notification operation. Although you can set this string using the **snmp-server host** command by itself, it is recommended that you define this string using the **snmp-server community** command prior to using the **snmp-server host** command.
udp-port *port*	(Optional) UDP port of the host to use. The default is 162.
notification-type	(Optional) Type of notification to be sent to the host. If no type is specified, all notifications are sent. The notification type can be one or more of the following keywords: **bgp**—Sends Border Gateway Protocol (BGP) state change notifications. **calltracker**—Sends Call Tracker call-start/call-end notifications. **config**—Sends configuration notifications. **dspu**—Sends downstream physical unit (DSPU) notifications. **entity**—Sends Entity MIB modification notifications. **envmon**—Sends Cisco enterprise-specific environmental monitor notifications when an environmental threshold is exceeded. **frame-relay**—Sends Frame Relay notifications. **hsrp**—Sends Hot Standby Routing Protocol (HSRP) notifications.

continues

Table 3-3   **snmp-server host** *Command (Continued)*

Syntax Description	Meaning
notification-type *(Continued)*	**isdn**—Sends Integrated Services Digital Network (ISDN) notifications. **llc2**—Sends Logical Link Control, type 2 (LLC2) notifications. **repeater**—Sends standard repeater (hub) notifications. **rsrb**—Sends remote source-route bridging (RSRB) notifications. **rsvp**—Sends Resource Reservation Protocol (RSVP) notifications. **rtr**—Sends SA Agent (RTR) notifications. **sdlc**—Sends Synchronous Data Link Control (SDLC) notifications. **sdllc**—Sends SDLLC notifications. **snmp**—Sends any enabled RFC 1157 SNMP linkUp, linkDown, authenticationFailure, warmStart, and coldStart notifications. **stun**—Sends serial tunnel (STUN) notifications. **syslog**—Sends error message notifications (Cisco Syslog MIB). Specify the level of messages to be sent with the **logging history level** command. **tty**—Sends Cisco enterprise-specific notifications when a Transmission Control Protocol (TCP) connection closes. **voice**—Sends SNMP poor quality of voice traps when used with the **snmp enable peer-trap poor qov** command. **x25**—Sends X.25 event notifications.

*   Table 3-3 is sourced from the Cisco Documentation website, www.cisco.com/univercd/cc/td/doc/product/
software/ios121/121cgcr/fun_r/frprt3/frd3001.htm#xtocid655917.

SNMP is disabled by default on Cisco IOS routers.

SNMP Examples

The following example assigns the SimonisCool string to SNMP, allowing read-only access, and specifies that IP access list 4 can use the community string:

```
R1(config)# snmp-server community SimonisCool ro 4
R1(config)# access-list 4 permit 131.108.1.0 0.0.0.255
```

The hosts on network 131.108.1.0/24 are permitted SNMP access if the read-only string is set to SimonisCool. This enables an added feature to ensure that devices that source SNMP information are from a trusted or internal network.

The following example assigns the string SnR to SNMP, allowing read-write access to the objects in the restricted view (read only):

```
R1(config)# snmp-server community SnR view restricted ro
```

The following example disables all versions of SNMP:

```
R1(config)# no snmp-server
```

The following example enables the router to send all traps to the host, host.cisco.com, using the community string public:

```
R1(config)# snmp-server enable traps
R1(config)# snmp-server host host.cisco.com public
```

In the following example, the BGP traps are enabled for all hosts, but only the ISDN traps are enabled to be sent to an actual host named simon:

```
R1(config)# snmp-server enable traps bgp
R1(config)# snmp-server host simon public isdn
```

The following example enables the router to send all inform requests to the host test.cisco.com using the community string publiC:

```
R1(config)# snmp-server enable traps
R1(config)# snmp-server host test.cisco.com informs publiC
```

Simple Mail Transfer Protocol

The Simple Mail Transfer Protocol (SMTP) mechanism is used for providing e-mail services to IP devices over the Internet. SMTP is defined in RFC 821. Typically, two mail servers will talk SMTP to exchange mails. After the mails are exchanged, the users can read/retrieve their mail from the mail server. This can be done using any mail client, such as Pine, Eudore, Outlook, and so on, which use different protocols, such as Post office protocol or POP3, to connect to the server. SMTP uses well-known ports TCP port 25 and UDP port 25.

A process or daemon running on a server will use SMTP to send mail to clients. A program called Sendmail is a common tool used for SMTP mail transfer. Recently, a new release of SMTP, called Enhanced SMTP (ESMTP), was developed. You are not required to know this protocol for the written exam.

NOTE   The client and SMTP server send various commands when communicating. The most common command is **HELO check**.

The **HELO Check** command introduces the calling machine to the receive machine; the client will advertise the mail server its host name. There are numerous other commands. A great resource if you are interested in further details on the Sendmail application is the book "Sendmail," by Bryan Costales and Eric Allman (O'Reilly and Associates, ISBN 1-56592-839-3).

To test if a remote host's SNMP mail is operational and active, you can use Telnet with the defined **HELO** command.

A summary of other useful SMTP commands is presented for your reference in case you are questioned on these commands during the exam:

HELLO (HELO)—Identifies the sender.

MAIL (MAIL)—Initiates a mail transaction in which the mail data is delivered to mailboxes.

RECIPIENT (RCPT)—Identifies an individual recipient of the mail data; multiple use of the command is needed for multiple users.

DATA (DATA)—The lines following the command are the mail data in ASCII character codes.

SEND (SEND)—Initiates a mail transaction in which the mail data is delivered to one or more terminals.

SEND OR MAIL (SOML)—Initiates a mail transaction in which the mail data is delivered to one or more terminals or mailboxes.

SEND AND MAIL (SAML)—Initiates a mail transaction in which the mail data is delivered to one or more terminals and mailboxes.

RESET (RSET)—The current mail transaction is to be aborted. Any stored sender, recipients, and mail data must be discarded, and all buffers and state tables cleared. The receiver must send an OK reply.

VERIFY (VRFY)—This is to verify if a user exists; a fully specified mailbox and name are returned.

NOOP (NOOP)—Specifies no action other than that the receiver sent an OK reply.

QUIT (QUIT)—The receiver must send an OK reply and then close the transmission channel.

Network Time Protocol

Network Time Protocol (NTP) is used for accurate time keeping and can reference atomic clocks that are present on the Internet, for example. NTP is capable of synchronizing clocks within milliseconds and is a useful protocol when reporting error logs (for instance, from Cisco routers).

For NTP, the defined ports are UDP port 123 and TCP 123. NTP can support a connection-orientated server (TCP guarantees delivery) or connectionless (UDP for non-critical applications).

An NTP network usually gets its time from an authoritative time source, such as a radio clock or an atomic clock attached to a time server. NTP then distributes this time across the network. NTP is extremely efficient; no more than one packet per minute is necessary to synchronize two machines to within a millisecond of one another.

NOTE   NTP uses the concept of a stratum to describe how many NTP hops away a machine is from an authoritative time source. A stratum 1 time server has a radio or atomic clock directly attached; a stratum 2 time server receives its time via NTP from a stratum 1 time server, and so on. Cisco routers cannot support stratum 1 (in other words, you cannot connect a Cisco router to an atomic clock source) and need to derive an atomic clock source from the Internet. NTP can also authenticate sessions.

Figure 3-7 displays a simple two-router network where Router R1 will be configured to supply a clock source to the Router R2. In this example, you will configure authentication and ensure that the NTP peer between the two routers is secure.

Figure 3-7   *NTP Sample Configuration*

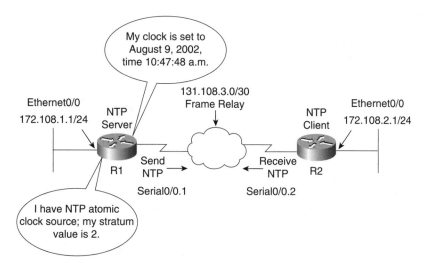

The following steps are required when enabling NTP on a Cisco router:

1 Define the time zone with the following command:

```
clock timezone zone hours [minutes]
```

2 Configure the master NTP router (this router will supply a clock to other routers) with the following command:

```
ntp master [stratum value]
```

The stratum value is 1 to 15, with 1 representing the best clock source.

3 To configure a remote NTP peer to a Cisco router with a better stratum value, use the following IOS command:

```
ntp peer ip-address [version number] [key keyid] [source interface] [prefer]
```

Table 3-4 displays the required parameters for the **ntp peer** command.

4 To define NTP to authenticate the NTP session, use the following IOS commands:

```
ntp trusted-key key-number
```

The *key-number* is the authentication key to be trusted.

```
ntp authentication-key number md5 value
```

Table 3-4 **ntp peer** *Command Defined*

Syntax	Description
ip-address	IP address of the peer providing, or being provided, the clock
version	(Optional) Defines the Network Time Protocol (NTP) version number
number	(Optional) NTP version number (1 to 3)
key	(Optional) Defines the authentication key
keyid	(Optional) Authentication key to use when sending packets to this peer
source	(Optional) Names the interface
interface	(Optional) Name of the interface from which to pick the IP source address
prefer	(Optional) Makes this peer the preferred peer to provide synchronization

To ensure that R1 sends R2 a clock source via NTP, R1 must be configured to send NTP traffic over the Frame Relay cloud with the command **ntp broadcast**. To specify that a specific interface should send NTP broadcast packets, use the **ntp broadcast** interface configuration command. Similarly, R2 must receive NTP traffic and is considered an NTP client with the IOS command **ntp broadcast client.**

R2's Serial 0/0 interface is configured with the command **ntp broadcast client**.

Example 3-8 configures Router R1 in Figure 3-7 to supply a clock source to Router R2.

Example 3-8 *NTP Configuration on R1*

```
clock set 10:20:00 9 August 2002
clock timezone UTC 10
!Interface configuration
interface serial0/0
ntp broadcast
!Global configuration
ntp authentication-key 1 md5 121A061E17 7
ntp authenticate
ntp trusted-key 1
ntp master 2
ntp peer 131.108.2.1 key 1
```

Notice that the router is set to the correct time first with the IOS command **clock set**.

The router is configured for the UTC time zone and 10 hours behind UTC time. The authentication key is set to 1.

Example 3-9 configures R2 to get the clock from R1 using the same MD5 password (set to ccie) from Example 3-8.

Example 3-9 *NTP Configuration on R2*

```
interface serial0/0
ntp broadcast client
!Global configuration
ntp authentication-key 1 md5 ccie
ntp authenticate
ntp trusted-key 1
ntp trusted-key
ntp peer 131.108.1.1 key 1
```

Example 3-10 displays the two clocks on Routers R1 and R2 confirming that R1 is sending R2 the correct time via NTP.

Example 3-10 **show clock** *on R1 and R2*

```
R1#show clock
10:47:48.508 UTC Fri Aug 9 2002
R2#show clock
10:47:48.508 UTC Fri Aug 9 2002
```

Example 3-11 confirms that NTP is authenticated (the remote stratum value is 2) by viewing the output of the IOS command **show ntp associations detail**.

Example 3-11 **show ntp associations detail** *Command on R2*

```
R2# show ntp associations detail
131.108.1.1 configured, authenticated, selected, sane, valid, stratum 2
ref ID .LOCL., time C0FD8D45.0B1C72E0 (10:37:25.043 UTC Fri Aug 9 2002)
our mode active, peer mode passive, our poll intvl 64, peer poll intvl 64
root delay 0.00 msec, root disp 0.03, reach 1, sync dist 15878.372
delay 6.67 msec, offset 297909193935.7106 msec, dispersion 15875.02
precision 2**16, version 3
org time C0FD8D45.BA55E231 (10:37:25.727 UTC Fri Aug 9 2002)
rcv time AF3BD17B.CBA5DDF0 (10:04:11.795 UTC Mon Mar 1 1993)
xmt time AF3BD17B.C9CB2BA2 (10:04:11.788 UTC Mon Mar 1 1993)
filtdelay =     6.67    0.00    0.00    0.00    0.00    0.00    0.00
filtoffset = 2979091    0.00    0.00    0.00    0.00    0.00    0.00
filterror =     0.02 16000.0 16000.0 16000.0 16000.0 16000.0 16000.0 16000.0
131.108.255.1 dynamic, authenticated, our_master, sane, valid, stratum 2
ref ID .LOCL., time C0FD8D05.0AE0774C (10:36:21.042 UTC Fri Aug 9 2002)
our mode passive, peer mode active, our poll intvl 64, peer poll intvl 64
root delay 0.00 msec, root disp 0.03, reach 2, sync dist 1.007
delay 0.00 msec, offset 0.0000 msec, dispersion 16000.00
precision 2**16, version 3
org time C0FD8D43.0B54AAFA (10:37:23.044 UTC Fri Aug 9 2002)
rcv time AF3BD179.1C9F231D (10:04:09.111 UTC Mon Mar 1 1993)
xmt time AF3BD186.C9CB3361 (10:04:22.788 UTC Mon Mar 1 1993)
filtdelay =    0.00    0.00    0.00    0.00    0.00    0.00    0.00    0.00
filtoffset =   0.00    0.00    0.00    0.00    0.00    0.00    0.00    0.00
filterror = 16000.0 16000.0 16000.0 16000.0 16000.0 16000.0 16000.0 16000.0
```

Example 3-11 displays that R2 is dynamically peered to R1 and is authenticated.

Secure Shell

Secure Shell (SSH) is a protocol that provides a secure connection to a router. Cisco IOS supports version 1 of SSH, which enables clients to make a secure and encrypted connection to a Cisco router. Before SSH was implemented, the only form of security available when accessing devices such as routers was Telnet username/password authentication, which is clearly visible with a network sniffer. Telnet is insecure because a protocol analyzer can view the information in clear text form. Figure 3-8 displays a simple protocol analyzer viewing information between a source address, 10.66.32.5, and the destination address 192.168.1.13 after a Telnet session is initiated by the address (PC) 192.168.1.13/24.

Figure 3-8 *Sniffer Capture of a Telnet Connection*

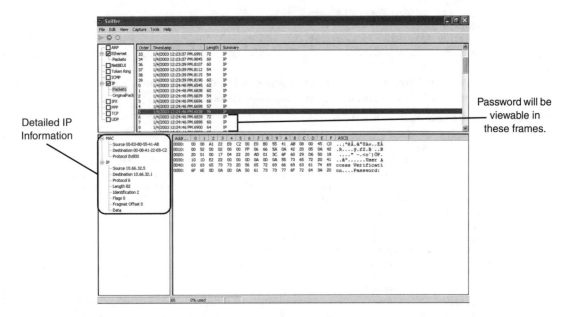

Figure 3-8 displays a simple Telnet connection between a PC and a remote router. Figure 3-8 is a packet trace from a client PC Telnet connection to a Cisco IOS router with the IP address 10.32.66.5. The packet trace clearly captures the password prompt sent by the router. Therefore, the prompt is viewable in clear text. If you scrolled down the next few frames (frames numbered 98-103 in Figure 3-8), the password would be clearly visible. An intruder or hacker can piece together the password and gain unauthorized access. For security reasons, these frames are not shown, but it is clear that the Telnet application protocol is not a secure protocol; all data is sent as clear text (including the password exchanged).

SSH is implemented with TCP port 22 and UDP port 22, and ensures that data is encrypted and untraceable by a network sniffer. SSH can be configured on both Cisco IOS routers and Catalysts switches.

Figure 3-9 displays the SSH protocol layers.

Figure 3-9   *SSH Protocol Layers*

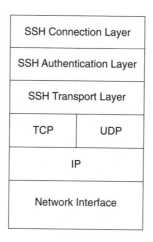

NOTE   Lightweight Directory Access Protocol (LDAP) is an Internet protocol that e-mail programs use to look up contact information from a server. For more details on LDAP, visit www.gracion.com/server/whatldap.html.

Active Directory is a Windows-defined application that stores and manages network services, resources, and information about where computers and printers are located. Active Directory allows network administrators of 2000 servers the ability to allocate and control how network resources are accessed by clients' PCs. For more information on Active Directory, visit www.microsoft.com.

SSH sits on top of the TCP/IP layers, protecting the hosts from unknown devices. The SSH transport layer is responsible for securing the data using strong encryption authentication. There are currently two versions of SSH: SSHv1 and SSHv2. Cisco IOS only supports SSHv1.

UNIX devices support SSH clients and Cisco routers can be configured to allow SSH between the UNIX device and Cisco router to ensure a secure Telnet connection. Currently, Cisco IOS 12.2 supports SSH and a number of hardware platforms, including the 2600 and 3600 series routers.

For more detailed information on SSH and the Cisco IOS functional matrix, visit www.ssh.com/products/ssh/ and www.cisco.com/warp/public/707/ssh.shtml, respectively.

Foundation Summary

The "Foundation Summary" is a condensed collection of material for a convenient review of this chapter's key concepts. If you are already comfortable with the topics in this chapter and decided to skip most of the "Foundation Topics" material, the "Foundation Summary" will help you recall a few details. If you just read the "Foundation Topics" section, this review should help further solidify some key facts. If you are doing your final preparation before the exam, the "Foundation Summary" offers a convenient and quick final review.

Table 3-5   *DNS Concepts*

Concept	Description
Well-known port numbers	UDP Port 53, TCP Port 53
ip host *name* [*tcp-port-number*] *ip address1* [*ip address2...ip address8*]	Configured locally to assign a host name with up to 8 IP addresses
no ip domain-lookup	Disables the IP DNS-based host name-to-address translation
ip domain-name *name*	Defines a default domain name that the Cisco IOS Software uses to complete unqualified host names
ip domain-list *name*	Defines a list of default domain names to complete unqualified host names
ip name-server *ip address*	Specifies the address of one or more name servers to use for name and address resolution; up to six name servers permitted

Table 3-6   *TFTP Concepts*

Concept	Description
Well-known port numbers	UDP Port 69 (UDP is typically the only supported protocol for TFTP produced by vendors) and TCP Port 69
copy tftp flash	Cisco IOS command to copy images from a TFTP server
Security	Only filename and directory name are methods used to secure transfers

Table 3-7   *Secure Shell (SSH) Concepts*   ✗ Wrong ID) is HTTPs

Concept	Description
Well-known port number	TCP port 443.
HTTPS	HTTP traffic runs over a secure connection.
Service/client authentication ✗	SSH uses a client server model where clients request secure connections to a host device, such as with a credit card transaction over the World Wide Web.

Table 3-8   *SNMP Concepts*

Concept	Description
Well-known port numbers	UDP 161 (SNMP servers) and UDP 162 (SNMP clients).
SNMP managed devices	An SNMP managed device is a network node that contains an SNMP agent and resides on a managed network. Managed devices collect and store management information and make this information available to Network Management System using SNMP.
SNMP agent	SNMP Agent is a network management software module that resides in a managed device. An agent has local knowledge of management information and translates that information into a form compatible with SNMP.

Table 3-9   *SMTP Concepts*

Concept	Description
Well-known port numbers	TCP 25 and UDP 25
HELO command	Used in communications between host and client

Table 3-10   *NTP Concepts*

Concept	Description
Well-known port numbers	TCP 123 and UDP 123.
ntp master *1-15*	Defines stratum value between 1 and 15.
clock set *hh***:***mm***:***ss day month year*	Manually sets clock on a Cisco router.
ntp peer *ip-address* [**version** *number*] [**key** *keyid*] [**source** *interface*] [**prefer**]	Defines NTP peers.
ntp authenticate	Enables authentication.
ntp authentication-key *number* **md5** *value*	Defines NTP authentication key and password.
ntp trusted-key *key-number*	Defines NTP to authenticate NTP session; *key-number* is the authentication key to be trusted.

Q & A

The Q & A questions are designed to help you assess your readiness for the topics covered on the CCIE Security written exam and those topics presented in this chapter. This format should help you assess your retention of the material. A strong understanding of the answers to these questions will help you on the CCIE Security written exam. You can also look over the questions at the beginning of the chapter again for review. As an additional study aid, use the CD-ROM provided with this book to take simulated exams, which draw from a database of over 300 multiple-choice questions—all different from those presented in the book. Select the best answer. Answers to these questions can be found in Appendix A, "Answers to Quiz Questions."

1 According to RFC 1700, what is the well-known TCP/UDP port used by DNS?

2 What does the IOS command **no ip domain-lookup** accomplish?

3 What is the correct IOS syntax to specify local host mapping on a Cisco router?

4 TFTP uses what well-known, defined TCP/UDP port?

5 What is the correct IOS command to copy a file from a TFTP server to the system flash?

6 Define the two modes of FTP.

_____

_____

_____

7 FTP uses what TCP port numbers?

_____

_____

_____

8 What well-known port do Secure Socket Layer (SSL) and Secure Shell (SSH) use?

_____

_____

_____

9 Define SNMP and give an example.

_____

_____

_____

10 What well-known UDP ports are used by SNMP?

_____

_____

_____

11 What IOS command enables SNMP on a Cisco IOS router?

_____

_____

_____

12 Which TCP/UDP port numbers are defined for use by Network Time Protocol or NTP?

_____

_____

_____

13 When defining a stratum value on a Cisco router, what is the range and what value is closest to an atomic clock?

_____

_____

_____

14 Secure Shell (SSH) allows what to be accomplished when in use?

_____

_____

_____

15 What is the difference between an SNMP inform request and an SNMP trap?

_____

_____

_____

16 What does the SNMP MIB refer to?

_____

_____

_____

17 What is the SNMP read-write community string for the following router configuration?

```
snmp-server community simon ro
snmp-server community Simon rw
```

_____

_____

_____

18 Before you can TFTP a file from a Cisco router to a UNIX- or Windows-based system, what is the first step you must take after enabling the TFTP server daemon on both platforms?

_____

_____

_____

19 What IOS command can be implemented to restrict SNMP access to certain networks by applying access lists? Can you apply standard, extended, or both?

---

20 Does TFTP have a mechanism for username and password authentication?

---

21 Can you use your Internet browser to configure a Cisco router? If so, how?

---

22 A network administrator defines a Cisco router to allow HTTP requests but forgets to add the authentication commands. What is the default username and password pairing that allows HTTP requests on the default TCP port 80? Can you predefine another TCP port for HTTP access other than port 80?

Scenario

Scenario 3-1: Configuring DNS, TFTP, NTP, and SNMP

This scenario uses a configuration taken from a working Cisco IOS router and tests your skills with DNS, TFTP, NTP, and SNMP. Example 3-12 displays the configuration of a Cisco router named R1.

Example 3-12 *R1 Running Configuration*

```
version 12.1
hostname R1
clock timezone UTC 10
!
no ip domain-lookup
ip domain-name cisco.com
ip host CCIE 131.108.1.1
ip host Router3 131.108.1.3
ip host Router2 131.108.1.2
ip host Router1 131.108.1.1
ip name-server 131.108.255.1
ip name-server 131.108.255.2
interface Ethernet0/0
 ip address 131.108.1.1 255.255.255.0
!
interface Serial0/0
 ip address 131.108.255.1 255.255.255.252
 ntp broadcast
!
no ip http server
snmp-server community public RO
snmp-server community publiC RW
snmp-server host 131.108.255.254 isdn
line con 0
!
ntp authentication-key 1 md5 121A061E17 7
ntp authenticate
ntp trusted-key 1
ntp master 1
ntp peer 131.108.2.1 key 1
end
```

1 What happens when a network administrator types the host name Router1 at the router prompt? (Select the best two answers.)

    a. DNS queries are disabled; nothing will be translated.

    b. The name Router1 is mapped to the IP address 131.108.1.1.

    c. The administrator could also type CCIE to reach the same IP address (131.108.1.1).

    d. Because DNS is disabled with the command **no ip domain-lookup**, the router assumes this is an invalid IOS command and returns the error "% Unknown command or computer name, or unable to find computer address."

    e. Local DNSs are case-sensitive so you can only type Router1 to map to 131.108.1.1.

2 The following commands are entered on the router named R1. What are the TFTP server address and TFTP filename stored on the router on board flash?

```
R1#copy tftp flash
Address or name of remote host []? 150.100.1.253
Source filename []? c2600-jo3s56i-mz.121-5.T10.bin
Destination filename [c2600-jo3s56i-mz.121-5.T10.bin]? c2600-c1
```

3 R1 supplies an NTP clock source to a remote router. What is the NTP's peer IP address, and what is the MD5 password used to ensure that NTP sessions are authenticated?

4 What is the SNMP read-write access community string for the following configuration?

```
snmp-server community public RO
snmp-server community publiC RW
```

Scenario Answers

Scenario 3-1 Solutions

1 **Answers: b and c.** The host name Router1 (not case-sensitive) is mapped to 131.108.1.1 with the command ip host Router1 131.108.1.1. Also, the IOS command CCIE is mapped to the same name with the IOS command ip host CCIE 131.108.1.1. If you look at the IP address assigned to the Ethernet 0/0, it's the local IP address. Therefore, if a user types Router1 or CCIE, they will be return to the same router. The following sample display demonstrates this fact:

```
R1#router1
Translating "router1"
Trying Router1 (131.108.1.1)... Open
User Access Verification
Password:
R1>quit
! quit commands exit Telnet session and you return
! to the first Telnet connection on R1
[Connection to router1 closed by foreign host]
R1#ccie
Translating "ccie"
Trying CCIE (131.108.1.1)... Open
User Access Verification
Password:
R1>
```

Both the DNS names, CCIE and Router1, are translated to the same IP address, 131.108.1.1.

2 **Answer:** The TFTP server address is 150.100.1.253 and the filename requested is c2600-jo3s56i-mz.121-5.T10.bin. However, the last command entered is the destination filename, which defines the names stored locally on the system flash. In this case, the network administrator types the filename c2600-c1.

3 **Answer:** R1 is configured statically to peer to the remote NTP IP address, 131.108.2.1 (ntp peer 131.108.2.1 key 1). The MD5 password is configured but, unfortunately, the configuration will not display the MD5 passwords (encrypted), so it cannot be derived.

4 **Answer:** The read-only (RO) community string is named public, and the read-write (RW) community string is set to publiC. Community strings are case-sensitive.

Exam Topics in this Chapter

CHAPTER 4

Cisco IOS Specifics and Security

This chapter covers the CCIE IOS Specifics blueprint. Unfortunately, the blueprint does not detail the exact requirements, and IOS in general could mean the entire range of topics. We cover topics that are actually possible topics in the written exam and common to the Routing and Switching blueprint.

This chapter covers the following topics:

- **Cisco Hardware**—This section covers the hardware components on a Cisco router, namely the System Flash, nonvolatile RAM (NVRAM), and how files are saved to and from a TFTP server.

- **show and debug Commands**—This section covers the most common **show** and **debug** commands used on Cisco routers to manage an IP network.

- **Password Recovery**—This section covers how password recovery is completed on Cisco IOS routers.

- **Basic Security on Cisco Routers**—This section reviews some commands used to ensure that Cisco routers are secured with basic passwords.

- **IP Access Lists**— This section covers both standard and extended IP access lists and their formats.

"Do I Know This Already?" Quiz

This assessment quiz's purpose is to help you determine how to spend your limited study time. If you can answer most or all these questions, you might want to skim the "Foundation Topics" section and return to it later, as necessary. Review the "Foundation Summary" section and answer the questions at the end of the chapter to ensure that you have a strong grasp of the material covered. If you already intend to read the entire chapter, you do not necessarily need to answer these questions now. If you find these assessment questions difficult, you should read through the entire "Foundation Topics" section and review it until you feel comfortable with your ability to answer all these and the Q & A questions at the end of the chapter.

Answers to these questions can be found in Appendix A, "Answers to Quiz Questions."

1 What IOS command will display the System Flash?

    a. **show flash**

    b. **show system flash**

    c. **show memory**

    d. **show process flash**

2 The network administrator has forgotten the enable password and all passwords are encrypted. What should the network administrator do to recover the password without losing the current configuration?

    a. Call the TAC and ask for a special back door password.

    b. Call the TAC and raise a case to supply the engineering password.

    c. Reboot the router, press the break key during the reload, and enter ROM mode and change the configuration register.

    d. Reboot the router, press the break key during the reload, enter ROM mode and change the configuration register, and when the router reloads, remove the old configuration.

3 What is the enable password for the following router?

```
enable password Simon
```

    a. More data required

    b. Simon

    c. simon or Simon

    d. You cannot set the password to a name; it must also contain digits.

4 If the configuration register is set to 0x2101, where is the IOS image booted from?

    a. slot0:

    b. slot1:

    c. Flash

    d. ROM

    e. TFTP server

5 What IOS command will copy the running configuration to a TFTP server? (Select the best two answers.)

    a. **copy running-config to tftp**

    b. **write network**

    c. **copy running-config tftp**

    d. **write erase**

6 What **debug** command allows an administrator to debug only packets from the network 131.108.0.0/16?

    a. **debug ip packet**

    b. **terminal monitor**

    c. **debug ip packet 1**

    d. **access-list 1 permit 131.108.0.0**

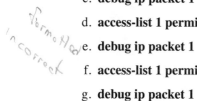

    e. **debug ip packet 1**

    f. **access-list 1 permit 131.108.0.0 0.0.255.255**

    g. **debug ip packet 1**

    h. **access-list 1 permit 131.108.0.0 255.255.0.0**

7 After entering **debug ip packet**, no messages appear on your Telnet session. What is the likely cause?

    a. OSPF routing is required.

    b. The console port does not support **debug** output.

    c. The **terminal monitor** command is required.

    d. IP packets are not supported with the **debug** command.

8 To change the configuration register to 0x2141, what is the correct IOS command?

    a. **copy running-config register**

    b. **configuration 0x2141**

    c. **config 0x2141 register**

    d. **config-register 0x2142**

    e. **config-register 0x2141**

9 Where is the startup configuration stored on a Cisco router?

    a. In the cam table

    b. NVRAM

    c. RAM

    d. Flash

    e. slot0:

10 Which of the following statements is true?

    a. The **enable secret** command overrides the **enable password** command.

    b. The **enable** command overrides the **enable secret** *password* command.

    c. Enable passwords cannot be used when the secret password is used.

    d. Both a and c are true.

11 A Cisco router has the following configuration:

```
line vty 0 4
login
```

What will happen when you Telnet to the router?

    a. You will be prompted for the login password.

    b. You will enter EXEC mode immediately.

    c. You cannot access the router without the password set.

    d. More configuration required.

12 A Cisco router has the following configuration:

```
line vty 0 4
no login
password cIscO
```

When a Telnet user tries to establish a remote Telnet session to this router, what will happen?

    a. You will be prompted for the login password cIscO.

    b. You will enter EXEC mode immediately.

    c. You cannot access the router without the password set.

    d. More configuration required.

    e. You will be prompted for the login password; password case does not matter.

13 A Cisco router has the following configuration:

```
line vty 0 1
no login
password cisco
line vty 2 4
login
password ciSco
```

When a third Telnet session is established to a remote router with the preceding configuration, what will happen?

a. You will be prompted for the login password, which is set to cisco.

b. You will be prompted for the login password, which is set to ciSco.

c. You will enter EXEC mode immediately.

d. You cannot access the router without the password set.

e. More configuration required.

14 Which of the following access lists will deny any IP packets sourced from network 131.108.1.0/24 and destined for network 131.108.2.0/24 and permit all other IP-based traffic?

a. access-list 1 deny 131.108.1.0

b. access-list 1 deny 131.108.1.0 0.0.0.255

c. access-list 100 permit/deny ip 131.108.1.0 0.0.0.255 131.108.2.0 0.0.0.255

d. access-list 100 deny ip 131.108.1.0 0.0.0.255 131.108.2.0 0.0.0.255

e. access-list 100 permit ip any any

15 An administrator notices a router's CPU utilization has jumped from 2 percent to 100 percent, and that a CCIE engineer was debugging. What IOS command can the network administrator enter to stop all debugging output to the console and vty lines without affecting users on the connected router?

a. **no logging console debugging**

b. **undebug all**

c. **line vty 0 4**

d. **no terminal monitor**

e. **reload the router**

Foundation Topics

Cisco Hardware

Cisco routers consist of many hardware components. The main components of a Cisco router include the following:

- RAM
- NVRAM
- Flash
- CPU
- ROM
- Configuration registers
- Interfaces

Figure 4-1 illustrates the hardware components on Cisco routers.

Figure 4-1 *Components of a Cisco Router*

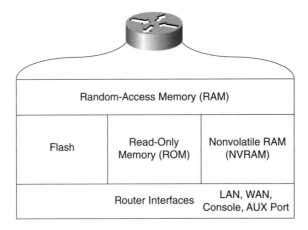

Each hardware component is vital for Cisco routers to operate properly. To help you prepare for the CCIE Security written exam, the next few sections present the main concepts you need to know about Cisco hardware components.

Random-Access Memory (RAM)

Routers use random-access memory (RAM) to store the current configuration file and other important data collected by the router. This data includes the IP routing table and buffer information. Buffers temporarily store packets before they are processed. All IOS processes, such as routing algorithms (OSPF or BGP, for example), also run in RAM.

RAM information is lost if the router power cycles (when a router loses and regains power) or is restarted by an administrator. To view a router's current configuration, use the **show running-config** IOS command. Before IOS version 10.3, administrators used the **write terminal** command to show a router's configuration. The **write terminal** command is still valid in today's IOS releases.

Cisco IOS is hardware-specific, and the image loaded on various router platforms varies from platform to platform. For example, the image on a Cisco 4500 will not run on a Cisco 3600. Also, IOS images contain certain features, such as IPX or DES encryption. For example, you can load only IOS software that supports IP or IP plus DES encryption and so forth.

Please visit the following Cisco website for more details on Cisco IOS images and platform requirements: www.cisco.com/warp/customer/130/choosing_ios.shtml.

Nonvolatile RAM (NVRAM)

Nonvolatile RAM (NVRAM) stores a copy of the router's configuration file. The NVRAM storage area is retained by the router in the event of a power cycle. When the router powers up from a power cycle or a reboot (**reload** command), the IOS copies the stored configuration file from the NVRAM to RAM. To view the configuration file stored in NVRAM, issue the **show startup-config** command. In earlier versions of IOS (before version 10.3), the **show config** command was used to view the configuration file stored in NVRAM. In IOS versions 11.0+, both the **show config** and **show startup-config** commands will work.

System Flash

The System Flash is an erasable and programmable memory used to store the router's IOS image. Although Flash memory is always limited in size, it can contain multiple versions of IOS. Therefore, you can delete, retrieve, and store new versions of IOS in the Flash memory system. To view the Flash on a Cisco router, use the **show flash** IOS command. Example 4-1 displays the Flash filename on a router named R1.

NOTE   On a high-performance router, such as Cisco 4500 series and 7500 series routers, you can make the Flash system look like a file system and store many versions of IOS. The IOS command to partition the System Flash is **partition flash** *number-of-partition size-of-each-partition*.

Example 4-1   **show flash** *Command*

```
R1>show flash
System flash directory:
File  Length   Name/status
  1   9558976  c2500-ajs40-l.12-17.bin
[9559040 bytes used, 7218176 available, 16777216 total]
16384K bytes of processor board System flash
```

Example 4-1 shows that the IOS image, c2500-ajs40-l.12-17.bin, is currently stored on the router's on-board System Flash.

The Cisco 7500 series router provides the option of installing additional PCMCIA Flash memory. If this additional memory is installed, the **dir slot0**: IOS command displays the IOS image stored in slot0.

NOTE   The IOS image's name conveys a lot of information, including the platform and feature sets. For more information, go to www.cisco.com and search for "software naming convention."

Central Processing Unit

The central processing unit (CPU) is the heart of a router, and every Cisco router has a CPU. A CPU manages all the router's processes, such as IP routing, and new routing entries, such as remote IP networks learned through a dynamic routing protocol.

To view a CPU's status, use the **show process** IOS command.

Example 4-2 shows a sample display taken from a Cisco IOS router.

Example 4-2   *(Truncated)* **show process** *Command*

```
R1>show process
CPU utilization for five seconds: 9%/7%; one minute: 9%;
five minutes: 10%
PID QTy   PC      Runtime (ms)  Invoked  uSecs    Stacks TTY Proc
  1 Csp  318F396  24456    1043   234   732/1000  0     Load Meter
  2 M*        0      28      28  1000  3268/4000  0     EXEC
  3 Lst  317D1FC   1304     175  5257  1724/2000  0     Check heap
...
```

The **show process** command displays the router utilization within the past five seconds, the past one minute, as well as the average over the last five minutes. Details about specific processes follow the CPU utilization statistics.

Read-Only Memory

Read-only memory (ROM) stores a scaled-down version of a router's IOS in the event that the Flash system becomes corrupted or no current IOS image is stored in Flash. ROM also contains the bootstrap program (sometimes referred to as the rxboot image in Cisco documentation) and a device's power up diagnostics. You can perform only a software upgrade (that is, perform a software image upgrade on the ROM) by replacing ROM chips because the ROM is not programmable.

The bootstrap program enables you to isolate or rule out hardware issues. For example, you might have a faulty Flash card and, subsequently, the router cannot boot the IOS image. The power diagnostics program tests all the hardware interfaces on the router. ROM mode contains a limited number of IOS commands, which enables the administrator or the Technical Assistance Center (TAC) to help troubleshoot and ascertain any hardware or configuration issues on a Cisco router. Cisco TAC is available 24 hours a day, seven days a week. You must pay Cisco for this service and have a valid contract number to open any cases.

Unfortunately, not all Cisco routers have the same ROM code, so the commands might vary but the principle remains the same. You can always issue the **?** command in ROM mode to identify the available commands used to troubleshoot a Cisco IOS-based router. Newer Cisco hardware models now contain a new boot program stored in Boot Flash rather than in the ROM. The program is a little more user-friendly. Menu-driven options are available to change the configuration register, for example.

Example 4-3 provides all the available options on a Cisco 4000 router when the **?** command is used in ROM mode.

Example 4-3   **?** *Command When in ROM Mode*

```
> ?
?            Types this display
$            Toggle cache state
B [filename] [TFTP Server IP address | TFTP Server Name]
      Load and excutute system image from ROM or from TFTP server
C [address]  Continue [optional address]
D /S M L V   Deposit value V of size S into location L with
      modifier M
E /S M L     Examine location L with size S with modifier M
G [address]  Begin execution
H            Help for commands
I            Initialize
K            Displays Stack trace
L [filename] [TFTP Server IP address | TFTP Server Name]
```

continues

Example 4-3   ? *Command When in ROM Mode (Continued)*

```
        Load system image from ROM or from TFTP server, but do not
        begin execution
O               Show software configuration register option settings
P               Set break point
S               Single step next instruction
T function      Test device (? for help)
```

The options in Example 4-3 include the ability to initialize a router with the **i** command after you have finished ROM mode. ROM mode enables you to recover lost passwords by altering the configuration registers (covered later in this chapter).

Configuration Registers

The configuration register is a 16-bit number that defines how a router operates on a power cycle. These options include if the IOS will be loaded from Flash or ROM. Configuration registers advise the CPU to load the configuration file from the NVRAM or to ignore the configuration file stored in memory, for example. The default configuration register is displayed as 0x2102. Table 4-1 displays the binary conversion from 0x2102.

Table 4-1   *0x2102 Binary Conversion*

Bit Number	Value
15	0
14	0
13	1
12	0
11	0
10	0
9	0
8	1
7	0
6	0
5	0
4	0
3	0
2	0
1	1
0	0

The bits are numbered from right to left. In the preceding example, the value is displayed as 0x2102 (0010.0001.0000.0010). The function of the configuration register bits is determined by their position, as follows:

- **Bits 0 through 3**—Determines the boot option whether the router loads the IOS from the Flash (binary value is 010) or from ROM (binary value is 000).
- **Bit 4**—Reserved.
- **Bit 5**—Reserved.
- **Bit 6**—Tells the router to load the configuration from NVRAM if set to 1 and to ignore the NVRAM if set to 0.
- **Bit 7**— Referred to as the OEM (OEM = original equipment manufacturer) bit in Cisco documentation and is not used.
- **Bit 8**—Specifies whether to enter ROM mode without power cycling the router. If bit 8 is set to 1 and the break key is issued while the router is up and running normally, the router will go into ROM mode. This is a dangerous scenario because if this occurs, your router immediately stops functioning.
- **Bit 9**—Reserved.
- **Bit 10**—Specifies the broadcast address to use, where 1 equals the use of all 0s for broadcast at boot (in conjunction with bit 14). Bit 10 interacts with bit 14.
- **Bits 11 and 12**—Set the console port's baud rate. For example, if bits 11 and 12 are set to 00, the baud rate is 9600 bps. A baud rate of 4800 bps can be set when these bits are set to 01. 10 sets the baud rate to 2400 bps, and 11 sets the baud rate to 1200 bps.
- **Bit 13**—Tells the router to boot from ROM if the Flash cannot boot from a network, such as a TFTP server. If bit 13 is set to 0 and no IOS is found, the router will hang. If bit 13 is set to 1 and no IOS is found, the router boots from ROM.
- **Bit 14**—Interacts with Bit 10 to define broadcast address.
- **Bit 15**—Specifies to enable diagnostics display on startup and ignore the NVRAM.

To view the current configuration register, use the **show version** IOS command.

Example 4-4 displays the configuration register of a router, R1.

Example 4-4 *(Truncated)* **show version** *Command*

```
R1>show version
Cisco Internetwork Operating System Software
IOS (tm) 2500 Software (C2500-AJS40-L), Version 11.2(17)
, RELEASE SOFTWARE (fc1)
Copyright (c) 1986-1999 by Cisco Systems, Inc.
Compiled Tue 05-Jan-99 13:27 by ashah
Image text-base: 0x030481E0, data-base: 0x00001000
ROM: System Bootstrap, Version 5.2(8a), RELEASE SOFTWARE
```

continues

Example 4-4 *(Truncated)* **show version** *Command (Continued)*

```
BOOTFLASH: 3000 Bootstrap Software (IGS-RXBOOT),
Version 10.2(8a), RELEASE SOFTWARE
R1 uptime is 6 days, 1 hour, 36 minutes
System restarted by reload
System image file is "flash:c2500-ajs40-l.112-17.bin", ..
..booted via flash
cisco 2520 (68030) processor (revision E) with 8192K/2048K byte
Processor board ID 02956210, with hardware revision 00000002
Bridging software.
SuperLAT software copyright 1990 by Meridian Technology Corp.
X.25 software, Version 2.0, NET2, BFE and GOSIP compliant.
TN3270 Emulation software.
Basic Rate ISDN software, Version 1.0.
1 Ethernet/IEEE 802.3 interface(s)
2 Serial network interface(s)
2 Low-speed serial(sync/async) network interface(s)
1 ISDN Basic Rate interface(s)
32K bytes of non-volatile configuration memory.
16384K bytes of processor board System flash (Read ONLY)
Configuration register is 0x2102
```

The output from Example 4-4 displays the configuration register as 0x2102. The **show version** command also displays other useful router information, such as the router's uptime, the IOS image in use, and the hardware configuration. To change the configuration register, use the global configuration command, **configure-register** *register-value*. When a configuration register is changed, use the **show version** command to ensure that the register has been changed to the new value.

Table 4-2 displays common configuration register values you can use in day-to-day troubleshooting of Cisco IOS routers.

Table 4-2   *Common Registers and Descriptions*

Register Value	Description
0x2100	Boots the router using the system bootstrap found in ROM.
0x2102	Boots the router using Flash and NVRAM. This is the default setting.
0x2142	Boots the router using Flash and ignores NVRAM. This value is used to recover passwords or modify configuration parameters.

Cisco Interfaces

Interfaces provide connections to a network. Interfaces include LANs, WANs, and management ports (that is, console and auxiliary ports).

To view the current LAN or WAN interface, issue the **show interface** command. The **show interface** command displays all LAN and WAN interfaces. To display information regarding console or auxiliary ports, use the **show line** command. Figure 4-2 summarizes the available IOS commands that administrators can use to view a router's current configuration.

Figure 4-2   *Interface IOS Commands*

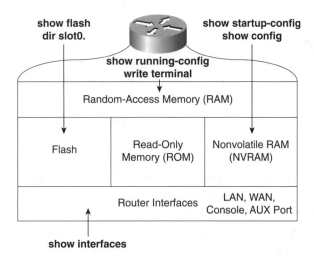

Now that you have reviewed Cisco routers' hardware basics, it's time to review how routers operate. In addition to router operation, this chapter covers how administrators can manage Cisco routers by saving and loading files to and from a TFTP server.

NOTE   Cisco routers can operate in a number of modes. Cisco defines them as follows:

- **ROM boot mode**—When the router is in boot mode and loaded with a subset of the IOS image, only a limited number of commands are available.

- **Configuration mode**—Where you can make configuration changes. An example prompt is **Router1(config)#**.

- **Interface configuration mode**—Where you make configuration changes to interfaces such as the Ethernet or Serial connections. Example prompt is **Router1(config-if)#**.

- **Initial configuration mode**—When a router first boots up out of the box with no initial configuration, you are prompted for basic system configuration details, such as name and IP address assignment. The prompt looks like this:

  Would you like to answer the initial configuration dialog? [yes/no]

- **User EXEC mode**—Basic IOS commands are permitted from the command-line interface (CLI). An example prompt is R1>.

- **Privileged EXEC mode (also referred to as enabled mode)**—Advance IOS commands are permitted when the enable password or secret password is entered from the CLI. An example prompt is R1#.

Saving and Loading Files

The configuration file can reside on the router's NVRAM, RAM, or on a TFTP server. When a router boots with the default configuration register (0x2102), the configuration file is copied from NVRAM to RAM.

Network administrators typically save the configuration files to a TFTP server as a backup, in case of a router failure.

To save a configuration file from RAM to NVRAM (after configuration changes are made), the IOS command is **copy running-config startup-config**. The **write terminal** command will also copy the running configuration to startup configuration. The **write** command is a legacy command from earlier releases of IOS still valid in today's versions of IOS software.

Example 4-5 displays a successful configuration change on Ethernet 0/0, followed by a network administrator in PRIV EXEC (privilege EXEC mode) mode saving the new configuration file to NVRAM.

Example 4-5 *Saving IOS Configurations Files*

```
R1#configure terminal
Enter configuration commands, one per line.  End with CNTL/Z.
R1(config)#interface ethernet 0/0
R1(config-if)#ip address 131.108.1.1 255.255.255.0
R1(config-if)#exit
R1#copy running-config startup-config
Destination filename [startup-config]?
Building configuration...
[OK]
R1#
```

Table 4-3 summarizes the configuration file manipulation that can be performed on Cisco IOS routers.

Table 4-3   *Cisco IOS File Manipulations*

IOS Command	Meaning
copy running-config startup-config	Copies the configuration file from RAM to NVRAM.
write memory	Copies the running configuration to NVRAM. (Superseded by the new command, **copy running-config startup-config**.)
copy startup-config running-config	Copies the configuration file from NVRAM to RAM.
write terminal	Displays the current configuration file in RAM. (Superseded by the new command, **show running-config**.)
show config	Displays the current configuration file in NVRAM. (Superseded by the new command, **show startup-config**.)
copy running-config tftp	Copies the configuration file stored in RAM to a TFTP server. Can also be copied to an FTP or RCP server.
copy tftp running-config	Copies a configuration file from a TFTP server to the running configuration.

show and debug Commands

Cisco IOS CLI has an enormous amount of **show** and **debug** commands available to the privileged EXEC user. This section covers the **show** and **debug** commands most often used to manage Cisco IOS devices.

Router CLI

Cisco IOS routers allow network administrators access to a wide range of **show** and **debug** commands. The **show** command displays various information about the router's state of play, such as the Ethernet collisions on a particular interface or a router's configuration file. Only a subset of **show** commands is available when in User EXEC mode. The full range is available when in privilege EXEC mode (PRIV EXEC mode).

The **debug** command is a more advanced IOS command that allows the administrator to view the router's analyses of packets or buffering mechanisms and is used only to troubleshoot a device or complete network. The **debug** command is very CPU-intensive.

show Commands

The best method to appreciate the use of **show** commands is to display sample output from a Cisco IOS router.

Example 4-6 displays a list of truncated **show** commands available from the CLI on a Cisco router in PRIV EXEC mode.

Example 4-6   **show** *Commands*

```
R1#show ?
  access-expression      List access expression
  access-lists           List access lists
  accounting             Accounting data for active sessions
  adjacency              Adjacent nodes
  aliases                Display alias commands
  arp                    ARP table
  async                  Information on terminal lines used as router
                         interfaces
  backup                 Backup status
  bgp                    BGP information
  bridge                 Bridge Forwarding/Filtering Database [verbose]
  buffers                Buffer pool statistics
  caller                 Display information about dialup connections
  cef                    Cisco Express Forwarding
  class-map              Show QoS Class Map
  clock                  Display the system clock
  configuration          Contents of Non-Volatile memory
  connection             Show Connection
  context                Show context information
  controllers            Interface controller status
  cops                   COPS information
  crypto                 Encryption module
  debugging              State of each debugging option
  derived-config         Derived operating configuration
  dhcp                   Dynamic Host Configuration Protocol status
  diag                   Show diagnostic information for port
                         adapters/modules
  dial-peer              Dial Plan Mapping Table for, e.g. VoIP Peers
  dialer                 Dialer parameters and statistics
  dialplan               Voice telephony dial plan
  diffserv               Differentiated services
  dlsw                   Data Link Switching information
  dnsix                  Shows Dnsix/DMDP information
  docsis                 Show DOCSIS
  drip                   DRiP DB
  dspu                   Display DSPU information
  dxi                    atm-dxi information
  entry                  Queued terminal entries
  environment            Environmental monitor statistics
  exception              exception informations
  file                   Show filesystem information
  flash:                 display information about flash: file system
  frame-relay            Frame-Relay information
  fras                   FRAS Information
  fras-host              FRAS Host Information
  gateway                Show status of gateway
  history                Display the session command history
```

Example 4-6 show *Commands (Continued)*

```
          hosts                 IP domain-name, lookup style, nameservers, and host
                                table
          html                  HTML helper commands
          idb                   List of Hardware Interface Descriptor Blocks
          interfaces            Interface status and configuration
          ip                    IP information (show ip route follows)
        ipv6                    IPv6 information
          key                   Key information
          line                  TTY line information
          llc2                  IBM LLC2 circuit information
          lnm                   IBM LAN manager
          local-ack             Local Acknowledgement virtual circuits
          location              Display the system location
          logging               Show the contents of logging buffers
          memory                Memory statistics
          mgcp                  Display Media Gateway Control Protocol information
          microcode             show configured microcode for downloadable hardware
          modemcap              Show Modem Capabilities database
          mpoa                  MPOA show commands
          ncia                  Native Client Interface Architecture
          netbios-cache         NetBIOS name cache contents
          ntp                   Network time protocol
          num-exp               Number Expansion (Speed Dial) information
          parser                Display parser information
          pas                   Port Adaptor Information
          pci                   PCI Information
          policy-map            Show QoS Policy Map
          ppp                   PPP parameters and statistics
          printers              Show LPD printer information
          privilege             Show current privilege level
          processes             Active process statistics
          protocols             Active network routing protocols
          registry              Function registry information
          reload                Scheduled reload information
          rmon                  rmon statistics
          route-map             route-map information
          running-config        Current operating configuration
        sessions                Information about Telnet connections
          sgbp                  SGBP group information
          snmp                  snmp statistics
          spanning-tree         Spanning tree topology
          srcp                  Display SRCP Protocol information
          ssh                   Status of SSH server connections
          ssl                   Show SSL command
          stacks                Process stack utilization
          standby               Hot standby protocol information
          startup-config        Contents of startup configuration
          tcp                   Status of TCP connections
          tech-support          Show system information for Tech-Support
          terminal              Display terminal configuration parameters
          traffic-shape         traffic rate shaping configuration
```

continues

Example 4-6 show *Commands (Continued)*

```
    users                  Display information about terminal lines
    version                System hardware and software status
    vlans                  Virtual LANs Information
    vtemplate              Virtual Template interface information
    whoami                 Info on current tty line
```

This section briefly covers the highlighted commands in Example 4-6.

Example 4-7 displays sample output from the most widely used IOS command, **show ip route**.

Example 4-7 **show ip route** *Command*

```
R1#show ip route
Codes: C - connected, S - static, I - IGRP, R - RIP, M - mobile, B - BGP
       D - EIGRP, EX - EIGRP external, O - OSPF, IA - OSPF inter area
       N1 - OSPF NSSA external type 1, N2 - OSPF NSSA external type 2
       E1 - OSPF external type 1, E2 - OSPF external type 2, E - EGP
       i - IS-IS, L1 - IS-IS level-1, L2 - IS-IS level-2, ia - IS-IS inter area
       * - candidate default, U - per-user static route, o - ODR
       P - periodic downloaded static route
Gateway of last resort is not set
     131.108.0.0/16 is variably subnetted, 3 subnets, 2 masks
C       131.108.255.0/30 is directly connected, Serial0/0
O       131.108.2.0/24 [110/400] via 131.108.255.2, 00:00:03, Serial0/0
C       131.108.1.0/24 is directly connected, Ethernet0/0
R1#show ip route ?
  Hostname or A.B.C.D  Network to display information about or hostname
  bgp                  Border Gateway Protocol (BGP)
  connected            Connected
  egp                  Exterior Gateway Protocol (EGP)
  eigrp                Enhanced Interior Gateway Routing Protocol (EIGRP)
  igrp                 Interior Gateway Routing Protocol (IGRP)
  isis                 ISO IS-IS
  list                 IP Access list
  mobile               Mobile routes
  odr                  On Demand stub Routes
  ospf                 Open Shortest Path First (OSPF)
  profile              IP routing table profile
  rip                  Routing Information Protocol (RIP)
  static               Static routes
  summary              Summary of all routes
  supernets-only       Show supernet entries only
  vrf                  Display routes from a VPN Routing/Forwarding instance
  |                    Output modifiers
  <cr>

R1#show ip route ospf
     131.108.0.0/16 is variably subnetted, 3 subnets, 2 masks
O       131.108.2.0/24 [110/400] via 131.108.255.2, 00:00:30, Serial0/0
R1#
```

Example 4-7 displays three IP routing entries. The more specific command, **show ip route ospf**, only displays remote OSPF entries. Every IOS command can be used with the **?** character to display more options. In this case, the network administer used it to identify the **ospf** option and then typed **show ip route ospf** to view only remote OSPF entries.

Example 4-8 displays the output from the **show ip access-lists** IOS command.

Example 4-8 show ip access-lists

```
R1#show ip access-lists ?
  <1-199>      Access list number
  <1300-2699>  Access list number (expanded range)
  WORD         Access list name
  |            Output modifiers
  <cr>
R1#show ip access-lists
Standard IP access list 1
    permit 131.108.0.0, wildcard bits 0.0.255.255
Extended IP access list 100
    permit tcp any host 131.108.1.1 eq telnet
```

Example 4-8 enables the network administrator to quickly verify any defined access lists. Example 4-8 includes two access lists numbered 1 and 100.

Use the **show debugging** command to display any **debug** commands in use. This verifies if any debugging is currently enabled.

Example 4-9 displays the sample output when d**ebug ip routing** is enabled.

Example 4-9 show debugging *Command*

```
R1#show debugging
IP routing:
  IP routing debugging is on
R1#undebug all
All possible debugging has been turned off
```

Currently, the router in Example 4-9 is enabled for debugging IP routing. To turn off the debugging, apply the **undebug all** command, as shown in Example 4-9. This command ensures all debug options are disabled. You can specify the exact debug option you want to disable with the **no** options; for example, to disable the IP packet option, the IOS command is **no debug ip packet**.

To display the hardware interfaces on the router, use the **show interfaces** command to explore the physical and statistical state.

Example 4-10 displays the **show interfaces** command on a router named R1.

Example 4-10 show interfaces

```
R1#show interfaces
Ethernet0/0 is up, line protocol is up  --physical status
  Hardware is AmdP2, address is 0002.b9ad.5ae0 (bia 0002.b9ad.5ae0)
  Internet address is 131.108.1.1/24
  MTU 1500 bytes, BW 10000 Kbit, DLY 1000 usec,
     reliability 255/255, txload 1/255, rxload 1/255
  Encapsulation ARPA, loopback not set
  Keepalive set (10 sec)
  ARP type: ARPA, ARP Timeout 04:00:00
  Last input 00:00:00, output 00:00:01, output hang never
  Last clearing of "show interface" counters 00:00:05
  Queueing strategy: fifo
  Output queue 0/40, 0 drops; input queue 0/75, 0 drops
  5 minute input rate 0 bits/sec, 0 packets/sec
  5 minute output rate 0 bits/sec, 0 packets/sec
     1 packets input, 366 bytes, 0 no buffer
     Received 1 broadcasts, 0 runts, 0 giants, 0 throttles
     0 input errors, 0 CRC, 0 frame, 0 overrun, 0 ignored
     0 input packets with dribble condition detected
     3 packets output, 202 bytes, 0 underruns(0/0/0)
     0 output errors, 0 collisions, 0 interface resets
     0 babbles, 0 late collision, 0 deferred
     0 lost carrier, 0 no carrier
     0 output buffer failures, 0 output buffers swapped out
Serial0/0 is up, line protocol is up
  Hardware is PowerQUICC Serial
  Internet address is 131.108.255.1/30
  MTU 1500 bytes, BW 256 Kbit, DLY 20000 usec,
     reliability 255/255, txload 1/255, rxload 1/255
  Encapsulation FRAME-RELAY, loopback not set
  Keepalive set (10 sec)
  LMI enq sent  0, LMI stat recvd 0, LMI upd recvd 0, DTE LMI up
  LMI enq recvd 0, LMI stat sent  0, LMI upd sent  0
  LMI DLCI 0  LMI type is ANSI Annex D  frame relay DTE
  Broadcast queue 0/64, broadcasts sent/dropped 1/0, interface broadcasts 1
  Last input 00:00:02, output 00:00:00, output hang never
  Last clearing of "show interface" counters 00:00:07
  Input queue: 0/75/0/0 (size/max/drops/flushes); Total output drops: 0
  Queueing strategy: weighted fair
  Output queue: 0/1000/64/0 (size/max total/threshold/drops)
     Conversations  0/1/256 (active/max active/max total)
     Reserved Conversations 0/0 (allocated/max allocated)
     Available Bandwidth 192 kilobits/sec
  5 minute input rate 0 bits/sec, 0 packets/sec
  5 minute output rate 0 bits/sec, 0 packets/sec
     2 packets input, 86 bytes, 0 no buffer
```

Example 4-10 show interfaces *(Continued)*

```
     Received 0 broadcasts, 0 runts, 0 giants, 0 throttles
     0 input errors, 0 CRC, 0 frame, 0 overrun, 0 ignored, 0 abort
     2 packets output, 86 bytes, 0 underruns
     0 output errors, 0 collisions, 0 interface resets
     0 output buffer failures, 0 output buffers swapped out
     0 carrier transitions
     DCD=up  DSR=up  DTR=up  RTS=up  CTS=up

Ethernet0/1 is administratively down, line protocol is down
  Hardware is AmdP2, address is 0002.b9ad.5ae1 (bia 0002.b9ad.5ae1)
  MTU 1500 bytes, BW 10000 Kbit, DLY 1000 usec,
     reliability 255/255, txload 1/255, rxload 1/255
  Encapsulation ARPA, loopback not set
  Keepalive set (10 sec)
  ARP type: ARPA, ARP Timeout 04:00:00
  Last input never, output never, output hang never
  Last clearing of "show interface" counters 00:00:10
  Queueing strategy: fifo
  Output queue 0/40, 0 drops; input queue 0/75, 0 drops
  5 minute input rate 0 bits/sec, 0 packets/sec
  5 minute output rate 0 bits/sec, 0 packets/sec
     0 packets input, 0 bytes, 0 no buffer
     Received 0 broadcasts, 0 runts, 0 giants, 0 throttles
     0 input errors, 0 CRC, 0 frame, 0 overrun, 0 ignored
     0 input packets with dribble condition detected
     0 packets output, 0 bytes, 0 underruns(0/0/0)
     0 output errors, 0 collisions, 0 interface resets
     0 babbles, 0 late collision, 0 deferred
     0 lost carrier, 0 no carrier
     0 output buffer failures, 0 output buffers swapped out
```

Example 4-10 displays a router with two Ethernet interfaces and one serial interface. Interface Ethernet 0/0 is enabled and is currently running packets over the wire, while Ethernet 0/1 is not enabled. Interface Serial 0/0 is configured for Frame Relay and the physical layer (Layer 1) details are displayed. Other possible physical states are as follows:

Ethernet0/1 is up, line protocol is up—The Ethernet Interface is active, sending and receiving Ethernet frames.

Ethernet0/1 is up, line protocol is down—The Ethernet Interface is cabled but no keepalives are received, and no Ethernet frames are sent or received (possible cable fault).

Ethernet0/1 is administratively down, line protocol is down—Ethernet Interface is not enabled administratively; typically an interface not configured as yet.

Ethernet 0/1 is down, line protocol is up—A physical condition is not possible, for example.

To display the system log (syslog), use the **show logging** command. Example 4-11 displays a sample output taken from a router name R1.

Example 4-11 **show logging** *Command*

```
R1#show logging
Syslog logging: enabled (0 messages dropped, 0 messages rate-limited, 0 flushes,
 0 overruns)
    Console logging: level debugging, 27 messages logged
    Monitor logging: level debugging, 0 messages logged
    Buffer logging: level debugging, 1 messages logged
    Logging Exception size (4096 bytes)
    Trap logging: level debugging, 31 message lines logged
        Log Buffer (60000 bytes):
2d20h: %SYS-5-CONFIG_I: Configured from console by console
2d20h: %CLEAR-5-COUNTERS: Clear counter on all interfaces by console
```

Example 4-11 shows that 27 message have been logged and the logging level is debugging, which entails the following log message types:

- **Emergencies**—System is unusable (severity = 0)
- **Alerts**—Immediate action needed (severity = 1)
- **Critical**—Critical conditions (severity = 2)
- **Errors**—Error conditions (severity = 3)
- **Warnings**—Warning conditions (severity = 4)
- **Notifications**—Normal but significant conditions (severity = 5)
- **Informational**—Informational messages (severity = 6)
- **Debugging**—Debugging messages (severity = 7)

Two messages have also been displayed on the terminal: the first message is a configuration change, and the second appears when a PRIV EXEC user cleared the counters on all the interfaces.

The **show route-map** command displays any policy route maps configured. Policy route maps override routing decisions on Cisco routers. Route maps basically allow an administrator to access the route manipulation.

The **show version** command displays the system's hardware configuration, the software version, the names and sources of configuration files, and the boot images. Issue the **show version** EXEC command to accomplish this.

Example 4-12 displays a sample output.

Example 4-12 **show version** *Command on R1*

```
R1#show version
Cisco Internetwork Operating System Software
IOS (tm) C2600 Software (C2600-IK8O3S-M), Version 12.2(2)T,  RELEASE SOFTWARE (f
c1)
TAC Support: http://www.cisco.com/cgi-bin/ibld/view.pl?i=support
Copyright (c) 1986-2001 by cisco Systems, Inc.
Compiled Sat 02-Jun-01 15:47 by ccai
Image text-base: 0x80008088, data-base: 0x813455F8
ROM: System Bootstrap, Version 11.3(2)XA4, RELEASE SOFTWARE (fc1)
ROM: C2600 Software (C2600-IK8O3S-M), Version 12.2(2)T,  RELEASE SOFTWARE (fc1)
R1 uptime is 2 days, 20 hours, 15 minutes
System returned to ROM by reload at 14:57:18 UTC Mon Mar 1 1993
System restarted at 10:00:02 UTC Mon Mar 1 1993
System image file is "flash:c2600-ik8o3s-mz.122-2.T.bin"
cisco 2611 (MPC860) processor (revision 0x203) with 61440K/4096K bytes of memory
Processor board ID JAD043000VK (1947766474)
M860 processor: part number 0, mask 49
Bridging software.
X.25 software, Version 3.0.0.
2 Ethernet/IEEE 802.3 interface(s)
32K bytes of non-volatile configuration memory.
16384K bytes of processor board System flash (Read/Write)
Configuration register is 0x2102
```

Example 4-12 displays a number of key hardware data about the router. For example, the IOS software version is 12.2T, the router's uptime is 2 days, 20 hours, 15 minutes, and the memory installed on the router is 64 MB. There is 16 MB of System Flash, and the current configuration register is 0x2102.

NOTE   The **alias** command creates a custom shortcut to IOS commands so the EXEC user does not have to type the complete IOS command. For example, **show ip route** is already defined in IOS with the shortcut **sh ip ro** (not an **alias** command but rather a **shortcut** command). You can define your own alias with the global IOS command:

```
alias EXEC alias-name IOS-command
```

View the predefined aliases with the following command:

```
Router#show aliases
EXEC mode aliases:
  h                     help
  lo                    logout
  p                     ping
  r                     resume
  s                     show
  u                     undebug
  un                    undebug
  w                     where
```

For example, you could make the command **ospf** display only OSPF routes by issuing the following command:

```
alias EXEC ospf show ip route ospf
```

Debugging Cisco Routers

The **debug** command is one of the best set of tools you will encounter on Cisco routers. The **debug** command is available only from privilege mode.

Cisco IOS router's debugging includes hardware and software to aid in troubleshooting internal problems and problems with other hosts on the network. The **debug** privileged EXEC mode commands start the console display of several classes of network events.

For **debug** output to display on a console port, you must ensure that debugging to the console has not been disabled or sent to the logging buffer with the **logging console debug** command.

If you enable any **debug** commands through a console and no debug output is displayed, it might be because logging has been disabled.

Check the running configuration for the line **no logging debugging console**, and remove this line (by typing **logging debugging console**) to enable debug messages to be viewed by the console port.

Remember to turn off console logging when you are done troubleshooting the problem. The router will continue to send to the console even if nobody is there, tying up valuable CPU resources.

On virtual lines (VTY lines), you must enable the **terminal monitor** command to view the **debug** output. You use VTY lines when you telnet to a remote Cisco router.

NOTE   Refer to the *Cisco IOS Debug Command Reference* at the following URL for the most updated **debug** command information:
www.cisco.com/univercd/cc/td/doc/product/software/ios122/122sup/122debug/index.htm.

When debugging data, you must also be aware of the switching method used by the router (for example, fast or process switches) because the CPU will use the same method when sending **debug** output to the console or vty line.

The **ip route-cache** IOS command with no additional keywords enables fast switching. When **debug ip packet flow** is enabled, make sure you disable fast switching so you can view packet-by-packet flow through the router. Search the Cisco website for the keywords "Process" and "fast switching" for more details on switching methods. The following URL provides quality information on switching methods available on Cisco 7200 routers:

www.cisco.com/en/US/customer/products/sw/iosswrel/ps1831/products_configuration_
guide_chapter09186a00800ca6c7.html#xtocid6.

Table 4-4 displays the **debug** commands and the system debug message feature.

Table 4-4   **debug** *Command Summary*

IOS Command	Purpose
show debugging	Displays the state of each debugging option
debug ?	Displays a list and brief description of all the **debug** command options
debug *command*	Begins message logging for the specified debug command
no debug *command* (or **undebug all**)	Turns message logging off for the specified **debug** command or turns off all debug messages with the **undebug all** command

Example 4-13 displays the list of **debug** command options covered in this section.

Example 4-13 debug *Command Options*

```
R1#debug ?
  all                 Enable all debugging
  ip                  IP information
  list                Set interface or/and access list for the next debug
                      command
R1#debug ip ?
  audit               IDS audit events
  auth-proxy          Authentication proxy debug
  bgp                 BGP information
  cache               IP cache operations
  cef                 IP CEF operations
  cgmp                CGMP protocol activity
  dhcp                Dynamic Host Configuration Protocol
  drp                 Director response protocol
  dvmrp               DVMRP protocol activity
  egp                 EGP information
  eigrp               IP-EIGRP information
  error               IP error debugging
  flow                IP Flow switching operations
  ftp                 FTP dialogue
  html                HTML connections
  http                HTTP connections
  icmp                ICMP transactions
  igmp                IGMP protocol activity
  igrp                IGRP information
  inspect             Stateful inspection events
  interface           IP interface configuration changes
  mbgp                MBGP information
  mcache              IP multicast cache operations
  mhbeat              IP multicast heartbeat monitoring
  mobile              IP Mobility
```

continues

Example 4-13 debug *Command Options (Continued)*

```
mpacket                       IP multicast packet debugging
mrm                           IP Multicast Routing Monitor
mrouting                      IP multicast routing table activity
msdp                          Multicast Source Discovery Protocol (MSDP)
mtag                          IP multicast tagswitching activity
nat                           NAT events
nbar                          StILE - traffic classification Engine
ospf                          OSPF information
packet                        General IP debugging and IPSO security transactions
peer                          IP peer address activity
pim                           PIM protocol activity
policy                        Policy routing
postoffice                    PostOffice audit events
rgmp                          RGMP protocol activity
rip                           RIP protocol transactions
routing                       Routing table events
rsvp                          RSVP protocol activity
rtp                           RTP information
scp                           Secure Copy
sd                            Session Directory (SD)
security                      IP security options
socket                        Socket event
ssh                           Incoming ssh connections
tcp                           TCP information
tempacl                       IP temporary ACL
trigger-authentication        Trigger authentication
udp                           UDP based transactions
urd                           URL RenDezvous (URD)
wccp                          WCCP information
```

This section covers the **debug** commands highlighted in Example 4-13.

CAUTION   The CPU system on Cisco routers gives the highest priority to debugging output. For this reason, debugging commands should be turned on only for troubleshooting specific problems or during troubleshooting sessions with technical support personnel. Excessive debugging output can render the system inoperable.

Try to use the most specific **debug** command possible to reduce the load on the CPU. For example, the **debug all** command will surely disable a router. You should use only the **debug all** command in a lab environment.

Typically, the console port is used for debugging major faults because the CPU places debugging messages to the console port as the highest priority. Sometimes, debugging messages can overwhelm a network administrator's ability to monitor the router, and the IOS command, **logging synchronous**, can limit the messages to the console.

When synchronous logging of unsolicited messages and **debug** output is turned on (the line console is configured with the **logging synchronous** IOS command), unsolicited Cisco IOS Software output is displayed on the console or printed after solicited Cisco IOS Software output is displayed or printed. Unsolicited messages and **debug** output is displayed on the console after the prompt for user input is returned. This keeps unsolicited messages and **debug** output from being interspersed with solicited software output and prompts. After the unsolicited messages are displayed, the console displays the user prompt again. The IOS commands logging trap can be used to limit the logging of error messages sent to syslog servers to only those messages at the specified level (levels range from 0 to 7). The lowest level is 7 (debugging messages, greatest level of messages, as level 7 encompasses all levels possible from 0 to 7), and the highest level is 0, or emergencies (system is unusable).

The **debug all** command turns on all possible debug options available to a Cisco router. This will crash any router in a busy IP network, so we strongly recommended that you never apply this command in a working network environment.

Example 4-14 displays the options when enabling IP packets through a Cisco router.

Example 4-14 debug ip packet ?

```
R1#debug ip packet ?
  <1-199>      Access list
  <1300-2699>  Access list (expanded range)
  detail       Print more debugging detail
  <cr>
```

You can define an access list so that only packets that satisfy the access list are sent through to the console or vty line.

Figure 4-3 displays a typical example where Simon, a user on one Ethernet (Ethernet 0/0), is advising you that packets from users on Ethernet 0/1 (Melanie's PC) are not reaching each other. To view the routing packet flow through Router R1, you can debug the IP packets and use a standard access list or an extended one (access lists are covered later in this chapter).

To view the IP packet flow and ensure that you view only packets from Melanie's PC to Simon's PC, you can define an extended access list matching the source address, 131.108.2.100 (Melanie's PC), to the destination address, 131.108.1.100 (Simon's PC).

Figure 4-3 *IP Data Flow from One Segment to Another*

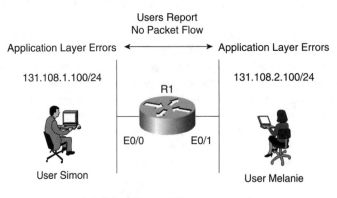

```
interface Ethernet0/0
ip address 131.108.1.1 255.255.255.0
interface Ethernet0/1
ip address 131.108.2.1 255.255.255.0
```

Example 4-15 displays the **debug** command configuration on Router R1.

Example 4-15 *Enabling* **debug ip packet** *with Access-list 100*

```
R1#config terminal
Enter configuration commands, one per line.  End with CNTL/Z.
R1(config)#access-list 100 permit ip host 131.108.2.100 host 131.108.1.100
R1#debug ip packet ?
  <1-199>      Access list
  <1300-2699>  Access list (expanded range)
  detail       Print more debugging detail
  <cr>
R1#debug ip packet 100 ?
  detail  Print more debugging detail
  <cr>
R1#debug ip packet 100 detail
IP packet debugging is on (detailed) for access list 100
```

Applying the exact **debug** command for only traffic generated from one device to another ensures that the router is not using too many CPU cycles to generate the **debug** output to the console. When a ping request is sent from Melanie's PC to Simon's PC, **debug** output displays a successful ping request.

Example 4-16 displays the sample **debug** output matching access-list 100 when 5 ping packets are sent.

NOTE	When debugging with a specific IP access list, be sure to stop all debugging options with the **undebug all** IOS command before removing IP access lists; Cisco IOS routers are prone to failure if the access list is removed before the debugging options are disabled. For example, no **debug** output will be captured and sent to the console if no access list is defined but referenced by a **debug** command (for example, **debug ip packet 100**, when access-list 100 is not defined). Also, remember that the default, deny not specifically permitted, is the default behavior for Cisco IOS access lists. Make sure you permit only traffic for which you are interested in viewing debug messages like the example shown in Figure 4-3.

Example 4-16 *Ping Request*

```
R1#ping 131.108.1.100
2d22h: IP: s=131.108.2.100 (local), d=131.108.1.100 (Ethernet0/0), len 100,
    sending
2d22h:    ICMP type=8, code=0
2d22h: IP: s=131.108.2.100 (Ethernet0/0), d=131.108.1.100 (Ethernet0/0),
    len 100, rcvd 3
2d22h:    ICMP type=8, code=0
2d22h: IP: s=131.108.2.100 (local), d=131.108.1.100 (Ethernet0/0), len 100,
    sending
2d22h:    ICMP type=8, code=0
2d22h: IP: s=131.108.2.100 (Ethernet0/0), d=131.108.1.100 (Ethernet0/0),
    len 100, rcvd 3
2d22h:    ICMP type=8, code=0
2d22h: IP: s=131.108.2.100 (local), d=131.108.1.100 (Ethernet0/0), len 100,
    sending
2d22h:    ICMP type=8, code=0
2d22h: IP: s=131.108.2.100 (Ethernet0/0), d=131.108.1.100 (Ethernet0/0),
    len 100, rcvd 3
2d22h:    ICMP type=8, code=0
2d22h: IP: s=131.108.2.100 (local), d=131.108.1.100 (Ethernet0/0), len 100,
    sending
2d22h:    ICMP type=8, code=0
2d22h: IP: s=131.108.2.100 (Ethernet0/0), d=131.108.1.100 (Ethernet0/0),
    len 100, rcvd 3
2d22h:    ICMP type=8, code=0
2d22h: IP: s=131.108.2.1 (local), d=131.108.1.1 (Ethernet0/0), len 100,
    sending
2d22h:    ICMP type=8, code=0
2d22h: IP: s=131.108.2.100 (Ethernet0/0), d=131.108.1.100 (Ethernet0/0),
    len 100, rcvd 3
2d22h:    ICMP type=8, code=0
```

The **debug** output demonstrates that five packets were successfully routed from Ethernet 0/1 to Ethernet 0/0. Therefore, the network fault reported by the users points to an application error rather than a network error.

Table 4-5 displays the meaning of the codes in Example 4-16.

Table 4-5   **debug ip packet 100 detail** *Explanation*

Field	Meaning
IP:	Indicates an IP packet
s=131.108.2.100 (Melanie's PC)	Indicates the packet's source address
d=131.108.1.100 (Simon's PC)	Indicates the packet's destination address
ICMP type 8 code 0	Ping request
Len 100	The length of the IP packet (100 bytes)

NOTE   The **detail** option allows for further detail in the **debug** output.

Using the route cache is often called *fast switching*. The route cache allows outgoing packets to be load-balanced on a *per-destination* basis, rather than on a per-packet basis.

NOTE   The output modifier | (pipe) is a great time saver. For example, the command, **show running-config | begin router ospf 100**, shows only the running configuration starting from the **router ospf 100** part instead of the entire output.

Password Recovery

Sometimes, the Cisco-enable or secret password is unknown and you must use password recovery to attain or change the enable/secret password.

Password recovery allows the network administrator to recover a lost or unknown password on a Cisco router. For password recovery, an administrator must have physical access to the router through the console or auxiliary port. When an EXEC user enters an incorrect enable password, the user receives an error message similar to the message shown in Example 4-17; the password entered is Cisco which is displayed as *****.

Example 4-17 *Incorrect Password Error Message*

```
R1>enable
Password: ******
Password: *****
Password: *****
% Bad passwords
R1>
```

When a user receives a *% Bad passwords* message, the user can neither access the advanced command set (in this case, enable mode), nor make any configuration changes. Fortunately, Cisco provides the following 10-step method to recover a lost password without losing configuration files:

Step 1   Power cycle the router.

Step 2   Issue a Control Break or the Break key command on the application (for Windows 2000, it is Control-Pause) to enter into boot ROM mode. The Control Break key sequence must be entered within 60 seconds of the router restarting after a power cycle.

Step 3   After you are in ROM mode, change the configuration register value to ignore the startup configuration file that is stored in NVRAM. Use the **o/r 0x2142** command.

Step 4   Allow the router to reboot by entering the **i** command.

Step 5   After the router has finished booting up without its startup configuration, look at the **show startup-config** command output. If the password is encrypted, move to Step 6, which requires you to enter the enable mode (type **enable** and you will not be required to enter any password) and copy the startup configuration to the running configuration with the **copy startup-config running-config** command. Then, change the password. If the password is not encrypted and the enable secret command is not used, simply document the plain text password and go to Step 8.

Step 6   Copy the startup configuration to RAM.

Step 7   Enable all active interfaces.

Step 8   Change the configuration register to 0x2102 (default).

Step 9   Reload the router.

Step 10 Check the new password.

NOTE	These are the generic steps for password recovery on a Cisco router. Some commands and steps might be slightly different depending on the hardware platform. Refer to the Password Recovery Procedures Index (www.cisco.com/warp/public/474/) for more information on each platform.

To review, look at an example. Assume you are directly connected to Router R1 and you do not know the enable password. You power cycle the router and press the Control Break key (the Esc key) to enter boot mode.

Example 4-18 shows the dialog displayed by the router after a break is issued.

Example 4-18 *Password Recovery Dialog on a Cisco Router*

```
System Bootstrap, Version 5.2(8a), RELEASE SOFTWARE
Copyright (c) 1986-1995 by cisco Systems

Abort at 0x10EA882 (PC)
!control break issued followed by ? to view help options
>>?
----------->control break issued followed by ? to view help options
$            Toggle cache state
B [filename] [TFTP Server IP address I TFTP Server Name]
             Load and EXECute system image from ROM
             or from TFTP server
C [address]  Continue EXECution [optional address]
D /S M L V   Deposit value V of size S into location L with
             modifier M
E /S M L     Examine location L with size S with modifier M
G [address]  Begin EXECution
H            Help for commands
I            Initialize
K            Stack trace
L [filename] [TFTP Server IP address I TFTP Server Name]
             Load system image from ROM or from TFTP server,
             but do not begin EXECution
O            Show configuration register option settings
P            Set the break point
S            Single step next instruction
T function   Test device (? for help)
```

As you can see in Example 4-18, the **?** symbol can display all the available options. To view the current configuration register, issue the **e/s 2000002** command, which displays the value of the configuration register. Example 4-19 displays the current configuration register.

Example 4-19 *e/s 200002 Command in Boot Rom Mode*

```
>e/s 2000002
! This command will display the current configuration register
2000002: 2102
! Type q to quit
>
```

The default value for the configuration register on Cisco IOS routers is 2102. For illustrative purposes, change the register to 0x2142, which tells the IOS to ignore the configuration in NVRAM.

The command to change the configuration register in Boot ROM mode is **0/r 0x2142** followed by the **initialize** (**i**) command, which will reload the router. Example 4-20 displays the configuration change and initializing of the router from boot ROM mode.

Example 4-20 *Changing the Configuration Register to 0x2142*

```
>0/r 0x2142
>i
```

The **i** command reboots the router and ignores your startup configuration because the configuration register has been set to 0x2142. The aim here is to change the password without losing your original configuration. Example 4-21 shows a truncated display by the Cisco IOS after the router is reloaded.

Example 4-21 *Dialog After Reload*

```
System Bootstrap, Version 5.2(8a), RELEASE SOFTWARE
Copyright (c) 1986-1995 by Cisco Systems
2500 processor with 6144 Kbytes of main memory
F3: 9407656+151288+514640 at 0x3000060


                 Restricted Rights Legend
Cisco Internetwork Operating System Software
IOS (tm) 2500 Software (C2500-AJS40-L), Version 11.2(17)
Copyright (c) 1986-1999 by cisco Systems, Inc.
Compiled Tue 05-Jan-99 13:27 by ashah
Image text-base: 0x030481E0, data-base: 0x00001000
Basic Rate ISDN software, Version 1.0.
1 Ethernet/IEEE 802.3 interface(s)
2 Serial network interface(s)
2 Low-speed serial(sync/async) network interface(s)
1 ISDN Basic Rate interface(s)
32K bytes of non-volatile configuration memory.
16384K bytes of processor board System flash (Read ONLY)
```

continues

Example 4-21 *Dialog After Reload (Continued)*

```
            --- System Configuration Dialog ---
At any point you may enter a question mark '?' for help.
Use ctrl-c to abort configuration dialog at any prompt.
Default settings are in square brackets '[]'.
Would you like to enter the initial configuration dialog? [yes]:No
Press RETURN to get started!
......
Router>ena  !(no password required or entered)
Router#
```

Notice that the router reverts to the default configuration. Enter the **enable** command to enter privilege EXEC mode. In this example, you will not be prompted for the enable password because there isn't one; by default, no enable password is configured when a Cisco IOS router boots from the default configuration (no passwords are configured in this default state).

You can view the startup config by using the **show startup-config** command (or **show config** in IOS versions predating version 10.3), as shown in Example 4-22.

Example 4-22 **show startup-config** *Command*

```
Router#show startup-config
Using 1968 out of 32762 bytes
! Last configuration change at 16:35:50 UTC Tue May 18 2002
! NVRAM config last updated at 16:35:51 UTC Tue May 18 2002
version 2.2
service password-encryption
hostname R1
! Note there is no secret password either
enable password 7 05080F1C2243
...
```

As you can see in Example 4-22, the enable password is encrypted. In instances where the password is not encrypted, you could view the password using the **show startup-config** command. When a password is encrypted, you must copy the startup configuration to the running configuration and change the password manually by using the following IOS command:

```
copy startup-config running-config
```

At this point, you are still in privileged mode, so you can now enter global configuration mode to change the password back to its original setting (cisco, in this instance).

Example 4-23 displays the password change in global configuration mode set to the new password of cisco.

Example 4-23 *Changing a Password and Setting the Configuration Registry Commands*

```
hostname#copy startup-config running-config
Destination filename [running-config]?
2818 bytes copied in 1.475 secs (2818 bytes/sec)
R1#config terminal
R1(config)#enable password cisco
R1(config)#config-register 0x2102
R1(config)#exit
R1#reload
```

You complete password recovery by changing the configuration register back to the default value (0x2102).

NOTE   If a secret password is also configured, you must use the **enable secret** *password* IOS command because the secret password overrides the enable password. Example 4-23 includes no secret password, so you can use the **enable password** command.

When the Cisco IOS router reloads, it will load the new configuration file with the password set to **cisco**.

Basic Security on Cisco Routers

You can access a Cisco router in a number of ways. You can physically access a router through the console port, or you can access a router remotely through a modem via the auxiliary port. You can also access a router through a network or virtual terminal ports (VTY lines), which allow remote Telnet access.

If you do not have physical access to a router—either through a console port or an auxiliary port via dialup—you can access a router through the software interface, called the virtual terminal (also referred to as a VTY port). When you telnet to a router, you might be required to enter the VTY password set by the network administrator. For example, on Router R1, the administrator types R2's remote address and tries to telnet to one of the VTY lines.

Example 4-24 provides the session dialog when a user telnets to the router with the IP address 131.108.1.2.

Example 4-24 *Using a VTY Port to Establish a Telnet Connection*

```
R1#Telnet 131.108.1.2
Trying 131.108.1.2 ... Open
User Access Verification
Password: xxxxx
R2>
```

Cisco routers can have passwords set on all operation modes, including the console port, privilege mode, and virtual terminal access. To set a console password to prevent unauthorized console access to the router, issue the commands shown in Example 4-25.

NOTE   All passwords are case-sensitive.

Example 4-25 *Setting a Console Password*

```
R1(config)#line con 0
R1(config-line)#password cisco
!You can also set a password on the auxiliary port
R1(config)#line aux 0
R1(config-line)#password cisco
```

To set the privilege mode password, you have two options: the enable and secret password. To set these passwords, use the respective commands listed in Example 4-26.

Example 4-26 *Setting Enable and Secret Password*

```
R1(config)#enable password cisco
R1(config)#enable secret ccie
```

The command to set an enable password is **enable password** *password*. You can also set a more secure password, called a secret password, which is encrypted when viewing the configuration with the **enable secret** *password* command.

The secret password IOS command overrides the enable password. Cisco IOS does not permit you to configure the same password if you apply both commands.

In Example 4-26, the secret password will always be used. Now, issue the **show running-config** command to display the configuration after entering the enable and secret passwords in Example 4-26.

Example 4-27 displays the output from the **show running-config** IOS command after entering enable and secret passwords.

Example 4-27 **show running-config** *Command on R1*

```
R1#show running-config
Building configuration
Current configuration:
!
version 12.2
```

Example 4-27 **show running-config** *Command on R1 (Continued)*

```
!
hostname R1
!
enable secret 5 $1$Aiy2$GGSCYdG57PdRiNg/.D.XI.
enable password cisco
```

Example 4-27 shows that the secret password is encrypted (using Cisco's proprietary algorithm), while the enable password is readable. This setup enables you to hide secret passwords when the configuration is viewed. If you want, you can also encrypt the enable password by issuing the **service password-encryption** command, as displayed in Example 4-28. Cisco uses the MD5 algorithm to hash the secret password. You cannot reverse engineer the hashed password (for example, 1Aiy2$GGSCYdG57PdRiNg/.D.XI.).

Example 4-28 **service password-encryption** *Command*

```
R1(config)#service password-encryption
```

The **service password-encryption** command encrypts all passwords issued to the router using the MD5 encryption algorithm. Example 4-29 shows an example of how these passwords appear when the configuration is viewed after all passwords have been encrypted.

Example 4-29 displays the **show running-config** command output after encrypting all passwords.

Example 4-29 **show running-config** *Command on R1 After Encrypting All Passwords*

```
R1#show running-config
Building configuration...
Current configuration:
!
service password-encryption
version 11.2
hostname R1
!
enable secret 5 $1$Aiy2$GGSCYdG57PdRiNg/.D.XI.
enable password 7 0822455D0A16
```

NOTE   Note the digits, 5 and 7, before the encrypted passwords. The number 5 signifies that MD5 Hash algorithm is used for encryption, whereas the number 7 signifies a weaker algorithm. You are not expected to know this for the written exam, but it is valuable knowledge for troubleshooting complex networks. In fact, a great network engineer is measured by his well-defined troubleshooting techniques, and not by how many CCIE lab exams he has passed.

Notice in Example 4-29 that both the secret and enable passwords are encrypted. If you enable the **service password-encryption** command in global configuration mode, all passwords will be encrypted and will not be viewable when displaying the configuration on the Cisco router.

The final Cisco password you can set is the virtual terminal password. This password verifies remote Telnet sessions to a router. Example 4-30 displays the commands necessary to set the virtual terminal password on a Cisco router.

Example 4-30 **password** *Command to Set a Virtual Terminal Password to ccie*

```
R4(config)#line vty 0 4
R4(config-line)#password ccie
```

If you issue the **no login** command below the virtual terminal command (**line vty 0 4**), remote Telnet users will not be asked to supply a password and will automatically enter EXEC mode. Example 4-31 displays the Telnet session dialogue when the **no login** command is entered.

Example 4-31 *Dialogue Display When No Login Is Enabled*

```
R1#telnet 1.1.1.1
Trying 1.1.1.1 ... Open
R2>
```

Why no mention of AAA

Keep in mind that the preceding setup is not a secure access method for a router network.

IP Access Lists

Standard and extended access lists filter IP traffic. An access list is basically a set of permit or deny statements. *Standard access lists* control IP traffic based on the source address only. *Extended access lists* can filter on source and destination addresses. Extended access lists can also filter on specific protocols and port numbers. This section covers how a Cisco router handles access lists.

Access Lists on Cisco Routers

By default, a Cisco router permits all IP and TCP traffic unless an access list is defined and applied to the appropriate interface. Figure 4-4 illustrates the steps taken if an access list is configured on a Cisco router.

Figure 4-4   *Access List Decision Taken by a Cisco Router*

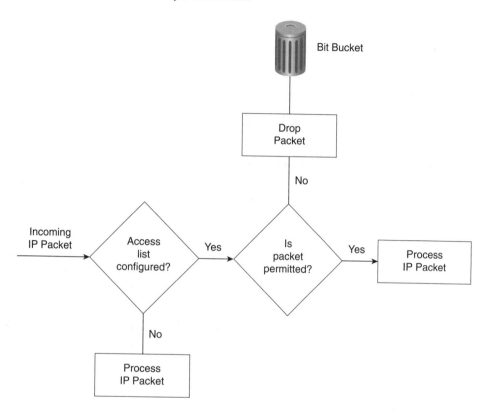

If an incoming IP packet is received on a router and no access list is defined, the packet is forwarded to the IP routing software. If an access list is defined and applied, the packet is checked against the access list, and the appropriate permit or deny action is taken. The default action taken by any access list is to permit any explicitly defined statements and explicitly deny everything else. You will not see the explicitly deny statement when you issue the **show ip access-lists** because that is the default behavior.

NOTE

If the keyword **out** or **in** is not applied by the administrator when defining an IP filter on an interface, the default action is to apply the filter on the outbound traffic.

Standard IP access lists range from 1 through 99 and 1300 through 1999.

Extended IP access lists range from 100 through 199 and 2000 through 2699.

Standard IP access lists filter on the source address only. The Cisco IOS syntax is as follows:

```
access-list access-list-number {deny I permit} [source-address]
    [source-wildcard]
```

Table 4-6 describes the purpose of each field.

Table 4-6   *Standard IP* **access-list** *Command Syntax Description*

Command Field	Description
access-list-number	A number from 1 through 99 that defines a standard access list number. Versions of IOS 12.0 or later also have standard access lists ranging from 1300-1999.
deny	IP packet is denied if a match is found.
permit	IP packet is permitted if it matches the criteria, as defined by the administrator.
source-address	Source IP address or network. Any source address can be applied by using the keyword **any**.
source-wildcard (optional)	Wildcard mask that is to be applied to the source address. This is an inverse mask, which is further explained with a few examples later in this section. The default is 0.0.0.0, which specifies an exact match.

After creating the access list as described in Table 4-6, you must apply the access list to the required interface using the following command:

```
ip access-group {access-list-number I name} {in I out}
```

Table 4-7 describes the purpose of each field.

Table 4-7   **ip access-group** *Command Syntax Description*

Command Field	Description
access-list-number	A number in the range from 1 through 99 and 1300 through 1999 that defines a standard access list number.
name	If you are using named access lists, that name will be referenced here.
in	Keyword that designates the access list as an inbound packet filter.
out	Keyword that designates the access list as an outbound packet filter. This is the default action.

The wildcard mask previously mentioned in the **access-list** command matches the source address. When the wildcard mask is set to binary 0, the corresponding bit field must match; if it is set to binary 1, the router does not care to match any bit or it is an insignificant bit. For example, the mask 0.0.255.255 means that the first two octets must match, but the last two octets do not need to match—hence, the commonly used phrases *care bits* (0s) and *don't care bits* (1s).

For further clarification, look at some examples of using access lists.

Suppose you have found a faulty NIC card with the address 141.108.1.99/24. You have been asked to stop packets from being sent out Serial 0 on your router but to permit everyone else. In this situation, you need to deny the host address 141.108.1.99 and permit all other host devices. Example 4-32 displays the access list that fulfills this requirement.

Example 4-32 *Access List Configuration*

```
access-list 1 deny 141.108.1.99 0.0.0.0
access-list 1 permit 141.108.1.0 0.0.0.255
```

Next, you would apply the access list to filter outbound (the keyword **out** is supplied) IP packets on the Serial 0 interface. Example 4-33 applies the access list number 1 to the Serial interface (outbound packets). You can be a little wiser and filter the incoming packets on the Ethernet interface. This ensures that the packet is immediately dropped before it is processed by the CPU for delivery over the serial interface. Both examples are displayed in Example 4-33.

Example 4-33 *Applying the Access-list*

```
Interface Ethernet0
ip access-group 1 in
interface Serial 0
ip access-group 1 out
```

Now look at a more complex example of using a standard access list. Suppose you have 16 networks ranging from 141.108.1.0 to 141.108.16.0, as shown in Figure 4-5.

You have assigned even subnets (2, 4, 6, 8, 10, 12, 14, and 16) to the Accounting department and odd subnets (1, 3, 5, 7, 9, 11, 13, and 15) to the Sales department. You do not want the Sales department to access the Internet, as shown in Figure 4-5. To solve this issue, you configure a standard access list. Figure 4-5 displays a simple requirement to block all odd networks from accessing the Internet.

You could configure the router to deny all the odd networks, but that would require many configuration lines.

NOTE   Access lists are CPU-process-intensive because the router has to go through every entry in the access list for each packet until a match is made. If you want to determine the actual effect an access list has on your router, compare the CPU processes before and after activating an access list. Remember to check on a regular basis to see the big picture.

Figure 4-5   *Standard Access List Example*

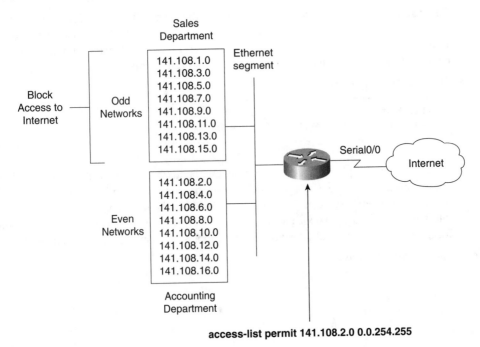

Sales
Department

Block
Access to
Internet

Odd
Networks

141.108.1.0
141.108.3.0
141.108.5.0
141.108.7.0
141.108.9.0
141.108.11.0
141.108.13.0
141.108.15.0

Ethernet
segment

Even
Networks

141.108.2.0
141.108.4.0
141.108.6.0
141.108.8.0
141.108.10.0
141.108.12.0
141.108.14.0
141.108.16.0

Accounting
Department

Serial0/0

Internet

access-list permit 141.108.2.0 0.0.254.255

Instead, permit only even networks (2, 4, 6, 8, 10, 12, 14, and 16) with one IOS configuration line. To accomplish this, convert all networks to binary to see if there is any pattern that you can use in the wildcard mask.

Table 4-8 displays numbers 1 through 16 in both decimal and binary format.

Table 4-8   *Example Calculation of Numbers in Binary*

Decimal	Binary
1	00000001
2	00000010
3	00000011
4	00000100
5	00000101
6	00000110
7	00000111
8	00001000

Table 4-8   *Example Calculation of Numbers in Binary (Continued)*

Decimal	Binary
9	00001001
10	00001010
11	00001011
12	00001100
13	00001101
14	00001110
15	00001111
16	00010000

Notice that odd networks always end in the binary value of 1, and even networks end with 0. Therefore, you can apply your access lists to match on the even network and implicitly deny everything else. Even numbers will always end in binary 0. You do not care about the first seven bits, but you must have the last bit set to 0. The wildcard mask that applies this condition is 111111110 (1 is don't care and 0 is must match; the first 7 bits are set to 1, and the last bit is set to 0).

This converts to a decimal value of 254. The following access list will permit only even networks:

```
access-list 1 permit 141.108.2.0 0.0.254.255
```

The preceding access list will match networks 2, 4, 6, 8, 10, 12, 14, and 16 in the third octet. The default action is to deny everything else, so only even networks will be allowed, and odd networks are blocked by default. Next, you would apply the access list to the outbound interface. Example 4-34 describes the full configuration.

Example 4-34 *Applying the Access List*

```
Hostname R1
interface Serial0/0
ip access-group 1 out
access-list 1 permit 141.108.2.0 0.0.254.255
```

Extended Access Lists

Extended access lists range from 100 through 199 and 2000 through 2699. Alternatively, you can use a named access list with IOS release 12.0 or later. As mentioned earlier in this chapter, extended access lists can be applied to both source and destination addresses, as well as filter protocol types and port numbers. Look at some examples of extended access lists that allow you to filter several different types of traffic.

For Internet Control Message Protocol (ICMP), use the syntax shown in Example 4-35.

Example 4-35 *Access List Syntax for ICMP Traffic*

```
access-list access-list-number [dynamic dynamic-name
[timeout minutes]] {deny | permit} icmp source source-wildcard
destination destination-wildcard [icmp-type [icmp-code]
[icmp-message] [precedence precedence] [tos tos] [log]
```

For Internet Group Management Protocol (IGMP), use the syntax shown in Example 4-36.

Example 4-36 *Access List Syntax for IGMP Traffic*

```
access-list access-list-number [dynamic dynamic-name
[timeout minutes]] {deny | permit} igmp source source-wildcard
destination destination-wildcard [igmp-type]
[precedence precedence] [tos tos] [log]
```

For TCP, use the syntax shown in Example 4-37.

Example 4-37 *Access List Syntax for TCP Traffic*

```
access-list access-list-number [dynamic dynamic-name
[timeout minutes]] {deny | permit} tcp source source-wildcard
[operator port [port]] destination destination-wildcard
[operator port [port]] [established] [precedence precedence]
[tos tos] [log]
```

For User Datagram Protocol (UDP), use the syntax shown in Example 4-38.

Example 4-38 *Access List Syntax for UDP Traffic*

```
access-list access-list-number [dynamic dynamic-name
[timeout minutes]] {deny | permit} udp source source-wildcard
[operator port [port]] destination destination-wildcard
[operator port [port]] [precedence precedence] [tos tos] [log]
```

As you can see, extended access lists have a range of options to suit any requirement. The most often used extended access list options are as follows:

- *access-list-number*—Provides a number ranging from 100 through 199 that defines an extended access list. Also numbers ranging from 2000 through 2699.

- **deny**—Denies access if the conditions are matched.

- **permit**—Permits access if the conditions are matched.

- *protocol*—Specifies the protocol you are filtering. Some common options include **eigrp**, **gre**, **icmp**, **igmp**, **igrp**, **ip**, **ospf**, **tcp**, and **udp**.

- *source*—Specifies the source address.

- *source-wildcard*—Specifies the wildcard mask.

- *destination*—Identifies the destination network.

- *destination-wildcard*—Identifies the destination mask.

You are expected to demonstrate your understanding of standard and extended access lists. You are not expected to memorize the available options in an extended access list. The options are provided in this chapter for your reference only. When constructing access lists, the built-in help feature (**?**) is extremely useful.

Here are a few more complex examples of access lists.

Example 4-39 permits Domain Naming System (DNS) packets, ICMP echo and echo replies, OSPF, and BGP packets. (BGP runs over TCP using port 179.)

Example 4-39 *Extended Access List Example*

```
access-list 100 permit tcp any any  eq smtp
! Permits Simple Mail Transfer Protocols
access-list 100 permit udp any any eq domain
! Permits DNS queries
access-list 100 permit icmp any any echo
! Permits ICMP ping requests
access-list 100 permit icmp any any echo-reply
! Permits ICMP replies
access 100 permit ospf any any
! Permits OSPF packets
access 100 permit tcp any any eq bgp
! Permits BGP to any device
```

In Example 4-39, the access list numbered 100 is not concerned with specific host addresses or networks, but rather ranges of networks.

The **any** keyword is shorthand for 0.0.0.0 255.255.255.255, which means that the device's address is irrelevant. This address can be entered in shorthand as **any**. If any IP packet arrives to the router and does not match the specified criteria, the packet is dropped.

The Cisco CD documentation provides additional quality examples of access lists. You should take some time to study Cisco's examples available on the CD and at www.cisco.com under the technical documents link.

Access lists are difficult to manage because you cannot explicitly delete a specific line; you must first remove the entire access list and re-enter the new access list with the correct order for numbered access lists. For a large access list that might contain over 1000 lines of code, any variations are completed on a TFTP server and copied to the startup configuration. I have worked with some access lists that were 2500 lines in length and took over 5 minutes to load on Cisco routers. On the other hand, named access-lists lists allow you to determine where in the access list the new line will be placed. For more detail on named access-list, please visit, www.cisco.com/en/US/customer/products/sw/iosswrel/ps1831/products_configuration_guide _chapter09186a00800d9817.html.

It might be a likely scenario for the CCIE security lab exam so please ensure you are fully comfortable with named and numbered access lists for the laboratory exam.

Foundation Summary

The "Foundation Summary" is a condensed collection of material for a convenient review of key concepts in this chapter. If you are already comfortable with the topics in this chapter and decided to skip most of the "Foundation Topics" material, the "Foundation Summary" will help you recall a few details. If you just read the "Foundation Topics" section, this review should help further solidify some key facts. If you are doing your final preparation before the exam, the "Foundation Summary" offers a convenient and quick final review.

Table 4-9   *Cisco Device Commands and Information*

Command	Description
show flash	Displays the content of the System Flash
Standard IP access list range	1-99, 1300-1999
Extended access list range	100-199, 2000-2699
copy running-config startup-config	IOS command to save running configuration from RAM to NVRAM
copy startup-config running-config	IOS command to save running configuration from NVRAM to RAM
0x2102 IOS syntax: **config-register** *value*	0x2102 is the standard default configuration register, which is a 16-bit number defining how the router loads To ignore the startup configuration, use 0x2142
show version	Displays detailed information about IOS and hardware configuration on a Cisco router

Table 4-10   *Advanced Cisco Device Operation*

IOS Command	Description
show debugging	Displays the current **debug** commands processed by the CPU
debug ?	Displays a list of available **debug** options
undebug all	Turns off all possible debugging commands
debug ip packet *access-list*	Allows debugging of specific network address without burdening the router with every IP packet processed by the CPU

Table 4-11 *Password Recovery Steps*

Step	Description
1	Power cycle the router.
2	Issue a control break or the break key command on the application to enter into boot ROM mode. The control break key sequence must be entered within 60 seconds of the router restarting after a power cycle.
3	Once you are in ROM mode, change the configuration register value to ignore the startup configuration file that is stored in NVRAM. Use the **o/r 0x2142** command.
4	Allow the router to reboot by entering the **i** command.
5	After the router has finished booting up without its startup configuration, look at the **show startup-config** command output. If the password is encrypted, move to Step 6, which requires you to enter the enable mode (type **enable** and you will not be required to enter any password) and copy the startup configuration to the running configuration with the **copy startup-config running-config** command. Then, change the password.
	If the password is not encrypted and the secret password is not used, you can simply read the password. Skip Steps 6 and 7 and go to Step 8.
6	Copy the startup configuration to RAM.
7	Enable all active interfaces.
8	Change the configuration register to 0x2102 (default).
9	Reload router.
10	Check the new password.

Table 4-12 *Basic Password Security*

IOS Command	Description
enable password *password*	Defines the enable password (case-sensitive) to allow EXEC user to Privilege mode where configuration changes can be made. Typically not encrypted, and it is viewable when the configuration is displayed.
enable secret *password*	Sets the secret password to enable EXEC user to Privilege mode where configuration changes can be made. Overrides an enable password and is encrypted by default.
service password-encryption	Encrypts all passwords on Cisco routers.

Q & A

The Q & A questions are designed to help you assess your readiness for the topics covered on the CCIE Security written exam and those topics presented in this chapter. This format helps you assess your retention of the material. A strong understanding of the answers to these questions will help you on the CCIE Security written exam. You can also look over the questions at the beginning of the chapter again for additional review. Use the CD-ROM provided with this book to take simulated exams, which draw from a database of over 300 multiple-choice questions—all different from those presented in the book.

Select the best answer. Answers to these questions can be found in Appendix A, "Answers to Quiz Questions."

1 Where is the running configuration stored on a Cisco router?

_____

_____

_____

2 What IOS command displays the startup configuration?

_____

_____

_____

3 What IOS command provides the following output?

```
System flash directory:
File  Length    Name/status
   1  9558976   c2500-ajs40-l.12-17.bin
[9559040 bytes used, 7218176 available, 16777216 total]
16384K bytes of processor board System flash
```

_____

_____

_____

4 What configuration register will enable a Cisco router to ignore the startup configuration?

_____

_____

_____

5 To copy the startup configuration to the running configuration, what IOS command or commands are used?

_____

_____

_____

6 What is the range for standard and extended IP access lists on Cisco IOS routers?

_____

_____

_____

7 What command display the IP access lists configured on a Cisco router?

_____

_____

_____

8 How do you disable all **debug** commands currently enabled on a Cisco router, assuming you are not sure what debug commands are enabled?

_____

_____

_____

9 What must you be very careful of when enabling any form of debugging on a Cisco router?

_____

_____

_____

10 What are the required steps when performing password recovery on a Cisco router?

_____

_____

_____

11 What is the enable password for the following configuration?

```
enable password CiscO
```

_____

_____

_____

Scenario

Scenario 4-1: Configuring Cisco Routers for Passwords and Access Lists

Figure 4-6 displays a simple one-router network with two Ethernet LAN interfaces connecting users on subnet 131.108.1.0/24 to the server IP network, 131.108.2.0/24.

Figure 4-6   *Scenario Physical Topology*

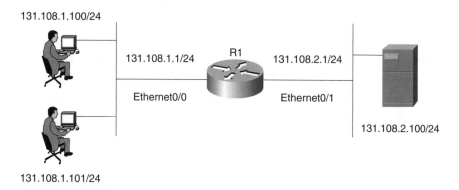

Example 4-40 displays the working configuration file on R1 numbered from line 1 to 25.

Example 4-40 *R1's Full Configuration*

```
1. version 12.2
2. no service password-encryption
3. hostname R1
4. no logging console debugging
5. enable secret 5 $1$TBUV$od27CrEfa4UVICBtwvqol/
6. enable password ciscO
7.interface Ethernet0/0
8. ip address 131.108.1.1 255.255.255.0
9.interface Ethernet0/1
10. ip address 131.108.2.1 255.255.255.0
11.no ip http server
12.access-list 1 permit 131.108.0.0 0.0.255.255
13.access-list 100 permit tcp any host 131.108.1.1 eq telnet
14.access-list 100 permit ip host 131.108.2.100 host 131.108.1.1
15.alias EXEC test show ip route ospf
16.alias EXEC eth0 show interface ethernet0/0
17.alias EXEC eth1 show interface ethernet0/1
```

continues

Example 4-40 *R1's Full Configuration (Continued)*

```
18.line con 0
19.EXEC-timeout 0 0
20.login
21.line aux 0
22.line vty 0 4
23.EXEC-timeout 0 0
24.no login
25.end
```

1   The network administrator enables the **debug ip packet** command on Router R1, but no output is seen when connected to the console. IP traffic is following correctly from Ethernet0/0 to Ethernet0/1. What is the likely problem? What IOS configuration change is required to rectify the fault?

2   There are a number of configured aliases. What alias will display the Ethernet interface statistics for the Ethernet interface labeled Ethernet0/1?

3   When the following command is entered at the privilege EXEC prompt, what will the output be?

```
R1#eth0
```

4   What is the password of Router 1 that enables a network administrator to make configuration changes?

5   What **debug** command can be used to debug IP packets' source from the address 131.108.2.100 to the PC with the IP address of 131.108.1.100.

6   A user telnets to Router R1 and runs the debug command, **debug ip packet**.

   IP data travels from the PC to the server but no output is displayed on the router.

   What is the likely problem?

```
R2#R1
Trying 131.108.255.1 ... Open

R1>debug ip packet
        ^
% Invalid input detected at '^' marker.

R1>
```

7   What is the configuration register of the router in Figure 4-6?

8   What is the VTY password required for Telnet clients logging into R1?

9   What does access list 1 accomplish in line 12?

10 What Global IOS command would encrypt all passwords configured on R1 in Figure 4-6?

Scenario Answers

1 Line 4 in Example 4-39 has disabled the **debug** output from being visible. To enable debug messages to be sent to the console port, the command **logging console debugging** must be configured in global configuration mode. Alternatively, telneting to the router and enabling the **terminal monitor** command via the VTY line enables the network administrator to view the **debug** output.

2 Line 17 displays the alias, **eth1**, which is the command **show interface ethernet0/1**.

3 Line 16 defines an alias, **eth0**, which will be used as a shortcut to the **show interface ethernet0/0** command. This IOS command displays the statistics of interface Ethernet0/0.

4 Line 6 (**enable password ciscO**) defines the enable password as ciscO. However, because a secret password exists on line 5, that is the password required to enter enable mode, and because the secret password is encrypted, you cannot decipher the password.

5 Access list 100 defines an **Access-list** with the source address 131.108.2.100 to the destination IP address 131.108.1.100. You can apply the debug command, **debug ip packet 100**, with the optional keyword **detail** to view IP packets sent from the server to the IP address 131.108.1.100.

6 The Telnet user must be in privilege EXEC mode and must enable the **terminal monitor** command to ensure **debug** output is sent to the VTY line.

7 The configuration in Example 4-38 does not include a configuration register, so the default register (0x2102) is enabled.

8 Line 24 configures the router for no VTY login, so there is no password; any Telnet users will be directed to the router at the EXEC prompt level.

9 Access list 1 is not defined on any interface and can be used when **debug ip packet** is turned on. Because it is a standard access list, it can be used to debug packets' source from network 131.108.0.0 to 131.108.255.255.

10 The Global IOS command, **service password-encryption**, encrypts all passwords, including the enable and VTY password, if any.

Exam Topics in This Chapter

CHAPTER 5

Security Protocols

This chapter covers some of today's most widely used technologies that give network administrators the ability to ensure sensitive data is secure from unauthorized sources.

Standards such as IP security (IPSec) and encryption standards are covered, as are all the fundamental foundation topics you need to master the topics covered in the security written exam.

This chapter covers the following topics:

- **Security protocols**—This section covers the security protocols authentication, authorization, and accounting (AAA), RADIUS, Terminal Access Controller Access Control System Authentication Plus (TACACS+) protocol, and Kerberos.

- **Virtual private dial-up networks**—This section covers VPDNs and their use in dialup IP networks.

- **Date encryption**—This section covers encrypting IP using standard encryption, such as Triple Data Encryption Standard (DES) and IPSec. The mechanism used to authenticate encryption tunnels is also covered.

- **Certificate Enrollment Protocol**—This section briefly covers the Cisco-defined certificate management protocol, CEP, and how a device communicates with a certificate authority.

"Do I Know This Already?" Quiz

This assessment quiz's purpose is to help you determine how to spend your limited study time. If you can answer most or all these questions, you might want to skim the "Foundation Topics" section and return to it later, as necessary. Review the "Foundation Summary" section and answer the questions at the end of the chapter to ensure that you have a strong grasp of the material covered. If you already intend to read the entire chapter, you do not necessarily need to answer these questions now. If you find these assessment questions difficult, read through the entire "Foundation Topics" section and review it until you feel comfortable with your ability to answer all these and the Q & A questions at the end of the chapter.

Answers to these questions can be found in Appendix A, "Answers to Quiz Questions."

1 What are the three components of AAA? (Choose the three best answers.)

    a. Accounting

    b. Authorization

    c. Adapting

    d. Authentication

2 What IOS command must be issued to start AAA on a Cisco router?

    a. **aaa old-model**

    b. **aaa model**

    c. **aaa new model**

    d. **aaa new-model**

    e. **aaa new_model**

3 What algorithm initiates and encrypts a session between two routers' exchange keys between two encryption devices?

    a. Routing algorithm

    b. Diffie-Hellman algorithm

    c. The switching engine

    d. The stac compression algorithm

4 Can you configure RADIUS and TACACS+ concurrently on a Cisco IOS router?

    a. No.

    b. Yes, provided you have the same lists names applied to the same interfaces.

    c. Yes, provided you have the different lists names applied to the same interfaces.

    d. Yes, provided you have the different lists names applied to different interfaces.

5 How do you enable a RADIUS server to debug messages for Cisco Secure on a UNIX server?

    a. Terminal monitor.

    b. Edit the configuration file on the router.

    c. Edit the syslog.conf and csu.cfg files.

    d. Not possible, as UNIX does not run IOS.

6 What RADIUS attribute is used by vendors and not predefined by RFC 2138?

a. 1

b. 2

c. 3

d. 4

e. 13

f. 26

g. 333

h. 33

7 RADIUS can support which of the following protocols?

a. PPP

b. OSPF

c. AppleTalk

d. IPX

e. NLSP

8 When a RADIUS server identifies the wrong password entered by the remote users, what packet type is sent?

a. Accept-user

b. Reject-users

c. Reject-deny

d. Reject-accept

e. Reject-Error

f. Access-reject

9 Identify the false statement about RADIUS.

a. RADIUS is a defined standard in RFC 2138/2139.

b. RADIUS runs over TCP port 1812.

c. RADIUS runs over UDP port 1812.

d. RADIUS accounting information runs over port 1646.

10 What is the RADIUS key for the following configuration? If this configuration is not valid, why isn't it?

```
aaa authentication login use-radius group radius local
aaa authentication ppp user-radius if-needed group radius
aaa authorization exec default group radius
aaa authorization network default group radius
radius-server 3.3.3.3
radius-server key IlovemyMum
```

a. IlovemyMum

b. Ilovemymum

c. This configuration will not work because the command **aaa new-model** is missing.

d. 3.3.3.3

11 What is the RADIUS key for the following configuration?

```
Aaa new-model
aaa authentication login use-radius group radius local
aaa authentication ppp user-radius if-needed group radius
aaa authorization exec default group radius
aaa authorization network default group radius
radius-server 3.3.3.3
radius-server key IlovemyMum
```

a. IlovemyMum

b. Ilovemymum

c. This configuration will not work.

d. 3.3.3.3

12 What versions of TACACS does Cisco IOS support? (Select the best three answers.)

a. TACACS+

b. TACACS

c. Extended TACACS

d. Extended TACACS+

13 TACACS+ is transported over which TCP port number?

a. 520

b. 23

c. 21

d. 20

e. 49

14 What is the predefined TACACS+ server key for the following configuration?

```
radius-server host 3.3.3.3
radius-server key CCIEsrock
```

a. 3.3.3.3

b. Not enough data

c. CCIESROCK

d. CCIEsRock

e. CCIEsrock

15 What does the following command accomplish?

```
tacacs_server host 3.3.3.3
```

a. Defines the remote TACACS+ server as 3.3.3.3

b. Defines the remote RADIUS server as 3.3.3.3

c. Not a valid IOS command

d. 3.3.3.3

e. Host unknown; no DNS details for 3.3.3.3 provided

16 Which of the following protocols does TACACS+ support?

a. PPP

b. AppleTalk

c. NetBIOS

d. All the above

17 Kerberos is defined at what layer of the OSI model?

a. Layer 1

b. Layer 2

c. Layer 3

d. Layer 4

e. Layer 5

f. Layer 6

g. Layer 7

18 What definition best describes a key distribution center when Kerberos is applied to a network?

a. A general term that refers to authentication tickets

b. An authorization level label for Kerberos principals

c. Applications and services that have been modified to support the Kerberos credential infrastructure

d. A domain consisting of users, hosts, and network services that are registered to a Kerberos server

e. A Kerberos server and database program running on a network host

19 What definition best describes a Kerberos credential?

a. A general term that refers to authentication tickets

b. An authorization level label for Kerberos principals

c. Applications and services that have been modified to support the Kerberos credential infrastructure

d. A domain consisting of users, hosts, and network services that are registered to a Kerberos server

e. A Kerberos server and database program running on a network host

20 What definition best describes Kerberized?

a. A general term that refers to authentication tickets

b. An authorization level label for Kerberos principals

c. Applications and services that have been modified to support the Kerberos credential infrastructure

d. A domain consisting of users, hosts, and network services that are registered to a Kerberos server

e. A Kerberos server and database program running on a network host

21 What definition best describes a Kerberos realm?

a. A general term that refers to authentication tickets

b. An authorization level label for the Kerberos principals

c. Applications and services that have been modified to support the Kerberos credential infrastructure

d. A domain consisting of users, hosts, and network services that are registered to a Kerberos server

e. A Kerberos server and database program running on a network host

22 What IOS command enables VPDN in the global configuration mode?

   a. **vpdn-enable**

   b. **vpdn enable**

   c. **vpdn enable in interface mode**

   d. Both a and c are correct

23 What is the number of bits used with a standard DES encryption key?

   a. 56 bits

   b. 32 bits; same as IP address

   c. 128 bits

   d. 256 bits

   e. 65,535 bits

   f. 168 bits

24 What is the number of bits used with a 3DES encryption key?

   a. 56 bits

   b. 32 bits; same as IP address

   c. 128 bits

   d. 256 bits

   e. 65,535 bits

   f. 168 bits

25 In IPSec, what encapsulation protocol encrypts only the data and not the IP header?

   a. ESP

   b. AH

   c. MD5

   d. HASH

   e. Both a and b are correct.

26 In IPSec, what encapsulation protocol encrypts the entire IP packet?

   a. ESH

   b. AH

   c. MD5

   d. HASH

   e. Both a and b are correct.

27 Which of the following is AH's destination IP port?

   a. 23

   b. 21

   c. 50

   d. 51

   e. 500

   f. 444

28 Which of the following is ESP's destination IP port?

   a. 23

   b. 21

   c. 50

   d. 51

   e. 500

   f. 444

29 Which of the following is not part of IKE phase I negotiations?

   a. Authenticating IPSec peers

   b. Exchanges keys

   c. Establishes IKE security

   d. Negotiates SA parameters

30 Which of the following is not part of IKE phase II?

   a. Negotiates IPSec SA parameters

   b. Periodically updates IPSec SAs

   c. Rarely updates SAs (at most, once a day)

   d. Established IPSec security parameters

31 Which is the faster mode in IPSEC?

   a. Main mode

   b. Fast mode

   c. Aggressive mode

   d. Quick mode

32 Certificate Enrollment Process (CEP) runs over what TCP port number? (Choose the best two answers.)

    a. Same as HTTP

    b. Port 80

    c. Port 50

    d. Port 51

    e. Port 333

    f. Port 444

Foundation Topics

Authentication, Authorization, and Accounting (AAA)

Authentication, authorization, and accounting, (pronounced triple A) provides security to Cisco IOS routers and network devices beyond the simple user authentication available on IOS devices.

AAA provides a method to identify which users are logged into a router and each user's authority level. AAA also provides the capability to monitor user activity and provide accounting information.

In today's IP networks, access to network data is available in a variety of methods, including the following:

- PSTN Dialup modems

- ISDN dialup

- Access through the Internet through virtual private networks (VPNs)

The AAA model is defined as follows:

- Authentication—Who are you?

- Authorization—What resources are you permitted to use?

- Accounting—What resources were accessed, what time, by whom were they used, and what commands were issued?

The three phases ensure that legitimate users are permitted access. A remote user must be authenticated before being permitted access to network resources.

Authentication allows the user to submit a username and password and permit challenges and responses. After the user is authenticated, authorization defines what services or resources in the network are permitted access. The operations permitted here can include IOS privileged exec commands. For example, a user might type commands but be permitted to type only certain **show** and **debug** commands, which are being authorized.

Accounting allows the network administrator to log and view what was actually performed (for example, if a Cisco router was reloaded or the configuration was changed). Accounting ensures that an audit will allow network administrators the ability to view what was performed and at what time it was performed. Accounting keeps track of auditing and reporting network resource usage information. This typically includes the username, the start and stop time of login, and the commands typed by the user.

NOTE	To start AAA on a Cisco router, issue the following IOS command:

        `aaa new-model`

        On a PIX Firewall, the command syntax is as follows:

        `aaa-server`

Figure 5-1 displays a typical secure network scenario.

Figure 5-1   *Secure Network Access*

The users could be dialup users running Async (in this case PSTN) or using ISDN with Point-to-Point Protocol (PPP). The Network Access Server (NAS) ensures that only authenticated users have access to the secure network; it maintains resources and accounting information.

Authorization tells which resources, or host devices, are authorized to be accessed (such as FTP servers). The NAS implements the AAA protocols and also collects data regarding what network resources were accessed. The NAS can also ensure that devices in the secured network require authentication. For example, the users in Figure 5-1 who are accessing Router R1 will require a valid username/password pairing to enter any IOS commands.

The following sections further define what authentication, authorization, and accounting are by discussing a common Cisco IOS router example.

Authentication

Authentication allows administrators to identify who can connect to a router by including the user's username and password. Normally, when a user connects to a router remotely by Telnet, the user must supply only a password and the administrator has no way of knowing the user's username. You can, however, configure local usernames and passwords on a Cisco IOS router, but this does not scale well and it is not very secure. Configuring a small set of routers with individual usernames and passwords (IOS syntax **username** *username* **password** *password*) is fine, but doing so for large networks would be a difficult exercise to manage. Centrally locating the usernames and passwords is a better solution because only a few devices need to be updated and maintained. Also, users are not logged, and their configuration changes are not monitored without further configuration changes made on each individual router.

Example 5-1 displays a sample code snippet of a remote user accessing an AAA-configured Cisco router by Telnet.

Example 5-1   *Username/Password Pair Entry*

```
Sydney>telnet San-Fran
Trying san-fran (10.99.1.1)... Open User Access Verification
Username: benjamin
Password: xxxxxxxx
San-Fran>
```

As you can see in Example 5-1, the user must enter a valid username and password to gain access to the router. Typically, a database containing the valid usernames resides locally on the router or on a remote security server.

Authorization

Authorization comes into play after authentication. Authorization allows administrators to control the level of access users have after they successfully gain access to the router. Cisco IOS allows certain access levels (called *privilege levels*) that control which IOS commands the user can issue. For example, a user with a privilege level of 0 cannot issue any IOS commands. A user with a privilege level of 15 can perform all valid IOS commands. The local database or remote security server can grant the required privilege levels.

Remote security servers, such as RADIUS and TACACS+, authorize users for specific rights by associating attribute-value (AV) pairs, which define those rights with the appropriate user. AAA authorization assembles a set of attributes that describes what the user is authorized to perform.

These attributes are compared with the information contained in a database for a given user, and the result is returned to AAA to determine the user's actual permissions and restrictions.

You can display the user's privilege level on a Cisco router with the **show privilege** command. Example 5-2 displays the privilege level when the enable password has already been entered.

Example 5-2   **show privilege** *Command*

```
R1#show privilege
Current privilege level is 15
```

The higher the privilege, the more capabilities a user has with the IOS command set.

Accounting

Accounting occurs after authentication and authorization have been completed. Accounting allows administrators to collect information about users. Specifically, administrators can track which user logged into which router, which IOS commands a user issued, and how many bytes were transferred during a user's session. For example, accounting enables administrators to monitor which routers have had their configurations changed. Accounting information can be collected by a router or by a remote security server.

To display local account information on a Cisco router collecting accounting information, issue the **show accounting** IOS command. Example 5-3 displays sample output when the command is issued on Router R1.

Example 5-3   **show accounting** *Command*

```
R1#show accounting
Active Accounted actions on Interface Serial0:1, User jdoe Priv 1
 Task ID 15, Network Accounting record, 00:00:18 Elapsed
 task_id=15 timezone=PDT service=ppp mlp-links-max=4 mlp-links-current=4
protocol=ip addr=119.0.0.2 mlp-sess-id=1
        Overall Accounting Traffic
           Starts   Stops   Updates   Active   Drops
Exec          0        0        0        0        0
Network       8        4        0        4        0
Connect       0        0        0        0        0
Command       0        0        0        0        0
Rsrc-mgmt     1        0        0        1        0
System        0        0        0        0        0
 User creates:21, frees:9, Acctinfo mallocs:15, frees:6
Users freed with accounting unaccounted for:0
Queue length:0
```

Table 5-1 describes the fields contained in Example 5-3.

Table 5-1 show accounting Fields

Field	Description
User	The user's ID
Priv	The user's privilege level (0-15)
Task ID	Each accounting session's unique identifier
Accounting Record	Type of accounting session
Elapsed	Length of time (hh:mm:ss) for this session type

Rather than maintain a separate database with usernames, passwords, and privilege levels, you can use external security servers to run external security protocols—namely RADIUS, TACACS+, and Kerberos.

These security server protocols stop unauthorized access to your network. The following sections review these three security protocols.

Security Server Protocols

In many circumstances, AAA uses security protocols to administer its security functions. If your router or access server is acting as a NAS, AAA is the means through which you establish communication between your network access server and your RADIUS, TACACS+, or Kerberos security server.

Remote Authentication Dial-In User Service (RADIUS)

RADIUS is a client/server-based system that secures a Cisco network against intruders. Implemented in IOS, RADIUS sends authentication requests to a RADIUS server. Radius was created by Livingston Enterprises and is now defined in RFC 2138/2139.

A RADIUS server is a device that has the RADIUS daemon or application installed. RADIUS must be used with AAA to enable the authentication, authorization, and accounting of remote users when using Cisco IOS routers.

When a RADUIS server authenticates a user, the following events occur:

1 The user is prompted for and enters a username and password.

2 The username and encrypted password are sent over the network to the RADIUS server.

3 The user receives one of the following responses from the RADIUS server:

ACCEPT—The user is authenticated.

ACCEPT-REJECT—The user is not authenticated and is prompted to re-enter the username and password, or access is denied. The RADIUS server sends this response when the user enters an invalid username/password pairing.

CHALLENGE—A challenge is issued by the RADIUS server. The challenge collects additional data from the user.

CHANGE PASSWORD—The RADIUS server issues a request asking the user to select a new password.

An ACCEPT or REJECT response can contain additional information for services that the user can access, including Telnet, rlogin, or local-area transport (LAT) connections, and PPP, Serial Line Internet Protocol (SLIP), or EXEC services.

RADIUS is commonly used when PPP is used. Figure 5-2 displays a typical PPP connection request to a RADIUS server.

Figure 5-2   *RADIUS Sequence Example*

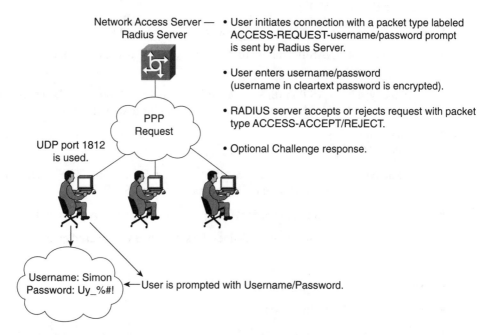

The RADIUS server accepts or rejects a username and password pair. In some instances, a user might be asked to enter more information (this is called a challenge response). For example, if a user's password has expired, a RADUIS server will prompt the user for a new password.

Transactions between the client (end user) and the RADIUS server are authenticated through a shared secret. The username is sent as clear text. RADIUS supports both Password Authentication Protocol (PAP) and Challenge Handshake Authentication Protocol (CHAP). PAP and CHAP are security protocols that allow users to gain access to remote devices with PPP. A RADIUS server will never send the user's password over the network in any circumstance. If the username/password pairing is entered incorrectly, the RADIUS server will send an ACCESS_REJECT response. The end user must re-enter the pairings or the connection will be rejected.

RADIUS supports a number of predefined attributes that can be exchanged between client and server, such as the client's IP address. RADIUS attributes carry specific details about authentication.

RFC 2138 defines a number of attributes. The following bulleted list provides details from the most common attributes:

- Attribute type 1—Username (defines usernames, such as numeric, simple ASCII characters, or a Simple Mail Transfer Protocol [SMTP] address)

- Attribute type 2—User Password (defines the password, which is encrypted using Message Digest 5 [MD5])

- Attribute type 3—CHAP Password (used only in access-request packets)

- Attribute type 4—NAS IP address (defines the NAS's IP address; used only in access-request packets)

- Attribute type 5—NAS Port (this is not the User Datagram Protocol (UDP) port number; it indicates the NAS's physical port number, ranging from 0 to 65,535)

- Attribute type 6—Service-Type (Type of service requested or type of service to be provided). Not supported by Cisco IOS.

- Attribute type 7—Protocol (defines required framing; for example, PPP is defined when this attribute is set to 1 and Serial Line Internet Protocol [SLIP] is set to 2)

- Attribute type 8—IP address (defines the IP address to be used by the remote user)

- Attribute type 9—IP subnet mask (defines the subnet mask to be used by the remote user)

- Attribute type 10—Routing

- Attribute type 13—Compression

- Attribute type 19—Callback ID

- Attribute type 26—Vendor-specific. Cisco (vendor-ID 9) uses one defined option: vendor type 1 named cisco-avpair; this attribute transmits TACACS+ A/V pairs

- Attribute type 61—NAS port type

Table 5-2 summarizes RADIUS protocol's main features

Table 5-2   *Summary of Radius Protocol Features*

Attribute	Features
UDP	Packets sent between client and server are UDP primarily because TCP's overhead does not allow for significant advantages. Typically, the user can wait for a username/password prompt.
UDP destination PORT	1812, port 1646 used for accounting. RADIUS is an industry standard defined in RFC 2138.
Attributes	Attributes are used to exchange information between the NAS and client.
Model	Client/server-based model where packets are exchanged in a unidirectional manner.
Encryption method	Password is encrypted using MD5; the username is not. RADIUS encrypts only the password in the access-request packet, from the client to the server. The remainder of the packet is transmitted in clear text. A third party can capture other information, such as username, authorized services, and accounting.
Multiprotocol support	Does not support protocols such as AppleTalk, NetBIOS, or IPX. IP is the only protocol supported.

Now, examine the RADIUS configuration tasks required on a Cisco router.

RADIUS Configuration Task List

A RADIUS server is usually software that runs on a variety of platforms, including Microsoft NT servers or a UNIX host. RADIUS can authenticate router users and vendors, and even validate IP routes.

To configure RADIUS on your Cisco router or access server, perform the following tasks:

Step 1   Enable AAA with the **aaa new-model** global configuration command. AAA must be configured if you plan to use RADIUS.

Step 2   Use the **aaa authentication** global configuration command to define method lists for RADIUS authentication.

Step 3   Use **line** and **interface** commands to enable the defined method lists to be used.

Step 4   Define the RADIUS server and secret key with the following IOS commands:

radius-server *ip address*

radius-server key *secret key*

NOTE   There are two optional RADIUS commands:

Use the **aaa authorization** global command to authorize specific user functions.

Use the **aaa accounting** command to enable accounting for RADIUS connections.

Examples are the best method to show the enormous IOS command set that is available for use when configuring RADIUS support with AAA.

Example 5-4 configures a Cisco IOS router with AAA and RADIUS support.

Example 5-4 *AAA and RADIUS*

```
aaa new-model
aaa authentication login use-radius group radius local
aaa authentication ppp user-radius if-needed group radius
aaa authorization exec default group radius
aaa authorization network default group radius
radius-server 3.3.3.3
radius-server key IlovetheMotheroftheEucharist
```

The command lines in this RADIUS authentication and authorization configuration are defined as follows:

- The **aaa authentication login use-radius group radius local** command configures the router to use RADIUS for authentication at the login prompt. If RADIUS returns an error, the user is authenticated using the local database. In this example, **use-radius** is the name of the method list, which specifies RADIUS and then local authentication. If the RADIUS server returns the REJECT response, the user is denied access and the router will not check its local database.

- The **aaa authentication ppp user-radius if-needed group radius** command configures the Cisco IOS Software to use RADIUS authentication for lines using PPP with CHAP or PAP, if the user is not already authorized. If the EXEC facility has authenticated the user, RADIUS authentication is not performed. In this example, **user-radius** is the name of the method list defining RADIUS as the if-needed authentication method.

- The **aaa authorization exec default group radius** command sets the RADIUS information used for EXEC authorization, autocommands, and access lists.

- The **aaa authorization network default group radius** command sets RADIUS for network authorization, address assignment, and access lists.

- The radius-server commands define the NAS.

- The radius-server key commands define the shared secret text string between the network access server and the RADIUS server host.

Example 5-5 displays an example in which AAA is enabled on a Cisco IOS router.

Example 5-5 *AAA and RADIUS Example*

```
Hostname R1
username simon password SimonisisAgreatdrummeR
aaa new-model
aaa authentication ppp dialins group radius local
```

Example 5-5   *AAA and RADIUS Example (Continued)*

```
aaa authorization network default group radius local
aaa accounting network default start-stop group radius
aaa authentication login simon local
aaa authorization exec default local
radius-server host 3.3.3.3
radius-server key CCIEsrock
```

The Example 5-5 line configurations are defined as follows:

- The **radius-server host** command defines the RADIUS server host's IP address.

- The **radius-server key** command defines the shared secret text string between the network access server and the RADIUS server host.

- The **aaa authentication ppp dialins group radius local** command defines the authentication method list, dialins, which specifies that RADIUS authentication and then (if the RADIUS server does not respond) local authentication will be used on serial lines using PPP.

- The **aaa authorization network default group radius local** command assigns an address and other network parameters to the RADIUS user.

- The **aaa accounting network default start-stop group radius** command tracks PPP usage. This command is used for all network services. Can be PPP, but also SLIP or ARAP.

- The **aaa authentication login simon local** command defines method list, simon, for local authentication.

- The **aaa authentication login simon** command applies the simon method list for login authentication.

NOTE   A method list simply defines the authentication methods to be used, in sequence, to authenticate a user. Method lists enable you to designate one or more security protocols to be used for authentication, ensuring a backup system for authentication in case the initial method fails. Cisco IOS Software uses the first method listed to authenticate users; if that method does not respond, the Cisco IOS Software selects the next authentication method listed. This process continues until there is successful communication with a listed authentication method or the authentication method list is exhausted, in which case authentication fails.

TIP   Cisco's website provides a long list of configuration examples. To view more detailed configurations, visit the following web address and follow the link to Security:

www.cisco.com/kobayashi/technotes/serv_tips.shtml

Terminal Access Controller Access Control System Plus (TACACS+)

Cisco IOS supports three versions of TACACS—TACACS, extended TACACS, and TACACS+. All three methods authenticate users and deny access to users who do not have a valid username/password pairing.

Cisco has also developed Cisco Secure Access Control Server (CSACS), a flexible family of security servers that supports both RADIUS and TACACS+. You can even run debugging commands on the Cisco Secure ACS software. In UNIX, you can modify files, such as syslog.conf and csu.cfg, to change the output to your screen. For more details on how to debug on a UNIX server, see www.cisco.com/warp/public/480/cssample2x.html#debug.

TACACS+ has the following features:

- TCP packets (port 49) ensure that data is sent reliably across the IP network.
- Supports AAA architectures and, in fact, separates each of the three mechanisms (authentication, authorization, and accounting).
- The data between the user and server is encrypted.
- Supports both PAP/CHAP and multiprotocols, such as IPX and X.25.
- Access lists can be defined on a user basis.

Figure 5-3 displays a typical TACACS+ connection request (Authentication).

Figure 5-3 *TACACS+ Authentication Example Sequence*

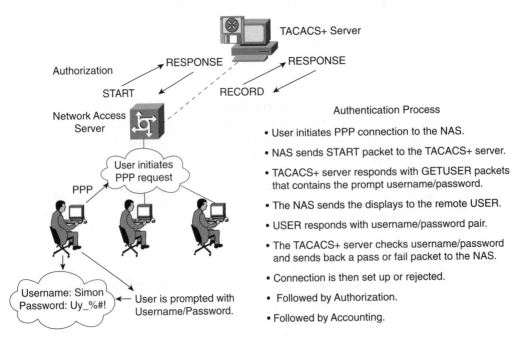

TACACS+ Server

Authorization

RESPONSE   RESPONSE

START   RECORD

Network Access Server

Authentication Process

- User initiates PPP connection to the NAS.
- NAS sends START packet to the TACACS+ server.
- TACACS+ server responds with GETUSER packets that contains the prompt username/password.
- The NAS sends the displays to the remote USER.
- USER responds with username/password pair.
- The TACACS+ server checks username/password and sends back a pass or fail packet to the NAS.
- Connection is then set up or rejected.
- Followed by Authorization.
- Followed by Accounting.

User initiates PPP request

PPP

Username: Simon
Password: Uy_%#!   User is prompted with Username/Password.

When a TACACS+ server authenticates a remote user, the following events occur:

1 When the connection is established, the NAS contacts the TACACS+ daemon to obtain a username prompt, which is then displayed to the user. The user enters a username and the NAS and contacts the TACACS+ daemon to obtain a password prompt. The NAS displays the password prompt to the user, the user enters a password, and the password is sent to the TACACS+ daemon.

2 The NAS eventually receives one of the following responses from the TACACS+ daemon:

   - ACCEPT—The user is authenticated and service can begin. If the NAS is configured to require authorization, authorization will begin at this time.

   - REJECT—The user has failed to authenticate. The user can be denied further access or will be prompted to retry the login sequence, depending on the TACACS+ daemon.

   - ERROR—An error occurred at some time during authentication. This can be either at the daemon or in the network connection between the daemon and the NAS. If an ERROR response is received, the NAS typically tries to use an alternative method for authenticating the user.

   - CONTINUE—The user is prompted for additional authentication information.

3 A PAP login is similar to an ASCII login, except that the username and password arrive at the NAS in a PAP protocol packet instead of being typed in by the user, so the user is not prompted. PPP CHAP logins are also similar, in principle.

4 Following authentication, the user is required to undergo an additional authorization phase, if authorization has been enabled on the NAS. Users must first successfully complete TACACS+ authentication before proceeding to TACACS+ authorization.

5 If TACACS+ authorization is required, the TACACS+ daemon is again contacted and it returns an ACCEPT or REJECT authorization response. If an ACCEPT response is returned, the response will contain data in the form of attributes used to direct the EXEC or NETWORK session for that user, determining services that the user can access.

   Services include the following:

   - Telnet, rlogin, Point-to-Point Protocol (PPP), Serial Line Internet Protocol (SLIP), or EXEC services

   - Connection parameters, including the host or client IP address, access list, and user timeouts

The TACACS+ authorization process is defined as the packet flow between the NAS and the TACACS+ server. The packets exchanged between the NAS and server contain attribute pairs (AV pairs). The NAS sends Start packets and the TACACS+ server responds with Response packets. The server can permit, deny, or modify commands requested by the end user. The data (that contains the full list of all username/password pairs) is stored on a local file defining what commands are permitted by the end user, for example.

TACACS+ accounting provides an audit record of what commands were completed. The NAS sends a record of any commands, and the TACACS+ server sends a response acknowledging the accounting record.

Table 5-3 summarizes the main features of TACACS+.

Table 5-3   *Summary of TACACS+ Protocol*

Feature	Feature
TCP	Packets sent between client and server are TCP. Typically, the user can wait for a username/password prompt.
TCP destination port	Port 49.
Attributes	Packet types are defined in TACACS+ frame format as follows: Authentication 0x01 Authorization 0x02 Accounting 0x03
Seq_no	The sequence number of the current packet flow for the current session. The Seq_no starts with 1, and each subsequent packet will increment by one. The client sends only odd numbers. TACACS+ server sends only even numbers.
Encryption method	Entire packet is encrypted. Data is encrypted using MD5 and a secret key that matches both on the NAS (for example, a Cisco IOS router) and the TACACS+ server.
Multiprotocol support	Support protocols, such as AppleTalk, NetBIOS, or IPX, along with IP.

Now, examine the TACACS+ configuration tasks required when enabling TACACS+ on a Cisco IOS router.

TACACS+ Configuration Task List

To configure your router to support TACACS+, you must perform the following tasks:

Step 1   Use the **aaa new-model** global configuration command to enable AAA, which must be configured if you plan to use TACACS+. For more information about using the **aaa new-model** command, refer to the link, www.cisco.com/univercd/cc/td/doc/product/software/ios121/121cgcr/secur_c/scprt1/index.htm.

Step 2   Use the **tacacs-server host** command to specify the IP address of one or more TACACS+ daemons. The command is as follows:

```
tacacs-server host hostname [single-connection] [port integer] [timeout
integer] [key string]
```

Step 3 Use the **tacacs-server key** command to specify an encryption key to encrypt all exchanges between the network access server and the TACACS+ daemon. This same key must also be configured on the TACACS+ daemon. The actual command is as follows:

```
tacacs-server key key
```

The key should match the one used on the TACACS+ daemon.

Step 4 Use the **aaa authentication** global configuration command to define method lists that use TACACS+ for authentication.

Step 5 Use **line** and **interface** commands to apply the defined method lists to various interfaces.

Step 6 To enable authorization, use the **aaa authorization** global command to configure authorization for the NAS. Unlike authentication, which can be configured per line or per interface, authorization is configured globally for the entire NAS.

Step 7 To enable accounting for TACACS+ connections, use the **aaa accounting** command. Optional commands include the following:

— Configuring AAA server groups (Optional)

— Configuring AAA server group selection based on DNIS (Optional)

— Specifying TACACS+ authentication (Required)

— Specifying TACACS+ authorization (Optional)

— Specifying TACACS+ accounting (Optional)

Example 5-6 displays a sample configuration of a Cisco router with TACACS+ authentication for PPP.

Example 5-6 *TACACS+ Authentication for PPP Example*

```
aaa new-model
aaa authentication ppp CCIE group tacacs+ local
tacacs-server host 10.1.2.3
tacacs-server key cciesarecool
interface serial 0
 ppp authentication chap pap CCIE
```

The configuration lines in Example 5-6 are defined as follows:

- The **aaa new-model** command enables the AAA security services.

- The **aaa authentication** command defines a method list, CCIE, to be used on serial interfaces running PPP. The keyword **group tacacs+** means that authentication is done through TACACS+. If TACACS+ returns an ERROR during authentication, the keyword **local** indicates that authentication will be attempted using the local database on the NAS. Note that the local database is not used if a REJECT response is received from the security server.

- The **tacacs-server host** command identifies the TACACS+ daemon as having an IP address of 10.1.2.3. The **tacacs-server key** command defines the shared encryption key as cciesarecool.

- The **interface** command selects the line, and the **ppp authentication** command applies the test method list to this line.

Example 5-7 shows how to configure TACACS+ as the security protocol for PPP authentication using the default method list; it also shows how to configure network authorization through TACACS+.

Example 5-7 *Authorization and TACACS+ Example*

```
aaa new-model
aaa authentication ppp default if-needed group tacacs+ local
aaa authorization network default group tacacs+
tacacs-server host 3.3.3.3
tacacs-server key simoniscool
interface serial 0
 ppp authentication default
```

The lines in the preceding sample configuration are defined as follows:

- The **aaa new-model** command enables the AAA security services.

- The **aaa authentication** command defines a method list, default, to be used on serial interfaces running PPP. The keyword **default** means that PPP authentication is applied by default to all interfaces. The **if-needed** keyword means that if the user has already authenticated by going through the ASCII login procedure, PPP authentication is not necessary and can be skipped. If authentication is needed, the keyword **group tacacs+** means that authentication is done through TACACS+. If TACACS+ returns an ERROR during authentication, the keyword **local** indicates that authentication will be attempted using the local database on the NAS.

- The **aaa authorization** command configures network authorization via TACACS+.

- The **tacacs-server host** command identifies the TACACS+ daemon as having an IP address of 3.3.3.3.

- The **tacacs-server key** command defines the shared encryption key as simoniscool.

- The **interface** command selects the line, and the **ppp authentication** command applies the default method list to this line.

Example 5-8 displays a sample configuration where accounting is also enabled.

Example 5-8   *Accounting Example*

```
aaa new-model
aaa authentication ppp default if-needed group tacacs+ local
aaa accounting network default stop-only group tacacs+
tacacs-server host 3.3.3.3
tacacs-server key andrewiscool
interface serial 0
 ppp authentication default
```

The lines in the Example 5-8 configuration are defined as follows:

- The **aaa new-model** command enables the AAA security services.

- The **aaa authentication** command defines a method list, default, to be used on serial interfaces running PPP. The keyword **default** means that PPP authentication is applied by default to all interfaces. The **if-needed** keyword means that if the user has already authenticated through the ASCII login procedure, PPP authentication is not necessary. If authentication is needed, the keyword **group tacacs+** means that authentication is done through TACACS+. If TACACS+ returns an ERROR during authentication, the keyword **local** indicates that authentication will be attempted using the local database on the NAS.

- The **aaa accounting** command configures network accounting through TACACS+. In this example, accounting records stop-only, meaning that the session that just terminated will be sent to the TACACS+ daemon whenever a network connection terminates.

- The **interface** command selects the line, and the **ppp authentication** command applies the default method list to this line.

NOTE   You can define a group of TACACS+ servers by defining the servers with the IOS command, **tacacs-server** *<ip address of server>*. For example, to define six servers you would use the IOS configuration:

```
tacacs-server host 1.1.1.1
tacacs-server host 2.2.2.2
tacacs-server host 3.3.3.3
tacacs-server host 4.4.4.4
tacacs-server host 5.5.5.5
tacacs-server host 6.6.6.6
tacacs-server key ccie
```

If the first server does not respond within a timeout period (default 5 seconds), the next server is queried, and so forth.

Typically, the console port is not configured for authorization.

TACACS+ Versus RADIUS

Table 5-4 compares the main differences between TACACS+ and RADIUS.

Table 5-4 *TACACS+/RADIUS Comparison*

	RADIUS	TACACS+
Packet delivery	UDP	TCP
Packet encryption	RADIUS encrypts only the password in the access-request packet from the client to the server.	TACACS+ encrypts the entire body of the packet but leaves a standard TACACS+ header.
AAA support	RADIUS combines authentication and authorization.	TACACS+ uses the AAA architecture, separating authentication, authorization, and accounting.
Multiprotocol support	None.	TACACS+ supports other protocols, such as AppleTalk, NetBIOS, and IPX.
Router management	RADIUS does not allow users to control which commands can be executed on a router.	TACACS+ allows network administrators control over which commands can be executed on a router.

NOTE You can configure both RADIUS and TACACS+ concurrently on a Cisco router provided that you have defined different list names and applied the list to different interfaces.

NOTE You can download and install a trial copy of Cisco Secure ACS for Windows NT/2000 or UNIX. This comes with a built-in RADIUS and TACACS+ server. You also need a Cisco router with IOS 12.X with one working Ethernet port. This will reinforce your understanding of the AAA concept. For more information, visit the Cisco Secure Software center at www.cisco.com.

The AAA configuration options are numerous, and those presented in this guide are only a small subset of a larger set you can view online at Cisco's website. Visit the following URL for more quality examples of how AAA, along with RADIUS or TACACS, can be implemented on Cisco IOS routers:

www.cisco.com/cgi-bin/Support/browse/index.pl?i=Technologies&f=1408

The IOS debug command set for RADIUS and TACACS is extensive. Presented here are some common RADIUS and TACACS debug outputs found in real networks.

Example 5-9 displays a sample output from the **debug aaa authentication** command for a RADIUS login attempt that failed. The information indicates that TACACS is the authentication method used.

Example 5-9   **debug aaa authentication**

```
R1# debug aaa authentication
14:02:55: AAA/AUTHEN (164826761): Method=RADIUS
14:02:55: AAA/AUTHEN (164826761): status = GETPASS
14:03:01: AAA/AUTHEN/CONT (164826761): continue_login
14:03:01: AAA/AUTHEN (164826761): status = GETPASS
14:03:04: AAA/AUTHEN (164826761): status = FAIL
```

Example 5-10 displays a sample output from the **debug radius** command that shows a successful login attempt, as indicated by an Access-Accept message:

Example 5-10   **debug radius Failure**

```
R1# debug radius
 13:59:02: Radius: IPC Send 0.0.0.0:1645, Access-Request, id 0xB, len 56
13:59:02:        Attribute 4 6 AC150E5A
13:59:02:        Attribute 5 6 0000000A
13:59:02:        Attribute 1 6 62696C6C
13:59:02:        Attribute 2 18 0531FEA3
13:59:04: Radius: Received from 131.108.1.1:1645, Access-Accept, id 0xB, len 26
13:59:04:        Attribute 6 6 00000001
```

Example 5-11 displays a sample output from the **debug radius** command that shows an unsuccessful login attempt, as indicated by an Access-Reject message.

Example 5-11   **debug radius** *Command*

```
R1# debug radius
13:57:56: Radius: IPC Send 0.0.0.0:1645, Access-Request, id 0xA, len 57
13:57:56:        Attribute 4 6 AC150E5A
13:57:56:        Attribute 5 6 0000000A
13:57:56:        Attribute 1 7 62696C6C
13:57:56:        Attribute 2 18 49C28F6C
13:57:59: Radius: Received from 171.69.1.152:1645, Access-Reject, id 0xA, len 20
```

Kerberos

Kerberos is a trusted third-party authentication application layer service (Layer 7 of the OSI model).

Kerberos is a secret-key network authentication protocol developed at the Massachusetts Institute of Technology (MIT) that uses the Data Encryption Standard (DES) cryptographic algorithm for encryption and authentication. In the Kerberos protocol, this trusted third party is called the key distribution center (KDC).

Figure 5-4 displays the Kerberos authentication process when a remote client initiates a remote Telnet session. (Kerberos supports Telnet, rlogin, rsh, and rcp.)

Figure 5-4 *Authentication Service with Kerberos*

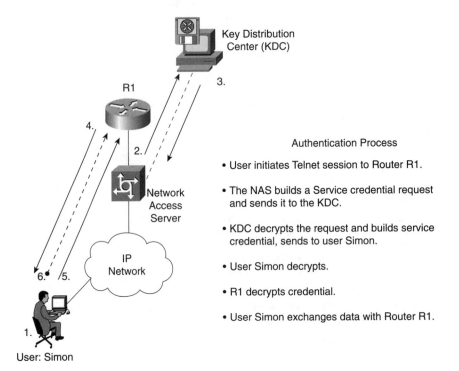

Key Distribution Center (KDC)

R1

3.

4.

2.

Network Access Server

Authentication Process

- User initiates Telnet session to Router R1.

- The NAS builds a Service credential request and sends it to the KDC.

- KDC decrypts the request and builds service credential, sends to user Simon.

- User Simon decrypts.

- R1 decrypts credential.

- User Simon exchanges data with Router R1.

IP Network

6. 5.

1.

User: Simon

Kerberos's primary use is to verify that users and the network services they employ are really who and what they claim to be. To accomplish this, a trusted Kerberos server issues tickets to users. These tickets, which have a limited lifespan, are stored in a user's credential cache and can be used in place of the standard username/password authentication mechanism.

The Kerberos credential scheme embodies a concept called *single logon*. This process requires authenticating a user once, and then allows secure authentication (without encrypting another password) wherever that user's credential is accepted.

Timestamps (large numbers representing the current date and time) have been added to the original Kerberos model to aid in the detection of replay attacks. Replay attacks basically reply to data flow with an unauthorized source attempting to gain access to a host. During the packet flow exchange, critical parameters exchanged are the client's name, the IP address, and the current workstation time. System time must be accurate to ensure replay attacks are avoided or, at the very least, detected, and the Kerberos session terminated.

NOTE   Starting with Cisco IOS Release 11.2, Cisco IOS Software includes Kerberos 5 support, which allows organizations already deploying Kerberos 5 to use the same Kerberos authentication database on their routers that they already use on their other network hosts (such as UNIX servers and PCs).

Table 5-5 summarizes the key concepts of Kerberos.

Table 5-5   *Features of the Kerberos Protocol*

Feature	Description
Packet delivery	A number of ports are defined: TCP/UDP ports 88, 543, 749, and TCP ports 754, 2105, and 4444.
Packet encryption	Supports username/password encryption.
Telnet support	Telnet sessions can be encrypted.

Table 5-6 defines common Kerberos terminology.

Table 5-6   *Kerberos Terminology*

Term	Definition
Credential	A general term that refers to authentication tickets, such as ticket granting tickets (TGTs) and service credentials. Kerberos credentials verify the identity of a user or service. If a network service decides to trust the Kerberos server that issued a ticket, it can be used in place of retyping in a username and password. Credentials have a default lifespan of eight hours.
Instance	An authorization level label for Kerberos principals. Most Kerberos principals are of the form user@REALM (for example, smith@EXAMPLE.COM). Note that the Kerberos realm name must be in uppercase characters.
Kerberized	Applications and services that have been modified to support the Kerberos credential infrastructure.
Kerberos realm	A domain consisting of users, hosts, and network services that are registered to a Kerberos server. The Kerberos server is trusted to verify a user's or network service's identity to another user or network service. Kerberos realms must always be in uppercase characters. TCP fragmentation must also be defined on the key distribution center (KDC) server. The Kerberos realm is also used to map a DNS domain to a Kerberos realm.

continues

Table 5-6   *Kerberos Terminology (Continued)*

Term	Definition
Kerberos server	A daemon running on a network host. Users and network services register their identities with the Kerberos server. Network services query the Kerberos server to authenticate to other network services. Also known as the Master Kerberos server.
Key Distribution Center (KDC)	A Kerberos server and database program running on a network host.
Principal	Also known as a Kerberos identity, this is who you are or what a service is according to the Kerberos server.
Service credential	A credential for a network service. When issued from the KDC, this credential is encrypted with the password shared by the network service and the KDC, and with the user's TGT.
SRVTAB	A password that a network service shares with the KDC. The network service authenticates an encrypted service credential using the SRVTAB (also known as a KEYTAB) to decrypt it.
Ticket Granting Ticket (TGT)	A credential that the KDC issues to authenticated users. When users receive a TGT, they can authenticate to network services within the Kerberos realm represented by the KDC.

Kerberos Configuration Task List

To configure Kerberos support on a Cisco router, complete the following tasks:

Step 1   Define the default realm for the router:

```
kerberos local-realm kerberos-realm
```

Step 2   Specify to the router which KDC to use in a given Kerberos realm and, optionally, the port number that the KDC is monitoring. (The default port number is 88.)

```
kerberos server kerberos-realm {hostname | ip-address} [port-number]
```

Step 3   Map a host name or DNS domain to a Kerberos realm (optional):

```
kerberos realm {dns-domain | host} kerberos-realm
```

NOTE   The **kerberos local-realm**, **kerberos realm**, and **kerberos server** commands are equivalent to the UNIX *krb.conf* file.

Example 5-12 displays a sample Kerberos configuration.

Example 5-12 *Kerberos Configuration*

```
kerberos local-realm CISCO.COM
kerberos server CISCO.COM 3.3.3.3
kerberos realm.cisco.com CISCO.COM
```

RADIUS and TACACS+ are far more common than Kerberos in today's networks. Microsoft 2000, for example, uses Kerberos for internal authentication in Active Directory.

NOTE

For a complete guide to Kerberos, a defined and open standard, please visit the following: http://web.mit.edu/is/help/kerberos/

For UNIX experts, some of the most common UNIX executable commands when configuring and enabling Kerberos are as follows:

- Kdb5_util—Allows the UNIX administrator to create the Kerberos database

- Kadmin—Allows the administrator to administer the Kerberos database

- Krb5kdc/kadmin—Starts the KDC daemon on the server

Cisco routers support encryption and Kerberos is used.

Another way for users to open a secure Telnet session is to use Encrypted Kerberized Telnet, which authenticates users by their Kerberos credentials before a Telnet session is established. The IOS command is **connect** *host* [*port*] **/encrypt Kerberos** and the exec prompt.

Virtual Private Dial-Up Networks (VPDN)

A VPDN is a network that extends remote access dialup clients to a private network. VPDN tunnels use either Layer 2 forwarding (L2F) or Layer 2 Tunnel Protocol (L2TP).

Cisco introduced L2F in RFC 2341. It is also used to forward PPP sessions for Multichassis Multilink PPP.

L2TP, introduced in RFC 2661, combines the best of the Cisco L2F protocol and Microsoft Point-to-Point Tunneling Protocol (PPTP). Moreover, L2F supports only dial-in VPDN, while L2TP supports both dial-in and dial-out VPDN.

Both protocols use UDP port 1701 to build a tunnel through an IP network to forward link-layer frames.

For L2F, the setup for tunneling a PPP session consists of two steps:

Step 1   Establish a tunnel between the NAS and the home gateway (HWY). The HWY is a Cisco router or access server (for example, an AS5300) that terminates VPDN tunnels and PPP sessions. This phase takes place only when no active tunnel exists between both devices.

Step 2   Establish a session between the NAS and the home gateway.

For L2TP, the setup for tunneling a PPP session consists of two steps:

Step 1   Establish a tunnel between the L2TP access concentrator (LAC) and the L2TP network server (LNS). The LAC acts as one side of the L2TP tunnel endpoint and has a peer to the LNS. This phase takes place only when no active tunnel exists between both devices.

Step 2   Establish a session between the LAC and the LNS.

Figure 5-5 displays the tunnel termination points between a remote point of presence (POP) (typically an ISP router) and the home gateway router.

Figure 5-5   *L2F or L2TP Tunnel Termination*

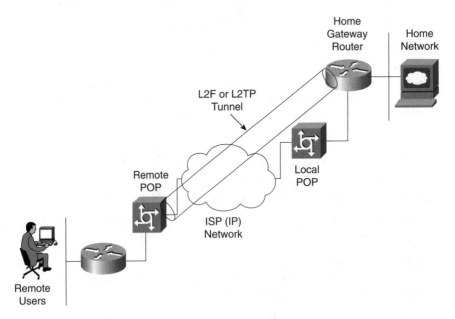

The remote POP accepts frames encapsulated in L2F or L2TP and forwarded over the tunnel.

The LAC and LNS are hardware devices, such as Cisco's AS 5300 series router platform. The LAC's function is to sit between the LNS and the remote system and forward packets to and from each device. The LNS logically terminates the PPP connection.

VPDNs are implemented so that users connected through ISPs in any part of the world can take advantage of the connection to the ISP and tunnel the company's remote access traffic through the ISP network.

VPDNs include the following benefits:

- Access to the corporate network from a remote location.

- Offload remote access services to the ISP, which already has the infrastructure place.

- End system transparency because the remote user does not require any hardware or software to use VPDN. Cisco IOS routers performs all the requirements.

- Allows for accounting, which is sent from the home gateway router.

Figure 5-6 displays a typical VPDN scenario where a PC or router dials the NAS/LAC to request a VPDN connection to the private network.

Figure 5-6 *VPDN Network Scenario*

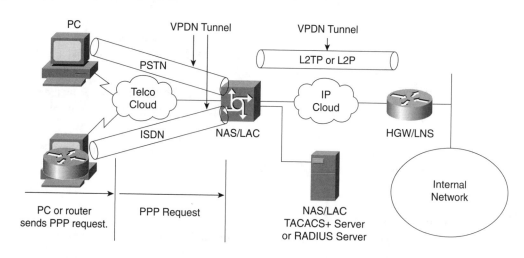

To implement the VPDN configuration, you need the following:

- A Cisco router or access server for client access (NAS/LAC) and a Cisco router for network access (HGW/LNS) with IP connectivity between them.

- Host names of the routers or local names to use on the VPDN groups.

- A tunneling protocol, either the L2TP or L2F Protocol. L2TP is an industry standard, and L2F is a Cisco-proprietary protocol.

- A password for the routers to authenticate the tunnel.

- A tunneling criteria, either domain name or Dialed Number Identification Service (DNIS).

- Username and password for the user (client dialing in).

- IP addresses and keys for your TACACS+ servers.

A VPDN connection between a remote user (router or through PSTN) and the corporate LAN is accomplished in the following steps:

Step 1 The remote user initiates a PPP connection to the ISP using the analog telephone system or ISDN.

Step 2 The ISP's NAS accepts the connection.

Step 3 The ISP NAS authenticates the end user with CHAP or PAP. The username determines whether the user is a VPDN client. If the user is not a VPDN client, the client accesses the Internet or other contacted service.

Step 4 The tunnel endpoints—the NAS and the home gateway—authenticate each other before any sessions are attempted within a tunnel.

Step 5 If no L2F tunnel exists between the NAS and the remote users' home gateway, a tunnel is created. Then, an unused slot within the tunnel is allocated.

Step 6 The home gateway accepts or rejects the connection. Initial setup can include authentication information required to allow the home gateway to authenticate the user.

Step 7 The home gateway sets up a virtual interface. Link-level frames can now pass through this virtual interface through the L2F tunnel.

VPDN Configuration Task List

To configure VPDNs on the home gateway router, complete the following steps:

Step 1 Create a virtual template interface, and enter the interface configuration mode:

```
interface virtual-template number
```

Step 2 Identify the virtual template interface type and number on the LAN:

```
ip unnumbered interface number
```

Step 3 Enable PPP encapsulation on the virtual template interface:

```
encapsulation ppp
```

Step 4 Enable PPP authentication on the virtual template interface:

```
ppp authentication {chap | ppp}
```

Step 5 Enable the global configuration command to allow virtual private networking on the NAS and home gateway routers:

```
vpdn enable
```

Step 6 Specify the remote host (the NAS), the local name (the home gateway) to use for authenticating, and the virtual template to use:

Home gateway router:

```
vpdn incoming nas-name hgw-name virtual-template number
```

NAS configuration:

```
vpdn outgoing domain-name NAS-nameip ip ip-address
```

NOTE You can also enable the NAS to authenticate users via TACACS+ or RADIUS using AAA commands.

A typical configuration file on a UNIX server has a configuration similar to the following configuration:

```
LAC Radius Configuration - Sample
Sanjose.cisco.com   Password = "cisco"
Service-Type = Outbound-User,
cisco-avpair = "vpdn:tunnel-id=DEFGH",
cisco-avpair = "vpdn:tunnel-type=l2tp",
cisco-avpair = "vpdn:ip-addresses=10.31.1.9",
cisco-avpair = "vpdn:l2tp-tunnel-password=ABCDE"
```

The configuration on the LAC defines the specific av-pairs, namely the tunnel-id, tunnel-type, ip-address, and l2tp password.

Example 5-13 displays a typical NAS/LAC configuration using TACACS+.

Example 5-13 *Sample NAS/LAC Configuration*

```
hostname NAS-LAC
!
aaa new-model
aaa authentication login default local
aaa authentication login CONSOLE none
aaa authentication ppp default if-needed group tacacs+
aaa authorization network default group tacacs+
enable password cciesarecool
!
username Melanie password 0 verysecretpassword
```

continues

Example 5-13 *Sample NAS/LAC Configuration (Continued)*

```
!
vpdn enable
!
interface Ethernet0
ip address 131.108.1.1 255.255.255.0
interface Dialer1
Description USER dials in and is assigned this interface
 ip unnumbered Ethernet0
 encapsulation ppp
 dialer-group 1
 peer d\efault ip address pool IPaddressPool
 ppp authentication chap
!
ip local pool IPaddressPool 10.10.10.1 10.10.10.254
!
tacacs-server host 3.3.3.3
tacacs-server key extremelysecrtetpassword
dialer-list 1 protocol ip permit
line con 0
 login authentication CONSOLE
 transport input none
line 1 96
 autoselect during-login
 autoselect ppp
 modem Dialin
line aux 0
line vty 0 4
```

Example 5-13 displays the ISP router that typically supplies the tunnel-id to the HGW and IP address to the dial users.

Example 5-14 displays a typical configuration the home gateway router.

Example 5-14 *Sample HGY/LNS Configuration*

```
hostname HGY-LNS
!
aaa new-model
aaa authentication login default local
aaa authentication login CONSOLE none
aaa authentication ppp default if-needed group tacacs+
aaa authorization network default group tacacs+
enable password cciesarecool
vpdn enable
!
vpdn-group DEFAULTcanbeanyname
! Default L2TP VPDN group
 accept-dialin
  protocol any
  virtual-template 1
```

Example 5-14 *Sample HGY/LNS Configuration (Continued)*

```
 local name LNS
 lcp renegotiation always
 l2tp tunnel password 0 secretpwd
interface Virtual-Template1
 ip unnumbered FastEthernet0/0
 peer default ip address pool IPaddressPool
 ppp authentication chap
ip local pool IPaddressPool 11.11.11.1 11.11.11.254
 !
tacacs-server host 3.3.3.3
tacacs-server key easypwd
 !
end
```

NOTE   You are not expected to demonstrate your IOS syntax knowledge for VPDN. They are presented here for completeness, along with the two sample configuration files. For more quality examples, please visit www.cisco.com/warp/public/471/#vpdn.

Encryption Technology Overview

When prominent Internet sites, such as www.cnn.com, are exposed to security threats, the news reaches all parts of the globe. Ensuring that data across any IP network is secure and not prone to vulnerable threats is one of today's most challenging topics in the IP storage arena (so much so that Cisco released an entirely new CCIE certification track).

Major problems for network administrators include the following:

- Packet snooping (eavesdropping)—When intruders capture and decode traffic obtaining usernames, passwords, and sensitive data, such as salary increases for the year

- Theft of data—When intruders use sniffers, for example, to capture data over the network and steal that information for later use

- Impersonation—When an intruder assumes the role of a legitimate device but, in fact, is not legitimate

The solution to these and numerous other problems is to provide encryption technology to the IP community and allow network administrators the ability to ensure that data is not vulnerable to any form of attack or intrusion. This ensures that data is confidential, authenticated, and has not lost any integrity during the routing of packets through an IP network.

Encryption is defined as the process by which plain data is converted into ciphered data (a system in which plain text is arbitrarily substituted according to a predefined algorithm) so that only the intended recipient(s) can observe the data. Encryption ensures data privacy, integrity, and authentication.

Figure 5-7 displays the basic methodology behind data encryptions.

Figure 5-7 *Encryption Methodologies*

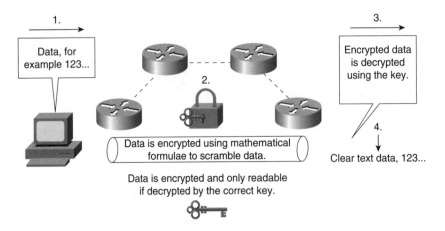

Figure 5-7 demonstrates the basic principles of data encryption, including the following:

Step 1 User data is forwarded over the network.

Step 2 Data (clear text) is modified according to a key. The key is a sequence of digits that decrypts and encrypts messages. Typically, each device has three keys:

— A private key used to sign messages that is kept secret and never shared

— A public key that is shared (used by others to verify a signature)

— A shared secret key that is used to encrypt data using a symmetric encryption algorithm, such as DES

Step 3 A mathematical formula is applied to scramble the data. In Figure 5-7, the mathematical formula is applied during Step 2.

Step 4 The data flows throughout the network and can be decrypted only if the correct key is applied.

Encryption can take place at the application layer, the network layer, or the data link layer. Be aware of the following encryption technologies for the written exam:

• Data Encryption Standard (DES)

• Triple DES (DES3)

• IP Secure (IPSec)

Cisco IOS routers support the following industry standards to accomplish network layer encryption:

- DES/3DES
- Digital signature standard (DSS)
- Diffie-Hellman exchange
- MD5
- IPSec

Data Encryption Standard (DES) and Triple Data Encryption Standard (3DES)

DES is one of the most widely used encryption methods. DES turns clear text data into cipher text with an encryption algorithm. The receiving station will decrypt the data from cipher text into clear text. The encryption key is a shared secret key used to encrypt and decrypt messages.

Figure 5-8 demonstrates DES encryption.

Figure 5-8   *DES Encryption Methodologies*

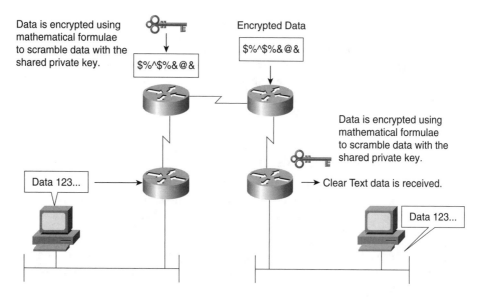

Figure 5-8 demonstrates the PC's clear text generation. The data is sent to the Cisco IOS router where it is encrypted with a shared key, sent over the IP network in unreadable format until the receiving router decrypts the message and forwards in clear text form.

DES is a block cipher algorithm, which means that DES performs operations on fixed-length data streams. DES uses a 56-bit key to encrypt 64-bit datagrams.

DES is a published, U.S. Government-approved encryption algorithm.

3DES is the DES algorithm that performs three times sequentially. Three keys are used to encrypted data, resulting in a 168-bit encryption key.

3DES is an improved encryption algorithm standard and is summarized as follows:

- The sending device encrypts the data with the first 56-bit key.

- The sending device decrypts the data with the second key, also 56 bits in length.

- The sending device encrypts for a final time with another 56-bit key.

- The receiving device decrypts the data with the first key.

- The receiving device then encrypts the data with the second key.

- Finally, the receiving devices decrypt the data with the third key.

A typical hacker uses a Pentium III computer workstation and takes approximately 22 hours to break a DES key. In 3DES's case, the documented key-breaking times are approximately 10 billion years when one million PC III computers are used. Encryption ensures that information theft is difficult.

Encryption can be used to enable secure connections over the LAN, WAN, and World Wide Web.

The end goal of DES/3DES is to ensure that data is confidential by keeping data secure and hidden. The data must have integrity to ensure that it has not been modified in any form, and be authenticated by ensuring that the source or destination is indeed the proper host device. The following section describes one method of making sure that data has not been tampered with—Digital Signature Standard (DSS).

Digital Signature Standard (DSS)

Hashing data is one method used to ensure that data has not been tampered with. Hashing involves taking a variable length of data and producing a fixed output. A HASH is defined as a one-way mathematical summary of a message (data) such that the hash value cannot be easily reconstructed into the original message.

DSS is a mechanism that protects data from an undetected change while traversing the network. DSS verifies the identity of the person sending the data just as you verify your signature to a bank manager.

For example, consider routing updates sent from one router to another as clear text; they are clearly visible to network sniffers or probes. Hashing and DSS can ensure that the routing updates are unreadable, except to the protected sources.

Figure 5-9 displays the DSS signature generation that ensures data is protected from an unsecured device. Cisco IOS Router R1 is configured to send all routing updates using a hash function.

Figure 5-9   *DSS Signature Generation*

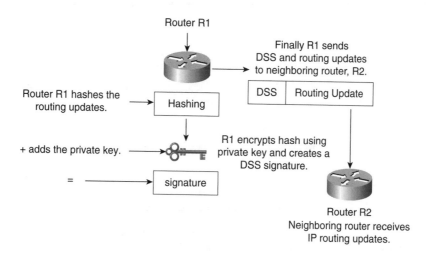

Routing updates are prone to network sniffers. By hashing the routing updates, as shown in Figure 5-9, the routing networks exchanged between Cisco IOS routers can be protected from unsecured devices.

The steps to ensure that network routing updates (in Figure 5-9) are secure follow:

Step 1   Router R1 hashes the routing update. (Cisco IOS routers can use MD5).

Step 2   R1 encrypts the hashed routing update using its own private key.

Step 3   R1 appends the routing update with the DSS.

Step 4   The DSS is verified by neighboring router, R2.

Step 5   R2 decrypts the DSS using R1's own public key and obtains the hash that was originally generated by R1.

Step 6   R2 compares the hash received from R1 with the hash it just generated. If they are the same, the routing update is assured legitimate and was not modified by any network intruder.

Message Digest 5 (MD5) and Secure Hash Algorithm (SHA)

Several hashing algorithms are available. The two discussed here are MD5 and SHA (sometimes called SHA-1).

Message hashing is an encryption technique that ensures a message or data has not be tampered with or modified.

MD5 Message hashing is supported on Cisco IOS routers. A variable-length message is taken, the MD5 algorithm is performed (for example, the **enable secret passwords** command), and a final fixed-length hashed output message is produced. MD5 is defined in RFC 1321.

Figure 5-10 displays the MD5 message operation.

Figure 5-10 *MD5 Operation*

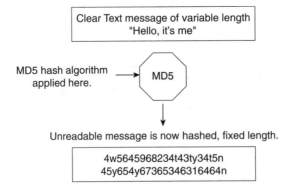

Figure 5-10 displays the simple clear text message, "Hello, it's me," which can be of any variable length. This message is sent to the MD5 process, where the clear text message is hashed and a fixed-length, unreadable message is produced. The data can include routing updates or username/password pairings, for example. MD5 produces a 128-bit hash output.

Secure Hash Algorithm (SHA) is the newer, more secure version of MD5, and Hash-based Message Authentication (HMAC) provides further security with the inclusion of a key exchange. SHA produces a 160-bit hash output, making it even more difficult to decipher. SHA follows the same principles as MD5 and is considered more CPU-intensive.

For more details on Cisco IOS encryption capabilities, please visit the following website:

www.cisco.com/en/US/tech/tk583/tk209/tech_protocol_family_home.html

Diffie-Hellman

The Diffie-Hellman protocol allows two parties to establish a shared secret over insecure channels, such as the Internet. This protocol allows a secure shared key interchange over the public network, such as the World Wide Web, before any secure session and data transfer is initiated. The Diffie-Hellman ensures that by exchanging just the public portions of the key, both devices can generate a session and ensure data is encrypted and decrypted by valid sources only. Only public keys (clear text) are exchanged over the public network. Using each device's public key and running the key through the Diffie-Hellmann algorithm generates a common session key. Only public keys will ever be exchanged.

Figure 5-11 displays the Diffie-Hellman exchange between Cisco routers, R1 and R2.

Figure 5-11 *Diffie-Hellman Key Exchange*

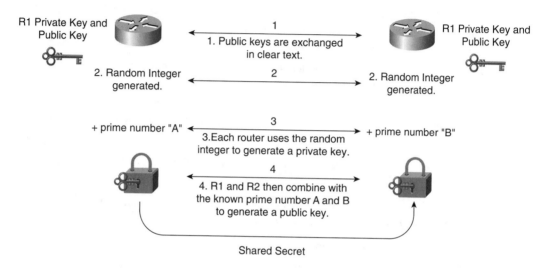

R1 Private Key and Public Key

1
1. Public keys are exchanged in clear text.

R1 Private Key and Public Key

2. Random Integer generated.

2

2. Random Integer generated.

+ prime number "A"

3
3.Each router uses the random integer to generate a private key.

+ prime number "B"

4
4. R1 and R2 then combine with the known prime number A and B to generate a public key.

Shared Secret

The Diffie-Hellman key exchange takes place over a public domain. With the private key secret, it is very difficult for an outside intruder to generate the same key, and the private key is never exchanged over the public domain, making the process very secure.

The shared prime numbers (mathematically, this means any positive integer greater than 1 and divisible without a remainder only by 1 and itself) have a special relationship that makes agreeing on a shared secret possible. An analogy would be to have two milkshake blenders making a chocolate milkshake, but with one blender supplied with apples and the other with oranges. The Diffie-Hellman algorithm is the secret ingredient that, when mixed in with both blenders, produces the chocolate milkshake. Remember, it really is a superb algorithm.

NOTE   RSA is another public key cryptographic algorithm (named after its inventors, Rivest, Shamir, and Adleman) with a variable key length. RSA's main weakness is that it is significantly slow to compute compared to popular secret-key algorithms, such as DES or 3DES. Cisco's IKE implementation uses a Diffie-Hellman exchange to get the secret keys. This exchange can be authenticated with RSA (or pre-shared keys). With the Diffie-Hellman exchange, the DES key never crosses the network, which is not the case with the RSA encryption and signing techniques. RSA is not public domain like DES/3DES, and to apply RSA, you must be licensed from RSA Data Security. An RSA signature is defined as the host (for example PC or routers) public and private key, which is bound with a digital certificate.

IP Security IPSec

IPSec provides security services at the IP layer by enabling a system to select required security protocols, determine the algorithm(s) to use for the service(s), and put in place any cryptographic keys required to provide the requested services. RFC 2401 for IP

IPSec is a defined encryption standard that encrypts the upper layers of the OSI model by adding a new predefined set of headers. A number of RFCs defined IPSec. IPSec is a mandatory requirement for IP version 6. (IPV6 is not covered in the examination.) IPSec ensures that the network layer of the OSI model is secured. In TCP/IP's case, this would be the IP network layer.

IPSec can be configured in two protection modes, which are commonly referred to as Security Association (SA). These modes provide security to a given IP connection. The modes are as follows:

- **Transport mode**—Protects payload of the original IP datagram; typically used for end-to-end sessions

- **Tunnel mode**—Protects the entire IP datagram by encapsulating the entire IP datagram in a new IP datagram

SA is required for inbound and outbound connection. In other words, IPSec is unidirectional. IKE, discussed in this chapter, allows for bidirectional SAs.

Figure 5-12 displays the extension to the current IP packet frame format for both transport and tunnel modes.

Figure 5-12 *IPSec Protection Modes*

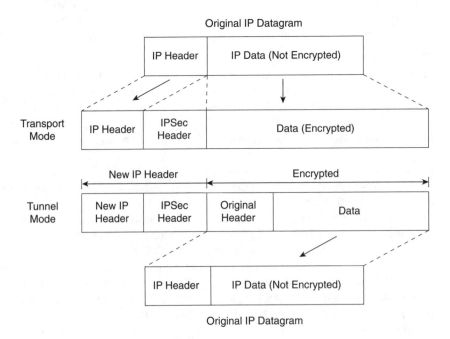

The encapsulation security payload (labeled IPSec header in Figure 5-12) can be of two forms:

- Encapsulation Security Payload (ESP)
- Authentication Header (AH)

Each of these is discussed in the following sections.

Encapsulation Security Payload (ESP)

The ESP security service is defined in RFC 2406. ESP provides a service to the IP data (payload), including upper-layer protocols such as TCP. The destination IP port number is 50. The ESP header is located between the user data and original IP header, as displayed in Figure 5-13.

Figure 5-13 displays the ESP header.

Figure 5-13 *ESP Header*

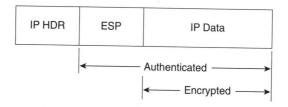

ESP does not encrypt the original IP header, and encrypts only the IP data by placing a header in between the original IP header and data. ESP provides data confidentiality, data integrity, and data origin authentication. ESP also prevents replay attacks. Replay attacks can include intruders capturing a valid packet and replaying it over the network in an attempt to get a packet conversation between an illegal and legal host.

ESP does not protect the IP header and cannot ESP detect any alternations during packet delivery.

Figure 5-14 displays the frame formats when ESP is applied.

The Security Parameters Index (SPI) is an arbitrary 32-bit value that, in combination with the destination IP address and security protocol (ESP), uniquely identifies the Security Association for this datagram.

The sequence number, an unsigned 32-bit field, contains a monotonically increasing counter value. It is mandatory and is always present, even if the receiver does not elect to enable the antireplay service for a specific SA. Pad or padding is used when the frame needs to meet the minimum frame size formats. The pad length defines the length of padding used. Padding is used for a number of reasons. For example, padding can ensure that the minimum frame size is set so that packets are not discarded because they are too small. Padding is typically all binary ones (1111. . .) or zeros (0000. . .). The sequence number ensures that no intruder or intruders can replay data transactions by using any form of attack mechanisms.

Figure 5-14 *ESP Frame Format*

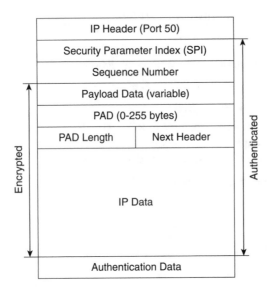

The Next Header is an 8-bit field that identifies the type of data contained in the Payload Data field. The IP data field contains the data to be sent. The Authentication Data field is a variable-length field containing an Integrity Check Value (ICV) computed over the ESP packet minus the Authentication Data.

Authentication Header (AH)

AH is described in RFC 2402. The IP protocol destination port is 51. Figure 5-15 highlights the fields in the IP datagram that are encrypted and authenticated. Note that not all fields, such as the Time to Live fields, are encrypted.

NOTE   AH provides data origin authentication and optional replay-detection services. AH doesn't provide data confidentiality (or encryption). Authentication is done by applying one-way hash to create a message digest of the packet. Replay detection can be implemented using the sequence number in the IP packet header.

Figure 5-15 *AH Header*

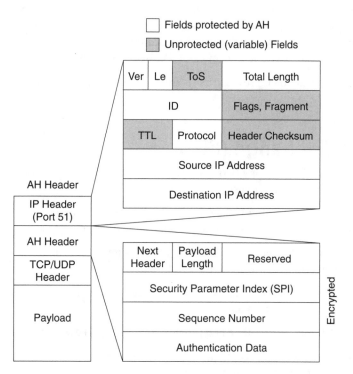

Following is a description of an AH packet:

- Next Header, an 8-bit field, identifies the type of the next payload after the Authentication Header.

- The Payload Length field is an 8-bit field specifying AH's length in 32-bit words (4-byte units), minus 2.

- The Reserved field is a 16-bit field reserved for future use. It MUST be set to 0.

- The SPI is an arbitrary 32-bit value that, in combination with the destination IP address and security protocol (AH), uniquely identifies the Security Association for this datagram.

AH can operate in transport or tunnel mode; however, contrary to ESP, AH also protects fields in the outer IP Header (in transport mode, this is the original IP header; in tunnel mode, this is the newly added IP header), which are normally considered nonvariable. AH ensures that if the original IP header has been altered, the packet is rejected.

Before you take a look at how IPSec is enabled on Cisco routers, you need to understand how keys are exchanged between secure devices to ensure that data is not comprised. IPSec ensures that once an IPSec tunnel is created, that the keys are modified so intruders cannot replicate the keys and create IPSec tunnels to insecure locations. A recent study showed that a network of computer hackers was able to decipher a DES-encrypted message in just a day.

In IPSec, this function is provided by Internet Key Exchange (IKE). IKE is discussed in the next section.

Internet Key Exchange (IKE)

In IPSec, a SA between any two devices will contain all relevant information such, as the cryptographic algorithm in use.

A cryptographic algorithm is the science of cryptography. This field of science includes the exact details of encryption algorithms, digital signatures, and key agreement algorithms.

A simple two-router network requires four SAs, two for each router. (IPSec requires two SAs on each router for two-way communication.)

Clearly, for a large network, this would not scale. IKE offers a scalable solution to configuration, and key exchange management.

IKE was designed to negotiate and provide authenticated keys in a secure manner.

IKE has two phases. In phase I, the cryptographic operation involves the exchange of a master secret where no security is currently in place. IKE phase I is primarily concerned with establishing the protection suite for IKE messages. Phase I operations are required infrequently and can be configured in two modes of operation—aggressive and main mode.

Aggressive mode eliminates several steps during IKE authentication negotiation phase I between two or more IPSec peers. Aggressive mode is faster than main mode but not as secure. Aggressive mode is a three-way packet exchange, while main mode is a six-way packet exchange.

IKE can be configured in aggressive mode or main mode (not both). Aggressive mode is a less intensive process that requires only three messages to establish a tunnel rather than six in main mode. Aggressive mode is typically used in dialup environments.

NOTE   Cisco devices use main mode but can respond to peers using aggressive mode.

IKE Phase I Messages Types 1-6

IKE phase I completes the following tasks:

- Negotiates IKE policy (message types 1 and 2). Information exchanges in these message types include IP addresses. Proposals, such as Diffie-Hellman group number and encryption algorithm, are also exchanged here. All messages are carried in UDP packets with a destination UDP port number of 500. The UDP payload comprises a header, an SA payload, and one or more proposals. Message type 1 offers many proposals, and message type 2 contains a single proposal.

- Performs authenticated Diffie-Hellman exchange (message types 3 and 4). Messages type 3 and 4 carry out the Diffie-Hellman (DH) exchange. Messages type 3 and 4 contain the key exchange payload, which is the DH public value and a random number. Messages type 3 and 4 also contain the remote peer's public key hash and the hashing algorithm. A common session key created on both ends, and the remaining IKE messages exchanged from here are encrypted. If perfect forward secrecy (PFS) is enabled, another DH exchange will be completed.

- Protects IKE peers' identities — identities are encrypted. Message types 5 and 6 are the last stage before traffic is sent over the IPSec tunnel. Message type 5 allows the responder to authenticate the initiating device. Message type 6 allows the initiator to authenticate the responder. These message types are not sent as clear text. Messages type 5 and 6 will now be encrypted using the agreed upon encryption methods established in message types 1 and 2.

After IKE phase I is completed, each peer or router has authenticated itself to the remote peer, and both have agreed on the characteristics of all the SA parameters.

Figure 5-16 summarizes the key components of IKE phase I and some of the possible permutations available on Cisco IOS routers.

The first message exchanged offers the remote router a choice of IPSec parameters, such as encryption algorithm, 3DES, MD5, and DH group number, for example. The first message's aim is to negotiate all SA policies and generate the shared secret.

In the second message (type 2), the responding device indicates which of the IPSec parameters it wants to use in the tunnel between the two devices, including the information required to generate the shared secret and provide authentication details. The final message (type 3; until now no encryption is enabled), which might or might not be encrypted, authenticates the initiator.

After IKE phase I is complete, IKE phase II is initiated. As discussed in the following section, IKE phase II negotiation has three message types.

Figure 5-16 *IKE Phase I Summary*

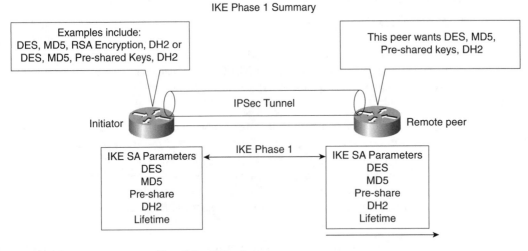

IKE Phase 1 Summary

Examples include:
DES, MD5, RSA Encryption, DH2 or
DES, MD5, Pre-shared Keys, DH2

This peer wants DES, MD5,
Pre-shared keys, DH2

IPSec Tunnel

Initiator

Remote peer

IKE SA Parameters
DES
MD5
Pre-share
DH2
Lifetime

IKE Phase 1

IKE SA Parameters
DES
MD5
Pre-share
DH2
Lifetime

- Negotiates IKE policy
- Performs authenticated Diffie-Hellman exchange
- Provides protection of identities of IKE peers
- Finally data can be transferred

IKE Phase II Message Types 1-3

IKE phase II negotiates the SA and the keys that will be used to protect the user data. IKE phase II messages occur more frequently and typically every few minutes, where IKE phase I messages might occur once a day.

IP datagrams that exchange IKE messages use UDP (connectionless) destination port 500.

Phase II negotiations occur in a mode called Oakley quick mode and have three different message exchanges. Quick mode can be the following:

- Without key exchange—No PFS enabled.

- With Key exchange—When PFS is enabled, the DH algorithm is run once more to generate the shared secret.

Message type I allows the initiator to authenticate itself and selects a random (nonce) number and proposes a security association to the remote peer. Additionally, a public key is provided (can be different than a key exchanged in IKE phase I). IKE phase II message type II allows the responding peer to generate the hash. Message type 2 allows the responder to authenticate itself, and selects a random number and accepts the SA offered by the initiating IPSec peer.

IKE Message type III acknowledges information sent from quick mode message 2 so that the phase II tunnel can be established.

NOTE   Perfect forward secrecy can be requested as part of the IKE security association. PFS ensures that a given IPSec SA key was not derived from any other secret (like some other keys). In other words, if someone were to break a key or get the key used between two peers, PFS ensures that the attacker would not be able to derive any other key. If PFS was not enabled, someone could hypothetically break the IKE SA secret key, copy all the IPSec protected data, and use knowledge of the IKE SA secret to compromise the IPSec Sa's setup by this IKE SA. With PFS, breaking IKE would not give an attacker immediate access to IPSec. The attacker would have to break each IPSec SA individually.

Changing the secret key being used for encryption after some period of time (or after a specified number of bytes have been encrypted) is a good idea. Changing keys makes it more difficult for an attacker to derive the key or the new created key.

Now that all the required data has been exchanged, the initiating IPSec router, or peer, sends a final phase I message with the hash of the two random numbers generated and the message ID.

Figure 5-17 summarizes the key components of IKE phase II.

Figure 5-17 *IKE Phase II Summary*

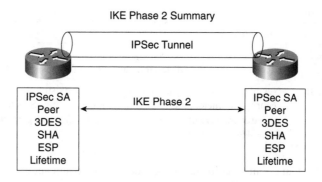

IKE Phase 2 Summary

IPSec Tunnel

IKE Phase 2

IPSec SA
Peer
3DES
SHA
ESP
Lifetime

IPSec SA
Peer
3DES
SHA
ESP
Lifetime

- Negotiates IPSec SA parameters protected by an existing IKE SA (during IKE phase 1)
- Establishes IPSec security associations, SA
- Periodically renegotiates IPSec SAs to ensure security
- Optionally performs an additional Diffie-Hellman exchange if PFS enabled

Figure 5-18 displays a typical IKE phase I/II completion.

IKE negotiates policy to protect the communication authenticated key exchange and SAs for IPSec.

Figure 5-18 *IKE Phase I/II*

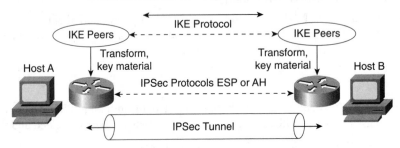

Steps Phase I/II
- Establish ISAKMP SA
- Negotiate ISAKMP SA policies such as encryption
  (MD5, 3DES, DSS)
- Exchange information needed to generate shared key
- Perform Diffie-Hellman calculation (shared secret)
- Generate the keys (pre-shared, DSS public keys)
- Communication can now begin by testing decryption

Table 5-7 summarizes the key components of IKE phase I and II.

Table 5-7   *IKE Phase I/II*

Phase	Components
IKE phase I	Authenticates IPSec peers, negotiates matching policy to protect IKE exchange, exchanges keys via Diffie-Hellman, and establishes the IKE SA.
IKE phase II	Negotiates IPSec SA parameters by using an existing IKE SA. Establishes IPSec security parameters. Periodically renegotiates IPSec SAs to ensure security and that no intruders have discovered sensitive data. Can also perform optional additional Diffie-Hellman exchange.

IKE requires that all information exchanges be encrypted and authenticated. In addition, IKE is designed to prevent the following attacks:

- **Denial of Service**—When messages are constructed with unique cookies that can be used to identify and reject invalid messages.

- **Man in the middle**—Prevents the intruder from modifying messages and reflecting them back to the source or replaying old messages.

NOTE   Access lists determine what traffic to encrypt. For example, you can specify that certain networks are to be encrypted and other networks are not. The permit statement encrypts data, and the deny statement (implicit) in an ACL does not send traffic encrypted. An ACL applied to IPSec configuration parameters does not stop IP routing on a Cisco IOS router.

Table 5-8 summarizes the key terms and concepts used in IPSec terminology.

Table 5-8   *Summary IPSec Terms and Concepts*

Attribute	Meaning
IKE	The IKE protocol provides utility services for IPSec, such as authentication of peers, negotiation of IPSec SAs, and encryption algorithms. IKE operates over the assigned UDP port 500.
SA	Security associations are connections between IPSec peers. Each IPSec peer maintains an SA database containing parameters, such as peer address, security protocol, and security parameter index (SPI).
DES	Data Encryption Standard. DES encrypts and decrypts data. Not considered a strong algorithm and replaced by 3DES. DES only supports a 56-bit key. 3DES supports 3×56, or a 168-bit key.
3DES	A variant of DES and much stronger encryption method that uses a 168-bit key.
MD5	Message Digest version 5 is a hash algorithm that takes an input message (of variable length) and produces a fixed-length output message. IKE uses MD5 for authentication purposes.
SHA-1	Secure Hash Algorithm that signs and authenticates data. It is stronger than MD5 but more CPU-intensive and, therefore, slower.
RSA signatures	RSA is a public-key encryption system used for authentication. Users are assigned both private and public keys. The private key is not available to the public and decrypts messages created with the public key.
CA	Certification authority is an entity that provides digital certificates and binds data items within a certificate.

Figure 5-19 displays the flow chart before any data can be transferred between two IPSec peers.

Figure 5-19   *IPSec flow*

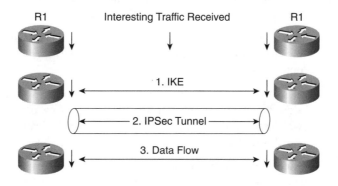

In Figure 5-19, interesting traffic (or traffic from an end user, for example) triggers the IKE phases I/II followed by the establishment of the IPSec tunnel. After the IPSec tunnel is established, the data can be transferred. After the data is transferred, the IPSec tunnel is closed. You can tunnel any form of data across the IPSec tunnel, such as IP, Novel IPX, or AppleTalk.

Cisco IOS IPSec Configuration

To enable IPSec between Cisco IOS routers, the following steps are required:

Step 1   Enable ISAKMP with the IOS command **crypto isakmp enable**.

This step globally enables or disables ISAKMP at your peer router.

ISAKMP is enabled by default (optionally, define what interesting traffic will be encrypted using defined access lists).

Step 2   Define an ISAKMP policy, a set of parameters used during ISAKMP negotiation:

```
crypto isakmp policy priority
```

You will enter **config-isakmp** command mode.

Options available include the following:

```
Router(config-isakmp)#?
authentication {rsa-sig | rsa-encr | pre-share}
  default
  encryption {des}
  exit
  group
  hash {md5 | sha}
  lifetime seconds
  no
```

This command invokes the Internet Security Association Key Management Protocol policy configuration (**config-isakmp**) command mode. While in the ISAKMP policy configuration command mode, the following commands are available to specify the parameters in the policy:

— Encryption (IKE policy)—The default is 56-bit DES-CBC. To specify the encryption algorithm within an Internet Key Exchange policy, options are des or 3des.

— Hash (IKE policy)—The default is SHA-1. To specify the hash algorithm within an Internet Key Exchange policy, options are sha, which specifies SHA-1 (HMAC variant) as the hash algorithm, or md5, which specifies MD5 (HMAC variant) as the hash algorithm.

— Authentication (IKE policy)—The default is RSA signatures. To specify the authentication method within an Internet Key Exchange policy, options are rsa-sig, which specifies RSA signatures as the authentication method, rsa-encr, which specifies RSA encrypted as the authentication method, or pre-share, which specifies pre-shared keys as the authentication method.

— Group {1|2}—The default is 768-bit Diffie-Hellman. To specify the Diffie-Hellman group identifier within an Internet Key Exchange policy, options are 1, which specifies the 768-bit Diffie-Hellman group, or 2, which specifies the 1024-bit Diffie-Hellman group.

— Lifetime (IKE policy)—The default is 86,400 seconds (once a day). To specify the lifetime of an Internet Key Exchange security association (SA), use the Lifetime Internet Security Association Key Management Protocol policy configuration command. If two IPSec peers share different lifetime values, the chosen value is the shortest lifetime.

Step 3 Set the ISAKMP identity (can be IP address or host name based).

```
crypto isakmp identity {address | hostname}
```

Step 4 Define transform sets.

A transform set represents a combination of security protocols and algorithms. During the IPSec security association negotiation, the peers agree to use a particular transform set for protecting a particular data flow.

To define a transform set, use the following commands starting in global configuration mode:

```
crypto ipsec transform-set
  transform-set-name transform1 [transform2 [transform3]]
```

This command puts you into the crypto transform configuration mode. Then define the mode associated with the transform set.

```
Router(cfg-crypto-tran)# mode [tunnel | transport]
```

Step 5 Define crypto maps. Crypto maps tie the IPSec policies and SAs together.

```
crypto map name seq method [dynamic dynamic-map-name]
```

NOTE Crypto map entries created for IPSec pull together the various parts used to set up IPSec SAs, including the following:

- Which traffic should be protected by IPSec (per a crypto access list)

- The granularity of the flow to be protected by a set of SAs

- Where IPSec-protected traffic should be sent (who the remote IPSec peer is)

- The local address to be used for the IPSec traffic

- What IPSec security should be applied to this traffic

- Whether SAs are manually established or are established through IKE

- Other parameters that might be necessary to define an IPSec SA

A dynamic crypto map entry is essentially a crypto map entry without all the parameters configured. It acts as a policy template where the missing parameters are later dynamically configured (as the result of an IPSec negotiation) to match a remote peer's requirements. This allows remote peers to exchange IPSec traffic with the router even if the router does not have a crypto map entry specifically configured to meet all the remote peer's requirements. Dynamic crypto maps are typically used to ensure security between a dialup IPSec client and Cisco IOS router, for example.

The following typical configuration scenario illustrates the IPSec configuration tasks with a two-router network. Figure 5-20 displays two routers configured with the networks 131.108.100.0/24 and 131.108.200.0/24, respectively. Suppose the Frame relay cloud is an unsecured network and you want to enable IPSec between the two routers, R1 and R2.

The network administrator has decided to define the following ISAKMP parameters:

- MD5

- Authentication will be pre-share

- The shared key phrase is CCIE

- IPSec mode is transport mode

Figure 5-20 *Typical IPSec Topology Between Two Remote Routers*

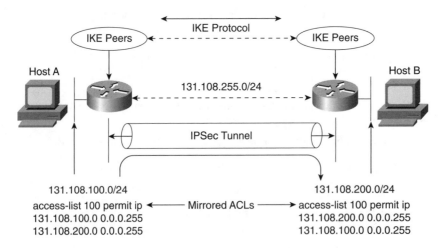

To start, configure IKE on Router R1. Example 5-15 displays the IKE configuration on R1. Remember that IKE policies define a set of parameters to be used during IKE negotiation.

Example 5-15 *R1 IKE Configuration*

```
crypto isakmp policy 1
  hash md5
  authentication pre-share
crypto isakmp key CCIE address 131.108.255.2
```

R1 is configured to use the MD5 algorithm, and the authentication method is defined as pre-shared. The pre-share key value (password) is CCIE, and the remote IPSec peer's address is 131.108.255.2 (R2 Serial Link to R1 in Figure 5-20).

Pre-shared Keys Versus Manual Keys

The example shown here is an example of pre-shared keys whereby IKE is used to negotiate all SA parameters. You can also define IPSec not to use IKE, and this is referred to as *manual IPSec* or *manual keys*. Cisco strongly recommends that you use IKE or pre-shared keys because it is very difficult to ensure that all SA parameters are matching between remote peers. The Diffie-Hellman algorithm is a more secure method when generating secret keys between peers. Manual keys are prone to intruders and unauthorized sources that gain entry to Cisco configuration files. Another major disadvantage of manual keys is that the IOS **crypto map** command used to establish SAs does not expire.

Following the IKE configuration, you can configure IPSec parameters. Example 5-16 enables the IPSec configuration parameters.

Example 5-16 *IPSec Configuration*

```
crypto ipsec transform-set anyname esp-des esp-sha-hmac  mode transport
!
crypto map anyname1 1 ipsec-isakmp
  set peer 131.108.255.2
  set security-association lifetime seconds 180
  set transform-set anyname
  match address 100
!
access-list 100 permit ip 131.108.100.0 0.0.0.255 131.108.200.0 0.0.0.255
```

The transform set command defines an acceptable combination of security protocols and algorithms. This example applies ESP-DES (ESP with the 56-bit DES encryption algorithm) and ESP with the SHA (HMAC variant) authentication algorithm. The next-hop peer address is defined and access-list 100 defines what traffic will be encrypted. In Figure 5-20, only IP traffic sourced from 131.108.100.0 destined for 131.108.200.0/24 is sent across the IPSec tunnel.

Example 5-17 displays the configuration on R2.

Example 5-17 *R2 IKE and IPSec Configuration*

```
! IKE configuration
crypto isakmp policy 1
 hash md5
 authentication pre-share
crypto isakmp key CCIE address 131.108.255.1
!
crypto ipsec transform-set anyname esp-des esp-sha-hmac
 mode transport
!IPSec configuration
crypto map anyname1 1 ipsec-isakmp
 set peer 131.108.255.1
 set security-association lifetime seconds 180
 set transform-set anyname
 match address 100
!Access list defines traffic to be encrypted
access-list 100 permit ip 131.108.200.0 0.0.0.255 131.108.100.0 0.0.0.255
```

Notice that the routers have mirrored access lists. This ensures that when encrypted data is received from a source, such as R1, the corresponding IPSec peer router, R2, enables encryption in the reverse direction. For example, when traffic from the network 131.108.100.0/24 residing on Router R1 is sent across destined for R2's Ethernet network, the IP subnet 131.108.200.0/24, R2 must have a corresponding ACL permitting traffic from the locally-connected Ethernet segment, 131.108.200.0/24, to the remote network, the IP subnet on R1, 131.108.100.0/24.

This is referred to as mirrored access lists.

Example 5-17 configures R2 to peer to R1 and only encrypt traffic sourced from 131.108.200.0/24 destined for R1's Ethernet network, 131.108.100.0/24. The crypto predefined map name is anyname1.

Finally, you must apply a previously defined crypto map (in our example the name defined is anyname1) in Example 5-16. The defined crypto map name is anyname1, so apply that configuration to the interface. The IOS command that applies the crypto map to an interface is as follows:

```
crypto map anyname1
```

Example 5-18 assigns the serial links on R1 and R2 the crypto map name anyname1.

Example 5-18 assigns the crypto map to interface Serial 0/0 on R1/R2.

Example 5-18 *Serial Links and* **crypto map** *on R1/R2*

```
Hostname R1
!
interface Serial0/0
 ip address 131.108.255.1 255.255.255.252
 crypto map anyname1
!
Hostname R2
!
interface Serial0/0
 ip address 131.108.255.2 255.255.255.252
 crypto map anyname1
```

To display the status of all crypto engine active connections, use the IOS command **show crypto engine connections active**.

Example 5-19 displays the current active crypto engines on R1.

Example 5-19 **show crypto engine connections active** *on R1*

```
R1#show crypto engine connections active
  ID Interface      IP-Address      State  Algorithm                Encrypt  Decrypt
   1 Serial0/0      131.108.255.1   set    HMAC_MD5+DES_56_CB             5        5
```

R1 has an IPSec peer connection to R2, through the Serial0/0 interface (131.108.255.1). The algorithm in use is defined and displayed, as well.

To view the crypto map configuration from the privilege prompt, use the IOS command **show crypto map**.

Example 5-20 displays the configuration present on R1.

Example 5-20 **show crypto map** *on R1*

```
R1#show crypto map
Crypto Map "anyname1" 1 ipsec-isakmp
        Peer = 131.108.255.2
        Extended IP access list 100
access-list 100 permit ip 131.108.100.0 0.0.0.255 131.108.200.0 0.0.0.255
        Current peer: 131.108.255.2
        Security association lifetime: 4608000 kilobytes/180 seconds
        PFS (Y/N): N
        Transform sets={ anyname, }
        Interfaces using crypto map anyname1:
                Serial0/0
```

Example 5-20 displays the fact that the crypto map named "MAP1" is peered to a remote router, 131.108.255.2, and the access-list 100 defines what traffic will be encrypted across the tunnel.

IPSec is a large field, and to define every possible scenario would require a book in itself. What is presented here in this guide is a conceptual overview of IPSec and a common configuration example.

For more extensive details, visit www.cisco.com/univercd/cc/td/doc/product/software/ios122/122cgcr/fsecur_c/index.htm.

For the written exam, expect to see scenarios of the variant presented in Figure 5-20 and questions on terminology and the main characteristics of IPSec.

NOTE   IPSec can also be supported over the Cisco software tunnel interface. Typically, the tunnel (IP tunnel; GRE, for example) can be configured to carry non-IP traffic by defining a crypto map to the tunnel interface and a crypto control list.

Table 5-9 defines some key configuration show and debug IPSec commands available on Cisco IOS routers.

Table 5-9   *IOS IPSec Configuration, Show, and Debug Commands*

Command	Description
crypto map *map-name seq-num* **ipsec-isakmp** [**dynamic** *dynamic-map-name*] [**discover**]	Creates a crypto map entry.
crypto ipsec transform-set *transform-set-name transform1* [*transform2* [*transform3*]]	Defines a transform set, an acceptable combination of security protocols and algorithms.
match address [*access-list-id* | *name*]	This command is required for all static crypto map entries.
crypto dynamic-map *dynamic-map-name dynamic-seq-num*	Use dynamic crypto maps to create policy templates that can be used when processing negotiation requests for new SAs from a remote IP Security peer, even if you do not know all the crypto map parameters.
crypto ca authenticate *name*	This command is required when you initially configure CA support at your router.
crypto ca identity *name*	Use this command to declare a CA.
crypto isakmp enable	Globally enables Internet Key Exchange (IKE) at your peer router.
Show crypto engine connection active	View phase II SA and traffic sent.

Table 5-9   *IOS IPSec Configuration, Show, and Debug Commands (Continued)*

Command	Description
authentication {rsa-sig I rsa-encr I pre-share}	Specifies the authentication method within an IKE policy.
show crypto ipsec sa	Use this command to view the settings used by current SAs to declare a CA.
show crypto map	This command views the crypto map configuration.
show crypto isakmp sa	This command views all current IKE SAs at a peer.
debug crypto engine	Use this command to display debug messages about crypto engines, which perform encryption and decryption.
debug crypto ipsec	Use this command to display IPSec events.
debug crypto pki messages	This command displays debug messages for the details of the interaction (message dump) between the CA and the router.

NOTE   A number of PC-based applications are available to the public that allow application layer encryptions.

An excellent e-mail encryption application is a product called Pretty Good Privacy (PGP).

Designed and freely available on the Internet (www.pgp.com/), PGP allows users to authenticate files and e-mail text, allowing only the intended recipient the ability to decrypt the message. Users who send and receive encrypted data exchange keys. With encrypted data, the remote user's key is used to encrypt clear text data or files. This ensures that the data is authenticated and not forged.

Microsoft Outlook 2000 supports PGP and allows the client to encrypt and decrypt data using the pre-shared private keys.

Certificate Enrollment Protocol (CEP)

CEP is a protocol jointly developed by Cisco and Verisign, Inc. CEP is an early implementation of Certificate Request Syntax (CRS), a proposed standard to the IETF. CEP specifies how a device communicates with the CA, how to retrieve the CA's public key, and how to enroll a device with the CA. CEP uses Public Key Cryptography Standards (PKCS).

CEP uses HTTP as a transport mechanism and uses the same TCP port (80) used by HTTP.

To declare the CA that a Cisco IOS router should use, use the **crypto ca identity** *<name>* command in global configuration mode. The CA might require a particular name, such as the domain name.

Foundation Summary

The "Foundation Summary" is a condensed collection of material for a convenient review of key concepts in this chapter. If you are already comfortable with the topics in this chapter and decided to skip most of the "Foundation Topics" material, the "Foundation Summary" will help you recall a few details. If you just read the "Foundation Topics" section, this review should help further solidify some key facts. If you are doing your final preparation before the exam, the "Foundation Summary" offers a convenient and quick final review.

Table 5-10   *AAA Terminology*

Attribute	Meaning
Authentication	Who are you? A remote user must be authenticated before being permitted access to network resources. Authentication allows users to submit their usernames and passwords, and permit challenges and responses. Username/Password pairs are a common form of authentication.
Authorization	What resources are you permitted? Once the user is authenticated, authorization defines what services in the network are permitted access. The operations permitted here can include IOS privileged exec commands.
Accounting	What resources were accessed, what times were they accessed, by whom were they accessed, and what commands were issued to access them? Accounting allows the network administrator to log and view what was actually performed. For example, if a Cisco router was reloaded or the configuration was changed. Accounting ensures that an audit will allow network administrators the ability to view what was performed and at what time.

Table 5-11   *RADIUS Summary*

Feature	Meaning
UDP	Packets sent between clients and servers are UDP primarily because TCP's overhead does not allow for significant advantages. Typically, the user can wait for a username/password prompt.
UDP destination port	1812, port 1646 used for accounting. RADIUS is an industry standard defined in RFC 2138.
Attributes	Attributes are used to exchange information between the NAS and client.
Model	Client/server-based model where packets are exchanged in a unidirectional manner.
Encryption method	Password is encrypted using MD5; the username is not. RADIUS encrypts only the password in the access-request packet from the client to the server. The remainder of the packet is in clear text. A third party could capture other information, such as username, authorized services, and accounting.
Multiprotocol support	Does not support protocols such as AppleTalk, NetBIOS, or IPX. IP is the only protocol supported.

Table 5-12   *TACACS+ Summary*

Feature	Meaning
TCP	Packets sent between client and server are TCP. Typically, the user can wait for a username/password prompt.
TCP destination port	Port 49.
Attributes	Packet types are defined in TACACS+ frame format as: Authentication 0x01 Authorization 0x02 Accounting 0x03
Seq_no	The sequence number of the current packet flow for the current session. The Seq_no starts with 1 and each subsequent packet will increment by one. The client only sends odd numbers. TACACS+ servers only send even numbers.
Encryption method	The entire packet is encrypted. Data is encrypted using MD5 and a secret key that matches both on the NAS (for example, a Cisco IOS router) and the TACACS+ server.
Multiprotocol support	Supports protocols such as AppleTalk, NetBIOS, or IPX. IP-supported only.

Table 5-13   *RADIUS Versus TACACS+*

	RADIUS	TACACS+
Packet delivery	UDP	TCP
Packet encryption	RADIUS encrypts only the password in the access-request packet from the client to the server.	TACACS+ encrypts the entire body of the packet, but leaves a standard TACACS+ header.
AAA support	RADIUS combines authentication and authorization.	TACACS+ uses the AAA architecture, separating authentication, authorization, and accounting.
Multiprotocol support	None.	Supports other protocols, such as AppleTalk, NetBIOS, and IPX.
Router management	RADIUS does not allow users to control which commands can be executed on a router.	TACACS+ allows network administrators control over which commands can be executed on a router.

Table 5-14 *Summary of Kerberos Protocol*

Attribute	Meaning
Packet delivery	A number of ports are defined: TCP/UDP ports 88, 543, and 749 TCP ports 754, 2105, and 4444
Packet encryption	Supports username/password encryption. Telnet sessions are encrypted, for example.
AAA support	RADIUS combines authentication and authorization.
Server support	Typically runs on a UNIX-based host system.
Router management	RADIUS does not allow users to control which commands can be executed on a router.

Following is a summary of the VPDN process when users are authenticated:

Step 1 The remote user initiates a PPP connection to the ISP using the analog telephone system or ISDN.

Step 2 The ISP NAS accepts the connection.

Step 3 The ISP NAS authenticates the end user with CHAP or PAP. The username determines whether the user is a VPDN client. If the user is not a VPDN client, the client accesses the Internet or other contacted service.

Step 4 The tunnel endpoints—the NAS and the home gateway—authenticate each other before any sessions are attempted within a tunnel.

Step 5 If no L2F tunnel exists between the NAS and the remote user's home gateway, a tunnel is created. Once the tunnel exists, an unused slot within the tunnel is allocated.

Step 6 The home gateway accepts or rejects the connection. Initial setup can include authentication information required to allow the home gateway to authenticate the user.

Step 7 The home gateway sets up a virtual interface. Link-level frames can now pass through this virtual interface through the L2F tunnel.

Table 5-15 *Encryption Methods*

Encryption	Description
DES	DES is a block cipher algorithm, which means that DES performs operations on fixed-length data streams. DES uses a 56-bit key to encrypt 64-bit datagrams. DES is a published, U.S. Government-approved encryption algorithm.
3DES	3DES is a variant of DES, which iterates (encrypt with one 56-bit key, decrypts with another 56-bit key, and then, finally, encrypts with another 56-bit key) three times with three separate keys. Three keys are used to encrypted data resulting in a 168-bit encryption key.

Table 5-16 *IKE Phase I/II*

Phase	Components
IKE phase I	Authenticates IPSec peers Negotiates matching policy to protect IKE exchange Exchanges keys using Diffie-Hellman Establishes IKE security association
IKE phase II	Negotiates IPSec SA parameters by using an existing IKE SA Establishes IPSec security parameters Periodically renegotiates IPSec SAs to ensure security and that no intruders have discovered sensitive data Can also perform optional additional Diffie-Hellman exchange

Table 5-17 *IPSec Terminology*

Attribute	Meaning
IKE	IKE is a protocol that provides utility services for IPSec, such as authentication of peers, negotiation of IPSec SAs, and encryption algorithms.
SA	A security association is a connection between IPSec peers.
MD5	Message Digest version 5, is a hash algorithm that takes an input message (of variable length) and produces a fixed-length output message. IKE uses MD5 for authentication purposes.
SHA-1	Secure Hash Algorithm that signs and authenticates data.
RSA signatures	RSA is a public-key encryption system used for authentication. Users are assigned both private and public keys. The private key is not available to the public and is used to decryption messages created with the public key.

continues

Table 5-17   *IPSec Terminology (Continued)*

Attribute	Meaning
CA	A certification authority is an entity that provides digital certificates and binds data items within a certificate.
AH	Authentication header used to authenticated data. AH provides data origin authentication and optional replay-detection services.
ESP	ESP does not encrypt the original IP header, and only encrypts the IP data by placing a header in between the original IP header and data. ESP provides data confidentiality, data integrity, and data origin authentication
DH	Diffie-Hellman algorithm. This algorithm is used to initiate and secure the session between two hosts, such as routers.
DSS	Digital Signature Standard is a mechanism that protects data from an undetected change while traversing the network. DSS verifies the identity of the person sending the data just as when you verify your signature to a bank manager.

Q & A

The Q & A questions help you assess your readiness for the topics covered on the CCIE Security written exam and those topics presented in this chapter. This format is intended to help you assess your retention of the material. A strong understanding of the answers to these questions will help you on the CCIE Security written exam. You can also look over the questions at the beginning of the chapter again for further review. As an additional study aid, use the CD-ROM provided with this book to take simulated exams, which draw from a database of over 300 multiple-choice questions—all different from those presented in the book.

Answers to these questions can be found in Appendix A, "Answers to Quiz Questions."

1 Define the AAA model and a typical application on a Cisco IOS router.

2 Can you allow a remote user authorization before the user is authenticated with AAA?

3 What IOS command is required when enabling AAA for the first time?

4 What is the privilege level of the following user? Assume AAA is not configured.

```
R2>
R2>show priv
Current privilege level is 1
```

5 Define four possible RADIUS responses when authenticating the user through a RADIUS server.

_____

_____

_____

6 What are RADIUS attributes? Supply five common examples.

_____

_____

_____

7 What protocols does RADIUS use when sending messages between the server and client?

_____

_____

_____

8 What predefined destination UDP port number is RADIUS accounting information sent to?

_____

_____

_____

9 What does the following command accomplish on a Cisco IOS router?

```
aaa authentication ppp user-radius if-needed group radius
```

_____

_____

_____

10 What is the RADIUS server IP address and key for the following configuration?

```
radius-server host 3.3.3.3
radius-server key GuitarsrocKthisplaneT
```

_____

_____

_____

11 TACACS+ is transported over what TCP destination port number?

_____

_____

_____

12 What information is encrypted between a Cisco router and a TACACS+ server?

_____

_____

_____

13 What are the four possible packet types from a TACACS+ server when a user attempts to authenticate a Telnet session to a Cisco router configured for AAA, for example?

_____

_____

_____

14 What is the significance of the sequence number in the TACACS+ frame format?

_____

_____

_____

15 What does the following IOS command accomplish?

```
aaa authentication ppp default if-needed group tacacs+ local
```

_____

_____

_____

16 What IOS command defines the remote TACACS+ server?

_____

_____

_____

17 What are the major difference between TACACS+ and RADIUS?

_____

_____

_____

18 Kerberos is a third-party authentication protocol operating at what layer of the OSI model?

_____

_____

_____

19 What delivery methods and destination ports does Kerberos support?

_____

_____

_____

20 What does the Kerberos realm define?

_____

_____

_____

21 Applications that have been modified to support Kerberos credential infrastructures are known as what?

_____

_____

_____

22 Define the two steps required in an L2F connection terminating a PPP connection?

_____

_____

_____

23 Define the two steps for setting up L2TP for tunneling a PPP connection.

_____

_____

_____

24 What are the steps taken for a VPDN connection between a remote user and a remote LAN?

_____

_____

_____

25 What are the three most common threats from intruders that network administrators face?

_____

_____

_____

26 What does the Digital Signature standard provides

_____

_____

_____

27 What is hash in encryption terminology?

_____

_____

_____

28 Name the two modes of operation in IPSec and their characteristics.

_____

_____

_____

29 What does IKE accomplish?

_____

_____

_____

30 Certificate Enrollment Protocol is transported over what TCP port?

Scenario

Scenario 5-1: Configuring Cisco Routers for IPSec

Figure 5-21 displays a simple two-router topology where traffic from network 131.108.100.0/24 is encrypted when it is sent to the remote network 131.108.200.0/24.

Figure 5-21 *Scenario Topology*

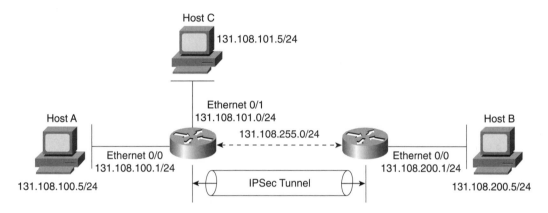

Example 5-21 displays the working configuration of R1 numbered from 1 to 31.

Example 5-21 *R1's Full Configuration*

```
1. version 12.2
2.hostname R1
3.enable password cisco
4.crypto isakmp policy 1
5.   hash md5
6.   authentication pre-share
7.   crypto isakmp key CCIE address 131.108.255.2
8. crypto ipsec transform-set anyname esp-des esp-sha-hmac
9. mode transport
10.crypto map anyname1 1 ipsec-isakmp
11.   set peer 131.108.255.2
12.   set security-association lifetime seconds 180
13.   set transform-set anyname
14.   match address 100
15. interface Ethernet0/0
16.   ip address 131.108.100.1 255.255.255.0
17. interface Serial0/0
18. ip address 131.108.255.1 255.255.255.252
19.   encapsulation frame-relay
```

continues

Example 5-21 *R1's Full Configuration (Continued)*

```
20.  ip split-horizon
21.  ip ospf network point-to-point
22.  frame-relay map ip 131.108.255.2 102 broadcast
23.  frame-relay interface-dlci 102
24.  frame-relay lmi-type ansi
25.  crypto map anyname1
26. interface Ethernet0/1
27.  ip address 131.108.101.1 255.255.255.0
28. router ospf 1
29.  network 131.108.0.0 0.0.255.255 area 0
30.  access-list 100 permit ip 131.108.100.0 0.0.0.255 131.108.200.0 0.0.0.255
31. end
```

Example 5-22 displays the working configuration of R2 numbered from 1 through 29.

Example 5-22 *R2's Full Configuration*

```
1. Version 12.2
2. hostname R2
3. enable password cisco
4. crypto isakmp policy 1
5. hash md5
6. authentication pre-share
7. crypto isakmp key CCIe address 131.108.255.1
8.crypto ipsec transform-set anyname esp-des esp-sha-hmac
9. mode transport
10. crypto map anyname1 1 ipsec-isakmp
11. set peer 131.108.255.1
12. set security-association lifetime seconds 180
13. set transform-set anyname
14. match address 100
15.interface Ethernet0/0
16.ip address 131.108.200.1 255.255.255.0
17. interface Serial0/0
18.  ip address 131.108.255.2 255.255.255.252
19.  encapsulation frame-relay
20.  ip split-horizon
21.  ip ospf network point-to-point
22.  frame-relay map ip 131.108.255.1 201 broadcast
23.  frame-relay interface-dlci 201
24.  frame-relay lmi-type ansi
25.  crypto map anyname1
26.  router ospf 1
27.  network 131.108.0.0 0.0.255.255 area 0
28.  access-list 100 permit ip 131.108.200.0 0.0.0.255 131.108.100.0 0.0.0.255
29. end
```

1 The following debug output is seen on R1 after the network administrator pings remote network 131.108.100.1 from Router R2's console port.

Why will the IPSec tunnel not negotiate properly?

```
R2#debug crypto engine
Crypto Engine debugging is on
R2#ping
Protocol [ip]:
Target IP address: 131.108.100.1
Repeat count [5]:
Datagram size [100]:
Timeout in seconds [2]:
Extended commands [n]: y
Source address or interface: 131.108.200.1
Type of service [0]:
Set DF bit in IP header? [no]:
Validate reply data? [no]:
Data pattern [0xABCD]:
Loose, Strict, Record, Timestamp, Verbose[none]:
Sweep range of sizes [n]:
Type escape sequence to abort.
Sending 5, 100-byte ICMP Echos to 131.108.100.1, timeout is 2 seconds:
22:58:55: CryptoEngine0: generate alg parameter
22:58:55: CRYPTO_ENGINE: Dh phase 1 status: 0
22:58:55: CRYPTO_ENGINE: Dh phase 1 status: 0
22:58:55: CryptoEngine0: generate alg parameter
22:58:55: CryptoEngine0: create ISAKMP SKEYID for conn id 1
22:58:55: CryptoEngine0: generate hmac context for conn id 1.
22:58:55: %CRYPTO-4-IKMP_BAD_MESSAGE: IKE message from 131.108.255.1   failed it
s sanity check or is malformed....
Success rate is 0 percent (0/5)
R2#
```

2 What subnets will be encrypted between Routers R1 and R2?

3 What IOS command produced the following display and from which router?

```
Crypto Map "anyname1" 1 ipsec-isakmp
        Peer = 131.108.255.2
        Extended IP access list 100
    access-list 100 permit ip 131.108.100.0 0.0.0.255 131.108.200.0 0.0.0.255
        Current peer: 131.108.255.2
        Security association lifetime: 4608000 kilobytes/180 seconds
        PFS (Y/N): N
        Transform sets={ anyname, }
        Interfaces using crypto map anyname1:
                Serial0/0
```

4 Will Host A be able to communicate with Host B or Host C? The following displays are the IP routing tables on R1 and R2. (Assume the gateway configurations on the PCs are correct.)

R1's IP routing table:

```
R1>show ip route
Codes: C - connected, , O - OSPF,
     131.108.0.0/16 is variably subnetted, 4 subnets, 2 masks
C       131.108.255.0/30 is directly connected, Serial0/0
O       131.108.200.0/24 [110/400] via 131.108.255.2, 00:52:00, Serial0/0
C       131.108.101.0/24 is directly connected, Ethernet0/1
C       131.108.100.0/24 is directly connected, Ethernet0/0
```

R2's IP routing table:

```
R2>show ip route
Codes: C - connected, , O - OSPF
       131.108.0.0/16 is variably subnetted, 4 subnets, 2 masks
C         131.108.255.0/30 is directly connected, Serial0/0
C         131.108.200.0/24 is directly connected, Ethernet0/0
O         131.108.101.0/24 [110/58] via 131.108.255.1, 00:52:09, Serial0/0
       131.108.100.0/24 [110/58] via 131.108.255.1, 00:52:09, Serial0/0
```

5 To allow the IP subnet 131.108.101.0/24 attached to R1 Ethernet 0/1 interface to be encrypted over the IPSec tunnel and to communicate with the remote PC IP address 131.108.200.5, what configuration changes are required on which router?

Scenario Answers

Scenario 5-1 Solutions

1 The following debug output advises the network administrator of the problem:

```
22:58:55: %CRYPTO-4-IKMP_BAD_MESSAGE: IKE message from 131.108.255.1   failed it
s sanity check or is malformed....
```

During the IKE negotiation, the router reports a message that identifies the fault as the share password. R2 is configured with the password, CCIe (should match R1's pre-shared password set to CCIE). See example 5-21, and code line 7.

Changing the IKE password to CCIE with the IOS command, **crypto isakmp key CCIE address 131.108.255.1**, the following debug output confirms the IPSec connections by pinging from R2 Ethernet 0/0 IP address to R1 Ethernet 0/0 IP address:

```
R2#ping
Protocol [ip]:
Target IP address: 131.108.100.1
Repeat count [5]:
Datagram size [100]:
Timeout in seconds [2]:
Extended commands [n]: y
Source address or interface: 131.108.200.1
Type of service [0]:
Set DF bit in IP header? [no]:
Validate reply data? [no]:
Data pattern [0xABCD]:
Loose, Strict, Record, Timestamp, Verbose[none]:
Sweep range of sizes [n]:
Type escape sequence to abort.
Sending 5, 100-byte ICMP Echos to 131.108.100.1, timeout is 2 seconds:
23:12:21: CryptoEngine0: generate alg parameter
23:12:21: CRYPTO_ENGINE: Dh phase 1 status: 0
23:12:21: CRYPTO_ENGINE: Dh phase 1 status: 0
23:12:21: CryptoEngine0: generate alg parameter
23:12:21: CryptoEngine0: create ISAKMP SKEYID for conn id 1
23:12:21: CryptoEngine0: generate hmac context for conn id 1
23:12:21: CryptoEngine0: generate hmac context for conn id 1
23:12:21: CryptoEngine0: generate hmac context for conn id 1
23:12:21: CryptoEngine0: clear dh number for conn id 1
23:12:22: CryptoEngine0: generate hmac context for conn id 1
23:12:22: validate proposal 0
23:12:22: validate proposal request 0
23:12:22: CryptoEngine0: generate hmac context for conn id 1.!!!!
Success rate is 80 percent (4/5), round-trip min/avg/max = 12/13/16 ms
R2#
```

The first Ping packet fails because the IPSec tunnel has not yet been created. Then, the IPSec tunnel is successfully brought up between R1 and R2.

2 Access-list 100 on both routers defines the IP subnets that need to be encrypted between R1 and R2. Packets flowing between subnets 131.108.100.0/24 and 131.108.200.0/24 will be encrypted.

R1's ACL is as follows:

```
access-list 100 permit ip 131.108.100.0 0.0.0.255 131.108.200.0 0.0.0.255
```

R2's ACL is as follows:

```
access-list 100 permit ip 131.108.100.0 0.0.0.255 131.108.100.0 0.0.0.255
```

3 The **show crypto map** IOS command displays the remote peer address and the transform set. The previous displays are taken from R1 because the remote peer address is displayed as 131.108.255.2 (R2's serial 0/0 IP address).

4 Yes, because IPSec has nothing to do with routing IP data, IPSec will encrypt only data as configured. R1 has a remote entry to the network residing on R2 and R2 has a remote entry to the network residing on R1.

Here is a sample ping request from R2 to R1 and Host A and Host C:

```
R2>ping 131.108.100.1

Type escape sequence to abort.
Sending 5, 100-byte ICMP Echos to 131.108.100.1, timeout is 2 seconds:
!!!!!
Success rate is 100 percent (5/5), round-trip min/avg/max = 4/6/8 ms
R2>ping 131.108.101.1
Type escape sequence to abort.
Sending 5, 100-byte ICMP Echos to 131.108.101.1, timeout is 2 seconds:
!!!!!
Success rate is 100 percent (5/5), round-trip min/avg/max = 4/6/8 ms
R2>
R2>ping 131.108.100.5
Type escape sequence to abort.
Sending 5, 100-byte ICMP Echos to 131.108.100.5, timeout is 2 seconds:
!!!!!
Success rate is 100 percent (5/5), round-trip min/avg/max = 4/6/8 ms
R2>
R2>ping 131.108.101.5
Type escape sequence to abort.
Sending 5, 100-byte ICMP Echos to 131.108.105.1, timeout is 2 seconds:
!!!!!
Success rate is 100 percent (5/5), round-trip min/avg/max = 4/6/8 ms
```

5 Because the source network is located on R1, Access-list 100 on R1 needs to be modified, remembering that, by default, an implicit deny is defined on ACL 100. Network 131.108.101.0/24 is only permitted to encrypt traffic to the static ip address 131.108.200.5, hence the ACL line required on R1 becomes the following:

```
access-list 100 permit ip 131.108.100.0 0.0.0.255 131.108.200.0 0.0.0.255
access-list 100 permit ip 131.108.101.0 0.0.0.255 131.108.200.5 0.0.0.0
or:
access-list 100 permit ip 131.108.100.0 0.0.0.255 131.108.200.0 0.0.0.255
access-list 100 permit ip 131.108.101.0 0.0.0.255 host 131.108.200.5
On R2 the access-list becomes:
access-list 100 permit ip 131.108.200.0 0.0.0.255 131.108.101.0 0.0.0.255
access-list 100 permit ip 131.108.200.0 0.0.0.255 131.108.100.0 0.0.0.255
```

IP routing is already configured and working. IPSec will ensure only that IP data is encrypted.

Exam Topics in This Chapter

CHAPTER 6

Operating Systems and Cisco Security Applications

This chapter reviews two of today's most common end user applications, UNIX and Windows NT systems. Cisco security applications are also covered.

This chapter covers the following topics:

- **UNIX**—The UNIX operating system and some of the most widely used operating commands. The section looks at the files that are manipulated in UNIX to monitor and maintain usernames and passwords.

- **Microsoft NT Systems**—Windows NT 4.0 and some of the concepts used to manage users and domains.

- **Cisco Secure for Windows and UNIX**—Cisco Secure Access Control Server (ACS), the Cisco security application that is available on Windows and UNIX platforms.

- **NetSonar and NetRanger**—Cisco supported applications, NetSonar (Cisco Secure Scanner) and NetRanger (Cisco Secure Intrusion Detection System), to ensure that networks are secured and tested for vulnerabilities.

"Do I Know This Already?" Quiz

The purpose of this assessment quiz is to help you determine how to spend your limited study time. If you can answer most or all these questions, you might want to skim the "Foundation Topics" section and return to it later, as necessary. Review the "Foundation Summary" section and answer the questions at the end of the chapter to make sure that you have a strong grasp of the material covered. If you intend to read the entire chapter, you do not necessarily need to answer these questions now. If you find these assessment questions difficult, you should read through the entire "Foundation Topics" section and review it until you feel comfortable with your ability to answer all these and the "Q & A" questions at the end of the chapter.

Answers to these questions can be found in Appendix A, "Answers to Quiz Questions."

1 What UNIX command implements a trace route to the remote network www.guitar.com?

   a. **trace www.guitar.com** if DNS is enabled with the IOS **command dns server** *ip-address*.

   b. **traceroute www.guitar.com**

   c. **trace guitar.com**

   d. UNIX does not support the **traceroute** command.

2 What UNIX command copies a file?

   a. **copy**

   b. **cpy**

   c. **cp**

   d. **pc**

3 A Cisco router network manager wants to copy the configuration in RAM to a UNIX server. What needs to be accomplished before this can occur?

   a. Issue **copy run tftp**.

   b. Modify the .rhosts file.

   c. Modify the rcmd.allow file.

   d. Erase the .rhosts.allow file.

   e. Enable TFTP on the UNIX server.

4 Which of the following is not a UNIX file flag parameter?

   a. Execute

   b. Write

   c. Read

   d. Read/Write

   e. Authenticate

5 Which of the following is not a UNIX file type?

   a. Normal

   b. Directories

   c. Special

   d. Link

   e. Medium

6 NetBIOS over TCP/IP operates at what layer of the OSI model?

   a. 1

   b. 2

   c. 3

   d. 4

   e. 5

   f. 6

   g. 7

7 In Windows NT, what is a domain that is trusted by all remote domains called?

   a. Local

   b. Remote

   c. Single

   d. Global

   e. Master

   f. Slave

8 In Windows NT, what is a domain that is trusted automatically called?

   a. Local

   b. Remote

   c. Single

   d. Global

   e. Master

   f. Slave

9 Which of the following is not an NTFS permission type?

   a. R

   b. W

   c. D

   d. P

   e. O

   f. M

10 In Windows NT, when in a DOS command window, what command displays the local IP ARP entries?

a. **arp**

b. **rarp**

c. **rarp –b**

d. **arp –n**

e. **arp –a**

11 What devices can the Cisco Secure Policy Manager remotely manage? (Select the best three answers.)

a. Routers

b. Switches

c. NMS workstations

d. PIX Firewalls

12 NetRanger LAN interface supports all but which one of the following?

a. Ethernet

b. Fast Ethernet

c. Token Ring

d. Serial WAN interfaces

e. FDDI

13 Which of the following is not a component of the security wheel?

a. Develop

b. Secure

c. Monitor

d. Manage

e. Increase

14 Which of the following is false in regards to NetRanger?

a. NetRanger examines the IP header.

b. NetRanger examines the TCP header.

c. NetRanger examines the entire IP frame.

d. NetRanger monitors TCP or UDP port scans.

15 How many phases are completed with NetSonar?

    a. 1

    b. 2

    c. 3

    d. 4

    e. 5

    f. 6

Foundation Topics

UNIX

The UNIX operating system was developed in 1969 at Bell Laboratories. UNIX has continued to develop since its inception. AT&T, for example, released UNIX 4.0.

UNIX was designed to be a multiuser system (more than one user can connect to the host at one time), and it is used usually for multiuser systems and networks.

Because most engineers are more familiar with DOS (and Windows NT) than UNIX, this section presents some analogies to demonstrate the UNIX command structure.

The operating system DOS used in the early days is similar to UNIX in terms of architecture. For example, the command syntax to list the directories in DOS is **dir**, and in UNIX, it is **ls**.

Table 6-1 displays some of the common commands between UNIX and DOS.

Table 6-1 *DOS Versus UNIX Commands*

DOS/Windows NT Command	UNIX Command	Purpose
attrib +h/-h	All files starting with a dot (for example .hosts) are hidden automatically. The UNIX command **mv** renames a file. For example, **mv hosts .hosts** hides the file named hosts.	Either hides (**+h**) or uncovers (**-h**) files from directory lists when the command **dir** is used. The **attrib** command also displays the file attributes. In UNIX, the . (dot) automatically hides files.
cd *dirname*	**cd** *dirname*	Moves the user to a specific directory.
chkdsk	**Df**	Checks the disk for logical problems; only admin users can perform this command in UNIX. UNIX commands are case-sensitive.
copy/xcopy *dirname/filename*	**cp** *dirname/filename*	Allows you to copy files.
del/erase *filename*	**rm** *filename*	Erases files from the disk.
dir	**ls**	Lists the files in the current directory.
help *command name*	**man** *command name*	Displays information about the specified command.
rename *oldfilename newfilename*	**mv** *oldfilename newfilename*	Renames a file. In UNIX, it can also be used to move the file to a different directory.

Table 6-1   *DOS Versus UNIX Commands (Continued)*

DOS/Windows NT Command	UNIX Command	Purpose
ping *ip-address*	**ping** *ip-address*	Pings a local or remote host.
tracert	**traceroute**	Windows sends ICMP requests with varying time to live (TTL) values. UNIX sends UDP probes, varies the TTL values, and watches for any ICMP messages returned.

NOTE   The Windows DOS-based **attrib** command is a widely used command that modifies file attributes. In a Windows environment, the options include the following:

```
C:\ >help attrib
Displays or changes file attributes.
ATTRIB [+R ¦ -R] [+A ¦ -A ] [+S ¦ -S] [+H ¦ -H] [[drive:] [path] filename]
      [/S [/D]]
    +   Sets an attribute.
    -   Clears an attribute.
    R   Read-only file attribute.
    A   Archive file attribute.
    S   System file attribute.
    H   Hidden file attribute.
    /S  Processes matching files in the current folder
        and all subfolders.
    /D  Processes folders as well
```

The **attrib** command allows files to be read only, archived, made a system file, or hidden.

In UNIX, you use the **man** command for command syntax help:

```
Simonunixhost% man
Usage: man [-M path] [-T macro-package] [ section ] name ...
or: man -k keyword ...
or: man -f file ...
```

UNIX Command Structure

UNIX servers and hosts are managed using files. To manage the files, you need to be aware of the UNIX command structure.

A UNIX command contains three basic parts:

- Command
- Flags
- Arguments

Figure 6-1 displays the parts of a UNIX command.

Figure 6-1   *Three Parts of a UNIX Command*

Figure 6-1 displays the copy request command (**cp**). Notice that most UNIX commands are abbreviations of English words. For example, the copy command is defined by **cp**. The first part of any UNIX command tells the device to run a specific program or process, such as the copy function. The second part identifies any flags, which directly follow the UNIX process commands; dashes (-) identify flags. The flags in Figure 6-1 are defined as the **-i** flag, telling the UNIX host to confirm before it overwrites any files in this process, and the **-r** flag, telling the UNIX host to copy any files in subdirectories if you are copying directories.

Finally, the last part is the argument, which, in most cases, is the name of a file or directory. In Figure 6-1, for example, the old filename and the new filename must be specified.

Table 6-2 displays some common UNIX commands and their meanings.

Table 6-2   *Common UNIX Commands*

Command	Description	Example
cp -i/-r *oldfile newfile*	Makes a copy of a file. You must specify the name of the file to be copied and the name of the new file to be created. The **-i** flag tells the computer to ask before it overwrites any files in this process. The **-r** flag copies any files in subdirectories if you are copying directories.	**cp -i simon.doc henry.doc**
rm -i/-r *filename*	Erases the specified file. The **-i** flag asks you for confirmation before a file is deleted. The **-r** flag erases directories/subdirectories and all the files they might contain.	**rm -i cisco**

Table 6-2   *Common UNIX Commands (Continued)*

Command	Description	Example
rmdir -p *directoryname*	Erases directories. The **-p** flag allows you to erase a directory and all its contents. Without this flag, the directory must be empty before you erase it.	**rmdir –ptomII**
mv -i *filename1 filename2*	Renames a file. The **-i** flag asks for confirmation before overwriting a file if you attempt to use a filename that is already taken. Without the flag, the original file with the same name is automatically erased.	**mv 2002ccie 10000ccie**
mv -i *filename directoryname/filename*	Moves a file to another directory. The flag serves the same purpose as in the other **mv** command.	**mv index.html index1.html**
man *command*	Displays a description and usage instructions for a specified command. This command is similar to **help** in a Windows environment.	**man ls**
grep -i	Allows you to search for a string in files. The flag **–i** tells the UNIX server to ignore upper- or lowercase.	**grep -i myword *.txt** Searches for the keyword myword in all files that end in .txt.
netstat -s	Displays a description and usage instructions for a specified command. The **netstat -s** displays statistics for network interfaces and protocols, such as TCP.	**netstat -s**
ifconfig -a	Displays the current interfaces that are configured. Displays the IP address and subnet mask.	**ifconfig –a**

NOTE   All UNIX commands are in lowercase and are case-sensitive. For a free tutorial on UNIX, visit www.ee.surrey.ac.uk/Teaching/Unix/.

UNIX Permissions

UNIX allows certain users access to files and commands by setting permissions to ensure that only legitimate users are permitted access to files and directories.

To view information about each file, use the **-l** flag with the UNIX command **ls** (for example, **ls –l**). The command **ls –s** lists the current UNIX permissions. To display both the file permissions and file information, combine the flags –s and –l with the command **ls** (for example, **ls –sl** or **ls –ls**). Figure 6-2 displays a sample output for the command **ls -ls** for a UNIX host named Simon.

Figure 6-2 also displays a sample output of the command **ls -sl** and explains the meaning of this output.

Figure 6-2   **ls -sl** *Command Output*

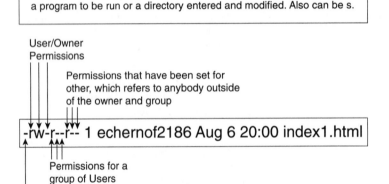

When a new file is created in UNIX, the default is to define read and write access to the owner. To set new or modify permissions, use the command **chmod** *flag filename*.

The **chmod** flag is always three numbers. The first number affects the owner permissions (U), the second number affects the group permissions (g), and the third number affects the other (o) permissions. Each number can be a number between 0 and 7; Table 6-3 displays the possible values for each flag.

Table 6-3   **chmod** *Flag Definitions*

Number	Value
0	No permissions
1	Execute only
2	Write only
3	Write and execute
4	Read only
5	Read and execute
6	Read and write
7	Read, write, and execute

NOTE   The network administrator is typically given the root password allowing configuration changes, program execution, and file management. For example, to connect a new hard drive, the installation engineer requires the root password. The administrator types in the root password first. After entering the root password, the administrator types the UNIX command **mount** to attach or detach a file system, also known as the super user.

UNIX File Systems

UNIX can consist of four main files types:

- **Normal files**—Contain user data
- **Directories**—Containers that hold files
- **Special files**—Input and output devices, such as a disk drive, printer, or CD-ROM
- **Links**—Pointers to another file

UNIX stores files and important information in directories. The following are some common examples (might vary according to the UNIX version):

- **/bin/**—Executable system utilities, such as **sh**, **cp**, and **rm**.
- **/etc/**—System configuration files and databases.

- **/lib/**—Operating system and programming libraries.
- **/tmp/**—System scratch files (all users can write here).
- **/lost+found/**—Where the file system checker puts detached files.
- **/usr/bin/**—Additional user commands.
- **/usr/include/**—Standard system header files.
- **/usr/lib/**—More programming and system call libraries.
- **/usr/local/**—Typically a place where local utilities go.
- **/usr/man**—The manual pages are kept here.

NOTE   Certain system files created by UNIX store important details about the operational characteristics, such as the password lists for all users.

The file named shadow in the /etc directory is a read only, protected file referenced by the program login.

The file named passwd contains the passwords for all users.

The file named wtmp contains an account of all users that logged into the UNIX host.

The file named lastlog contains details of when a user logged out of a UNIX host.

The file .rhosts contains information permitting remote devices, such as routers, the capability to TFTP or Remote Copy Protocol (RCP) files to a UNIX host.

Microsoft NT Systems

This section briefly covers Windows NT 4.0. Cisco Systems requires you to have no more than a conceptual overview on Windows NT systems, so the detail in the next section is only provided to give you the required foundations to pass the CCIE Security written exam.

Windows NT allows clients and servers to be grouped into domains or workgroups. A *domain* is typically a large group of devices under a common administration. A *workgroup* usually describes a smaller group of Windows devices or any logical collection of computers. A domain is managed by a primary domain controller (PDC), which is a Windows-based server that stores and controls security and user account information for an entire domain. Each domain must have at least one PDC. A backup domain controller (BDC) maintains a copy of the database in the event the PDC is unavailable.

NetBEUI was first developed by IBM in the mid 1980s to provide an interface for applications that were currently using Network Basic Input/Output System (NetBIOS).

Before routing became popular, NetBEUI was developed as a Layer 2 protocol that allowed devices, such as PCs, to communicate over a broadcast medium, such as Ethernet. NetBEUI was also designed for earlier versions of Windows (Windows 3.1 and MS-DOS-based clients).

NetBEUI is not routable and must be bridged when networks are not locally reachable. NetBEUI is still used today.

NetBIOS is a session layer protocol that allows communication between PCs in domains or workgroups.

NetBIOS provides the following functions:

- Authentication
- Connection management
- Error control
- File sharing
- Flow control
- Full-duplex transmissions
- Name resolution
- Print sharing
- Session management

NOTE   NetBIOS over IPX is called NWLink, and NetBIOS over TCP/IP is called NetBT.

Next, you learn how Windows devices can find network resources by browsing and using Windows name resolution.

Browsing and Windows Names Resolution

Network Neighborhood, Windows NT's browsing service, provides end users with a list of all devices available in their network. Before a user's PC can browse the network or Network Neighborhood, the Windows-based PC must register its name periodically by sending a broadcast to the master browser. The master browser contains a list of all devices available on the network. This service, called *browsing*, is supported by three methods—NetBEUI, NWLink, and NetBT. In addition to accessing the Network Neighborhood services, Windows devices require name resolution so that network names can be translated to protocol addresses, either IP or IPX.

Networking administrators have four options for name resolution, which are similar to the Domain Name System (DNS) provided by TCP/IP. These four name resolution options for Windows NT network administrators are as follows:

- **Broadcasts**—This method enables end stations to broadcast their names to a designated master browser (typically a Windows NT server). The master browser collects the names of available devices and maintains a list. The list is then sent to all devices that request it. This allows communication between servers and clients.

- **LMhosts file**—This simple method enables local PCs to maintain a static list of all Windows computers available in the network. The file typically contains the name and protocol addresses of all servers available in the domain. For large networks, the file might become too large and unusable, so a service called Windows Internet Naming Services (WINS) was developed (as described in the next entry).

- **Windows Internet Naming Services (WINS)**—This was developed so Windows network administrators could avoid dealing with a large amount of broadcasts or statically defined lists. WINS allows client PCs to dynamically register and request name resolution by a specific server running the WINS services. Instead of sending broadcasts, the client sends unicasts. WINS typically runs on a Windows NT server and has an IP address. Clients are statically or dynamically configured to use the server's IP address.

- **Dynamic Host Configuration Protocol (DHCP)**—In large networks (which contain thousands of PCs), a static IP address configuration can cause scalability issues because all devices in the network would require file modification. DHCP was developed to dynamically allocate IP addresses and many other parameters, such as subnet masks, gateways, and WINS server addresses. When you use DHCP, a Windows client sends out a broadcast for an IP address, and the DHCP server (a Windows NT server or compatible device) provides all the necessary TCP/IP information. The client then registers its names with the WINS server so browsing can take place. Cisco IOS routers can relay DHCP clients' requests (because Cisco IOS routers drop broadcast packets by default) with the **ip helper-address** *remote dhcp servers ip address* command.

NOTE   DHCP is an IP address assignment and management solution rather than a name resolution. The DHCP server pushes the WINS/DNS/Gateway addresses to the client making it easier for the client to resolve names.

Scaling Issues in Windows NT

In larger Windows NT environments, you can have many domains. Windows NT allows information sharing between domains with the use of trusted domains. A *trusted domain* grants or denies access to clients without having to manage each user individually. Each domain can exchange information and form a trust relationship. Based on these trust relationships, end users from each domain can be allowed or denied access. Creating trust relationships allows secure data to flow between different domains and ensures adequate security for data files and application files in any Windows-based network.

Windows NT supports several domain models, including the following:

- **Single domain**—Used in small networks.
- **Global domain**—Automatically trusts every domain.
- **Master domain**—Trusted by all remote domains but does not trust the remote domains.
- **Multiple master domains**—Used in large networks where the master domain is trusted by other master domains, which in turn trust smaller domains.

Login and Permissions

NT users must log in to the domain. Pressing Control-Alt-Delete together displays the login utility.

After a valid username and password pair are entered, the verification process starts by comparing the username/password pair with the data stored in the Security Accounts Manager (SAM), which is stored on the NT server in the form of a database.

This database also contains a list of privileges for each user. For example, the database might contain the following permissions:

- User_1 is permitted access to group Cisco_Icon.
- User_2 is permitted access to group APAC.
- Directory d:\data has read and write access to both groups Cisco_Icon and APAC.
- The Word documents stored in d:\data\word are owned by group APAC only.
- The Excel documents stored in d:\data\excel are owned by group APAC, and read access is granted to all other users.

When a user or client attempts to access objects shared by other users in the domain, permissions are used to authorize or deny services.

The Windows NT file system is called New Technology File System (NTFS). NTFS is a naming file system that allows extra security. Earlier versions of Windows, such as 95, did not support NTFS and do not support file permissions.

The following are six NTFS permissions:

- **R**—Read only. The data or object can only be viewed.
- **W**—Write access. The data can be changed.
- **X**—Execute. The data can be executed. (For example, a directory can be viewed or a program can be executed.)

- **D**—Delete. The data can be deleted.
- **P**—Change Permissions. The data access permissions can be altered.
- **O**—Take Ownership. The ownership can be altered.

The NTFS permissions can also be combined for certain files and directories. For example, RX (read/execute) allows a client to view and execute the data.

NOTE   Computers running DOS/Windows 3.X, 95, 98, or ME/Windows NT with FAT partition do not provide any file permissions. They can provide only share-level permission. (Remote users can be permitted or denied access.) File permissions for local users can be implemented only in an NTFS file system.

Windows NT Users and Groups

The following is an explanation of the groups:

- **Global Groups**—A global group contains only individual user accounts (no groups) from the domain in which it is created. It can be added to a local group. After created, a global group can be assigned permissions and rights, either in its own domain or in any trusting domain. Global groups are available only on Windows NT Server domains. Domain Admins and Domain Users are two built-in groups.

- **Local Groups**—Local groups are created on a Windows NT Server or Workstation computer and are available only on that computer. A local group can contain user accounts or global groups from one or more domains. They cannot contain other local groups. Backup Operator and Guests are examples of built-in local groups.

The permissions for a user of multiple groups will be additive of all permissions except for NO PERMISSION, which overrides all other permissions.

Windows NT Domain Trust

Setting up trust among multiple NT domains allows the users of one domain to use resources from another domain. The trusting domain trusts the trusted domain to manage users, groups, and resources. The trusting domain contains the resources that validated users need to access. Trust relationships aren't transitive. In other words, if the A domain trusts B, and B trusts C, A doesn't necessarily trust C. A domain's administrator must explicitly grant a trust to another domain to establish a trust relationship. Trust is one way; if A trusts B, B does not necessarily trust A.

Common Windows DOS Commands

The following are some of the most widely used DOS operating commands in Windows environments along with sample displays:

- **ipconfig**—Displays IP address and subnet mask:

```
C:\>ipconfig
Ethernet adapter Local Area Connection:

        Connection-specific DNS Suffix  . : cisco.com
        IP Address. . . . . . . . . . . : 150.100.1.253
        Subnet Mask . . . . . . . . . . : 255.255.255.0
        Default Gateway . . . . . . . . : 150.100.1.240
```

- **ipconfig /all**—Displays more detailed information about TCP/IP configurations, such as DNS and domain names:

```
C:\>ipconfig /all

Windows 2000 IP Configuration

        Host Name . . . . . . . . . . . : c03298157693425
        Primary DNS Suffix  . . . . . . : cisco.com
        Node Type . . . . . . . . . . . : Hybrid
        IP Routing Enabled. . . . . . . : No
        WINS Proxy Enabled. . . . . . . : No
        DNS Suffix Search List. . . . . : cisco.com

Ethernet adapter Local Area Connection:

        Connection-specific DNS Suffix  . : cisco.com
        Description . . . . . . . . . . : 3Com 10/100 Mini PCI Ethernet Adaptr
        Physical Address. . . . . . . . : 00-00-86-48-7B-35
        DHCP Enabled. . . . . . . . . . : No
        IP Address. . . . . . . . . . . : 150.100.1.253
        Subnet Mask . . . . . . . . . . : 255.255.255.0
        Default Gateway . . . . . . . . : 150.100.1.240
        DNS Servers . . . . . . . . . . : 64.104.200.116
                                          171.68.10.70
        Primary WINS Server . . . . . . : 64.104.193.200
```

- **arp –a**—Displays ARP entries on the local machine:

```
C:\>arp  -a

Interface: 150.100.1.253 on Interface 0x1000003
  Internet Address      Physical Address      Type
  150.100.1.240         00-60-09-c4-34-17     dynamic
  150.100.1.254         00-b0-64-46-a8-40     dynamic
```

- **hostname**—Displays the local host name:

```
C:\>hostname
c03298157693425
```

- **nbtstat**—Displays the NetBIOS over TCP/IP statistics. A number of options are displayed:

```
C:\>nbtstat

Displays protocol statistics and current TCP/IP connections using NBT
(NetBIOS over TCP/IP).
```

```
NBTSTAT [ [-a RemoteName] [-A IP address] [-c] [-n]
        [-r] [-R] [-RR] [-s] [-S] [interval] ]

  -a   (adapter status) Lists the remote machine's name table given its name
  -A   (Adapter status) Lists the remote machine's name table given its
                        IP address.
  -c   (cache)          Lists NBT's cache of remote [machine] names and their
                        IP addresses
  -n   (names)          Lists local NetBIOS names.
  -r   (resolved)       Lists names resolved by broadcast and via WINS
  -R   (Reload)         Purges and reloads the remote cache name table
  -S   (Sessions)       Lists sessions table with the destination IP addresses
  -s   (sessions)       Lists sessions table converting destination IP
                        addresses to computer NETBIOS names.
  -RR  (ReleaseRefresh) Sends Name Release packets to WINs and then starts
                        Refresh

  RemoteName   Remote host machine name.
  IP address   Dotted decimal representation of the IP address.
  interval     Redisplays selected statistics, pausing interval seconds
               between each display. Press Ctrl+C to stop redisplaying
               statistics.
```

- **ping**—Provides a means to test and verify remote locations. An example ping to www.cisco.com follows:

```
C:\>ping www.cisco.com
Pinging www.cisco.com [198.133.219.25] with 32 bytes of data:
Reply from 198.133.219.25: bytes=32 time=182ms TTL=248
Reply from 198.133.219.25: bytes=32 time=180ms TTL=248
Reply from 198.133.219.25: bytes=32 time=180ms TTL=248
Reply from 198.133.219.25: bytes=32 time=181ms TTL=248
Ping statistics for 198.133.219.25:
    Packets: Sent = 4, Received = 4, Lost = 0 (0% loss),
Approximate round trip times in milli-seconds:
    Minimum = 180ms, Maximum = 182ms, Average = 180ms
C:\>
```

- **tracert**—Provides a method to list next hop addresses for remote networks. The following is a sample Windows output when **tracert** routing to the URL www.smh.com.au:

```
C:\>tracert www.smh.com.au
Tracing route to smh.com.au [203.26.51.42]
over a maximum of 30 hops:
  1   <1 ms    <1 ms    <1 ms  c6k-bbn1-vlan105.cisco.com [64.105.208.2]
  2   <1 ms    <1 ms    <1 ms  c6k-bbn1-msfc-v161.cisco.com [10.66.2.2]
  3   <1 ms    <1 ms    <1 ms  sydneycisco-wall-1-f0-1.cisco.com [10.166.128.15]
  4   41 ms   236 ms    <1 ms  telstra-gw.cisco.com [103.141.98.141]
  5    1 ms     1 ms    <1 ms  FastEthernet6-1-0.chw12.Sydney.telstra.net
[149.130.85.3]
  6    1 ms     1 ms     1 ms  FastEthernet1-0-0.ken4.Sydney.telstra.net
[203.50.19.14]
```

- **route**—Provides a method to define static routing entries (Windows NT supports RIP and 2000 supports OSPF). The following example adds a static route for the network 150.100.100.0/24 via the next hop address 131.108.1.1:

```
c:\>route add 150.100.100.0 mask 255.255.255.0 131.108.1.1
```

- **nslookup**—Provides a DNS query for any host names. The following displays the use of **nslookup** for the host name www.cisco.com:

```
C:\>nslookup www.cisco.com
Server:  dns-sydney.cisco.com
Address:  64.104.200.248

Name:    www.cisco.com
Address:  198.133.219.25
```

Cisco Secure for Windows and UNIX

Cisco Systems has developed a number of scalable security software products to help protect and ensure a secured network in relation to Cisco products.

Cisco Secure Access Control Server (ACS), commonly referred to as Cisco Secure, provides additional network security when managing IP networks designed with Cisco devices.

Cisco Secure can run on Windows NT/2000 and UNIX platforms.

Three versions of Cisco Secure are listed here:

- **Cisco Secure ACS for NT**—This powerful ACS application for NT servers runs both TACACS+ and RADIUS. It can use NT username/password database or Cisco Secure ACS database.

- **Cisco Secure ACS for UNIX**—This powerful ACS application for UNIX includes support for TACACS+ and RADIUS. It supports SQL applications such as Oracle and Sybase.

- **Cisco Secure Global Roaming Server**—This performs TACACS+ and RADIUS proxy functions. It is a standalone server for large ISP networks.

NOTE	Cisco also has a UNIX-based freeware TACACS+ server available for download.

NOTE	Cisco Secure topics are tested in the CCIE Security lab exam (particularly Cisco Secure for Windows 2000 server). The written exam does not require you to have a detailed understanding of this application.

The main features of Cisco Secure ACS include the following:

- Supports centralization of AAA access for all users, including routers and firewalls
- Can manage Telnet access to routers and switches

- Can support an unlimited number of network access servers
- Supports many different Cisco platforms, including PIX access servers and routers

Figure 6-3 displays a typical centralized Cisco Secure ACS performing functions such as user authentication, authorization, and accounting.

Figure 6-3   *Cisco Secure Example*

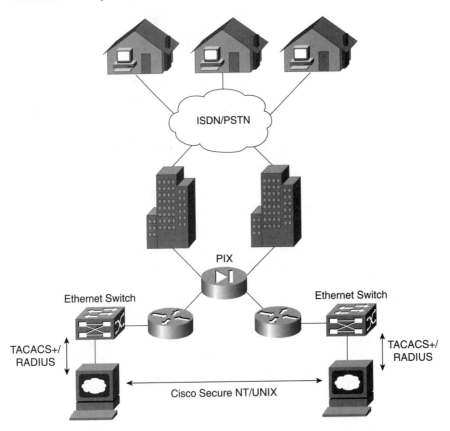

Figure 6-3 displays a typical application where ISDN/PSTN users are authenticated by RADIUS or TACACS+ via the Cisco Secure ACS server.

In addition to simultaneous support for RADIUS/TACACS+, Cisco Secure also supports the following AAA features:

- TACACS+ support for the following:
  - Access lists
  - Privilege level support
  - Time restrictions where access to network is controlled during the day and night

- RADIUS support for the following:
  - Cisco RADIUS AV pairs
  - IETF support (RADIUS is a defined standard)
- Others include the following:
  - Support for virtual private networking
  - The ability to disable accounts after a set number of failed attempts

Further description of the Cisco ACS application and screenshots are shown in the sample CCIE Security lab in Chapter 9, "CCIE Security Self-Study Lab."

Cisco Secure Policy Manager

Cisco Secure Policy Manager (CSPM) provides a scalable and comprehensive security management system for Cisco Secure PIX Firewalls and Cisco Secure Integrated Systems.

Cisco Secure Policy Manager, formerly known as the Cisco Security Manager, is a policy-based security management system for Cisco security technologies and network devices.

Policy-based management allows a network administrator to define a set of high-level rules that control the deployment of and access to services, such as FTP and HTTP.

CSPM enables the management of remote Cisco Secure PIX and IOS Firewalls. CSPM allows you to configure and edit configurations remotely. CSPM only runs over Microsoft Windows operating systems.

NOTE	Cisco PIX Firewalls running version 6.2 and above have a built-in, Java-based PIX Device Manager (PDM). PDM allows browser-based management and configuration of PIX Firewalls.

Cisco Secure Intrusion Detection System and Cisco Secure Scanner

This section covers network security tools that are useful for managing network security. Cisco Secure Intrusion Detection System (IDS), formerly known as NetRanger, and Cisco Secure Scanner, formerly known as NetSonar, are two security applications that allow network monitoring.

NOTE	The CCIE Security written exam still refers to the terms NetRanger and NetSonar, so this guide refers to NetRanger and NetSonar as well.

NetRanger (Cisco Secure Intrusion Detection System)

NetRanger is an enterprise intrusion detection system designed to detect, report, and, in the event of unauthorized access, terminate data sessions between users and host devices.

NetRanger is an application designed to detect unauthorized access. Users are not aware that NetRanger is watching data across the network; it is transparent to all systems.

NetRanger has two components:

- **NetRanger Sensor**—High-speed device that analyzes the contents of data being transported across a network and determines whether that traffic is authorized or unauthorized. Unauthorized traffic includes ping requests from intruders. Traffic detected from unauthorized sources is sent directly to the NetRanger Director, and the intruder is removed from the network (optional setting to remove host).

- **NetRanger Director**—Provides real-time response to intruders in the network by blocking access to the network and terminating any active data sessions. The Director collects the real-time information from the Sensor.

Figure 6-4 displays the typical network placement of NetRanger products.

NetRanger Sensors can be located anywhere in the network. They are typically located close to hosts or entry points to a network, such as dial-in users or Internet connections. Alarms are logged on the Sensor and Director. The alarms are displayed or viewed on the Director. Optional configuration settings include killing an active TCP session or reconfiguring access lists (termed shunning).

The sensor can detect the intruder's IP address and destination ports, and buffer up to 256 characters entered by the illegal devices. NetRanger supports Ethernet (10/100), Token Ring, and FDDI LAN interfaces. NetRanger Sensors can modify predefined access lists on Cisco IOS routers and change the definitions of permitted networks in response to an attack. NetRanger Sensors cannot modify the IP routing table nor reload or shutdown interfaces. When illegal activity is discovered, an alarm is sent directly to configured directors, including multiple directors. The software used on the sensors can be loaded from a central director, allowing easier software upgrades. The GUI interface on the Director also allows network monitoring from one central location, ensuring that one central group within an organization can be directly responsible for monitoring and acting on alarms. GUI interfaces and colored alarms indicate possible vulnerabilities.

Figure 6-4   *Typical NetRanger Design*

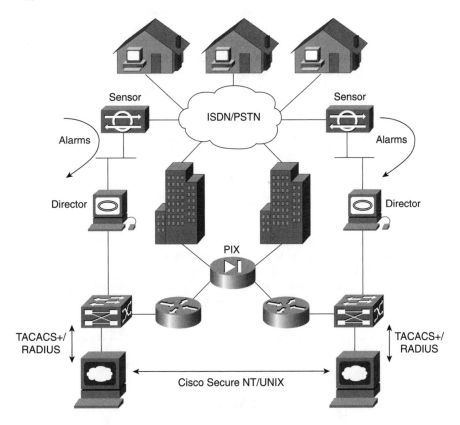

The following platforms support NetRanger Sensor applications:

- IBM PC Pentium II or higher with the following specifications:
    - 32 MB RAM
    - At least 2 GB hard drive
    - Ethernet, Token Ring, or FDDI
    - Windows-based software
- Ultra Sparc Based UNIX station with the following specifications:
    - 167 MHz Clone or higher
    - 64 MB RAM
    - 2 GB hard drive
    - Ethernet or FDDI
    - Solaris version 2.6 or higher software; and HP OpenView installed prior to loading NetRanger software

NetRanger Director can send out an alarm when certain configuration changes are made on Cisco routers, can send e-mail messages when particular alarm levels are reached, and can ensure a TCP attack is thwarted by sending TCP reset segments to unauthorized sources. When a NetRanger Sensor communicates with the Director, if the network is down, up to 255 alternate route paths can be attempted. Packets can be buffered and sent when the network is restored and communications occur (there are no keepalive communications; rather, one device sends and the other waits and listens) to ensure that alarms are sent.

The following platforms support NetRanger Director applications:

- HP UNIX, Ultra UNIX workstations (not PC-based)
- Software: Solaris 2.6, HP UNIX
- 128 MB RAM, CD-ROM drive, 4 GB of hard disk space
- Example machines include Sun Ultra 170 and HP 725

NOTE NetRanger examines only the IP or TCP header and not actual data. Intruders usually use an attack based on large ICMP traffic, typically fragmented, to discover the behavior of routers in a network. When a router that is set for a particular MTU size receives a fragmented packet, it sends all fragments to the destination, assuming that the end device can reassemble the packet. Intruders typically also use context-based attacks by scanning TCP or UDP ports in use.

For more details on how Cisco IOS supports NetRanger, visit

www.cisco.com/univercd/cc/td/doc/product/iaabu/csids/csids3/index.htm

NetSonar (Cisco Secure Scanner)

NetSonar is a Cisco Systems-developed product, now named Cisco Secure Scanner. NetSonar is a software tool designed to investigate vulnerable systems within a network and report the vulnerabilities to the network administrator.

NetSonar scans the network to uncover systems that might be vulnerable to security threats by performing a number of predefined steps:

- **Network mapping**—NetSonar compiles an electronic inventory of all host devices on the network.
- **Security assessment**—NetSonar identifies potential security holes by probing and confirming vulnerabilities in the network.

- **Reports**—NetSonar communicates results to the administrator detailing the assessment, such as detailing what operating systems are in use, what the host addresses are, and the associated vulnerabilities.
- **Network security database**—This database lists the critical problems and organizes them by operating system, system services, and device types.

Figure 6-5 displays the process completed by NetSonar.

Figure 6-5 *NetSonar Phase Functions*

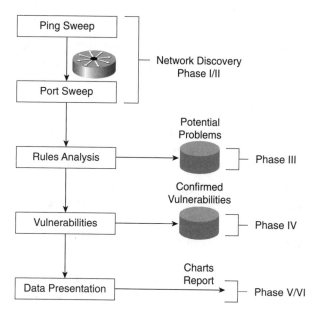

Figure 6-5 displays the six phases completed by NetSonar:

Phase I—NetSonar sends out ICMP echo requests (pings) to query hosts.

Phase II—All live hosts are collected and stored on particular port numbers.

Phase III—NetSonar identifies the hardware devices that might be vulnerable, such as routers, switches, firewalls, printers, desktops, and hosts that responded to ping requests. Operating systems and network services are documented and labeled as potential vulnerabilities.

Phase IV—Vulnerabilities are confirmed. This phase is intrusive.

Phase V—The data is charted for presentation. The data can also be charted graphically as line or 3D bar graphs.

Phase VI—The data is reported in a number of different formats, including a summary report, a short and detailed report, or a full technical report.

NetSonar software has the following hardware requirements:

- Intel Pentium I or higher
- 64 MB RAM
- 2 GB hard drive
- TCP/IP software or Sun Sparc Solaris with version 2.5 and higher

Any HTTP browser can be used to manage the NetSonar server, which can be located anywhere in the IP network.

Cisco Systems details more security products at the following URLs:

> www.cisco.com/en/US/netsol/ns110/ns129/net_solution_home.html
> www.cisco.com/univercd/cc/td/doc/product/vpn/ciscosec/index.htm

Cisco Security Wheel

Cisco defines a *Security Wheel* concept that outlines the critical steps to ensuring that data and networks are secured correctly. The Security Wheel revolves around a strong, well-defined corporate policy. The Security Wheel consists of the following:

- **Secure**—After defining a strong corporate policy, you should secure your network by deploying the products necessary in the appropriate places to achieve your corporate security goals.
- **Monitor and respond**—Continuously monitor using NetRanger tools at strategic points in the network to discover new vulnerabilities.
- **Test**—On a regular and formal basis, test all network components.
- **Manage and improve**—Analyze all the reports and metrics supplied by NetSonar and continue to cycle through the Security Wheel by going through all these steps continuously.

Figure 6-6 displays the Cisco Security Wheel graphically.

Figure 6-6 *Cisco Security Wheel*

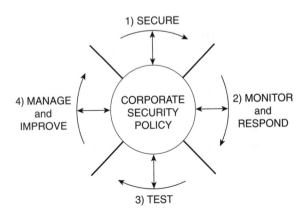

Foundation Summary

The Foundation Summary is a condensed collection of material for a convenient review of key concepts in this chapter. If you are already comfortable with the topics in this chapter and decided to skip most of the "Foundation Topics" material, the "Foundation Summary" section can help you recall a few details. If you just read the "Foundation Topics" section, this review should help further solidify some key facts. If you are doing your final preparation before the exam, the "Foundation Summary" section offers a convenient way to do a quick final review.

Table 6-4 summarizes important UNIX commands.

Table 6-4   *UNIX Commands*

Command	Description
cp -i/-r *oldfile newfile*	Makes a copy of a file. You must specify the name of the file to be copied and the name of the new file to be created.
	The **-i** flag tells the computer to ask before it overwrites any files in this process.
	The **-r** flag copies any files in subdirectories if you are copying directories.
rm -i/-r *filename*	Erases the specified file.
	The **-i** flag asks you for confirmation before a file is deleted.
	The **-r** flag erases directories or subdirectories and all the files they contain.
rmdir -p *directoryname*	Erases directories.
	The **-p** flag allows you to erase a directory and all its contents. Without this flag, the directory must be empty before you can erase it.
mv -i *filename1 filename2*	Renames a file.
	The **-i** flag asks for confirmation before overwriting a file if you attempt to use a filename that is already taken. Without the flag, the original file with the same name will be automatically erased.
mv -i *filename directoryname/ filename*	Moves a file to another directory. The flag serves the same purpose as in the other **mv** command.
man *command*	Displays a description and usage instructions for a specified command. This command is similar to **help** in a Windows environment.

continues

Table 6-4   *UNIX Commands (Continued)*

Command	Description
grep -i	Allows you to search for a string in files. The flag **–i** tells the UNIX server to ignore upper- or lowercase.
netstat -s	Displays a description and usage instructions for a specified command. The **netstat -s** displays statistics for network interfaces and protocols, such as TCP.
ifconfig -a	Displays the current interfaces that are configured (displays the IP address and subnet mask).

Table 6-5 summarizes the main Windows DOS commands.

Table 6-5   *DOS Commands*

Command	Meaning
ping	Provides a means to test and verify remote locations.
nslookup	Provides a DNS query for any host names.
route	Provides a method to define static routing entries (Windows NT supports RIP and 2000 supports OSPF).
tracert	Provides a method to list next hop addresses for remote networks.

Table 6-6 Summarizes NetRanger's two components.

Table 6-6   *NetRanger Components*

Component	Meaning
NetRanger Sensor	High-speed device that analyzes the contents of data being transported across a network and determines whether that traffic is authorized or unauthorized. Unauthorized traffic includes ping requests from intruders.
NetRanger Director	Provides real-time response to intruders in the network by blocking access to the network and terminating any active data sessions. The director collects the real-time information from the sensor.

Table 6-7 defines the NetSonar Phase functions.

Table 6-7   *NetSonar Phase Functions*

Phase Number	Function
I	Sends ICMP echo requests (ping) to query hosts.
II	Collects and stores all live hosts on particular port numbers.
III	Identifies the hardware devices that might be vulnerable, such as routers, switches, firewalls, printers, desktops, and hosts that responded to ping requests.

Table 6-7   *NetSonar Phase Functions (Continued)*

Phase Number	Function
IV	Confirms vulnerabilities. This phase is intrusive.
V	Charts data for presentation. The data can also be charted graphically as line or three-dimensional bar graphs.
VI	Reports data in a number of different formats, including a summary report, a short and detailed report, or a full technical report.

Table 6-8 displays the Cisco Security Wheel model and functions.

Table 6-8   *Cisco Security Wheel*

Cisco Security Wheel	Meaning
Secure	After defining a strong corporate policy, you should secure your network by deploying the products necessary in the appropriate places to achieve your corporate security goals.
Monitor and respond	Continuously monitor using NetRanger tools at strategic points in the network to discover new vulnerabilities.
Test	On a regular and formal basis, test all network components.
Manage and improve	Analyze all the reports and metrics supplied by NetSonar and cycle through the Security Wheel by going through all these steps continuously.

Q & A

The Q & A questions are designed to help you assess your readiness for the topics covered on the CCIE Security written exam and those topics presented in this chapter. This format is intended to help you assess your retention of the material. A strong understanding of the answers to these questions can help you on the CCIE Security written exam. You can also look over the questions at the beginning of the chapter again for additional review. As an additional study aid, use the CD-ROM provided with this book to take simulated exams, which draw from a database of over 300 multiple-choice questions—all different from those presented in the book.

Select the best answer. Answers to these questions can be found in Appendix A, "Answers to Quiz Questions."

1 What UNIX command displays the files in the current directory?

_____

_____

_____

2 What UNIX command changes a directory from etc/ to bin/?

_____

_____

_____

3 What does the following UNIX command accomplish?

```
cp -i simon.doc henry.doc
```

_____

_____

_____

4 To define a permission for a UNIX file, what command line interface is required?

_____

_____

_____

5 The **chmod** UNIX command can define what levels of access or permissions on a UNIX host?

_____

_____

_____

6 In a Windows NT environment, what is a domain, primary domain controller, and backup domain controller?

_____

_____

_____

7 What functions does the protocol NetBIOS provide in a Window NT environment?

_____

_____

_____

8 What is the function of the lmhosts file on a Windows platform device?

_____

_____

_____

9 Name and define the six NTFS permission types.

_____

_____

_____

10 In Windows NT 4.0, what DOS command displays any local ARP entries?

_____

_____

_____

11 Define the terms NetRanger Sensor and Director and their uses?

_____

_____

_____

12 What LAN interfaces can be supported on a NetRanger Sensor?

_____

_____

_____

13 What are the six phases completed by Cisco NetSonar?

_____

_____

_____

14 What is the meaning of the term Security Wheel?

_____

_____

_____

Scenarios

Scenario 6-1: NT File Permissions

A group of users in a Windows NT environment are members of the domain CISCO_CCIE. You are supplied the following details regarding file permissions:

- PC1 and PC2 are authenticated in domain CISCO.

- The CISCO domain is trusted by the CISCO_CCIE domain.

- The directory d:\data has a file named ccielab35.doc and has access for users in the CISCO domain set to read only access.

- A user named hbenjamin in the CISCO domain owns the Word document ccielab3.doc.

With these details, can PC1 open and read the file named ccielab35.doc?

Scenario 6-2: UNIX File Permissions

A newly created program file is on a UNIX server in the etc/bin named simon.exe directory. The root user creates the file simon.exe after compiling some UNIX C-based code. The root user password is set to guitar. How can you allow all users who are authenticated and authorized to view the etc/bin directory access to the file named simon.exe?

Scenario Answers

Scenario 6-1 Solution

The CISCO domain is part of the large domain CISCO_CCIE. Because the directory d:\data is set to read only, users from the CISCO domain are permitted to open the document in read-only mode. User hbenjamin is permitted to open and write to the document because Windows NT sets the privilege for the owner as read/write by default.

Scenario 6-2 Solution

If the users know the root password, they can enter the root mode by typing **root** and then the password **guitar**. This allows the user access. If the root password is not known, the file permissions can be modified with the command **chmod 777 simon.exe**, and because users can already view the directory etc/bin, access to the file named simon.exe is now permitted.

Exam Topics in This Chapter

CHAPTER 7

Security Technologies

This chapter covers some of today's most widely used technologies that enable Network administrators to ensure that sensitive data is secured from unauthorized sources.

Cisco's support for security is also covered, as are all the fundamental foundation topics you will need to master the security CCIE written exam.

This chapter covers the following topics:

- **Advanced security concepts**—This section covers some the of the advanced security policies in demilitarized zones (DMZs).

- **Packet filtering, proxies, NAT, and PAT**—This section covers some packet filtering, proxies, and how to hide addresses using Network Address Translation (NAT) and Port Address Translation (PAT).

- **Cisco Firewall routers and IOS feature set**—This section covers the Cisco PIX Firewall and the IOS Firewall feature set available on Cisco routers.

- **Public Key infrastructure (PKI)**—This section covers the Public Key infrastructure (PKI), followed by a description of VPN networks and a typical design example.

"Do I Know This Already?" Quiz

The purpose of this assessment quiz is to help you determine how to spend your limited study time. If you can answer most or all these questions, you might want to skim the "Foundation Topics" section and return to it later, as necessary. Review the "Foundation Summary" section and answer the questions at the end of the chapter to ensure that you have a strong grasp of the material covered. If you already intend to read the entire chapter, you do not necessarily need to answer these questions now. If you find these assessment questions difficult, read through the entire "Foundation Topics" section and review it until you feel comfortable with your ability to answer all these and the Q & A questions at the end of the chapter.

Answers to these questions can be found in Appendix A, "Answers to Quiz Questions."

1 DMZ stands for what?

    a. Demilitarized zone

    b. Demitted zone

    c. Domain main zone

    d. Domain name

2 When defining an extended access list, what TCP port numbers can you use?

    a. Only predefined Cisco keywords

    b. 0 to –65,000

    c. 0 to –65,535

    d. 1 to 65,534

    e. None of the above

3 When defining an extended access list, what UDP port numbers can you use?

    a. Only predefined Cisco keywords

    b. 0 to 65000

    c. 0 to 65535

    d. 1 to 65534

    e. None of the above

4 Which of the following is *not* a TCP service?

    a. who

    b. whois

    c. finger

    d. ftp

    e. pop3

5 Which of the following is *not* a UDP service?

    a. BGP

    b. echo

    c. domain

    d. discard

    e. rip

    f. snmp

6 For how many translations does PAT allow you to use one IP address?

   a. 32,000

   b. 64,000

   c. 96,000

   d. 128,000

   e. 256,000

7 PAT translates all private addresses based on what?

   a. Source port

   b. Destination port

   c. Both source and destination

   d. None

8 NAT is which of the following?

   a. Network Architectural Language

   b. National anthem of Latvia

   c. Network translation

   d. Network Address Translation

9 NAT is defined in which RFC?

   a. 1700

   b. 1701

   c. 2002

   d. 1631

   e. 1613

10 The following defines which NAT terminology: "A legitimate registered IP address as assigned by the InterNIC?"

   a. Inside local address

   b. Outside global address

   c. Inside global address

   d. Outside local address

11 What IOS command defines a pool of addresses that will be translated to a registered IP address?

   a. **ip nat inside**

   b. **ip nat outside**

   c. **ip nat pool**

   d. **ip nat inside pool**

   e. **ip nat outside pool**

12 PIX stands for what?

   a. Protocol interchange

   b. Cisco Private Internet

   c. Private Internet Exchange

   d. Public Internet Exchange

13 To define how a PIX will route IP data, what is the correct syntax for a PIX 520?

   a. **ip route**

   b. **route**

   c. **ip route enable**

   d. **default-network**

14 What is the alias command's function on a PIX Firewall?

   a. To define a local host name

   b. To define the DNS server

   c. Used in NAT environments where one IP address is translated into another

   d. Only applicable to Cisco IOS

15 CBAC stands for what?

   a. CBAC is not a valid term

   b. Cisco Business architectural centre

   c. Context-based Access Control

   d. Context-based Accelerated controller

   e. Content-based arch. Centre

16 What is IKE used to accomplish?

   a. NAT translations

   b. Ensures that data is not sourced by the right sources

   c. Ensures that data is not sourced by the wrong sources

   d. No use

   e. Both a and c

17 To create a simple VPN tunnel (unencrypted) between two sites, what must you do on a Cisco router?

   a. Create a GRE tunnel

   b. Create a routing map

   c. Nothing, use a PIX

   d. Create an IPSec tunnel

Foundation Topics

Advanced Security Concepts

A wealth of security concepts have been covered and now some of the techniques used in areas of your network will be covered that are vulnerable to attacks, in particular, the Demilitarized Zone (DMZ).

The DMZ is defined as an isolated part of the network that is easily accessible to hosts outside of the network, such as the Internet.

Figure 7-1 displays a typical network design where a DMZ is defined with a number of bastion hosts (first line of defense or hosts that can be scarified in case of a network attack or attacks).

Figure 7-1 *DMZ Design*

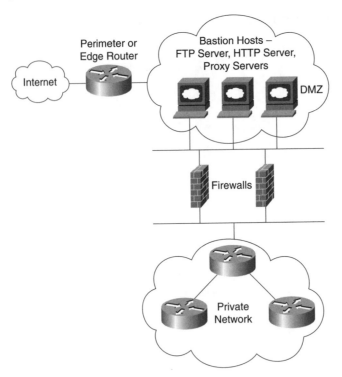

Figure 7-1 displays a typical perimeter network where the DMZ is separated by a firewall. *Firewalls* are network devices such as Private Internet Exchange (PIX), which are discussed later in this chapter. Firewalls are designed to protect the internal (or private) parts of a network from the public domain.

The aim of all firewalls is to accomplish the following:

- **Serve as a traffic point**—The traffic from inside and outside the network must pass through the traffic point.

- **Authorize traffic**—Permits only authorized traffic.

- **Designed to be immune from penetration**—Firewalls are designed to be immune from attacks. Firewalls are still often devices that are attacked by outside hosts.

- **Invisibility**—Ensures that the private network is invisible to the outside world.

As shown in Figure 7-1, the perimeter router sits between the DMZ and the public domain. Typically, a high performance router or routers will be located here, performing a number of duties including the following:

- Ensuring that access to the Internet Protocol (IP) is restricted using access lists

- Restricting Transmission Control Protocol (TCP) services

- Preventing attacks on firewall systems

- Preventing Denial of Service (DoS) attacks on bastion hosts and the private network

- Permitting only authorized traffic to the bastion hosts

- Logging all network events to external or internal systems

- Performing Address translation (NAT/PAT)

- Running static or dynamic routing protocols; Cisco PIX is limited to RIP and static routing.

NOTE   Proxy servers are designed to shield internal devices from outside intruders by replacing the internal hosts' IP addresses with its own IP address. Most new vendors now allow routers to act as proxy servers. Proxy servers have scalability and speed issues, as all packets must be examined and IP headers modified for packet delivery.

Firewalls and perimeter routers have the additional function of packet filtering. A *packet filter* is a device that inspects all incoming and outgoing packets based on IP source address, destination IP address, and protocol type, such as TCP or UDP. Based on configurable options, the filter decides whether to reject or allow traffic to pass through the device.

Table 7-1 summarizes the main functions of a perimeter and firewall router.

Table 7-1   *Perimeter/Firewall Router Functions*

Protection Service	Method
Sniffer or snooping capabilities	Control eavesdropping with the TCP/IP service and network layer encryption (IPSec).
Control unauthorized access	Use authentication, authorization, accounting (AAA), and Cisco Secure. Also, access-list filtering and PIX Firewall.
Controlling session replay	Control what TCP/IP sessions are authorized. Block SNMP, IP source routing, and finger services to outside hosts.
Controlling inbound connections	Filter internal address as the source from the outside world. Filter all private addresses. Filter Bootp, Trivial File Transfer Protocol (TFTP), and trace route commands. Allow TCP connections established from the inside network. Permit inbound traffic to DMZ only.
Controlling outbound connections	Allow only valid IP addresses to the outside world and filter remaining illegal addresses.
Packet filtering	Use predefined access lists that control the transmission of packets from any given interface, controlling Virtual Terminal lines, VTY, and access, and ensuring that routing updates are authenticated.

Cisco IOS routers can filter TCP or UDP protocol types. Example 7-1 displays the number of TCP services you can filter on a Cisco IOS router using extended access lists.

Example 7-1   *TCP Services Filtered on Cisco IOS Routers*

```
R1(config)#access-list 100 permit tcp any any eq ?
  <0-65535>    Port number
  bgp          Border Gateway Protocol (179)
  chargen      Character generator (19)
  cmd          Remote commands (rcmd, 514)
  daytime      Daytime (13)
  discard      Discard (9)
  domain       Domain Name Service (53)
  echo         Echo (7)
  exec         Exec (rsh, 512)
  finger       Finger (79)
  ftp          File Transfer Protocol (21)
  ftp-data     FTP data connections (used infrequently, 20)
  gopher       Gopher (70)
  hostname     NIC hostname server (101)
  ident        Ident Protocol (113)
  irc          Internet Relay Chat (194)
  klogin       Kerberos login (543)
  kshell       Kerberos shell (544)
```

Example 7-1 *TCP Services Filtered on Cisco IOS Routers (Continued)*

```
login          Login (rlogin, 513)
lpd            Printer service (515)
nntp           Network News Transport Protocol (119)
pim-auto-rp    PIM Auto-RP (496)
pop2           Post Office Protocol v2 (109)
pop3           Post Office Protocol v3 (110)
smtp           Simple Mail Transport Protocol (25)
sunrpc         Sun Remote Procedure Call (111)
syslog         Syslog (514)
tacacs         TAC Access Control System (49)
talk           Talk (517)
telnet         Telnet (23)
time           Time (37)
uucp           Unix-to-Unix Copy Program (540)
whois          Nicname (43)
www            World Wide Web (HTTP, 80)
```

Example 7-2 displays the extended access list when filtering services based on the UDP protocol suite of services.

Example 7-2 *UDP Services Filtered on Cisco IOS Routers*

```
R1(config)#access-list 101 permit udp any any eq ?
  <0-65535>     Port number
  biff          Biff (mail notification, comsat, 512)
  bootpc        Bootstrap Protocol (BOOTP) client (68)
  bootps        Bootstrap Protocol (BOOTP) server (67)
  discard       Discard (9)
  dnsix         DNSIX security protocol auditing (195)
  domain        Domain Name Service (DNS, 53)
  echo          Echo (7)
  isakmp        Internet Security Association and Key Management Protocol (500)
  mobile-ip     Mobile IP registration (434)
  nameserver    IEN116 name service (obsolete, 42)
  netbios-dgm   NetBios datagram service (138)
  netbios-ns    NetBios name service (137)
  netbios-ss    NetBios session service (139)
  ntp           Network Time Protocol (123)
  pim-auto-rp   PIM Auto-RP (496)
  rip           Routing Information Protocol (router, in.routed, 520)
  snmp          Simple Network Management Protocol (161)
  snmptrap      SNMP Traps (162)
  sunrpc        Sun Remote Procedure Call (111)
  syslog        System Logger (514)
  tacacs        TAC Access Control System (49)
  talk          Talk (517)
  tftp          Trivial File Transfer Protocol (69)
  time          Time (37)
  who           Who service (rwho, 513)
  xdmcp         X Display Manager Control Protocol (177)
```

Examples 7-1 and 7-2 clearly allow a network administrator flexibility when designing perimeter security based on particular port numbers, as defined in RFC 1700.

Network Address Translation and Port Address Translation

NAT is a router function, which allows it to translate the addresses of hosts behind a firewall. This also helps to overcome IP address shortage. It also provides security by hiding the entire network and their real IP addresses.

NAT is typically used for internal IP networks that have unregistered (not globally unique) IP addresses. NAT translates these unregistered addresses into legal addresses on the outside (public) network.

PAT provides additional address expansion but is less flexible than NAT. With PAT, one IP address can be used for up to 64,000 hosts by mapping several IP port numbers to one IP address. PAT is secure because the inside hosts' source IP addresses are hidden from the outside world. The perimeter router typically provides the NAT or PAT function.

NAT is defined in RFC 1631, www.ietf.org/rfc/rfc1631.txt. Cisco devices started supporting NAT in IOS versions 11.2 and higher. NAT basically provides the capability to retain your network's original IP addressing scheme while translating that scheme into a valid Internet IP address to ensure that intruders never view your private address.

NOTE	IOS 12.0 and higher support full NAT functionality in all images. Version 11.2 and higher need "PLUS" image for a NAT feature set.

NAT changes the Layer 3 address when the packet is sent out to the Internet. This is a function no other protocol will do (that is, alter the Layer 3 source address).

For your review to fully prepare you for the exam, Table 7-2 explains some of the terminology used in a NAT environment.

Table 7-2   *NAT Terminology*

Term	Meaning
Inside local address	An IP address that is assigned to a host on the internal network; that is, the logical address that is not being advertised to the Internet. A local administrator generally assigns this address. This address is NOT a legitimate Internet address.
Inside global address	A legitimate registered IP address, as assigned by the InterNIC.
Outside local address	The IP address of a network's outside host that is being translated as it appears to the inside network.
Outside global address	The IP address assigned to a host on the outside of the network that is being translated by the host's owner.

Figure 7-2 displays a typical scenario where a private address space is deployed that requires Internet access. The Class A 10.0.0.0/8 is not routable in the Internet.

Figure 7-2   *Typical NAT Scenario*

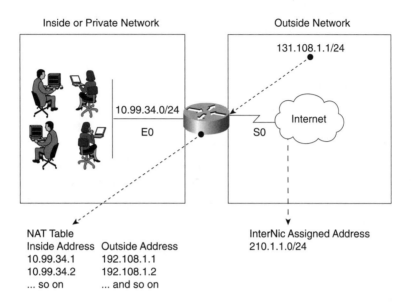

The users in Figure 7-2 are configured with the inside local addresses ranging from 10.99.34.1/24 to 10.99.34.254/24. To allow Internet access, NAT (PAT could also be configured if only one IP address was allocated by InterNIC) is configured on Router R1 to permit the inside local addresses access to the Internet. Advantages of using NAT include the following:

- You can hide the Class A address space 10.99.34.0/24

  To view the NAT translation table on the Cisco router, apply the exec command **show ip nat translations** on the CLI interface.

- It gives you the capability to connect a nonroutable network to the Internet.

- You can use unregistered address space and NAT to the Internet.

- You can use both NAT/PAT on the same router.

- You can have 64,000 inside hosts per allocated IP address.

The InterNic is an Internet authority assigned the task of allocating IP address space to the public. In Figure 7-2, assume that the InterNIC assigned the address space 210.1.1.1/24 for use.

NOTE   Disadvantages of NAT/PAT include the following:

- CPU processing power.

- Layer 3 header and source address changes.

- Voice over IP is not supported yet.

- Some Multimedia-intensive applications do not support NAT, especially when the data stream inbound is different from the outbound path (for example, in multicast environments).

NAT Operation on Cisco Routers

When a packet leaves the inside network, NAT translates the inside address to a unique InterNIC address for use on the outside network, as shown in Figure 7-2.

The R1 router in Figure 7-2 will be configured for an address translation and will maintain a NAT table. When an IP packet returns from the outside network, the NAT router will then perform an address translation from the valid InterNIC address to the original local inside address.

Dynamic NAT Configuration Task List

Look at the steps required to configure Dynamic NAT on a Cisco router. Dynamic NAT maps any unregistered IP addresses to a registered IP address from a group of registered IP addresses.

The basic configuration tasks are as follows:

1 Determine the network addresses to be translated.

2 Configure the inside network with the following IOS command:

```
ip nat inside
```

3 Configure the outside network with the following IOS command:

```
ip nat outside
```

4 Define a pool of addresses to be translated with the following IOS command:

ip nat pool *<pool-name>* *<start ip address> <end ip address> <mask>*

5 Define the addresses that are allowed to access the Internet with the following IOS command:

ip nat inside source list *<access list number>* **pool** *<pool name>*

For a more specific illustration, configure NAT on Router R1. In Figure 7-2, the NAT pool name is going to be CCIE. (You can use any name you want.) Assume that the InterNIC has assigned you the Class C address of 210.1.1.0/2424.

Your Internet service provider (ISP) has also supplied you the unique address 131.108.1.1/30 to use on your serial connection.

Example 7-3 provides a sample NAT configuration for this setup.

Example 7-3 *Sample NAT Configuration on R1*

```
hostname R1
ip nat pool CCIE 210.1.1.1 210.1.1.254 netmask 255.255.255.0
ip nat inside source 1 pool CCIE
interface ethernet0
ip address 10.99.34.1 255.255.255.0
ip nat inside
interface serial 0
ip address 131.108.1.1 255.255.255.252
ip address 210.1.1.1 255.255.255.0 secondary
ip nat outside
access-list 1 permit 10.99.34.0 0.0.0.255
```

It is assumed that you have an IP routing protocol to advertise the IP networks shown in the sample, which are 131.108.1.0/30 and 210.1.1.0/24, to the remote ISP router through R1's Serial 0 interface.

The configuration shown in Example 7-3 translates the inside addresses 10.99.34.0/24 into globally unique addresses ranging from 210.1.1.1/24 to 210.1.1.254.

Monitoring NAT Operations with **show** Commands

To monitor the operation of NAT, you can use the following commands:

```
show ip nat translation [verbose]
show ip nat statistics
```

The **show ip nat translation** command displays the current active transactions. The **show ip nat statistics** command displays NAT statistics, such as how many translations are currently taking place.

There are four different versions of NAT translations:

- **Static NAT**—Maps an unregistered IP address to a registered IP address on a one-to-one basis. This is particularly useful when a device needs to be accessible from outside the network to an internal unregistered address.

- **Dynamic NAT**—Maps an unregistered IP address to a registered IP address from a group of registered IP addresses.

- **Overloading**—A form of dynamic NAT that maps multiple, unregistered IP addresses to a single registered IP address by using different ports.

- **Overlapping**—When the IP addresses used on your internal network are registered IP addresses in use on another network, the router must maintain a lookup table of these addresses so that it can intercept them and replace them with registered unique IP addresses.

For more quality examples on NAT, visit the following URL:

- www.cisco.com/warp/customer/556/index.shtml

- www.cisco.com/warp/customer/707/overload_private.shtml demonstrates when you can NAT over an IPSec tunnel. The following URLs give examples of when you can use NAT over an IPSec tunnel:

    www.cisco.com/warp/public/556/index.shtml

    www.cisco.com/warp/public/707/overload_private.shtml

NOTE   TCP load distribution is typically used in large IP networks that have server farms. You might want to distribute the network load across many servers but advise users to use only one IP address to target. TCP load distribution ensures that all servers are equally loaded.

Cisco Private Internet Exchange (PIX)

Cisco Private Internet Exchange (PIX) and Cisco IOS feature sets are designed to further enhance a network's security. The Private Internet Exchange (PIX) Firewall prevents unauthorized connections between two or more networks. The latest versions of Cisco code for the PIX Firewall also perform many advanced security features, such as AAA services, access lists, VPN Configuration (IPSec), FTP logging, and Cisco IOS-like interface commands. In addition, the PIX Firewall can support multiple outside or perimeter networks in the DMZs.

NOTE   When reading Cisco documentation about PIX Firewalls, realize that inside networks and outside networks both refer to networks to which the PIX is connected.

For example, inside networks are protected by the PIX, but outside networks are considered the "bad guys." Consider them as trusted and untrusted, respectively.

A PIX Firewall permits a connection-based security policy. For example, you might allow Telnet sessions from inside your network to be initiated from within your network but not allow them to be initiated into your network from outside your network.

The PIX Firewall's popularity stems from the fact that it is solely dedicated to security. A router is still required to connect to WANs, such as the Internet. Some companies use PIX Firewalls for internal use only where they might have sensitive networks, such as a payroll or human resources department.

Figure 7-3 shows a typical network scenario where a PIX Firewall is implemented between an inside network and an outside network.

Figure 7-3   *PIX Location*

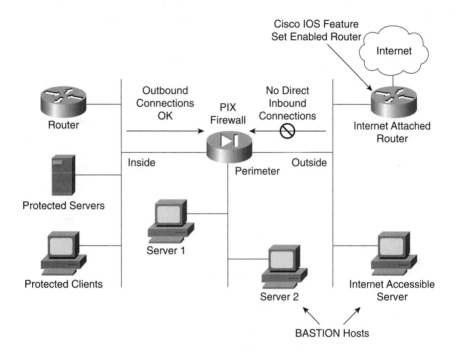

Although optional, it is recommended that you install the Cisco IOS Firewall software on the router directly connected to the Internet. The Cisco IOS Firewall feature is discussed later in this chapter.

Each connection through a PIX Firewall requires memory. You can support up to 32,768 connections with 16 MB of RAM installed on a PIX; 32 MB of memory can support up to 65,536 connections and support up to 260,000 connections with 128 MB.

NOTE   Demilitarized zones (DMZs) usually exist as part of a network that the Internet community or general public can access, such as a Web, FTP, or SMTP servers. For example, FTP servers allow external users access to public files, such as Cisco IOS Software, which are available online at ftp.cisco.com. Your remaining servers are protected by the firewall.

The PIX Firewall logic is engineered around the Adaptive Security Algorithm (ASA). Every inbound packet is checked against the ASA and against connection state information in memory. This stateful approach to security is regarded in the industry as being far more secure than a stateless packet-screening approach.

Examples of the stateful approach to security include the following:

- No packets can traverse the PIX Firewall without a connection and state.

- Outbound connections or states are allowed, except those specifically denied by access control lists. An outbound connection is one where the originator, or client, is on a higher security interface than the receiver, or server. The highest security interface is always the inside interface (value 100), and the lowest is the outside interface (value 0). Any perimeter interfaces can have security levels between the inside and outside values (for example, 50).

- Inbound connections or states are denied, except those specifically allowed. An inbound connection or state is one where the originator, or client, is on a lower security interface/ network than the receiver, or server. You can apply multiple exceptions to a single xlate (translation). This lets you permit access from an arbitrary machine, network, or any host on the Internet to the host defined by the xlate.

- All Internet Control Message Protocol (ICMP) packets are denied unless specifically permitted.

- All attempts to circumvent the previous rules are dropped and a message is sent to syslog.

When an outbound packet arrives at a PIX Firewall higher-security-level interface (security levels can be viewed with the **show nameif** command; by default, the outside interface has a security level set to 100, or untrusted, and the inside interface is set to 0, or trusted), the PIX Firewall checks to see if the packet is valid based on the ASA, and whether or not previous packets have come from that host. If not, the packet is for a new connection, and the PIX Firewall creates a translation slot in its state table for the connection. The information that the PIX Firewall stores in the translation slot includes the inside IP address and a globally unique IP address assigned by NAT, PAT, or Identity (which uses the inside address as the outside address). The PIX Firewall then changes the packet's source IP address to the globally unique address, modifies the checksum and other fields as required, and forwards the packet to the lower-security-level interface.

When an inbound packet arrives at an external interface such as the outside interface, it must first pass the PIX Firewall Adaptive Security criteria. If the packet passes the security tests, the PIX Firewall removes the destination IP address, and the internal IP address is inserted in its place. The packet is forwarded to the protected interface.

NOTE   The PIX Firewall supports NAT, which provides a globally unique address for each inside host, and PAT, which shares a single globally unique address for up to 64 K, simultaneously accessing inside hosts. The following is a list of current models that Cisco supports:

- PIX 501

- PIX 506/506E

- PIX 515/515E

- PIX 520

- PIX 525

- PIX 535

For a full feature list of the PIX, visit the following:

www.cisco.com/univercd/cc/td/doc/product/iaabu/pix/pix_v51/config/intro.htm#xtocid0

Figure 7-4 displays the PIX 520, which is used in the current CCIE Security lab exam. PIX Firewall devices are based on the Intel Pentium process, which is basically a PC with Cisco-installed PIX software.

Figure 7-4   *Cisco PIX 520*

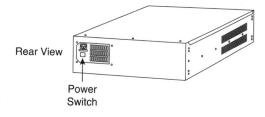

Rear View

Power
Switch

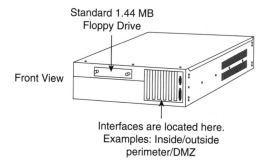

Standard 1.44 MB
Floppy Drive

Front View

Interfaces are located here.
Examples: Inside/outside
perimeter/DMZ

Configuring a PIX

Take a look at configuring the PIX software and the six basic commands used to configure a PIX Firewall.

Figure 7-5 *Typical PIX Logical Setup*

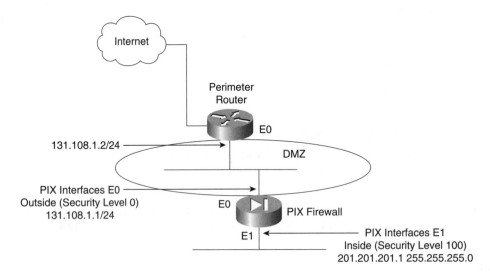

Figure 7-5 displays a typical DMZ and perimeter network between the inside (protected) and outside (public) networks.

PIX Firewall Configuration Task List

The following steps show you how the PIX software is configured for the scenario in Figure 7-5:

Step 1   Name the inside and outside interfaces.

Step 2   Name interfaces and assign the security levels. (Configuration mode):

```
nameif hardware_id if_name security_level
```

The **nameif** command lets you assign a name to an interface. You can use this command to assign interface names if you have more than two network interface circuit boards in your PIX Firewall. The first two interfaces have the default names **inside** and **outside**. The **inside** interface has default security level 100, and the **outside** interface has default security level 0.

Table 7-3 describes the PIX command **nameif** as documented on the Cisco documentation CD.

Table 7-3   **nameif** *Command and Required Fields*

Syntax	Description
hardware_id	The hardware name for the network interface that specifies the interface's slot location on the PIX Firewall motherboard. Interface boards are numbered from the leftmost slot nearest the power supply as slot 0. The internal network interface must be in slot 1. The lowest security_level external interface board is in slot 0, and the next lowest security_level external interface board is in slot 2.
	Possible choices are **Ethernet** for Ethernet or **Token-ring** for Token Ring. The internal interface is **ethernet1**. These names can be abbreviated with any leading characters in the name; for example, **ether1**, **e2**, **token0**, or **t0**.
if_name	A name for the internal or external network interface of up to 48 characters in length. This name can be uppercase or lowercase. By default, the PIX Firewall names the inside interface **inside**, the outside interface **outside**, and any perimeter interface **intfn**, where n is 2 through 5.
security_level	Either **0** for the outside network or **100** for the inside network. Perimeter interfaces can use any number between **1** and **99**. By default, the PIX Firewall sets the security level for the inside interface to **security100**, and the outside interface to **security0**. The first perimeter interface is initially set to **security10**, the second to **security15**, the third to **security20**, and the fourth perimeter interface to **security25** (a total of 6 interfaces are permitted, with a total of 4 perimeter interfaces permitted).

Step 3   Identify the hardware interfaces, speed, and duplex type installed with the following interface command:

```
interface hardware_id [hardware_speed] [shutdown]
```

In Figure 7-5, the following commands are configured:

```
interface ethernet0 10full
interface ethernet1 10full
```

Table 7-4 defines and describes the options for the **interface** command, as documented on the Cisco documentation CD.

Table 7-4 **interface** *Command Options*

Option	Description
hardware_id	Identifies the network interface type. Possible values are **ethernet0**, **ethernet1** to **ethernet***n*, **gb-ethernet***n*, **fddi0** or **fddi1**, **token-ring0**, and **token-ring1** to **token-ring***n*, depending on how many network interfaces are in the firewall.
hardware_speed	Network interface speed (optional). Do not specify a *hardware_speed* for a Fiber Distributed Data Interface (FDDI) interface.
	Possible Ethernet values are as follows:
	10baset—Set for 10 Mbps Ethernet half-duplex communication.
	10full—Set for 10 Mbps Ethernet full-duplex communication.
	100basetx—Set for 100 Mbps Ethernet half-duplex communication.
	100full—Set for 100 Mbps Ethernet full-duplex communication.
	1000sxfull—Set for 1000 Mbps Gigabit Ethernet full-duplex operation.
	1000basesx—Set for 1000 Mbps Gigabit Ethernet half-duplex operation.
	1000auto—Set for 1000 Mbps Gigabit Ethernet to auto-negotiate full or half duplex.
	Aui—Set 10 for Mbps Ethernet half-duplex communication with an AUI cable interface.
	Auto—Set Ethernet speed automatically. The **auto** keyword can be used only with the Intel 10/100 automatic speed sensing network interface card, which shipped with the PIX Firewall units manufactured after November 1996.
	Bnc—Set for 10 Mbps Ethernet half-duplex communication with a BNC cable interface.
	Possible Token Ring values are as follows:
	4mbps—4 Mbps data transfer speed. You can specify this as **4**.
	16mbps—(Default) 16 Mbps data transfer speed. You can specify this as **16**.
shutdown	Disables an interface.

Step 4 Define the inside and outside IP addresses.

The **ip address** *if_name ip_address* [*netmask*] command lets you assign an IP address to each interface.

Use the **show ip** command to view which addresses are assigned to the network interfaces.

In Figure 7-5, the IP address assignment is defined as follows:

```
ip address inside 201.201.201.1 255.255.255.0
ip address outside 131.108.1.1 255.255.255.0
```

Table 7-5 defines the options and meaning of the **interface** command.

Table 7-5   **interface** *Command*

Option	Description
if_name	The internal or external interface name designated by the **nameif** command
ip_address	PIX Firewall unit's network interface IP address
netmask	Network mask of *ip_address*

Step 5   Define the NAT with the **nat** command.

The **nat** command lets you enable or disable address translation for one or more internal addresses. Address translation means that when a host starts an outbound connection, the IP addresses in the internal network are translated into global addresses. NAT lets your network have any IP addressing scheme, and the firewall protects these addresses from visibility on the external network.

The command syntax is as follows:

```
nat [(if_name)] nat_id local_ip [netmask [max_conns [em_limit]]] [norandomseq]
```

In Figure 7-5, the following pool is assigned to the PIX:

```
nat  (inside) 1 0.0.0.0 0.0.0.0
```

This command enables all inside hosts to access the Internet.

Table 7-6 defines the options of the **nat** command, as documented on the Cisco documentation CD.

Table 7-6   **nat** *Command Options*

Option	Description
if_name	Any internal network interface name.
nat_id	The *nat_id* is an arbitrary positive number between 0 and 2 billion. Specify **0** with IP addresses and netmasks to identify internal networks that desire only outbound identity address translation. Use **0** with the **access-list** option to specify traffic that should be exempt from NAT. The access list should already be defined, otherwise PIX gives an error message.
access-list	Associate an **access-list** command statement to the **nat 0** command.
local_ip	Internal network IP address to be translated. You can use **0.0.0.0** to allow all hosts to start outbound connections. The **0.0.0.0** *local_ip* can be abbreviated as **0**.
netmask	Network mask for *local_ip*. You can use **0.0.0.0** to allow all outbound connections to translate using IP addresses from the global pool.

continues

Table 7-6   **nat** *Command Options (Continued)*

Option	Description
max_conns	The maximum TCP connections permitted from the interface you specify.
em_limit	The embryonic connection limit. The default is 0, which means unlimited connections. Set it lower for slower systems and higher for faster systems.
Norandomseq	Do not randomize the TCP packet's sequence number. Only use this option if another inline firewall is also randomizing sequence numbers and the result is scrambling the data. Use of this option opens a security hole in the PIX Firewall.

Step 6   Define the global pool.

The **global** command defines a pool of global addresses. The global addresses in the pool provide an IP address for each outbound connection, and for those inbound connections resulting from outbound connections.

If the **nat** command is used, you must also use the global command. Basically, when an outbound IP packet is sent from the inside network, the PIX will extract the source address and compare that address to the list of current NAT translations. If there is no entry, a new entry is created. If a NAT translation entry already exists, the packet is forwarded.

The PIX syntax for the global command is defined as follows:

```
global [if_name] nat_id global_ip [-global_ip] [netmask global_mask]
```

In Figure 7-5, the pool of address is defined as follows:

```
global (outside) 1 192.192.1.2-192.192.1.30 netmask 255.255.255.224
```

The pool of addresses is typically assigned to you by the InterNIC or your ISP.

Table 7-7 defines the options of the **global** command, as documented on the Cisco documentation CD.

Table 7-7   **global** *Command Options*

Option	Description
if_name	The external network where you use these global addresses.
nat_id	A positive number shared with the **nat** command that groups the **nat** and **global** command statements together. The valid ID numbers can be any positive number up to 2,147,483,647.
global_ip	One or more global IP addresses that the PIX Firewall shares among its connections.
	If the external network is connected to the Internet, each global IP address must be registered with the Network Information Center (NIC). You can specify a range of IP addresses by separating the addresses with a dash (-).

Table 7-7   **global** *Command Options (Continued)*

Option	Description
global_ip (*Continued*)	You can create a PAT **global** command statement by specifying a single IP address. You can have one PAT **global** command statement per interface. A PAT can support up to 65,535 xlate objects.
netmask	Reserved word that prefaces the network global_mask variable.
global_mask	The network mask for global_ip. If subnetting is in effect, use the subnet mask; for example, 255.255.255.128. If you specify an address range that overlaps subnets, **global** will not use the broadcast or network addresses in the pool of global addresses. For example, if you use 255.255.255.224 and an address range of 209.165.201.1 to 209.165.201.30, the 209.165.201.31 broadcast address and the 209.165.201.0 network address will not be included in the pool of global addresses.

Step 7   Finally, define how to route IP data with the route command.

Use the route command to enter a default or static route for an interface. The PIX syntax is as follows:

```
route if_name ip_address netmask gateway_ip [metric]
```

Configuring Static Routing on a PIX Firewall

Figure 7-5 defines all routes via the perimeter router as follows:

```
route outside 0.0.0.0 0.0.0.0 131.108.1.2
```

Table 7-8 defines the options of the **route** command, as documented on the Cisco documentation CD.

Table 7-8   **route** *Command Options*

Option	Description
if_name	The internal or external network interface name.
ip_address	The internal or external network IP address. Use **0.0.0.0** to specify a default route. You can abbreviate the **0.0.0.0** IP address as **0**.
netmask	Specify a network mask to apply to ip_address. Use **0.0.0.0** to specify a default route. The **0.0.0.0** netmask can be abbreviated as **0**.
gateway_ip	Specify the gateway router's IP address (the next hop-address for this route).
metric	Specify the number of hops to gateway_ip. In Figure 7-5, this is 1.

Example 7-4 displays the full working configuration of the PIX in Figure 7-5. The highlighted portions of this display are configuration commands we have entered, and the nonhighlighted portions are default configurations. One of the advantages of the PIX Firewall, like the Catalysts

Ethernet switch, is that you can view the full working and default configuration, unlike Cisco
IOS routers where the default configuration is not displayed.

Example 7-4 *PIX Full Working Configuration*

```
pix# write terminal
 nameif ethernet0 outside security0
 nameif ethernet1 inside security100
hostname pixfirewall
 fixup protocol ftp 21
 fixup protocol http 80
 fixup protocol smtp 25
 fixup protocol h323 1720
 fixup protocol rsh 514
 fixup protocol sqlnet 1521
 names
 name 1.1.1.1 abcd
 name 1.1.1.2 a123456789
 name 1.1.1.3 a123456789123456
 pager lines 24
 logging timestamp
 no logging standby
 logging console debugging
 no logging monitor
 logging buffered debugging
 no logging trap
 logging facility 20
 logging queue 512
 interface ethernet0 10full
 interface ethernet1 10full
 mtu outside 1500
 mtu inside 1500
ip address inside 201.201.201.1 255.255.255.0
ip address outside 131.108.1.1 255.255.255.0
 no failover
 failover timeout 0:00:00
 failover ip address outside 0.0.0.0
 failover ip address inside 0.0.0.0
 arp timeout 14400
global (outside) 1 192.192.1.2-192.192.1.30 netmask 255.255.255.0
nat  (inside) 1 0.0.0.0 0.0.0.0
 no rip outside passive
 no rip outside default
 no rip inside passive
 no rip inside default
 route outside 0.0.0.0 0.0.0.0 131.108.1.2 1
 timeout xlate 3:00:00 conn 1:00:00 half-closed 0:10:00 udp 0:02:00
 timeout rpc 0:10:00 h323 0:05:00
 timeout uauth 0:00:00 absolute
 no snmp-server location
```

Example 7-4   *PIX Full Working Configuration (Continued)*

```
no snmp-server contact
snmp-server community public
no snmp-server enable traps
telnet timeout 5
terminal width 80
: end
```

Miscellaneous PIX Firewall Commands   Three other important commands that are commonly used in PIX configurations are the **static**, **conduit**, and **alias** commands.

The **static** command creates a permanent mapping (Cisco documentation names or calls this a translation slot or xlate) between a local IP address and a global IP address. Use the **static** and **conduit** commands when you are accessing an interface of a higher security level from an interface of a lower security level; for example, when accessing the inside from the outside interface.

The command syntax is as follows:

```
static [(internal_if_name, external_if_name)] global_ip local_ip [netmask network_mask]
[max_conns [em_limit]] [norandomseq]
```

Table 7-9 defines the options of the **route** command, as documented on the Cisco documentation CD.

Table 7-9   **route** *Command Options*

Option	Description
internal_if_name	The internal network interface name. The higher-security-level interface you are accessing.
external_if_name	The external network interface name. The lower-security-level interface you are accessing.
global_ip	A global IP address. This address cannot be a PAT IP address. The IP address on the lower-security-level interface you are accessing.
local_ip	The local IP address from the inside network. The IP address on the higher-security-level interface you are accessing.
netmask	Reserve word required before specifying the network mask.
network_mask	The network mask pertains to both global_ip and local_ip. For host addresses, always use 255.255.255.255. For network addresses, use the appropriate class mask or subnet mask; for example, for Class A networks, use 255.0.0.0. An example subnet mask is 255.255.255.224.

continues

Table 7-9 route *Command Options (Continued)*

Option	Description
max_conns	The maximum number of connections permitted through the static connection at the same time.
em_limit	The embryonic connection limit. An embryonic connection is one that has started but not yet completed. Set this limit to prevent attack by a flood of embryonic connections. The default is 0, which means unlimited connections.
norandomseq	Do not randomize the TCP/IP packet's sequence number. Use only this option if another inline firewall is also randomizing sequence numbers and the result is scrambling the data. Use of this option opens a security hole in the PIX Firewall.

An example of the command is as follows:

```
static (inside,outside) 192.192.1.33  201.201.201.10
```

The **static** command should be used in conjunction with either **conduit** or **access-list.**

A **conduit** command statement creates an exception to the PIX Firewall Adaptive Security mechanism by permitting connections from one firewall network interface to access hosts on another.

The **clear conduit** command removes all conduit command statements from your configuration.

The command syntax is defined as follows:

```
conduit {permit I deny} protocol global_ip global_mask [operator port [port]]
    foreign_ip foreign_mask [operator port [port]]
```

Table 7-10 displays the options and command syntax for the **conduit** command, as documented on the Cisco documentation CD.

Table 7-10 conduit *Command Options*

Option	Description
permit	Permits access if the conditions are matched.
deny	Denies access if the conditions are matched.
protocol	Specifies the transport protocol for the connection. Possible literal values are **icmp**, **tcp**, **udp**, or an integer in the range 0 through 255, representing an IP protocol number. Use **ip** to specify all transport protocols.
global_ip	A global IP address previously defined by a **global** or static command. You can use **any** if the *global_ip* and *global_mask* are 0.0.0.0 0.0.0.0. The **any** option applies the **permit** or **deny** parameters to the global addresses.

Table 7-10   **conduit** *Command Options (Continued)*

Option	Description
global_mask	Network mask of *global_ip*. The *global_mask* is a 32-bit, four-part dotted decimal, such as 255.255.255.255. Use 0s in a part to indicate bit positions to be ignored. Use subnetting, if required. If you use 0 for *global_ip*, use 0 for the *global_mask*; otherwise, enter the *global_mask* appropriate to *global_ip*.
foreign_ip	An external IP address (host or network) that can access the *global_ip*. You can specify 0.0.0.0 or 0 for any host. If both the *foreign_ip* and *foreign_mask* are 0.0.0.0 0.0.0.0, you can use the shorthand **any** option.
foreign_mask	Network mask of *foreign_ip*. The *foreign_mask* is a 32-bit, four-part dotted decimal, such as 255.255.255.255. Use 0s in a part to indicate bit positions to be ignored. Use subnetting, if required.
operator	A comparison operand that lets you specify a port or a port range. Use without an operator and port to indicate all ports. For example, **conduit permit tcp any any**. By default, all ports are denied until explicitly permitted.
port	Service(s) you permit to be used while accessing *global_ip or foreign_ip*. Specify services by the port that handles them, such as smtp for port 25, www for port 80, and so on. You can specify ports by either a literal name or a number in the range of 0 to 65535. You can specify all ports by not specifying a port value (for example: **conduit deny tcp any any**).
icmp_type	The type of ICMP message.

The **alias** command translates one address into another. The **alias** command is used when nonregistered addresses have been used in a private network and access is required to the registered address space in the Internet. Consider the following example: the inside network contains the IP subnet address 64.236.16.0/24. Assume this belongs to the website on www.cnn.com.

When inside clients try to access www.cnn.com, the packets do not go to the firewall because the client thinks 64.236.16.0/24 is on the local inside network. To correct this, a net **alias** is created as follows with the **alias** command:

```
alias (inside) 64.236.16.0 131.108.2.0 255.255.255.0
```

When the inside network client 64.236.16.0 connects to www.cnn.com, the DNS response from an external DNS server to the internal client's query would be altered by the PIX Firewall to be 131.108.1.1-254/24.

Advanced Cisco PIX Commands

Table 7-11 summarizes some of the other useful features on a Cisco PIX Firewall, as documented on the Cisco Documentation CD.

Table 7-11 *PIX Firewall Advanced Features*

Command	Description
ca	Configure the PIX Firewall to interoperate with a Certification Authority (CA).
clear xlate	Clears the contents of the translation slots.
show xlate	Displays NAT translations. The **show xlate** command displays the contents of only the translation slots.
crypto dynamic-map	Create, view, or delete a dynamic crypto map entry.
failover [*active*]	Use the **failover** command without an argument after you connect the optional failover cable between your primary firewall and a secondary firewall.
fixup protocol	The fixup protocol commands let you view, change, enable, or disable the use of a service or protocol through the PIX Firewall.
kill	Terminate a Telnet session. Telnet sessions to the PIX must be enabled.
telnet ip_address [**netmask**] [*if_name*]	Specify the internal host for PIX Firewall console access via Telnet from inside hosts only.

Cisco PIX Firewall Software Features

A list of the current features of the Cisco PIX Firewall product follows:

- State-of-the-art Adaptive Security Algorithm (ASA) and stateful inspection firewalling.
- Cut-through proxy authenticates and authorizes connections, while enhancing performance.
- Easy-to-use web-based interface for managing PIX Firewalls remotely; the web-based interface is not a suggested practice by Cisco for medium to large networks.
- Support for up to 10 Ethernet interfaces ranging from 10-BaseT, 10/100 Fast Ethernet to Gigabit Ethernet.
- Stateful firewall failover capability with synchronized connection information and product configurations.
- True Network Address Translation (NAT), as specified in RFC 1631.

- Port Address Translation (PAT) further expands a company's address pool—one IP address supports 64,000 hosts.

- Support for IPsec and L2TP/PPTP-based VPNs.

- Support for high-performance URL filtering via integration with Websense-based URL filtering solutions.

- Mail Guard removes the need for an external mail relay server in perimeter network.

- Support for broad range of authentication methods via TACACS+, RADIUS, and Cisco Access Control Server (ACS) integration.

- Domain Name System (DNS) Guard transparently protects outbound name and address lookups.

- Flood Guard and Fragmentation Guard protect against denial-of-service attacks.

- Support for advanced Voice over IP (VoIP) standards.

- Java blocking eliminates potentially dangerous Java applets (not compressed or archived), extending authentication, authorization, and accounting capabilities.

- Net Aliasing transparently merges overlapping networks with the same IP address space.

- Capability to customize protocol port numbers.

- Integration with Cisco Intrusion Detection Systems for shunning connections of known malicious IP addresses.

- Enhanced customization of syslog messages.

- Simple Network Management Protocol (SNMP) and syslog for remote management.

- Reliable syslogging using either TCP or UDP.

- Extended transparent application support (both with and without NAT enabled) includes the following:

  - Sun remote procedure call (RPC)

  - Microsoft Networking client and server communication (NetBIOS over IP) using NAT

  - Multimedia, including RealNetworks' RealAudio, Xing Technologies' Streamworks, White Pines' CuSeeMe, Vocal Tec's Internet Phone, VDOnet's VDOLive, Microsoft's NetShow, VXtreme Web Theatre 2; and Intel's Internet Video Phone and Microsoft's NetMeeting (based on H.323 standards)

  - Oracle SQL*Net client and server communication

Cisco will also publish loopholes found in PIX software, such as the PIX mail guard feature, which was designed to limit SMTP messages but can be exploited by intruders. You can find the Cisco publications at www.cisco.com/warp/public/707/PIXfirewallSMTPfilter-pub.shtml.

NOTE   When troubleshooting why certain applications, such as SMTP mail or L2TP (TCP 1071) tunnels are not working, a good starting point is always to look at which TCP or UDP ports are filtered by the PIX because, by default, you must configure any TCP/UDP ports you will permit through the PIX with the conduit or static translations commands.

Cisco Secure PIX Firewalls, published by Cisco Press (ISBN 1-58705-035-8 by David W. Chapman Jr., Andy Fox), is an excellent resource if you want to learn more about the PIX Firewall.

Cisco IOS Firewall Security Feature Set

Cisco systems software has developed a version of IOS with security-specific features integrated in current IOS software. It is available only on some Cisco IOS devices.

NOTE   The need to provide firewall functionally in existing router models led Cisco down a path of enabling IOS to be security aware. Not many folks think of Cisco as a software company but, in fact, they sell more software than hardware.

The Cisco IOS features set consists of the following:

- Context-based Access Control (CBAC) provides internal users secure, per-application-based access control for all traffic across perimeters, such as between private enterprise networks and the Internet.

- Java blocking protects against unidentified, malicious Java applets.

- Denial-of-service detection and prevention defends and protects router resources from common attacks, checking packet headers and dropping suspicious packets.

- Audit trail details transactions, recording time stamp, source host, destination host, ports, duration, and the total number of bytes transmitted.

- Real-time alerts log alerts in case of denial-of-service attacks or other preconfigured conditions.

You can use the Cisco IOS Firewall feature set to configure your Cisco IOS router as follows:

- An Internet firewall or part of an Internet firewall

- A firewall between groups in your internal network

- A firewall providing secure connections to or from branch offices

- A firewall between your company's network and your company's partners' networks

For example, when a user authenticates from the Cisco IOS Firewall proxy, authentication is completed by HTTP and access lists are downloaded from AAA server to authorized or rejected connections. The IOS Firewall feature set has many different applications for today's IP networks.

CBAC provides secure, per-application access control across the network. CBAC is designed to enhance security for TCP and UDP applications, and supports protocols such as H.323, RealAudio, and SQL-based applications, to name a few.

CBAC can filter TCP/UDP packets based on application layer, transport, and network layer protocol information. Traffic is inspected for sessions that originate on any given interface and also inspect traffic flowing through a firewall. CBAC can inspect FTP, TFTP, or SMTP traffic, but does not inspect ICMP packet flows.

CBAC can even manually open and close openings in the firewall to test security in a network.

The following list provides samples of protocols supported by CBAC:

- Telnet
- SNMP
- TFTP
- SMTP
- Finger
- Java Blocking
- Oracle SQL
- RealAudio
- H.323

The other major benefits of the Cisco IOS feature set include the following:

- Integrated solutions and no need for a PIX Firewall for investments already made in Cisco IOS routers.
- No new hardware is required (just a software upgrade).
- Allows for full IP routing capabilities.
- Cisco customers are already aware of IOS command structure.
- Low cost.

Cisco IOS Security feature-enabled routers should always maintain the same secure polices described in Chapter 8, "Network Security Policies, Vulnerabilities, and Protection," such as password encryption and disabling nonessential service, such as Hypertext Transfer Protocol (HTTP) or Dynamic Host Configuration Protocol (DHCP).

CBAC Configuration Task List

Configuring CBAC requires the following tasks:

- Picking an interface: internal or external
- Configuring IP access lists at the interface
- Configuring global timeouts and thresholds
- Defining an inspection rule
- Applying the inspection rule to an interface
- Configuring logging and audit trail
- Other guidelines for configuring a firewall
- Verifying CBAC (Optional)

Example 7-5 shows a router named R1 with two Ethernet interfaces, one defined as the inside interface (Ethernet0) and one as the outside interface (Ethernet1). For this example, CBAC is being configured to inspect RTSP and H.323 protocol traffic inbound from the protected network on a router with two Ethernet interfaces. Interface Ethernet0 is the protected network, and interface Ethernet1 is the unprotected network. The security policy for the protected site uses access control lists (ACLs) to inspect TCP/UDP protocol traffic. Inbound access for specific protocol traffic is provided through dynamic access lists, which are generated according to CBAC inspection rules.

ACL 199 permits TCP and UDP traffic from any source or destination, while denying specific ICMP protocol traffic and permitting ICMP trace route and unreachable messages. The final deny statement is not required but is included for explicitness—the final entry in any ACL is an implicit denial of all IP protocol traffic. Example 7-5 defines the Access-list 199 on Router R1, which has two Ethernet interfaces: Ethernet0 and ethernet1.

Example 7-5 **Access-list** *Definition*

```
R1(config)# access-list 199 permit tcp any any  eq telnet
R1(config)# access-list 199 deny udp any any  eq  syslog
R1(config)# access-list 199 deny any any echo-reply
R1(config)# access-list 199 deny any any echo
R1(config)# access-list 199 deny any any time-exceeded
R1(config)# access-list 199 deny any any packet-too-big
R1(config)# access-list 199 permit any any traceroute
R1(config)# access-list 199 permit any any unreachable
R1(config)# access-list 199 permit deny ip any any
```

ACL 199 is applied inbound at interface Ethernet 1 to block all access from the unprotected network to the protected network. Example 7-6 configures the inbound ACL on R1.

Example 7-6 *R1 ACL Inbound Configuration*

```
R1(config)#interface ethernet1
R1(config-if)# ip access-group 199 in
```

An inspection rule is created for "users" that covers two protocols: RTSP and H.323. Example 7-7 configures R1 to inspect RTSP and H.323 traffic.

Example 7-7 *Inspected Traffic*

```
R1(config)# ip inspect name users rtsp
R1(config)# ip inspect name users h323
```

The inspection rule is applied inbound at interface Ethernet1 to inspect traffic from users on the protected network. When CBAC detects multimedia traffic from the protected network, CBAC creates dynamic entries in Access-list 199 to allow return traffic for multimedia sessions. Example 7-8 configures the R1 unprotected network to inspect traffic on interface ethernet1.

Example 7-8 *Inspects Traffic on R1 Protected Interface*

```
R1(config)# interface Ethernet1
R1(config-if)# ip inspect users in
```

You can view the CBAC logs by three methods:

- Debugging output (refer to the Cisco Documentation CD for full details)
- Syslog messages (show logging)
- Console messages (system messages)

After you complete the inspection of traffic, you can turn off CBAC with the global IOS command **no ip inspect**. The Cisco Systems IOS feature set also supports AAA, TACACS+, and Kerberos authentication protocols.

NOTE   Active audit and content filters are used with NetRanger and NetSonar products to allow administrators to decipher or reply to networks when an intruder has accessed the network. CBAC is just another useful tool in IOS that allows a quick audit of an IP network.

Public Key Infrastructure

In the new digital environment, a Public Key Infrastructure (PKI) ensures that sensitive electronic communications are private and protected from tampering. It provides assurances of the identities of the participants in those transactions, and prevents them from later denying participation in the transaction.

PKI provides the following assurances:

- Protects privacy by ensuring the data is not read but can't stop someone from intercepting it (If you can't read something, what's the use of that data?)

- Assures the integrity of electronic communications by ensuring that they are not altered during transmission

- Verifies the identity of the parties involved in an electronic transmission

- Ensures that no party involved in an electronic transaction can deny involvement in the transaction

Before you send data over the public Internet, you want to make sure that the data, no matter how sensitive, won't be read by the wrong source. PKI enables data to be sent encrypted by use of a public key, cryptography, and digital signatures.

Public key cryptography ensures the confidentiality of sensitive information or messages using a mathematical algorithm, or key, to scramble (encrypt) data, and a related mathematical key to unscramble (decrypt) it. In public key cryptography, authorized users receive special encryption software and a pair of keys, one an accessible public key, and the other a private key, which the user must keep secret.

A digital signature (DSS) is an electronic identifier comparable to a traditional, paper-based signature—it is unique and verifiable, and only the signer can initiate it.

Before any communication can take place, both parties involved in the data communication must obtain a Certificate of Authority from a Certification Authority (CA), a trusted third party responsible for issuing digital certificates and managing them throughout their lifetime.

Consider the following example: a user named Simon wants to communicate with a user named Sharon. Simon already has his digital certificate but Sharon has yet to obtain one. Sharon must identify herself to the CA to obtain a certificate. This is analogous to a passport when you travel the world. When Sharon obtains her digital certificate, it contains a copy of her public key, the certificate's expiration date, and the CA's digital signature. Each of these details is public.

Sharon also receives a private key, which is not shared with anyone. Now that both parties have a DSS, they can communicate and encrypt data using their public key, but they can decrypt only the data using their respective private keys. Pretty Good Privacy (application layer tool) is an excellent example of this type of communication. I suggest you install the software (free demonstration version) and try PKI for yourself. You can find the free software at www.pgp.com.

Virtual Private Networks

A virtual private network (VPN) enables IP traffic to travel securely over a public TCP/IP network by encrypting all traffic from one network to another. A VPN uses "tunneling" to encrypt all information at the IP level.

VPN is very loosely defined as a network in which a customer or end user connects to one or more sites through a public infrastructure, such as the Internet or World Wide Web.

We have already discussed dialup VPNs or Virtual Private Dialup Network (VPDN) in Chapter 5, "Security Protocols."

VPNs are typically set up permanently between two or more sites. Figure 7-6 displays a typical VPN design.

Figure 7-6   *VPN Model*

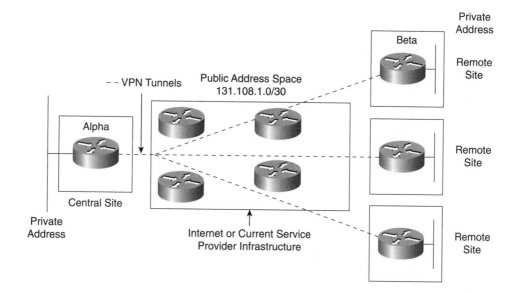

Figure 7-6 displays a typical hub (central site) to spoke (remote site) model, where all existing public infrastructure transports data. IP generic routing encapsulation (GRE) tunnels can be set up between the hub and spoke routers, and any protocol can run over the IP tunnel.

Consider an example where the router, Alpha, needs to communicate with the remote site, Router Beta.

At no time should the private address space be advertised to any public domain. Assuming that IP routing is enabled and configured, we can configure an IP GRE tunnel between Alpha and Beta.

Assume that you have a client who wants to create a VPN across your network. The client's main network is attached via Alpha over the Internet IP cloud. The client has a group of employees in their own IP space on the Ethernet interface. The client has a classless inter-domain routing (CIDR) block of 192.1.64.0/20 for the network attached to the Alpha router, and the CIDR block 141.108.32.0/20 to the network attached to the Beta router. The network 131.108.1.0/30 is assigned between the routers and is pingable.

Example 7-9 configures Alpha with a GRE tunnel pointing to the remote IP address 131.108.1.2/30 (Beta's Serial IP address) and uses 131.108.1.5 for the loopback interface.

Example 7-9 *Alpha GRE Tunnel*

```
hostname Alpha
!
interface Loopback0
 ip address 131.108.1.1 255.255.255.255
! IP GRE tunnel configuration follows
interface Tunnel0
 ip address 192.1.64.1 255.255.255.0
 tunnel source Loopback0
 tunnel destination 131.108.1.2
!
interface Ethernet0/0
 ip address 192.1.65.1 255.255.248.0
!
interface Serial0
Description Link to Beta via Internet Cloud
ip address 131.108.1.1 255.255.255.252
!
router ospf 1
network 192.1.64.0.0 0.0.240.255 area 0

End
```

Example 7-10 configures Beta with a GRE tunnel pointing to the remote IP address 131.108.1.1/30 and 131.108.1.6/32 for loopback use.

Example 7-10 *Beta GRE Tunnel*

```
hostname Beta
!
interface Loopback0
 ip address 131.108.1.2 255.255.255.255
! IP GRE tunnel configuration follows
interface Tunnel0
 ip address 192.1.64.2 255.255.255.0
 tunnel source Loopback0
 tunnel destination 131.108.1.1
!
interface Ethernet0/0
```

Example 7-10 *Beta GRE Tunnel (Continued)*

```
 ip address 141.108.32.1 255.255.240.0
!
router ospf 1
network 141.108.0.0 0.0.255.255 area 0
interface Serial0
Description Link to Alapha via Internet Cloud
ip address 131.108.1.2 255.255.255.252
!
End
```

The IP GRE tunnel is now configured between the routers Alpha and Beta. While using public address space for the source and destination of the VPN tunnel, the reserved CIDR block 192.1.64.0/20 will not be advertised or routable over the public domain. The private traffic can now flow between both hub site and remote site securely. You can also transport other non-IP protocols over the VPN tunnel, such as Internetwork Packet Exchange (IPX) or AppleTalk. IP GRE tunnels support only IPX or AppleTalk.

Foundation Summary

The "Foundation Summary" is a condensed collection of material for a convenient review of this chapter's key concepts. If you are already comfortable with the topics in this chapter and decided to skip most of the "Foundation Topics" material, the "Foundation Summary" will help you recall a few details. If you just read the "Foundation Topics" section, this review should help further solidify some key facts. If you are doing your final preparation before the exam, the "Foundation Summary" offers a convenient way to do a quick final review.

Table 7-12   *Perimeter or Firewall Router Functions*

To Protect	Method
Sniffer or snooping capabilities	Control eavesdropping with TCP/IP service and network layer encryption (IPSec).
Control unauthorized access	Use AAA and Cisco Secure. Also, access-list filtering and PIX Firewall.
Controlling session replay	Control what TCP/IP sessions are authorized. Block SNMP, IP source routing, and finger services to outside hosts.
Controlling inbound connections	Filter the internal address as the source from the outside world. Filter all private addresses. Filter Bootp, TFTP, and trace route commands. Allow TCP connections established from the inside network. Permit inbound traffic to DMZs only.
Controlling outbound connections	Allow only valid IP addresses to the outside world; filter remaining illegal addresses.
Packet filtering	Use predefined access lists that control the transmission of packets from any given interface, control VTY access, and ensure routing updates are authenticated.

Table 7-13   *NAT Configuration Steps*

Step	Description
1	Determine the network addresses to be translated.
2	Configure the inside network with the IOS **ip nat inside** command.
3	Configure the outside network with the IOS **ip nat outside** command.
4	Define a pool of addresses to be translated with the following IOS command: **ip nat pool** *pool-name start ip address end ip address mask*
5	Define the addresses allowed to access the Internet with the following IOS command: **ip nat inside source list** *access list number* **pool** *pool name*

Table 7-14   *Cisco PIX Model Numbers*

PIX 501
PIX 506/506E
PIX 515/515E
PIX 520 (in current CCIE lab)
PIX 525
PIX 535

Table 7-15   *PIX Configuration Steps*

Step	Description
1	Name the inside/outside interfaces and security levels.
2	Identify the hardware interfaces and speed/duplex.
3	Define the IP address for inside and outside interfaces.
4	Define NAT/PAT.
5	Define the global pool.
6	Define the IP route path.
7	Define static/conduits or static/access lists (for outside networks to access inside hosts or networks).

Table 7-16   *PIX Command Options*

Option	Description
ca	Configures the PIX Firewall to interoperate with a Certification Authority (CA).
clear xlate	Clears the contents of the translation slots.
show xlate	Displays NAT translations. The **show xlate** command displays the contents of only the translation slots.
crypto *dynamic-map*	Create, view, or delete a dynamic crypto map entry with this command.
failover *[active]*	Use the **failover** command without an argument after you connect the optional failover cable between your primary firewall and a secondary firewall.
fixup protocol	The **fixup protocol** commands let you view, change, enable, or disable the use of a service or protocol through the PIX Firewall.
kill	Terminate a Telnet session. Telnet sessions to the PIX must be enabled and are sent as clear text.
telnet *ip_address* [**netmask**] [*if_name*]	Specify the internal host for PIX Firewall console access through Telnet.

Table 7-17 *Cisco IOS Feature Set*

Feature	Function
CBAC	Provides internal users secure, per-application-based access control for all traffic across perimeters, such as between private enterprise networks and the Internet. CBAC supports the following: Telnet SMNPSNMP-GDL TFTP SMTP Finger Java Blocking Oracle SQL RealAudio H.323
Java blocking	Java blocking protects against unidentified, malicious Java applets.
Denial-of-service detection and prevention	Defends and protects router resources against common attacks, checking packet headers and dropping suspicious packets.
Audit trail	Details transactions, recording time stamp, source host, destination host, ports, duration, and total number of bytes transmitted.
Real-time alerts	Log alerts in case of denial-of-service attacks or other preconfigured conditions (intrusion detection).
Firewall	An Internet firewall or part of an Internet firewall.

Q & A

The Q & A questions are designed to help you assess your readiness for the topics covered on the CCIE Security written examination and those topics presented in this chapter. This format helps you assess your retention of the material. A strong understanding of the answers to these questions will help you on the CCIE Security written exam. You can also look over the questions at the beginning of the chapter again for review. As an additional study aid, use the CD-ROM provided with this book to take simulated exams, which draw from a database of over 300 multiple-choice questions — all different from those presented in the book.

Select the best answer. Answers to these questions can be found in Appendix A, "Answers to Quiz Questions."

1 What does the term DMZ refer to?

2 What is the perimeter router's function in a DMZ?

3 What two main transport layer protocols do extended access lists filter traffic through?

4 Which of the following is *not* a TCP service?

   a. Ident

   b. ftp

   c. pop3

   d. pop2

   e. echo

5 Name five UDP services that can be filtered with an extended access-list.

_____

_____

_____

6 What RFC defines NAT?

_____

_____

_____

7 In NAT, what is the inside local address used for?

_____

_____

_____

8 What does the IOS command **ip nat inside source list** accomplish?

_____

_____

_____

9 What are the four possible NAT translations on a Cisco IOS router?

_____

_____

_____

10 How many connections can be translated with a PIX Firewall for the following RAM configurations: 16 MB, 32MB, or 128MB?

_____

_____

_____

11 When the **alias** command is applied to a PIX, what does it accomplish?

_____

_____

_____

12 What security features does the Cisco IOS Firewall feature set allow a network administrator to accomplish?

_____

_____

_____

13 What does CBAC stand for?

_____

_____

_____

14 Name the eight possible steps to take when configuring CBAC.

_____

_____

_____

15 What is a virtual private network?

_____

_____

_____

Scenario

Scenario 7-1: Configuring a Cisco PIX for NAT

The following configuration is installed on a PIX 520. Users from the inside network 10.0.0.0/8 report to you that they cannot browse the Internet. What is the problem, and what command or commands will rectify the problem?

```
pix# write terminal
 nameif ethernet0 outside security0
 nameif ethernet1 inside security100
hostname pix
 fixup protocol ftp 21
 fixup protocol http 80
 fixup protocol smtp 25
 fixup protocol h323 1720
 fixup protocol rsh 514
 fixup protocol sqlnet 1521
  logging timestamp
 no logging standby
 logging console debugging
 no logging monitor
 logging buffered debugging
 no logging trap
 logging facility 20
 logging queue 512
 interface ethernet0 10full
 interface ethernet1 10full
 mtu outside 1500
 mtu inside 1500
ip address inside 201.201.201.1 255.255.255.
ip address outside 131.108.1.1 255.255.255.0
route inside 10.0.0.0 255.0.0.0 201.201.201.2
route outside 0.0.0.0 0.0.0.0 131.018.1.2
 no failover
 failover timeout 0:00:00
 failover ip address outside 0.0.0.0
 failover ip address inside 0.0.0.0
 arp timeout 14400
global (outside) 1 192.192.1.2-192.192.1.30 netmask 255.255.255.224
 no rip outside passive
 no rip outside default
 no rip inside passive
 no rip inside default
timeout xlate 3:00:00 conn 1:00:00 half-closed 0:10:00 udp 0:02:00
 timeout rpc 0:10:00 h323 0:05:00
 timeout uauth 0:00:00 absolute
 no snmp-server location
 no snmp-server contact
 snmp-server community public
 no snmp-server enable traps
 telnet timeout 5
 terminal width 80
: end
```

Scenario Answer

Scenario 7-1 Solution

Cisco PIX Firewalls need to NAT any nonregistered IP address space. In particular, the Class A 10.0.0.0/8 is not routable in the Internet, so you must use NAT to permit access, or you could re-address your entire network, which clearly is not an exercise you will do often.

The following command will NAT all inside addresses:

```
nat  (inside) 1 0.0.0.0 0.0.0.0
```

Before you can access the Internet, you must also tell the PIX (remember the PIX is not as intelligent as a router; RIP can be configured by the network administrator), and you must route IP data with the command shown here:

```
route outside 0.0.0.0 0.0.0.0 <default-gateway>
```

This command installs a default route where IP datagrams will be sent, typically, the perimeter router or ISP router.

Exam Topics in This Chapter

CHAPTER 8

Network Security Policies, Vulnerabilities, and Protection

This chapter reviews today's most common Cisco security policies and mechanisms available to the Internet community to combat cyber attacks. The standard security body, CERT/CC, is covered along with descriptions of Cisco IOS-based security methods that ensure that all attacks are reported and acted upon. Cisco Security applications, such as Intrusion Detection System, are covered to lay the foundations you need to master the topics in the CCIE Security written exam.

This chapter covers the following topics:

- **Network security policies**—Standard security policies that should be deployed in any IP network**.**

- **Standards bodies and incident response teams**—Some of the standard bodies designed to help the Internet community tackle intrusion; the forums and e-mail aliases that can help a network security architect.

- **Vulnerabilities, Attacks, and Common Exploits**—Some of the vulnerabilities and methods that exploit IP networks; some common attacks that exploit data and how that data is retrieved and modified.

- **Intrusion Detection System (IDS)**—How IDS (Cisco IDS strategies, in particular) can be implemented to help deter intruders from gaining access to secure data.

- **Protecting Cisco IOS from Intrusion**—Some of the standard configurations that every IOS-enabled router connected to the Internet should consider to avoid intruders gaining access to unauthorized material.

"Do I Know This Already?" Quiz

The purpose of this assessment quiz is to help you determine how to spend your limited study time. If you can answer most or all these questions, you might want to skim the "Foundation Topics" section and return to it later, as necessary. Review the "Foundation Summary" section and answer the questions at the end of the chapter to ensure that you have a strong grasp of the material covered. If you intend to read the entire chapter, you do not necessarily need to answer these questions now. If you find these assessment questions difficult, you should read through the entire "Foundation Topics" section and review it until you feel comfortable with your ability to answer all these and the "Q & A" questions at the end of the chapter.

Answers to these questions can be found in Appendix A, "Answers to Quiz Questions."

1 A remote user tries logging into a remote network but fails after three additional tries and is disconnected. What useful information should the network administrator gather? (Select the best two answers.)

   a. Username

   b. Invalid password

   c. Invalid username

   d. Valid username

2 What is the first step that should be implemented in securing any network?

   a. Create a database of secure passwords.

   b. Create the IP address scheme.

   c. Run NetRanger or NetSonar.

   d. Define a security policy.

   e. Configure access lists on all routers.

3 What primary security method can be designed and deployed to secure and protect any IP network after an attack has been documented?

   a. Security policy

   b. IP policy

   c. Countermeasures

   d. Measurement

   e. Logging passwords

4 A security administrator notices that a log file stored on a local router has increased in size from 32 k to 64 k in a matter of seconds. What should the network administrator do?

   a. Increase the buffer to 64 k.

   b. Decrease the buffer to 16 k.

   c. Log the event as suspicious and notify the incident response team.

   d. Nothing, this is normal.

   e. Both a and b are correct.

5 What is the primary responsibility of CERT/CC?

    a. Define access lists for use on routers

    b. Set security standards

    c. Coordinate attacks on secure networks

    d. Maintain a security standard for networks

    e. Nothing to do with security

6 Who can use network scanners and probes? (Select the best two answers.)

    a. Intruders

    b. Security managers

    c. End users

    d. Cable service providers

7 What is a bastion host?

    a. Firewall device supported by Cisco only

    b. Network's last line of defense

    c. Network's first line of defense

    d. IP host device designed to route IP packets

8 A TCP SYN attack is what type of attack?

    a. ICMP

    b. DoS

    c. Telnet/Kerberos attack

    d. Ping attack only

9 When an intruder sends a large amount of ICMP echo (ping) traffic using IP broadcasts, this type of DoS attack is known as what?

    a. Bastion

    b. Land.C

    c. Man in the middle

    d. Smurf

    e. Ping of death

10 What kind of attack sends a large ICMP echo request packet with the intent of overflowing the input buffers of the destination machine and causing it to crash?

a. Ping of death

b. Smurf

c. Land.C

d. Man in the middle

e. Birthday attack

11 In the context of intrusion detection, what is an exploit signature?

a. DoS attack

b. An attack that is recognized and detected on the network

c. The same as a Smurf attack

d. The same as a man in the middle attack

12 To stop spam e-mail from overwhelming an e-mail server, what step can you take?

a. Ask the ISP for help.

b. Nothing, because spam e-mail is too difficult to stop to be worth the effort.

c. Install an intrusion detection system that has a signature for spam e-mail.

d. Nothing, because the client software takes care of this.

e. Change the IOS code.

f. Configure the bastion host to stop spam e-mail.

Foundation Topics

Network Security Policies

IP networks are susceptible to unsecured intruders using a number of different methods. Through the campus, by dialup, and through the Internet, an intruder can view IP data and attack vulnerable network devices.

IP networks must provide network security for the following reasons:

- **Inherent technology weaknesses**—All network devices and operating systems have inherent vulnerabilities.

- **Configuration weaknesses**—Common configuration mistakes can be exploited to open up weaknesses.

- **Network policy**—The lack of a network policy can lead to vulnerabilities, such as password security.

- **Outside/inside intruders**—Internal and external people always want to exploit network resources and retrieve sensitive data.

Every IP network architecture should be based on a sound security policy designed to address all these weaknesses and threats. Every network should have a sound security policy before allowing remote access, for example. Network vulnerabilities must be constantly monitored, found, and addressed because they define points in the network that are potential security weak points (or loopholes) that can be exploited by intruders or hackers.

Technologies, such as TCP/IP, which is an open and defined standard, allow intruders to devise programs to send IP packets looking for responses and act on them. Countermeasures can be designed and deployed to secure and protect a network.

Intruders are typically individuals who have a broad skill set. Intruders can be skilled in coding programs in Java, UNIX, DOS, C, and C++. Their knowledge of TCP/IP can be exceptional, and they can be very experienced when using the Internet and searching for security loopholes. Sometimes, the biggest security threat comes from within an organization from disgruntled former employees, in particular, who would have access to usernames and passwords.

An intruder's motivation can be based on a number of reasons that make any network a possible target:

- Cash profit
- Revenge
- Vandalism
- Cyber terrorism
- Challenge to gain prestige or notoriety
- Curiosity, to gain experience, or to learn the tools of trade

Countermeasures against vulnerabilities attacks ensure that a policy, procedure, or specific technology is implemented so that networks are not exploited.

The ever-changing nature of attacks is another major challenge facing network administrators. Intruders today are well organized and trained, and Internet sites are easy targets and offer low risk to intruders. The tools used by intruders (see the section, "Vulnerabilities, Attacks, and Common Exploits," in this chapter) are increasingly sophisticated, easy to use, and designed for large-scale attacks.

Now that you are aware of some of the reasons a network must have a sound security policy and the reason intruders (hackers) want to exploit a poorly designed network, consider some of the standards bodies that are designed to help network administrators.

Standards Bodies and Incident Response Teams

A number of standards bodies today help a network administrator design a sound security policy. The two main entities that are helpful are the Computer Emergency Response Team Coordination Center (CERT/CC) and the various newsgroups that enable you to share valuable security information with other network administrators.

The CERT/CC is a U.S. federally funded research and development center at Carnegie Mellon University in Pittsburgh, Pennsylvania. Following the infamous worm incident (a virus developed to halt IP networks), which brought 10 percent of Internet systems to a halt in November 1988, the CERT/CC has helped to establish incident handling practices that have been adopted by more than 200 response teams around the world.

CERT/CC works with the Internet community to facilitate responses to incidents involving the Internet and the hosts that are attacked. CERT/CC is designed to take proactive steps to ensure that future attacks and vulnerabilities are communicated to the entire Internet community. CERT/CC also conducts research aimed at improving the security of existing systems.

CERT/CC also helped technology managers with Y2K compliance and various other well-known viruses, such as the Melissa virus. CERT/CC does not focus on the intruders themselves, or on the arrest of individuals responsible for causing havoc; rather, it ensures that vulnerabilities and loopholes are closed as soon as possible. CERT/CC does not maintain any security standards (these are left for RFCs); also, it does not provide any protocols to help network administrators.

CERT/CC has a number of relationships with other organizations, such as law enforcement, Internet security experts, and the general public, so that any information gathered by the teams involved in stifling attacks is communicated.

Examples of intruders actually overcoming network security include the famous Barclay Bank attack in July 2001, where the company's home page was defaced. *The New York Times* website was altered in September 1998. In February 2000, Yahoo also came under attack. In response to attacks like these and the increased concern brought about by them, Cisco Systems decided to release a new CCIE Security certification.

Cisco Systems also provides a website (for the Cisco Product Security Incident Response Team) where customers can report any security concerns regarding flaws in Cisco IOS products:

www.cisco.com/warp/public/707/sec_incident_response.shtml

You can also e-mail the Cisco Product Security Incident Response Team directly for emergency issues at securityalert@cisco.com, and for nonemergencies at psirt@cisco.com.

NOTE   *Social engineering* is a widely used term that refers to the act of tricking or coercing employees into providing information, such as usernames or mail user identifications and even passwords. First-level phone support personnel are individuals typically called by intruders pretending to work for the company to gain valuable information.

In 1998, CERT/CC handled 4942 incidents involving intruders. In 2001, CERT/CC handled over 52,000 incidents resulting is 2437 incidents reports.

If you have never heard of CERT/CC, now is the time to read more and ensure that you are alerted to vulnerabilities. For more details on CERT/CC, visit www.cert.org. CERT/CC claims that over 95 percent of intrusions can be stopped with countermeasures in place and monitoring tools.

Incident Response Teams

Incident response teams are too often set up only after an incident or intrusion occurs. However, sound security administration should already have teams set up to monitor and maintain network security.

Incident responses teams do the following:

- Verify the incident.
- Determine the magnitude of the incident (hosts affected and how many).
- Assess the damage (for example, determine if public servers have been modified).
- Gather and protect the evidence.

After this data has been collected, the incident response team determines whether there is enough trace data to track the intruders. The actual data you discover might be only a small part of the entire puzzle. For example, initially, you might have only a log file or notice that a log file size increased or decreased during the incident.

The data should be sent to upper management, to the operations groups within an organization, to all affected sites, and to organizations such as CERT/CC or the press. Organizations like Cisco are typically not going to release a statement to the press detailing any attacks.

After the information flows to all parts of an organization, the incident response team restores programs and data from the vendor-supplied media and backup device storage media. The data restored needs to be securely configured (such as routers; see the example in the section, "Protecting Cisco IOS from Intrusion" later in this chapter), including installing all relevant patches for all application-based programs.

Finally, the incident response team prepares a report and provides that information to the law enforcement organization if prosecution is required.

Internet Newsgroups

Another important body for both network administrators and intruders themselves is Internet newsgroups. Newsgroups are mailing list type forums where individuals can share ideas and past incidents to keep current with the latest security concerns and protection policies. As a network administrator, you must be aware of both standards and what intruders are discussing.

For example, CERT/CC recommends the following newsgroups:

- **alt.security**—Lists computer security issues as well as other security issues, such as car locks and alarm systems

- **comp.risks**—Moderated forum on the risks to the public in computers and related systems

- **comp.security.announce**—Computer security announcements, including new CERT advisories, summaries, and vendor-initiated bulletins

- **comp.security.misc**—A variety of issues related to computer and network security

- **comp.security.unix**—Security information related to the UNIX operating system

- **comp.virus**—Computer viruses and related topics

NOTE   The following sites also contain a great wealth of information. Although not security specific, they can help you identify the mechanism used to infiltrate technologies such as TCP/IP:

- Internet Domain Survey (www.isc.org/ds/)—Includes Host Count History and pointers to other sources of Internet trend and growth information

- Internet Engineering Task Force (IETF) (www.ietf.org/)—Offers technical papers, best practices, standards, and more

- Internet Society (ISOC) (www.isoc.org/internet/)—Provides an overview of the Internet, including its history and how it works

---

Vulnerabilities, Attacks, and Common Exploits

This section covers some of the vulnerabilities in TCP/IP and the tools used to exploit IP networks.

TCP/IP is an open standard protocol, which means that both network administrators and intruders are aware of the TCP/IP architecture and vulnerabilities.

NOTE   There are a number of network vulnerabilities, such as password protection, lack of authentication mechanism, use of unprotected routing protocols, and firewall holes. This section concentrates on TCP/IP vulnerabilities.

Network intruders can capture, manipulate, and replay data. Intruders typically try to cause as much damage to a network as possible by using the following methods:

- **Vandalizing**—Accessing the web server and altering web pages.

- **Manipulating data**—Altering the files on a network device.

- **Masquerading**—Manipulating TCP/IP segments to pretend to be at a valid IP address.

- **Session replay**—Capturing, altering, and replaying a sequence of packets to causes unauthorized access. This method identifies weaknesses in authentication.

- **Session hijacking**—Defining himself with a valid IP address after a session has been established to the real IP address by spoofing IP packets and manipulating the sequence number in IP packets.

- **Rerouting**—Routing packets from one source to an intruder source; altering routing updates to send IP packets to an incorrect destination, allowing the intruder to read and use the IP data inappropriately.

The following are some of the attacking methods intruders use:

- Probes and scans

- Denial-of-Service (DoS) attacks (covered in more detail later)

- Compromises

- Malicious code (such as viruses)

As described in Chapter 6, "Operating Systems and Cisco Security Applications," network scanners and tools are available to both network administrators and intruders. These tools can be used and placed at strategic points in the network to gain access to sensitive data. NetSonar, for example, can be used to find network vulnerabilities and can, therefore, be used by intruders to do as much harm as it does network administrators good if you aren't aware of these vulnerabilities.

DoS attacks are the most common form of attack used by intruders and can take many forms. The intruder's goal is to ultimately deny access to authorized users and tie up valuable system resources.

Figure 8-1 displays several techniques deployed in DoS attacks.

Figure 8-1   *Forms of Denial of Service Attack*

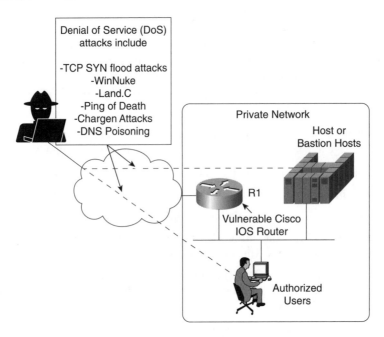

Figure 8-1 displays a typical network scenario with a router connected to the Internet and all users have access to hosts in a public domain. A *bastion host* is a computer or host, such as a UNIX host, that plays a critical role in enforcing any organization's network security policy. Bastion hosts are typically highly secured (including physically in secure computer rooms), as these hosts are vulnerable to attacks because they are exposed to untrusted or unknown networks and are the first line of defense. Bastion hosts often provide services to Internet users, such as Web services (WWW), and public access systems, such as FTP or SMTP mail. Because these computers are likely to be attacked, they are often referred to as *sacrificial hosts*.

The intruder in Figure 8-1 attacks the authorized users and hosts (or bastion host) behind a router by a number of methods, including the following:

- **Ping of death**—Attack that sends an improperly large ICMP echo request packet with the intent of overflowing the input buffers of the destination machine and causing it to crash. The IP protocol header field is set to 1, the last fragment bit is set, and the data length is greater than 65,535, which is greater than the maximum allowable IP packet size.

- **TCP SYN Flood attacks**—This form of DoS attack randomly opens up a number of TCP ports ensuring that network devices are using CPU cycles for bogus requests. By tying up valuable resources on the remote host, the CPU is tied up with bogus requests, and legitimate users experience poor network response or are denied access. This type of attack can make the host unusable.

- **E-mail attacks**—This form of DoS attack sends a random number of e-mails to a host. E-mail attacks try to fill an inbox with bogus e-mails, ensuring that the end user cannot send mail while thousands (or an e-mail bomb) of e-mails are received.

- **CPU-intensive attacks**—This DoS attack ties up systems' resources by using programs such as TROJAN (a program designed to capture username/passwords from a network), or enabling viruses to disable remote systems.

- **Teardrop**—Exploits an overlapping IP fragment implementation bug in various operating systems. The bug causes the TCP/IP fragmentation reassembly code to improperly handle overlapping IP fragments causing the host to hang or crash.

- **DNS poisoning**—The attacker exploits the DNS server, causing the server to return a false IP address to a domain name query.

- **UDP Bomb**—Sends illegal length field in the packet header, causing Kernel panic and crash.

- **Distributed Denial Of Service (DDoS)**—These DoS attacks are run by multiple hosts. The attacker first compromises vulnerable hosts using various tools and techniques. Then, the actual DOS attack on a target is run from the pool of all the compromised hosts.

- **Chargen attacks**—Establish a User Datagram Protocol (UDP) service by producing a high-character input. This can cause congestion on a network.

- **Attacks via dialup (out of band)**—Applications such as Windows 95 have built-in vulnerabilities on data port 139 (known as WinNuke) if the intruders can ascertain the IP address.

- **Land.C attacks**—A program designed to send TCP SYN packets (TCP SYN is used in the TCP connection phase) that specifies the target's host address as both source and destination. This program can use TCP port 113 or 139 (source/destination), which can also cause a system to stop functioning.

DoS attacks are designed to send traffic to host systems so that they cannot respond to legitimate traffic by overwhelming the end device through a number of incomplete and illegal connections or requests. DoS attacks send more traffic than is possible to process and can send excessive mail requests, excessive UDP packets, and excessive Internet Control Message Protocol (ICMP) pings with very large data packet sizes to render a remote host unusable.

Many other known and unknown attacking methods and terms exist. Here are a few more you should be aware of for the written exam:

- **Spoof attack**—The attacker creates IP packets with an address found (or spoofed) from a legitimate source. This attack is powerful in situations where a router is connects to the Internet with one or more internal addresses. The real solution to this form of attack is to track down the source device and stop the attack.

- **Smurf attack**—Named after its exploit program and one of the most recent in the category of network-level attacks against hosts. In this attack, an intruder sends a large amount of ICMP echo (ping) traffic to IP broadcast addresses, which all have a victim's spoofed source address. For more details, go to www.cert.org/advisories/CA-1998-01.html.

  Smurf attacks include a primary and secondary victim and are extremely potent damaging to any IP network. Smurf attacks result in a large number of broadcast ICMP networks, and if routers are configured to forward, broadcasts can result in a degraded network and poor performance between the primary and secondary device. A quick solution is to disable IP-directed broadcasts.

- **Man in the middle attack**—Just as with packet sniffers and IP spoofing attacks, a brute-force password attack can provide access to accounts that can be used to modify critical network files and services. An example that compromises your network's integrity is an attacker modifying your network's routing tables. By doing so, the attacker ensures that all network packets are routed to him before they are transmitted to their final destination. In such a case, an attacker can monitor all network traffic, effectively becoming a man in the middle.

- **Birthday attack**—Refers to a class of brute-force attacks. It gets its name from the surprising fact that the probability that two or more people in a group of 23 share the same birthday is greater than 50 percent; such a result is called a birthday paradox.

Intrusion Detection System

Intrusion detection systems (IDS) are designed to detect and thwart network attacks. Based on their location, they can be either of the following:

- **Network IDS**—Examines or sniffs every packet flowing across the network and generates an alarm upon detection of a network attack signature.

- **Host IDS**—Examines operating system information such as logs or system process, against a base line. When the system deviates from the normal values because of an attack, alarms are generated.

Chapter 6 defines some of the intrusion detection mechanisms you can use in an IP network, namely NetRanger.

Cisco IDS delivers a comprehensive, pervasive security solution for combating unauthorized intrusions, malicious Internet worms, and bandwidth and e-Business application attacks.

Recently, Cisco announced a number of new products to support IDS:

- **Cisco IDS Host Sensor 2.5**—Bolsters enterprise security by delivering unparalleled levels of protection and customization to customers

- **Cisco IDS 4250 Appliance Sensor**—Raises the performance bar for high-throughput gigabit protection in a performance-upgradable IDS chassis

- **Cisco IDS 4235 Appliance Sensor**—Provides enterprise-class intrusion protection at new price/performance levels

- **Cisco IDS 3.1 Sensor Software**—Delivers powerful web-based, embedded device management, graphical security analysis, and data mining capabilities

---

NOTE   In addition to the Cisco IDS 4200 series of IDS appliances, Cisco also has the following IDS sensors:

- IOS with IDS feature set for routers

- Catalyst 6500 IDS module for switch-based sensor

- PIX Firewall with version 6.x with built-in IDS sensor

- Cisco IDS Host sensor for Windows, Solaris OS, and web servers, such as IIS and Apache

You are not expected to know these details for the written exam; they are presented here for completeness only.

Each Cisco IDS sensor can be configured to support a number of different signatures. A *Signature Engine* is a component of the Cisco IDS sensor designed to support many signatures in a certain category. An engine is composed of a parser and an inspector. Each engine has a set of legal parameters that have allowable ranges or sets of values. Exploit signatures are an identifiable pattern of attack detected by your network device, such as a Cisco IDS Host sensor.

Table 8-1 displays the signature lists and descriptions available with Cisco IDS version 3.1.

IDS can be used, for example, to detect spam e-mail and still allow regular e-mail. Most ISPs do not detect or remove spam e-mail, so it is up to the security administrator to ensure that spam e-mail is not permitted or used as a DoS attack.

Table 8-1 *Cisco IDS Signature Engines**

Signature Engine	Description
ATOMIC.ICMP	Simple ICMP alarms based on the following parameters: type, code, sequence, and ID
ATOMIC.IPOPTIONS	Simple alarms based on the decoding of Layer 3 options
ATOMIC.L3.IP	Simple Layer 3 IP alarms
ATOMIC.TCP	Simple TCP packet alarms based on the following parameters: port, destination, and flags
ATOMIC.UDP	Simple UDP packet alarms based on the following parameters: port, direction, and data length
FLOOD.HOST.ICMP	ICMP floods directed at a single host
FLOOD.HOST.UDP	UDP floods directed at a single host
FLOOD.NET	Multiprotocol floods directed at a network segment
FLOOD.TCPSYN	Connections to multiple ports using TCP SYN
SERVICE.DNS.TCP	Domain Name Service (DNS) packet analyzer on TCP port 53 (includes compression handler)
SERVICE.DNS.UDP	UDP-based DNS signatures
SERVICE.PORTMAP	Remote Procedure Call (RPC) program number sent to port mapper
SERVICE.RPC	Simple RPC alarms based on the following parameters: program, procedure, and length
STATE.HTTP	Stateful HTTP protocol decode-based string search (includes anti-evasive URL deobfuscation)
STRING.HTTP	Specialized STRING.TCP alarms for Web traffic (includes anti-evasive URL deobfuscation)
STRING.ICMP	Generic ICMP-based string search engine
STRING.TCP	Generic TCP-based string search engine
STRING.UDP	Generic UDP-based string search engine
SWEEP.HOST.ICMP	A single host sweeping a range of nodes using ICMP
SWEEP.HOST.TCP	A single host sweeping a range of nodes using TCP
SWEEP.PORT.TCP	TCP connections to multiple destination ports between two nodes
SWEEP.PORT.UDP	UDP connections to multiple destination ports between two nodes
SWEEP.RPC	Connections to multiple ports with RPC requests between two nodes

* The information in Table 8-1 is from Table 1 at the Cisco web page, www.cisco.com/en/US/partner/products/sw/ secursw/ps2113/prod_technical_reference09186a00800d9dd5.html#56785.

Protecting Cisco IOS from Intrusion

Now that you have a snapshot of modern security concerns, this section looks at Cisco IOS and the configuration commands you can use to deny intruders the ability to harm valuable network resources that are typically connected behind a Cisco router. In particular, this section covers how you can stop DoS attacks.

Figure 8-2 displays a typical network scenario. You see how to configure the router, separating the public and private networks so that the private network is not vulnerable.

Figure 8-2   *Typical Internet Connection on R1*

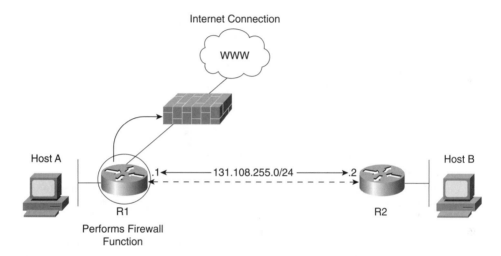

Example 8-1 configures the Router R1 to enable the Nagle algorithm defined in RFC 896.

Example 8-1   *Enable Nagle*

```
service nagle
service tcp-keepalives-in
service tcp-keepalives-out
```

Cisco Connection Online defines the NAGLE algorithm (www.cisco.com/univercd/cc/td/doc/product/software/ios100/rpcg/36053.htm):

> The algorithm developed by John Nagle (RFC 896) helps alleviate the small-packet problem in TCP. In general, it works this way: The first character typed after connection establishment is sent in a single packet, but TCP holds any additional characters typed until the receiver acknowledges the previous packet. Then the second, larger packet is sent, and additional typed characters are saved until the acknowledgment comes back. The effect is to accumulate characters into larger chunks, and pace them out to the network at a rate matching the round-trip time of the given connection. This method is usually effective for all TCP-based traffic. However, do not use the **service nagle** command if you have X Remote users on X Window system sessions.

Enabling this algorithm along with the **service tcp keepalive** command ensures that no TCP connections on any router get hung.

To generate keepalive packets on idle incoming network connections (initiated by the remote host), use the **service tcp-keepalives-in** global configuration command.

To generate keepalive packets on idle outgoing network connections (initiated by a user), use the **service tcp-keepalives-out** global configuration command.

Example 8-2 configures R1 to disable (on by default) TCP/UDP small servers.

Example 8-2   *Disable TCP/UDP Small Servers*

```
no service udp-small-servers
no service tcp-small-servers
```

By default, the TCP servers for Echo, Discard, Chargen, and Daytime services are disabled.

When the minor TCP/IP servers are disabled, access to the Echo, Discard, Chargen, and Daytime ports causes the Cisco IOS Software to send a TCP Reset packet to the sender and discard the original incoming packet. When the commands in Example 8-2 are entered, they do not display when you view the configuration because the default is to disable TCP/UDP servers.

NOTE   When a Cisco IOS router is configured to disable the UDP small servers' access to Echo, Discard and Chargen ports enable the router to send ICMP port unreachable messages to the source device, and the incoming packet is discarded. It is up to the source station to act on the unreachable ICMP messages. In other words, if this is from an unauthorized host, you will be sending information to the same device.

Example 8-3 configures R1 to encrypt all passwords configured on a Cisco router.

Example 8-3   *Encrypting All Passwords*

```
service password-encryption
enable secret 5 $1$CNqo$C4bT4/zR.iJF0YEpqMhPF/
enable password 7 13061E010803
```

This ensures that if anyone (intruder or insider) views the configuration file, the passwords are hidden. Then, define the secret password, because it is hidden using a stronger authentication (md5) than the enable password.

Example 8-4 configures R1 to disable DHCP, which is enabled by default.

Example 8-4 *Disable DHCP*

```
no service dhcp
```

Cisco has enabled routers to act as DHCP servers to clients by default. This is not a necessary service to have running, so it should be disabled to stop any intruder from receiving a valid IP address.

Example 8-5 enables the Router R1 to log any debug output and define each entry with a timestamp.

Example 8-5 *Logging Router System Changes and Events*

```
service timestamps debug
service timestamps log
logging buffered 64000 debugging
logging rate-limit console 10 except errors
no logging console
logging trap debugging
logging 1.1.1.1
logging 141.108.1.1
logging 5.5.5.5
```

Make sure the router's clock is set to the correct time via NTP or manual entry with the **clock set** command. This allows you to look at the log after any incident has occurred. Also, because you are logging to a remote host or hosts and locally to the buffer, you can disable the debug output to the console port so that messages do not overwhelm the router. You are logging to three different remote hosts. You also buffer and output the log file for viewing at a time favorable to the network administrator. You can enable a Cisco IOS router to log messages with the command, **logging on**. The command **logging buffered** enables the router to store logged messages, such as configuration to a local file stored in NVRAM, for later viewing. To view a logging message buffered to memory, use the **show logging** command.

Example 8-6 configures R1 with the service sequence.

Example 8-6 *Enable Sequence Numbering*

```
service sequence-numbers
```

The service category is quite useful. Essentially, enabling it means your syslog entries will be numbered to ensure that they are not tampered with. R1 is configured for TACACS via the remote host 131.108.1.1.

Example 8-7 configures R1 for AAA.

Example 8-7 *AAA Configuration*

```
username cisco pass ciSc0
aaa new-model
aaa authentication login default group tacacs+ local-case
aaa authentication enable default group tacacs+ enable
aaa authorization commands 15 default group tacacs+ local
aaa accounting exec default stop-only group tacacs+
aaa accounting commands 15 default stop-only group tacacs+
aaa accounting network default stop-only group tacacs+
tacacs-server host 131.108.1.1
tacacs-server key myguitarrocksthisworld
```

Example 8-7 configures R1 for AAA authentication in the event TACACS+ fails to use local authentication with a case-sensitive password to keep hackers guessing.

By default, Cisco IOS permits a number of default services. Example 8-8 disables some common services.

Example 8-8 *Disable Services on by Default*

```
no ip http server
no ip finger
no service pad
no ip source-route
no ip bootp server
```

Example 8-8 disables R1 for an HTTP server. The **finger** command service allows remote users to view the output (equivalent to the **show users** [**wide**] command). When **ip finger** is configured, the router responds to a **telnet** *a.b.c.d* **finger** command from a remote host by immediately displaying the output of the **show users** command and then closing the connection. You should turn this service off. The **service pad** enables all packets to be assembled or disassembled (PAD) between PAD devices and access servers. The command **no ip source-route** causes the system to discard any IP datagram containing a source-route option. When you disable the BOOTP server, access to the BOOTP ports causes the Cisco IOS Software to send an "ICMP port unreachable" message to the sender and discard the original incoming packet.

Example 8-9 enables TCP intercept.

Example 8-9 *TCP Intercept*

```
ip tcp intercept list 100
ip tcp intercept connection-timeout 60
ip tcp intercept watch-timeout 10
ip tcp intercept one-minute low 1800
ip tcp intercept one-minute high 5000
access-list 100 permit ip any any
```

TCP intercept helps prevent SYN-flooding attacks by intercepting and validating TCP connection requests. In intercept mode, the TCP intercept software intercepts TCP synchronization (SYN) packets from clients to servers that match an extended access list. The router responds; if it is a valid connection, the devices are allowed to communicate.

The low and high identifies when TCP intercept should deactivate or activate (TCP aggressive mode).

In this case, the IOS command **ip tcp intercept one-minute high 5000** defines the number of connection requests (5000) received in the minute before the IOS enters aggressive mode. The IOS command **ip tcp intercept one-minute low 1800** defines the number of connection requests (1800) below which the software leaves aggressive mode.

Example 8-10 configures R1 to dump the router's memory contents in case of a router crash.

Example 8-10 *Allowing Core Dumps*

```
ip ftp username rooter
ip ftp password $%&#*&^$$%&$
exception core-file secure-r01-core-dump
exception protocol ftp
exception dump 3.3.3.3
```

It is important to be able to look at why a router crashed, especially a router that provides a security wall to the outside world. Core dumps can be given to Cisco personnel who can decipher the main reason the router crashed. The IOS command **exception core-file secure-r01-core-dump** sets the filename generated when the router actually crashes. The IOS command **exception protocol ftp** defines the protocol used to send the memory dump. The IOS command **exception dump 3.3.3.3** defines the remote host where the file will be copied; in this case, the file will be copied via FTP to remote host 3.3.3.3. Cisco Systems TAC engineers will use the memory dump to try and decipher why the router crashed.

Example 8-11 shows R1 configured for some common parameters for packets sent to unknown destinations and networks that do not exist.

Example 8-11 *IP Unreachables and Routes to Null0*

```
interface loopback0
 ip address 3.3.3.3 255.255.255.255
 no ip redirects
 no ip unreachables
interface null0
 no ip unreachables
ip route 131.0.0.0 255.0.0.0 null0
```

The IOS command **no ip redirects** disables the Cisco router from sending ICMP redirect messages to a device's source from the same interface.

The IOS command **no ip unreachables** disables the router from sending ICMP unreachables for packets it is not configured for. The **ip route** command ensures that packets received for the network 131.0.0.0/8 are thrown away and not acted on. This can stop a routing loop and an intruder trying to spoof (pretending) to belong to network 131.0.0.0/8.

Loopback interfaces are the source of log messages. Loopbacks are often used for routing protocols, as well, because a logical interface does not go down and is reliable. Assign an IP address that uniquely identifies this router. Then, configure and activate the null0 interface as a place to send unknown destination packets. This becomes the trap for packets; they can route in but they can't route out in case an intruder is spoofing networks from valid IP networks.

The configurations shown in Examples 8-1 through 8-11 are just some of the techniques you can use to ensure vulnerable routers are secure. Just imagine all the routers in the Internet that do not contain this level of security, and you will be aware of the challenges faced in the day-to-day running of the WWW and reasons why organizations like CERT/CC are an invaluable resource.

For more details on security configurations visit www.cisco.com/warp/public/707/index.shtml.

Foundation Summary

The Foundation Summary is a condensed collection of material for a convenient review of key concepts in this chapter. If you are already comfortable with the topics in this chapter and decided to skip most of the Foundation Topics material, the "Foundation Summary" section can help you recall a few details. If you just read the "Foundation Topics" section, this review should help further solidify some key facts. If you are doing your final preparation before the exam, the "Foundation Summary" section offers a convenient way to do a quick final review.

Table 8-2 summarizes the key reasons that networks should be secured.

Table 8-2   *Security Policies*

Policy Reason	Meaning
Inherent technology weaknesses	All network devices and operating systems have inherent vulnerabilities.
Configuration weaknesses	Common configurations mistakes can be exploited to open weaknesses.
Network policy vulnerabilities	The lack of network policies can lead to vulnerabilities such as password security.
Outside/inside intruders	There are always internal and external people wanting to exploit network resources and retrieve sensitive data.

Table 8-3 summarizes the key motivation factors behind intruders attacking secure and unsecured networks.

Table 8-3   *Intruder/Hackers Motivations*

Intruder/Hackers Motivation	Explanation
Cash profit	To make money from attacks, such as by transferring funds
Revenge	To get back at employers or individuals
Vandalism	To cause damage for personal satisfaction
Cyber terrorism	To gain an advantage or notoriety for an organization's ideology
For a challenge	Peer pressure or challenges set by other hackers to gain notoriety
Curiosity	Learning the tools of trade, possibly to gain experience for bigger challenges

Table 8-4 summarizes the actions taken by incident response teams.

Table 8-4 *Incident Response Team Actions*

Step		Explanation
1	Verify the incident.	Verify and gather details on the incident.
2	Determine the magnitude of the problem.	Verify hosts and how they might have been affected.
3	Assess the damage.	Determine what data has been manipulated.
4	Gather and protect the evidence.	Restore the data and any software patches.

Table 8-5 summarizes the methods used in common network attacks.

Table 8-5 *Network Attacks*

Attack	Meaning
Ping of death	Attack that sends an improperly large ICMP echo request packet with the intent of overflowing the destination machine's input buffers and causing it to crash. The IP protocol header field is set to 1, the last fragment bit is set, and the data length is greater than 65,535, greater than the maximum allowable IP packet size.
TCP SYN Flood attacks	This DoS attack randomly opens a number of TCP ports ensuring that network devices are using CPU cycles for bogus requests and denying other legitimate users access.
Teardrop	Exploits an overlapping IP fragment implementation bug in various operating systems. The bug causes the TCP/IP fragmentation re-assembly code to improperly handle overlapping IP fragments, causing the host to hang or crash.
Land.C attacks	A program designed to send TCP SYN packets (remember TCP SYN is used in the TCP connection phase) that specifies the target's host address as both source and destination. This program can use TCP port 113 or 139 (source/destination), which can also cause a system to stop functioning.
DNS poisoning	The attacker exploits the DNS server, causing the server to return a false IP address to a domain name query.
UDP Bomb	Sends illegal length field in the packet header, causing Kernel panic and crash.
E-mail attacks	This DoS attack sends a random number of e-mails to a host.
CPU-Intensive attacks	This DoS attack ties up systems resources by using programs, such as TROJAN (a program designed to capture username or passwords from a network) or enables viruses to disable remote systems.
Chargen attacks	Establishes UDP services by producing a high character input. This can cause congestion on a network.

Table 8-5   *Network Attacks (Continued)*

Attack	Meaning
Attacks via dialup (out of band)	Applications, such as Windows 95, have built-in vulnerabilities on data port 139 (known as WinNuke), if the intruders can ascertain the IP address.
Distributed Denial of Service	A DDoS attack is a DoS attack run by multiple hosts. The attacker first compromises vulnerable hosts using various tools and techniques. Then, the actual DoS attack on a target is run from the pool of all these compromised hosts.

Table 8-6 summarizes some of the critical IOS commands used to protect IOS-enabled routers.

Table 8-6   *Protecting Cisco IOS Routers*

IOS Command	Meaning
service nagle	Enables the Nagle algorithm.
no service udp-small-servers and **no service tcp-small-servers**	By default, the TCP/UDP servers for Echo, Discard, Chargen, and Daytime services are disabled.
service password-encryption	Ensures that all passwords are encrypted and not viewable when viewing the IOS configuration file.
service timestamps debug **service timestamps log**	Enables the router to log any debug output and define each entry with a timestamp.
service sequence-numbers	Allows the syslog entries to be numbered to ensure that they are not tampered with.

Q & A

The Q & A questions are designed to help you assess your readiness for the topics covered on the CCIE Security written exam and those topics presented in this chapter. This format is intended to help you assess your retention of the material. A strong understanding of the answers to these questions can help you on the CCIE Security written exam. You can also look over the questions at the beginning of the chapter again for additional review. As an additional study aid, use the CD-ROM provided with this book to take simulated exams, which draw from a database of over 300 multiple-choice questions—all different from those presented in the book.

Select the best answer. Answers to these questions can be found in Appendix A, "Answers to Quiz Questions."

1 Define four reasons networks should be secured.

_____

_____

_____

2 What is the function of the CERT/CC organization, and what are its primary objectives?

_____

_____

_____

3 What are the primary steps completed by incident response teams?

_____

_____

_____

4 Name common methods used by intruders to disrupt a secure network.

_____

_____

_____

5 In security, what is session hijacking?

_____

_____

_____

6 In security terms, what is a man in the middle attack?

_____

_____

_____

7 What is a Signature Engine?

_____

_____

_____

8 What is social engineering?

_____

_____

_____

9 Describe a ping of death attack.

_____

_____

_____

10 What is a Land.C attack?

_____

_____

_____

11 What does the following IOS code accomplish on a Cisco IOS router?

```
no service udp-small-servers
no service tcp-small-servers
```

_____

_____

_____

12 What is the secret password for the following IOS configuration?

```
enable secret %$@$%&^$@*$^*@$^*
enable pass cisco
```

_____

_____

_____

13 What is the purpose of the command **service sequence-numbers**?

_____

_____

_____

Scenario

Scenario 8-1: Defining IOS Commands to View DoS Attacks in Real Time

Figure 8-3 displays a typical two-router topology with an external connection to the Internet via R1.

Figure 8-3   *Two-Router Network Attacked by External Intruder*

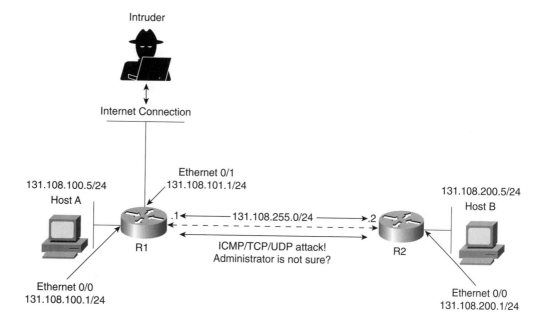

In this scenario, a Cisco IOS router is subjected to ICMP, TCP, or UDP IP packets. The network administrator is not sure of what type but notices the log file that is buffered to the Router R2 has just increased from 1 MB to 2.5 MB in less than 5 seconds. What can be done to characterize the traffic and detect the type of denial-of-service attack?

Scenario Answer

Scenario 8-1 Solution

The network administrator can quickly configure an extended access list permitting all ICMP, UDP, or TCP, as shown in Example 8-12, applying the access list to the inbound interface on R2, Serial 0/0. (The configuration is truncated to focus on the critical configuration.)

Example 8-12 *Access List Configuration on R2*

```
Hostname R2
!
interface Serial0/0
 ip address 131.108.255.2 255.255.255.252
 ip access-group 100 in
!
access-list 100 permit icmp any any log-input
access-list 100 permit tcp any any log-input
access-list 100 permit udp any any log-input
!
End
```

To determine the traffic type, access list 100 allows ICMP, UDP, and TCP inbound on Serial 0/0. Logging is also enabled with the keyword **log-input**. Assuming the DoS attack is taking place by viewing the access list 100 with the command **show ip access-list 100**, you can get an idea for which protocol type is being used. The displays in Example 8-13 are taken from R2 while the DoS attack is taking place. The command **show ip access-list 100** is entered a few times on Router R2 to view the statistics and crucial bits of data that enable you to verify the source of the attack and the method, whether it is ICMP, TCP, or UDP. Logging has been enabled so the display in Example 8-13 describes what packet matches have been made and incremented each time a packet match is made on access list 100.

Example 8-13 **show ip access-list 100** *on R2 (Repeated Five Times in Real Time)*

```
r2#show ip access-lists 100
Extended IP access list 100
    permit icmp any any log-input (5000 matches)
    permit tcp any any log-input (100 matches)
    permit udp any any log-input (23 matches)
r2#show ip access-lists 100
Extended IP access list 100
    permit icmp any any log-input (25000 matches)
    permit tcp any any log-input (100 matches)
    permit udp any any log-input (24 matches)
r2#show ip access-lists 100
```

Example 8-13 **show ip access-list 100** *on R2 (Repeated Five Times in Real Time) (Continued)*

```
Extended IP access list 100
    permit icmp any any log-input (35500 matches)
    permit tcp any any log-input (100 matches)
    permit udp any any log-input (25 matches)
r2#show ip access-lists 100
Extended IP access list 100
    permit icmp any any log-input (45500 matches)
    permit tcp any any log-input (100 matches)
    permit udp any any log-input (26 matches)
r2#show ip access-lists 100
Extended IP access list 100
    permit icmp any any log-input (67000 matches)
    permit tcp any any log-input (100 matches)
    permit udp any any log-input (26 matches)
r2#
```

Example 8-13 clearly shows that ICMP packets are increasing at an alarming rate. This indicates that an intruder could be attempting a Smurf attack (by sending a large number of ICMP requests). Now that you have identified the protocol type, you can take steps to stop ICMP packets from being sent to R2 by configuring the access list 100 on R1's outbound interface to R2, as displayed in Example 8-14.

Example 8-14 *R1's Access List 100 Configuration*

```
Hostname R1
!
interface Serial0/0
 ip address 131.108.255.2 255.255.255.252
 ip access-group 100 out
!
access-list 100 deny icmp any any log-input
access-list 100 permit tcp any any log-input
access-list 100 permit udp any any log-input
!
End
```

You can also configure the Router R1 from the inbound Internet connection with the same access list denying ICMP inbound requests.

This scenario is a simple one that clearly demonstrates the power of extended access lists and the simplest use of show commands that can be deployed in any medium or large IP network to quickly and safely identify and prevent some DoS attacks.

CHAPTER 9

CCIE Security Self-Study Lab

This chapter is designed to assist you in your final preparation for the CCIE Security exam by providing you with an extensive lab that incorporates many of the technologies and concepts covered throughout this book. This lab requires a broad perspective and knowledge base. Any knowledge you have acquired through the practical examples presented in this guide and real-life network implementations will help you achieve the end goal: a *routable* network according to the security design criteria.

This sample lab is presented in sections. A solution appears following each section.

At the end of the lab, the final configurations are presented for your reference. If you have any questions on this lab, e-mail me at hbenjamin@optusnet.com.au, and I will try to help clarify any questions you might have.

NOTE This lab draws together much of the content covered throughout this book. Keep in mind that there is not always one right or wrong way to accomplish many of the tasks presented here, but you should follow the parameters that are stipulated.

How to Use This Chapter

This lab contains a five-router network with a PIX Firewall 520 (ISP) providing a connection to the Internet. This lab is designed to ensure that you have all the practical skills to achieve almost any IP routing and security requirements in real-life networks, and to test your practical skill set so you can confidently pass the CCIE Security exam.

Goal of This Lab

This lab should assist you in your final preparation for the CCIE Security exam.

Sample solutions are provided here, but you need to research other various solutions on your own. Feel free to modify the questions to suit any design scenario and discover new IOS commands by using the Cisco Universe CD. This lab is not the only tool you should use and is provided here to demonstrate the minimum level of difficulty you will encounter when attempting the CCIE Security lab.

This lab builds on the sample Routing and Switching lab in Appendix C. This is intentional because the CCIE Security Lab Exam builds on your routing skills and requires you to build a secure IP network. The CCIE Security lab exam is a difficult examination because the routing and switching topics are assumed knowledge. You can think of the CCIE Security lab exam as two lab examinations built into one difficult security examination.

The end goal of any CCIE lab is a working solution, although you might be restricted by certain parameters.

Candidates often ask me how best to prepare for the CCIE Security lab. My answer is to practice and configure every feature available and then practice some more. Of course, not every feature will be tested, and you are encouraged to read the most up-to-date information on the web at www.cisco.com/warp/customer/625/ccie/certifications/security.html for the latest information regarding the CCIE Security certification. In particular, always look for new details on new IOS technologies and hardware.

As of August 15, 2002, the hardware types you can expect to see in the CCIE Security Lab, as documented by Cisco, are as follows:

- 2600 series routers
- 3600 series routers
- Catalyst 3550 series switches
- PIX (running Pix software version 5.2)

You can also expect to see the following applications:

- Services/applications
- Certificate authority support
- Cisco Secure Access Control System (NT server version only)
- Cisco Secure Intrusion Detection System

NOTE   The CCIE Security Lab doesn't require you to configure any Token Ring devices or Token Ring interfaces, nor any non-IP protocols, such as IPX or DLSW.

Effective November 4, 2002, CCIE labs worldwide employ Catalyst 3550 with IOS v12.1 using the Enhanced Multilayer Image. The CCIE team does not regularly change hardware because of budget concerns with Cisco in general.

CCIE Security Self-Study Lab Part I Goals

The goal of Part I of this sample lab is to ensure you provide a working IP network solution quickly and adhere to the guidelines given. You should take no longer than 4 hours to complete Part I.

CCIE Security Self-Study Lab Part II Goals

Part II builds on the working IP network and requires security features, such as IPSec and PIX. RIP routing is required. You should take no longer than 4 hours to complete Part II.

General Lab Guidelines and Setup

Follow these general guidelines during this lab:

- Static and default routes are not permitted unless directly stated in a task. This includes floating static routes.
- Routes to Null0 generated by any routing protocol are permitted.
- Full access to the two AAA servers from your workstation is permitted. The user ID is admin, and the password is cisco.
- The Class B address 144.254.0.0/16 will be used throughout the network.

Figure 9-1 displays the topology of the routed network.

Figure 9-1   *Lab Topology*

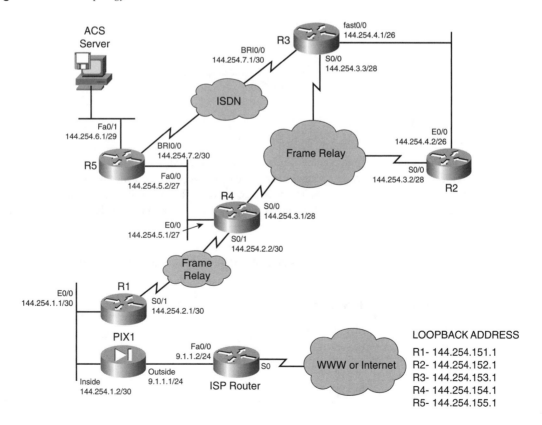

Figure 9-2 displays the Frame relay topology setup.

Figure 9-2   *Frame Relay DLCI Assignment*

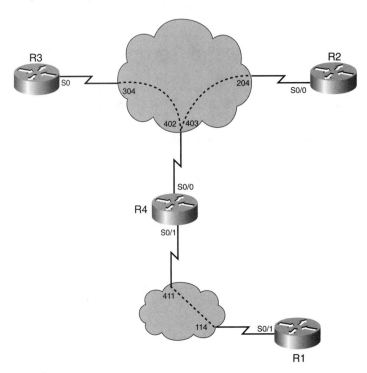

Table 9-1 displays the IP address assignment for the network topology in Figure 9-1.

Table 9-1   *IP Address Assignment*

Router Interface	IP Address
R1 E0/0	144.254.1.1/24
R1 S0/1	144.254.2.1/30
R2 E0/0	144.254.4.2/26
R2 S0/0	144.254.3.2/28

Table 9-1   *IP Address Assignment (Continued)*

Router Interface	IP Address
R3 E0/0	144.254.4.1/26
R3 S0/0	144.254.3.3/28
R3 BRI0/0	144.254.7.1/30
R4 E0/0	144.254.5.1/27
R4 S0/0	144.254.3.1/28
R4 S0/1	144.254.2.2/30
R5 FaEth0/0	144.254.5.2/27
R5 FaEth0/1	144.254.6.1/29
R5 BRI0/0	144.254.7.2/30
PIX inside	144.254.1.2/24
PIX outside	9.1.1.1/24
ISP router E0/0	9.1.1.2/24

Each router, R1-R5, is to be configured for a loopback interface. Table 9-2 displays the IP address assignment for each router.

Table 9-2   *Loopback IP Address Assignment*

Router	Loopback IP address
R1	144.254.151.1/24
R2	144.254.152.1/24
R3	144.254.153.1/24
R4	144.254.154.1/24
R5	144.254.155.1/24

After your have completed your IGP confirmation, you must be able to ping or telnet to each router loopback from any given router.

NOTE   Because of recent changes to the CCIE Security exam, the candidate is not required to configure IP addressing. However, the subject is presented here to ensure potential CCIE candidates have a good understanding of IP address spaces and subnetting. Quickly perform a spot check on all your routers to ensure that the CCIE Security exam documentation matches what is configured on your CCIE lab rack.

Communications Server

Configure the communication server (R1) so that when you type the host name of a router on the communications server, you are connected across the console port to that router:

- Disable the break command on R1 so that R1 will not permit an intruder to issue a break command and perform password recovery. (Hint: change the configuration register to 0x2002.)

- Set up the routers, as shown in Figure 9-1.

- Configure R1 as the communication server using the **ip host** command.

- Communication server ports 2 to 5 are connected to Routers R2 to R5, respectively.

- Communication server port 8 connects to the Catalyst.

Communications Server Solution

Router R1 is configured for reverse Telnet. To enable reverse Telnet on the async lines 1 through 16, you must first enable Telnet. Example 9-1 allows reverse Telnet through lines 1 through 16.

Example 9-1 *Enable Reverse Telnet on R1*

```
Line 1 16
Transport input all
```

After allowing for reverse Telnet on the async lines, define the reverse Telnet name and TCP port number. Line 1 uses TCP port 2001, line 2 TCP port 2002, and so on.

R2 is connected to Line 2, TCP port 2002, so the IOS command is as follows:

ip host R2 2002 *local ip address*

R3 is connected to Line 3, TCP port number 2003, so the IOS command is as follows:

ip host R3 2003 *local ip address*

The local IP address must be an active interface, so choose the loopback IP address. If the local IP address is assigned to a LAN or WAN interface and that interface happens to fail, your reverse Telnet connection will not work. R3 is assigned the loopback address 144.254.151.1/24. The full configuration for R1 is displayed in Example 9-2. The PIX is connected to line 15, or TCP port 2015; the Ethernet switch is on line 8, or TCP port 2008 on the local router, R1. Example 9-2 configures R2 for local name lookup.

Example 9-2 *Communication Server Solution on R1*

```
ip host R2 2002 144.254.151.1
ip host R3 2003 144.254.151.1
ip host R4 2004 144.254.151.1
ip host R5 2005 144.254.151.1
```

Example 9-2 *Communication Server Solution on R1 (Continued)*

```
ip host CAT5K 2008 144.254.151.1
ip host PIX 2015 144.254.151.1
line 1 16
transport input telnet
```

Example 9-3 displays a reverse Telnet connection on R1 to the Router R2.

Example 9-3 *Reverse Telnet to R2 on R1*

```
R1>R2
Trying 144.254.151.1 2002 ... Open
User Access Verification

Password: cisco
R2>
```

CCIE Security Self-Study Lab Part I: Basic Network Connectivity (4 Hours)

Mimicking the real CCIE Security lab exam, Part I requires you to enable physical and logical connectivity. The section requires full network connectivity between all routers and switches, including the PIX Firewall. You can test this by pinging the assigned loopbacks from any given routers, switch, or PIX.

Basic Frame Relay Setup

Configure the network in Figure 9-2 for basic physical Frame Relay connectivity. The following are the parameters:

You must use static Frame Relay maps for IP and disable Frame Relay inverse ARP. (Hint: Use **no frame-relay inverse-arp** on all frame-enabled interfaces.)

- For the connection between R1 and R4, you are not permitted the keyword **broadcast** when mapping IP between the R1/R4 Frame Relay link.
- No dynamic mapping is permitted.
- No Frame Relay subinterfaces are permitted on any router.
- Assume that RIP or IGRP will be configured over this link sometime in the next month (Hint: Use the keyword BROADCAST).
- Assign a subnet to each link from your Class B range, as described in Table 9-1.
- Use LMI type ANSI only. You can rely on auto sensing the LMI type on all routers.

- All router interface types are set to DTE. The Frame Relay switch interface type is DCE.

- Ensure that you can also ping the local and remote IP interfaces from each router configured for Frame Relay.

- Table 9-1 displays the IP address assignments for the Frame Relay network in Figure 9-1.

Users in VLAN D are sending large IP packets across the Frame Relay circuit. The Frame Relay provider has asked you to set the discard eligibility when any IP packets larger than 768 bytes are sent to R4 across the Frame Relay connection.

(Hint: Set the discard eligibility, DE, bit to packets greater than 768 Bytes on R2/R3.)

Basic Frame Relay Setup Solution

The topology in Figure 9-2 defines a number of Frame Relay PVCs. R1 is connected to R4 through the local DLCI number 114. Example 9-4 configures R1 to map the remote IP address 144.254.2.2 through DLCI 114.

Example 9-4 *Frame Relay Configuration R1*

```
interface Serial0/1
 ip address 144.254.2.1 255.255.255.252
 encapsulation frame-relay
 ip split-horizon
 frame-relay map ip 144.254.2.1 114
 frame-relay map ip 144.254.2.2 114
 frame-relay interface-dlci 114
 no frame-relay inverse-arp
```

Example 9-4 displays the configuration on R1 to enable Frame Relay encapsulation on R1 followed by static Frame Relay map statements (no **broadcast** keyword is permitted, as requested). The DLCI interface is defined as 114, and the command, **no frame-relay inverse-arp**, ensures that no dynamically learned mapping will be discovered. Make sure you use the **clear frame-relay-inarp** IOS command to remove any dynamically learned Frame Relay inverse ARP mappings. Another option to clear all dynamically learned Frame Relay mappings is to reload all your routers.

By default, on a main Cisco Frame Relay interface, Cisco IOS routers disable split horizon. You need to enable split horizon so that routing updates are not received from the originating router.

Example 9-5 displays the Frame Relay configuration required on R4.

Example 9-5 *R4 Frame Relay Configuration*

```
interface Serial0/1
 ip address 144.254.2.2 255.255.255.252
 encapsulation frame-relay
 ip split-horizon
```

Example 9-5 *R4 Frame Relay Configuration (Continued)*

```
frame-relay map ip 144.254.2.1 411
frame-relay map ip 144.254.2.2 411
frame-relay interface-dlci 411
```

R4 is configured for Frame Relay encapsulation for interface Serial 0/1 and Frame Relay map statements for the local and remote IP addresses. Frame Relay inverse ARP is disabled with the **no frame-relay inverse-arp** command.

Example 9-6 confirms IP connectivity between R1 and R4, and that there are only static Frame Relay circuits.

Example 9-6 *IP Connectivity Between R1 and R4*

```
R1#show frame-relay map
Serial0/1 (up): ip 144.254.2.1 dlci 114(0x72,0x1C20), static,
              CISCO, status defined, active
Serial0/1 (up): ip 144.254.2.2 dlci 114(0x72,0x1C20), static,
              CISCO, status defined, active
R1#ping 144.254.2.1
Type escape sequence to abort.
Sending 5, 100-byte ICMP Echos to 144.254.2.1, timeout is 2 seconds:
!!!!!
Success rate is 100 percent (5/5), round-trip min/avg/max = 8/10/12 ms
R1#ping 144.254.2.2
Type escape sequence to abort.
Sending 5, 100-byte ICMP Echos to 144.254.2.2, timeout is 2 seconds:
!!!!!
Success rate is 100 percent (5/5), round-trip min/avg/max = 4/5/8 ms
R1#
```

As requested by the lab parameters, both local and remote IP connectivity are active. Subinterfaces have not been used either.

Example 9-7 confirms the interface statistics on R1 and the LMI type setting at ANSI; because of LMI auto sense, you do not need to define the LMI type explicitly.

Example 9-7 **show interface serial 0/1** *on R1*

```
R1#show interfaces serial0/1
Serial0/1 is up, line protocol is up
  Hardware is PowerQUICC Serial
  Internet address is 144.254.2.1/30
  MTU 1500 bytes, BW 1544 Kbit, DLY 20000 usec,
     reliability 255/255, txload 1/255, rxload 1/255
  Encapsulation FRAME-RELAY, loopback not set
  Keepalive set (10 sec)
  LMI enq sent  111797, LMI stat recvd 111798, LMI upd recvd 0, DTE LMI up
```

continues

Example 9-7 **show interface serial 0/1** *on R1 (Continued)*

```
LMI enq recvd 0, LMI stat sent  0, LMI upd sent  0
LMI DLCI 0  LMI type is ANSI Annex D  frame relay DTE

FR SVC disabled, LAPF state down
Broadcast queue 0/64, broadcasts sent/dropped 2/0, interface broadcasts 0
Last input 00:00:02, output 00:00:02, output hang never
Last clearing of "show interface" counters 1w5d
Input queue: 0/75/0/0 (size/max/drops/flushes); Total output drops: 0
Queueing strategy: weighted fair
Output queue: 0/1000/64/0 (size/max total/threshold/drops)
    Conversations  0/1/256 (active/max active/max total)
    Reserved Conversations 0/0 (allocated/max allocated)
    Available Bandwidth 1158 kilobits/sec
5 minute input rate 0 bits/sec, 0 packets/sec
5 minute output rate 0 bits/sec, 0 packets/sec
    378917 packets input, 17810137 bytes, 0 no buffer
    Received 0 broadcasts, 0 runts, 0 giants, 0 throttles
    0 input errors, 0 CRC, 0 frame, 0 overrun, 0 ignored, 0 abort
    409981 packets output, 28541580 bytes, 0 underruns
    0 output errors, 0 collisions, 1 interface resets
    0 output buffer failures, 0 output buffers swapped out
    2 carrier transitions
    DCD=up  DSR=up  DTR=up  RTS=up  CTS=up
```

Example 9-7 confirms the interface state as active (Serial0/1 is up, line protocol is up) and that the LMI type is set to ANSI (LMI type is ANSI). The physical state, signals DCD/DSR/DTR/RTS/CTS, indicates that the interface is operational at Layer 1 of the OSI model.

The same configuration steps are completed on the remaining routers. In this case, you are not restricted with Frame Relay static map statements. Use the keyword **broadcast** with remote IP addresses so that routing protocols, such as OSPF, can establish neighbor adjacencies.

Example 9-8 displays the Frame Relay configuration for R2.

Example 9-8 *R2 Frame Relay Configuration*

```
interface Serial0/0
 ip address 144.254.3.2 255.255.255.248
 encapsulation frame-relay
ip split-horizon
 frame-relay map ip 144.254.3.1 204 broadcast
 frame-relay map ip 144.254.3.2 204 broadcast
 frame-relay map ip 144.254.3.3 204 broadcast
 frame-relay interface-dlci 204
 no frame-relay inverse-arp
 frame-relay lmi-type ansi
```

R2 has three Frame Relay map statements: one is to remote Router R4, another to remote Router R3, and one to the local IP address on R2 itself. Also, in this configuration, the LMI type is manually set.

Example 9-9 displays the Frame Relay configuration for R3.

Example 9-9 *R3 Frame Relay Configuration*

```
interface Serial0/0
 ip address 144.254.3.3 255.255.255.248
 encapsulation frame-relay
 ip split-horizon
 frame-relay map ip 144.254.3.1 304 broadcast
 frame-relay map ip 144.254.3.2 304 broadcast
 frame-relay map ip 144.254.3.3 304 broadcast
 frame-relay interface-dlci 304
 no frame-relay inverse-arp
```

R3 is configured for Frame Relay, and the three map statements to maintain connectivity to R4, R2, and the local IP address are assigned to Serial 0/0. R2 and R3 have been configured for split horizon in case a distance vector protocol is deployed in the future.

R4 is the hub router between R2 and R3. Because a subinterface is not permitted, you must define the two local DLCIs, 402 and 403. By default, when Frame Relay is enabled on a main Cisco IOS interface, split horizon is disabled. Because R4 is connected to R2 and R3, Router R4 must send information it receives from R2 to R3 and from R3 to R2. If a distance vector protocol is used, you must leave split horizon disabled. Because R2 and R3 have split horizon enabled, you will not have a routing loop because both R2 and R3 will reject any networks advertised by R4 that are local (as split horizon is enabled and this is the main purpose, to reject networks advertised by local router). In this lab, OSPF is configured between R4, R2, and R3, and you do not need to be concerned about split horizon; it is added here to bring the possibility of routing loops when distance vector routing protocols, such as RIP, are used in Frame Relay networks to your attention.

Example 9-10 displays the Frame Relay working configuration on R4.

Example 9-10 *R4 Frame Relay Configuration*

```
interface Serial0/0
 ip address 144.254.3.1 255.255.255.248
 encapsulation frame-relay
 frame-relay map ip 144.254.3.1 402
 frame-relay map ip 144.254.3.2 402 broadcast
 frame-relay map ip 144.254.3.3 403 broadcast
 frame-relay interface-dlci 402
 frame-relay interface-dlci 403
 no frame-relay inverse-arp
 frame-relay lmi-type ansi
 no ip split-horizon
```

Now that R2, R3, and R4 have been configured for Frame Relay, ensure that IP connectivity is enabled by pinging all the interfaces on each router.

Example 9-11 displays a successful ping request on R4 to R2 and R3, as well as the local interface on R4.

Example 9-11 *Ping Request to R2, R3, and Local IP Address*

```
R4#show frame map
Serial0/0 (up): ip 144.254.3.1 dlci 402(0x192,0x6420), static,
               CISCO, status defined, active
Serial0/0 (up): ip 144.254.3.2 dlci 402(0x192,0x6420), static,
               broadcast,
               CISCO, status defined, active
Serial0/0 (up): ip 144.254.3.3 dlci 403(0x193,0x6430), static,
               broadcast,
               CISCO, status defined, active
Serial0/1 (up): ip 144.254.2.1 dlci 411(0x19B,0x64B0), static,
               CISCO, status defined, active
Serial0/1 (up): ip 144.254.2.2 dlci 411(0x19B,0x64B0), static,
               CISCO, status defined, active
R4#ping 144.254.3.1
Type escape sequence to abort.
Sending 5, 100-byte ICMP Echos to 144.254.3.1, timeout is 2 seconds:
!!!!!
Success rate is 100 percent (5/5), round-trip min/avg/max = 8/9/12 ms
R4#ping 144.254.3.2
Type escape sequence to abort.
Sending 5, 100-byte ICMP Echos to 144.254.3.2, timeout is 2 seconds:
!!!!!
Success rate is 100 percent (5/5), round-trip min/avg/max = 4/4/8 ms
R4#ping 144.254.3.3
Type escape sequence to abort.
Sending 5, 100-byte ICMP Echos to 144.254.3.3, timeout is 2 seconds:
!!!!!
Success rate is 100 percent (5/5), round-trip min/avg/max = 4/6/8 ms
R4#
```

R4 has only static Frame Relay statements, as required by the lab.

The final step is to enable Routers R2 and R3 to set the discard eligibility (DE) when users from VLAN_D send frames larger than 768. The ISP typically sets and acts on the DE.

Example 9-12 enables R2 and R3 to set the DE bit when frames larger than 768 are received from VLAN_D. This is a global configuration command.

Example 9-12 *DE Set on R2 and R3*

```
frame-relay de-list 5 protocol ip gt 768
```

This completes the Frame Relay configuration.

Physical Connectivity

Your network is already physically patched. Construct your network, as shown in Figure 9-1 and Figure 9-2.

Configure the following characteristics for the topology in Figure 9-1 and 9-2:

- Routers R3 and R5 are connected to an ISDN service with the switch type defined as basic-5ess. R3 connects to number plan 7775010 and R5 connects to number plan 7775020.

- Routers R1 through R5 are connected to the Catalyst Ethernet switch (Catalyst 5505 series switch) as follows:

    — R1 Ethernet0/0—2/1

    — R2 Ethernet0/0—2/2

    — R3 FastEthernet0/0—2/3

    — R4 Ethernet0/0—2/4

    — R5 FastEthernet0/0—2/5

    — R5 FastEthernet0/1—2/6

    — PIX inside—2/8

    — PIX outside—2/9

No solution is provided on the physical setup. In the lab, all physical connections are precabled; this section is provided for readers who have access to real Cisco equipment and want to practice.

Catalyst Ethernet Switch Setup I

Configure the Ethernet switch for 5 VLANs:

- VLAN 2, named VLAN_A, is connected to R1 and PIX inside.
- VLAN 3, named VLAN_B, is connected to R4 and R5 FastEth0/0.
- VLAN 4, named VLAN_C, is connected to R5 FastEth0/1.
- VLAN 5, named VLAN_D, is connected to R2 and R3.
- VLAN 6, named VLAN_E, is connected to the PIX outside interface and the ISP managed router.

Using VLAN_D, configure the management interface sc0 with the address 144.254.4.3/26. Ensure that all devices in your network can ping the switch even if R2 or R3 is down.

Make sure the switch is configured in the VTP domain, SecCCIE.

The switch will never be permitted to create any more VLANS, so ensure that after you set up these VLANs, only a VTP server configuration change will allow VLAN additions to this switch.

Ensure that the only routers that can telnet to the switch are the loopback IP interfaces on R1 through R5 and the directly attached networks on R2 and R3.

Catalyst Ethernet Switch Setup I Solution

Creating VLANs on a Catalyst 5000 switch requires the VTP domain name setup first.

Example 9-13 configures the Catalyst 5000 in the VTP domain, SecCCIE, and mode server. You must enable new VLANs.

Example 9-13 *Enable VTP Domain Name and Server Mode*

```
set vtp domain SecCCIE mode server
```

Now that the switch is enabled for VTP and VLAN creation, you can create the five VLANs. Example 9-14 configures the switch for the five VLANs.

Example 9-14 *VLAN Creation*

```
set vlan 2 name VLAN_A
set vlan 3 name VLAN_B
set vlan 4 name VLAN_C
set vlan 5 name VLAN_D
set vlan 6 name VLAN_E
```

After you create all the VLANs, you must disable VLAN creation by configuring the switch as a VTP client only. The central switch in the network (VTP server) creates and deletes VLANs, as required in the future.

Example 9-15 disables local VLAN creation on the Catalyst switch.

Example 9-15 *VTP Client Setup*

```
set vtp domain SecCCIE mode client
```

The Catalyst command, **set vlan,** configures port assignments for each VLAN.

Example 9-16 configures the VLAN assignment on the Ethernet switch.

Example 9-16 *VLAN Port Assignment*

```
set vlan 1    2/7,
set vlan 2    2/1,2/8
set vlan 3    2/4-5
set vlan 4    2/6
set vlan 5    2/2-3,
set vlan 6    2/9,2/10
```

Configure the management interface (sc0) on the Catalyst switch with the following Catalyst command:

```
set interface sc0 [vlan] [ip_addr [netmask [broadcast]]]
```

The configuration of the sc0 interface in VLAN_D (or number 5) is defined in Example 9-17.

Example 9-17 *Defining the sc0 Interface*

```
set interface sc0 5 144.254.4.3 255.255.255.192
```

Example 9-18 confirms the sc0 IP address assignment and correct VLAN.

Example 9-18 **show interface** *Command on the Ethernet Switch*

```
C5K> (enable) show interface
sl0: flags=51<UP,POINTOPOINT,RUNNING>
        slip 0.0.0.0 dest 0.0.0.0
sc0: flags=63<UP,BROADCAST,RUNNING>
vlan 5 inet 144.254.4.3 netmask 255.255.255.192 broadcast 144.254.4.63
C5K> (enable)
```

You can ping the interface (sc0) and the local routers (R2/R3) to ensure connectivity to the rest of the network; you must also enable a default route. The Catalyst switch on VLAN_D is connected to R2 and R3, so you can provide two default gateways, one through R2 and another through R3; in case of network failure, the switch will still be managed either by R2 or R3.

Example 9-19 configures a default gateway point to R2 and R3 Ethernet address and also displays a successful ping request to R2 and R3.

Example 9-19 *Default Gateway Configuration and Ping Request*

```
C5K> (enable) set ip route 0.0.0.0 144.254.4.1
Route added
C5K> (enable) set ip route 0.0.0.0 144.254.4.2
Route added
C5K> (enable) ping 144.254.4.1
! Primary gateway
144.254.4.1 is alive
C5K> (enable) ping 144.254.4.2
! Secondary gateway
144.254.4.2 is alive
C5K> (enable)
```

Example 9-20 confirms the default routes with the Catalyst command, **show ip route**.

Example 9-20 **show ip route** *on the Catalyst Switch*

```
C5K> (enable) show ip route
Fragmentation   Redirect   Unreachable
-------------   --------   -----------
enabled         enabled    enabled
The primary gateway: 144.254.4.1
Destination       Gateway            Flags   Use          Interface
default           144.254.4.2        G           0         sc0
default           144.254.4.1        UG         39         sc0
144.254.4.0       144.254.4.3        U         119         sc0
default           default            UH          0         sl0
C5K> (enable)
```

The final configuration request is to permit only the VLAN_D users and the assigned loopbacks on R1 through R5. To complete this on a Catalyst switch, you need to enable an IP permit list, which defines what IP addresses are permitted access to the management interface.

Example 9-21 displays the options you can enable when the **set ip permit** command is set on the Catalyst switch.

Example 9-21 *Enabling IP permit*

```
C5K> (enable) set ip permit ?
Usage: set ip permit <enable | disable>
       set ip permit <addr> [mask]
       (mask is in dotted decimal format e.g. 255.255.0.0)
C5K> (enable) set ip permit enable
IP permit list enabled.
C5K> (enable) set ip permit 144.254.4.0 255.255.255.192
144.254.4.0 with mask 255.255.255.192 added to IP permit list.
C5K> (enable) set ip permit 144.254.151.1 255.255.255.255
144.254.151.1 with mask 255.255.255.255 added to IP permit list.
C5K> (enable) set ip permit 144.254.152.1 255.255.255.255
144.254.152.1 with mask 255.255.255.255 added to IP permit list
C5K> (enable) set ip permit 144.254.153.1 255.255.255.255
144.254.153.1 with mask 255.255.255.255 added to IP permit list
C5K> (enable) set ip permit 144.254.154.1 255.255.255.255
144.254.154.1 with mask 255.255.255.255 added to IP permit list
C5K> (enable) set ip permit 144.254.155.1 255.255.255.255
144.254.155.1 with mask 255.255.255.255 added to IP permit list
```

Example 9-21 configures an IP permit list with the subnet. To define IP addresses, you must first enable IP permit with the Catalyst command, **set ip permit enable**.

Example 9-22 confirms the IP permit list with the Catalyst command, **show ip permit**.

Example 9-22 show ip permit *Command*

```
C5K> (enable) show ip permit
IP permit list feature enabled.
Permit List         Mask
----------------    ----------------
144.254.4.0         255.255.255.192
144.254.151.1
144.254.152.1
144.254.153.1
144.254.154.1
144.254.155.1

Denied IP Address   Last Accessed Time    Type
----------------    ------------------    ------
144.254.2.1         09/30/02,15:13:44     Telnet
C5K> (enable)
```

The default mask on the loopback is actually 255.255.255.255 but is not displayed in Example 9-22.

Example 9-23 displays a successful Telnet from R2 to the SC0 management interface.

Example 9-23 *Telnet to 144.254.4.3 or R3 from R2*

```
R2#144.254.4.3
Trying 144.254.4.3 ... Open

Cisco Systems Console

Enter password: cisco
C5K> quit
[Connection to 144.254.4.3 closed by foreign host]
```

Example 9-24 displays an unsuccessful Telnet when the source interface is changed to an IP address not listed on the IP permit list on the Catalyst 5000.

Example 9-24 *Denied Telnet Example to Catalyst 5000*

```
R2#telnet 144.254.4.3 /source-interface ?
  Ethernet   IEEE 802.3
  Loopback   Loopback interface
  Null       Null interface
  Serial     Serial
  TokenRing  IEEE 802.5
R2#telnet 144.254.4.3 /source-interface serial 0/0
Trying 144.254.4.3 ... Open
Access not permitted. Closing connection...
[Connection to 144.254.4.3 closed by foreign host]
R2#
```

NOTE	The Cisco Catalyst 5000 series switch is no longer tested in any of the three CCIE lab exams and is used here to ensure that Cisco's strict nondisclosure agreement (NDA) is not violated. The 3550 is similar to the 5000 but also has Layer 3 connectivity, or routing capabilities. In the exam, you are required to configure two Catalyst 3550s; make sure you are familiar with the command structure. You can even apply this task with a Catalyst 3550 and add Layer 3 connectivity. For details on the 3550, please visit www.cisco.com/en/US/products/hw/switches/ps646/index.html.

Catalyst Ethernet Switch Setup II

Configure the following spanning tree parameters on the Catalyst 5505:

- Ensure that the switch will never become the root bridge on VLAN_D.
- Ensure that the switch will have the best possible chance of becoming the root bridge in VLAN_E.
- Set the Ethernet ports 2/1-12 to forward data immediately after a device is plugged in or activated.
- Set the hello time on VLAN_B to 5 seconds.
- Set the maxage on VLAN_B to 10 seconds.
- Configure the following miscellaneous parameters:
    - Enable Cisco Discovery Protocol on ports 2/1-12 only.
    - Ensure the only MAC address permitted to access the switch on port 2/9 is the MAC address 40-00-00-00-40-00.

You have a client who wants to run network tests. The client has a traffic generator on port 2/10 and a sink device to collect and count packets on port 2/9. The network sniffer device does not transmit packets but has a MAC address of 00-00-33-33-33-33 and an IP address of 144.254.4.1. Configure the Ethernet switch so that the client can run tests. Ensure that if the switch is rebooted, this configuration will not be lost.

Catalyst Ethernet Switch Setup II Solution

The MAC address and priority are the two critical spanning tree parameters used in determining which switch is the root bridge. To ensure that the switch will never become the root for VLAN_D, you can set the priority to the highest possible value, 65535. Example 9-25 configures VLAN_D with the highest priority setting.

Example 9-25 Set Spanning Tree Priority to 65535

```
C5K> (enable) set spantree priority ?
Usage: set spantree priority <bridge_priority> [vlan]
       (bridge_priority = 0..65535, vlan = 1..1005)
C5K> (enable) set spantree priority 65535 5
Spantree 5 bridge priority set to 65535.
C5K> (enable)
```

To view the root bridge on VLAN 5 (VLAN_D), use the **show spantree** command. Example 9-26 displays the spanning tree parameters on VLAN_D with the command, **show spantree**.

Example 9-26 show spantree ? *Command*

```
C5K> (enable) show spantree ?
Usage: show spantree [vlan] [active]
       show spantree <mod_num/port_num>
       show spantree backbonefast
       show spantree blockedports [vlan]
       show spantree portstate <trcrf>
       show spantree portvlancost <mod_num/port_num>
       show spantree statistics <mod_num/port_num> [vlan]
       show spantree statistics <trcrf> <trbrf>
       show spantree summary
       show spantree uplinkfast
C5K> (enable) show spantree 5
VLAN 5
Spanning tree enabled
Spanning tree type         ieee
Designated Root     00-00-54-ab-c5-aa
Designated Root Priority   32268
Designated Root Cost       0
Designated Root Port       1/0
Root Max Age    20 sec    Hello Time 2  sec   Forward Delay 15 sec
Bridge ID MAC ADDR         00-50-a2-5a-c8-04
Bridge ID Priority         65535
Bridge Max Age 20 sec    Hello Time 2  sec   Forward Delay 15 sec
Port      Vlan  Port-State    Cost   Priority  Fast-Start  Group-Method
 2/2      5     forwarding    100         32   enabled
 2/3      5     forwarding     19         32   enabled
 2/10     5     not-connected 100         32   enabled
C5K> (enable)
```

The root bridge in Example 9-26 is defined with the MAC address, 00-00-54-ab-c5-aa. The local priority is set to 65,535.

To ensure a switch will become the root bridge, you can set the priority to 0. Example 9-27 sets the priority on VLAN_E to 0 and displays the spanning tree state after the change.

Example 9-27 *Setting Spanning Tree to 0 and* **show spantree 6**

```
C5K> (enable) set spantree priority 0 6
Spantree 6 bridge priority set to 0.
C5K> (enable) show spantree 6
VLAN 6
Spanning tree enabled
Spanning tree type        ieee
Designated Root           00-50-a2-5a-c8-05
Designated Root Priority  0
Designated Root Cost      0
Designated Root Port      1/0

Root Max Age   20 sec    Hello Time 2  sec   Forward Delay 15 sec

Bridge ID MAC ADDR        00-50-a2-5a-c8-05
Bridge ID Priority        0
Bridge Max Age 20 sec     Hello Time 2  sec   Forward Delay 15 sec

Port     Vlan  Port-State     Cost   Priority  Fast-Start  Group-Method
-------- ----  ------------   -----  --------  ----------  ------------
 2/6      6    forwarding      100      32      enabled
 2/12     6    forwarding       19      32      enabled
```

Example 9-27 confirms the root bridge in VLAN 6 is the Catalyst switch with the MAC address of 00-50-a2-5a-c8-05.

To enable all Ethernet ports to forward data immediately means you must enable spantree portfast. Some PCs are too fast for IEEE spanning tree (listening, learning, forwarding) when connected to an Ethernet switch. Configuring the Ethernet ports to forward immediately allows for connection immediately. Example 9-28 configures ports 2/1-12 for portfast.

Example 9-28 set spantree portfast 2/1-12 enable

```
C5K> (enable) set spantree portfast 2/1-12 enable
Warning: Spantree port fast start should only be enabled on ports connected
to a single host.  Connecting hubs, concentrators, switches, bridges, etc. to
a fast start port can cause temporary spanning tree loops.  Use with caution.
Spantree ports 2/1-12 fast start enabled.
C5K> (enable)
```

The hello time and maxage parameters are always taken from the root spanning tree bridge, so before you set these parameters, make sure the root bridge in VLAN_B (numbered 3) is the root bridge.

Example 9-29 configures VLAN_B on the Catalyst switch as the root bridge and confirms the root bridge as the local Catalyst switch.

Example 9-29 *Setting VLAN_B as the Root Bridge*

```
C5K> (enable) set spantree priority ?
Usage: set spantree priority <bridge_priority> [vlan]
       (bridge_priority = 0..65535, vlan = 1..1005)
C5K> (enable) set spantree priority  0 3
Spantree 3 bridge priority set to 0.
C5K> (enable) show spantree 3
VLAN 3
Spanning tree enabled
Spanning tree type        ieee
Designated Root           00-50-a2-5a-c8-02
Designated Root Priority  0

Designated Root Cost      0
Designated Root Port      1/0
Root Max Age   20 sec    Hello Time 2  sec   Forward Delay 15 sec
Bridge ID MAC ADDR        00-50-a2-5a-c8-02
Bridge ID Priority        0
Bridge Max Age 20 sec    Hello Time 2  sec   Forward Delay 15 sec
Port      Vlan  Port-State    Cost   Priority  Fast-Start Group-Method
2/4       3     forwarding    100        32    enabled
2/5       3     forwarding     19        32    enabled
```

Example 9-30 configures the maxage and hello parameters for VLAN_B, numbered 3.

Example 9-30 *Maxage and Hello Time Configuration*

```
C5K> (enable) set spantree  maxage 10 ?
Usage: set spantree maxage <agingtime> [vlans]
       (agingtime = 6..40, vlan = 1..1005)
C5K> (enable) set spantree  maxage 10 3
Spantree 3 max aging time set to 10 seconds.
C5K> (enable) set spantree hello ?
Usage: set spantree hello <interval> [vlans]
       (interval = 1..10, vlan = 1..1005)
C5K> (enable) set spantree hello  5 3
Spantree 3 hello time set to 5 seconds.
C5K> (enable)
```

Example 9-31 confirms the correct spanning tree parameters of 10 and 5, respectively.

Example 9-31 show spantree 3 *Command*

```
C5K> (enable) show spantree 3
VLAN 3
Spanning tree enabled
```

Example 9-31 **show spantree 3** *Command (Continued)*

```
Spanning tree type          ieee
Designated Root             00-50-a2-5a-c8-02
Designated Root Priority    0
Designated Root Cost        0
Designated Root Port        1/0
Root Max Age   10 sec    Hello Time 5  sec   Forward Delay 15 sec
Bridge ID MAC ADDR          00-50-a2-5a-c8-02
Bridge ID Priority          0
Bridge Max Age 10 sec    Hello Time 5  sec   Forward Delay 15 sec
Port     Vlan  Port-State    Cost   Priority  Fast-Start  Group-Method
 2/4     3     forwarding     100       32     enabled
 2/5     3     forwarding      19       32     enabled
C5K> (enable)
```

To define CDP, Cisco's proprietary discovery protocol that is used to discover other Cisco devices, use the **set cdp** command.

Example 9-32 enables CDP on ports 2/1-12. Use the **show cdp** command to confirm the port enabled for CDP.

Example 9-32 **set cdp** *and* **show cdp** *Commands*

```
C5K> (enable) set cdp  enable  2/1-12
CDP enabled on ports 2/1-12.
C5K> (enable) show cdp interface
Port     CDP Status  Message-Interval
-------- ----------- ----------------
 1/1     disabled    60
 1/2     disabled    60
 2/1     enabled     60
 2/2     enabled     60
 2/3     enabled     60
 2/4     enabled     60
 2/5     enabled     60
 2/6     enabled     60
 2/7     enabled     60
 2/8     enabled     60
 2/9     enabled     60
 2/10    enabled     60
 2/11    enabled     60
 2/12    enabled     60
C5K> (enable)
```

Port 2/9 is permitted to connect only to a device with the MAC address 40-00-00-00-40-00. Catalyst port security will accomplish this. Example 9-33 configures port security on port 2/9.

Example 9-33 *Enable Port Security on 2/9*

```
C5K> (enable) set port security   2/9   enable 40-00-00-00-40-00
Port 2/9 port security enabled with 40-00-00-00-40-00 as the secure mac address
Trunking disabled for Port 2/9 due to Security Mode
C5K> (enable)
```

Example 9-34 confirms port security with the **show port 2/9** command.

Example 9-34 *Show port 2/9 on the Catalyst 5000 Switch*

```
C5K> (enable) show port 2/9
Port  Name               Status    Vlan      Level  Duplex Speed Type
2/9                      connect   1         normal  auto  auto 10/100BaseTX
Port  Security Secure-Src-Addr   Last-Src-Addr    Shutdown Trap    IfIndex
2/9   enabled  40-00-00-00-40-00                  No       disabled 13
Last-Time-Cleared
------------------------truncated display for clarity
Fri Sep 13 2002, 13:36:14
C5K> (enable)
```

Alternatively, you can use **show port security** to display this feature.

The final task requests that a network sniffer that does not transmit packets be set up so packets can be monitored. Cisco switches build CAM tables based on packets sourced from each port; for the switch to send packets to the source address, 00-00-33-33-33-33, you must set up a permanent CAM entry on port 2/10. This will tell the switch to send packets to the MAC address 00-00-33-33-33-33 via port 2/10. Example 9-35 configures a permanent CAM entry and enables port monitoring (span port in Cisco terminology).

Example 9-35 *CAM Entry and Port Span*

```
C5K> (enable) set cam permanent 00-00-33-33-33-33 2/10
Permanent unicast entry added to CAM table.
C5K> (enable) set span 2/9 2/10
Enabled monitoring of Port 2/9 transmit/receive traffic by Port 2/10
C5K> (enable)
```

If a static CAM entry was entered and the switch is rebooted, the CAM entry is lost; therefore, in Example 9-35, a permanent CAM entry is stored and will not be lost in case of a power failure or reset on the switch.

IP Host Lookup and Disable DNS

Configure local IP host addresses on each router (R1 through R5) so that when an exec or privilege user types the router name (R1, R2, R3, R4, or R5), the user can ping or telnet without having to type the full IP address.

Do not configure a DNS server on any router, and disable DNS lookup entries so that incorrect commands on the exec or priv prompt are not sent to any DNS server. (Hint: This saves you time as well; IOS command, **no ip domain-lookup,** disables DNS queries.)

IP Host Lookup and Disable DNS Solution

To configure local host lookups, use the IOS command, **ip host** *name ip address*.

Example 9-36 configures Router R2 for IP host lookup for all routers, including itself.

Example 9-36 ip host *Command on R2*

```
R2#configure terminal
Enter configuration commands, one per line.  End with CNTL/Z.
R2(config)#ip host r5 144.254.155.1
R2(config)#ip host r4 144.254.154.1
R2(config)#ip host r3 144.254.153.1
R2(config)#ip host r2 144.254.152.1
R2(config)#ip host r1 144.254.151.1
```

Example 9-37 disables DNS lookups for remote DNS server.

Example 9-37 no ip domain-lookup *on R2*

```
R2(config)#no ip domain-lookup
```

The same commands are installed on R1, R3, R4, and R5. See the full working configuration at the end of this chapter.

This completes the physical setup for this sample lab. You can now start configuring IP network routing on the PIX followed by the routers.

PIX Configuration

PIX1 is connected to R1 by the inside interface, and the outside interface is connected to a managed router through a 10 Mbps connection on the outside interface. Use the IP address 144.254.1.2/30 for the inside interface, and the outside interface should be set to 9.1.1.1/24.

PIX1 should use RIPv2 to communicate to R1 and supply a default route to R1.

Ensure that all RIP updates are authenticated using MD5.

You can configure a static default route on the PIX to network 144.254.0.0/16 through R1 and the Internet through 9.1.1.2.

All inside hosts should be able to ping, but only R1 is permitted to telnet to the PIX.

Configure NAT on the PIX so that inside users can reach the Internet.

PIX Configuration Solution

Example 9-38 configures the inside and outside IP address on the PIX1. The host name is set to PIX1.

Example 9-38 *Inside/Outside IP Address Configuration*

```
pixfirewall# config terminal
pixfirewall(config)# hostname PIX1
! Set the name and security level for the PIX interfaces
PIX1(config)# nameif ethernet0 outside security0
PIX1(config)# nameif ethernet1 inside security100
! enable the interfaces and set the speed
PIX1(config)# interface ethernet0 auto
PIX1(config)# interface ethernet1 auto
! configure the interface IP address
PIX1(config)# ip address outside 9.1.1.1 255.255.255.0
PIX1(config)# ip address inside 144.254.1.2 255.255.255.252
```

Example 9-39 confirms the IP address configuration with the PIX command, **show interface**.

Example 9-39 show interface *Command on the PIX*

```
PIX1# show interface
interface ethernet0 "outside" is up, line protocol is up
  Hardware is i82558 ethernet, address is 0090.2742.ff83
  IP address 9.1.1.1, subnet mask 255.255.255.0
  MTU 1500 bytes, BW 100000 Kbit full duplex
        166 packets input, 52434 bytes, 0 no buffer
        Received 80 broadcasts, 0 runts, 0 giants
        0 input errors, 0 CRC, 0 frame, 0 overrun, 0 ignored, 0 abort
        83 packets output, 5872 bytes, 0 underruns
        0 output errors, 0 collisions, 0 interface resets
        0 babbles, 0 late collisions, 0 deferred
        0 lost carrier, 0 no carrier
interface ethernet1 "inside" is up, line protocol is up
  Hardware is i82558 ethernet, address is 0090.2743.01ab
  IP address 144.254.1.2, subnet mask 255.255.255.252
  MTU 1500 bytes, BW 100000 Kbit full duplex
        34046 packets input, 2265846 bytes, 0 no buffer
        Received 33958 broadcasts, 0 runts, 0 giants
        0 input errors, 0 CRC, 0 frame, 0 overrun, 0 ignored, 0 abort
```

continues

Example 9-39 show interface *Command on the PIX (Continued)*

```
                92 packets output, 6508 bytes, 0 underruns
                0 output errors, 0 collisions, 0 interface resets
                0 babbles, 0 late collisions, 0 deferred
                0 lost carrier, 0 no carrier
    PIX1#
```

To enable RIPv2 on the PIX, enter the following command on the PIX:

```
rip inside passive version 2 authentication md5 secret-key text
```

Example 9-40 configures the PIX Firewall for RIP version 2 and MD5 authentication. Two static routes are configured, also pointing to network 144.254.0.0/8 and the Internet.

Example 9-40 *RIP Version 2 Configuration on the PIX*

```
rip inside passive version 2 authentication md5 ccie 1
rip inside default version 2 authentication md5 ccie 1
route outside 0.0.0.0 0.0.0.0 9.1.1.2
route inside 144.254.0.0 255.255.0.0 144.254.1.1
```

The MD5 password is set to ccie. The second configuration line supplies a default RIP route to R1. The final two commands enable static routes for the internal network and the Internet through 144.254.1.1 and 9.1.1.2, respectively.

You must now configure Router R1 for RIP authentication.

Example 9-41 configures a key chain named cisco and the MD5 password is ccie. RIP is enabled on the Ethernet 0/0 interface connecting to the inside interface on the PIX Firewall.

Example 9-41 *Key Chain Configuration on R1*

```
Hostname R1
key chain cisco
 key 1
  key-string ccie
interface Ethernet0/0
 ip rip authentication mode md5
 ip rip authentication key-chain cisco
```

To enable inside hosts to ping and telnet to the PIX, allow ICMP and Telnet to the PIX on the inside interface only. By default, the PIX will not permit ICMP and Telnet to any interface.

Example 9-42 permits ICMP and Telnet from the inside hosts.

Example 9-42 *Allowing ICMP and Telnet on the PIX*

```
icmp permit any echo inside
```

Example 9-43 permits R1 to telnet to the PIX with the **telnet** command.

Example 9-43 **telnet** *Command on the PIX for R1 Only*

```
telnet  144.254.1.1 255.255.255.255 inside
```

Example 9-44 displays the Telnet request from R1 to the PIX Firewall; the enable password has not been set, so you simply press return.

Example 9-44 *Telnet to 144.254.1.2 from R1*

```
R1#telnet 144.254.1.2
Trying 144.254.1.2 ... Open

PIX passwd: cisco
Welcome to the PIX firewall

Copyright (c) 1996-2000 by Cisco Systems, Inc.

                Restricted Rights Legend

Use, duplication, or disclosure by the Government is
subject to restrictions as set forth in subparagraph
(c) of the Commercial Computer Software - Restricted
Rights clause at FAR sec. 52.227-19 and subparagraph
(c) (1) (ii) of the Rights in Technical Data and Computer
Software clause at DFARS sec. 252.227-7013.

                Cisco Systems, Inc.
                170 West Tasman Drive
                San Jose, California 95134-1706

Type help or '?' for a list of available commands.
PIX1> enable
Password:
PIX1#
```

The **telnet** command is used on the PIX to enable which hosts are permitted to telnet to the PIX. By default, inside hosts do not require IPSec to remotely manage the PIX, but outside hosts do. In earlier versions of PIX code, it was possible to telnet only from an inside interface. By default, the Telnet password is set to cisco.

All outside hosts (hosts that are untrusted, such as Internet devices) need to be configured for IPSec to the PIX to enter the management console by Telnet.

To NAT all inside hosts on the PIX, the following command is first required on the PIX:

```
nat (inside) 1 0.0.0.0 0.0.0.0 0 0
```

The NAT command associates a network with a pool of global IP addresses. The following is the full PIX OS syntax:

```
nat [(if_name)] nat_id local_ip [netmask [max_conns [em_limit]]] [norandomseq]
nat [(if_name)] 0 access-list acl_name
nat [(if_name)] 0 local_ip [netmask [max_conns [em_limit]]] [norandomseq]
no nat [[(if_name)] nat_id local_ip [netmask [max_conns [em_limit]]]]
    [norandomseq]
no nat [(if_name)] 0 access-list acl_name
```

Table 9-3 summarizes the available options with the **nat** command.

Table 9-3   **nat** *Command Syntax Description*

Syntax	Description
if_name	The internal network interface name.
	If the interface is associated with an access list, the *if_name* is the higher security level interface name.
nat_id	All **nat** command statements with the same *nat_id* are in the same NAT group. Use the *nat_id* in the global command statement; for example:
	nat (inside) 1 0 0
	global (outside) 1 10.1.1.0 10.1.1.254 netmask 255.255.255.224
	This example associates the **nat** command with the global command by the *nat_id*.
	The *nat_id* is an arbitrary positive number between 0 and 2 billion. This number can be the same as the ID used with the **outbound** and **apply** commands.
	Specify **0** with IP addresses and netmasks to identify internal networks that desire only outbound identity address translation. Specify **0** with the **access-list** option to specify traffic that should be exempted from NAT.
access-list	Associates an **access-list** command statement with the **nat 0** command.
local_ip	Internal network IP address to be translated. You can use **0.0.0.0** to allow all hosts to start outbound connections. The **0.0.0.0** *local_ip* can be abbreviated as **0**.
netmask	Network mask for *local_ip*. You can use **0.0.0.0** to allow all outbound connections to translate with IP addresses from the global pool.
max_conns	The maximum TCP connections permitted from the interface you specify.
em_limit	The embryonic connection limit. The default is 0, which means unlimited connections. Set it lower for slower systems and higher for faster systems.
norandomseq	Do not randomize the TCP packet's sequence number. Only use this option if another inline firewall is also randomizing sequence numbers and the result is scrambling the data. Use of this option opens a security hole in the PIX Firewall.

See the Cisco website for more details on how NAT/PAT can be configured on a Cisco PIX:

www.cisco.com/univercd/cc/td/doc/product/iaabu/pix/pix_sw/index.htm

More PIX tasks appear later in this CCIE Security self-study lab.

IGP Routing

After this section is completed, all routers must have full IP connectivity between every routing domain, including the ISDN backup interfaces when operational.

RIP Configuration

Configure RIP on Router R1 and the PIX only:

- Authenticate RIP between R1 and the PIX.
- VLAN_A resides in a RIP Version II domain only.
- Redistribute the RIP routes into the IGP network.
- Make sure you can see distributed RIP routes throughout your topology and that the OSPF cost metric is set to 1000 for all RIP routes redistributed from R1.
- Use a route-map to set the cost.

RIP Configuration Solution

Example 9-45 enables RIPv2 only on R1 and redistributes the EIGRP routes into RIP.

Example 9-45 *Enable RIP on R1*

```
router rip
 version 2
 redistribute eigrp 333 metric 5
 passive-interface Serial0/1
 network 144.254.0.0
```

R1 is configured for RIPv2 only; notice that only Serial0/1 (link to R4 through EIGRP) is configured in a passive state where no RIP route will be sent to R4, as this link resides in EIGRP only.

Example 9-46 configures MD5 authentication between the R1 and the PIX Firewall.

Example 9-46 *MD5 RIP Authentication on R1*

```
interface Ethernet0/0
 ip rip authentication mode md5
 ip rip authentication key-chain cisco
```

Example 9-47 confirms RIP connectivity (**show ip route rip** command) between the PIX and R1. Notice the default route supplied by the PIX.

Example 9-47 show ip route rip *on R1*

```
R1#show ip route rip
R*   0.0.0.0/0 [120/1] via 144.254.1.2, 00:00:10, Ethernet0/0
R1#
```

Example 9-47 displays a default RIP route via 144.254.1.2 on the PIX inside interface.

EIGRP Configuration

Configure EIGRP between R1 and R4 Frame Relay connections only:

- Configure EIGRP in AS 333.
- Ensure that EIGRP is authenticated across the Frame Relay connections.
- Redistribute the EIGRP routes into OSPF domain with a varying OSPF cost metric.
- Configure R1 with the following additional loopback interfaces and corresponding IP addresses:
    - Loopback 1 131.108.1.1/24
    - Loopback 2 131.108.2.1/24
    - Loopback 3 131.108.3.1/24

Configure the above loopbacks to be in EIGRP domain 333. Ensure that all routers in your network can ping these loopbacks.

EIGRP Configuration Solution

EIGRP is to be enabled on the link between R1 and R4 only, so you must make all other interfaces passive. The real problem here, though, is the fact that you are not permitted to use the Frame Relay **broadcast** keyword when mapping IP across the frame cloud. EIGRP sends updates as broadcasts, so even if you enable EIGRP on the serial link, no updates will be sent, as broadcasts have been disabled. Remember that by default a Cisco router interface drops all broadcast frames. To enable EIGRP to maintain a neighbor relationship in this scenario, you can tunnel EIGRP over an IP GRE tunnel.

Example 9-48 configures R1 for EIGRP and an IP GRE tunnel to obtain EIGRP neighbors to R4.

Example 9-48 *Enable EIGRP and Tunnel Interface on R1*

```
Hostname R1

interface Tunnel0
 ip unnumbered Serial0/1
 tunnel source Serial0/1
```

Example 9-48 *Enable EIGRP and Tunnel Interface on R1 (Continued)*

```
    tunnel destination 144.254.2.2
 router eigrp 333
   passive-interface Ethernet0/0
   network 144.254.0.0
```

Example 9-49 configures R4 for EIGRP and the IP GRE tunnel to obtain EIGRP neighbors to R1.

Example 9-49 *Enable EIGRP and Tunnel Interface on R4*

```
 Hostname R4
 interface Tunnel0
  ip unnumbered Serial0/1
  tunnel source Serial0/1
  tunnel destination 144.254.2.1
 router eigrp 333
 passive-interface Ethernet0/0
  passive-interface Serial0/0
  passive-interface Loopback0
  network 144.254.0.0
```

Example 9-50 confirms the EIGRP relationship over the newly created tunnel interface.

Example 9-50 **show ip eigrp neighbor** *Command on R1 and R4*

```
 R1#show ip eigrp neighbors
 IP-EIGRP neighbors for process 333
 H    Address                 Interface     Hold Uptime     SRTT   RTO  Q  Seq Type
                                            (sec)           (ms)       Cnt Num
 0    144.254.2.2             Tu0            12 1w6d          15  5000  0  155
 R1#

 R4#show ip eigrp neighbors
 IP-EIGRP neighbors for process 333
 H    Address                 Interface     Hold Uptime     SRTT   RTO  Q  Seq Type
                                            (sec)           (ms)       Cnt Num
 0    144.254.2.1             Tu0            13 1w6d          62  5000  0  165
 R4#
```

To enable authentication of EIGRP packets, use the following **ip authentication key-chain eigrp** interface configuration command:

```
ip authentication key-chain eigrp as-number key-chain
```

To specify the type of authentication used in EIGRP packets, use the following **ip authentication mode eigrp** interface configuration command:

```
ip authentication mode eigrp as-number md5
```

Example 9-51 configures R1 with a new key chain and EIGRP authentication. First, the key chain is defined, and then the authentication is applied to the Interface tunnel 0, not the serial link, as the EIGRP neighbors are established over the tunnel interface and not the nonbroadcast Serial interface.

Example 9-51 *EIGRP Authentication on R1*

```
R1(config)#key chain  ?
  WORD  Key-chain name
R1(config)#key ?
  chain      Key-chain management
  config-key  Set a private configuration key
R1(config)#key chain eigrp
R1(config-keychain)#key 1
R1(config-keychain-key)#key-string ccie
R1(config-keychain-key)#exit
R1(config-keychain)#interface tunnel0
R1(config-if)#ip authentication key-chain eigrp 333 eigrp md5
R1(config-if)# ip authentication key-chain ?
  eigrp  Enhanced Interior Gateway Routing Protocol (EIGRP)

R1(config-if)# ip authentication key-chain eigrp ?
  <1-65535>  Autonomous system number

R1(config-if)# ip authentication key-chain eigrp 333 ?
  LINE  name of key-chain

R1(config-if)# ip authentication key-chain eigrp 333 eigrp ?
LINE     <cr>

R1(config-if)# ip authentication key-chain eigrp 333 eigrp md5
```

The secret key is set to ccie.

Example 9-52 configures R4 for the same parameters.

Example 9-52 *R4 EIGRP Authentication*

```
R4(config)#key chain eigrp
R4(config-keychain)# key 1
R4(config-keychain-key)#  key-string ccie
R4(config-keychain-key)#interface Tunnel0
R4(config-if)# ip unnumbered Serial0/1
R4(config-if)# ip authentication mode eigrp 333 md5
R4(config-if)# ip authentication key-chain eigrp 333 eigrp  md5
```

Example 9-53 confirms EIGRP neighbor relations after the changes.

Example 9-53 show ip eigrp neighbors *Command on R1*

```
R1#show ip eigrp neighbors
IP-EIGRP neighbors for process 333
H   Address                  Interface    Hold Uptime    SRTT   RTO   Q  Seq Type
                                          (sec)          (ms)         Cnt Num
0   144.254.2.2              Tu0            10 00:00:36   687   5000   0  161
R1#
```

The final section requires three additional loopbacks configured on R1 and redistribution into OSPF. Example 9-54 enables the three additional loopbacks on R1.

Example 9-54 *Loopback Addition on R1*

```
interface Loopback1
  ip address 131.108.1.1 255.255.255.0
!
interface Loopback2
  ip address 131.108.2.1 255.255.255.0
!
interface Loopback3
  ip address 131.108.3.1 255.255.255.0
router eigrp 333
  network 131.108.0.0
```

Notice in Example 9-54 that the networks (the three loopbacks) are placed into EIGRP AS 333.

Example 9-55 enables R4 to redistribute the EIGRP routes into OSPF with a metric type 1, or varying metric type.

Example 9-55 *R4 Redistribution into OSPF*

```
router ospf 1

 redistribute eigrp 333 metric 100 metric-type 1 subnets
```

R4 is configured to redistribute the EIGRP networks with a cost metric of 100, metric type E1, and the keyword **subnets** allows the subnetted routes (131.108.0.0 and 144.254.0.0) to be injected into the OSPF domain.

You will confirm IP routing connectivity after all IGP routing protocols are configured.

OSPF Configuration

Configure OSPF, as described in Figure 9-3. Do not create any nonspecified OSPF areas. There are two OSPF backbones.

Figure 9-3   *OSPF Area Assignments*

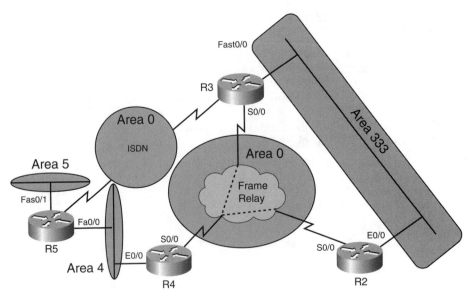

For loopback interfaces, place the interfaces in the appropriate OSPF area already assigned to the router. For Example, R4 resides in areas 0 and 4; place R4 Loopback 0 in area 0, and so forth.

When applying an inverse mask, apply the following on all interfaces configured in OSPF, 0.0.0.0:

- Configure the OSPF backbone over the Frame Relay network between the three Routers R2, R3, and R4.
- Do not change the network type on any Frame Relay interface.
- The ISDN link between R3 and R5 resides in area 0.0.0.0.
- The Ethernet link between R4 and R5 is in area 4.
- The Ethernet segment named VLAN_C will reside in area 5.
- Ensure that all OSPF routes are redistributed and reachable in the RIP and EIGRP domains.
- Make sure the OSPF backbone in the frame cloud is authenticated using the strongest authentication possible.
- Ensure that R2 will never be the DR on all segments.
- Ensure the ISDN link is active only if OSPF neighbors are lost between R3 and R4. Do not use the **backup** command or **dialer-watch** commands to accomplish this task. Only IP traffic is permitted across the ISDN link. See the ISDN section before completing the ISDN setup.

- Ensure that R4 is the DR in the OSPF Frame Relay backbone network.

- Ensure that the router ID of all OSPF-enabled routers is the loopback address. Do not assume this will be the case, but make sure no matter what IP address is assigned, the router-id is set to Loopback 0.

- Advertise the loopbacks as 24-bit subnets; do not use the command **redistributed connected** to accomplish this task.

- Do not create any additional areas.

- Set dead interval between the R2 and R4 link to 100 seconds. Do not use the **ip ospf dead-interval** command to accomplish this task.

- Set the Hello interval on R2 Ethernet segment to 20 seconds.

The Ethernet connection between R5 and R4 has been experiencing packet loss. Configure the OSPF process such that the neighbor relationship between R4 and R5 will remain established if at least one OSPF HELLO packet is received every 60 seconds.

OSPF security is a concern on VLAN B. Configure the strongest form of OSPF security on VLAN B so that someone with a packet tracer cannot read OSPF packet exchanges between R4 and R5.

OSPF Configuration Solution

The first part of any OSPF design is the need for all areas to be connected to area 0 or the backbone. In Figure 9-3, there are two backbones, but the ISDN link is used only in the event that R3 loses OSPF neighbor connectivity to R5. Area 5 is not connected to the backbone under normal OSPF operation (In other words, you need a virtual link between area 5 and area 0.)

Start by enabling OSPF on Router R2 followed by R3, R4, and R5.

Example 9-56 configures OSPF on R2.

Example 9-56 *Enabling OSPF on R2*

```
Hostname R2
interface Loopback0
 ip address 144.254.152.1 255.255.255.0
 ip ospf network point-to-point
interface Ethernet0/0
 ip address 144.254.4.2 255.255.255.192
 ip ospf priority 0
ip ospf hello-interval 20
interface Serial0/0
 ip address 144.254.3.2 255.255.255.248

 ip ospf authentication message-digest-key 1 md5 cisco
 ip ospf authentication-key cisco
ip ospf hello-interval 25
```

continues

Example 9-56 *Enabling OSPF on R2 (Continued)*

```
! Four times this value give 100 sec
 ip ospf priority 0
router ospf 1
 router-id 144.254.152.1
 log-adjacency-changes
 area 0 authentication message-digest
 network 144.254.3.2 0.0.0.0 area 0
 network 144.254.4.2 0.0.0.0 area 333
 network 144.254.152.1 0.0.0.0 area 0
```

As per requirements in the question, the network mask applied to all interfaces in OSPF is 0.0.0.0, or exact match, which means you must also supply the actual IP address. The loopback interface is configured for point-to-point so the interface is advertised as a /24 subnet and not a stub host (/32) by default. R2 serial link to R4 is configured for MD5 authentication, and the OSPF priority is set to 0 so that R4 is the designated router. MD5 is the strongest authentication mechanism available to OSPF. R2 priority on Ethernet 0/0 is also set to 0 so that R2 will never be the DR on any LAN or WAN segment. R2 router ID is manually set to the loopback interface. The dead interval needs to be set to 100 seconds, but the use of the **ip ospf dead-interval** command is not allowed. Because, by default, the dead interval is four times the Hello interval, set the Hello interval to 25 seconds. This will make the dead interval 100 seconds. The command, **ip ospf hello-interval,** accomplishes this. In any exam, you should always think outside the square for questions such as this one if you are familiar with how each routing protocol is designed.

Also, R4 and R3 require the same command, as R2, R3, and R4 are part of the same nonbroadcast network. All OSPF routers require the same change of the Hello interval to 25 seconds. The same applies to OSPF authentication, as R2, R3, and R4 reside in area 0, and OSPF requires all routers in the same area configured for authentication to be enabled with the secret key. (In this case, MD5 encrypts or hashes the password ccie.) Similarly, you are asked to change the Hello interface on the R2 segment to 20 seconds; this requires R3 to be changed, as well, so that OSPF neighbor adjacency is maintained. OSPF will not become adjacent if the Hello intervals are not the same.

Example 9-57 enables OSPF on Router R3.

Example 9-57 *R3 OSPF Configuration*

```
Hostname R3
interface Loopback0
 ip address 144.254.153.1 255.255.255.0
 ip ospf network point-to-point
 !
interface fastethernet0/0
ip ospf hello-interval 20
interface Serial0/0
 ip address 144.254.3.3 255.255.255.248
```

Example 9-57 *R3 OSPF Configuration (Continued)*

```
 ip split-horizon
  ip ospf authentication message-digest-key 1 md5 cisco
  ip ospf authentication-key cisco
  ip ospf hello-interval 25
  ip ospf priority 0
  router ospf 1
  router-id 144.254.153.1
  area 0 authentication message-digest
  network 144.254.3.3 0.0.0.0 area 0
  network 144.254.4.1 0.0.0.0 area 333
 network 144.254.7.1 0.0.0.0 area 0
  network 144.254.153.1 0.0.0.0 area 0
```

The OSPF configuration for the ISDN BRI interface is covered in the ISDN section below. R3 requires the loopback interface advertised as /24 and the manual router-id setup to the loopback 0 interface.

Example 9-58 configures OSPF on R4.

Example 9-58 *R4 OSPF Configuration*

```
 Hostname R4
 !
 interface Loopback0
  ip address 144.254.154.1 255.255.255.0
  ip ospf network point-to-point
 !
 !
 interface Ethernet 0/0
 ip ospf hello-interval 60
 interface Serial0/0
  ip address 144.254.3.1 255.255.255.248
  encapsulation frame-relay
  ip ospf authentication message-digest-key 1 md5 cisco
  ip ospf authentication-key cisco
  ip ospf hello-interval 25
  ip ospf priority 255
 !
 !
 router eigrp 333
  redistribute ospf 1 metric 1544 20000 255 1 1500

 router ospf 1
  router-id 144.254.154.1
  log-adjacency-changes
  area 0 authentication message-digest-key 1 md5 cisco
  area 4 virtual-link 144.254.155.1
  redistribute eigrp 333 metric 100 metric-type 1 subnets
  network 144.254.3.1 0.0.0.0 area 0
```

continues

Example 9-58 *R4 OSPF Configuration (Continued)*

```
 network 144.254.5.1 0.0.0.0 area 4
 network 144.254.154.1 0.0.0.0 area 0
 neighbor 144.254.3.3
 neighbor 144.254.3.2
```

Example 9-58 displays the fact that R4 is the DR to R2/R3, and because you are not permitted to change the network type in the core Frame Relay backbone network, you must configure OSPF for neighbors using the **neighbor** command. R4 also redistributes EIGRP routes into OSPF. R4 Ethernet 0/0 segment has an OSPF Hello interval set to 60 seconds so that only one Hello packet every minute is sufficient to maintain OSPF adjacencies to R5, as requested by the question. The virtual link between R4 and R5 is required so that area 5 is visible to the backbone when the ISDN link is not in operation.

Example 9-59 displays the OSPF configuration on R5.

Example 9-59 *OSPF Configuration on R5*

```
Hostname R5
interface Loopback0
 ip address 144.254.155.1 255.255.255.0
 ip ospf network point-to-point
!
interface FastEthernet0/0
 ip ospf hello-interval 60
ip ospf authentication-message-digest
ip ospf message-digest-key 1 md5 cisco

 !
 !
interface FastEthernet0/1
 ip address 144.254.6.1 255.255.255.248
 !
interface Serial0/1
 no ip address
 shutdown
!
router ospf 1
 router-id 144.254.155.1
area 0 authentication message-digest
 area 4 virtual-link 144.254.154.1
network 144.254.5.2 0.0.0.0 area 4
 network 144.254.6.1 0.0.0.0 area 5
 network 144.254.7.2 0.0.0.0 area 0
 network 144.254.155.1 0.0.0.0 area 4
```

R5 is configured for a virtual link over transit area 4. Notice that good OSPF design always sets the router ID so that virtual links can be configured by network administrators knowing that a failure of any physical interface will not bring down a virtual link. Area 0 on R5 is configured for authentication because the core Frame Relay network between R2, R3, and R4 in area 0 is configured for authentication ; in particular, R3 will not become adjacent because R3 is part of the core backbone where MD5 authentication is configured.

Now that all IGP routing protocols are completed and redistribution is enabled, ensure that there is IP connectivity between all routers by viewing the IP routing tables and pinging all loopback interfaces from Router R4.

Example 9-60 displays the IP routing table on R4.

Example 9-60 show ip route *on R4*

```
R4#show ip route
Codes: C - connected, S - static, I - IGRP, R - RIP, M - mobile, B - BGP
       D - EIGRP, EX - EIGRP external, O - OSPF, IA - OSPF inter area
       N1 - OSPF NSSA external type 1, N2 - OSPF NSSA external type 2
       E1 - OSPF external type 1, E2 - OSPF external type 2, E - EGP
       i - IS-IS, L1 - IS-IS level-1, L2 - IS-IS level-2, ia - IS-IS inter area
       * - candidate default, U - per-user static route, o - ODR
       P - periodic downloaded static route

Gateway of last resort is 144.254.2.1 to network 0.0.0.0

     144.254.0.0/16 is variably subnetted, 12 subnets, 5 masks
O IA    144.254.6.0/29 [110/11] via 144.254.5.2, 00:04:11, Ethernet0/0
O       144.254.7.0/30 [110/1572] via 144.254.5.2, 00:04:42, Ethernet0/0
O IA    144.254.4.0/26 [110/49] via 144.254.3.3, 00:04:11, Serial0/0
C       144.254.5.0/27 is directly connected, Ethernet0/0
C       144.254.2.0/30 is directly connected, Serial0/1
C       144.254.3.0/29 is directly connected, Serial0/0
D       144.254.1.0/30 [90/297270016] via 144.254.2.1, 00:49:09, Tunnel0
C       144.254.154.0/24 is directly connected, Loopback0
O       144.254.155.0/24 [110/11] via 144.254.5.2, 00:04:13, Ethernet0/0
O       144.254.152.0/24 [110/49] via 144.254.3.2, 00:04:43, Serial0/0
O       144.254.153.0/24 [110/49] via 144.254.3.3, 00:04:43, Serial0/0
D       144.254.151.0/24 [90/297372416] via 144.254.2.1, 00:49:09, Tunnel0
     131.108.0.0/24 is subnetted, 3 subnets
D       131.108.3.0 [90/297372416] via 144.254.2.1, 00:49:09, Tunnel0
D       131.108.2.0 [90/297372416] via 144.254.2.1, 00:49:09, Tunnel0
D       131.108.1.0 [90/297372416] via 144.254.2.1, 00:49:09, Tunnel0
D*EX 0.0.0.0/0 [170/302364416] via 144.254.2.1, 00:49:09, Tunnel0
R4#
```

R4 has OSPF, EIGRP, and connected routes to all parts of the network. By pinging all the loopback interfaces from any given router, you can be sure that IP routing is configured correctly. Notice that the EIGRP routes from R1 are learned over the tunnel interface. A default router is advertised by the PIX to the World Wide Web.

Example 9-61 pings all the remote loopbacks from R4 to ensure IP connectivity.

Example 9-61 *Ping Loopbacks from R4*

```
R4#ping 144.254.151.1

Type escape sequence to abort.
Sending 5, 100-byte ICMP Echos to 144.254.151.1, timeout is 2 seconds:
!!!!!
Success rate is 100 percent (5/5), round-trip min/avg/max = 4/7/8 ms
R4#ping 144.254.152.1

Type escape sequence to abort.
Sending 5, 100-byte ICMP Echos to 144.254.152.1, timeout is 2 seconds:
!!!!!
Success rate is 100 percent (5/5), round-trip min/avg/max = 4/5/8 ms
R4#ping 144.254.153.1

Type escape sequence to abort.
Sending 5, 100-byte ICMP Echos to 144.254.153.1, timeout is 2 seconds:
!!!!!
Success rate is 100 percent (5/5), round-trip min/avg/max = 4/4/8 ms
R4#ping 144.254.154.1

Type escape sequence to abort.
Sending 5, 100-byte ICMP Echos to 144.254.154.1, timeout is 2 seconds:
!!!!!
Success rate is 100 percent (5/5), round-trip min/avg/max = 1/1/4 ms
R4#ping 144.254.155.1

Type escape sequence to abort.
Sending 5, 100-byte ICMP Echos to 144.254.155.1, timeout is 2 seconds:
!!!!!
Success rate is 100 percent (5/5), round-trip min/avg/max = 1/2/4 ms
R4#
```

Example 9-62 pings all the remote loopbacks from R1 to ensure IP connectivity.

Example 9-62 *Ping loopbacks from R1*

```
R1#ping 144.254.151.1
Type escape sequence to abort.
Sending 5, 100-byte ICMP Echos to 144.254.151.1, timeout is 2 seconds:
!!!!!
Success rate is 100 percent (5/5), round-trip min/avg/max = 1/2/4 ms
R1#ping 144.254.152.1
Type escape sequence to abort.
Sending 5, 100-byte ICMP Echos to 144.254.152.1, timeout is 2 seconds:
!!!!!
Success rate is 100 percent (5/5), round-trip min/avg/max = 8/11/12 ms
R1#ping 144.254.153.1
Type escape sequence to abort.
```

Example 9-62 *Ping loopbacks from R1 (Continued)*

```
Sending 5, 100-byte ICMP Echos to 144.254.153.1, timeout is 2 seconds:
!!!!!
Success rate is 100 percent (5/5), round-trip min/avg/max = 8/10/12 ms
R1#ping 144.254.154.1
Type escape sequence to abort.
Sending 5, 100-byte ICMP Echos to 144.254.154.1, timeout is 2 seconds:
!!!!!
Success rate is 100 percent (5/5), round-trip min/avg/max = 4/7/8 ms
R1#ping 144.254.155.1
Type escape sequence to abort.
Sending 5, 100-byte ICMP Echos to 144.254.155.1, timeout is 2 seconds:
!!!!!
Success rate is 100 percent (5/5), round-trip min/avg/max = 4/7/8 ms
R1#
```

Now, test IP connectivity from R2, but use host names you configured earlier. Example 9-63 pings the remote and local loopbacks from R2.

Example 9-63 *R2 Ping Test Connectivity*

```
R2#ping r1
Type escape sequence to abort.
Sending 5, 100-byte ICMP Echos to 144.254.151.1, timeout is 2 seconds:
!!!!!
Success rate is 100 percent (5/5), round-trip min/avg/max = 8/10/12 ms
R2#ping r2
Type escape sequence to abort.
Sending 5, 100-byte ICMP Echos to 144.254.152.1, timeout is 2 seconds:
!!!!!
Success rate is 100 percent (5/5), round-trip min/avg/max = 1/1/4 ms
R2#ping r3
Type escape sequence to abort.
Sending 5, 100-byte ICMP Echos to 144.254.153.1, timeout is 2 seconds:
!!!!!
Success rate is 100 percent (5/5), round-trip min/avg/max = 8/9/12 ms
R2#ping r4
Type escape sequence to abort.
Sending 5, 100-byte ICMP Echos to 144.254.154.1, timeout is 2 seconds:
!!!!!
Success rate is 100 percent (5/5), round-trip min/avg/max = 4/5/8 ms
R2#ping r5
Type escape sequence to abort.
Sending 5, 100-byte ICMP Echos to 144.254.155.1, timeout is 2 seconds:
!!!!!
Success rate is 100 percent (5/5), round-trip min/avg/max = 4/5/8 ms
R2#
```

Example 9-64 confirms OSPF neighbor adjacencies between R4 and R2 and R4 and R5.

Example 9-64 show ip ospf neighbor *on R4*

```
R4#show ip ospf neighbor
Neighbor ID     Pri   State          Dead Time   Address        Interface
144.254.153.1    0    FULL/DROTHER   00:01:17    144.254.3.3    Serial0/0
144.254.152.1    0    FULL/DROTHER   00:01:22    144.254.3.2    Serial0/0
144.254.155.1    1    FULL/DR        00:03:47    144.254.5.2    Ethernet0/0
R4#
```

This completes the IP routing requirement. In a typical CCIE security lab, you are expected to have this sort of network active in a short period (less than four hours is ideal). At this stage, no security technologies have been extensively covered except for routing algorithm-based authentication with RIP, OSPF, and EIGRP. The remainder of this CCIE Security self-study lab concentrates on security topics and some miscellaneous IOS features, such as DHCP and ISDN.

Basic ISDN Configuration

The basic ISDN configuration task information is as follows:

- ISDN switch information:
  - ISDN switch type: basic-5ess
- ISDN numbering:
  - R3: 7775010
  - R5: 7775020
- SPIDs are not required.

Configure the ISDN interfaces on R3 and R5 as follows:

- Ensure that only R3 can call R5, and R3 should never challenge R5 for a username or password pairing.
- ISDN switch type is basic-5ess. Do not configure any SPIDs.
- If Traffic exceeds more than 65 percent, the second ISDN B-channel will be used. (Hint: Enable **ppp multilink**.)
- If there is an error-rate of 20 percent or higher, the interface on R3 should show only a "down" status when the command **show interface bri0/0** is displayed. (Hint: Use the **ppp quality** command.)
- R5 cannot call R3 under any circumstance. If R3 OSPF adjacency goes down, make sure the ISDN link is operational and all OSPF routing is accomplished through the ISDN link. Use **OSPF demand circuit** and not **static** or **dialer-watch** statements.
- Use PPP encapsulation and the strongest authentication available.

- When the ISDN is active, all routers must be able to ping and telnet the local ISDN interfaces on R3 and R5.

- Ensure that OSPF neighbors are not keeping the ISDN call active unless the neighbor over the frame link is not adjacent. (Hint: Apply the **no peer neighbor-route** IOS command on R3 and R5.)

- Use the command **show isdn status** to confirm when any ISDN calls are activated or deactivated.

Basic ISDN Configuration Solution

R3 and R5 are connected to an ISDN switch. All the ISDN parameters are provided so you can configure them easily. OSPF demand circuit is enabled between R3 and R5.

Example 9-65 configures R3 for ISDN connectivity to R5.

Example 9-65 *ISDN Configuration for R3*

```
Hostname R3
!
username R5 password 0 cisco
!
isdn switch-type basic-5ess
interface BRI0/0
 description 7775010
 ip address 144.254.7.1 255.255.255.252
 encapsulation ppp
 ip ospf authentication message-digest-key 1 md5 cisco
 ip ospf authentication-key cisco
ip ospf demand-circuit
 ppp quality 80
 dialer map ip 144.254.7.2 name R5 broadcast 7775020
 dialer load-threshold 165 either
no peer neighbor-route
 dialer-group 1
 isdn switch-type basic-5ess
ppp authentication chap callin
ppp multilink
!Global command below permits IP traffic only
dialer-list 1 protocol ip permit
```

In Example 9-65, R3 is configured for OSPF demand circuit. Only when OSPF is adjacent to R3 and R4 is down will R3 make an outgoing ISDN call to R5. IP data is permitted to cross the ISDN link via the **dialer** group command. OSPF authentication is enabled because area 0 requires all interfaces configured for authentication to have authentication configured and enabled with the correct secret key. PPP CHAP authentication is used because CHAP encrypts all passwords with MD5. The **ppp quality** command ensures that if error rates on the interface reaching 20 percent of errors (80 percent or less is good traffic), the interface will be brought down. This is a specific IOS command.

Example 9-66 enables R5 to receive the call.

Example 9-66 *R5 ISDN Configuration*

```
hostname R5
!
username R5 password 0 cisco
!
interface BRI0/0
 description 7775020
 ip address 144.254.7.2 255.255.255.252
 encapsulation ppp
 ip ospf authentication message-digest
 ip ospf authentication-key cisco-key 1 md5 cisco dialer load-threshold 165 either

 dialer map ip 144.254.7.1 name R3 broadcast
dialer-group 1
 isdn switch-type basic-5ess
 no peer neighbor-route
 ppp authentication chap callin
ppp multilink
 !
dialer-list 1 protocol ip permit
```

R5 cannot make an outgoing call because the dial map statement contains no valid ISDN number. The **ppp multilink** command is enabled so that two B channels can be active when R3 outbound traffic reaches 65 percent or more. The **ppp authentication chap callin** command checks only for R3 username and password, and ensures that R3 does not challenge R5 for a username or password. Notice that R5 is not configured for OSPF demand circuit because R3 makes the outgoing call and, to obtain OSPF adjacency, only the remote edge router needs to have demand circuit enabled.

Example 9-67 displays the OSPF exchange when the frame link is not active or when the OSPF dead interval expires between R3 and R4.

Example 9-67 *ISDN Call on R3*

```
R3#show debug
Dial on demand:
  Dial on demand events debugging is on
IP routing:
  OSPF adjacency events debugging is on
  OSPF events debugging is on
3w6d: OSPF: 144.254.153.1 address 144.254.3.3 on Serial0/0 is dead, state DOWN
3w6d: OSPF: Neighbor change Event on interface Serial0/0
3w6d: OSPF: DR/BDR election on Serial0/0
3w6d: OSPF: Elect BDR 0.0.0.0
3w6d: OSPF: Elect DR 144.254.154.1
3w6d:        DR: 144.254.154.1 (Id)   BDR: none
3w6d: OSPF: 144.254.154.1 address 144.254.3.1 on Serial0/0 is dead, state DOWN
3w6d: %OSPF-5-ADJCHG: Process 1, Nbr 144.254.154.1 on Serial0/0 from FULL to DOW
```

Example 9-67 *ISDN Call on R3 (Continued)*

```
N, Neighbor Down: Interface down or detached^Z
R3#
3w6d: OSPF: Neighbor change Event on interface Serial0/0
3w6d: OSPF: DR/BDR election on Serial0/0
3w6d: OSPF: Elect BDR 0.0.0.0
3w6d: OSPF: Elect DR 0.0.0.0
3w6d:        DR: none    BDR: none
3w6d: OSPF: Remember old DR 144.254.154.1 (id)
3w6d: OSPF: Build router LSA for area 0, router ID 144.254.153.1, seq 0x80000269
3w6d: OSPF: Send with youngest Key 0
3w6d: BR0/0 DDR: Dialing cause ip (s=144.254.7.1, d=224.0.0.5)
3w6d: BR0/0 DDR: Attempting to dial 7775020
3w6d: %LINK-3-UPDOWN: Interface BRI0/0:2, changed state to up
3w6d: %LINK-3-UPDOWN: Interface Virtual-Access1, changed state to up
3w6d: Vi1 DDR: Dialer statechange to up
3w6d: Vi1 DDR: Dialer call has been placed
3w6d: %LINEPROTO-5-UPDOWN: Line protocol on Interface BRI0/0:2, changed state to
up
3w6d: %LINEPROTO-5-UPDOWN: Line protocol on Interface Virtual-Access1, changed s
tate to up
3w6d: %LINEPROTO-5-UPDOWN: Line protocol on Interface Serial0/0, changed state t
o down
3w6d: OSPF: Send with youngest Key 0
3w6d: %ISDN-6-CONNECT: Interface BRI0/0:2 is now connected to 7775020 R5
```

Example 9-67 displays the debug when an ISDN call is made to R5 after OSPF neighbor adjacencies between R3 and R4 are terminated. The debug shows the neighbor adjacency state to R4 failing and an outgoing call to R3 being made followed by a successful OSPF adjacency.

Example 9-68 confirms OSPF neighbor adjacency to R5 and the fact that IP routing is now over the ISDN interface BRI0/O.

Example 9-68 show ip ospf neighbor *on R3*

```
R3#show ip ospf neighbor
Neighbor ID     Pri   State        Dead Time   Address        Interface
144.254.155.1    1   FULL/  -          -        144.254.7.2    BRI0/0
144.254.152.1    0   FULL/DROTHER  00:01:19    144.254.4.2    FastEthernet0/
0
R3#show ip route ospf
     144.254.0.0/16 is variably subnetted, 12 subnets, 5 masks
O IA    144.254.6.0/29 [110/1563] via 144.254.7.2, 00:03:29, BRI0/0
O IA    144.254.5.0/27 [110/1563] via 144.254.7.2, 00:03:29, BRI0/0
O E1    144.254.2.0/30 [110/1663] via 144.254.7.2, 00:03:29, BRI0/0
O       144.254.3.0/29 [110/1611] via 144.254.7.2, 00:03:29, BRI0/0
O E1    144.254.1.0/30 [110/1663] via 144.254.7.2, 00:03:29, BRI0/0
O       144.254.154.0/24 [110/1564] via 144.254.7.2, 00:03:29, BRI0/0
O IA    144.254.155.0/24 [110/1563] via 144.254.7.2, 00:03:29, BRI0/0
O       144.254.152.0/24 [110/1612] via 144.254.7.2, 00:03:29, BRI0/0
```

continues

Example 9-68 show ip ospf neighbor *on R3 (Continued)*

```
O E1    144.254.151.0/24 [110/1663] via 144.254.7.2, 00:03:29, BRI0/0
        131.108.0.0/24 is subnetted, 3 subnets
O E1    131.108.3.0 [110/1663] via 144.254.7.2, 00:03:29, BRI0/0
O E1    131.108.2.0 [110/1663] via 144.254.7.2, 00:03:29, BRI0/0
O E1    131.108.1.0 [110/1663] via 144.254.7.2, 00:03:29, BRI0/0
R3#
```

Finally, ensure that when ISDN is active, the ISDN subnet, 144.254.7.0/30, is reachable from all parts of the network.

Example 9-69 confirms the subnet in the routing table on the furthest router from R3, namely R1.

Example 9-69 show ip route *on R1*

```
R1#show ip route
Codes: C - connected, S - static, I - IGRP, R - RIP, M - mobile, B - BGP
       D - EIGRP, EX - EIGRP external, O - OSPF, IA - OSPF inter area
       N1 - OSPF NSSA external type 1, N2 - OSPF NSSA external type 2
       E1 - OSPF external type 1, E2 - OSPF external type 2, E - EGP
       i - IS-IS, L1 - IS-IS level-1, L2 - IS-IS level-2, ia - IS-IS inter area
       * - candidate default, U - per-user static route, o - ODR
       P - periodic downloaded static route

Gateway of last resort is 144.254.1.2 to network 0.0.0.0

     144.254.0.0/16 is variably subnetted, 12 subnets, 5 masks
D EX    144.254.6.0/29 [170/302364416] via 144.254.2.2, 02:06:49, Tunnel0
D EX    144.254.7.0/30 [170/302364416] via 144.254.2.2, 00:16:26, Tunnel0
D EX    144.254.4.0/26 [170/302364416] via 144.254.2.2, 01:26:04, Tunnel0
D       144.254.5.0/27 [90/297270016] via 144.254.2.2, 02:06:49, Tunnel0
C       144.254.2.0/30 is directly connected, Serial0/1
D       144.254.3.0/29 [90/297756416] via 144.254.2.2, 02:06:49, Tunnel0
C       144.254.1.0/30 is directly connected, Ethernet0/0
D       144.254.154.0/24 [90/297372416] via 144.254.2.2, 02:06:50, Tunnel0
D EX    144.254.155.0/24 [170/302364416] via 144.254.2.2, 01:23:27, Tunnel0
D EX    144.254.152.0/24 [170/302364416] via 144.254.2.2, 02:06:50, Tunnel0
D EX    144.254.153.0/24 [170/302364416] via 144.254.2.2, 00:16:17, Tunnel0
C       144.254.151.0/24 is directly connected, Loopback0
     131.108.0.0/16 is variably subnetted, 4 subnets, 2 masks
C       131.108.3.0/24 is directly connected, Loopback3
C       131.108.2.0/24 is directly connected, Loopback2
C       131.108.1.0/24 is directly connected, Loopback1
D       131.108.0.0/22 is a summary, 02:57:04, Null0
R*   0.0.0.0/0 [120/1] via 144.254.1.2, 00:00:01, Ethernet0/0
```

Example 9-70 displays a successful ping request from R1 to R3 BRI0/0 and R5 BRI0/0.

Example 9-70 *Ping 144.254.7.1 and 144.254.7.2 from R1*

```
R1#ping 144.254.7.1
Type escape sequence to abort.
Sending 5, 100-byte ICMP Echos to 144.254.7.1, timeout is 2 seconds:
!!!!!
Success rate is 100 percent (5/5), round-trip min/avg/max = 36/38/40 ms
R1#ping 144.254.7.2
Type escape sequence to abort.
Sending 5, 100-byte ICMP Echos to 144.254.7.2, timeout is 2 seconds:
!!!!!
Success rate is 100 percent (5/5), round-trip min/avg/max = 4/6/8 ms
R1#
```

NOTE   The IOS command **show isdn status** details if any calls are active. R3 must have only a call active when the frame connection to R4 is not routing IP.

The following display is taken when the frame link is operational:

```
R3#show isdn status
Global ISDN Switchtype = basic-5ess
ISDN BRI0/0 interface
        dsl 0, interface ISDN Switchtype = basic-5ess
    Layer 1 Status:
        ACTIVE
    Layer 2 Status:
        TEI = 64, Ces = 1, SAPI = 0, State = MULTIPLE_FRAME_ESTABLISHED
    Layer 3 Status:
        0 Active Layer 3 Call(s)
    Active dsl 0 CCBs = 0
    The Free Channel Mask:  0x80000003
    Total Allocated ISDN CCBs = 0
R3#
```

Currently, there are no Layer 3 calls. When the ISDN interface is operational, you should see, at most, two calls. The following display is taken when one ISDN B channel is active:

```
R3#show isdn status
Global ISDN Switchtype = basic-5ess
ISDN BRI0/0 interface
        dsl 0, interface ISDN Switchtype = basic-5ess
    Layer 1 Status:
        ACTIVE
    Layer 2 Status:
        TEI = 64, Ces = 1, SAPI = 0, State = MULTIPLE_FRAME_ESTABLISHED
    Layer 3 Status:
        1 Active Layer 3 Call(s)
        CCB:callid=803F, sapi=0, ces=1, B-chan=1, calltype=DATA
    Active dsl 0 CCBs = 1
    The Free Channel Mask:  0x80000002
    Total Allocated ISDN CCBs = 1
R3#
```

You should also use **show** commands in any CCIE lab to make sure you have satisfied the questions, as just seen, in the case of ensuring ISDN is active only when a failure occurs.

DHCP Configuration

A number of Windows XP users on VLAN D support DHCP and the ability to receive more than one IP gateway. Configure R2 to provide only a pool of DHCP address with the following criteria:

- IP addresses pool ranges from 144.254.4.0/26 shared between R2 and R3.
- DNS servers 139.134.2.2 and 139.134.1.1.
- Domain name cisco.com.
- Default gateway of 144.254.4.1 or 144.254.4.2 only.
- Hosts must retain DHCP assigned addresses forever.
- The predefined addresses 144.254.4.1, 144.254.4.2, and 144.254.4.3 are never allocated to DHCP clients.

You can assume you have Windows XP clients only and support more than one gateway in the event any one router fails.

DHCP Configuration Solution

VLAN D contains the subnet 144.254.4.0/26 with the allocated IP addresses, one to R2 E0/0, R3 Fast0/0, and the Catalyst 5000 management interface. You must ensure that any DHCP servers (R2, in this case) do not allocate these three preassigned address.

Example 9-71 configures R2 for DHCP pool allocation.

Example 9-71 *DHCP Configuration on R2*

```
ip dhcp excluded-address 144.254.4.1
ip dhcp excluded-address 144.254.4.2
ip dhcp excluded-address 144.254.4.3
!
ip dhcp pool ccie
   network 144.254.4.0 255.255.255.192
   domain-name cisco.com
   dns-server 139.134.2.2 139.134.1.1

default-router 144.254.4.1 144.254.4.2
   lease infinite
```

R2 provides DNS domain name and two default gateways. Notice that the lease is enabled to be used forever by DHCP clients with the IOS command, **lease infinite**. In the event that R2 fails, all DHCP clients with existing IP address will route through Router R3 with the default gateway 144.254.4.1.

BGP Routing Configuration

After finishing this section, make sure all configured interfaces and subnets are consistently visible on all pertinent routers, even in the event of network failure of any one router.

Basic IBGP Configuration

Configure IBGP on all routers in your network:

- Do not use any WAN IP interfaces for IBGP sessions because your network is prone to failures across the Frame Relay cloud.

- Configure R4 as the route reflector and ensure that remote routers peer to R4 only.

- Minimize IBGP configurations as much as possible.

- The IBGP connection between R2 and R4 must use MD5 authentication to authenticate the IBGP peer.

- You can disable BGP synchronization.

- Use AS 333 on all IBGP routers.

- As long as there is IP connectivity in your network, ensure that BGP is active in all routers.

- Using the **network** command only, make sure only the loopback interfaces on Routers R1 through R5 are advertised by BGP to the route reflector, R4. Ensure that each router has a corresponding BGP table entry for all loopbacks.

- Do not change the BGP administrative distance to complete this task.

- Make sure you have full IBGP connectivity.

- Ensure that all routers have BGP routing entries in their respective BGP tables.

NOTE   R4's BGP table (not IP routing table) should look like this:

```
R4#show ip bgp
BGP table version is 11, local router ID is 144.254.154.1
Status codes: s suppressed, d damped, h history, * valid, > best, i - internal
Origin codes: i - IGP, e - EGP, ? - incomplete

   Network          Next Hop          Metric LocPrf Weight Path
*>i144.254.151.0/24 144.254.151.1          0    100      0 i
*>i144.254.152.0/24 144.254.152.1          0    100      0 i
*>i144.254.153.0/24 144.254.153.1          0    100      0 i
*>  144.254.154.0/24 0.0.0.0               0           32768 i
```

Basic IBGP Configuration Solution

Router R4, the hub of this network, is to provide BGP (internal) information to R1, R2, R3, and R5.

Example 9-72 configures R4 as the route reflector to remote peers R1, R2, R3, and R5 using the loopback interface as the source address. Next-hop address could be used, but in the event of a WAN failure (in particular for R3), the BGP session would be inactive, so it is better to use the loopback.

Example 9-72 *IBGP Configuration on R4*

```
router bgp 333
 no synchronization
 network 144.254.154.0 mask 255.255.255.0
 neighbor 144.254.151.1 remote-as 333
 neighbor 144.254.151.1 update-source Loopback0
 neighbor 144.254.151.1 route-reflector-client
 neighbor 144.254.152.1 remote-as 333
 neighbor 144.254.152.1 password cisco
 neighbor 144.254.152.1 update-source Loopback0
 neighbor 144.254.152.1 route-reflector-client
 neighbor 144.254.153.1 remote-as 333
 neighbor 144.254.153.1 update-source Loopback0
 neighbor 144.254.153.1 route-reflector-client
 neighbor 144.254.155.1 remote-as 333
 neighbor 144.254.155.1 update-source Loopback0
 neighbor 144.254.155.1 route-reflector-client
```

R4 is configured as the route reflector to four remote routers in AS 333. Notice that MD5 authentication is enabled between R4 and R2, as stated in the question criteria. The **network** command is used to inject Loopback 0 on R4 into the BGP routing table.

Example 9-73 enables IBGP on R2 with MD5 authentication to R4.

Example 9-73 *IBGP Configuration on R2*

```
router bgp 333
 no synchronization
 network 144.254.152.0 mask 255.255.255.0
 neighbor 144.254.154.1 remote-as 333
 neighbor 144.254.154.1 password cisco
 neighbor 144.254.154.1 update-source Loopback0
```

R2 is configured as an IBGP peer to R5 with MD5 authentication to ensure the IBGP session is authenticated. The **network** command is used to inject the loopback of R2 into the BGP table.

Example 9-74 confirms the BGP table on R2 with the command, **show ip bgp**.

Example 9-74 show ip bgp *on R2*

```
R2#show ip bgp
BGP table version is 22, local router ID is 144.254.152.1
Status codes: s suppressed, d damped, h history, * valid, > best, i - internal
```

Example 9-74 show ip bgp *on R2 (Continued)*

```
Origin codes: i - IGP, e - EGP, ? - incomplete

  Network          Next Hop         Metric LocPrf Weight Path
*>i144.254.151.0/24 144.254.151.1        0    100      0 i
*> 144.254.152.0/24 0.0.0.0             0         32768 i
*>i144.254.153.0/24 144.254.153.1        0    100      0 i
*>i144.254.154.0/24 144.254.154.1        0    100      0 i
*>i144.254.155.0/24 144.254.155.1        0    100      0 i
R2#
```

Example 9-75 confirms the BGP table on R4 with the command **show ip bgp**.

Example 9-75 show ip bgp *on R4*

```
R4#show ip bgp
BGP table version is 14, local router ID is 144.254.154.1
Status codes: s suppressed, d damped, h history, * valid, > best, i - internal
Origin codes: i - IGP, e - EGP, ? - incomplete

  Network          Next Hop         Metric LocPrf Weight Path
*>i144.254.151.0/24 144.254.151.1        0    100      0 i
*>i144.254.152.0/24 144.254.152.1        0    100      0 i
*>i144.254.153.0/24 144.254.153.1        0    100      0 i
*> 144.254.154.0/24 0.0.0.0             0         32768 i
*>i144.254.155.0/24 144.254.155.1        0    100      0 i
R4#
```

Example 9-76 confirms the IBGP on R4, as established with the summary BGP command **show ip bgp summary**.

Example 9-76 how ip bgp summary *on R4*

```
R4#show ip bgp summary
BGP router identifier 144.254.154.1, local AS number 333
BGP table version is 14, main routing table version 14
5 network entries and 5 paths using 665 bytes of memory
2 BGP path attribute entries using 120 bytes of memory
0 BGP route-map cache entries using 0 bytes of memory
0 BGP filter-list cache entries using 0 bytes of memory
BGP activity 8/31 prefixes, 8/3 paths, scan interval 15 secs
Neighbor        V    AS MsgRcvd MsgSent   TblVer  InQ OutQ Up/Down  State/PfxRcd
144.254.151.1   4   333   14192   14204       14    0    0 1w2d            1
144.254.152.1   4   333   14191   14202       14    0    0 1w2d            1
144.254.153.1   4   333   14189   14198       14    0    0 1w2d            1
144.254.155.1   4   333   14189   14199       14    0    0 1w2d            1
R4#
```

Five networks are installed in the BGP table, one local (next hop 0.0.0.0) and four remote (next hops for R1, R2, R3, and R5 loopbacks IP addresses).

NOTE   For more examples of CCIE questions on BGP, refer to Appendix C for a sample routing and switching lab endorsed by the CCIE content management team.

CCIE Security Self-Study Lab Part II: Advanced Security Design (4 Hours)

The final section, Part II, concentrates on the advanced security topics that are possible in the CCIE Security exam. Now that Part I has been configured and all devices are communicating, you can add security to the network and ensure that the network is safe from intruders or hackers.

IP Access List

On R5, configure an access list that meets the following criterion and contains the *fewest* configuration lines as possible:

- Apply the access list on the outbound interface on R5's Fast Ethernet link to R4.
- Deny any TCP packet with source address 129.57.204.0/24.
- Deny any TCP packet with source address 129.57.140.0/24.
- Deny any TCP packet with source address 225.133.29.0/24.
- Deny any TCP packet with source address 161.133.29.0/24.
- Deny every even subnet in 182.133.0.0/16.
- Deny every odd subnet in 182.133.0.0/16.
- Permit all other IP traffic.

Confirm access to the network after applying the access list. (Hint: Use at most four lines of access list configuration.)

How can you review any access violations?

IP Access List Solution

The access list required here is somewhat tricky. The requirement that you use the least number of lines possible means that you should start looking for similarities in the subnets so you can configure the correct mask.

Because you are denying TCP, you must use an extended access list because standard access lists are based on IP only.

The first two subnets (129.57.140.0/24 and 129.57.204.0/24), when displayed in binary, look like the following. Notice that the first two octets are the same:

140 in binary is 10001100

204 in binary is 11001100

Only one bit (bit 2) is different, so you can apply the mask as follows (remember, 0 means match and 1 means do not care):

10001100 (140 in decimal)

11001100 (204 in decimal)

01000000 (64 in decimal)

Example 9-77 configures the first access list line code to encompass the two networks, 129.57.140.0/24 and 129.57.204.0/24, with one line of IOS code.

Example 9-77 *First Access List Line*

```
access-list 100 deny  tcp 129.57.140.0 0.0.64.255 any log
```

The inverse mask, 0.0.64.255, means the first two octets (129 and 57) must match followed by either 140 or 204 and you do not care about the last octet (255 or all 111111111).

The same principle of binary bit notation is followed with the second pair of networks:

11100001 (225 in decimal)

1000001 (161 in decimal)

01000000 (64 in decimal)

Example 9-78 configures the second access list line code to encompass the two networks, 225.133.29.0/24 and 161.133.29.0/24, with one line of IOS code.

Example 9-78 *Second Access List Line*

```
access-list 100 deny tcp 161.133.29.0 64.0.0.0 any log
```

The final two conditions are met with a deny statement for all networks on 182.133.0.0/16 and an implicit permit on all other networks. Example 9-79 displays the final two IOS coded lines.

Example 9-79 *Final Two Statements*

```
access-list 100 deny  tcp 182.133.0.0 0.0.255.255 any log
access-list 100 permit ip any any log
```

The **log** keyword ensures any packets matching the access list are logged and available for further investigation when required. Ensure all other legitimate IP data, such as OSPF routing updates, is encompassed in the last statement by implicitly allowing all other traffic.

Finally, apply the access list to the outbound interface on R5. Example 9-80 applies the access number 100 on the outbound interface to R5.

Example 9-80 *Access List Applied to R5 Serial 0/0*

```
R5(config)#interface fastEthernet 0/0
R5(config-if)# ip access-group 100 out
```

Telnet to R5 and review the access list log, and you should see the number of access list violations that were entered as a result of the failed access.

To view access list violations, use the IOS command **show ip access-list 100**.

Prevent Denial-of-Service Attacks

Legitimate user from Company A no longer has access to their internal website on VLAN_A. A network sniffer analyzer advises that attacks have taken place on VLAN A in your network subnet 144.254.1.0/30. E-mail server and FTP services (VLAN 2) are unavailable because a hacker is flooding the server with a number of requests for connections. Configure your router to prevent TCP servers from TCP SYN flooding attacks from flooding VLAN A.

Prevent Denial-of-Service Attacks Solution

TCP intercept will stop this DoS attack. The IOS command syntax is as follows:

```
ip tcp intercept mode intercept
ip tcp intercept list 100

access-list 100 permit ip any subnet-being-attacked
```

R1 is configured with TCP intercept mode. Example 9-81 enables R1 for TCP intercept mode.

Example 9-81 *TCP Intercept on R1*

```
R1(config)# ip tcp intercept mode intercept
R1(config)#ip tcp intercept list 100
R1(config)#access-list 100 permit ip any 144.254.1.0 0.0.0.3
```

Example 9-82 displays the output of a sample **show tcp intercept connections** EXEC command.

Example 9-82 show tcp intercept connections *Command*

```
R1# show tcp intercept connections
 Incomplete:
Client                    Server              State    Create   Timeout  Mode
172.19.160.17:58190       10.1.1.30:23        SYNRCVD  00:00:09 00:00:05 I
172.19.160.17:57934       10.1.1.30:23        SYNRCVD  00:00:09 00:00:05 I

Established:
Client                    Server              State    Create   Timeout  Mode
171.69.232.23:1045        10.1.1.30:23        ESTAB    00:00:08 23:59:54 I
```

Table 9-4 describes significant fields shown in the display.

Table 9-4 **show tcp intercept connections** *Description*

Output	Description
Incomplete:	Rows of information under "Incomplete" indicate connections that are not yet established.
Client	The client's IP address and port.
Server	IP address and port of the server being protected by TCP intercept.
State	SYNRCVD—establishing with client. SYNSENT—establishing with server. ESTAB—established with both, passing data.
Create	Hours:minutes:seconds since the connection was created.
Timeout	Hours:minutes:seconds until the retransmission timeout.
Mode	I—intercept mode. W—watch mode.
Established:	Rows of information under "Established" indicate connections that are established. The fields are the same as those under "Incomplete," except for the Timeout field.
Timeout	Hours:minutes:seconds until the connection will timeout, unless the software sees a FIN exchange, in which case, this indicates the hours:minutes:seconds until the FIN or RESET timeout.

Table 9-5 displays other useful TCP intercept configuration and monitoring commands.

Table 9-5 *TCP Intercept Related Commands*

Command	Description
ip tcp intercept connection-timeout	Changes how long a TCP connection will be managed by the TCP intercept after no activity
ip tcp intercept first-timeout	Changes how long after receipt of a reset or FIN-exchange the software ceases to manage the connection
ip tcp intercept list	Enables TCP intercept
show tcp intercept statistics	Displays TCP intercept statistics

NOTE   You can find more details on TCP intercept at the following:

www.cisco.com/univercd/cc/td/doc/product/software/ios122/122cgcr/fsecur_c/ftrafwl/scfdenl.htm.

Time-Based Access List

Employees connected to VLAN_C on R5 don't need web access while at work. Block web traffic from Monday through Friday between the hours of 7:00 a.m. and 5:00 p.m.

Time-Based Access List Solution

On Fast Ethernet 0/1 VLAN C, you need to apply an extended access list. Example 9-83 displays the extended access list configuration on R5 Fast0/1. Use a named access list to make things a little more interesting and easy to read.

Example 9-83 *Access List Configuration on R5*

```
R5(config)#interface fastethernet 0/1
R5(config-if)#ip access-group web-traffic out
R5(config-if)#exit
```

Example 9-84 configures and defines the extended access list named web-traffic.

Example 9-84 *Extended Access List Configuration*

```
R5(config)#ip access-list extended web-traffic
R5(config-ext-nacl)#deny ?
  <0-255>  An IP protocol number
  ahp      Authentication Header Protocol
  eigrp    Cisco's EIGRP routing protocol
  esp      Encapsulation Security Payload
```

Example 9-84 *Extended Access List Configuration (Continued)*

```
gre       Cisco's GRE tunneling
icmp      Internet Control Message Protocol
igmp      Internet Gateway Message Protocol
igrp      Cisco's IGRP routing protocol
ip        Any Internet Protocol
ipinip    IP in IP tunneling
nos       KA9Q NOS compatible IP over IP tunneling
ospf      OSPF routing protocol
pcp       Payload Compression Protocol
pim       Protocol Independent Multicast
tcp       Transmission Control Protocol
udp       User Datagram Protocol
```

After you select the TCP option (HTTP runs over TCP port 80), you are presented with the time range options. Example 9-85 configures R5 to set a time range for World Wide Web access.

Example 9-85 *Specify Time Range for WWW Access*

```
R5(config-ext-nacl)#deny tcp any any ?
 ack          Match on the ACK bit
 dscp         Match packets with given dscp value
 eq           Match only packets on a given port number
 established  Match established connections
 fin          Match on the FIN bit
 fragments    Check non-initial fragments
 gt           Match only packets with a greater port number
 log          Log matches against this entry
 log-input    Log matches against this entry, including input interface
 lt           Match only packets with a lower port number
 neq          Match only packets not on a given port number
 precedence   Match packets with given precedence value
 psh          Match on the PSH bit
 range        Match only packets in the range of port numbers
 rst          Match on the RST bit
 syn          Match on the SYN bit
 time-range   Specify a time-range
 tos          Match packets with given TOS value
 urg          Match on the URG bit
 <cr>

R5(config-ext-nacl)#deny tcp any any eq 80 time-range ?
WORD  Time-range entry name

R5(config-ext-nacl)#deny tcp any any eq 80 time-range web-timing
R5(config-ext-nacl)#permit ip any any
R5(config-ext-nacl)#exit
R5(config)#time-range  ?
  WORD  Time range name
```

Finally, the **time-range** global configuration command defines specific times of the day and week. Example 9-86 enables the time-range command on R5.

Example 9-86 time-range *Command on R5*

```
R5(config)#time-range  web-timing
R5(config-time-range)#?
Time range configuration commands:
  absolute  absolute time and date
  default   Set a command to its defaults
  exit      Exit from time-range configuration mode
  no        Negate a command or set its defaults
  periodic  periodic time and date
R5(config-time-range)#periodic weekdays  7:00 to 17:00
```

Dynamic Access List/Lock and Key Feature

Make sure that during normal operation it is not possible to ping from R2 (Ethernet0/0) to R3 (FastEthernet0/0). After a Telnet login from R2 to R3, pings are allowed, but reassure that after 5 minutes of inactivity normal operation is restored. Routing should still be in place in both circumstances.

Dynamic Access List/Lock and Key Feature Solution

This is an example where dynamic access lists are used to allow access only after a valid username/password has been entered. Access is denied again after a period (5 minutes, in this case) of inactivity.

Example 9-87 configures R3 with an extended access-list, 100.

Example 9-87 *Extended Access List Configuration on R3*

```
R3(config)#access-list 100 ?
  deny     Specify packets to reject
  dynamic  Specify a DYNAMIC list of PERMITs or DENYs
  permit   Specify packets to forward
  remark   Access list entry comment
R3(config)#access-list 100 dynamic ?
  WORD  Name of a Dynamic list
R3(config)#access-list 100 dynamic blockping ?
  deny     Specify packets to reject
  permit   Specify packets to forward
  timeout  Maximum time for dynamic ACL to live
R3(config)#access-list 100 dynamic blockping timeout 5 ?
  deny     Specify packets to reject
  permit   Specify packets to forward
R3(config)#$access-list 100 dynamic blockping timeout 5 permit icmp host
     144.254.4.2 host 144.254.4.1
R3(config)#access-list 100 deny icmp host 144.254.4.2 host 144.254.4.1 echo
R3(config)#access-list 100 permit ip any any
```

After the access list is defined, you must apply the access list to the VTY lines on R3. Example 9-88 displays the VTY line configuration.

After the ACL is defined, you must apply the ACL to the interface, followed by the **auto command** under VTY lines on R3. Example 9-88 displays applying the ACL to the interface and the VTY line configuration.

Example 9-88 *VTY Configuration*

```
R3(config)#line vty 0 4
R3(config-line)#autocommand ?
  LINE                     Appropriate EXEC command
  no-suppress-linenumber  Display service linenumber message
R3(config-line)#autocommand access-enable-after-ping  ?
LINE    <cr>
R3(config-line)#autocommand access-enable-after-ping  host timeout 5
```

Example 9-89 displays a failed ping request from R2 to R3.

Example 9-89 *Ping 144.254.4.1 from R2*

```
R2#ping 144.254.4.1

Type escape sequence to abort.
Sending 5, 100-byte ICMP Echos to 144.254.4.1, timeout is 2 seconds:
U.U.U
Success rate is 0 percent (0/5)
```

The ping requests are not permitted because a successful Telnet connection is required before ICMP pings are permitted.

Example 9-90 telnets from R2 to R3, passes authentication, and is automatically dropped out by R3.

Example 9-90 *Telnet from R2 to R1*

```
R2#telnet 144.254.4.1
Trying 144.254.4.1 ... Open
User Access Verification
Password: cisco
[Connection to 144.254.4.1 closed by foreign host]
```

Example 9-91 now pings R3 from R2 successfully.

Example 9-91 ping **144.254.4.1** *from R2*

```
R2#ping 144.254.4.1
Type escape sequence to abort.
Sending 5, 100-byte ICMP Echos to 144.254.4.1, timeout is 2 seconds:
!!!!!
Success rate is 100 percent (5/5), round-trip min/avg/max = 1/2/4 ms
R2#ping 144.254.4.1
Type escape sequence to abort.
Sending 5, 100-byte ICMP Echos to 144.254.4.1, timeout is 2 seconds:
!!!!!
Success rate is 100 percent (5/5), round-trip min/avg/max = 1/2/4 ms
R2#
```

To monitor the access violations, use the IOS command **show ip access-list 100**.

Example 9-92 displays the accesses and violations on R3.

Example 9-92 **show ip access-list 100** *Command on R3*

```
R3#show ip access-lists
Extended IP access list 100
    Dynamic blockping permit icmp host 144.254.4.2 host 144.254.4.1
        permit icmp host 144.254.4.2 host 144.254.4.1 (30 matches) (time left 269)
    deny icmp host 144.254.4.2 host 144.254.4.1 echo (8 matches)
    permit ip any any (260 matches)
R3#
```

IOS Firewall Configuration on R5

Translate the following policy into a working CBAC configuration on R5 (assuming this router's FastEth0/1 is connected to another ISP):

- Allow all TCP and UDP traffic initiated on the inside from network 144.254.5.0 to access the Internet. ICMP traffic will also be allowed from the same network. Other networks (inside) must be denied. For traffic initiated on the outside, allow everyone to access only HTTP to host 144.254.5.3.

- All other traffic must be denied.

IOS Firewall Configuration on R5 Solution

CBAC intelligently filters TCP and UDP packets based on application layer protocol session information. You can configure CBAC to permit specified TCP and UDP traffic through a firewall only when the connection is initiated from within the network you want to protect. CBAC can inspect traffic for sessions that originate from either side of the firewall, and CBAC can be used for intranet, extranet, and Internet perimeters of your network.

To configure CBAC, perform the following tasks:

- Pick an interface: internal or external (required).
- Configure IP access lists at the interface (required).
- Configure global timeouts and thresholds (required).
- Define an inspection rule (required).
- Apply the inspection rule to an interface (required).
- Configure logging and audit trail (required).
- Follow other guidelines for configuring a firewall (required).
- Verify CBAC (optional).

Example 9-93 configures R5 for CBAC outbound connections.

Example 9-93 *R5 Outbound Connections*

```
R5(config)#ip inspect name OUTBOUND tcp
R5(config)#ip inspect name OUTBOUND udp
R5(config)#access-list 101 permit ip 144.254.5.0 255.255.255.192 any
R5(config)#interface FastEthernet0/0
R5(config-if)#ip inspect OUTBOUND in
R5(config-if)#ip access-group 101 in
```

Example 9-94 configures R5 for inbound connections.

Example 9-94 *Inbound Connections from the Internet*

```
R5(config)#access-list 102 permit icmp any host 144.254.5.3
R5(config)#access-list 102 permit tcp any host 144.254.5.3 eq www
R5(config)#interface FastEthernet0/1
R5(config-if)#ip access-group 102 in
```

Monitoring and Maintaining CBAC

To assist CBAC debugging, you can turn on audit trail messages that will be displayed on the console after each CBAC session closes. The IOS command **ip inspect audit-trail** turns on CBAC audit trail messages.

Many other debug commands are available, including the following:

- Generic **debug** Commands
- Transport level **debug** commands
- Application protocol **debug** commands

For more details on CBAC visit:

www.cisco.com/univercd/cc/td/doc/product/software/ios122/122cgcr/fsecur_c/ftrafwl/
scfcbac.htm#xtocid21

IPSec Configuration

The Frame Relay network between R2, R3, and R4 requires IPSec to ensure all data between these routers is not susceptible to intruders.

Set up IPSec using pre-shared keys between R2, R3, and R4, and ensure the following points are taken into account:

- Use MD5 as the hashing algorithm.
- Authentication will be pre-shared.
- The authentication key is CciE; use a 56-bit key.
- Use SHA to calculate the hashes on the actual packet payloads in ESP.
- Set up IPSec in transport mode.
- Set the security association lifetime to 300 seconds.
- Ensure all IP data between the R2, R3, and R4 are encrypted using IPSec (over the Frame Relay network only).
- (Hint: Apply the crypto map to the Serial links only and not the ISDN link.)
- Use one transform set on each router.

IPSec Configuration Solution

To start, configure IKE on Routers R4, R2, and R3. Example 9-95 displays the IKE configuration on R4. Remember that IKE policies define a set of parameters to be used during IKE negotiation. The shaded portion in Example 9-95 matches the criteria in the question.

Example 9-95 *IKE Configuration on R4*

```
R4(config)#crypto isakmp policy 1
R4(config-isakmp)#hash ?
  md5  Message Digest 5
  sha  Secure Hash Standard
R4(config-isakmp)#hash md5
R4(config-isakmp)#authentication ?
  pre-share  Pre-Shared Key
  rsa-encr   Rivest-Shamir-Adleman Encryption
  rsa-sig    Rivest-Shamir-Adleman Signature
R4(config-isakmp)#authentication pre-share
```

Example 9-96 configures the pre-share key set to CCiE.

Example 9-96 *Pre-Shared Key on R4 Set to CCiE*

```
R4(config)#crypto isakmp key ?
  WORD  pre-shared key
R4(config)#crypto isakmp key CCiE ?
  address   define shared key with IP address
  hostname  define shared key with hostname
R4(config)#crypto isakmp key CCiE address 144.254.3.2 ?
  A.B.C.D  Peer IP subnet mask
  <cr>
R4(config)#crypto isakmp key CCiE address 144.254.3.2
R4(config)#crypto isakmp key CCiE address 144.254.3.3
```

The pre-share key value (password) is CciE, and the peer address of the remote IPSec peer is 144.254.3.2 (R2) and 144.254.3.3 (R3).

Pre-Shared Keys Versus Manual Keys

This is an example of pre-shared keys where IKE is used to negotiate all SA parameters. You can also define IPSec not to use IKE; this is referred to as manual IPSec or manual keys. Cisco strongly recommends that you use IKE or pre-shared keys because it is very difficult to ensure that all SA parameters are matching between remote peers. The DH algorithm is a more secure method when generating secret keys between peers. Manual keys are prone to in traders and unauthorized sources that gain entry to Cisco configuration files. Another major disadvantage of manual keys is that the IOS **crypto map** command that is used to establish security associations (SAs) does not expire.

Example 9-97 defines the transform set, which indicates to use transport mode and SHA and ESP encapsulation.

Example 9-97 *SHA/ESP and Transport Mode Configuration on R4*

```
R4(config)#crypto ipsec transform-set anyname1 ?
  ah-md5-hmac   AH-HMAC-MD5 transform
  ah-sha-hmac   AH-HMAC-SHA transform
  comp-lzs      IP Compression using the LZS compression algorithm
  esp-des       ESP transform using DES cipher (56 bits)
  esp-md5-hmac  ESP transform using HMAC-MD5 auth
  esp-null      ESP transform w/o cipher
  esp-sha-hmac  ESP transform using HMAC-SHA auth
  <cr>
R4(config)#crypto ipsec transform-set anyname1 esp-des ?
```

continues

Example 9-97 *SHA/ESP and Transport Mode Configuration on R4 (Continued)*

```
  ah-md5-hmac   AH-HMAC-MD5 transform
  ah-sha-hmac   AH-HMAC-SHA transform
  comp-lzs      IP Compression using the LZS compression algorithm
  esp-md5-hmac  ESP transform using HMAC-MD5 auth
  esp-sha-hmac  ESP transform using HMAC-SHA auth
  <cr>
R4(config)#crypto ipsec transform-set anyname1 esp-des esp-sha-hmac
R4(cfg-crypto-trans)#mode ?
  transport  transport (payload encapsulation) mode
  tunnel     tunnel (datagram encapsulation) mode

R4(cfg-crypto-trans)#mode transport
```

The **transform set** command defines an acceptable combination of security protocols and algorithms; this example applies ESP-DES (ESP with the 56-bit DES encryption algorithm) and ESP with the SHA (HMAC variant) authentication algorithm.

You need to define the crypto map and the access list to encompass the networks you want to encrypt. On R4 only, the network 144.254.3.0/28 is encrypted. Example 9-98 configures R4 with a crypto map and access list 150.

Example 9-98 *Crypto Map and Access List Configuration on R4*

```
crypto map anyname 1 ipsec-isakmp
 set peer 144.254.3.2
 set peer 144.254.3.3
 set security-association lifetime seconds 300
 set transform-set anyname1
 match address 150
access-list 150 permit ip any any
```

Access list 150 ensures that all IP data is encrypted from R4 to R2 and R3.

Finally, on R4, you must apply the crypto map to the physical interface Serial 0/0 on R4. Example 9-99 applies the crypto map to Serial0/0 on R4.

Example 9-99 *Crypto Map Interface Configuration on R4*

```
R4#config terminal
Enter configuration commands, one per line.  End with CNTL/Z.
R4(config)#interface serial0/0
R4(config-if)#crypto map anyname
```

R2 and R3 need to be configured exactly the same way.

Example 9-100 displays the full IPSec configure on R2.

Example 9-100 *R2 IPSec Configuration*

```
crypto isakmp policy 1
 hash md5
 authentication pre-share
crypto isakmp key CCiE address 144.254.3.1
!
!
crypto ipsec transform-set anyname1onR2 esp-des esp-sha-hmac
 mode transport
!
crypto map anyname 1 ipsec-isakmp
 set peer 144.254.3.1
 set security-association lifetime seconds 300
 set transform-set anyname1onR2
 match address 150
interface Serial0/0
crypto map anyname
access-list 150 permit ip any any
```

Example 9-101 displays the full IPSec configure on R3.

Example 9-101 *R3 IPSec Configuration*

```
crypto isakmp policy 1
 hash md5
 authentication pre-share
crypto isakmp key CCiE address 144.254.3.1
!
crypto ipsec transform-set anyname1onR3 esp-des esp-sha-hmac
 mode transport
!
crypto map anyname 1 ipsec-isakmp
 set peer 144.254.3.1
 set security-association lifetime seconds 300
 set transform-set anyname1onR3
 match address 150
interface Serial0/0
crypto map anyname
access-list 150 permit ip any any
```

To display the status of all crypto engine active connections, use the IOS command, **show crypto engine connections active**.

Example 9-102 displays the current active crypto engines on R4.

Example 9-102 show crypto engine connections active *on R4*

```
R4#show crypto engine connections active
   ID Interface       IP-Address       State  Algorithm             Encrypt  Decrypt
    3 <none>          <none>           set    HMAC_MD5+DES_56_CB          0        0
    6 Serial0/0       144.254.3.1      set    HMAC_MD5+DES_56_CB          0        0
    7 Serial0/0       144.254.3.1      set    HMAC_MD5+DES_56_CB          0        0
 2008 Serial0/0       144.254.3.1      set    HMAC_SHA+DES_56_CB          0    27531
 2009 Serial0/0       144.254.3.1      set    HMAC_SHA+DES_56_CB      27529        0
 2010 Serial0/0       144.254.3.1      set    HMAC_SHA+DES_56_CB          0      988
 2011 Serial0/0       144.254.3.1      set    HMAC_SHA+DES_56_CB       1243        0

R4#
```

Example 9-103 displays the current active crypto engines on R2.

Example 9-103 show crypto engine connections active *on R2*

```
R2#show crypto engine connections active

   ID Interface       IP-Address       State  Algorithm             Encrypt  Decrypt
    1 <none>          <none>           set    HMAC_MD5+DES_56_CB          0        0
 2006 Serial0/0       144.254.3.2      set    HMAC_SHA+DES_56_CB          0    71250
 2007 Serial0/0       144.254.3.2      set    HMAC_SHA+DES_56_CB      60250        0

R2#
```

Example 9-104 displays the current active crypto engines on R3.

Example 9-104 show crypto engine connections active *on R3*

```
R3#show crypto  engine connections active
   ID Interface       IP-Address       State  Algorithm             Encrypt  Decrypt
    2 <none>          <none>           set    HMAC_MD5+DES_56_CB          0        0
 2006 Serial0/0       144.254.3.3      set    HMAC_SHA+DES_56_CB          0     1243
 2007 Serial0/0       144.254.3.3      set    HMAC_SHA+DES_56_CB        988        0

R3#
```

The preceding examples confirm that R2, R3, and R4 maintain an IPSec connection.

There are a number of Cisco IOS **show** commands when monitoring IPSec. Here are a few examples.

To view the parameters for each Internet key exchange policy, use the **show crypto isakmp policy** EXEC command.

Example 9-105 displays the sample output when issued on R4.

Example 9-105 show crypto isakmp policy *on R4*

```
R4#show crypto isakmp policy
Protection suite of priority 1
        encryption algorithm:   DES - Data Encryption Standard (56 bit keys).
        hash algorithm:         Message Digest 5
        authentication method:  Pre-Shared Key
        Diffie-Hellman group:   #1 (768 bit)
        lifetime:               86400 seconds, no volume limit
Default protection suite
        encryption algorithm:   DES - Data Encryption Standard (56 bit keys).
        hash algorithm:         Secure Hash Standard
        authentication method:  Rivest-Shamir-Adleman Signature
        Diffie-Hellman group:   #1 (768 bit)
        lifetime:               86400 seconds, no volume limit
R4#
```

To view the crypto map configuration, use the **show crypto map** EXEC command.

Example 9-106 displays a sample output of the command **show crypto map** when applied to R2.

Example 9-106 show crypto map *on R2*

```
R2#show crypto map
Crypto Map "anyname" 1 ipsec-isakmp
        Peer = 144.254.3.1
        Extended IP access list 150
            access-list 150 permit ip any any
        Current peer: 144.254.3.1
        Security association lifetime: 4608000 kilobytes/300 seconds
        PFS (Y/N): N
        Transform sets={ anyname1onR2, }
        Interfaces using crypto map anyname:
                Serial0/0
```

You can also verify the crypto map configuration by viewing the configuration with the command **show running-config**. Example 9-107 displays configured crypto map configurations when viewing the running configuration.

Example 9-107 show running-config *(Truncated) on R2*

```
Hostname R2
!
crypto map anyname 1 ipsec-isakmp
 set peer 144.254.3.1
 set security-association lifetime seconds 300
 set transform-set anyname1onR2
 match address 150
```

Refer to Chapter 5, "Security Protocols," for more crypto commands or the following URL:

www.cisco.com/univercd/cc/td/doc/product/software/ios122/122cgcr/fsecur_r/fipsencr/index.htm

Advanced PIX Configuration

In any security exam, you can be sure that the PIX will be a core device (only one the exam), so the next few question highlight the areas of the PIX you should be proficient with to ensure you are ready for the many scenarios that you might be asked to configure. The next section concentrates on a sample PIX topology to guide you in areas you should concentrate on in your study preparation.

Configuring SSH on the PIX

Configure the PIX to accept SSH connections. Make sure sessions are killed after two hours of inactivity. Limit only VLAN D hosts to SSH to the PIX. The domain name is cisco.com. Set all passwords to cisco.

Configuring SSH on the PIX Solution

Four steps are required when enabling SSH on a Cisco PIX Firewall:

Step 1   Assign a host name and a domain name. This is required so that an RSA key is generated. The PIX commands are as follows:

```
hostname PIX1
domain-name cisco.com
```

Step 2   Generate the RSA key with the following PIX command:

```
ca generate any-key-name rsa
```

Step 3   Define the hosts that are permitted access with the following PIX command:

```
ssh ip_address [netmask] [interface_name]
```

Step 4   Set the enable and Telnet password (optional).

Example 9-108 configures the PIX firewall for SSH connections from VLAN_D or network 144.254.4.0/26. To set a timeout value, use the PIX command **ssh timeout** *seconds* in this case, 2 minutes or 120 seconds.

Example 9-108   *SSH Configuration on the PIX*

```
Pixfirewall(config)#hostname PIX1
PIX1(config)#domain-name cisco.com
PIX1(config)#ca generate rsa key 2048
PIX1(config)#ssh 144.254.4.0 255.255.255.192 inside
PIX1(config)#ssh timeout 120
```

Configuring the PIX for Intrusion Detection

Configure the PIX according to the following Intrusion Detection System (IDS) policy:

- For the outside interface, enable all informational signatures but drop the packet, and send a message to the syslog server. Attack signatures should be enabled on both the outside and inside interface. More specifically, for the outside interface, drop the packet, send a syslog message, and generate TCP resets in both directions.

- For the inside interface, drop the packet and send an alert to the syslog server.

Configuring the PIX for Intrusion Detection Solution

The PIX command syntax to enable IDS is as follows:

```
ip audit attack [action [alarm] [drop] [reset]]
ip audit info [action [alarm] [drop] [reset]]
ip audit interface if_name audit_name
ip audit name audit_name attack [action [alarm] [drop] [reset]]
ip audit name audit_name info [action [alarm] [drop] [reset]]
ip audit signature signature_number disable
```

Table 9-6 summarizes the command's syntax.

Table 9-6   *IP Audit Syntax Description*

Syntax	Description
audit attack	Specify the default actions to be taken for attack signatures.
audit info	Specify the default actions to be taken for informational signatures.
audit interface	Apply an audit specification or policy (using the **ip audit name** command) to an interface.
audit name	Specify informational signatures, except those disabled or excluded by the **ip audit signature** command, as part of the policy.
audit signature	Specify which messages to display, attach a global policy to a signature, and disable or exclude a signature from auditing.
action *actions*	The **alarm** option indicates that when a signature match is detected in a packet, the PIX Firewall reports the event to all configured syslog servers. The **drop** option drops the offending packet. The **reset** option drops the offending packet and closes the connection if it is part of an active connection. The default is **alarm**.
audit_name	Audit policy name viewed with the **show ip audit name** command.
signature_number	IDS signature number.

Example 9-109 enables the PIX for IDS matching the conditions outlined in the task.

Example 9-109 *IDS Configuration on the PIX Named PIX1*

```
PIX1(config)# ip audit name Attack-outside attack action alarm drop
PIX1(config)# ip audit name Information-inside info action alarm drop
PIX1(config)# ip audit name Attack-inside attack action alarm reset
PIX1(config)# ip audit interface inside Attack-inside
PIX1(config)# ip audit interface inside Information-inside
PIX1(config)# ip audit interface outside Attack-outside
PIX1(config)# ip audit info action alarm
PIX1(config)# ip audit attack action alarm
```

Table 9-7 displays the available **show** commands that monitor IDS on a Cisco PIX Firewall.

Table 9-7   **show ip audit** *Commands and Output*

show Command	show Command Output
show ip audit attack	Displays the default attack actions PIX1# **show ip audit attack** ip audit attack action alarm
show ip audit info	Displays the default informational actions PIX1# **show ip audit info** ip audit info action alarm
show ip audit interface	Displays the interface configuration PIX1# **show ip audit interface** ip audit interface outside Attack-inside ip audit interface inside Information-inside ip audit interface inside Attack-outside
show ip audit name [name [info | attack]]	Displays all audit policies or specific policies referenced by name and possibly type PIX1# **show ip audit name** ip audit name Attack-inside attack action alarm reset ip audit name Information-inside info action alarm drop ip audit name Attack-outside attack action alarm drop

NOTE   For more details on IDS, go to:

www.cisco.com/cgi-bin/Support/PSP/psp_view.pl?p=Software:Cisco_Secure_IDS.

ACS Configuration

The AAA ACS server is located on the R5 network with the IP address 144.254.6.2, and the server key is set to ccie.

Non-AAA Authentication Methods

Configure the Router R2 so that it provides a TACACS-like username and encrypted password authentication system for networks that cannot support TACACS. Limit this only to users on VLAN_D.

Non-AAA Authentication Methods Solution

Cisco IOS routers can be configured to authorize usernames with the following command:

username *name* **password** *encryption-type*

This IOS command establishes username authentication with encrypted passwords.

To define an access list so that only VLAN_D users can access the router, use the following command:

username *name* **access-class** *number*

Example 9-110 configures Router R2 for local-based authentication for users from VLAN_D only.

Example 9-110 *Configuring Non-AAA Authentication Methods on R2*

```
R2#show running
hostname R2
aaa new-model
aaa authentication login default local

enable password cisco
!
username Erik access-class 1 password 0 Erik
ip subnet-zero
!

!
access-list 1 permit 144.254.4.0
!
R2#
```

Example 9-111 displays the debug when an EXEC user on Router R3 telnets to Router R3.

Example 9-111 debug aaa authentication *on R2*

```
R2#debug aaa authentication
AAA Authentication debugging is on
R2#show debugging
General OS:
  AAA Authentication debugging is on
Oct 11 16:27:41: AAA: parse name=tty130 idb type=-1 tty=-1
Oct 11 16:27:41: AAA: name=tty130 flags=0x11 type=5 shelf=0 slot=0 adapter=0 por
t=130 channel=0
Oct 11 16:27:41: AAA/MEMORY: create_user (0x62C7BDA8) user='' ruser='' port='tty
130' rem_addr='144.254.4.3' authen_type=ASCII service=LOGIN priv=1
Oct 11 16:27:41: AAA/AUTHEN/START (4131783264): port='tty130' list='' action=LOG
IN service=LOGIN
Oct 11 16:27:41: AAA/AUTHEN/START (4131783264): using "default" list
Oct 11 16:27:41: AAA/AUTHEN/START (4131783264): Method=LOCAL
Oct 11 16:27:41: AAA/AUTHEN (4131783264): status = GETUSER
Oct 11 16:27:47: AAA/AUTHEN/CONT (4131783264): continue_login (user='(undef)')
Oct 11 16:27:47: AAA/AUTHEN (4131783264): status = GETUSER
Oct 11 16:27:47: AAA/AUTHEN/CONT (4131783264): Method=LOCAL
Oct 11 16:27:47: AAA/AUTHEN (4131783264): status = GETPASS
Oct 11 16:27:49: AAA/AUTHEN/CONT (4131783264): continue_login (user='Erik')
Oct 11 16:27:49: AAA/AUTHEN (4131783264): status = GETPASS
Oct 11 16:27:49: AAA/AUTHEN/CONT (4131783264): Method=LOCAL
Oct 11 16:27:49: AAA/AUTHEN (4131783264): status = PASS
R2#
```

NOTE   When using this form of authentication, usernames are sent in plain text (Erik, in this example).

Login Authentication Methods

Configure R2 so that when a user is prompted to enter a password when trying to connect via the VTY lines, the following display is visible: "Enter your password within 15 seconds:"

Login Authentication Methods Solutions

To define a message on R2 for Telnet (VTY users), use the following IOS command:

```
aaa authentication password-prompt "Enter your password within 15 seconds:"
```

Example 9-112 displays the configurations commands on R2.

Example 9-112 *R2 Message Banner*

```
hostname R2
!
logging rate-limit console 10 except errors
aaa new-model
```

Example 9-112 *R2 Message Banner (Continued)*

```
aaa authentication password-prompt "Enter your password within 15 seconds:"
aaa authentication login default local
enable password cisco
!
username gert password 0 gert
username Erik password 0 Erik
```

Example 9-113 displays the message banner when a PRIV user on R3 Telnets to R2.

Example 9-113 *Telnet from R3 to R2*

```
R3#telnet 144.254.4.2
Trying 144.254.4.2 ... Open


User Access Verification

Username: Erik
Enter your password within 15 seconds:
Password:*****
R2>
```

Example 9-114 displays the debug output once the Telnet connection is made to R2. Notice you have 15 seconds to enter a valid password; otherwise, the Telnet connection is closed.

Example 9-114 *Debugging tacacs Operation on R2*

```
R2#debug tacacs ?
  events  TACACS+ protocol events
  <cr>
R2#debug tacacs events
TACACS+ events debugging is on
R1#debug tacacs
TACACS access control debugging is on
R2#debug aaa authentication
AAA Authentication debugging is on
R2#show debugging
General OS:
  TACACS access control debugging is on
  TACACS+ events debugging is on
  AAA Authentication debugging is on
R2#
R2#
Oct 11 16:40:44: AAA: parse name=tty130 idb type=-1 tty=-1
Oct 11 16:40:44: AAA: name=tty130 flags=0x11 type=5 shelf=0 slot=0 adapter=0 por
t=130 channel=0
Oct 11 16:40:44: AAA/MEMORY: create_user (0x62C7BDA8) user='' ruser='' port='tty
```

continues

Example 9-114 *Debugging tacacs Operation on R2 (Continued)*

```
130' rem_addr='144.254.4.3' authen_type=ASCII service=LOGIN priv=1
Oct 11 16:40:44: AAA/AUTHEN/START (1269435710): port='tty130' list='' action=LOGIN
service=LOGIN
Oct 11 16:40:44: AAA/AUTHEN/START (1269435710): using "default" list
Oct 11 16:40:44: AAA/AUTHEN/START (1269435710): Method=LOCAL
Oct 11 16:40:44: AAA/AUTHEN (1269435710): status = GETUSER
Oct 11 16:40:48: AAA/AUTHEN/CONT (1269435710): continue_login (user='(undef)')
Oct 11 16:40:48: AAA/AUTHEN (1269435710): status = GETUSER
Oct 11 16:40:48: AAA/AUTHEN/CONT (1269435710): Method=LOCAL
Oct 11 16:40:48: AAA/AUTHEN (1269435710): status = GETPASS
Oct 11 16:40:52: AAA/AUTHEN/CONT (1269435710): continue_login (user='Erik')
Oct 11 16:40:52: AAA/AUTHEN (1269435710): status = GETPASS
Oct 11 16:40:52: AAA/AUTHEN/CONT (1269435710): Method=LOCAL
Oct 11 16:40:52: AAA/AUTHEN (1269435710): status = PASS
```

Example 9-114 displays a successful Telnet from R3 to R2.

Login Authentication Using TACACS+

Configure R2 to use TACACS+ for authentication at the login prompt. If TACACS+ returns an error, the user is authenticated using the local database.

Login Authentication Using TACACS+ Solution

R2 must be configured for a login name and login method with the following IOS command:

```
aaa authentication login name tacacs+  local
```

Then, the VTY lines on R2 must be configured for authentication with the following IOS command:

```
line vty 0 4
login authentication name
```

Example 9-115 configures R2 for login authentication.

Example 9-115 *AAA Authentication on R2 (Truncated)*

```
hostname R2
aaa new-model
aaa authentication login default group tacacs+ local
enable password cisco
!
!
tacacs-server host 144.254.6.2
tacacs-server key ccie
end
```

Example 9-116 displays a successful login attempt when an exec user telnets from R3 to R2.

Example 9-116 *Login Authentication Using TACACS+*

```
Oct 11 12:26:56: TAC+: send AUTHEN/START packet ver=192 id=3375296121
Oct 11 12:26:56: TAC+: Using default tacacs server-group "tacacs+" list.
Oct 11 12:26:56: TAC+: Opening TCP/IP to 144.254.6.2/49 timeout=5
Oct 11 12:26:56: TAC+: Opened TCP/IP handle 0x62C8424C to 144.254.6.2/49
Oct 11 12:26:56: TAC+: periodic timer started
Oct 11 12:26:56: TAC+: 144.254.6.2 req=62C81284 Qd id=3375296121 ver=192 handl
e=0x62C8424C (ESTAB) expire=5 AUTHEN/START/LOGIN/ASCII queued
Oct 11 12:26:56: TAC+: 144.254.6.2 (3375296121) AUTHEN/START/LOGIN/ASCII queue
d
Oct 11 12:26:56: TAC+: 144.254.6.2 ESTAB id=3375296121 wrote 38 of 38 bytes
Oct 11 12:26:56: TAC+: 144.254.6.2 req=62C81284 Qd id=3375296121 ver=192 handl
e=0x62C8424C (ESTAB) expire=4 AUTHEN/START/LOGIN/ASCII sent
Oct 11 12:26:56: TAC+: 144.254.6.2 ESTAB read=12 wanted=12 alloc=12 got=12
Oct 11 12:26:56: TAC+: 144.254.6.2 ESTAB read=28 wanted=28 alloc=28 got=16
Oct 11 12:26:56: TAC+: 144.254.6.2 received 28 byte reply for 62C81284
Oct 11 12:26:56: TAC+: req=62C81284 Tx id=3375296121 ver=192 handle=0x62C8424C (
ESTAB) expire=4 AUTHEN/START/LOGIN/ASCII processed
Oct 11 12:26:56: TAC+: (3375296121) AUTHEN/START/LOGIN/ASCII processed
Oct 11 12:26:56: TAC+: periodic timer stopped (queue empty)
Oct 11 12:26:56: TAC+: ver=192 id=3375296121 received AUTHEN status = GETUSER
Oct 11 12:27:00: TAC+: send AUTHEN/CONT packet id=3375296121
Oct 11 12:27:00: TAC+: periodic timer started
Oct 11 12:27:00: TAC+: 144.254.6.2 req=62C81230 Qd id=3375296121 ver=192 handl
e=0x62C8424C (ESTAB) expire=5 AUTHEN/CONT queued
Oct 11 12:27:00: TAC+: 144.254.6.2 (3375296121) AUTHEN/CONT queued
Oct 11 12:27:00: TAC+: 144.254.6.2 ESTAB id=3375296121 wrote 21 of 21 bytes
Oct 11 12:27:00: TAC+: 144.254.6.2 req=62C81230 Qd id=3375296121 ver=192 handl
e=0x62C8424C (ESTAB) expire=4 AUTHEN/CONT sent
Oct 11 12:27:00: TAC+: 144.254.6.2 ESTAB read=12 wanted=12 alloc=12 got=12
Oct 11 12:27:00: TAC+: 144.254.6.2 ESTAB read=28 wanted=28 alloc=28 got=16
Oct 11 12:27:00: TAC+: 144.254.6.2 received 28 byte reply for 62C81230
Oct 11 12:27:00: TAC+: req=62C81230 Tx id=3375296121 ver=192 handle=0x62C8424C (
ESTAB) expire=4 AUTHEN/CONT processed
Oct 11 12:27:00: TAC+: (3375296121) AUTHEN/CONT processed
Oct 11 12:27:00: TAC+: periodic timer stopped (queue empty)
Oct 11 12:27:00: TAC+: ver=192 id=3375296121 received AUTHEN status = GETPASS
Oct 11 12:27:04: TAC+: send AUTHEN/CONT packet id=3375296121
Oct 11 12:27:04: TAC+: periodic timer started
Oct 11 12:27:04: TAC+: 144.254.6.2 req=62C81230 Qd id=3375296121 ver=192 handl
e=0x62C8424C (ESTAB) expire=5 AUTHEN/CONT queued
Oct 11 12:27:04: TAC+: 144.254.6.2 (3375296121) AUTHEN/CONT queued
Oct 11 12:27:04: TAC+: 144.254.6.2 ESTAB id=3375296121 wrote 21 of 21 bytes
Oct 11 12:27:04: TAC+: 144.254.6.2 req=62C81230 Qd id=3375296121 ver=192 handl
e=0x62C8424C (ESTAB) expire=4 AUTHEN/CONT sent
Oct 11 12:27:05: TAC+: 144.254.6.2 ESTAB read=12 wanted=12 alloc=12 got=12
Oct 11 12:27:05: TAC+: 144.254.6.2 ESTAB read=18 wanted=18 alloc=18 got=6
Oct 11 12:27:05: TAC+: 144.254.6.2 received 18 byte reply for 62C81230
```

continues

Example 9-116 *Login Authentication Using TACACS+ (Continued)*

```
Oct 11 12:27:05: TAC+: req=62C81230 Tx id=3375296121 ver=192 handle=0x62C8424C (
ESTAB) expire=3 AUTHEN/CONT processed
Oct 11 12:27:05: TAC+: (3375296121) AUTHEN/CONT processed
Oct 11 12:27:05: TAC+: periodic timer stopped (queue empty)
Oct 11 12:27:05: TAC+: ver=192 id=3375296121 received AUTHEN status = PASS
Oct 11 12:27:05: TAC+: Closing TCP/IP 0x62C8424C connection to 144.254.6.2/49
R2#
```

Example 9-116 displays a successful login attempt. Notice that TCP packets are exchanged because TACACS+ runs over TCP.

Figure 9-4 displays the ACS configuration for AAA and TACACS+. ACS is an intuitive software application.

Figure 9-4 *Configure Cisco ACS for TACACS+*

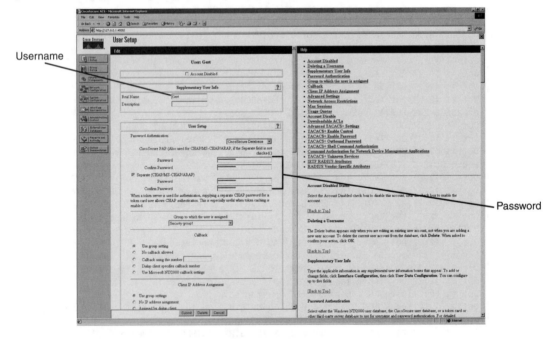

Figure 9-4 displays the creation of a remote username named "Gert" and password creation.

Figure 9-5 displays the ACS network configuration allowing Router R2 (IP address 144.254.152.1) to use the TACACS+ server daemon.

Figure 9-5   *TACACS+ Network Configuration*

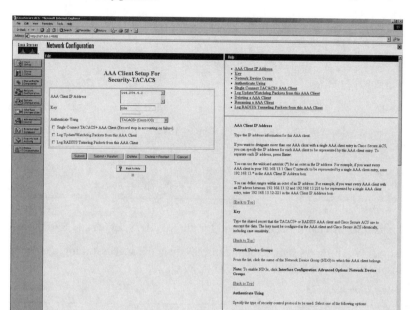

ACS Configuration: Login Authentication Using RADIUS

Configure R3 to use RADIUS for authentication at the login prompt. If RADIUS returns an error, the user is authenticated using the local database. Also, make sure the display, "Enter your name:" is visible when logging in.

ACS Configuration: Login Authentication Using RADIUS Solution

RADIUS commands (similar to previous tasks on TACACS+) are as follows:

```
aaa new-model
aaa authentication login name RADIUS local
aaa authentication username-prompt "Enter your name:"

vty 0 4
login authentication name
```

Example 9-117 configures R3 for RADIUS authentication.

Example 9-117 *Login Authentication Using RADIUS*

```
hostname R3
!

aaa new-model
```

continues

Example 9-117 *Login Authentication Using RADIUS (Continued)*

```
aaa authentication username-prompt "Enter your name:"
aaa authentication login radius group radius local
enable password cisco
!
username Gert password 0 gert
ip subnet-zero
!
<snip>
!
radius-server host 144.254.6.2 auth-port 1645 acct-port 1646
radius-server retransmit 3
radius-server key ccie
line vty 0 4
 login authentication radius
```

R3 must first be enabled for AAA and for the RADIUS server and RADIUS key.

Example 9-118 shows sample debug displays when a successful login attempt is made to R3. R2 is used to Telnet to R3.

Example 9-118 *Telnet from R2 to R3*

```
R3#debug aaa authentication
AAA Authentication debugging is on
R3#show debugging
General OS:
  AAA Authentication debugging is on
Radius protocol debugging is on
R3#
R2#144.254.4.3
Trying 144.254.4.3 ... Open

Enter your name:Gert
Password: *****

R3>enable
Password:****
! Debug output follows
2d23h: AAA: parse name=tty66 idb type=-1 tty=-1
2d23h: AAA: name=tty66 flags=0x11 type=5 shelf=0 slot=0 adapter=0 port=66 channe
l=0
2d23h: AAA/MEMORY: create_user (0x8271FE78) user='' ruser='' port='tty66' rem_ad
dr='144.254.4.2' authen_type=ASCII service=LOGIN priv=1
2d23h: AAA/AUTHEN/START (503012338): port='tty66' list='radius' action=LOGIN ser
vice=LOGIN
2d23h: AAA/AUTHEN/START (503012338): found list radius
2d23h: AAA/AUTHEN/START (503012338): Method=radius (radius)
2d23h: AAA/AUTHEN (503012338): status = GETUSER
```

Example 9-118 *Telnet from R2 to R3 (Continued)*

```
2d23h: AAA/AUTHEN/CONT (503012338): continue_login (user='(undef)')
2d23h: AAA/AUTHEN (503012338): status = GETUSER
2d23h: AAA/AUTHEN (503012338): Method=radius (radius)
2d23h: AAA/AUTHEN (503012338): status = GETPASS
2d23h: AAA/AUTHEN/CONT (503012338): continue_login (user='Gert')
2d23h: AAA/AUTHEN (503012338): status = GETPASS
2d23h: AAA/AUTHEN (503012338): Method=radius (radius)
2d23h: RADIUS: ustruct sharecount=1
2d23h: RADIUS: Initial Transmit tty66 id 2 144.254.6.2:1645, Access-Request, l
en 76
2d23h:         Attribute 4 6 96640115
2d23h:         Attribute 5 6 00000042
2d23h:         Attribute 61 6 00000005
2d23h:         Attribute 1 6 47657274
2d23h:         Attribute 31 14 3135302E
2d23h:         Attribute 2 18 74DEA58C
2d23h: RADIUS: Received from id 2 144.254.6.2:1645, Access-Accept, len 20
2d23h: RADIUS: saved authorization data for user 8271FE78 at 826F6E2C
2d23h: AAA/AUTHEN (503012338): status = PASS
```

The successful user in Example 9-118 was authenticated by the TACACS+ (ACS server) server.

Figure 9-6 displays the username creation on the ACS server.

Figure 9-6   *Username Creation on the ACS for RADIUS*

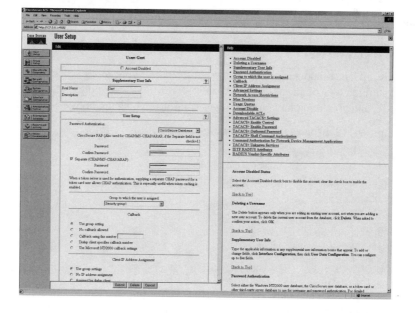

Figure 9-7 displays enabling RADIUS on the ACS server so that Router R3 can authenticate users.

Figure 9-7 *Radius Network Configuration*

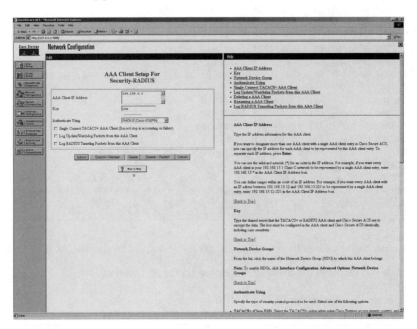

Final Configurations

Finally, all lab components have been completed. For your reference, here are the full working configuration files of all routers and the PIX Firewall. Please note that these configurations are a guide, and you might have found other solutions, which are correct, as well.

Example 9-119 displays the full working configuration for R1.

Example 9-119 *R1's Full Working Configuration*

```
Current configuration : 2627 bytes
version 12.1
no service single-slot-reload-enable
service timestamps debug uptime
service timestamps log uptime
no service password-encryption
hostname R1
!
ip host R2 2002 144.254.151.1
ip host R3 2003 144.254.151.1
ip host R4 2004 144.254.151.1
ip host R5 2005 144.254.151.1
```

Example 9-119 *R1's Full Working Configuration (Continued)*

```
ip host CAT5K 2008 144.254.151.1
ip host PIX 2015 144.254.151.1
enable password cisco
username cisco password 0 cisco
ip subnet-zero
no ip finger
ip tcp intercept list 100
no ip domain-lookup
ip domain-name cisco.com
ip host r1 144.254.151.1
ip host R2 2002 144.254.151.1
ip host R3 2003 144.254.151.1
ip host R4 2004 144.254.151.1
ip host R5 2005 144.254.151.1
ip host CAT5K 2008 144.254.151.1
ip host PIX 2015 144.254.151.1
!
ip audit notify log
ip audit po max-events 100
key chain cisco
 key 1
  key-string ccie
key chain eigrp
 key 1
  key-string ccie
call rsvp-sync
cns event-service server
!
interface Loopback0
 ip address 144.254.151.1 255.255.255.0
!
interface Loopback1
 ip address 131.108.1.1 255.255.255.0
!
interface Loopback2
 ip address 131.108.2.1 255.255.255.0
!
interface Loopback3
 ip address 131.108.3.1 255.255.255.0
!
interface Tunnel0
 ip unnumbered Serial0/1
 ip authentication mode eigrp 333 md5
 ip authentication key-chain eigrp 333 eigrp
 tunnel source Serial0/1
 tunnel destination 144.254.2.2
!
interface Ethernet0/0
 ip address 144.254.1.1 255.255.255.252
ip ospf authentication message-digest-key 1 md5 cisco
 ip ospf authentication-key cisco
```

continues

Example 9-119 *R1's Full Working Configuration (Continued)*

```
 half-duplex
!
interface Serial0/0
 no ip address
 shutdown
!
interface Ethernet0/1
 no ip address
 shutdown
 half-duplex
!
interface Serial0/1
 ip address 144.254.2.1 255.255.255.252
 encapsulation frame-relay
 ip split-horizon
 ip summary-address eigrp 333 131.108.0.0 255.255.252.0 5
 frame-relay map ip 144.254.2.1 114
 frame-relay map ip 144.254.2.2 114
 frame-relay interface-dlci 102
 no frame-relay inverse-arp
!
router eigrp 333
 redistribute rip metric 1500 20000 255 1 1500
 passive-interface Ethernet0/0
 network 131.108.0.0
 network 144.254.0.0
 no auto-summary
 no eigrp log-neighbor-changes
!
router rip
 version 2
 redistribute eigrp 333 metric 1
 passive-interface Serial0/1
 network 144.254.0.0
!
router bgp 333
 no synchronization
 bgp log-neighbor-changes
 network 144.254.151.0 mask 255.255.255.0
 neighbor 144.254.154.1 remote-as 333
 neighbor 144.254.154.1 update-source Loopback0
!
ip kerberos source-interface any
ip classless
no ip http server
!
access-list 100 permit ip any 144.254.1.0 0.0.0.3
!
line 1 16
transport input telnet
```

Example 9-119 *R1's Full Working Configuration (Continued)*

```
!
line con 0
 exec-timeout 0 0
 password cisco
 login
 transport input telnet
line aux 0
 exec-timeout 0 0
 password cisco
 login
 transport input telnet
line vty 0 4
 exec-timeout 0 0
 password cisco
 login local
 transport input telnet
!
end
```

Example 9-120 displays the full working configuration for R2.

Example 9-120 *R2's Full Working Configuration*

```
version 12.1
no service single-slot-reload-enable
service timestamps debug uptime
service timestamps log uptime
no service password-encryption
!
hostname R2
!
aaa new-model
username Erik access-class 1 password 0 Erik
username gert password 0 gert
aaa authentication login default local
aaa authentication password-prompt "Enter your password within 15 seconds:"
aaa authentication login default group tacacs+ local
enable password cisco
ip subnet-zero
no ip finger
no ip domain-lookup
ip host r1 144.254.151.1
ip host r2 144.254.152.1
ip host r3 144.254.153.1
ip host r4 144.254.154.1
ip host r5 144.254.155.1
ip dhcp excluded-address 144.254.4.1
ip dhcp excluded-address 144.254.4.2
ip dhcp excluded-address 144.254.4.3
```

continues

Example 9-120 *R2's Full Working Configuration (Continued)*

```
!
ip dhcp pool ccie
   network 144.254.4.0 255.255.255.192
   domain-name cisco.com
   default-router 144.254.4.1 144.254.4.2
   lease infinite
ip audit notify log
ip audit po max-events 100
frame-relay de-list 5 protocol ip gt 768
crypto isakmp policy 1
 hash md5
 authentication pre-share
crypto isakmp key CCiE address 144.254.3.1
crypto ipsec transform-set anyname1onR2 esp-des esp-sha-hmac
 mode transport
crypto map anyname 1 ipsec-isakmp
 set peer 144.254.3.1
 set security-association lifetime seconds 300
 set transform-set anyname1onR2
 match address 150
!
call rsvp-sync
cns event-service server
interface Loopback0
 ip address 144.254.152.1 255.255.255.0
 ip ospf network point-to-point
!
interface Ethernet0/0
 ip address 144.254.4.2 255.255.255.192
 ip ospf hello-interval 20
 ip ospf priority 0
 half-duplex
!
interface Serial0/0
 ip address 144.254.3.2 255.255.255.248
 encapsulation frame-relay
ip ospf authentication message-digest-key 1 md5 cisco
 ip ospf authentication-key cisco
 ip ospf hello-interval 25
 ip ospf priority 0
 frame-relay map ip 144.254.3.1 204 broadcast
 frame-relay map ip 144.254.3.2 204 broadcast
 frame-relay map ip 144.254.3.3 204 broadcast
 frame-relay interface-dlci 204
 no frame-relay inverse-arp
 frame-relay lmi-type ansi
 crypto map anyname
!
interface TokenRing0/0
 no ip address
 shutdown
 ring-speed 16
```

Example 9-120 *R2's Full Working Configuration (Continued)*

```
!
interface Serial0/1
 no ip address
!
router ospf 1
 router-id 144.254.152.1
 log-adjacency-changes
 area 0 authentication message-digest
 network 144.254.3.2 0.0.0.0 area 0
 network 144.254.4.2 0.0.0.0 area 333
 network 144.254.152.1 0.0.0.0 area 0
!
router bgp 333
 no synchronization
 bgp log-neighbor-changes
 network 144.254.152.0 mask 255.255.255.0
 neighbor 144.254.154.1 remote-as 333
 neighbor 144.254.154.1 password cisco
 neighbor 144.254.154.1 update-source Loopback0
!
ip kerberos source-interface any
ip classless
no ip http server
access-list 1 permit 144.254.4.0
access-list 150 permit ip any any
tacacs-server host 144.254
tacacs-server key ccie
dial-peer cor custom
line con 0
 exec-timeout 0 0
 password cisco
 login
 transport input telnet
line aux 0
 exec-timeout 0 0
 password cisco
 login
 transport input telnet
line vty 0 4
 exec-timeout 0 0
 password cisco
 login
 transport input telnet
!
end
```

Example 9-121 displays the full working configuration for R3.

Example 9-121 *R3's Full Working Configuration*

```
!
version 12.1
no service single-slot-reload-enable
service timestamps debug uptime
service timestamps log uptime
no service password-encryption
hostname R3
logging rate-limit console 10 except errors
enable password cisco
username Gert password 0 gert
username R5 password 0 cisco
ip subnet-zero
aaa new-model
aaa authentication username-prompt "Enter your name:"
aaa authentication login radius group radius local
no ip finger
no ip domain-lookup
ip host r5 144.254.155.1
ip host r4 144.254.154.1
ip host r3 144.254.153.1
ip host r2 144.254.152.1
ip host r1 144.254.151.1
ip audit notify log
ip audit po max-events 100
frame-relay de-list 5 protocol ip gt 768
crypto isakmp policy 1
 hash md5
 authentication pre-share
crypto isakmp key CCiE address 144.254.3.1
crypto ipsec transform-set anyname1onR3 esp-des esp-sha-hmac
 mode transport
crypto map anyname 1 ipsec-isakmp
 set peer 144.254.3.1
 set security-association lifetime seconds 300
 set transform-set anyname1onR3
 match address 150
isdn switch-type basic-5ess
call rsvp-sync
cns event-service server
interface Loopback0
 ip address 144.254.153.1 255.255.255.0
 ip ospf network point-to-point
!
interface FastEthernet0/0
 ip address 144.254.4.1 255.255.255.192
 ip access-group 100 in
 ip ospf hello-interval 20
 duplex auto
 speed auto
```

Example 9-121   *R3's Full Working Configuration (Continued)*

```
!
interface Serial0/0
 ip address 144.254.3.3 255.255.255.248
 encapsulation frame-relay
 ip split-horizon
ip ospf authentication message-digest-key 1 md5 cisco
 ip ospf authentication-key cisco
 ip ospf hello-interval 25
 ip ospf priority 0
 frame-relay map ip 144.254.3.1 304 broadcast
 frame-relay map ip 144.254.3.2 304 broadcast
 frame-relay map ip 144.254.3.3 304 broadcast
 frame-relay interface-dlci 304
 no frame-relay inverse-arp
 crypto map anyname
!
interface BRI0/0
 description 7775010
 ip address 144.254.7.1 255.255.255.252
 encapsulation ppp
ip ospf authentication message-digest-key 1 md5 cisco
ip ospf authentication-key cisco
 ip ospf demand-circuit
 dialer map ip 144.254.7.2 name R5 broadcast 7775020
 dialer load-threshold 165 either
 dialer-group 1
 isdn switch-type basic-5ess
 no peer neighbor-route
 ppp quality 80
 ppp authentication chap
 ppp multilink
!
interface FastEthernet0/1
 no ip address
 shutdown
 duplex auto
 speed auto
!
interface Serial0/1
 no ip address
!
router ospf 1
 router-id 144.254.153.1
 log-adjacency-changes
 area 0 authentication message-digest
 network 144.254.3.3 0.0.0.0 area 0
 network 144.254.4.1 0.0.0.0 area 333
 network 144.254.4.2 0.0.0.0 area 333
 network 144.254.7.1 0.0.0.0 area 0
 network 144.254.153.1 0.0.0.0 area 0
!
```

continues

Example 9-121 *R3's Full Working Configuration (Continued)*

```
router bgp 333
 no synchronization
 bgp log-neighbor-changes
 network 144.254.153.0 mask 255.255.255.0
 neighbor 144.254.154.1 remote-as 333
 neighbor 144.254.154.1 update-source Loopback0
!
ip kerberos source-interface any
ip classless
no ip http server
!
access-list 100 dynamic blockping timeout 5 permit icmp host 144.254.4.2 host 14
4.254.4.1
access-list 100 deny   icmp host 144.254.4.2 host 144.254.4.1 echo
access-list 100 permit ip any any
access-list 150 permit ip any any
dialer-list 1 protocol ip permit
radius-server host 144.254.6.2 auth-port 1645 acct-port 1646
radius-server retransmit 3
radius-server key ccie
!
line con 0
 exec-timeout 0 0
 password cisco
 logging synchronous
 login
 transport input none
line aux 0
 exec-timeout 0 0
 password cisco
 login
 transport input telnet
line vty 0 4
 exec-timeout 0 0
 password cisco
 login
 autocommand  access-enable host timeout 5
 transport input telnet
!
no scheduler allocate
end
```

Example 9-122 displays the full working configuration for R4.

Example 9-122 *R4's Full Working Configuration*

```
!
version 12.1
no service single-slot-reload-enable
service timestamps debug uptime
```

Example 9-122 *R4's Full Working Configuration (Continued)*

```
service timestamps log uptime
no service password-encryption
hostname R4
logging rate-limit console 10 except errors
enable password cisco
ip subnet-zero
no ip finger
no ip domain-lookup
ip host r1 144.254.151.1
ip host r2 144.254.152.1
ip host r3 144.254.153.1
ip host r4 144.254.154.1
ip host r5 144.254.155.1
ip audit notify log
ip audit po max-events 100
crypto isakmp policy 1
 hash md5
 authentication pre-share
crypto isakmp key CCiE address 144.254.3.2
crypto isakmp key CCiE address 144.254.3.3
crypto ipsec transform-set anyname1 esp-des esp-sha-hmac
 mode transport
crypto map anyname 1 ipsec-isakmp
 set peer 144.254.3.2
 set peer 144.254.3.3
 set security-association lifetime seconds 300
 set transform-set anyname1
 match address 150
key chain eigrp
 key 1
  key-string ccie
call rsvp-sync
cns event-service server
!
interface Loopback0
 ip address 144.254.154.1 255.255.255.0
 ip ospf network point-to-point
!
interface Tunnel0
 ip unnumbered Serial0/1
 ip authentication mode eigrp 333 md5
 ip authentication key-chain eigrp 333 eigrp
 tunnel source Serial0/1
 tunnel destination 144.254.2.1
!
interface Ethernet0/0
 ip address 144.254.5.1 255.255.255.224
 ip ospf hello-interval 60
 half-duplex
```

continues

Example 9-122 *R4's Full Working Configuration (Continued)*

```
!
interface Serial0/0
 ip address 144.254.3.1 255.255.255.248
 encapsulation frame-relay
 ip ospf authentication message-digest
 ip ospf authentication-key cisco
 ip ospf hello-interval 25
 ip ospf priority 255
 frame-relay map ip 144.254.3.1 402
 frame-relay map ip 144.254.3.2 402 broadcast
 frame-relay map ip 144.254.3.3 403 broadcast
 frame-relay interface-dlci 402
 frame-relay interface-dlci 403
 no frame-relay inverse-arp
 frame-relay lmi-type ansi
 crypto map anyname
!
interface TokenRing0/0
 ip address 135.7.24.4 255.255.255.0
 shutdown
 ring-speed 16
!
interface Serial0/1
 ip address 144.254.2.2 255.255.255.252
 encapsulation frame-relay
 ip split-horizon
 frame-relay map ip 144.254.2.1 411
 frame-relay map ip 144.254.2.2 411
 frame-relay interface-dlci 201
 no frame-relay inverse-arp
!
router eigrp 333
 redistribute ospf 1 metric 1544 20000 255 1 1500
 passive-interface Ethernet0/0
 passive-interface Serial0/0
 passive-interface Loopback0
 network 144.254.0.0
 no auto-summary
 no eigrp log-neighbor-changes
!
router ospf 1
 router-id 144.254.154.1
 log-adjacency-changes
 area 0 authentication message-digest
 area 4 virtual-link 144.254.155.1
 redistribute eigrp 333 metric 100 metric-type 1 subnets
 network 144.254.3.1 0.0.0.0 area 0
 network 144.254.5.1 0.0.0.0 area 4
 network 144.254.154.1 0.0.0.0 area 0
 neighbor 144.254.3.3
 neighbor 144.254.3.2
```

Example 9-122 *R4's Full Working Configuration (Continued)*

```
!
router bgp 333
 no synchronization
 bgp log-neighbor-changes
 network 144.254.154.0 mask 255.255.255.0
 neighbor 144.254.151.1 remote-as 333
 neighbor 144.254.151.1 update-source Loopback0
 neighbor 144.254.151.1 route-reflector-client
 neighbor 144.254.152.1 remote-as 333
 neighbor 144.254.152.1 password cisco
 neighbor 144.254.152.1 update-source Loopback0
 neighbor 144.254.152.1 route-reflector-client
 neighbor 144.254.153.1 remote-as 333
 neighbor 144.254.153.1 update-source Loopback0
 neighbor 144.254.153.1 route-reflector-client
 neighbor 144.254.155.1 remote-as 333
 neighbor 144.254.155.1 update-source Loopback0
 neighbor 144.254.155.1 route-reflector-client
 !
ip kerberos source-interface any
ip classless
no ip http server
access-list 150 permit ip any any
dial-peer cor custom
!
line con 0
 exec-timeout 0 0
 password cisco
 login
 transport input telnet
line aux 0
 exec-timeout 0 0
 password cisco
 login
 transport input telnet
line vty 0 4
 exec-timeout 0 0
 password cisco
 login
 transport input telnet
!
end
```

Example 9-123 displays the full working configuration for R5.

Example 9-123 *R5's Full Working Configuration*

```
version 12.1
no service single-slot-reload-enable
service timestamps debug uptime
service timestamps log uptime
no service password-encryption
hostname R5
logging rate-limit console 10 except errors
enable password cisco
username R5 password 0 cisco
username R3 password 0 cisco
ip subnet-zero
no ip finger
no ip domain-lookup
ip host r5 144.254.155.1
ip host r4 144.254.154.1
ip host r3 144.254.153.1
ip host r2 144.254.152.1
ip audit notify log
ip audit po max-events 100
isdn switch-type basic-5ess
interface Loopback0
 ip address 144.254.155.1 255.255.255.0
 ip ospf network point-to-point
interface FastEthernet0/0
 ip address 144.254.5.2 255.255.255.224
 ip access-group 100 out
 ip ospf hello-interval 60
 duplex auto
 speed auto
!
interface Serial0/0
 no ip address
 ip access-group 100 out
 shutdown
!
interface BRI0/0
 description 7775020
 ip address 144.254.7.2 255.255.255.252
 encapsulation ppp
ip ospf authentication message-digest-key 1 md5 cisco
 ip ospf authentication-key cisco
Ciscodialer load-threshold 165 either
 dialer map ip 144.254.7.1 name R3 broadcast
 dialer-group 1
 isdn switch-type basic-5ess
 no peer neighbor-route
 ppp authentication chap callin
 ppp multilink
!
interface FastEthernet0/1
 ip address 144.254.6.1 255.255.255.248
```

Example 9-123 *R5's Full Working Configuration (Continued)*

```
 ip access-group 101 in
 ip access-group web-traffic out
 ip inspect OUTBOUND in

 duplex auto
 speed auto
!
interface Serial0/1
 no ip address
 shutdown
!
router ospf 1
 router-id 144.254.155.1
 log-adjacency-changes
 area 0 authentication message-digest
 area 4 virtual-link 144.254.154.1
 network 144.254.5.2 0.0.0.0 area 4
 network 144.254.6.1 0.0.0.0 area 5
 network 144.254.7.2 0.0.0.0 area 0
 network 144.254.155.1 0.0.0.0 area 4
!
router bgp 333
 no synchronization
 bgp log-neighbor-changes
 network 144.254.155.0 mask 255.255.255.0
 neighbor 144.254.154.1 remote-as 333
!
ip kerberos source-interface any
ip classless
no ip http server
ip access-list extended web-traffic
 deny   tcp any any time-range web-timing
 permit ip any any
access-list 100 deny   tcp 129.57.140.0 0.0.64.255 any log
access-list 100 deny   tcp 161.133.29.0 64.0.0.0 any log
access-list 100 deny   tcp 182.133.0.0 0.0.255.255 any log
access-list 100 permit ip any any
access-list 100 permit ip any any log
access-list 101 permit ip 0.0.0.0 255.255.255.192 any
dialer-list 1 protocol ip permit
dial-peer cor custom
line con 0
 exec-timeout 0 0
 password cisco
 login
 transport input telnet
line aux 0
 exec-timeout 0 0
 password cisco
 login
 transport input telnet
```

continues

Example 9-123 *R5's Full Working Configuration (Continued)*

```
line vty 0 4
 exec-timeout 0 0
 password cisco
 login
 transport input telnet
!
no scheduler allocate
time-range web-timing
 periodic weekdays 7:00 to 17:00
!
end
```

Example 9-124 displays the full working configuration for the PIX Firewall.

Example 9-124 *PIX Firewall Full Working Configuration*

```
PIX Version 5.2(3)
nameif ethernet0 outside security0
nameif ethernet1 inside security100
enable password 8Ry2YjIyt7RRXU24 encrypted
passwd 2KFQnbNIdI.2KYOU encrypted
hostname PIX1
fixup protocol ftp 21
fixup protocol http 80
fixup protocol h323 1720
fixup protocol rsh 514
fixup protocol smtp 25
fixup protocol sqlnet 1521
fixup protocol sip 5060
names
pager lines 24
logging on
no logging timestamp
no logging standby
no logging console
no logging monitor
no logging buffered
no logging trap
no logging history
logging facility 20
logging queue 512
interface ethernet0 auto
interface ethernet1 auto
icmp permit any inside
mtu outside 1500
mtu inside 1500
ip address outside 9.1.1.1 255.255.255.0
ip address inside 144.254.1.2 255.255.255.252
ip audit name Attack-inside attack action alarm reset
ip audit name Information-inside info action alarm drop
```

Example 9-124   *PIX Firewall Full Working Configuration (Continued)*

```
ip audit name Attack-outside attack action alarm drop
ip audit interface outside Attack-inside
ip audit interface inside Information-inside
ip audit interface inside Attack-outside
ip audit info action alarm
ip audit attack action alarm
no failover
failover timeout 0:00:00
failover poll 15
failover ip address outside 0.0.0.0
failover ip address inside 0.0.0.0
arp timeout 14400
nat (inside) 1 0.0.0.0 0.0.0.0 0 0
rip outside passive version 1
rip inside passive version 2 authentication md5 ccie 1
rip inside default version 2 authentication md5 ccie 1
route outside 0.0.0.0 0.0.0.0 9.1.1.2
route inside 144.254.0.0 255.255.0.0 144.254.1.1
timeout xlate 3:00:00
timeout conn 1:00:00 half-closed 0:10:00 udp 0:02:00 rpc 0:10:00 h323 0:05:00 si
p 0:30:00 sip_media 0:02:00
timeout uauth 0:05:00 absolute
aaa-server TACACS+ protocol tacacs+
aaa-server RADIUS protocol radius
no snmp-server location
no snmp-server contact
snmp-server community public
no snmp-server enable traps
floodguard enable
no sysopt route dnat
isakmp identity hostname
telnet 144.254.1.1 255.255.255.255 inside
telnet timeout 5
ssh timeout 5
terminal width 80
Cryptochecksum:7827bfd3d2885989e9a789c8c9a4c6d6
: end
```

NOTE   The routers in this network were Cisco 2600 and 3600 but, in theory, you can use any Cisco IOS router and PIX Firewall. The Catalyst switch used in this lab was a Catalyst 5505 Ethernet switch running version 4.5.

Conclusion

You should be able to complete this CCIE Security self-study lab within eight hours. The difficulty level presented here is the very minimum of what you can expect in any CCIE lab exam. Focus your attention on time management and your ability to configure a number of IOS features quickly. If you can complete this lab successfully, modify the tasks and try again. Change the IP routing algorithm, for example, or configure the PIX for IPSec termination from the Internet. Make sure you are familiar with Cisco ACS and are comfortable with TACACS+ and RADIUS.

Your ability to complete any design scenario is what will ensure that you are a master of CCIE, rather than someone who has just passed an eight-hour exam. In today's environment, being a CCIE might not be marketable enough. Demonstrating to a prospective employer your skills of designing any network topology in any network condition will ensure you are ahead of the rest.

I would like to thank Gert De Laet for helping me write this chapter.

Best of luck to you in your endeavors to become a CCIE Security expert and beyond. When you do pass the exam, please e-mail me at hbenjamin@optusnet.com.au so I, too, can share in your great accomplishment.

Answers to Quiz Questions

Chapter 2 "Do I Know This Already?" Quiz Answers

1 Which layer of the OSI model is responsible for converting frames into bits and bits into frames?

   a. Physical

   b. Network

   c. Transport

   d. LLC sublayer

   e. Data link

   Answer: e

   The data link layer performs bit conversion to pass to the MAC sublayer.

2 Routing occurs at what layer of the OSI model?

   a. Physical

   b. Network

   c. Transport

   d. LLC sublayer

   e. Data link

   Answer: b

   Routing is a Layer 3 (network layer) function.

3 Bridging occurs at what layer of the OSI model?

   a. Physical

   b. Network

   c. Transport

   d. Data link

   Answer: d

   The data link layer is where bridging is performed.

4 Which of the following is *not* part of the OSI model?

    a. Network layer

    b. Physical layer

    c. Operational layer

    d. Application layer

Answer: c

The operational layer is not one of the seven OSI layers. The OSI model layers are physical, data link, network, transport, session, presentation, and application.

5 IP operates at what layer of the OSI model?

    a. Layer 1

    b. Layer 2

    c. Layer 3

    d. Layer 4

    e. Layer 5

    f. Layer 6

    g. Layer 7

Answer: c

IP operates at the network layer (Layer 3) and provides a path to a destination.

6 On which layer of the OSI model is data commonly referred to as segments?

    a. Layer 4

    b. Layer 3

    c. Layer 2

    d. Layer 1

Answer: a

The data on Layer 4 is commonly referred to as segments.

7 On which layer of the OSI model is data commonly referred to as packets?

   a. Layer 1

   b. Layer 2

   c. Layer 4

   d. Layer 3

Answer: d

The data on Layer 3 is commonly referred to as packets.

8 Which layer of the OSI model transmits raw bits?

   a. Layer 1

   b. Layer 2

   c. Layer 3

   d. Layer 4

Answer: a

At Layer 1, the lowest layer of the OSI model, bits are transferred across the wire.

9 Which of the following protocols is *not* routable?

   a. IP

   b. IPX

   c. NetBEUI

   d. NetBIOS

Answer: c

NetBEUI is not a routed protocol and must be bridged.

10 Which of the following is *not* a required step to enable FastEther Channel (FEC)?

   a. Ensure that all ports share the same speed at 10 Mbps.

   b. Ensure that all ports share the same parameter such as speed.

   c. Ensure that all ports operate at 100 Mbps.

   d. Only eight ports can be bundled into a logical link or trunk.

Answer: a

FEC uses full-duplex Fast Ethernet (100 Mbps) links.

11 How is FastEther Channel best defined?

   a. A bundle of 10-Mbps ports on a switch

   b. Another name for half duplex 100 Mbps

   c. Not available on Cisco Catalyst switches

   d. The ability to bundle 100 Mbps ports into a logical link

   e. Only supported with Gigabit ports

Answer: d

The FastEther Channel feature bundles 100 Mbps Fast Ethernet ports into a logical link between two devices, such as Catalyst switches.

12 On what OSI layer does bridging occur?

   a. Layer 1

   b. Layer 2

   c. Layer 3

   d. Both Layer 1 and 2

Answer: b

Bridging occurs at the data link layer (Layer 2) of the OSI model.

13 In spanning tree, what is a BPDU?

   a. A break protocol data unit

   b. A routable frame

   c. A bridge protocol data unit

   d. A frame sent out by end stations

Answer: c

BPDU is a bridge protocol data unit.

14 An incoming frame on a Layer 2 switch is received on port 10/1 on a Catalyst 5000. If the destination address is known through port 10/2, what happens?

   a. The frame is discarded.

   b. The frame is sent via port 10/2.

   c. The frame is broadcast to all ports on the switch.

   d. The frame is sent back via 10/1.

   e. None of the above.

Answer: b

The destination MAC address has already been discovered through port 10/2, so the frame will only be sent to the known port or slot 10, port 2.

15 Which of the following are the four possible states of spanning tree?

   a. Listening, learning, blocking, broadcasting

   b. Listening, learning, blocking, connecting

   c. Discovering, learning, blocking, connecting

   d. Listening, learning, blocking, forwarding

Answer: d

The four states of spanning tree are listening, learning, blocking, and forwarding.

16 How many bits make up an IP address?

   a. 64 bits

   b. 48 bits

   c. 32 bits

   d. 24 bits

   e. 8 bits

Answer: c

IP addresses for IPv4 are 32 bits in length.

17 Identify the broadcast address for the subnet 131.108.1.0/24.

    a. 131.108.1.1

    b. 131.108.1.254

    c. 131.108.1.255

    d. 131.108.1.2

    e. More data required

Answer: c

131.108.1.0/24 is a Class B address with a Class C mask, and the all (all binary 1s) broadcast address is 131.108.1.255 (11111111).

18 Convert the following address to binary:

131.1.1.1/24

    a. 10000011.1.1.1

    b. 10000011.00000010.1.1

    c. 10000011.1.1.01010101

    d. 10000011.1.1.11111111

Answer: a

131.108.1.1 in binary is 10000011.00000001.00000001.00000001 or 10000011.1.1.1

19 How many subnets are possible in VLSM if the Class C address 131.108.255.0 is used with the subnet mask 255.255.255.252 in the fourth octet field?

    a. None

    b. 100

    c. 255

    d. 254

    e. 253

    f. 252

    g. 64

    h. 62

Answer: h

$2^6 - 2 = 64 - 2 = 62.$

20 How many hosts are available when a /26 subnet mask is used?

   a. 254

   b. 62

   c. 64

   d. 126

Answer: b

$2^6-2 = 64-2 = 62.$

21 How many hosts are available in a Class C or /24 network?

   a. 255

   b. 254

   c. 253

   d. 0

   e. More data required

Answer: b

A Class C or /24 network has $2^8-2 = 256-2 = 254$ addresses available for host devices.

22 You require an IP network to support at most 62 hosts. What subnet mask will accomplish this requirement?

   a. 255.255.255.255

   b. 255.255.255.252

   c. 255.255.255.224

   d. 255.255.255.192

   e. 255.255.255.240

Answer: d

62 hosts require 62+2 = 64 addresses. This needs 6 bits borrowed from the subnet mask. In binary, that number is 11000000.

23 Which of the following are multicast addresses? (Choose all that apply.)

    a. 224.0.0.5

    b. 224.0.0.6

    c. 221.0.0.5

    d. 192.1.1.1

    e. 131.108.1.1

Answer: a and b

224.0.0.5 and 224.0.0.6 are multicast addresses.

24 Which of the following routing protocols does *not* support VLSM?

    a. RIPv1

    b. RIPv2

    c. OSPF

    d. EIGRP

    e. BGP

Answer: a

RIP version I is classful and does not carry subnet masks in routing updates.

25 What is the source TCP port number when a Telnet session is created by a PC to a Cisco router?

    a. 23

    b. Not a known variable

    c. 21

    d. 20

    e. 69

Answer: b

The source TCP port is a random number; the destination port is 23.

26 What best describes the ARP process?

a. DNS resolution

b. Mapping an IP address to a MAC address

c. Mapping a next-hop address to outbound interface on a Cisco router

d. Both a and b

Answer: b

ARP maps an IP address to a MAC address.

27 If two Cisco routers are configured for HSRP and one router has a default priority of 100 and the other 99, which router assumes the role of active router?

a. The default priority cannot be 100.

b. The router with a higher priority.

c. The router with the lowest priority.

d. Neither router because Cisco routers do not support HSRP; only clients do.

Answer: b

The highest priority assumes the role of active router.

28 A Cisco router has the following route table:

```
R1#show ip route
     131.108.0.0/16 is variably subnetted, 17 subnets, 2 masks
C       131.108.255.0/24 is directly connected, Serial0/0
C       131.108.250.0/24 is directly connected, Serial0/1
O       131.108.254.0/24 [110/391] via 131.108.255.6, 03:33:03, Serial0/1
                         [110/391] via 131.108.255.2, 03:33:03, Serial0/0
R       131.108.254.0/24 [120/1] via 131.108.255.6, 03:33:03, Serial0/1
                         [120/1] via 131.108.255.2, 03:33:03, Serial0/
```

What is the preferred path to 131.108.254.0/24? (Choose the best two answers.)

a. Via Serial 0/0

b. Via Serial 0/1

c. None

d. To null0

Answers: a and b

OSPF is chosen because of the lower administrative distance of 110 compared to RIP's 120. Also notice OSPF load balancing between Serial0/0 and Serial0/1. (The written examination always advises you how many answers to select. Practice on the CD provided.)

29 IP RIP runs over what TCP port number?

    a. 23

    b. 21

    c. 69

    d. 520

    e. None of the above

Answer: e

IP RIP does not use TCP port numbers; it uses UDP.

30 IP RIP runs over what UDP port number?

    a. 23

    b. 21

    c. 69

    d. 520

Answer: d

UDP 520

31 An OSPF virtual link should _____ .

    a. Never be used

    b. Allow nonpartitioned areas access to the backbone

    c. Allow partitioned areas access to the backbone

    d. Not be used in OSPF, but in ISDN

Answer: c

Virtual links allow access to areas not directly connected to the backbone or partitioned areas.

32 What is the BGP version most widely used today?

   a. 1

   b. 2

   c. 3

   d. 4

   e. 5

   f. 6

Answer: d

BGP4.

33 What is the destination port number used in a Telnet session?

   a. 23

   b. 69

   c. 21

   d. 161

Answer: a

Telnet, an application layer protocol, uses destination port 23.

34 In what fields does the IP checksum calculate the checksum value?

   a. Data only

   b. Header and data

   c. Header only

   d. Not used in an IP packet

Answer: c

The IP checksum calculation only covers the IP header.

35 The TCP header checksum ensures integrity of what data in the TCP segment?

   a. The data only.

   b. The header only.

   c. The data and header.

   d. There are no TCP header checksums; IP covers the calculation.

Answer: c

The TCP checksum calculation covers the TCP header and data.

36 ISDN BRI channels are made up of what?

    a. 1×64 kbps channel and one D channel at 64 kbps

    b. 2×64 kbps channels and one D channel at 64 kbps

    c. 2×64 kbps channels and one D channel at 16 kbps

    d. 32×64 kbps channels and one D channel at 16 kbps

Answer: c

ISDN basic rate interface (BRI) is two 64-kbps data channels and one signaling channel (D Channel at 16 Kb).

37 What services can ISDN carry?

    a. Data only

    b. Data and voice only

    c. Voice and video

    d. Data, voice, and video

Answer d.

ISDN supports data, video, and voice.

38 Place the following steps in the correct order for PPP callback, as specified in RFC 1570.

    1. A PC user (client) connects to the Cisco access server.

    2. The Cisco IOS Software validates callback rules for this user/line and disconnects the caller for callback.

    3. PPP authentication is performed.

    4. Callback process is negotiated in the PPP link control protocol (LCP) phase.

    5. The Cisco Access Server dials the client.

    a. 1, 2, 3, 4, 5

    b. 1, 3, 2, 5, 4

    c. 1, 4, 5, 3, 2

    d. 5, 4, 3, 2, 1

Answer d.

RFC 1570 dictates how PPP callback is to be followed. For more information, refer to www.cis.ohio-state.edu/cgi-bin/rfc/rfc1570.html.

39 What hardware port is typically designed to connect a Cisco router for modem access?

   a. The console port

   b. The vty lines

   c. The auxiliary port

   d. The power switch

   e. The Ethernet interface

Answer c.

The auxiliary port on Cisco routers can be used for modem access. The console port can also be used but, typically, the Aux port is applied for remote access or dialup access for network failures.

40 The AS5300 series router can support which of the following incoming connections?

   a. Voice

   b. Dialup users via PSTN

   c. ISDN

   d. All the above

Answer d.

The AS5300 series router can support both digital (ISDN) and analogue connections, and also supports voice traffic.

Chapter 2 Q & A Answers

1 What are the seven layers of the OSI model?

Answer: The seven layers of the OSI model are as follows:

- Application
- Presentation
- Session
- Transport
- Network
- Data link
- Physical

2 What layer of the OSI model is responsible for ensuring that IP packets are routed from one location to another?

Answer: The network layer is primarily responsible for routing IP packets from one destination to another.

3 What mechanism is used in Ethernet to guarantee packet delivery over the wire?

Answer: Carrier Sense Multiple Access/Collision Detection (CSMA/CD) is the Ethernet mechanism used to ensure that when devices detect collisions, other devices on the segment are sent a jam signal. CSMA/CD ensures that when collisions occur, other devices (such as PCs or routers) back off (do not transmit) for a specified period of time. When a device receives a jam signal, it will wait a random amount of time to retransmit. This lowers the chance of another collision. All devices that detect a jam signal can transmit up to 16 times before sending an error message to the application layer.

4 Name two physical characteristics of 10BaseT?

Answer: 10BaseT is an Ethernet physical layer standard that defines a maximum length of 100 m and a network speed of 10 Mbps.

5 What Catalyst command displays the bridging or CAM table on a Cisco 5000 series switch?

Answer: show cam dynamic

6 What are the possible states of spanning tree?

Answer: The possible states of spanning tree are as follows:

- **Disabled—The port is not participating in spanning tree and is not active.**
- **Listening—The port has received data from the interface and will listen for frames. In this state, the bridge only receives data and does not forward any frames to the interface or to other ports.**
- **Learning—In this state, the bridge still discards incoming frames. The source address associated with the port is added to the CAM table. BPDUs are sent and received.**
- **Forwarding—The port is fully operational; frames are sent and received.**
- **Blocking—The port has been through the learning and listening states and, because this particular port is a dual path to the root bridge, the port is blocked to maintain a loop-free topology.**

The order of spanning tree states is listening, then learning, and, finally, forwarding or blocking. Typically, each state takes around 15 seconds on Cisco Catalyst switches.

7 FastEther Channel (FEC) allows what to occur between Cisco Catalyst switches?

Answer: FEC is a Cisco method that bundles 100 MB/s fast Ethernet ports into a logical link between Cisco Catalysts switches, such as the Catalyst 5000 or 6000 series switches.

Up to four ports can be bundled together to scale bandwidth up to 800 Mbps.

8 What field in the IP packet guarantees data delivery?

Answer: The IP frame format has no settings that guarantee packet delivery, so IP is termed connectionless. The error check is only performed on the IP header fields, not the data in the packet.

9 Name some examples of connection-orientated protocols used in TCP/IP networks.

Answer: Connection-orientated protocols include TCP, FTP, and Telnet.

10 Given the address, 131.108.1.56/24, what are the subnet and broadcast addresses? How many hosts can reside on this network?

Answer: The subnet is 131.108.1.0 and the broadcast address is 131.108.1.255. The number of hosts is defined by the formula 2^8-2=256-2=254.

11 How many hosts can reside when the subnet mask applied to the network 131.108.1.0 is 255.255.255.128 (or 131.108.1.0/25)?

Answer: The number of hosts is 2^7-2=128-2=126.

12 Name five routing protocols that support VLSM.

Answer: Routing protocols that support VLSM include the following:

- **RIP Version II**
- **OSPF**
- **IS-IS**
- **EIGRP**
- **BGP4**

13 What is the destination port number used in a Telnet session?

Answer: The TCP port number is 23, and the source port is a random number generated by the host device.

14 What TCP/IP services are common in today's large IP networks?

Answer: TCP/IP has a number of applications or services in use:

- **Address Resolution protocol (ARP)**
- **Reverse Address Resolution protocol (RARP)**
- **Dynamic Host Configuration Protocol (DHCP)**
- **Hot Standby Router Protocol (HSRP)**
- **Internet Control Message Protocol (ICMP)**
- **Telnet**
- **File transfer protocol (FTP)**
- **Trivial File Transfer Protocol (TFTP)**

15 What IOS command displays the IP ARP table on a Cisco IOS router?

Answer: The IOS command is show ip arp. This command displays IP ARP entries only. IOS command, show arp, displays all ARP entries for all protocols in use.

16 Cisco routers use what mechanism to determine the routing selection policy for remote networks if more than one routing protocol is running?

Answer: Cisco IOS routers use administrative distance, which defines a set number for every routing protocol in use. The lower the AD, the more trustworthy the network. For example, a static route (AD is 1) is preferred to an OSPF (AD is 110) discovered route. A static route pointing to a directly connected interface, for example, via ethernet0, has an AD set to 0, the same as a directly connected interface even though a static route is enabled.

17 What is the administrative distance for OSPF, RIP, and external EIGRP?

Answer: The AD for RIP is 120, 110 for OSPF, and 170 for external EIGRP (internal EIGRP is 90).

18 Name five characteristics of distance vector routing protocols and provide two examples of routing protocols classified as distance vector.

Answer: Distance vector characteristics and example protocols are as follows:

Periodic updates	Periodic updates are sent at a set interval; for IP RIP, this interval is 30 seconds.
Broadcast updates	Updates are sent to the broadcast address 255.255.255.255. Only devices running routing algorithms will listen to these updates.
Full table updates	When an update is sent, the entire routing table is sent.
Triggered updates	Also known as Flash updates, triggered updates are sent when a change occurs outside the update interval.
Split horizon	This method stops routing loop. Updates are not sent out an outgoing interface from which the route was received. This also saves bandwidth.
Maximum Hop Count limit	For RIP, the limit is 15, and for IGRP it's 255.
Algorithm	An example is Bellman-Ford for RIP.
Examples	RIP and IGRP.

19 IP RIP runs over what protocol and port number when sending packets to neighboring routers?

Answer: UDP port number 520

20 How many networks can be contained in an IP RIP update?

Answer: Up to 25 networks

21 Specify three main differences between RIPv1 and RIPv2?

Answer: RIPv1 does not support VLSM, authentication, or multicast updates. RIPv2 supports VLSM, authentication, multicast updates, and unicast updates to remote routers.

22 What is an EIGRP Feasible Successor?

Answer: An EIGRP Feasible Successor is a neighboring EIGRP Cisco router with a lower AD.

23 What is the metric used by OSPF?

Answer: The metric used by OSPF is cost and is defined by the formula $10^8/$ Bandwidth for a given interface. The cost to a remote path is the sum of all the costs that a packet will transverse to reach the remote network.

24   If OSPF is configured for one area, what area assignment should be used?

Answer: Good OSPF design defines area 0, or the backbone, as the core area, and area 0 should always be used. If the OSPF network resides in one area only, theoretically, any area assignment is possible.

25   What LSA types are not sent in a total stubby area?

Answer: Totally stubby areas block LSA types 3, 4, and 5. Although similar to a stub area, a totally stubby area blocks LSAs of type 3, as well. This solution is Cisco proprietary and is used to further reduce a topological database. The only Link State Advertisement (LSA) type permitted is a specific type 3 LSA advertising a default router only.

26   What IOS command disables an interface from participating in the election of an OSPF DR/BDR router?

Answer: To disable an interface on a Cisco router when electing a DR, the IOS command is ip ospf priority 0. The router with the highest priority (range is between 0 and 255) will be elected the DR.

27   On an Ethernet broadcast network, a DR suddenly reboots. When the router recovers and discovers neighboring OSPF routers, will it be the designated router once more?

Answer: Once the router fails, the Backup DR (BDR) assumes the functions of the DR and another OSPF router (if it exists) is elected the BDR. After the failed router recovers, neighboring OSPF hello packets will advise that a DR/BDR already exists and there is no need to assume the functions of DR or BDR until another election process is initiated.

28   What Layer 4 protocol does BGP use to guarantee routing updates, and what destination port number is used?

Answer: BGP4 uses TCP and the destination port number is 179.

29   What are ISDN BRI and PRI?

Answer: ISDN can be supplied by a carrier in two main forms: Basic Rate Interface (BRI) and Primary Rate Interface (PRI). An ISDN BRI consists of two 64-kbps services (B channels) and one 16-kbps signaling channel (D channel). An ISDN PRI consists of 23 B or 30 B channels and a 64-kbps D channel, depending on the country. In North America and Japan, a PRI service consists of 23 B channels for a total bit rate of up to 1.544 Mbps. In Asia and Australia, a PRI delivers 30 B-channels and one 64-kbps D channel, delivering a total bit rate of 2.048 Mbps.

30 What are the three phases that occur in any PPP session?

Answer: The three phases that occur in any PPP session are

- **Link establishment—Link Control Program (LCP) packets are sent to configure and test the link.**

- **Authentication (optional)—After the link is established, authentication can be used to ensure that link security is maintained.**

- **Network layers—In this phase, NCP packets determine which protocols will be used across the PPP link. An interesting aspect of PPP is that each protocol (IP, IPX, and so on) supported in this phase is documented in a separate RFC that discusses how it operates over PPP.**

31 Define what BECN and FECN mean in a Frame Relay network?

Answer: Forward explicit congestion notification (FECN)—Bit set by a Frame Relay network device to inform DTE receiving the frame that congestion was experienced in the path from source to destination. DTE receiving frames with the FECN bit set can request that higher-level protocols take flow-control action, as appropriate.

Backward explicit congestion notification (BECN)—Bit set by a Frame Relay network device in frames traveling in the opposite direction of frames encountering a congested path. DTE receiving frames with the BECN bit set can request that higher-level protocols take flow-control action, as appropriate.

32 Frame Relay DLCI values are used for what purpose?

Answer: The data-link connection identifier (DLCI) value specifies a PVC or SVC in a Frame Relay network. DLCIs are locally significant. There are globally significant DLCIs used for LMI communication between Frame Relay switches.

33 What is the IP address range used in IP multicast networks?

Answer: The range of networks is from 224.0.0.0 to 239.255.255.255.

34 What type of network environment typically uses an AS5300?

Answer: The AS5300, or universal Access Server (AS), is a versatile data communications platform that provides the functions of an access server, router, and digital modems in a single modular chassis. Internet Service Providers typically use AS5300 to allow clients to use ISDN or PSTN when accessing the Internet. The AS5300 also supports voice communication.

Chapter 3 "Do I Know This Already?" Quiz Answers

 1 RFC 1700 defines what well-known ports for DNS?

   a. TCP port 21

   b. TCP port 23

   c. UDP port 21

   d. UDP port 53

   e. TCP/UDP port 53

   Answer: e

   DNS is permitted by RFC 1700 to use both TCP/UDP port 53. Typically UDP is vendor-configured for UDP port 53.

 2 What supplies DNS security?

   a. A default username/password pairing

   b. A TFTP directory

   c. A filename

   d. A domain name

   e. None of the above

   Answer: e

   DNS has no form of security, so any device can request name-to-IP address mappings.

 3 What IOS command will stop a Cisco router from querying a DNS server when an invalid IOS command is entered on the EXEC or PRIV prompt?

   a. **no ip domain-lookup**

   b. **no ip dns-lookup**

   c. **no ip dns-queries**

   d. **no exec**

   Answer: a

   To disable DNS query lookup, the IOS command in global configuration mode is no ip domain-lookup.

4 What does the following Global IOS configuration line accomplish?

```
ip host SimonisaCCIE 131.108.1.1 131.108.1.2
```

a. Defines the router name as SimonisaCCIE

b. Defines a local host name, SimonisaCCIE, mapped to IP addresses 131.108.1.1 and 131.108.1.2

c. Configures the IOS router for remote routing entries 131.108.1.1 and 131.108.1.2

d. Not a valid IOS command

e. Configures the local routers with the IP address 131.108.1.1 and 131.108.1.2 on boot up

Answer: b

The ip host *name ip address1* [*ipaddress2 ipaddress3 ipaddress4 ipaddress5 ipaddress6 ipaddress7 ipaddress8*] command configures a local address lookup for the name SimonisaCCIE. Up to 8 addresses can be used. The router will try 131.108.1.1 first and, if no response is made by the remote host, the second address, 131.108.1.2, will be attempted from the command-line interface (CLI).

5 TFTP uses what predefined UDP port number?

a. 21

b. 22

c. 23

d. 53

e. 69

Answer: e

TFTP uses UDP port number 69.

6 What IOS command will copy an IOS image from the current system flash to a TFTP server?

a. **copy tftp image:**

b. **copy flash tftp**

c. **copy tftp flash**

d. **copy tftp tftp**

Answer: b

To copy an IOS image from the routers to system flash, the correct IOS command is copy flash tftp.

7 Suppose a client calls and advises you that an FTP data transaction is not allowing him to view the host's directory structure. What are the most likely causes of the problem? (Choose all that apply.)

a. The client's username/password is wrong.

b. The client's FTP data port is not connected.

c. The host machine has denied him access because the password is wrong.

d. A serious network outage requires that you reload the router closest to the client.

e. An access list is stopping port 20 from detailing the directory list.

Answers: b and e

The FTP data port is used to view the directory and could be blocked because of an access list or a fault with the client's software when establishing the FTP 20 connection.

8 FTP runs over what Layer 4 protocol?

a. IP

b. TCP

c. TFTP

d. DNS

e. UDP

Answer: b

The FTP application is a connection-orientated protocol and is part of the TCP/IP protocol suite. FTP ensures data is delivered by running data with a TCP overhead.

9 HTTPS traffic uses what TCP port number?

a. 21

b. 443

c. 334

d. 333

e. 343

Answer: b

HTTPS runs over TCP port 443.

10 SNMP is restricted on Cisco routers by what IOS command?

   a. **snmp-server enable**

   b. **snmp-server community** *string*

   c. **snmp-server** *ip-address*

   d. **snmp-server no access permitted**

Answer: b

To restrict SNMP access, the correct IOS command is snmp-server community *string*. **Without the correct string, NMS stations will not be able to access a router with SNMP queries. You can disable SNMP on a router and restrict SNMP access with the IOS command no snmp-server.**

11 TFTP protocol uses which of the following?

   a. Username/password pairs to authorize transfers

   b. Uses TCP port 169

   c. Uses UDP port 169

   d. Can use UDP/TCP and port 69

   e. None of the above

Answer: d

TFTP is defined in RFC 1700 and is permitted to use TCP/UDP port 69 only.

12 Which of the following statements is true regarding SSL?

   a. Every packet sent between host and client is authenticated.

   b. Encryption is used after a simple handshake is completed.

   c. SSL uses port 2246.

   d. SSL is not a predefined standard.

   e. SSL does not perform any data integrity checks.

Answer: b

After the hosts have negotiated with valid username/password pairs, SSL will start to encrypt all data. After the handshake, packets are not authenticated. SSL uses TCP port 443. RFC 2246 defines SSL.

13 What is the **HELO** SMTP command used for?

    a. To authenticate SMTP clients

    b. To identify SMTP clients

    c. This is an unknown standard

    d. The **HELO** command is used in SNMP (not SMTP)

Answer: b

The HELO command identifies the client to the SMTP server.

14 POP3 clients can do what?

    a. Receive SNMP queries

    b. Send mail

    c. Send SNMP queries

    d. The POP3 protocol is a routing algorithm

Answer: b

POP3 clients send mail to POP3 servers. SMTP is not part of the POP3 standard.

15 NTP uses what well-known TCP port?

    a. 23

    b. 551

    c. 21

    d. 20

    e. 123

    f. 321

Answer: e

NTP uses UDP or TCP, and the port number is 123.

16 Secure Shell (SSH) is used to do what?

  a. Disable spanning tree on Catalyst 5000 switches

  b. Protect the data link layer only from attacks

  c. Protect the TCP/IP host

  d. Allow TCP/IP access to all networks without any security

  e. SSH is used only in the data link layer

Answer: c

SSH is used to protect TCP/IP hosts.

17 Which of the following protocols can be authenticated? (Select the best four answers.)

  a. Telnet

  b. HTTP

  c. HTTPS

  d. Spanning tree

  e. TFTP

  f. FTP

Answers: a, b, c, and f

18 What is the community string value when the following IOS commands are entered in global configuration mode?

```
snmp-server community publiC RO
snmp-server enable traps config
snmp-server host 131.108.255.254 isdn
```

  a. ISDN

  b. Config

  c. publiC

  d. public

  e. Public

  f. More data required

Answer: c

The community string is defined by the command snmp-server community *community string*, **which, in this case, is set to publiC. The community string is case sensitive.**

19 Which of the following best describes an SNMP inform request?

 a. Requires no acknowledgment

 b. Requires an acknowledgment from the SNMP agent

 c. Requires an acknowledgment from the SNMP manager

 d. Only SNMP traps can be implemented on Cisco IOS routers

Answer: c

SNMP inform requests require an acknowledgment from the SNMP manager. SNMP hosts will continue sending the SNMP inform request until an acknowledgment is received.

20 What UDP port number will SNMP traps be sent from?

 a. 21

 b. 22

 c. 161

 d. 162

Answer: d

SNMP traps are sent by SNMP agents (such as routers) over UDP port 162.

21 What TCP port number will an SNMP inform acknowledgment packet be sent to?

 a. 21

 b. 22

 c. 23

 d. 161

 e. 162

 f. None of the above

Answer: d

SNMP inform acknowledgments are sent over UDP (not TCP) port number 161.

22 To restrict SNMP managers from the source network 131.108.1.0/30, what IOS command is required?

a.

```
ip http enable 131.108.1.1 131.108.1.2
```

b.

```
snmp community  131.108.1.1 131.108.1.2
```

c.

```
snmp-server community SimonisCool ro 4
  access-list 4 permit 131.108.1.0 0.0.0.252
```

d.

```
snmp-server community SimonisCool ro 4
```

e.

```
snmp-server community SimonisCool ro 1
  access-list 11 permit 131.108.1.0 0.0.0.252
```

Answer: c

The SNMP server community name must be defined with the following command:

```
snmp-server community string ro access-list-number
```

The access list number definition must follow (in this case, number 4). The access list range is between 1 and 99 only.

Chapter 3 Q & A Answers

1 According to RFC 1700, what is the well-known TCP/UDP port used by DNS?

Answer: RFC 1700 defines the well-known ports for the whole TCP/IP protocol suite. For DNS, the well-known port for TCP/UDP is number 53.

2 What does the IOS command **no ip domain-lookup** accomplish?

Answer: This IOS command disables DNS queries for network administrators connected to a Cisco console or vty line.

3 What is the correct IOS syntax to specify local host mapping on a Cisco router?

Answer: Local host mappings to IP addresses are accomplished using the following IOS command:

```
ip host name [tcp-port-number] ip address1 [ip address2...ip address8]
```

Up to eight IP addresses can be assigned to one name.

4 TFTP uses what well-known, defined TCP/UDP port?

Answer: TFTP uses port number 69.

5 What is the correct IOS command to copy a file from a TFTP server to the system flash?

Answer: The IOS command is copy tftp flash. To copy a file from the system flash to the TFTP server, the IOS command is copy flash tftp.

6 Define the two modes of FTP.

Answer: FTP can be configured for the following two modes:

- **Active mode**
- **Passive mode**

7 FTP uses what TCP port numbers?

Answer: FTP uses well-known port numbers 20 and 21.

8 What well-known port do Secure Socket Layer (SSL) and Secure Shell (SSH) use?

Answer: SSL uses well-known port number 443. Secure Shell uses well-known TCP port 22.

9 Define SNMP and give an example.

Answer: Simple Network Management Protocol (SNMP) is an application layer protocol that is used to manage IP devices. SNMP is part of the TCP/IP application layer suite. SNMP allows network administrators the ability to view and change network parameters and monitor connections locally and remotely. Cisco routers can be configured to send SNMP traps to network managing stations to alert administrators. For example, SNMP traps may indicate a router with low memory or high CPU usage.

10 What well-known UDP ports are used by SNMP?

Answer: RFC 1700 defines the SNMP ports as 161 and 162. TCP can also be used, but vendors typically only implement SNMP with UDP. SNMP port 161 is used to query SNMP devices, and SNMP port 162 is used to send SNMP traps. SNMP runs over UDP and is secured by a well-known community string that is case sensitive.

11 What IOS command enables SNMP on a Cisco IOS router?

Answer: The command syntax is snmp-server community *string access-rights*. The *access-rights* options are RO and RW.

12 Which TCP/UDP port numbers are defined for use by Network Time Protocol or NTP?

Answer: NTP can use TCP and UDP port number 123.

13 When defining a stratum value on a Cisco router, what is the range and what value is closest to an atomic clock?

Answer: The stratum value ranges from 1 to 15. 1 represents an atomic clock, which is the most accurate clock available. The default stratum value on Cisco routers is 8.

14 Secure Shell (SSH) allows what to be accomplished when in use?

Answer: Secure Shell (SSH) is a protocol that provides a secure connection to a router. Cisco IOS supports version 1 of SSH. SSH enables clients to make a secure and encrypted connection to a Cisco router.

15 What is the difference between an SNMP inform request and an SNMP trap?

Answer: The major difference between a trap and an inform request is that an SNMP agent (when ending a trap) has no way of knowing if an SNMP trap was received by the SNMP manager. On the other hand, an SNMP inform request packet will be sent continually until the sending SNMP manager receives an SNMP acknowledgment.

16 What does the SNMP MIB refer to?

Answer: The Management Information Base (MIB) is a virtual information storage area for network management information, which consists of collections of managed objects. MIB modules are written in the SNMP MIB module language, as defined in STD 58, RFC 2578, RFC 2579, and RFC 2580.

17 What is the SNMP read-write community string for the following router configuration?

```
snmp-server community simon ro
snmp-server community Simon rw
```

Answer: The read-write community string is set to Simon (case sensitive). The read-only community attribute is set to simon.

18 Before you can TFTP a file from a Cisco router to a UNIX- or Windows-based system, what is the first step you must take after enabling the TFTP server daemon on both platforms?

Answer: On a UNIX server where the TFTP server daemon is installed, the file to be copied must have the appropriate access rights. In UNIX, the Touch command allows a TFTP request. In other words, to copy a file from a Cisco IOS router to a UNIX host, the file must already exist on the host. For a Windows-based platform, the software must be configured to permit file creation on the Windows-based file system.

19 What IOS command can be implemented to restrict SNMP access to certain networks by applying access lists? Can you apply standard, extended, or both?

Answer: The IOS command is as follows:

```
snmp-server community string [view view-name] [ro | rw] [number]
You can only apply a standard access-list list with the above command.
```

number **refers to a standard access list, ranging from 1 to 99 only, that defines the remote hosts or subnets that are permitted SNMP access. The correct SNMP community string must also be correctly configured on the SNMP manger and agent to allow SNMP communication.**

20 Does TFTP have a mechanism for username and password authentication?

Answer: TFTP is a connectionless protocol (UDP) that has no method to authenticate username or password. The TFTP packet format has no field enabling the username or password to be exchanged between two TCP/IP hosts. TFTP security (configurable on UNIX and Windows platforms) on the TFTP server is accomplished by allowing a predefined file on the server to be copied to the host TFTP server.

21 Can you use your Internet browser to configure a Cisco router? If so, how?

Answer: To view the router's home page, use a Web browser pointed to http://*a.b.c.d*, where *a.b.c.d* is the IP address of your router or access server. If a name has been set, use http://*router-name*, and use the DNS server to resolve the IP address.

To enable HTTP on a Cisco router, use the IOS command ip http in global configuration mode.

22 A network administrator defines a Cisco router to allow HTTP requests but forgets to add the authentication commands. What is the default username and password pairing that allows HTTP requests on the default TCP port 80? Can you predefine another TCP port for HTTP access other than port 80?

Answer: By default Cisco IOS routers configured for HTTP access use the router's local host name as the username and the enable or secret password as the password.

The IOS command ip http [0-65535] allows the network administrator to define a new port number other than 80, which is the default setting.

Chapter 4 "Do I Know This Already?" Quiz Answers

1 What IOS command will display the System Flash?

   a. **show flash**

   b. **show system flash**

   c. **show memory**

   d. **show process flash**

Answer: a

The show flash IOS command displays the System Flash:

```
R1#show flash

System flash directory:
File   Length    Name/status
  1    11600424  c2600-ik8o3s-mz.122-2.T.bin
[11600488 bytes used, 5176728 available, 16777216 total]
16384K bytes of processor board System flash (Read/Write)

R1#
```

2 The network administrator has forgotten the enable password and all passwords are encrypted. What should the network administrator do to recover the password without losing the current configuration?

   a. Call the TAC and ask for a special back door password.

   b. Call the TAC and raise a case to supply the engineering password.

   c. Reboot the router, press the break key during the reload, and enter ROM mode and change the configuration register.

   d. Reboot the router, press the break key during the reload, enter ROM mode and change the configuration register, and when the router reloads, remove the old configuration.

Answer: c

The TAC will not supply any passwords. The steps required include issuing the break key and modifying the configuration register, but the aim is to not lose the initial configuration, so answer d is incorrect.

3 What is the enable password for the following router?

   ```
   enable password Simon
   ```

   a. More data required

   b. Simon

   c. simon or Simon

   d. You cannot set the password to a name; it must also contain digits.

   Answer: b

   The enable password is case-sensitive, so the password is Simon.

4 If the configuration register is set to 0x2101, where is the IOS image booted from?

   a. slot0:

   b. slot1:

   c. Flash

   d. ROM

   e. TFTP server

   Answer: d

   0x2101 tells the router to load the IOS image from ROM.

5 What IOS command will copy the running configuration to a TFTP server? (Select the best two answers.)

   a. **copy running-config to tftp**

   b. **write network**

   c. **copy running-config tftp**

   d. **write erase**

   Answer: b and c

   Write network and copy running-config tftp will save the configuration stored in RAM to a TFTP server.

6 What **debug** command allows an administrator to debug only packets from the network 131.108.0.0/16?

   a. **debug ip packet**

   b. **terminal monitor**

   c. **debug ip packet 1**

   access-list 1 permit 131.108.0.0

   d. **debug ip packet 1**

   access-list 1 permit 131.108.0.0 0.0.255.255

   e. **debug ip packet 1**

   access-list 1 permit 131.108.0.0 255.255.0.0

Answer: d

To debug only packets from the source network 131.108.0.0/16, or networks ranging from 131.108.0.0 to 131.108.255.255, the correct access list is access-list 1 permit 131.108.0.0 0.0.255.255, followed by the debug ip packet 1 command in privilege EXEC mode.

7 After entering **debug ip packet**, no messages appear on your Telnet session. What is the likely cause?

   a. OSPF routing is required.

   b. The console port does not support **debug** output.

   c. The **terminal monitor** command is required.

   d. IP packets are not supported with the **debug** command.

Answer: c

Accessing a router via Telnet to enable debug messages to the terminal session requires the terminal monitor IOS command.

8 To change the configuration register to 0x2141, what is the correct IOS command?

   a. **copy running-config register**

   b. **configuration 0x2141**

   c. **config 0x2141 register**

   d. **config-register 0x2142**

   e. **config-register 0x2141**

Answer: e

9   Where is the startup configuration stored on a Cisco router?

a. In the cam table

b. NVRAM

c. RAM

d. Flash

e. slot0:

Answer: b

The startup configuration is usually stored in the NVRAM. You can store the file on a TFTP server, as well.

10   Which of the following statements is true?

a. The **enable secret** command overrides the **enable password** command.

b. The **enable** command overrides the **enable secret** *password* command.

c. Enable passwords cannot be used when the secret password is used.

d. Both a and c are true.

Answer: a

The enable secret command overrides the enable password command when configured concurrently.

11   A Cisco router has the following configuration:

```
line vty 0 4
login
```

What will happen when you Telnet to the router?

a. You will be prompted for the login password.

b. You will enter EXEC mode immediately.

c. You cannot access the router without the password set.

d. More configuration required.

Answer: c

Without the password configured, you cannot enter EXEC mode. The router will advise the Telnet user that the password is not set and disconnect the session, as follows:

```
R1#131.108.1.1
Trying 131.108.1.1 ... Open
Password required, but none set
[Connection to 131.108.1.1 closed by foreign host]
```

12 A Cisco router has the following configuration:

```
line vty 0 4
no login
password cIscO
```

When a Telnet user tries to establish a remote Telnet session to this router, what will happen?

   a. You will be prompted for the login password cIscO.

   b. You will enter EXEC mode immediately.

   c. You cannot access the router without the password set.

   d. More configuration required.

   e. You will be prompted for the login password; password case does not matter.

Answer: b

Because the no login command is configured, the VTY lines allow all Telnet sessions directly to the EXEC prompt even though a password is set.

13 A Cisco router has the following configuration:

```
line vty 0 1
no login
password cisco
line vty 2 4
login
password ciSco
```

When a third Telnet session is established to a remote router with the preceding configuration, what will happen?

   a. You will be prompted for the login password, which is set to cisco.

   b. You will be prompted for the login password, which is set to ciSco.

   c. You will enter EXEC mode immediately.

   d. You cannot access the router without the password set.

   e. More configuration required.

Answer: b

The first two telnet sessions (line vty 0 1) will directly enter EXEC mode because of no login. The third (line vty 2 4) requires the password, ciSco.

14 Which of the following access lists will deny any IP packets sourced from network
131.108.1.0/24 and destined for network 131.108.2.0/24 and permit all other IP-based
traffic?

    a. access-list 1 deny 131.108.1.0

    b. access-list 1 deny 131.108.1.0 0.0.0.255

    c. access-list 100 permit/deny ip 131.108.1.0 0.0.0.255 131.108.2.0 0.0.0.255

    d. access-list 100 deny ip 131.108.1.0 0.0.0.255 131.108.2.0 0.0.0.255

       access-list 100 permit ip any any

Answer: d

**The correct access list is an extended access list because both source and destination
addresses must be configured. To permit all other traffic, you must add the line
access-list permit ip any. Otherwise, all other IP-based traffic will be denied access
by default.**

15 An administrator notices a router's CPU utilization has jumped from 2 percent to 100
percent, and that a CCIE engineer was debugging. What IOS command can the network
administrator enter to stop all debugging output to the console and vty lines without
affecting users on the connected router?

    a. **no logging console debugging**

    b. **undebug all**

    c. **line vty 0 4**

       no terminal monitor

    d. **reload the router**

Answer: b

**IOS command undebug all stops all configured debug commands. Reloading the
router also stops debugs but will affect users because the router will be unavailable
during the reboot. Entering no logging debugging does not stop the router from
sending debug information nor processing the CPU-intensive requests to any
connecting users via Telnet.**

Chapter 4 Q & A Answers

1 Where is the running configuration stored on a Cisco router?

Answer: The configuration is stored in the Random Access Memory (RAM). For all newer Cisco hardware platforms, the memory location where the running configuration is stored is called the Dynamic Random-Access Memory (DRAM).

2 What IOS command displays the startup configuration?

Answer: The IOS command show startup-config or show config will display the configuration stored in NVRAM.

3 What IOS command provides the following output?

```
System flash directory:
File  Length   Name/status
  1   9558976  c2500-ajs40-l.12-17.bin
[9559040 bytes used, 7218176 available, 16777216 total]
16384K bytes of processor board System flash
```

Answer: The IOS command to display the System Flash is show flash.

4 What configuration register will enable a Cisco router to ignore the startup configuration?

Answer: 0x2142 will set the IOS to ignore the configuration stored in NVRAM; typically, this configuration register is used for password recovery.

5 To copy the startup configuration to the running configuration, what IOS command or commands are used?

Answer: copy startup-config running-config.

6 What is the range for standard and extended IP access lists on Cisco IOS routers?

Answer: Standard IP access lists range from 1-99 and 1300-1999. Extended access lists range from 100-199 and 2000-2699.

7 What command display the IP access lists configured on a Cisco router?

Answer: show ip access-lists will display all configured IP access lists. The show access-lists IOS command displays all configured access lists, not just IP access lists.

8 How do you disable all **debug** commands currently enabled on a Cisco router, assuming you are not sure what debug commands are enabled?

Answer: undebug all (or u all in shorthand). You can also use the [no] debug <specific debug-enabled commands> for each specific debug that has been enabled. To quickly disable all debug commands, undebug all is typically used.

9 What must you be very careful of when enabling any form of debugging on a Cisco router?

Answer: You should make the debug command as specific as possible and ensure that you enable the output to the console (if disabled) and VTY lines with the IOS command, terminal monitor; this command is entered in privilege EXEC mode only. By default, Cisco IOS will send all debug output to the console port.

The CPU system on Cisco routers gives the highest priority to debugging output. For this reason, debugging commands should be turned on only for troubleshooting specific problems or during troubleshooting sessions with technical support personnel. Excessive debugging output can render the router inoperable.

Try to use the most specific debug command possible to reduce the load on the CPU.

10 What are the required steps when performing password recovery on a Cisco router?

Answer: The password recovery steps are as follows:

Step 1 Power cycle the router.

Step 2 Issue a control break or the break key command on the application to enter into boot ROM mode. The control break key sequence must be entered within 60 seconds of the router restarting after a power cycle.

Step 3 Once you are in ROM mode, change the config register value to ignore the startup configuration file that is stored in NVRAM. Use the o/r 0x2142 command.

Step 4 Allow the router to reboot by entering the i command.

Step 5 After the router has finished booting up without its startup configuration, look at the show startup-config command output. If the password is encrypted, move to Step 6, which requires you to enter the enable mode (type enable and you will not be required to enter any password) and copy the startup configuration to the running configuration with the copy startup-config running-config command. Then, change the password. If the password is not encrypted and the secret password is not used, you can simply read the password. Skip Steps 6 and 7 and go to Step 8.

Step 6 Copy the startup configuration to RAM.

Step 7 Enable all active interfaces.

Step 8 Change the configuration register to 0x2102 (default).

Step 9 Reload the router.

Step 10 Check the new password.

11 What is the enable password for the following configuration?

```
enable password CiscO
```

Answer: Passwords are case-sensitive, so the password is CiscO. If the secret password was set, you would not be able to read the password in clear text because Cisco IOS hashes the password using the md5 encryption algorithm, as in the following example:

```
enable secret 5 $1$Aiy2$GGSCYdG57PdRiNg/.D.XI.
```

➠ **Password is not in clear text.**

You cannot reverse engineer the hashed password (1Aiy2$GGSCYdG57PdRiNg/ .D.XI.). Hashing occurs when plain text data is encrypted into cipertext (unreadable data) by some form of encryption algorithm.

Chapter 5 "Do I Know This Already?" Quiz Answers

1 What are the three components of AAA? (Choose the three best answers.)

a. Accounting

b. Authorization

c. Adapting

d. Authentication

Answers: a, b, and d

AAA is used for authentication, authorization, and accounting. Answer c is incorrect because adapting is not part of the security options available with AAA.

2 What IOS command must be issued to start AAA on a Cisco router?

a. **aaa old-model**

b. **aaa model**

c. **aaa new model**

d. **aaa new-model**

e. **aaa new_model**

Answer: d

The aaa new-model command starts authentication, authorization and accounting (AAA). Answers a, b, and c are incorrect because they represent invalid IOS commands.

3 What algorithm initiates and encrypts a session between two routers' exchange keys between two encryption devices?

   a. Routing algorithm

   b. Diffie-Hellman algorithm

   c. The switching engine

   d. The stac compression algorithm

Answer: b

When using encryption between two routers, the Diffie-Hellman algorithm is used to exchange keys. This algorithm initiates the session between two routers and ensures that it is secure. Answer a is incorrect because the routing algorithm is used for routing, not for encryption. Answer c is incorrect because a switching engine is used to switch frames and has nothing to do with encryption. Answer d is incorrect because the stac compression algorithm is used by PPP; it compresses data on a PPP WAN link.

4 Can you configure RADIUS and TACACS+ concurrently on a Cisco IOS router?

   a. No.

   b. Yes, provided you have the same lists names applied to the same interfaces.

   c. Yes, provided you have the different lists names applied to the same interfaces.

   d. Yes, provided you have the different lists names applied to different interfaces.

Answer: d

List names and interfaces must be different.

5 How do you enable a RADIUS server to debug messages for Cisco Secure on a UNIX server?

   a. Terminal monitor

   b. Edit the configuration file on the router

   c. Edit the syslog.conf and csu.cfg files

   d. Not possible, as UNIX does not run IOS

Answer: c

You can enable debugging on a UNIX host running Cisco Secure by editing the syslog.confg and csu.cfg files.

6 What RADIUS attribute is used by vendors and not predefined by RFC 2138?

   a. 1

   b. 2

   c. 3

   d. 4

   e. 13

   f. 26

   g. 333

   h. 33

Answer: f

Attribute 26 is a vendor-specific attribute. Cisco uses vendor ID 9.

7 RADIUS can support which of the following protocols?

   a. PPP

   b. OSPF

   c. AppleTalk

   d. IPX

   e. NLSP

Answer: a

RADIUS supports PPP and none of the multiprotocols listed in options b, c, d, or e.

8 When a RADIUS server identifies the wrong password entered by the remote users, what packet type is sent?

   a. Accept-user

   b. Reject-users

   c. Reject-deny

   d. Reject-accept

   e. Reject-Error

   f. Access-reject

Answer: f

RADIUS sends an access-reject error if the password entered is invalid.

9   Identify the false statement about RADIUS.

   a. RADIUS is a defined standard in RFC 2138/2139.

   b. RADIUS runs over TCP port 1812.

   c. RADIUS runs over UDP port 1812.

   d. RADIUS accounting information runs over port 1646.

   Answer: b

   RADIUS does not deploy TCP.

10   What is the RADIUS key for the following configuration? If this configuration is not valid, why isn't it?

```
aaa authentication login use-radius group radius local
aaa authentication ppp user-radius if-needed group radius
aaa authorization exec default group radius
aaa authorization network default group radius
radius-server 3.3.3.3
radius-server key IlovemyMum
```

   a. IlovemyMum

   b. Ilovemymum

   c. This configuration will not work because the command **aaa new-model** is missing.

   d. 3.3.3.3

   Answer: c

   Because aaa new-model is not configured, this is not a valid configuration and no requests will be sent to the RADIUS server.

11   What is the RADIUS key for the following configuration?

```
Aaa new-model
aaa authentication login use-radius group radius local
aaa authentication ppp user-radius if-needed group radius
aaa authorization exec default group radius
aaa authorization network default group radius
radius-server 3.3.3.3
radius-server key IlovemyMum
```

   a. IlovemyMum

   b. Ilovemymum

   c. This configuration will not work

   d. 3.3.3.3

   Answer: a

   The key is case-sensitive; the IOS command, radius-server *key IlovemyMum, defines* the key as IlovemyMum.

12 What versions of TACACS does Cisco IOS support? (Select the best three answers.)

  a. TACACS+

  b. TACACS

  c. Extended TACACS

  d. Extended TACACS+

Answers: a, b, and c

There is no Cisco Extended TACACS+ support.

13 TACACS+ is transported over which TCP port number?

  a. 520

  b. 23

  c. 21

  d. 20

  e. 49

Answer: e

14 What is the predefined TACACS+ server key for the following configuration?

```
radius-server host 3.3.3.3
radius-server key CCIEsrock
```

  a. 3.3.3.3

  b. Not enough data

  c. CCIESROCK

  d. CCIEsRock

  e. CCIEsrock

Answer: e

The key is case-sensitive and is defined by the IOS command, radius-server key CCIEsrock.

15 What does the following command accomplish?

```
tacacs_server host 3.3.3.3
```

a. Defines the remote TACACS+ server as 3.3.3.3

b. Defines the remote RADIUS server as 3.3.3.3

c. Not a valid IOS command

d. 3.3.3.3

e. Host unknown; no DNS details for 3.3.3.3 provided

Answer: c

The IOS command to define a remote TACACS+ server is tacacs-server host *ip-address*.

16 Which of the following protocols does TACACS+ support?

a. PPP

b. AppleTalk

c. NetBIOS

d. All the above

Answer: d

TACACS+ has multiprotocol support for PPP, AppleTalk, NetBIOS and IPX.

17 Kerberos is defined at what layer of the OSI model?

a. Layer 1

b. Layer 2

c. Layer 3

d. Layer 4

e. Layer 5

f. Layer 6

g. Layer 7

Answer: g

Kerberos is an application layer protocol defined at Layer 7 of the OSI model.

18 What definition best describes a key distribution center when Kerberos is applied to a network?

   a. A general term that refers to authentication tickets

   b. An authorization level label for Kerberos principals

   c. Applications and services that have been modified to support the Kerberos credential infrastructure

   d. A domain consisting of users, hosts, and network services that are registered to a Kerberos server

   e. A Kerberos server and database program running on a network host

Answer: e

The KDC is a server and database program running on a network host.

19 What definition best describes a Kerberos credential?

   a. A general term that refers to authentication tickets

   b. An authorization level label for Kerberos principals

   c. Applications and services that have been modified to support the Kerberos credential infrastructure

   d. A domain consisting of users, hosts, and network services that are registered to a Kerberos server

   e. A Kerberos server and database program running on a network host

Answer: a

A credential is a general term that refers to authentication tickets, such as ticket granting tickets (TGTs) and service credentials. Kerberos credentials verify the identity of a user or service. If a network service decides to trust the Kerberos server that issued a ticket, it can be used in place of retyping a username and password. Credentials have a default lifespan of eight hours.

20 What definition best describes Kerberized?

   a. A general term that refers to authentication tickets

   b. An authorization level label for Kerberos principals

   c. Applications and services that have been modified to support the Kerberos credential infrastructure

   d. A domain consisting of users, hosts, and network services that are registered to a Kerberos server

   e. A Kerberos server and database program running on a network host

Answer: c

Kerberized refers to applications and services that have been modified to support the Kerberos credential infrastructure.

21 What definition best describes a Kerberos realm?

   a. A general term that refers to authentication tickets

   b. An authorization level label for the Kerberos principals

   c. Applications and services that have been modified to support the Kerberos credential infrastructure

   d. A domain consisting of users, hosts, and network services that are registered to a Kerberos server

   e. A Kerberos server and database program running on a network host

Answer: d

The Kerberos realm is also used to map a DNS domain to a Kerberos realm.

22 What IOS command enables VPDN in the global configuration mode?

   a. **vpdn-enable**

   b. **vpdn enable**

   c. **vpdn enable in interface mode**

   d. **Both a and c are correct**

Answer: b

To Enable VPDN in global configuration mode, the correct IOS command is vpdn enable.

23 What is the number of bits used with a standard DES encryption key?

  a. 56 bits

  b. 32 bits; same as IP address

  c. 128 bits

  d. 256 bits

  e. 65,535 bits

  f. 168 bits

Answer: a

DES applies a 56-bit key. The documented time taken to discover the 56-bit key is 7 hours on a Pentium III computer, so DES is not a common encryption algorithm used in today's networks.

24 What is the number of bits used with a 3DES encryption key?

  a. 56 bits

  b. 32 bits; same as IP address

  c. 128 bits

  d. 256 bits

  e. 65,535 bits

  f. 168 bits

Answer: f

Triple DES (3DES) is today's standard encryption with a 168-bit key.

25 In IPSec, what encapsulation protocol only encrypts the data and not the IP header?

  a. ESP

  b. AH

  c. MD5

  d. HASH

  e. Both a and b are correct

Answer: a

ESP only encrypts the data, not the IP header.

26   In IPSec, what encapsulation protocol encrypts the entire IP packet?

   a. ESH

   b. AH

   c. MD5

   d. HASH

   e. Both a and b are correct

Answer: b

AH encrypts the entire IP packet. The time to live (TTL) is not encrypted because this value decreases by one (1) every time a router is traversed.

27   Which of the following is AH's destination IP port?

   a. 23

   b. 21

   c. 50

   d. 51

   e. 500

   f. 444

Answer: d

The AH destination port number is 51.

28   Which of the following is ESP's destination IP port?

   a. 23

   b. 21

   c. 50

   d. 51

   e. 500

   f. 444

Answer: c

The ESP destination IP port number is 50.

29 Which of the following is not part of IKE phase I negotiations?

   a. Authenticating IPSec peers

   b. Exchanges keys

   c. Establishes IKE security

   d. Negotiates SA parameters

   Answer: d

   IKE phase II negotiates SA parameters.

30 Which of the following is not part of IKE phase II?

   a. Negotiates IPSec SA parameters

   b. Periodically updates IPSec SAs

   c. Rarely updates SAs (at most, once a day)

   d. Established IPSec security parameters

   Answer: c

   IKE phase II updates SAs at periodically-defined intervals.

31 Which is the faster mode in IPSEC?

   a. Main mode

   b. Fast mode

   c. Aggressive mode

   d. Quick mode

   Answer: c

   Aggressive mode is faster than Main mode but is less secure. They can both occur in Phase I. Phase II only has Quick mode. Fast mode does not exist in the IPSec standard set of security protocols.

32 Certificate Enrollment Process (CEP) runs over what TCP port number? (Choose the best two answers.)

a. Same as HTTP

b. Port 80

c. Port 50

d. Port 51

e. Port 333

f. Port 444

Answers: a and b

CEP uses the same port as HTTP, port 80.

Chapter 5 Q & A Answers

1 Define the AAA model and a typical application on a Cisco IOS router.

Answer: Authentication, authorization, and accounting (pronounced triple A) provides security to Cisco IOS routers and network devices beyond the simple user authentication available on IOS devices.

AAA provides a method to identify which users are logged into a router and each user's authority level. AAA also provides the capability to monitor user activity and provide accounting information.

Typically, AAA is used to authenticate and authorize Cisco IOS commands, and provides accounting information to the network administrator.

2 Can you allow a remote user authorization before the user is authenticated with AAA?

Answer: Before authorization occurs, the remote user must be authenticated. Cisco IOS routers allow you to configure AAA authorization, but no access will be permitted until the remote user is authenticated.

3 What IOS command is required when enabling AAA for the first time?

Answer: aaa new-model must be entered globally before additional IOS commands are entered.

4 What is the privilege level of the following user? Assume AAA is not configured.

```
R2>
```

Answer: The privilege level ranges from 0 to 15 (the higher the level, the more commands are available). Because the user is not in PRIV exec mode, the default privilege level for an EXEC user is 1. Only basic show commands are available in priv level 1.

```
R2>show priv
Current privilege level is 1
```

5 Define four possible RADIUS responses when authenticating the user through a RADIUS server.

Answer: The four possible responses are as follows:

- **ACCEPT—The user is authenticated.**

- **REJECT—The user is not authenticated and is prompted to reenter the username and password, or access is denied. The RADIUS server sends this response when the user enters an invalid username/password pairing.**

- **CHALLENGE—The RADIUS server issues a challenge. The challenge collects additional data from the user.**

- **CHANGE PASSWORD—The RADIUS server issues a request asking the user to select a new password.**

6 What are RADIUS attributes? Supply five common examples.

Answer: RADIUS supports a number of predefined attributes that can be exchanged between client and server, such as the client's IP address. RADIUS attributes carry specific details about authentication.

RFC 2138 defines a number of RADIUS predefined attributes.

The following bulleted lists provides details from the most common attributes:

- **Attribute type 1—Username (defined usernames can be numeric, simple ASCII characters, or an SMTP address)**

- **Attribute type 2—Password (defines the password; passwords are encrypted using MD5)**

- **Attribute type 3—CHAP Password (only used in access-request packets)**

- **Attribute type 4—NAS IP address (defines the NAS server's IP address; only used in access-request packets)**

- **Attribute type 5—NAS port (not UDP port number); and indicates that the NAS's physical port number ranges from 0 to 65535**

- **Attribute type 6—Service-type (type of service requested or type of service to be provided); for Cisco devices is Callback and is not supported**

- **Attribute type 7—Protocol (defines what framing is required; for example, PPP is defined when this attribute is set to 1, SLIP is 2)**
- **Attribute type 8—IP address (defines the IP address to be used by the remote user)**
- **Attribute type 9—IP subnet mask (defines the subnet mask to be used by the remote user)**
- **Attribute type 10—Routing**
- **Attribute type 13—Compression**
- **Attribute type 19—Callback number**
- **Attribute type 20—Callback ID**
- **Attribute type 26—Vendor-specific (Cisco [vendor-ID 9] uses one defined option, vendor type 1, named cisco-avpair)**

7 What protocols does RADIUS use when sending messages between the server and client?

Answer: RADIUS transports through UDP destination port number 1812.

8 What predefined destination UDP port number is RADIUS accounting information sent to?

Answer: UDP port 1646

9 What does the following command accomplish on a Cisco IOS router?

```
aaa authentication ppp user-radius if-needed group radius
```

Answer: The aaa authentication ppp user-radius if-needed group radius command configures the Cisco IOS software to use RADIUS authentication for lines using PPP with CHAP or PAP, if the user has not already been authorized. If the EXEC facility has authenticated the user, RADIUS authentication is not performed. User-radius is the name of the method list that defines RADIUS as the if-needed authentication method.

10 What is the RADIUS server IP address and key for the following configuration?

```
radius-server host 3.3.3.3
radius-server key GuitarsrocKthisplaneT
```

Answer: The radius-server host command defines the RADIUS server host's IP address. The IP address is 3.3.3.3.

The radius-server key command defines the shared secret text string between the NAS and the RADIUS server host. The key is case-sensitive like all passwords on Cisco IOS devices, so the key is defined as GuitarsrocKthisplaneT.

11 TACACS+ is transported over what TCP destination port number?

Answer: TCP port 49

12 What information is encrypted between a Cisco router and a TACACS+ server?

Answer: All data communication between TACACS+ devices is encrypted, excluding the IP header.

13 What are the four possible packet types from a TACACS+ server when a user attempts to authenticate a Telnet session to a Cisco router configured for AAA, for example?

Answer: The four packets types are as follows:

- **ACCEPT—The user is authenticated and service can begin. If the network access server is configured to require authorization, authorization will begin at this time.**

- **REJECT—The user has failed to authenticate. The user can be denied further access or will be prompted to retry the login sequence, depending on the TACACS+ daemon.**

- **ERROR—An error occurred at some time during authentication. This can be either at the daemon or in the network connection between the daemon and the NAS. If an ERROR response is received, the network access server typically tries to use an alternative method for authenticating the user.**

- **CONTINUE—The user is prompted for additional authentication information.**

14 What is the significance of the sequence number in the TACACS+ frame format?

Answer: The sequence number is the number of the current packet flow for the current session. The sequence number starts with 1 and each subsequent packet will increment by one. The client only sends odd numbers. TACACS+ servers only send even numbers.

15 What does the following IOS command accomplish?

```
aaa authentication ppp default if-needed group tacacs+ local
```

Answer: The aaa authentication command defines a method list, "default," to be used on serial interfaces running PPP. The keyword default means that PPP authentication is applied by default to all interfaces. The if-needed keyword means that if the user has already authenticated through the ASCII login procedure, PPP authentication is not necessary and can be skipped. If authentication is needed, the keyword group tacacs+ means that authentication will be done through TACACS+. If TACACS+ returns an ERROR during authentication, the keyword local indicates that authentication will be attempted using the local database on the NAS.

16 What IOS command defines the remote TACACS+ server?

Answer: To define the TACACS+ server, the IOS command is tacacs-server host *ip address*.

17   What are the major difference between TACACS+ and RADIUS?

Answer: The following table lists the major differences between TACACS+ and RADIUS.

	RADIUS	TACACS+
Packet delivery	UDP	TCP
Packet encryption	RADIUS encrypts only the password in the access-request packet, from the client to the server.	TACACS+ encrypts the entire body of the packet, but leaves a standard TACACS+ header.
AAA support	RADIUS combines authentication and authorization.	TACACS+ uses the AAA architecture, separating authentication, authorization, and accounting.
Multiprotocol support	None.	TACACS+ supports other protocols, such as AppleTalk, NetBIOS, and IPX.
Router management	RADIUS does not allow users to control which commands can be executed on a router.	TACACS+ allows network administrators control over which commands can be executed on a router.

18   Kerberos is a third-party authentication protocol operating at what layer of the OSI model?

Answer: Kerberos is an application layer protocol, which operates at Layer 7 of the OSI model.

19   What delivery methods and destination ports does Kerberos support?

Answer: Kerberos supports both TCP and UDP, including the following port numbers:

- **TCP/UDP ports 88, 543, and 749**
- **TCP ports 754, 2105, and 4444**

20   What does the Kerberos realm define?

Answer: A Kerberos realm defines a domain consisting of users, hosts, and network services that are registered to a Kerberos server. The Kerberos server is trusted to verify the identity of a user or network service to another user or network service. Kerberos realms must always be in uppercase characters.

21 Applications that have been modified to support Kerberos credential infrastructures are known as what?

Answer: Kerberized.

22 Define the two steps required in an L2F connection terminating a PPP connection?

Answer: For L2F, the setup for tunneling a PPP session consists of two steps:

Step 1   Establish a tunnel between the NAS and the Home Gateway (HWY). The HWY is a Cisco router or access server (for example, an AS5300) that terminates VPDN tunnels and PPP sessions. This phase takes place only when no active tunnel exists between both devices.

Step 2   Establish a session between the NAS and the Home Gateway.

23 Define the two steps for setting up L2TP for tunneling a PPP connection.

Answer: For L2FP, the setup for tunneling a PPP session consists of two steps:

Step 1   Establish a tunnel between the LAC and the LNS. The LAC is an L2TP access concentrator that acts as one side of the L2TP tunnel endpoint and has a peer to the L2TP network server or LNS. This phase takes place only when no active tunnel exists between both devices.

Step 2   Establish a session between the LAC and the LNS.

24 What are the steps taken for a VPDN connection between a remote user and a remote LAN?

Answer: A VPDN connection between a remote user (router or via PSTN) and the remote LAN is accomplished in the following steps:

Step 1   The remote user initiates a PPP connection to the ISP using the analog telephone system or ISDN.

Step 2   The ISP network access server accepts the connection.

Step 3   The ISP network access server authenticates the end user with CHAP or PAP. The username determine whether the user is a VPDN client. If the user is not a VPDN client, the client accesses the Internet or other contacted service.

Step 4   The tunnel endpoints—the NAS and the home gateway—authenticate each other before any sessions are attempted within a tunnel.

Step 5   If no L2F tunnel exists between the NAS and the remote users' home gateway, a tunnel is created. Once the tunnel exists, an unused slot within the tunnel is allocated.

Step 6 The home gateway accepts or rejects the connection. Initial setup can include authentication information required to allow the home gateway to authenticate the user.

Step 7 The home gateway sets up a virtual interface. Link-level frames can now pass through this virtual interface through the L2F or L2TP tunnel.

25 What are the three most common threats from intruders that network administrators face?

Answer: The most common attacks are as follows:

- **Packet snooping (also known as *eavesdropping*)—When intruders capture and decode traffic obtaining usernames, passwords, and sensitive data, such as salary increases for the year.**

- **Theft of data—When intruders use sniffers, for example, to capture data over the network and steal that information for later use.**

- **Impersonation—When an intruder assumes the role of a legitimate device but, in fact, is not legitimate.**

26 What does the Digital Signature standard provides

Answer: DSS is a mechanism that protects data from an undetected change while traversing the network. DSS verifies the identity of the person sending the data just as you verify your license signature to the bank manager.

27 What is hash in encryption terminology?

Answer: A hash is defined as the one-way mathematical summary of a message (data) such that the hash value cannot be easily reconstructed back into the original message.

28 Name the two modes of operation in IPSec and their characteristics.

Answer: The two modes are transport and tunnel mode.

- **Transport mode—Protects payload of the original IP datagram; typically used for end-to-end sessions.**

- **Tunnel Mode—Protects the entire IP datagram by encapsulating the entire datagram in a new IP datagram.**

29 What does IKE accomplish?

Answer: IKE negotiates and provides authenticated keys in a secure manner. IKE was developed by the company previously known as ISAKMP Oakley Key Resolution.

30 Certificate Enrollment Protocol is transported over what TCP port?

Answer: CEP is transported over TCP port 80 (same as HTTP).

Chapter 6 "Do I Know This Already?" Quiz Answers

1 What UNIX command implements a trace route to the remote network www.guitar.com?

    a. **trace www.guitar.com** if DNS is enabled with the IOS **command dns server** *ip-address*.

    b. **traceroute www.guitar.com**

    c. **trace guitar.com**

    d. UNIX does not support the **traceroute** command.

Answer: b

2 What UNIX command copies a file?

    a. **copy**

    b. **cpy**

    c. **cp**

    d. **pc**

Answer: c

3 A Cisco router network manager wants to copy the configuration in RAM to a UNIX server. What needs to be accomplished before this can occur?

    a. Issue **copy run tftp**.

    b. Modify the .rhosts file.

    c. Modify the rcmd.allow file.

    d. Erase the .rhosts.allow file.

    e. Enable TFTP on the UNIX server.

Answer: b

4 Which of the following is not a UNIX file flag parameter?

    a. Execute

    b. Write

    c. Read

    d. Read/Write

    e. Authenticate

Answer: e

5 Which of the following is not a UNIX file type?

    a. Normal

    b. Directories

    c. Special

    d. Link

    e. Medium

Answer: e

6 NetBIOS over TCP/IP operates at what layer of the OSI model?

    a. 1

    b. 2

    c. 3

    d. 4

    e. 5

    f. 6

    g. 7

Answer: e

7 In Windows NT, what is a domain that is trusted by all remote domains called?

    a. Local

    b. Remote

    c. Single

    d. Global

    e. Master

    f. Slave

Answer: e

8 In Windows NT, what is a domain that is trusted automatically called?

a. Local

b. Remote

c. Single

d. Global

e. Master

f. Slave

Answer: d

9 Which of the following is not an NTFS permission type?

a. R

b. W

c. D

d. P

e. O

f. M

Answer: f

10 In Windows NT, when in a DOS command window, what command displays the local IP ARP entries?

a. **arp**

b. **rarp**

c. **rarp –b**

d. **arp –n**

e. **arp –a**

Answer: e

11 What devices can the Cisco Secure Policy Manager remotely manage? (Select the best three answers.)

a. Routers

b. Switches

c. NMS workstations

d. PIX Firewalls

Answers: a, b, and d

12 NetRanger LAN interface supports all but which one of the following?

a. Ethernet

b. Fast Ethernet

c. Token Ring

d. Serial WAN interfaces

e. FDDI

Answer: d

13 Which of the following is not a component of the security wheel?

a. Develop

b. Secure

c. Monitor

d. Manage

e. Increase

Answer: e

14 Which of the following is false in regards to NetRanger?

a. NetRanger examines the IP header.

b. NetRanger examines the TCP header.

c. NetRanger examines the entire IP frame.

d. NetRanger monitors TCP or UDP port scans.

Answer: c

15 How many phases are completed with NetSonar?

   a. 1

   b. 2

   c. 3

   d. 4

   e. 5

   f. 6

   Answer: f

Chapter 6 Q & A Answers

1 What UNIX command displays the files in the current directory?

Answer: ls

2 What UNIX command changes a directory from etc/ to bin/?

Answer:

```
cd ..          (takes you down one directory)
cd etc         (root directory to etc directory)
```

3 What does the following UNIX command accomplish?

```
cp -i simon.doc henry.doc
```

Answer: This command makes a copy of the files simon.doc and henry.doc. You must specify the name of the file to be copied and the name of the new file to be created. The -i flag tells the computer to ask before it overwrites any files in this process. The -r flag copies any files in subdirectories if you are copying directories.

4 To define a permission for a UNIX file, what command line interface is required?

Answer: chmod *flag filename*

5 The **chmod** UNIX command can define what levels of access or permissions on a UNIX host?

Answer: The *chmod* flag is always three numbers. The first number affects the owner permissions, the second number affects the group permissions, and the third number affects all other permissions. Each number can be a number between 0 and 7. See Table 6-3 for an explanation of these levels.

6 In a Windows NT environment, what is a domain, primary domain controller, and backup domain controller?

Answer: A domain is typically a large group of devices under a common administration. A domain is managed by a primary domain controller (PDC), which is a Windows-based server that stores and controls security and user account information for an entire domain. Each domain must have at least one PDC. A backup domain controller (BDC) maintains a copy of the database in the event the PDC is unavailable.

7 What functions does the protocol NetBIOS provide in a Window NT environment?

Answer: NetBIOS is a session layer protocol that is used to allow communication between PCs. NetBIOS provides the following functions:

Authentication

Connection management

Error control

File sharing

Flow control

Full-duplex transmissions

Name resolution

Print sharing

Session management

8 What is the function of the lmhosts file on a Windows platform device?

Answer: The lmhosts file enables local PCs to maintain a static list of all computers available in the network. The file typically contains the name and protocol addresses of all servers available in the domain. For large networks, the file might become too large and unusable, so a service called Windows Internet Naming Services (WINS) was developed to help network administrators who had to previously modify every Windows PC on the network via the lmhosts files. WINS allows NetBIOS Windows-based systems running TCP/IP to perform a name lookup for Windows resources, such as remote servers. An excellent white paper on WINS is available at www.lucent.com/livelink/09009403800049fc_White_paper.pdf.

9 Name and define the six NTFS permission types.

Answer: The six NTFS permissions are as follows:

R—Read only. The data or object can only be viewed.

W—Write access. The data can be changed.

X—Execute. The data can be executed; for example, a directory can be viewed or program executed.

D—Delete. The data can be deleted.

P—Change permissions. The data access permissions can be altered.

O—Take ownership. The ownership can be altered.

10 In Windows NT 4.0, what DOS command displays any local ARP entries?

Answer: arp -a

11 Define the terms NetRanger Sensor and Director and their uses?

Answer: NetRanger has two components:

NetRanger Sensor—High speed device that analyzes the content of data being transported across a network and determines whether that traffic is authorized or unauthorized. Unauthorized traffic includes ping requests from intruders. Traffic that is detected from unauthorized sources is sent directly to the NetRanger Director, and the intruder is removed from the network (optional and set by network administrator).

NetRanger Director—Provides real-time response to intruders in the network by blocking access to the network and terminating any active data sessions.

12 What LAN interfaces can be supported on a NetRanger Sensor?

Answer: NetRanger supports Ethernet (10 or 100 MB), Token Ring, and FDDI LAN interfaces.

13 What are the six phases completed by Cisco NetSonar?

Answer: The six phases completed by NetSonar are as follows:

Phase I—NetSonar sends out ICMP echo requests (ping) to query hosts.

Phase II—All live hosts are collected and stored on particular port numbers.

Phase III—NetSonar identifies the hardware devices that might be vulnerable, such as routers, switches, firewalls, printers, desktops, and hosts that responded to ping requests. Operating systems and network services are documented and labeled as potential vulnerabilities.

Phase IV—Vulnerabilities are confirmed. This phase is intrusive.

Phase V—The data is charted for presentation. The data can also be charted graphically as line or 3D bar graphs.

Phase VI—The data is reported in a number of different formats, including a summary report, a short and detailed report, or a full technical report.

14 What is the meaning of the term Security Wheel?

Answer: Cisco defines a Security Wheel concept that outlines the critical steps to ensuring that data and networks are secured correctly. The Security Wheel revolves around a strong, well-defined corporate policy. The Security Wheel consists of the following:

Secure—After defining a strong corporate policy, you should secure your network by deploying the products necessary in the appropriate places to achieve your corporate security policy.

Monitor and respond—Continuously monitor using NetRanger tools at strategic points in the network to discover new vulnerabilities.

Test—On a regular and formal basis, test all network components.

Manage and improve—Analyze all the reports and metrics supplied by NetSonar, and cycle through the Security Wheel by going through all these steps continuously.

Chapter 7 "Do I Know This Already?" Quiz Answers

1 DMZ stands for what?

   a. Demilitarized zone

   b. Demitted zone

   c. Domain main zone

   d. Domain name

   Answer: a

2 When defining an extended access list, what TCP port numbers can you use?

   a. Only predefined Cisco keywords

   b. 0 to –65,000

   c. 0 to –65,535

   d. 1 to 65,534

   e. None of the above

   Answer: c

   TCP port numbers from 0 to –65,535; devices such as PCs go from 1025 to 65535.

3 When defining an extended access list, what UDP port numbers can you use?

   a. Only predefined Cisco keywords

   b. 0 to 65000

   c. 0 to 65535

   d. 1 to 65534

   e. None of the above

Answer: c

UDP port numbers from 0 to 65535.

4 Which of the following is *not* a TCP service?

   a. who

   b. whois

   c. finger

   d. ftp

   e. pop3

Answer: a

who is a UDP service.

5 Which of the following is *not* a UDP service?

   a. BGP

   b. echo

   c. domain

   d. discard

   e. rip

   f. snmp

Answer: a

BGP runs over TCP port 179.

6 For how many translations does PAT allow you to use one IP address?

   a. 32,000

   b. 64,000

   c. 96,000

   d. 128,000

   e. 256,000

Answer: b

Port Address Translation (PAT) occurs when the local port number is modified, allowing more than one host the ability to share one public address, for example. The Port number in a TCP frame can be numbered from 0 to –65,535, so answer b is closet to the actual number of allowed translations.

7 PAT translates all private addresses based on what?

   a. Source port

   b. Destination port

   c. Both source and destination

   d. None

Answer: c

PAT is based on source port; the destination port is not altered. For example, a Telnet connection is based on the local port number (a random number generated by the device between 0 and –65,535) and the destination port number 23.

8 NAT is which of the following?

   a. Network Architectural Language

   b. National anthem of Latvia

   c. Network translation

   d. Network Address Translation

Answer: d

9 NAT is defined in which RFC?

   a. 1700

   b. 1701

   c. 2002

   d. 1631

   e. 1613

Answer: d

NAT is defined by Request for comment (RFC) number 1631.

10 The following defines which NAT terminology: "A legitimate registered IP address as assigned by the InterNIC?"

   a. Inside local address

   b. Outside global address

   c. Inside global address

   d. Outside local address

Answer: c

11 What IOS command defines a pool of addresses that will be translated to a registered IP address?

   a. **ip nat inside**

   b. **ip nat outside**

   c. **ip nat pool**

   d. **ip nat inside pool**

   e. **ip nat outside pool**

Answer: c

12 PIX stands for what?

   a. Protocol interchange

   b. Cisco Private Internet

   c. Private Internet Exchange

   d. Public Internet Exchange

Answer: c

13   To define how a PIX will route IP data, what is the correct syntax for a PIX 520?

a. ip route

b. route

c. ip route enable

d. default-network

Answer: b

A PIX can run RIP or be configured for static routing; a default route is typically required so that end-user data can be sent to the Internet, for example.

14   What is the alias command's function on a PIX firewall?

a. To define a local host name

b. To define the DNS server

c. Used in NAT environments where one IP address is translated into another.

d. Only applicable to Cisco IOS

Answer: c

The PIX alias command is used for NAT configurations. The alias command translates one IP address into another address. For example, one private network might be using unregistered IP address space, and to allow users access to outside address space, the alias command is used. This command is applied differently on a Cisco IOS router.

15   CBAC stands for what?

a. CBAC is not a valid term

b. Cisco Business architectural centre

c. Context-based Access Control

d. Context-based Accelerated controller

e. Content-based arch. Centre

Answer: c

16 What is IKE used to accomplish?

    a. NAT translations

    b. Ensures that data is not sourced by the right sources

    c. Ensures that data is not sourced by the wrong sources

    d. No use

    e. Both a and c

Answer: c

Internet Key Exchange (IKE) allows a network confidentially from unauthorized sources.

17 To create a simple VPN tunnel (unencrypted) between two sites, what must you do on a Cisco router?

    a. Create a GRE tunnel

    b. Create a routing map

    c. Nothing, use a PIX

    d. Create an IPSec tunnel

Answer: a

A simple VPN tunnel requires a generic routing encapsulation (GRE) tunnel between two Cisco routers.

Chapter 7 Q & A Answers

1 What does the term DMZ refer to?

Answer: The DMZ, or demilitarized zone, is defined as an isolated part of the network that is easily accessible to hosts on the outside (Internet, for example).

2 What is the perimeter router's function in a DMZ?

Answer: The perimeter router sits between the DMZ and the public domain. It is typically a high performance router or routers that perform a number of duties, including the following:

- **Access lists to ensure access to IP is restricted**
- **Restrictions to TCP services**
- **Restrictions on what applications can be run**
- **Routing protocols (typically, BGP)**

3 What two main transport layer protocols do extended access lists filter traffic through?

Answer: Extended access lists filter both TCP and UDP transport layer services.

4 Which of the following is *not* a TCP service?

    a. Ident

    b. ftp

    c. pop3

    d. pop2

    e. echo

Answer: e

Echo is part of the UDP protocol suite. Ident, ftp, and pop2/pop3 are TCP services.

5 Name five UDP services that can be filtered with an extended access-list.

Answer: Cisco IOS can filter a number of UDP services, including the following:

- **biff—Biff (mail notification, comsat, 512)**
- **bootpc—Bootstrap Protocol (BOOTP) client (68)**
- **bootps—Bootstrap Protocol (BOOTP) server (67)**
- **discard—Discard (9)**
- **dnsix—DNSIX security protocol auditing (195)**
- **domain—Domain Name Service (DNS, 53)**
- **echo—Echo (7)**
- **isakmp—Internet Security Association and Key Management Protocol (500)**
- **mobile-ip—Mobile IP registration (434)**
- **nameserver—IEN116 name service (obsolete, 42)**
- **netbios-dgm—NetBIOS datagram service (138)**
- **netbios-ns—NetBIOS name service (137)**
- **netbios-ss—NetBIOS session service (139)**
- **ntp—Network Time Protocol (123)**
- **pim-auto-rp—PIM Auto-RP (496)**
- **rip—Routing Information Protocol (router, in.routed, 520)**
- **snmp—Simple Network Management Protocol (161)**
- **snmptrap—SNMP traps (162)**
- **sunrpc—Sun Remote Procedure Call (111)**

- **syslog—System Logger (514)**
- **tacacs—TAC Access Control System (49)**
- **talk—Talk (517)**
- **tftp—Trivial File Transfer Protocol (69)**
- **time—Time (37)**
- **who—Who service (rwho, 513)**
- **xdmcp—X Display Manager Control Protocol (177)**

6 What RFC defines NAT?

Answer: Network Address Translation (NAT) is defined in RFC 1631.

7 In NAT, what is the inside local address used for?

Answer: The inside local address refers to the IP address that is assigned to a host on the internal network, that is, the logical address that is not being advertised to the Internet. A local administrator generally assigns this address. This address is NOT a legitimate Internet address.

8 What does the IOS command **ip nat inside source list** accomplish?

Answer: It defines the addresses that will be allowed to access the Internet. This command enables the network address translation of the inside source addresses. The "list" keyword helps define the access list to be used for determining the source addresses.

9 What are the four possible NAT translations on a Cisco IOS router?

Answer: The four NAT translation versions are as follows:

- **Static NAT—Maps an unregistered IP address to a registered IP address on a one-to-one basis.**
- **Dynamic NAT—Maps an unregistered IP address to a registered IP address from a group of registered IP addresses.**
- **Overloading—A form of dynamic NAT that maps multiple unregistered IP addresses to a single registered IP address using different ports. Known also as Port Address Translation (PAT), single address NAT, or port-level multiplexed NAT.**
- **Overlapping—When the IP addresses used on your internal network are registered IP addresses in use on another network, the router must maintain a lookup table of these addresses so that it can intercept them and replace them with registered unique IP addresses.**

10 How many connections can be translated with a PIX firewall for the following RAM configurations: 16 MB, 32MB, or 128MB?

Answer: You can support up to 260,000 connections with 128MB, 16MB can support up to 32,768 connections, and 32MB of memory can support up to 65,536 connections.

11 When the **alias** command is applied to a PIX, what does it accomplish?

Answer: The alias command translates one address into another, and is used for translating unregistered IP addresses in a NAT environment.

12 What security features does the Cisco IOS Firewall feature set allow a network administrator to accomplish?

Answer: The Cisco IOS features set consists of the following:

- **Context-based Access Control (CBAC) provides internal users secure, per-application-based access control for all traffic across perimeters, such as between private enterprise networks and the Internet.**

- **Java blocking protects against unidentified, malicious Java applets.**

- **Denial-of-service detection and prevention defends and protects router resources against common attacks, checking packet headers and dropping suspicious packets.**

- **Audit trail details transactions, recording time stamp, source host, destination host, ports, duration, and total number of bytes transmitted.**

- **Real-time alerts log alerts in case of denial-of-service attacks or other preconfigured conditions.**

13 What does CBAC stand for?

Answer: Context-based Access Control

14 Name the eight possible steps to take when configuring CBAC.

Answer: To configure CBAC, the following tasks are required or optional:

- **Pick an internal or external interface. (Required)**

- **Configure IP access lists at the interface. (Required)**

- **Configure global timeouts and thresholds. (Required)**

- **Define an inspection rule. (Required)**

- **Apply the inspection rule to an interface. (Required)**

- **Configure logging and audit trail. (Required)**

- **Follow other guidelines for configuring a firewall. (Required)**

- **Verify CBAC. (Optional)**

15 What is a virtual private network?

Answer: A virtual private network (VPN) enables IP traffic to travel securely over a public TCP/IP network by encrypting all traffic from one network to another. A VPN uses tunneling to encrypt all information at the IP level.

Chapter 8 "Do I Know This Already?" Quiz Answers

1 A remote user tries logging into a remote network but fails after three additional tries and is disconnected. What useful information should the network administrator gather? (Select the best two answers.)

a. Username

b. Invalid password

c. Invalid username

d. Valid username

Answer: b and c

Network administrators need the invalid username (because it is not an allowable username) and the invalid password used to see if the intruder is using a text-based algorithm to generate passwords.

2 What is the first step that should be implemented in securing any network?

a. Create a database of secure passwords.

b. Create the IP address scheme.

c. Run NetRanger or NetSonar.

d. Define a security policy.

e. Configure access lists on all routers.

Answer: d

The first step in securing any network must be to define the security policy.

3 What primary security method can be designed and deployed to secure and protect any IP network after an attack has been documented?

    a. Security policy

    b. IP policy

    c. Countermeasures

    d. Measurement

    e. Logging passwords

Answer: c

Countermeasures should be in placed in every IP network. For example, back up sensitive data or application software and apply all the required patches.

4 A security administrator notices that a log file stored on a local router has increased in size from 32 k to 64 k in a matter of seconds. What should the network administrator do?

    a. Increase the buffer to 64 k.

    b. Decrease the buffer to 16 k.

    c. Log the event as suspicious and notify the incident response team.

    d. Nothing, this is normal.

    e. Both a and b are correct.

Answer: c

Any log file that increases (more data to view) or decreases (for example, cleared by the intruder to hide his actions) should be regarded as suspicious activity.

5 What is the primary responsibility of CERT/CC?

    a. Define access lists for use on routers

    b. Set security standards

    c. Coordinate attacks on secure networks

    d. Maintain a security standard for networks

    e. Nothing to do with security

Answer: d

CERT/CC's primarily responsibility is to aid in the security of any public network; go to www.cert.org for more details.

6 Who can use network scanners and probes? (Select the best two answers.)

  a. Intruders

  b. Security managers

  c. End users

  d. Cable service providers

Answer: a and b

Network scanners are used by intruders just as network administrators use them.

7 What is a bastion host?

  a. Firewall device supported by Cisco only

  b. Network's last line of defense

  c. Network's first line of defense

  d. IP host device designed to route IP packets

Answer: c

Bastion hosts are typically the first line of defense. Sometimes, they are sacrificed because they are typically public domain servers and can be quickly restored using backup methods.

8 A TCP SYN attack is what type of attack?

  a. ICMP

  b. DoS

  c. Telnet/Kerberos attack

  d. Ping attack only

Answer: b

A TCP SYN attack is a form of denial-of-service attack.

9 When an intruder sends a large amount of ICMP echo (ping) traffic using IP broadcasts, this type of DoS attack is known as what?

   a. Bastion

   b. Land.C

   c. Man in the middle

   d. Smurf

   e. Ping of death

   Answer: d

   A Smurf attack sends large ICMP or ping requests via a broadcast address, ensuring that all devices on the remote network respond and enabling the intruder to list the IP address that is connected to the network for further DOS-based attacks.

10 What kind of attack sends a large ICMP echo request packet with the intent of overflowing the input buffers of the destination machine and causing it to crash?

   a. Ping of death

   b. Smurf

   c. Land.C

   d. Man in the middle

   e. Birthday attack

   Answer: a

   A ping of death sends a large number of ICMP echo request packets causing the end device to overflow, and can cause a remote server to stop functioning for legitimate requests.

11 In the context of intrusion detection, what is an exploit signature?

   a. DoS attack

   b. An attack that is recognized and detected on the network

   c. The same as a Smurf attack

   d. The same as a man in the middle attack

   Answer: b

   An exploit signature is an attack that is readily detected.

12 To stop spam e-mail from overwhelming an e-mail server, what step can you take?

    a. Ask the ISP for help.

    b. Nothing, because spam e-mail is too difficult to stop to be worth the effort.

    c. Install an intrusion detection system that has a signature for spam e-mail.

    d. Nothing, because the client software takes care of this.

    e. Change the IOS code.

    f. Configure the bastion host to stop spam e-mail.

Answer: c

Spam e-mail can be controlled with an IDS server.

Chapter 8 Q & A Answers

1 Define four reasons networks should be secured.

Answer: IP networks must provide a network security policy for the following reasons:

Inherent technology weaknesses—All network devices and operating systems have inherent vulnerabilities.

Configuration weaknesses—Common configuration mistakes can be exploited to open weaknesses.

Security policy vulnerabilities—The lack of security policies can lead to vulnerabilities, such as password security.

Outside/inside intruders—There are always internal and external people wanting to exploit network resources and retrieve sensitive data.

2 What is the function of the CERT/CC organization, and what are its primary objectives?

Answer: The CERT Coordination Center (CERT/CC) is a center of Internet security expertise, located at the Software Engineering Institute, a U.S. federally funded research and development center operated by Carnegie Mellon University. CERT/CC provides information ranging from protecting your networks from potential problems, to reacting to current problems, to predicting and preparing for future problems. Work involves handling computer security incidents and vulnerabilities, publishing security alerts, researching long-term changes in networked systems, developing information, and even providing training to help you improve security. CERT/CC does not concern itself with the individual or where the intruder is physically located, but ideally tries to restore and prevent similar attacks in the future. CERT/CC is regarded as the industry leader in security concerns.

3 What are the primary steps completed by incident response teams?

Answer: Incident responses teams do the following:

Verify the incident.

Determine the magnitude of the incident (hosts affected and how many).

Assess the damage (for example, if public servers have been modified).

Gather and protect the evidence.

4 Name common methods used by intruders to disrupt a secure network.

Answer: Intruders can use the following methods (and many more):

Session hijacking—The intruder defines himself with a valid IP address after a session has been established to the real IP address by spoofing IP packets and manipulating the sequence number in an IP packet.

Rerouting—Packets from one source are routed to an intruder source. Routing updates are altered to send IP packets to an incorrect destination, allowing the intruder to read and use the IP data inappropriately.

Denial-of-service (DoS) attacks—A service attack that is used in an attempt to deny legitimate users access to a network they have full rights to.

Probes and scans.

Malicious code.

5 In security, what is session hijacking?

Answer: Session hijacking is where the intruder defines himself with a valid IP address after a session has been established to the real IP address by spoofing IP packets and manipulating the sequence number in an IP packet.

6 In security terms, what is a man in the middle attack?

Answer: Just as with packet sniffers and IP spoofing attacks, a brute-force password attack can provide access to accounts that can be used to modify critical network files and services. An example that compromises your network's integrity is an attacker modifying your network's routing tables. By doing so, the attacker ensures that all network packets are routed to him before they are transmitted to their final destination. In such a case, an attacker can monitor all network traffic, effectively becoming a man in the middle.

7 What is a Signature Engine?

Answer: A Signature Engine is a component designed to support many signatures in a certain category. An engine is composed of a parser and an inspector. Each engine has a set of legal parameters that have allowable ranges or sets of values. Exploit signatures are an identifiable pattern of attack.

8 What is social engineering?

Answer: Social engineering is the act of tricking or coercing employees into providing information, such as usernames or mail user identifications and even passwords. First-level phone support personnel are typically called by intruders pretending to work for the company to gain valuable information.

9 Describe a ping of death attack.

Answer: A ping of death occurs when a large number of ICMP echo request packets cause the end device to overflow. For example, a ping of death can cause a remote server to stop functioning for legitimate requests.

10 What is a Land.C attack?

Answer: A Land.C attack is a program designed to send TCP SYN packets (TCP SYN is used in the TCP connection phase) that specify the target's host address as both source and destination. This program can use TCP port 113 or 139 (source/destination), which can also cause a system to stop functioning.

11 What does the following IOS code accomplish on a Cisco IOS router?

```
no service udp-small-servers
no service tcp-small-servers
```

Answer: These commands disable the minor TCP/UDP servers. When the minor TCP/IP servers are disabled, access to the Echo, Discard, Chargen, and Daytime ports causes the Cisco IOS Software to send a TCP Reset packet to the sender and discard the original incoming packet. When these commands are entered in global configuration, they do not display when you view the configuration (show running-config or write terminal) because the default is to disable TCP/UDP small servers. Unlike Cisco Switches, Cisco IOS Software does not display default configuration.

12 What is the secret password for the following IOS configuration?

```
enable secret %$@$%&^$@*$^*@$^*
enable pass cisco
```

Answer: Secret passwords are encrypted using the MD5 hashing algorithm, so you cannot decipher the secret password, which overrides the enable password.

13 What is the purpose of the command **service sequence-numbers**?

Answer: Essentially, this command enables your syslog entries to be numbered and ensures that they are not tampered with by external sources.

Study Tips for CCIE Security Examinations

This appendix describes some study tips and options for you to consider while preparing for the CCIE Security written and lab examinations.

CCIE is regarded as the most sought-after certification in the industry today; more and more vendors are devising their own certification programs and trying to catch up to the industry-leading Cisco Systems. Working in the CCIE program, I have seen many changes and challenges facing potential CCIEs every day for the past two years. As of August 22, 2002, there were approximately 9000 CCIEs, and the number is growing rapidly. Of the 9000 CCIEs, approximately 110 hold more than one CCIE certification. The majority of CCIEs are located in Europe and North America.

Before you decide to take this step, you need to be aware of the challenges in front of you. You cannot hope to become a CCIE by simply buying a book or a series of books. Hands-on experience is required, and at least two years of internetworking experience is critical; and even then, you must fully prepare for the difficult examinations. The current three varieties of CCIE certification follow:

- CCIE Routing and Switching (released 1993)
- CCIE Security (released August 2001)
- CCIE Communications and Services (released August 2001)

This discussion concentrates on the CCIE Security certification. The CCIE Security examination is one examination you should consider tackling, especially in today's climate of Internet firewall frailty and demand for security experts.

NOTE   For more information on the Security track, see the following:

www.cisco.com/en/US/learning/le3/le2/le23/le476/learning_certification_
type_home.html

Recently, four CCIE tracks were retired: ISP Dial, SNA, Design, and WAN Switching.

Steps Required to Achieve CCIE Security Certification

The CCIE Security certification requires a candidate to pass two exams:

- A 2-hour, computer-based written exam (#350-018) consisting of 100 questions. The pass mark is approximately 70 percent, but varies according to statistics and could float between 65 and 75 percent. This book is designed to help prepare you for this written exam.

- An 8-hour lab examination. The passing score is set at 80 percent. Historically, the lab examination was a full 2-day lab; that changed October 1, 2001. All CCIE lab exam versions are monitored closely and adapted where necessary to conform to the CCIE program standards, which are not publicly available. This book contains supplemental material intended to help you prepare for the lab exam, but that is not the focus of this book. The following URL provides a breakdown of CCIE numbers and geographic locations:

  www.cisco.com/en/US/learning/le3/le11/learning_ccie_population.html

CCIE Security Written Exam

The CCIE Security written exam uses the typical certification test format of asking multiple-choice questions with one or more correct answers per question. What makes some of the questions more difficult is that more than five answer choices are listed on some questions. This reduces the power of eliminating answers and choosing from those remaining. However, the number of required answers is given for each question. You might be required to give only one answer or select a couple of correct answers. Attempt to answer every question to give you the best chance of passing, even if you have to guess.

After completing the test, you will be given a percentage for each section. The following are the sections you will be scored in:

- Security Protocols
- Operating Systems
- Application Protocols
- General Networking
- Security Technologies
- Cisco Security Applications
- Security General
- Cisco General

If you do not receive a passing score, compare your results with Table 1-1 to identify the areas you need to concentrate on for your next attempt.

You will also be given the passing mark, your score, and your grade. The grade is either a pass or fail.

The examination is similar to other Cisco certifications, albeit it is a little more difficult with many more in-depth questions. You can view some sample questions from the similarly formatted CCIE Routing and Switching written exam at the following location (there are currently no available security questions):

www.cisco.com/warp/public/625/ccie/certifications/sample_routing.html

The CCIE Security written exam requires test-taking skills that many of us learned in high school or college. This section is a refresher for many and important for all.

The first thing to focus on is time management during the test. The CCIE exam allows 120 minutes to complete the test. You have 100 questions, so if you allow 1 minute per question and 20 minutes to review your answers, you will be doing well.

Some questions require more time, so you can mark and skip them if you want and complete them later. Be sure before moving on to the next question that the application on the testing device permits a review of questions; Cisco can change this at any time.

Remember that a wrong answer incurs no extra penalty, so answer all the questions. Another advantage of marking difficult questions and returning to them at the end is that the answer for a previously asked question will often appear in a later question. I have also found that at times when I can't remember an answer that I should know, my memory is later refreshed by another question. Remember to just mark questions that you can't answer and come back to them at the end.

Read every question and all the possible answers carefully. The CCIE Security written exam has many questions that are designed to be tricky, so they require careful examination of the syntax. Many of the questions refer to exact commands required to implement a function on a router. It is important to know the different syntax and to recognize small differences in commands. This book has similarly formatted questions in each chapter and in the sample questions on the CD-ROM. Go through these questions, study areas of weakness, and go through the questions again to ensure your understanding of a subject.

Make sure you read every answer before choosing one. One answer might sound great; however, another answer could be more correct than the first. The fact that on these exams one answer can be more or less correct than another is a concept you should keep in mind when taking any Cisco exam. In addition, saying questions out loud or writing them down on your scrap paper might help you understand the question easier than viewing it on a computer screen.

| NOTE | Occasionally, Cisco announces a beta trial for the written exams, and if you book the test, you pay only a small fee compared to the standard fee of approximately U.S.$250. The following link has more information: |

> www.cisco.com/en/US/learning/le3/le11/learning_beta_certifcation_exams_list.html

Decoding Ambiguity

Cisco exams have a reputation for including questions that can be difficult to interpret, confusing, or ambiguous. In my experience with numerous exams, consider this reputation to be completely justified. The Cisco exams are deliberately tough.

The only way to beat Cisco at its own game is to be prepared. You'll discover that many exam questions test your knowledge of things that are not directly related to the issue that a question raises. This means that the answers you must choose from—even incorrect ones—are just as much a part of the skill assessment as the question itself. If you don't know something about most aspects of the CCIE Security written exam topics, you might not be able to eliminate obvious wrong answers. In other words, the more you know about Cisco IOS Software and securing Cisco internetworks, the easier it will be for you to tell a right answer from a wrong one.

Questions often give away their answers, but you have to be Sherlock Holmes to see the clues. Often, subtle hints appear in the question text in such a way that they seem almost irrelevant to the situation. You must realize that each question is a test unto itself, and you must inspect and successfully navigate each question to pass the exam. Look for small clues, such as access list modifications, problem isolation specifics (such as which layers of the OSI model are not functioning correctly), and invalid Cisco IOS commands. Little things like these can point to the right answer if properly understood; if missed, they can leave you facing a blind guess.

Another trick is to watch out for keywords, such as *not* or choose the *best*; these words will define the required answer. If you miss keywords, your answer will be correct in your mind but might not be the correct answer. Read questions out loud or write them down to ensure you identify keywords and fully understand what the question is asking.

For questions requiring more than one answer, be sure to view how many answers are required and remove the obvious choices before making your selection. These questions are frequently ambiguous, and you need to be on your guard.

Another common difficulty with certification exams is vocabulary. Be sure to brush up on the key internetworking terms presented in this guide. You may also want to read through the Terms and Acronyms on the following Cisco website:

> www.cisco.com/univercd/cc/td/doc/cisintwk/ita/index.htm

The test questions appear in random order, and many elements or issues that receive mention in one question might also crop up in other questions. It's not uncommon to find that an incorrect answer to one question is the correct answer to another, or vice versa. Take the time to read every answer to each question, even if you recognize the correct answer to a question immediately.

Because you're taking a fixed-length test, you can revisit any question as many times as you like. If you're uncertain of the answer to a question, check the box that's provided to mark it for easy return later on. You should also mark questions you think might offer information that you can use to answer other questions. Candidates usually mark somewhere between 25 and 50 percent of the questions on exams. The testing software is designed to let you mark every question if you choose; use this framework to your advantage. Everything you want to see again should be marked; the testing software can help you return to marked questions quickly and easily. Be sure to check out the latest updates from Cisco because policies like these can change; see the following URL for more details:

www.cisco.com/en/US/partner/learning/le3/learning_ccie_written_exam.html

The best method to pass any Cisco written exam is to go through each question and answer the questions you are confident with in your first pass and mark the remaining questions. After you complete the 100 questions, review all your marked questions.

On your second pass, survey the questions you marked more thoroughly as you begin to answer them systematically and consistently. Try to eliminate the choices that are way off base and make an educated guess with the remaining choices. Continue to mark and ignore the clueless questions, and on pass three, attack the totally clueless ones; by then, you might be able to make a more educated guess from clues in the context of other questions you already answered.

If you have time, you can go back and check all your answers. Experience has shown me that your first reaction to a question is typically the best choice unless you see a glaring mistake.

Preparing for the Written Exam

The best way to prepare for the test—after you study—is to take practice exams until you feel comfortable with your results. This certification guide includes over 300 simulated test questions on the CD-ROM that allow you to take the sample examination (in study and exam simulation modes) as many times as you like until you are comfortable with the test format and your knowledge level. Try to identify subject areas where you are weak and use this book and other resources to study those areas more.

Give yourself 120 minutes to take the practice exam, keep yourself on the honor system, and don't look at text in the book or jump ahead to the answer key. When your time is up or you finish the questions, go back and review your correct and incorrect answers. You learn more by making mistakes in a simulation than from the real examination, which provides little feedback on incorrect answers. Study your incorrect answers very carefully. Practice the three-phase approach I mentioned earlier, or if you have your own strategy, practice this strategy a few times before attempting the real examination.

I have attempted to estimate the number of questions that are taken from each subject area to give you an idea of where to focus the majority of your time. Each chapter contains a weighted number of questions to match those on the examination, and similarly, the CD-ROM simulation examinations are weighted, as well. For example, 50 percent of the CD-ROM questions are based on Routing and Switching topics, 50 percent are on Security topics, and so forth to mimic the questions on the real exam. The percentage of questions you get for any topic will vary. The passing score will also vary. If you concentrate on the questions and think clearly, you will not need to worry about the passing score. Typically, the passing range is from 65 to 75 percent depending on the scoring rate for that month. Cisco will not release the passing score. As far as I have discovered, the passing score is static for the Security examination at 70 percent, but don't be surprised if this changes in the future.

Knowing how to recognize correct answers is good, but understanding why incorrect answers are wrong can be equally valuable.

I cannot stress how much getting hands-on experience with Cisco routers and switches will help you pass not only the written exam, but also the more difficult lab examination. A small test bed with two Cisco routers and a PC is the best way to learn and reinforce your theoretical knowledge. I strongly recommend it even for the written exam, which, in turn, aids your preparation for the lab examination.

Cisco provides a Cisco Documentation CD with every shipment with a wealth of documentation that you can implement on test equipment. The documentation CD is a great study tool. The documentation CD is not provided for the written exam but is provided for the laboratory exam. Understanding how a protocol works is only half of your goal; you need to appreciate how Cisco routers and switches operate when a certain protocol is activated with IOS.

Talk to all your colleagues or friends that attempted the written exam and find out what they studied to help them. Of course, all who have taken the exam are bound by the nondisclosure agreement, so you cannot share specific details about exam content, but you can share study tips and habits.

Taking the Written Exam

On exam-day eve, you should relax and spend a maximum of one hour studying. Don't sit up all night studying and worrying—if you want to do your best, you need to feel refreshed. Have a good meal, scan your study materials (such as the "Foundation Summary" sections in this book), and get a good night's sleep.

On the day of the exam, eat a well-balanced breakfast and briefly review your study notes. Make sure that you arrive at the testing center at least one hour before your scheduled time. Find a quiet corner to relax and mull over the main exam subjects.

When you're sitting in front of the testing computer, there's nothing more you can do to increase your knowledge or preparation. Take a deep breath, stretch, and read the first question.

Don't rush; you have plenty of time to complete each question. Both easy and difficult questions are intermixed throughout the test in random order. Don't cheat yourself by spending too much time on a hard question early in the test, depriving yourself of the time you need to answer the questions at the end of the test.

On a fixed-length test, you can read through the entire test and, before returning to marked questions for a second visit, figure out how much time you have per question. As you answer each question, remove its mark. Continue to review the remaining marked questions until you run out of time or you complete the test.

After you complete the exam, your test will be scored immediately. A few moments after you finish, the computer will indicate whether you passed or failed.

You Passed!

Passing the CCIE Security exam means that you're ready to take the lab examination. Within 48 to 72 hours, Cisco will be notified of your result. There is no need to fax your result, as was previously required. To set a lab exam date, visit tools.cisco.com/CCIE/Schedule_Lab/jsp/login.jsp and select the location and examination date you prefer. (Hopefully, seats will be available.) The lab exam is popular, and you might need to wait a month or more for an opening. Some locations have a waiting list of six months or more. For example, the Sydney, Australia CCIE lab is generally not fully booked, and you might get a seat at a time of your choice; in Brussels, Belgium, you might need to wait six months. Make sure you agree to a testing date that you feel comfortable with, and leave yourself plenty of time to study for the rigorous lab exam. After passing the written test, you have one full year to pass the lab examination, so, if necessary, you can study for a few months before taking it.

You Failed

If you fail the CCIE Security written exam, don't worry about the result. You can still take advantage of the situation. While the test is fresh in your mind, jot down problem areas on a notepad (the sooner you make notes for yourself the better). Try to remember questions you felt less comfortable with and study those areas before taking the exam again.

The CCIE Security written exam is not an easy exam to pass. In fact, this examination ranks among the toughest networking examinations in today's certification market. If you really want to be a CCIE, a first-attempt failure should not discourage you. A failed attempt should encourage you to invest in some serious study time so that you can pass on your next attempt. A number of candidates have noted that the second attempt is much easier than the first. Remember that the reason Cisco Systems makes the written examination hard is to ensure that you are fully prepared for the challenging lab examination.

That's it for pointers. Here are some frequently asked questions about the written examination followed by some bonus information on the lab examination.

FAQs About the CCIE Security Written Exam

This section answers some common questions about the written CCIE Security examination. These frequently asked questions should help dispel any confusion surrounding this exam.

1 How many questions are on the CCIE Security written examination?

   There are 100 questions. All questions are multiple choice. Some questions require a single answer, whereas other questions require more than one answer to earn a point.

2 What is a passing score?

   Cisco no longer publishes a set passing score for the written examination. Instead, Cisco supplies you with a pass or fail grade. The actual passing score (a percentage) is based on a statistical analysis system that checks the scores of all candidates over three months and adjusts the score needed to pass accordingly. For example, the passing score for one candidate might be 70 percent, but it might be 75 percent for another candidate, depending on what results candidates are attaining.

3 Can I change an answer after working through all the questions?

   Yes, as long as time remains, you can return to any question.

4 How long is the examination?

   The exam is two hours long. Make sure you use your time wisely—you want to have an opportunity to answer as many questions as possible. If you find you are spending too long on a single question, mark it and move on. If time permits, you can return to difficult questions later.

5 What happens when I finish the examination?

   The computer scores your test within minutes and indicates whether you passed or failed. You receive a printed score sheet with a grade for the entire exam and a percentage score for each of the topics. If you fail, you must wait at least 24 hours before retaking the exam.

6 Can I use the Windows calculator during the exam?

   No. You are not permitted to use any Windows tools. You are supplied with a pencil and some white paper or an erasable sheet.

7 How many times can I retake the written examination?

   You can retake the exam as many times as you like.

8 What do I do after I pass the written exam?

   You do not need to fax your test results to your nearest CCIE lab administrator. Visit the following URL to set a lab examination:

   tools.cisco.com/CCIE/Schedule_Lab/jsp/login.jsp

9 Where can I find further information about the CCIE Security exam?

Cisco provides additional information online:

www.cisco.com/en/US/learning/le3/le2/le23/le476/learning_certification_ type_home.html

CCIE Security Lab Exam

NOTE	Although the focus of this book is to prepare you for the CCIE Security written exam only, you can find bonus material, such as this section, that helps start your preparation for the lab exam.

Passing the written examination is the easier part of the CCIE Security certification journey. For the lab exam, your life needs to change dramatically, and you need to study on routers full time for at least three to six months. The good news is that the format of the lab examination has changed from two full days to one day. You are no longer required to troubleshoot a network (regarded as the true method to test a CCIE's ability to restore a network back to full IP connectivity); you are now required only to configure a set number of Cisco IOS, PIX, and Catalyst features. Upon entering the lab room, you will already have preconfigured router and switch host names and IP addressing, and the enable password and login commands will all be set on all devices to **cisco**.

After you pass the written exam, you are eligible to sit for the lab examination. You can book your lab examination online:

tools.cisco.com/CCIE/Schedule_Lab/jsp/login.jsp

The lab examination contains the following devices:

- 2600 Series Routers
- 3640 Series Routers
- 4000/4500 Series Routers (not all labs)
- PIX 520 running 5.2 or later
- Catalyst 5000 or 3550 Series switches
- Cisco ACS running on Windows 2000 server

Make sure you practice with and understand these devices. Practice configuring almost every IOS feature and fully understand what each IOS command actually enables, rather than just relying on limited experience with certain commands. Anyone can configure a Cisco router, but the ability to understand the full consequence of any Cisco IOS command is crucial to the CCIE Security lab examination.

CCIE Security Lab Exam FAQs

The following are some frequently asked questions about the difficult one-day CCIE Security lab examination.

1 When did the lab format change from two days to one day?

    October 2001. All CCIE certification labs worldwide now test candidates in the one-day format.

2 Where can I take the CCIE Security lab examination?

    Locations and contact information follow:

    - **San Jose, California**

        Tel: 1-800-829-6387 (select option 2) or 1-919-392-4525

        Fax: 1-919-392-0166

        E-mail: ccie_ucsa@cisco.com

    - **Chatswood, NSW, Australia (location of this author)**

        Tel: +61 2 8446 6135

        Fax: +61 2 8446 8440

        E-mail: ccie_apt@cisco.com

    - **Brussels Belgium**

        Tel: +32 2 704-5670

        Fax: +32 2 704-6000

        E-mail: ccie_emea@cisco.com

    Over time, you can expect the Security lab examination to be available in other locations worldwide. E-mail ccie-lab@cisco.com if you want to know more details.

3 What is the maximum score and what is a passing score?

    The total examination is worth 100 points and the passing grade is 80 percent. The passing rate for first attempts is very low, so expect the possibility of taking the examination more than once. Cisco will not release the passing rate.

4 What if I have a question and cannot find the answer?

E-mail your question to ccie-lab@cisco.com. All questions receive a response from the CCIE team within 72 hours.

5 What happens after the exam?

You will be escorted outside the lab. You receive an e-mail notification within 24 hours. The e-mail advises you to log on to Cisco's website (tools.cisco.com/CCIE/ Schedule_Lab/jsp/login.jsp) and login your written exam results, and you will be presented with a breakdown of the main sections and your percentage score in each section. You can fill in a critique regarding your lab experience; be sure to provide all the feedback you have—good or bad. Candidates can receive free lab attempts for valid excuses or lab incompetence. For the price, you want to make sure you have been given every opportunity to pass.

6 Can I use Notepad and Windows calculator?

Yes, you can, but you are not permitted to save any files. You can, however, cut and paste to and from Notepad. Calculator is very useful for determining subnets and bit boundaries or converting hexadecimal to decimal.

7 How many times can you take the lab examination?

You must allow 30 days between lab attempts. There is no limit on the number of lab attempts, and there are no minimum score requirements.

8 What happens if you pass?

In addition to becoming a CCIE, you also gain access to exclusive CCIE chat forums and merchandise, and you receive a CCIE medallion and certificate. Expect these to be mailed to you between 6 and 12 months after your test date.

The following URL provides more details on benefits CCIEs can expect:

www.cisco.com/en/US/learning/le3/learning_about_recertication.html

9 What happens if I fail? Am I told in which areas I scored poorly?

Cisco will not tell you specific areas of weakness; that is left to the candidate to decipher from the brief score report. You can, however, pay a fee (U.S.$250.00) to have your lab routers re-examined for accuracy. Unless you believe your score is close to 80 percent, I strongly recommend you keep studying and put those funds toward another attempt. Even with a regrade, no additional information is provided to you—only a brief score report by e-mail and your new grade (pass or fail).

10 What materials can you bring into the lab?

You are permitted to bring only necessary medication and a dictionary. No other materials are permitted. Cisco provides refreshments at all CCIE lab sites. Lunch is also provided during a lunch break (30 minutes). Lunch is mandatory and CCIE staff escort you.

11 What is the proctor's role?

You can seek clarification from a proctor if you do not understand a question or the objective of a question. The proctor cannot provide answers but can ensure that you understand the question. The proctor can also make any changes required in case of network hardware failures or examination mistakes. The proctor is there to ensure that you have the best possible chance of success and should not hinder your ability to pass the test. If you feel otherwise, you can e-mail your concerns to ccie-lab@cisco.com. The CCIE program manager's core responsibility is the welfare of the candidates, and you never know, your case might warrant a free future lab.

12 Where can I find out more about CCIE and all the different certification tracks?

The following URL provides information about the CCIE tracks:

www.cisco.com/en/US/learning/le3/le2/le23/learning_certification_level_home.html

13 How often do you need to recertify?

You must recertify every two years to maintain your CCIE status; otherwise, your CCIE status will be changed from active to inactive. An inactive CCIE means you cannot purchase CCIE merchanise or particiapte in the CCIE forum.

To view your CCIE status, visit the following URL:

www.cisco.com/en/US/learning/le3/le11/learning_ccie_online_verification_tool_launch.html

14 What examinations or alternative methods can I take to recertify my CCIE?

Currently, you can use a couple different methods to recertify your CCIE:

- **You can take any of a number of different written examinations.**

- **You can achieve a CCIE certification from a track you do not currently possess.**

For more information on recertification, visit www.cisco.com/en/US/learning/le3/learning_about_recertication.html.

Sample CCIE Routing and Switching Lab

NOTE   Although this book's aim is to help prepare you for the CCIE Security written exam, I include this appendix as bonus material for a few reasons. First, even though this is a sample lab for the CCIE Routing and Switching lab exam, it gives you an idea of the level of tasks involved in a CCIE lab examination. Second, being a triple CCIE myself, I recognize that if you are interested in attaining CCIE Security certification, you might be curious about the other CCIE options, as well.

This appendix is designed to assist you in your final preparation for the lab portion of the most popular CCIE certification to date, CCIE Routing and Switching (CCIE R&S).

Many books are published today on how CCIE R&S certification can be achieved but, in reality, no matter how many books you purchase, it all comes down to your level of hands-on experience. The strict Non-Disclosure Agreement (NDA) policed by Cisco ensures that candidates do not share any information about the lab exam content, so very little is known before your first attempt.

For the first time ever, the CCIE team has approved this sample CCIE Multiprotocol lab so that you can be aware of the level of difficulty involved in the lab exam and prepare. *Solutions are not provided at the request of the Cisco Systems CCIE department.* You are left to research the various solutions on your own. In researching the solutions, you learn more about each topic and commit the information to memory better. In the end, this ensures that you are as prepared as you can be for the lab if you decide to take it.

The end goal of any CCIE lab is a working solution. However, you might be restricted in the way you provide a working solution, as you discover in this sample CCIE R&S lab.

Candidates who prepare for the lab often ask me what is the best way to prepare. My answer to them is to practice and configure every feature available and then practice some more. Of course, not every feature will be tested on the lab. You are encouraged to read the most up-to-date information about Cisco exams and certifications at www.cisco.com/en/US/learning/le3/le2/le23/learning_certification_level_home.html.

You must be able to provide a working solution quickly and adhere to the guidelines stated in the question. A good analogy is going for your driving test; imagine you're asked to drive down a 100-mile road that is perfectly straight, but instead of going down the road the way you think is best, a sign every 100 feet indicates an action you must take. The exam designer does not always ask for the best solution or your favorite solution, but might ask you to solve the problem in a very specific way. For this reason, you must have a broad knowledge of all IOS features. The lab exam is designed to discover if you are capable of configuring more challenging and difficult scenarios.

The CCIE lab changed dramatically in format on October 1, 2001. The lab changed from a two-day lab to a one-day lab, which means that a candidate is no longer required to sit for a separate troubleshooting section but must configure a network in 8 hours. One of the most critical skills in the new format is time management. Troubleshooting is still regarded as a fundamental skill in today's most critical IP networks, and having CCIE certification does not necessarily mean you demonstrated troubleshooting skills to a perspective employer.

NOTE
Token Ring switching and legacy routing protocols, such as IPX and IGRP, are no longer tested in the CCIE R&S lab exam. DLSw over Ethernet remains a core test topic.

Each task in this sample CCIE R&S lab examination includes the time allocation you should allow to complete the task. This lab is designed to be completed within 8 hours. Sections that indicate 0 hours mean that in the real CCIE lab that particular section has already been completed for you. For example, this sample lab asks you to physically cable the network; no time allocation is provided because in the real CCIE lab, the physical cabling is already completed for you.

This sample lab's goal is a working IP network according to the set design criteria.

Figure C-1 displays the sample topology with nine Cisco IOS routers and the logical topology.

Figure C-2 displays the Frame Relay connections between the Cisco routers.

Figure C-1   *CCIE Lab Topology*

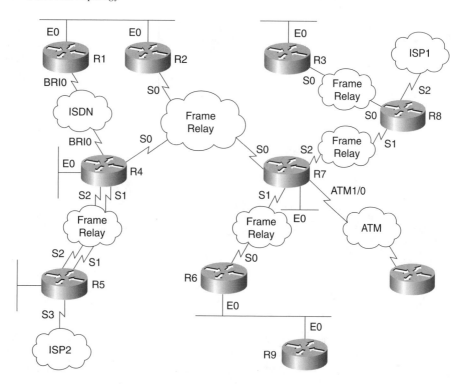

Figure C-2   *Frame Relay DLCI Assignment*

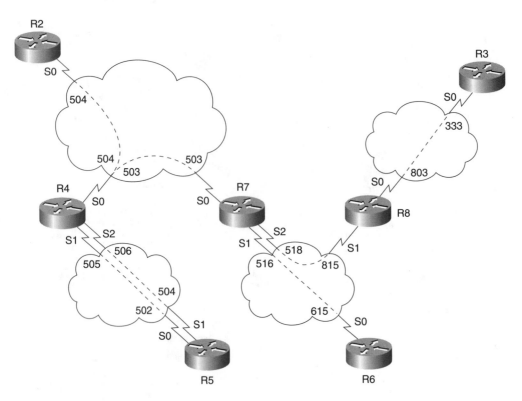

Basic Setup (1 Hour)

Configure the network in Figure C-1 for basic physical connectivity.

Communications Server (0.25 Hours)

NOTE	Not all CCIE R&S labs require you to configure a communication server.

Configure the communication server so that when you type the host name of a router on the server, you are connected across the console port to that router. Set up the routers in Figure C-1 with the following physical attributes:

- Set up the routers, as shown in Figure C-1.

- Configure R1 as the communication server with the **ip host** command.

- Communication server ports 2 to 8 are connected to Routers R2 to R8, respectively.

- Communication server port 9 connects to the Catalyst Ethernet switch.

- R9 is a Catalyst 6509 switch with a Multilayer Switch Feature Card (MSFC) module installed.

Physical Connectivity (No Time)

NOTE   From October 1, 2001 onward, a CCIE candidate is not required to physically cable up the lab network. Therefore, no time allocation is given to this section, which is added for completeness only.

Your network is already physically patched. Construct your network, as shown in Figure C-1.

Configure the following characteristics for the topology in Figure C-1:

- A Frame Relay switch connects all serial links between routers. Use only the indicated DLCIs in Figure C-2 and disable Frame Relay inverse ARP for IP only.

- Routers R1 and R4 are connected to an ISDN service with the switch type defined as basic-5ess. R1 connects to number plan 0298017705 and R4 connects to number plan 0296307050.

- Routers R1 through R9 are connected to the Catalyst Ethernet switch (Catalyst 6509 series switch), according to Table C-1.

Table C-1   *Ethernet Interface Connections to the 6509*

Router	Catalyst Port
R1 Ethernet 0	3/1
R2 Ethernet 0	3/2
R3 Ethernet 0	3/3
R4 Ethernet 0	3/4
R5 Ethernet 0	3/5
R6 Ethernet 0	3/6
R7 Ethernet 0	3/7
R8 Ethernet 0	3/8
R9 Ethernet 0	3/9

Catalyst Ethernet Switch Setup I (0.25 Hours)

Configure the Ethernet switch for six VLANs:

- VLAN 2 named VLAN_A is connected to R1 and R2.

- VLAN 3 named VLAN_B is connected to R3.

- VLAN 4 named VLAN_C is connected to R4.

- VLAN 5 named VLAN_D is connected to R5.

- VLAN 6 named VLAN_E is connected to R6 and R9.

- VLAN 7 named VLAN_F is connected to R7.

Using VLAN_A, configure the management interface sc0 with the address 131.108.0.2/25. Ensure that all devices in your network can Telnet to the switch even if R1 or R2 is down.

Make sure the switch is configured in the VTP domain Cisc0_vTp and the switch can create and delete VLANs in the future.

Catalyst Ethernet Switch Setup II (0.25 Hours)

Configure the following spanning tree parameters on the Catalyst 6509:

- Ensure the switch never becomes the root bridge on VLAN_D.

- Ensure the switch has the best possible chance of becoming the root bridge in VLAN_E.

- Set all the Ethernet ports to forward data immediately after a device is plugged in or activated.

- Set the hello time on VLAN_B to 10 seconds.

- Set the max age on VLAN_F to 10 seconds.

Configure the following miscellaneous parameters:

- Disable Cisco Discovery Protocol on ports 3/1-8.

- Ensure that any IP phones installed or connected to Card 3 are supplied inline power.

- Ensure that the switches get a clock source from R1 using NTP.

- Make sure the only MAC address permitted to access the switch on port 3/23 is the MAC address 2010-2010-2010 or 4000-0000-4000.

- Disable power redundancy on the switch.

- Warn all Telnet clients that any "unauthorized access is not permitted" by displaying a warning message when any Telnet session is activated to the SC0 interface only.

- If any ports become disabled because of hardware errors, ensure the switch automatically enables the affected ports after 10 minutes.

Catalyst Ethernet MSFC Setup (0.25 Hours)

NOTE   The CCIE R&S lab contains two Catalyst 3550s per candidate rack, and the 6500 is purposefully configured here so that the difficulty level is much higher.

Configure R9 (6509 with an MSFC card) for IP routing.

Example C-1 displays the hardware profile on the Catalyst 6509 switch.

Example C-1 **show module** *on R9 (MSFC)*

```
Cat6509> (enable) show module
Mod Slot Ports Module-Type              Model              Sub Status
--- ---- ----- ------------------------ ------------------ --- --------
 1   1    2    1000BaseX Supervisor     WS-X6K-SUP1A-2GE   yes ok
15   1    1    Multilayer Switch Feature WS-F6K-MSFC       no  ok
 3   3   48    10/100BaseTX Ethernet    WS-X6348-RJ-45     yes ok

 9   9    8    1000BaseX Ethernet       WS-X6408-GBIC      no  ok
Mod Module-Name          Serial-Num
--- -------------------- -----------
 1                       SAD0413022N
15                       SAD041501U6
```

continues

Example C-1 show module *on R9 (MSFC) (Continued)*

```
2                          SAD041501U6
3                          SAD04270A8A
9                          SAD03479837
Mod MAC-Address(es)                          Hw   Fw        Sw
1   00-30-96-33-21-7e to 00-30-96-33-21-7f 3.1   5.3(1)    5.5(4)
    00-30-96-33-21-7c to 00-30-96-33-21-7d
    00-d0-01-b0-4c-00 to 00-d0-01-b0-4f-ff
15  00-30-96-33-24-84 to 00-30-96-33-24-c3 1.4   12.1(1)E,  12.1(1)E,
3   00-30-96-34-9b-48 to 00-30-96-34-9b-77 1.1   5.3(1)    5.5(4)
9   00-30-96-2b-e1-f4 to 00-30-96-2b-e1-fb 2.3   4.2(0.24)V 5.5(4)
Mod Sub-Type              Sub-Model         Sub-Serial  Sub-Hw
1   L3 Switching Engine   WS-F6K-PFC        SAD04150DYL 1.1
3   Inline Power Module   WS-F6K-VPWR                   1
```

Using the information displayed in Example C-1, configure the MSFC for IP routing in VLAN 6 only using RIPv2 only.

Do not route between any other interfaces.

IP Configuration and IP Addressing (No Time)

NOTE   Because of recent changes to the CCIE exam, the candidate is not required to configure IP addressing. However, the subject is presented here to ensure potential CCIE candidates have a good understanding of IP address spaces and subnetting. No time is projected for this section.

Use the Class B subnetted IP addresses 131.108.0.0 to 131.108.255.255 to design your network. You must use this address space for all addresses unless specified in a particular question. Read the entire task before designing your IP address space.

After your IP address space and IP routing is completed, it must be possible to reach all your routers and switches. Set the enable password for all routers and switches to cisco.

Configure IP addresses on your remaining interfaces:

- Use a 25-bit mask for VLAN 2.
- Use a 27-bit mask for VLAN 3.
- Use a 28-bit mask for VLAN_D.
- Use a 24-bit mask for VLAN_E.
- Use a 24-bit mask for all other interfaces.

- Use a subnet with the least number of hosts for the ISDN link.
- Use a 29-bit mask for all Frame Relay connections running classless IP routing protocols.
- Use a 24-bit mask for all Frame Relay connections running classful IP routing protocols.
- Assign each router a 24-bit subnet to be used by the loopback address. It must be possible to ping and Telnet from any one router using the loopback address.
- Configure local IP host addresses on each router so that an exec or privilege user can type the router name to ping or Telnet without having to type the full IP address.

Frame Relay Setup (0.5 Hours)

Configure IP across your Frame Relay network, as displayed in Figure C-2:

- You have to use static maps for each protocol. No dynamic mapping is permitted.
- *No* subinterfaces are allowed on any router.
- Use the most efficient subnetwork for IP addresses on the Frame cloud.
- You can assign a subnet from your Class B range.
- Use LMI-type **Cisco only** and do not rely on auto sensing the LMI type on any routers. All router interface types are DTE. The Frame port type is DCE.
- Do not use the keyword **broadcast** for the Frame Relay link between R6 and R7 when mapping IP.
- Make sure you can also ping the local interface from each router configured for Frame Relay.

Basic ATM Configuration (0.5 hours)

Configure ATM on R7 to connect to the ATM cloud:

- Your IP address for the ATM cloud is 197.1.1.1/24.
- One PVC is configured between your Router R9 and the remote ATM router. Your end of the PVC is VPI = 0 and VCI = 100.
- Configure RFC 1577 on R9.
- You must be able to ping the remote ATM router address of 192.1.7.2/24.

IGP Routing (3 Hours)

After this section is completed, all routers must have full IP connectivity between every routing domain, including the ISDN backup interfaces when operational.

RIP Configuration (0.5 Hours)

Configure RIP on Routers R6 and R9 only:

- Configure RIP on R6 E0 and R9 E0.

- Make sure only unicast updates are sent and received.

- Authenticate any RIP packets.

- Redistribute the RIP route into the IGRP domain.

- Make sure you can see distributed RIP routes throughout your topology.

IS-IS Configuration (0.5 Hours)

Configure IS-IS on Routers R6 and R7 only:

- The MAC address of the respective routers are the following:

  — R6 0050.5460.98e8 net ID is 00.0001.0050.5460.98e8.00

  — R7 00b0.64fc.d7bd net ID is 00.0001.00b0.64fc.d7bd.00

- Configure all routers in IS-IS area 1.

- Configure R6 as an IS-IS level 2 router only.

- Redistribute the IS-IS routes into the OSPF domain.

- Make sure you can see distributed IS-IS routes throughout your topology as type 1 OSPF routes.

EIGRP Configuration (0.5 Hours)

Configure EIGRP on Routers R3, R7, and R8 only:

- Configure EIGRP in domain 333 between the serial link on R7 to R8, R3 to R8, and VLAN 3.

- Summarize as much as possible to reduce the redistributed routes into OSPF, but make sure all routes appear in the IS-IS and RIP domains.

- Ensure that EIGRP is authenticated across the Frame Relay connections.

- Redistribute the EIGRP routes into OSPF domain with a cost metric of 1000 seen on all OSPF routers.

- Ensure that R3 never sends any updates across the Ethernet (E0) segment.

OSPF Configuration (1.5 Hours)

Configure OSPF as described in Figure C-1. Do not create any nonspecified OSPF areas:

- Configure the OSPF backbone over the Frame Relay network between Routers R2, R4, and R7.

- The ISDN link between R1 and R4 resides in the area 0.0.0.0.

- The link between R4 and R5 is in area 4.

- The Ethernet segment between R1 and R2 resides in area 1.

- The Ethernet segment on R4 resides in area 0.0.0.40.

- Make sure all OSPF routes are redistributed and reachable in the IGRP, RIP, and EIGRP domains.

- Ensure that the OSPF backbone in the Frame cloud is authenticated.

- Ensure that R1 is never the designated router (DR) on all segments.

- Make sure R4 is the DR in the OSPF backbone network.

- Ensure that the router ID of all OSPF-enabled routers is the loopback address.

- Do not create any additional areas.

- Set the hello interval between links R1 and R4 to 25 seconds.

- Set the hello interval on R2 Ethernet segment to 20 seconds.

- Ensure that all loopbacks appear as /24-bit networks on all IP routing tables. Do not use the **redistribute connected** command on any router to accomplish this.

- Make sure area 0.0.0.40 is configured so that excessive CPU resources are not consumed on Router R4. You can assume no other areas or routers are attached to this segment.

Basic ISDN Configuration (0.5 Hours)

ISDN switch information:

- ISDN switch type: basic-5ess.
- ISDN numbering:
  - R1: 0298017705
  - R4: 0296307050
- SPIDs are not required.

Configure the ISDN interfaces on R1 and R4 as follows:

- When R1's S0 goes down, R1 should place an outgoing call to R4.
- R4 cannot call R1 under any circumstance.
- Use PPP encapsulation and the strongest authentication available.
- Never bring up more than one B channel to ensure that costs are kept to a minimum.
- When the Frame Relay link is restored, bring down the ISDN link after 25 minutes.
- When the ISDN is active, all routers must be able to ping and telnet the local ISDN interfaces on R1 and R4.

DLSw+ Configuration (0.75 Hours)

Configure DLSw+ on R1, R2, R5, and R6:

- VLANs 2, 5, and 6 should have DLSw configured to allow SNA devices to communicate between each other.
- Do not enable DLSw on R9, but allow any future segments connected to R9 reachability to VLAN 2 only.
- SNA/NetBIOS hosts reside on VLANs 2 and 5.
- Hosts on VLAN 2 are used only when VLAN 5 is not reachable.
- Make sure all routers peer to R1 and that only in a network failure will DLSw+ circuits terminate on R2 or R5.
- DLSw+ peers should only be active when user-based traffic (SNA/NetBIOS) is sent or received.
- If IP connectivity exists, ensure that DLSw+ remains established.
- Use a different virtual ring group on each router.

- Configure a filter that blocks NetBIOS packets with destination name SimonisaCCIE from leaving R5 and R8. Permit all other NetBIOS traffic starting with the name Simonis?***.

- Ensure that remote DLSw+ peers do not send too many queries for the destination MAC address 0200.0200.0200 on VLAN 6 or VLAN 2.

- Be sure the only SAPs enabled on R3 are null SAPs and SAP 08.

Flash Configuration (0.2 Hours)

The customer accidentally erased Router R1's system image in flash memory. The customer has no Cisco IOS Software or TFTP server on hand. There is no Internet access. Restore the IOS image to the Flash on R1 and then reload R1.

R1 and R2 are running the same IOS code and are the same router hardware type (Cisco 2503 routers).

VTY Changes (0.2 Hours)

Configure all VTY lines so that network administrators require no local authentication.

Administrators must still use the enable password ccieToBe on all routers to access privilege mode.

To allow nonprivileged users access to R1 and the ability to clear terminal server lines, ensure that all exec users can use the IOS command **clear** in exec mode on Router R1 only.

HTTP server (0.2 Hours)

Configure R1 to act as an HTTP server, but allow only clients from users on VLAN_A or VLAN_B.

Catalyst 6509 Password Recovery (0.2 Hours)

The enable password on the 6509 switch has been modified. Assuming you have access to the switch using password recovery on the switch, set the enable password to ccie and the access password to cisco.

Private Address Space Allocation (0.2 Hours)

Some users on VLAN_A have configured their PCs with the Class A addresses ranging from 10.10.1.1 to 10.10.1.255/24. Make sure the Class A address is never present in any routing table but R1, and allow the users to access the rest of the network.

Ensure that the remaining network can access the host with the IP address 10.10.1.100/24.

BGP Routing Configuration (0.75 Hours)

After finishing each of the following sections, make sure all configured interfaces/subnets are consistently visible on all pertinent routers, even in the event of network failure of any one router.

Basic IBGP Configuration (0.5 Hours)

Configure IBGP on all routers in your network:

- Do not use any WAN IP interfaces for IBGP sessions because your network is prone to failures across the Frame Relay cloud.

- Configure R5 and R8 as route reflectors and make sure that all traffic as a preferred path is via Router R5.

- Minimize IBGP configurations as much as possible.

- Do not disable BGP synchronization.

- Use AS 2002 on all IBGP routers.

- As long as there is IP connectivity in your network, ensure that BGP is active in all routers.

- Using the **network** command only, advertise all networks to route reflectors R5 and R3.

- Do not change the administrative distance on any interior routing protocol.

- Make sure you have full BGP connectivity.

- Be sure all routers have entries in their IP routing tables.

EBGP Configuration (0.25 Hours)

Configure EBGP on R5 and R8 as follows:

- R5's remote peer is 171.108.1.2/24 and remote AS is 1024.

- R8's remote peer is 191.200.1.2/30 and remote AS is 4345.

- ISP1 and ISP2 are advertising the full Internet routing table.

- The only route accepted is a default route and routes of the form 110.100.0.0 to 121.110.255.255.

- Set all routes in the range 110.100.0.0 to 121.110.255.255 with the following attributes:

  — BGP origin is set to IGP.

  — Prepend the AS paths 1000 999 100.

  — Set the weight to 1000 for all even networks and 2000 for all odd networks.

NOTE   At the request of the CCIE department, solutions to this sample lab are not provided in this book. Consider this lab a source for understanding the type of testing you can expect on a CCIE lab exam. The material in this appendix is in no way intended to represent the exact material you will see on the actual lab examination.

Conclusion

You should be able to complete the sample CCIE Routing and Switching lab in this appendix within eight hours. The difficulty level presented here is similar to what you can expect in any CCIE lab examination; in fact, the difficulty level here might be higher. Focus your attention on time management and the ability to configure a set number of IOS features very quickly. If you complete this lab successfully, try it again by modifying the questions and changing the IP routing algorithm. For example, configure multipoint Frame Relay connections or subinterfaces across the Frame Relay network in Figure C-2; try PPP over an ISDN connection.

Be familiar with Cisco IOS 12.1 and above. Also, be up to date with the latest features tested in the examination. Most candidates are intimidated by the recent CCIE content changes. You must have an overall conceptual view of all Cisco IOS features, because Cisco cannot possibly test all the more advanced features of all the content. Nor are there complex hardware models present in the lab. New content typically tests only the overall concepts. You must be able to competently search the Cisco Documentation CD, find any feature you need to configure, and quickly appreciate the use of any IOS command. Typically, a portion of any CCIE exam will be unknown to you, so you must be able to search the CD documentation provided in every lab quickly.

The ability to complete any design scenario efficiently, correctly, and per the given parameters ensures that you are a master of CCIE rather than someone who just passed an eight-hour exam by configuring a set number of IOS features. In today's environment, being a CCIE is not always marketable enough. Troubleshooting skills and an ability to demonstrate your skills to a prospective employer when designing any network topology in any network condition can place you ahead of the rest.

Symbols

.rhosts file (UNIX), 290
| (pipe), 174

Numerics

3DES (Data Encryption Standard), 238
10Base2, 28
10Base5, 28
10BaseT, 28
100BaseT, 28
802.1Q, 33
1000 GE, 28

A

AAA (authentication, authorization and accounting), 208-209
    accounting, 211-212
    authentication, 210
    authorization, 210-211
ABRs (Area Border Routers), 68
access lists, 250
    extended, 187-189
    filtering TCP services, 222-224
    IP packet debugging, 171-172
    standard, 182-187
    wildcard masks, 184
accessing Cisco routers, 179
accounting, 208, 211-212
ACKs (acknowledgments), 63
ACS (Cisco Secure Access Control Server).
    See Cisco Secure
Active Directory, 133
Active FTP, 115-117

adaptive cut-through switching, 30
address classes, 36
adjacencies, 67
administrative distances, 56-57
agents (SNMP), 123
Aggregator attribute (BGP), 78
Aggressive mode (IKE), 246
AH (Authentication Header), 244-246
alias command, 167
allocating IP addresses, InterNIC, 325
ambiguous test questions, decoding, 572-573
application layer (OSI model), 25
applications
    NetRanger, 300
        Director, 302
        sensors, 300
        supporting platforms, 301
        typical network placement, 300
    TFTP, 113
applying access lists to interfaces, 185-187
areas, 67
arguments (UNIX commands), 286
ARP (Address Resolution Protocol), 45-46
AS (autonomous system), 67
AS_Path attribute (BGP), 77
ASA (Adaptive Security Algorithm), 330
ASBRs (autonomous system boundary routers), 68
asynchronous communications, 84-85
Atomic Aggregate attribute (BGP), 78
attacks
    birthday attacks, 372
    chargen, 371
    CPU-intensive, 371
    DDoS, 371
    DNS poisoning, 371
    DoS, 370-372
    e-mail, 371
    incident response teams, 367

D

M

N

O

W-X-Y-Z

Why 700,000+ Cisco Employees, Customers & Partners Train with KnowledgeNet:

As the only Cisco Learning Solutions Partner with true, second-wave learning solutions, KnowledgeNet's advantage is unmistakable. We provide solid training that's in line with key Cisco initiatives — like voice over IP, security, and wireless, as well as multiple certification options including CCNA®, CCNP®, CCIE® and more. And we deliver your training in flexible, engaging live and self-paced formats that let you decide how, when, and where you want to train.

Try KnowledgeNet for yourself and find out why Cisco chose us to train so many of their employees, customers, and channel partners.

Visit us on the Web at
www.knowledgenet.com/ciscopress

NET®

Train with authorized Cisco Learning Partners.

Discover all that's possible on the Internet.

One of the biggest challenges facing networking professionals is how to stay current with today's ever-changing technologies in the global Internet economy. Nobody understands this better than Cisco Learning Partners, the only companies that deliver training developed by Cisco Systems.

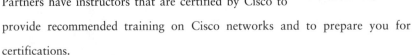

Just go to **www.cisco.com/go/training_ad**. You'll find more than 120 Cisco Learning Partners in over 90 countries worldwide.* Only Cisco Learning Partners have instructors that are certified by Cisco to provide recommended training on Cisco networks and to prepare you for certifications.

To get ahead in this world, you first have to be able to keep up. Insist on training that is developed and authorized by Cisco, as indicated by the Cisco Learning Partner or Cisco Learning Solutions Partner logo.

Visit **www.cisco.com/go/training_ad** today.

CISCO SYSTEMS

EMPOWERING THE
INTERNET GENERATION™

Cisco Press

Learning is serious business.

Invest wisely.

CCIE Security

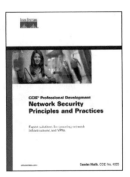

Network Security Principles and Practices (CCIE Professional Development)

Saadat Malik

1-58705-025-0 • **Available Now**

Network Security Principles and Practices is a comprehensive guide to network security threats and the policies and tools developed specifically to combat those threats. Starting with a general discussion of network security concepts and design philosophy, the book shows readers how they can build secure network architectures from the ground up. Taking a practical, applied approach to building security into networks, the book focuses on showing readers how to implement and verify security features and products in a variety of environments. Security aspects of routing protocols are discussed and various options for choosing and using them analyzed. The book goes into a detailed discussion of the security threats posed by increasingly prevalent LAN to LAN virtual private networks and remote access VPN installations and how to minimize large vulnerabilities caused by these non-traditional network portals. Firewalls, including the PIX and IOS® Firewalls, and underlying protocols are presented in depth. Intrusion detection is fully examined. The book shows the reader how to control dial-in access by setting up access servers with AAA, PPP, TACACS+, and RADIUS. Finally, protections at the service provider are discussed by showing the reader how to provision security at the service provider level.

CCIE® Practical Studies: Security (CCIE Self-Study)

Andrew Mason, Dmitry Bokotey

1-58705-110-9 • **Available June 2003**

The Cisco Certified Internetworking Expert (CCIE) Certification from Cisco Systems is the most prestigious certification in the networking industry. In 2001, Cisco exam with a one-day intensive lab exam is a highly sought after affirmation of a networkers security skills. A key to success in the intensive lab exam is hands-on understanding of how the security principles and concepts are executed in a real network. *CCIE Practical Studies: Security* provides a series of lab scenarios that help a CCIE candidate or advanced-level networker gain that expertise. The labs show how, with or without a lab of actual equipment, different concepts are applied. Chapters include background and technology overviews, directions on how to set up a practice lab, case study-based scenarios that show the step-by-step implementation of these concepts, and comprehensive labs that mimic those in the one-day lab exam. *CCIE Practical Studies: Security* serves as an invaluable guide in gaining networking security experience and in CCIE testing success.

Learning is serious buisiness. **Invest wisely.**

Cisco Press

Learning is serious business.

Invest wisely.

General CCIE

CCIE Routing and Switching
Exam Certification Guide

Anthony Bruno, CCIE

1-58720-053-8 • Available Now

CCIE Routing and Switching Exam Certification Guide covers the general networking topics listed in the Routing and Switching (#350-001) and Communications and Services CCIE Qualification Exams. This book will help the reader increase and reinforce their knowledge in each general networking area to prepare for the qualifying exam; it serves as a complete self-assessment tool for candidates to identify weak spots in their knowledge that require additional review. As with all Exam Certification Guides from Cisco Press, each chapter has a "Do I know this already?" pre-chapter quiz and other standard elements like the accompanying CD-ROM with exams that will help the reader practice for the test. In addition to building confidence as an exam preparation resource, this book provides network engineers, designers, and architects with an all-around reference to keep them on top of the latest and most important networking technologies and techniques.

CCIE Practical Studies, Volume 1

Karl Solie, CCIE

1-58720-002-3 • Available Now

While the popularity of the CCIE Exam grows amongst technology professionals, the fail rate is still quite high, over 80% (approx.). *CCIE™ Practial Studies, Volume I* focuses on the lab portion of the exam, where most fail. It includes in-depth coverage for over 70 labs scenarios as well as how to design and implement basic to complicated networks.

Learning is serious buisiness. **Invest wisely.**

Cisco Press Security

Troubleshooting IP Routing Protocols
(CCIE Professional Development)

Zaheer Aziz, CCIE; Johnson Liu, CCIE;
Abe Martey, CCIE; Faraz Shamin; CCIE

1-58705-019-6 • Available Now

As the Internet continues to grow exponentially, the need for
network engineers to build, maintain and troubleshoot the
growing number of component networks has also increased
significantly. Since network troubleshooting is a practical skill
that requires on-the-job experience, it has become critical that the
learning curve to gain expertise in internetworking technologies
be reduced to quickly fill the void of skilled network engineers
needed to support the fast growing internet.

Troubleshooting Remote Access Networks
(CCIE Professional Development)

Plamen Nedeltchev

1-58705-076-5 • Available Now

Troubleshooting Remote Access Networks helps you understand
underlying technologies and gain insight into the challenges,
issues, and best practices for supporting remote access networks.
Covering fundamental concepts, design issues, provisioning, DSL
and Cable connectivity options, central office operations,
authentication techniques, and troubleshooting, this book serves
as a comprehensive tool to resolving remote access issues. In-depth
analysis of essential remote access technologies provides greater
insight into Dial, ISDN, Frame Relay, and VPNs. With a focus
specifically on the more popular enterprise applications of these
technologies, each major section discusses troubleshooting
methodology and scenarios. The methodology walks readers
through the process of identifying, isolating, and correcting
common failures. This structured approach helps limit the
inclination to attack network failures in a more random fashion,
which is not nearly as efficient. Explanations of typical symptoms,
problems, show commands, and debug information are also
extensive.

ciscopress.com

Cisco Press Security

CCSP™ Cisco Secure PIX® Firewall Advanced Exam Certification Guide (CCSP Self-Study)

Christian Degu, Greg Bastien

1-58720-067-8 • **Available No**

The CSPFA exam is one of the five component exams to the CCSP certification. *CCSP Cisco Secure PIX Firewall Advanced Exam Certification Guide* provides CSPFA exam candidates with a comprehensive preparation tool for testing success. With pre- and post-chapter tests, a CD-ROM-based testing engine with more than 200 questions, and comprehensive training on all exam topics, this title brings the proven exam preparation tools from the popular Cisco Press Exam Certification Guide series to the CSPFA candidate. It also serves as a learning guide for networkers interested in learning more about working with the PIX Firewall line of products.

CCSP Cisco Secure VPN Exam Certification Guide

John Roland, Mark Newcomb

1-58720-070-8 • **Available Now**

As security demands continue to increase for enterprise and service provider networks, the number of employees working from remote locations requiring an efficient and rapid virtual private network connection grows as well. The Cisco Secure line of products and services are focused on providing the seamless operation of these remote networks with the maximum level of security available. Organizations using this suite of products and services need networking professionals with proven skills at getting the highest levels of both security and network operability. This need has created a booming demand for the Cisco Systems security certifications that verify those skills and abilities. The CSVPN exam is one of the components of the Cisco Systems security designation. CSS-1 Cisco Secure VPN Exam Certification Guide provides CSVPN exam candidates with a comprehensive preparation tool for testing success. With pre- and post-chapter tests, a CD-ROM-based testing engine with more than 200 questions, and comprehensive training on all exam topics, this title brings the proven exam preparation tools from the popular Cisco Press Exam Certification Guide series to the CSVPN candidate.

ciscopress.com

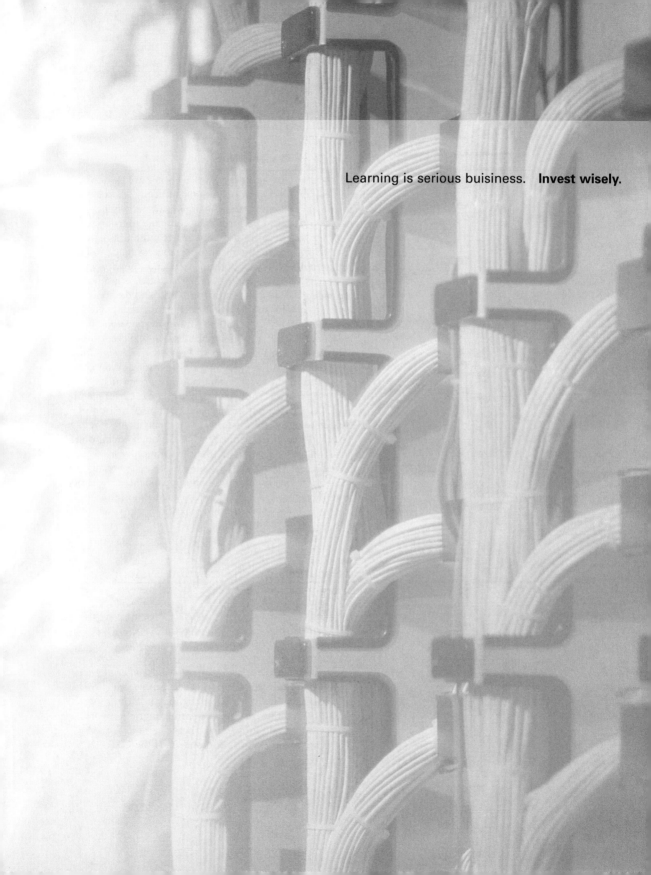

Learning is serious buisiness.   **Invest wisely.**

Cisco Press Security

Web Security Field Guide
Steve Kalman
1-58705-092-7 • **Available Now**

Networks are broken into every day. Websites are defaced.
Viruses shut down network operations and deny services to
both customers and employees. As organizations rely increasingly on the Internet to perform their company's business, the
impact of network security breaches grows more dramatic.
The task of securing an organization's resources tends to fall
on administrators who lack both the time and know-how to
properly secure a network. *Web Security Field Guide* is a how-to
book, providing the steps to securing networks and the conceptual
information to understand what these actions are doing. Network
administrators who have part time security responsibilities will
be able to take this book, follow the steps, and prevent the
vast majority of intrusion attempts. *Web Security Field Guide*
covers the techniques for hardening the operating system, the
web server and the browser. It then addresses firewalls, access
lists, ongoing security maintenance, and testing. Coverage of
these topics is focused not on the theoretical explanation of
how the technology works, but on how to apply the technology.
Most chapters introduce a topic, provide enough background
to understand the problem and how the solution works, and
then move on to a tutorial showing how to secure the component
under discussion or how to install and implement the security
tool being introduced. An essential workplace tool, this
portable guide is designed for the application of real-world
solutions.

Cisco Secure Intrusion Detection System
Earl Carter
1-58705-034-X • **Available Now**

Cisco Secure Intrusion Detection System provides a clear
explanation of why network security is crucial in today's
converged networking environment, how CSIDS improves
the security on a network, and how to install and configure
CSIDS. The Cisco Secure Intrusion Detection System (CSIDS)
is a real-time, network-based IDS designed to detect, report,
and terminate unauthorized activity throughout a network.
The industry's first and now the market-leading IDS, the
CSIDS is the dynamic security component of the Cisco
end-to-end security product line.

PACKET

PACKET